INTERNATIONAL ECONOMICS

THIRD EDITION

Ingo Walter
Kaj Areskoug

John Wiley and Sons

New York   Chichester   Brisbane   Toronto

Library of Congress Cataloging in Publication Data:

Walter, Ingo.
  International economics.

  Includes index.
  1.   International economic relations.   2.   Commerce.
I. Areskoug, Kaj, joint author.   II.   Title
HF1411.W32   1981   337   80-21541
ISBN 0-471-04957-3

Printed in the United States of America

10 9 8 7 6 5 4 3 2

ABOUT THE AUTHORS

Ingo Walter is Professor of Economics and Finance at the Graduate School of Business Administration, New York University, where he also serves as chairman of the International Business program. He holds A.B. and M.S. degrees from Lehigh University and a Ph.D. from New York University. He has written numerous articles in professional journals, and is author or editor of over a dozen books, including *Multinationals under Fire: Lessons in the Management of Conflict*, co-authored with Thomas N. Gladwin and published by John Wiley in 1980. He has held research grants from various foundations and has served as a consultant to a number of international organizations, government agencies, banks, and corporations.

Kaj Areskoug is Professor of Finance at the Graduate School of Business, Pace University. He holds a Ph.D. in economics from Columbia University and a law degree from the University of Lund, Sweden. He has also taught at New York University, Columbia University, the University of Texas at Dallas, and Fordham University and previously served as a research economist in banks and corporations. Among his publications are a number of journal articles and monographs on problems of international development finance, multinational corporate investment, international capital markets, exchange rates, and trade policy.

v

remaining deficiencies. No less important have been our undergraduate and M.B.A. students, who rarely hesitated to give us free advice. Marion Epps, Ligija Roze, and Mary Jaffee typed and retyped the manuscript. Rich Esposito of Wiley kept the heat on and in various ways facilitated completion of the manuscript. To all we owe sincere thanks.

New York City
October 1980

INGO WALTER
KAJ ARESKOUG

CONTENTS

1
INTRODUCTION

In the beginning, studying a new subject is like a voyage into unfamiliar territory. Travelers do not really know its size, contours, or characteristics. They may need a guide who can prepare them for the experience to come by pointing out unique features and relating them to broader, more familiar phenomena. This is, in part, the function of an introduction to a text such as this. The student who is taking his or her first course in international economics ought to know what the subject is about, how it is related to other branches of economics, and what kinds of things distinguish it.

WHAT IS INTERNATIONAL ECONOMICS?

Like all economic subjects, international economics deals with the allocation of scarce resources to competing ends for the satisfaction of human wants. It puts this very basic economic problem in the context of international relations—relations among economic "actors" located in separate nations. It attempts to explain how international economic relations affect the allocation of resources, both within nations and among nations.

International economics has a private aspect and a governmental, public-policy aspect. And so the economic "actors" we will be concerned with include both firms—and, occasionally, other private institutions and individuals—and government agencies of various types. They also include official international organizations that have assumed certain supranational functions in the world economy.

International economics owes its existence as a more or less distinct academic field to a particular political institution—the nation-state. Without this institution, there would still be ample reason to study economic relations

1

between different parts of the world. But that subject—perhaps called "global economics"—essentially would be just a geographic extension of the study of national economies; it could perhaps be characterized as *interregional* economics. In reality, *international* economic relations are generically quite distinct from interregional economic relations within any one nation, say between the American Northeast and the Sunbelt, or the north of Italy and the Mezzogiorno.

To be sure, both international and interregional economics share certain problems of distance and transportation. But the nation-state presents us with a much more important differentiating feature in the world economy. Each national government is politically sovereign, develops international economic relations on its own, and in many diverse ways injects itself into international relations among private parties. It initiates and administers economic policies, which sometimes—as in the case of trade and exchange-rate policy—directly aim at affecting international transactions. Other policies (such as pollution control and income taxation) may on the surface appear to be purely domestic, both in intent and in effects. But we will find that such policies, too, will usually have international economic consequences.

One traditional function of governments is the issue and regulation of money, often via a central bank that may or may not take direct instructions from the government itself. The world is divided into separate currency areas that mostly, but not entirely, coincide with national political boundaries. The creation and use of money, in turn, is closely connected with the structure and activities of national banking systems and national financial markets. National monies can be converted into one another in the *foreign exchange markets*, and many large firms can operate in foreign, as well as domestic, financial markets. Even so, economic relations between parties that use different types of currencies and rely on different financial markets will usually create special complications—problems that form an integral part of international economics.

Most economic transactions among private parties take the form of exchange, or trade. Firms buy certain goods and services and sell other goods or services in the marketplace, hoping to earn a profit in the process. This is the basis of *microeconomics*, as viewed from the perspective of the individual economic unit. *Macroeconomics* concerns itself, in part, with broad exchange relationships among entire sectors of the national economy and tries to determine how these relationships affect total national output, employment, and the price level. International economics contains major elements of both microeconomics and macroeconomics. International selling and buying— *exports* and *imports*—are the main topics of the theory of international trade. Such activities depend on conditions in the input and output markets of each firm, as shown in basic microeconomic analysis. At the same time, individual markets for goods or services will always be connected with one another—and this is where the macroeconomic aspects come into the picture.

In a dynamic economy, firms will grow or shut down, and new firms will be established. Workers may move from industry to industry, or from region to region. This occurs internationally as well as domestically. When a firm shifts part of its operations abroad, or when workers migrate to foreign countries in search of better jobs, we usually speak of *international factor movements*— the factors of production in these cases being capital and labor, perhaps combined with technology and entrepreneurship. International capital movements usually take place, not directly through shipments of capital goods, but indirectly through transfers of funds. International lending, borrowing, and transactions in securities can provide the means for an expansion of productive facilities in the receiving country. In such instances, international trade can acquire both a "real" and a financial dimension.

Sometimes there is no discernable link between financial transactions and the flow of physical goods or services. One can then regard financial activity as a separate form of economic behavior, with "inputs" and "outputs" consisting of different financial instruments (stocks, bonds, loans) and with analytical principles all its own. And so there is a special branch of international economics called the *theory of international capital movements* or, more broadly, *international financial theory*. Still, it helps to remember that most of the general rules that we shall develop about private economic behavior can be applied to both real and financial transactions. Lending and borrowing can be construed as trade in financial assets, internationally as well as domestically. Analogies of this sort can provide a useful shortcut to understanding.

At a private level, international economics thus draws on microeconomics, macroeconomics, money and banking, and financial economics. To a somewhat lesser extent, it embodies elements of the study of industrial organization, labor economics, and transport economics. When it addresses the special international problems of developing countries, it naturally enters the territory of development economics. And in studying the behavior of large contemporary firms with activities in many different countries, it incorporates much of the just-emerging theory of multinational enterprise.

At a governmental level, international economics naturally becomes an extension of the analysis of economic policy. We can divide economic policy into three chief segments: *money and credit policy*, usually executed by the central bank; *fiscal* (tax and expenditure) *policy*, in the hands of legislators and national administrators; and *regulatory policies* of many kinds, implemented by various specialized agencies under mandate from the authorities in power. Such a breakdown provides a useful perspective on international economic policy as well. Governments try to regulate exports and imports through various direct controls; this is the subject of *trade policy*, or *commercial policy*. They often impose controls and regulations on various types of international lending or borrowing, and on foreign-exchange market transactions; these matters come under the rubric of *international financial* (or monetary) *policy*.

But the most important and controversial international policy questions center on the effects of national monetary and fiscal measures on overall international economic-financial relations. How do such measures affect international trade and capital flows, and how might they have to be modified so as to take these effects into account? The fact is that all major trading nations must tailor their monetary and fiscal policies to both domestic and international circumstances. There is, for example, a significant amount of cooperation in the formulation and execution of monetary policies among the leading industrial countries, and elaborate efforts have been made to develop mutually acceptable exchange-rate policies and to set up intergovernmental credit facilities. These arrangements are part of what is loosely called the *international monetary system*. They clearly belong in the policy part of international financial analysis. Similarly, trade policies adopted by one country will clearly have an impact on others that buy from it or sell to it, and these, too, have to be coordinated if economic conflicts are to be avoided.

A SWEEP THROUGH HISTORY

International trade, in a strict sense, can be traced in history to the emergence of the true national state, with well-defined borders and a functioning central authority. In Europe, such states began to evolve during the sixteenth century, with France, England, Spain, and the Netherlands being the most prominent ones. By contrast, Germany and Italy did not really become national entities until the late nineteenth century. The United States, of course, assumed nationhood during the late eighteenth and early nineteenth centuries.

Trade that took place in earlier times was certainly important to the level and structure of economic activity at the time. But the development of the modern international economy really began with the period of rapid industrialization that more or less coincided with the emergence of national states. With the introduction of new manufactured products and specialized production techniques, and the need for raw materials to feed them, international commerce became increasingly crucial to producers and consumers alike.

The significance of international economic relationships in earlier times can be gauged by the government policies adopted during the so-called *mercantilist* era, which dates from about 1500 to the middle of the eighteenth century. The mercantilists felt that the accumulation of precious metals in national coffers was crucial to the welfare of the state, and that the prime function of international trade was to augment this particular form of wealth. Accordingly, their efforts were geared toward maximum export sales and minimum import purchases—that is, toward maximum trade "surpluses." These were to be settled through the importation of gold and other precious metals, which functioned as international money and were placed in the national treasury.

By necessity, international trade under the mercantilist system was subject to a great deal of government control. State trading monopolies were common, and there were administrative regulations on both exports and imports. Import taxes reduced purchases from abroad, or prevented the importation of certain goods completely. Concurrently, exports were subsidized.

Although mercantilist ideas, particularly the narrow concept of wealth, might seem irrational today, the accumulation of precious metals did in fact serve to stimulate, via exports, the growth of national economic activity. Also, there occurred an opening of many new trade routes and a state-fostered buildup of maritime industries—developments that created new opportunities for economic activity. The early phases of the mercantilist era were dominated by Spain and Portugal, which pioneered in exploring the Western Hemisphere, Africa, and Asia. But it was not long before the British and the Dutch began to expand their operations as well. Early exports by these nations included cloth, metalwares, ornaments, and gunpowder, whereas their imports comprised tobacco, spices, and other commodities often foreign to the European culture.

One institution that facilitated mercantilist policies was the *trading company*. Through this type of organization, merchants pooled their physical and financial resources and, under government charter, engaged in long-term and often risky trading ventures. The Dutch East India Company operated in parts of Asia and Africa, whereas the British East India Company concentrated on India, and the Hudson's Bay Company on North America. These trading companies established enclaves in their respective trading areas and thus became an important feature of the rapidly emerging colonial and imperial era. Simple manufactures were added to the list of imports as colonial production capabilities improved. Regions under colonial domination effectively supplemented the economy of the mother country, and of course aided in its acquisition of precious metals.

Eventually, the mercantilist era gave way to a more liberal conception of national and international economic activity. This coincided with a parallel transformation of political and religious thought, as well as with the rise to power of the bourgeois classes. But the strongest force for the liberalization of international economic transactions was probably the Industrial Revolution itself. By the late nineteenth century, in fact, international trade and capital movements among the then "advanced" countries were relatively unrestricted, and each of them benefited enormously from the existence of a stable, dependable international system of money and finance—the gold standard.

Despite the periodic ups and downs in economic activity that made themselves felt in international economic transactions, not until the onset of World War I was the relatively smooth operation of the international economy severely disrupted. Yet even the wartime emergency proved to be only a temporary setback. The period after World War I was marked by rapid recovery and a surge of economic activity throughout most of the Western world, despite the disastrous inflations in such countries as Austria and Germany. By 1928, the volume of international trade had expanded enormously, and the flow of people (migration) and capital (lending and investing) between nations had reached unprecedented levels.

The start of the Great Depression, in the early 1930s, was followed by a precipitous decline in international economic transactions, punctuated by the suspension of the international gold standard and mushrooming controls on trade. The demise of gold in international exchange, as well as the continuing problem of World War I reparations, intensified the recessionary forces in the world economy. A period of marked international economic disintegration and fragmentation followed. Each nation geared its policies more and more toward economic self-sufficiency, or *autarky*. This development by itself was not excessively painful for large nations such as the United States, but it had near-disastrous consequences for small countries that depended on foreign markets for a large portion of their product needs.

The rampant *economic* nationalism during the late 1930s coincided with the growth of virulent *political* nationalism that ultimately led to World War II. By contrast, the year 1946 marked the beginning of an international economic resurgence in the war-devastated nations of Europe and Japan in an atmosphere of economic cooperation. This led to a period of relatively continuous and rapid economic growth in these areas, supported by an expanding volume of international trade and by massive infusions of American financial aid. Major efforts were made to achieve a renewed liberalization of international trade and payments. The establishment of the International Monetary Fund (IMF), the International Bank for Reconstruction and Development (IBRD)—or World Bank—and the General Agreement on Tariffs and Trade (GATT) serve as prominent examples of these efforts. Still, the broad ideal of essentially free trade and free mobility of productive factors has never been fully attained.

The 1950s saw the rise of a number of regional economic blocs, of which the European Economic Community (EEC) is certainly the best known. To a degree, the emergence of *economic regionalism* underscores the failure to achieve trade and payments liberalization on a global scale. Although considerable progress was achieved during the 1960s and 1970s—particularly during the "Kennedy Round" and "Tokyo Round" of trade negotiations— economic regionalism seems here to stay. The EEC has helped to strengthen the relative economic and political power of Western Europe at the expense of the United States. Financially, this trend has manifested itself in a weakening in the official international status of the U.S. dollar, and in the rapid development of European money and capital markets, especially the so-called *Eurocurrency markets.*

Two additional recent changes in the organization of the world economy ought to be mentioned. The last few decades have seen an astonishing expansion of *multinational enterprise*. Large U.S.- and foreign-based corporations, engaged in businesses ranging from the manufacture of high-technology consumer or capital goods to the extraction, refining, and marketing of petroleum, have established networks of affiliates throughout the world. This development has had far-reaching consequences for the global patterns of trade and production, for the flow of labor, capital, and technology, and for the conduct of government policies. Also in the 1970s, the *Organization of Petroleum Exporting Countries* (OPEC) consolidated its cartel power and managed to bring about a tenfold increase in world prices of crude oil. Never before had there been such a drastic shift in relative commodity prices, or such a gross redistribution of income and wealth in favor of a particular bloc of exporting nations. We shall analyze such comparatively recent global economic developments at considerable length as we proceed from topic to topic.

HOW THE BOOK IS ORGANIZED

The purpose of this book is to explain and illustrate international economic concepts in as concise, systematic, and relevant a manner as possible. Its basic aim is to provide the reader with the tools for analyzing, interpreting, and predicting international economic events. We do not intend, however, to present an elaborate exposition of international economic or financial institutions, or of the historical evolution of the international economy—this has been done adequately elsewhere. The book is, primarily, a study in *methods* of international economic analysis, with as many applications of these methods to contemporary real-world problems as seem appropriate. We will rely heavily on somewhat abstract economic models, often with geometrical illustrations. These models are not ends in themselves. Instead, they should be considered simplified summary pictures of significant economic relationships among nations, industries, or firms.

Our guiding principle is first to develop simple, basic principles, and then to elaborate on them in successively greater depth—with pertinent illustrations drawn from actual or hypothetical situations. We proceed from an analysis of trade in goods and services to an analysis of capital flows and finance. Within both of these broad subject areas, the discussion starts out at the level of private individuals, firms, and markets, and goes on to problems of government policy and intergovernmental cooperation.

The text is divided into five distinct parts, two devoted to the trade and production aspects of international economic relations, and three to the financial aspects. Each part contains several relatively self-contained chapters that deal with particular analytical issues. Each chapter concludes with a brief summary of the main ideas, a list of concepts that the reader should have become familiar with, some review questions, and a selection of additional readings. In a few cases, we have, at the end of chapters, added Advanced Material sections that contain further theoretical or empirical elaborations, or restatements of major points in more precise terms.

Part I deals with the "pure" (nonfinancial) theory of international trade. It attempts to determine why nations engage in trade with one another, to predict the direction, volume, and composition of such trade, and to determine its effects on national economies. "Which nation trades what goods and services with what other nations and in what quantities?" is a fundamental question to which international trade theory is addressed. Clearly, the answers to these questions will depend on both supply and demand conditions in the international economy. And they will have implications for the economic welfare of the trading nations, which—as we shall see—tend to reap "gains from trade."

The main topic of Part II—trade policy—deals with governmental actions to influence or restrict the pattern and volume of international trade. Why are trade barriers deliberately set up, despite the generally favorable effects of trade on national output and consumer welfare? A special trade-policy issue focuses on economic integration—that is, the process of creating a single regional economic entity from several national economies. With the aid of theory and models, we shall show the chief advantages and disadvantages of such arrangements. We shall also examine the economic reasons for the international flow of factors of production, which in turn has a bearing on trade policy. To a large extent, such transactions are performed by multinational corporations, a relatively new and major force in the world economy; we shall attempt to appraise their role in world trade and in the global structure of production.

In all modern economies, production, investment, and commerce depend on the availability of credit and on methods for settling debts and storing purchasing power in a temporary monetary form. Part III demonstrates how these principles apply in international relationships. We shall develop the basic theoretical rationale for international lending or borrowing and analyze the facilities that exist today for intercountry financial transactions, especially via the foreign exchange markets.

Like other economic entities, nations have to live within their financial means—but there may be many different ways of arranging their economic affairs. We normally analyze a nation's overall economic relations with the rest of the world on the basis of its *balance-of-payments* record. And we treat the issue of how international trade and capital flows can and should accommodate themselves to international economic circumstances as a matter of "adjustment"—essentially, as a matter of international economic interdependence, obviously with a large policy content. These topics are covered in Part IV of the book.

To conclude the volume, we move the discussion of international financial policy to the plane of intergovernmental cooperation. We shall outline different approaches to the problems of settling international payments, maintaining international monetary "reserves," and, possibly, regulating the policies that nations can undertake for adjustment purposes. These are some of the main issues in the theory of international monetary and financial policy, and they involve fundamental conflicts between national economic independence and self-determination, on the one hand, and international cooperation and integration, on the other. The final chapter describes and evaluates the monetary system that has evolved in the present century. It remains in a state of flux.

In short, the book contains a box of analytical tools. We try to provide the hammers, screwdrivers, and wrenches as readily as possible. The tools are powerful indeed. Their effectiveness, however, depends on the user.

Important Concepts

macroeconomics	mercantilism
microeconomics	trading companies
exports	autarky
imports	economic regionalism
international factor movements	multinational enterprise

Questions

1. What differentiates interregional from international economic transactions?
2. What features of mercantilist thinking about international economic relations do you perceive exist today?
3. Offhand, what merits and demerits can you identify in economic regionalism as opposed to a more open, global economic system?

Further Readings

Adams, John, *International Economics* (New York: St. Martin's Press, 1972). A self-teaching guide to international economics.

Caves, Richard E., and Ronald W. Jones, *World Trade and Payments*, 2nd edition (Boston: Little, Brown, 1977). A good text, one level more advanced than ours.

Condliffe, J. B., *The Commerce of Nations* (New York: Norton, 1950). Contains an excellent historical treatment of the subject.

Heckscher, Eli F., *Mercantilism* (London: George Allen & Unwin, 1935).

Kreinin, Mordechai E., *International Economics: A Policy Approach*, 2nd edition (New York: Harcourt Brace Jovanovich, 1975). An introductory text, one level easier than ours.

Richardson, J. David, *Understanding International Economics* (Boston: Little, Brown, 1980). An up-to-date text providing an alternative explanation of some of the concepts used here.

Roepke, Wilhelm, *International Economic Disintegration* (London: Stevens, 1942).

Salvatore, Dominick, *International Economics* (New York: McGraw-Hill, 1975). Another good programmed learning book on the subject.

I

International Trade

2
WHY NATIONS TRADE

Since World War II, international trade has grown enormously. As a sign of the growing interdependence of national economies, trade has expanded at roughly twice the rate of economic growth. In the 1940s and 1950s, the United States dominated international trade, while Europe and Japan struggled to recover from the devastating effects of the war. But in the 1960s and 1970s the United States' share of trade declined steadily, as countries such as Germany, Japan, and Italy made bigger inroads on world markets. And in the 1980s we can see how some of the more advanced developing countries—for example, Hong Kong, Taiwan, Singapore, Brazil, and South Korea—are expanding their shares of global trade at the expense of the advanced industrial countries. The trading role of the developing countries will no doubt become still more pronounced as this century draws to a close.

The composition of trade has changed just as dramatically. Years ago it was dominated by agricultural commodities, industrial raw materials, and a narrow range of simple manufactured goods. With the Industrial Revolution, trade in manufactured products reached much higher levels, at the same time as textiles, steel, motor vehicles, ships, and machine tools became increasingly prominent items in the outputs of the trading nations. Further structural shifts in the postwar period are reflected in the growing trade in such advanced products as computers, aircraft, and consumer electronics, and also in an expanding international exchange of services such as banking, accounting, consulting, insurance, and technical knowhow. In short, the composition of trade reflects the evolving structures of the world's trading economies. (Examine Tables 2-1 and 2-2.)

What is the reason for the enormous volume and growth of trade? And why should nations trade with one another in the first place? What specific benefits can be obtained by engaging in international trade? And how does inter-

13

Table 2-1
Exports and Imports as a Percentage of GNP in the
United States and Other Major Industrialized Countries

Country	Year	Merchandise Only[a]		Goods and Services[b]	
		Exports	Imports	Exports	Imports
United States	1978	6.8%	8.2%	8.4%	9.8%
Canada	1978	23.6	22.1	25.8	25.7
Japan	1977	11.6	9.1	13.7	12.1
West Germany	1978	22.1	18.3	27.1	24.3
France	1976	16.3	17.5	19.1	20.3
Italy	1977	23.2	23.1	26.2	26.9
United Kingdom	1977	23.6	24.7	30.9	30.1

[a] Measured on a transactions basis.
[b] Measured on a national accounts basis.
Source: International Monetary Fund, *International Financial Statistics*.

national trade differ from interregional trade within a single nation, particularly with respect to the underlying causal forces? Let us begin by trying
to find some simple, commonsense explanations for these questions. We shall
then briefly review a few basic tools of microeconomics and develop
an elementary model of trade between two countries in a single product,
before embarking on a more formal and rigorous analysis of the theory of
international trade.

SUPPLY ELEMENTS

There are profits to be made in international trade—profits that in a typical
transaction result from the purchase of goods by traders at lower prices
in one country and their subsequent sale at higher prices in another country.
An American buys a Japanese camera because he finds it to be considerably
cheaper or better than a comparable item made in the United States.
There is a basic difference in camera prices between the United States and
Japan, even after quality differences have been taken into account. A general,
commonsense explanation of international trade, then, would appear to lie
in the differences in prices that are seen to prevail for various products
among the nations of the world. Put simply, it "pays" to trade.

But prices are partly a reflection of the costs of production, with
due allowance for the fact that market imperfections may somewhat distort
the cost-price link. Production costs, in turn, are a reflection of the wages
paid to labor, the cost of capital, the value of land, the cost of raw
materials, and, especially, the degree of efficiency of the productive process.

Table 2-2

Composition of United States' Merchandise Trade, 1972 and 1977

	1972		1977	
	Exports	Imports	Exports	Imports
Food, raw materials, ores, and other minerals	25.1%	20.5%	26.2%	15.1%
Fuels	3.3	8.6	3.7	29.9
Metals, chemicals, and other semimanufactures	16.1	19.1	16.2	15.4
Engineering products	47.9	36.0	47.4	28.6
Textiles, clothing, and other consumer goods	5.2	12.9	5.2	9.3
Unspecified	2.4	2.9	i.3	1.7
Total	100.0%	100.0%	100.0%	100.0%

Source: Adapted from GATT, *International Trade 1976/1977* and *1977/1978*, Table A.

The costs of production are a composite of all of these elements, although any one element may be powerful enough to be the determining factor in a particular international cost-price relationship.

It is often said that Taiwan exports great quantities of products that embody substantial amounts of labor in production—that is, *labor-intensive* goods. Since Taiwanese wage levels are relatively low, because of the abundance of workers in that country, one would expect its labor-intensive exports to compete effectively in countries where labor is relatively more scarce and wages are correspondingly higher. Similarly, a country such as Canada should logically export substantial quantities of wheat, a *land-intensive* good, given its greater abundance of land compared with most other countries. By the same reasoning the United States, clearly a *capital-abundant* country, should be selling to other nations those goods that require a great deal of capital in their manufacture or in research and development. Of course, when we say that a particular factor is "abundant" in a given nation, we mean that it is abundant in relation to the supplies of other productive factors in that country, as compared with similar factor availabilities in other countries and this should be reflected in relative factor prices—an important point to remember. A simple explanation, then, is that each country merely *exports* goods using productive factors that it possesses in abundance and *imports* goods requiring factors that are relatively scarce at home. But things are not quite that simple, even in a superficial examination of the subject.

Remember that the factors of production are not the *only* influences on costs and prices. The efficiency with which they are used—productivity—is also of importance. Certainly Canada is land abundant and should export grains, but so is Siberia. Canada indeed does export grains, yet if Siberia were a country, it is likely that its grain exports would be negligible.

Why? Because the *productivity* of land is much greater in Canada than in Siberia, even though both are about equally land abundant. Thus, climate and geographic differences are important influences on the productivity of land, and therefore on the patterns of international trade in agricultural commodities.

What has just been said about land is equally true of labor and capital. Not only are the wages of labor important, but so is the productivity of labor. Climate influences not only the productivity of land, but labor efficiency as well. And capital itself is of little value without the technology to use it efficiently. The character of the people—their dexterity, ingenuity, organizational ability, entrepreneurial orientation, and acquisitive behavior—is critical in the use of *all* resources in the productive process. No less significant is the economic, political, and social environment within which the productive process takes place. And technology—or, more broadly, *useful knowledge*—affects productivity both directly and, indirectly, by the way it is incorporated in physical and human capital—and so do the scale economies or diseconomies that are encountered as output expands.

The immediate cause of international trade, then, seems to be the existence of differences in the prices of goods among countries. Price differences are traceable to differences in production costs, which, in turn, hinge on relative endowments of productive factors *as well as* the degree of efficiency with which these factors are employed.

What about the availability of natural resources as yet another supply factor? Countries endowed with abundant natural resources of a certain kind can logically be expected to export quantities of that resource to other countries, or to export products requiring substantial inputs of that resource in the production process. But natural resource endowments alone need not be even a partial guide to trade patterns. A large deposit of iron ore is virtually useless without massive infusions of capital in the form of mines and equipment for extracting the ore. Even then, further capital investment in transport systems is needed to bring the ore to the point of shipment. A skilled work force is required to mine the ore and prepare it for shipment, and technology is necessary to enable any kind of process to function effectively. Once all of these elements are present, the foundation has been built in a country for a trade pattern characterized by exports of *resource-intensive products*.

On the other hand, countries *lacking* a certain natural resource will not necessarily be unable to export products requiring that resource in their manufacture: Japan has become the premier world steel exporter with virtually none of the required natural resources. Such countries will have to import the needed raw materials for processing into exportable finished goods. And the story becomes more complex in cases of products that depend on large amounts of several resources, as does aluminum (bauxite, electric power) and steel (coal, iron ore). So the presence or absence of a single natural resource provides us with insufficient information for predicting the composition or direction of a nation's international trade.

Just as in the case of natural resources, the availability of any one agent of production may not always be a good indicator of potential trade flows. Labor, capital, and technologies can all be acquired from abroad through migration, through foreign borrowing and investment inflows, or through the transfer of technology. And as long as international trade flows are relatively unrestricted, there is nothing to prevent the importation of *products* containing those productive agents that are lacking at home, for subsequent reexport in a more or less changed form.

Once again, trade, of whatever kind, is founded on international price differences that are based on divergences in overall production costs and reflect variations in all the relevant factor endowments and their productivities.

DEMAND ELEMENTS

In trying to find a commonsense explanation for trade between nations, we have considered a variety of factors operating on the *supply* side of the economic equation. But what about *demand?* Is it not possible to conceive of two countries producing given products at identical supply costs, yet with a substantial volume of trade between them? Indeed, differences in demand, also reflected in international price differentials, may be just as important as differences in costs of production.

Demand largely depends on tastes and incomes. Tastes can play a decisive role in the demand for products across national boundaries. If the domestic availability of a certain desired good is insufficient, the excess demand may be satisfied by means of imports. Also, there are sometimes significant qualitative differences between seemingly uniform products originating in different countries. The United States buys enormous quantities of French, German, and Italian wines, despite the domestic abundance of California and New York wines. Americans annually purchase large numbers of Japanese refrigerators, whereas the Japanese simultaneously buy a surprising number of U.S. refrigerators. Beer, automobiles, tobacco, aircraft, and textiles are other items for which tastes seem to be a strong causal demand force in international trade. Demand responds to changing tastes, prices reflect the demand shifts, and trade in turn follows international differences in product prices.

Demand for foreign, as well as domestic, goods depends also on the disposable incomes available to consumers, businesses, and governments. We would thus expect some sort of a relationship between a country's national income and its purchases from abroad. If our incomes rise, so, typically, does our demand for most categories of goods and services, and so do our imports. For one thing, we would expect low-income countries to import mainly necessities, whereas imports of high-income countries would be more heavily concentrated in luxury goods. A similar relation appears to exist between a country's exports and the respective national incomes of the foreign nations with which it trades. At the same time, a rise in incomes may cause a rise in domestic prices, thus making imported goods more competitive with domestic products. This trend will tend to result in a switching of purchases from domestic to foreign goods, which can cause an increase in trade quite apart from that which resulted from the initial income growth.

INTERNATIONAL AND INTERREGIONAL TRADE

Do the explanations for trade between nations apply equally well to commerce between different regions within a single country? Actually, there is no substantive difference between interregional and international flows of goods and services or the causes behind them.

Just as international trade is based on differences in prices between countries, so is interregional trade based on price differences between parts of the same country. The explanations for this domestic trade are also similar: Endowments of the factors of production may vary substantially among the regions of a country, and productivity, or efficiency, may be high in some regions and low in others for particular product lines. From a cost standpoint, therefore, there is ample justification for the large-scale interregional trade that we know exists in most countries.

The same analogy holds for demand. If incomes grow in a certain part of a nation, that stimulates demand not only for locally manufactured goods, but for products made in other parts of the country as well. Certain products for which there is a demand may simply not be available in some regions, and interregional trade is the mechanism through which this demand can be satisfied. Tastes also vary between different parts of a country. The consumption pattern of the Sicilian, for instance, is hardly the same as that of his Milanese compatriot, and the average Manhattan consumer buys different things than his Honolulu counterpart.

IMPORTANCE OF TRADE

We now have a rough idea of why nations trade with one another. But what is trade's importance for national economic well-being? And how does the world as a whole stand to benefit? One would think that the enormous volume of international trade today must be founded on some tangible economic benefits for the nations of the world. What, specifically, is the nature of these benefits?

For the answer we go back to one of the earliest and most renowned contributors to the study of economics, Adam Smith. In his famous example of the pin-making factory, Smith proposed a notion that has long been a fundamental principle of economics, one that is almost second nature to all economics students: If each individual or enterprise (or region) specializes in a certain limited aspect of the production process, total output will far exceed what would have been possible if each carried out the entire production process from beginning to end. Maximization of output—and therefore of personal economic well-being—is based on interdependence and specialization, not independence and self-sufficiency. Each producing entity should specialize in those particular tasks that it can perform relatively better than can others. Only in this way can output be maximized for the nation as a whole.

It is a simple task to carry Smith's idea one step further into the international arena. World output of goods and services can be maximized *only* if each nation concentrates on whatever tasks it can perform relatively better than other nations. Here, too, the principles of specialization, division of labor, and interdependence apply. If Adam Smith was correct, we would expect to observe an enormous volume of transactions between individuals, firms, and regions *within* a country—and we do. And internationally, we should observe an enormous volume of trade in goods and services *between* the individual countries of the world—and we do. Only the free movement of goods and services between countries will ensure that production is carried out by the most efficient of the world's enterprises, and that overall economic welfare, as we try to define it, is maximized. Trade thus plays a vital role in helping provide higher standards of living throughout the world.

If this is true, it seems hardly sensible for nations to impose any kind of barriers to international trade. Yet everyone knows that myriad restrictions, ranging from import tariffs to outright government control of international transactions, impede the flow of goods between countries. How to explain such an apparently contradictory state of affairs is the task of the *theory of commercial policy*, with which we will concern ourselves later. At this point it is sufficient to acknowledge that national restrictions on trade can under certain circumstances secure for a *country* or a *group* within a country a larger share of world output and income, at the expense of other nations and, usually, of the world economy as a whole.

TRADE AND INTERNATIONAL FACTOR FLOWS

In addition to international trade in goods and services, a closely related aspect of international economic relations is the flow of productive factors. The United States in the 1960s sent massive amounts of direct investment capital to Western Europe and Canada; in the 1970s such investment flows increasingly entered the United States. During the past two decades, millions of workers from Spain, Portugal, Yugoslavia, North Africa, Turkey, Greece, and elsewhere have found employment in the industrial areas of northern Europe. Immigration played a dominant role in the economic development of North America, and in the 1980s legal and illegal inflows of people are continuing to have a major impact on the U. S. economy. The Saudi Arabian and other Middle Eastern economies are fueled to a significant extent by Egyptian and other expatriate workers. Clearly, international flows of labor and capital have assumed major proportions. Why?

The supply forces are here virtually identical to those operating on international trade. Factors of production move—when they are allowed to—from countries where they are abundant, or their productivity is low, to countries where they are scarce, or their productivity is high. They move in response to differences in returns (yields on capital, wage rates), as long as these are wide enough to more than offset the economic and social cost of the relocation process itself. We conclude, therefore, that a country short of labor can either import labor-intensive goods or import labor itself, and may end up doing both. The same is true of capital flows and technology transfers. Hence international trade and factor flows seem to be substitutes for each other, and there are real gains associated with both.

We can now begin to formalize some of the ideas and concepts discussed rather casually above. There are four basic questions that the theory of international trade must attempt to answer: (1) What countries will trade how much of which products with whom? That is, what will be the geographic and commodity *pattern* and *volume* of trade in goods and services? (2) What are the *gains* from international trade, and how are they realized? (3) What impact does international trade have on the *economic structure* of a nation? (4) How does international trade affect the various *productive factors* within an economy, especially with regard to the returns earned by their owners? We shall proceed through a series of *models*—abstract but instructive representations of the real world, based on simplifying assumptions. To start, we shall develop a simple supply-and-demand framework that illustrates some of the points made in this chapter. The framework will utilize only the most elementary principles of microeconomics.

DETERMINANTS OF DEMAND

The concept of demand refers to the amount of a given product that consumers or users are able and willing to buy at each and every possible price. It may relate to a certain product category (automobiles), or simply to the output of a single enterprise (Volkswagen); the former is called *industry demand* and the latter, *firm demand*. Demand may pertain

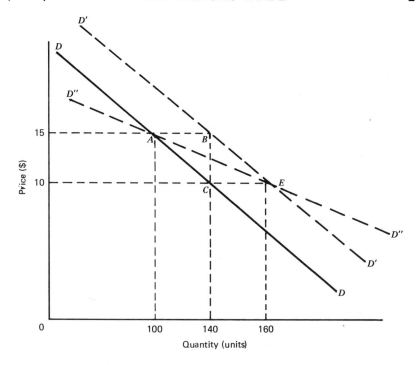

	Price ($)	Quantity (units)
Initial price (on DD)	15	100
Price reduction (along DD)	10	140
Shift in demand (to $D'D'$)	15	140
Initial price: higher elasticity (along $D''D''$)	15	100
Price reduction(along $D''D''$)	10	160

Figure 2-1. Demand.

to categories of goods or services of varying degrees of homogeneity or likeness. In fact, economists even talk about *aggregate demand* and *foreign demand* (the demand originating in the rest of the world for the entire range of goods and services produced by a given nation).

When applied to a single good, or a relatively homogeneous group of goods, the quantity demanded is generally related inversely to price. At high prices, very little will be bought, whereas at low prices the quantity demanded is likely to be quite large. Why? Because at lower prices consumers or users (*a*) find that their money income will buy more units of that particular product (and all other products as well), and (*b*) tend to substitute that product for other goods in their purchases.

The linear demand curve *DD* in Figure 2-1 is a graphical illustration of this relationship between quantity demanded and price, everything else being held constant. At a price of $15, 100 units will be demanded; at a lower price of $10, a larger quantity, 140 units, will be demanded.

Of course, the price of a good can be considered to be the sole determinant of quantity demanded *only* if we ignore all other factors that might influence consumer or user decisions to purchase. Clearly, per capita income, population, tastes, and prices of goods that are considered substitutes or complements will also affect demand. A change in any one of these will cause a *shift* in the demand curve; that is, more or less will be demanded at any stipulated price. In Figure 2-1, a decline in price from $15 to $10 brings forth an increase in quantity demanded from 100 to 140 units— a movement *along* the curve *DD*. But the same increase of 40 units in quantity demanded could be achieved without any decrease in price if incomes or tastes caused the entire demand curve to shift to the right. The relevant demand function is now *D′D′*, with 140 units demanded at the original price of $15. Thus, there is a crucial difference between changes in *quantity demanded*, which result from changes in price, and shifts in *demand*, which result from changes in variables other than the price of the product in question.

But how can we describe the *shape* of the initial demand curve? If the price of oranges declines by 10 percent, what will be the resultant change in the quantity of oranges demanded? This question involves the concept of *elasticity*, a quantitative measure of the response of the quantity demanded to given changes in price.

Referring once more to Figure 2-1, with the original demand curve *DD*, a decline in price of $5 brings forth an increase in quantity demanded of 40 units. Now suppose the demand curve had been *D″D″* instead. The same $5 price reduction would have resulted in an increase in quantity demanded of 60 units. Clearly, the quantity demanded is thus substantially more responsive to price changes under demand curve *D″D″* than under *DD*. We say that the demand described by curve *D″D″* is more *elastic* in the range of prices examined than that represented by curve *DD*.

Elasticity is measured in terms of relative changes in quantity and price, essentially by a ratio of percentages. If we define Δ (delta) as a "small change" in a variable, the formula for the elasticity of the demand curve is

$$e_p = \frac{\frac{\Delta Q}{Q}}{\frac{-\Delta P}{P}} = \frac{P \Delta Q}{Q(-\Delta P)} = \frac{\Delta Q}{-\Delta P} \times \frac{P}{Q}$$

In Figure 2-1, the elasticity of curve *DD* is 0.80 and the elasticity of curve *D″* is 1.20, for the prices examined. Whereas the *slope* of a linear demand function, defined as $\frac{-\Delta P}{\Delta Q}$, is constant, the *elasticity* changes throughout its length; the elasticity coefficient, *e*, is large (elastic) at its upper end and small (inelastic) at its lower end. By applying some numerical figures to the example, the reader can verify this. If the elasticity coefficient turns out to have a value of 1 at some point on the curve, we call it *unitary* elasticity; that is, a 1 percent decline in price will call forth exactly a 1 percent increase in quantity demanded. Only if the demand function is a rectangular hyperbola, convex to the origin, will it have unitary elasticity throughout its length.

Finally, and of particular importance to our later discussions, is the implicit change in total expenditure. If the demand for a certain good is elastic, a decline in price will result in a rise in total expenditure on that product, because the percentage increase in quantity bought is, by definition, greater than the percentage price reduction. Conversely, a price reduction in a product characterized by an inelastic demand will bring about a reduction in total expenditure on it. Exactly the opposite holds true for price *increases* with elastic and inelastic demand functions, respectively; that is, a price rise under inelastic demand conditions results in an expansion of expenditures, whereas elastic demand conditions will cause an expenditure decline.

There are other concepts of demand elasticity, notably those measuring demand responses to variables other than the price of the good itself; among them, the *cross-elasticity of demand* and the *income elasticity of demand* are two of special interest. If we let A and B represent two goods, then the cross-elasticity of demand for A can be defined as the responsiveness of the quantity demanded of good A to changes in the price of good B. Algebraically, this can be writtten as

$$e_{AB} = \frac{\frac{\Delta Q_A}{Q_A}}{\frac{\Delta P_B}{P_B}}$$

If the two products are complements to one another (e.g., nuts and bolts), the cross-elasticity of demand will have a *negative* sign; if they are substitutes (e.g., aluminum and steel), the sign will be *positive*.

Income elasticity of demand, on the other hand, measures the degree of responsiveness of quantity demanded to a change in income. Accordingly, this relation may be written as follows:

$$e_y = \frac{\frac{\Delta Q}{Q}}{\frac{\Delta Y}{Y}}$$

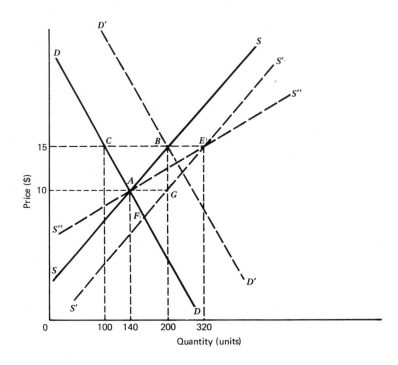

	Price ($)	Quantity (units)
Initial price (*SS*)	10	140
Increased price (*SS*)	15	200
Shift in supply (*S'S'*)	10	200
Initial price: higher elasticity (*S"S"*)	10	140
Increased price (*S"S"*)	15	320
Market surplus (*DD, SS*)	15	100
Market equilibrium (*DD, SS*)	10	140
Equilibrium with demand shift (*D'D', SS*)	15	200

Figure 2-2. Supply and equilibrium.

SUPPLY AND MARKET EQUILIBRIUM

An analysis similar to that just completed may be made of the supply of a given product or group of products. It seems natural that at low prices producers would be willing to provide the market with a smaller quantity of goods than at higher prices. Hence, we would expect the supply curve to be upward sloping, as, for instance, curve *SS* in Figure 2-2. That is, quantity supplied is directly related to price. But we do not have to rely on pure intuition to tell us that the supply curve should normally be upward sloping.

Without going very deeply into production theory, we can say that the short-run supply curve of a given firm is based on its *marginal cost*— the change brought about in its total variable costs as a result of a single additional unit of output. Up to a point, marginal cost falls with each additional unit of output because the efficiency with which variable inputs are used increases with output, and this results in successively lower variable costs per each *additional* unit of production. Thereafter, the degree of efficiency with which variable inputs are being used declines, and hence variable costs per each additional unit of production increase. We assume that most firms are operating under conditions of increasing marginal costs (on the upward-sloping part of the U-shaped marginal-cost curve), and that the supply curve for a firm is therefore upward sloping.

Although this justification for an upward-sloping supply curve is based on the economics of a single firm and holds only in the short run, it can be demonstrated that it is a more general phenomenon. It can apply as well, though for different reasons, to the long-run cost behavior of a firm, and possibly to the output of entire industries. Nevertheless, we cannot completely assume away the possible existence of constant costs or even decreasing costs (flat or downward-sloping supply curves) under certain circumstances, as we shall see later on.

Returning once more to the supply curve SS in Figure 2-2, we must make the same distinction between changes in quantity supplied in response to price changes on one hand, and shifts in the supply schedule on the other, as we made in the case of demand. A price increase of $5 causes producers to supply an additional amount of 60 units—a change in *quantity supplied*. The same 60-unit quantity increase would be achieved without any change in the price of $10, if the entire supply curve were to shift to the right, from SS to S'S'. Such supply shifts could result from changes in the cost and availability of inputs, or perhaps from the introduction of cost-saving technological innovations.

The question of elasticity also enters into the analysis of supply. If the market price of a good rises by 1 percent, by what percentage are producers willing to increase their output? Supply elasticity is defined as the degree of responsiveness of the output supplied by producers to changes in the price they receive. Given the supply function SS in Figure 2-2, an increase in price of $5 brings with it a rise in quantity supplied of 60 units. If, instead, the relevant supply function were S"S", then the same $5 price rise would cause quantity supplied to grow by 180 units. Quite obviously, 180 is very much greater than 60, and we say that S"S" is substantially more elastic than SS in the range of prices examined.

The coefficient of supply elasticity at a given point on a supply curve may be stated by the relation

$$e_s = \frac{\frac{\triangle Q}{Q}}{\frac{\triangle P}{P}}$$

This is the same formula given for the point elasticity of demand, apart from the minus sign in the demand elasticity formula. The computed supply elasticity of curve SS in this case is 0.86, and the corresponding elasticity of curve $S''S''$ is 2.57.

Given a linear supply function and a linear demand function, it is possible to determine a unique equilibrium price and quantity sold, since both supply and demand are functions of price. In Figure 2-2, this equilibrium is at point A, with a price of $10 and sales of 140 units. Any price above $10 will result in an excess quantity supplied over quantity demanded—a *surplus* on the market. The existence of a surplus causes sellers to strive for elimination of their unwanted excess inventories, which drives the price downward. With a declining price, the quantity producers are willing to supply also declines, while the quantity demanded rises until equilibrium is reached at A. Conversely, if for some reason the prevailing price happens to be below equilibrium, quantity demanded exceeds quantity supplied and a *shortage* exists. If prices are free to move, the shortage will cause consumers or users to bid up the price, and as the price rises, the quantity producers are willing and able to supply will increase; meanwhile, some potential buyers may drop out of the market or reduce their demand for the commodity, thereby causing overall quantity demanded to fall. Again, the movement is toward equilibrium at A, the only point at which the system has no further tendency to change.

Shifts in supply or demand may be easily applied to this simple model. If, for any reason, demand rises from DD to $D'D'$ in Figure 2-2, then equilibrium moves from A to B, with attendant increases in price and output. If, on the other hand, supply rises from SS to $S'S'$, equilibrium moves from A to F and results in a reduced price and expanded output.

A SIMPLE TRADE MODEL

We can now put these basic demand and supply concepts to work in a simple model of international trade. Suppose we have a product that is made and consumed in two countries, A and B, and there is no trade between these countries. We shall also assume that there are no transport costs. According to Figure 2-3a, domestic demand equals domestic supply in country I at a price of $100 per unit. At any price below $100, quantity demanded exceeds quantity supplied by the horizontal distance between the two curves: this is the hypothetical *import demand* defined by curve D_I^M in Figure 2-3b. At any price above $100 the reverse is true, and a hypothetical

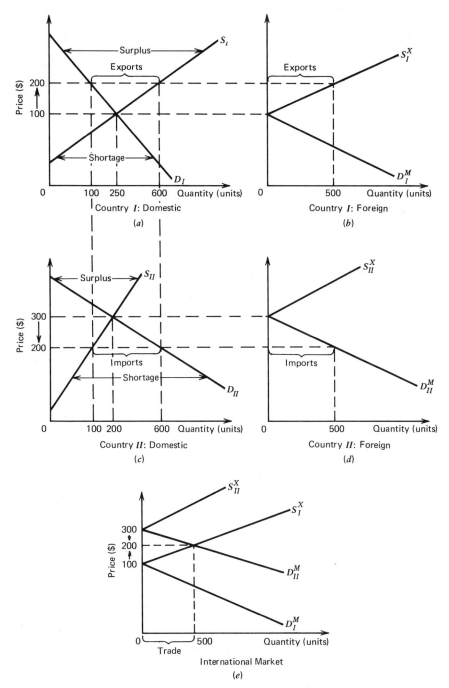

Figure 2-3. International trade in partial equilibrium. See legend on next page.

27

Variable	Without Trade	With Trade
Price in I	$100	$200
Price in II	$300	$200
Quantity supplied in I	250 units	600 units
Quantity demanded in I	250	100
Quantity supplied in II	200	100
Quantity demanded in II	200	600
Export supply in I	0	500
Export supply in II	0	0
Import demand in I	0	0
Import demand in II	0	500
Volume of trade	0	500

export supply is generated as domestic surpluses become available, defined by curve S_I^X in Figure 2-3b. At any given price, $S_I^X = S_I - D_I$ and $D_I^M = D_I - S_I$, with $S = D_I$ (zero import demand and export supply) at a price of $100. The corresponding domestic situation is depicted in Figure 2-3c for the second country, with an equilibrium price of $300; its export supply and import demand curves likewise are derived as D_{II}^M and S_{II}^X in Figure 2-3d.

Since country II's equilibrium price of $300 exceeds the $100 equilibrium price in country I, we know that when we open the system to trade, some quantity of the product will flow from country I to country II. As goods flow into II from I, the price in I will begin to rise and the price in II will begin to fall, until they become equal at $200 in Figure 2-3$e$ and there is no more profit or gain to be made by additional trade. At that price, I's export supply exactly equals II's import demand at 500 units. Once prices are equalized in the two countries, trade does not cease; it continues at that volume which in each time period serves to equalize prices.

Note that elasticities have a great deal to do with the volume of trade that develops. For instance, American demand for Swiss cheese (the real kind, imported from Switzerland) depends, in part, on the price of various types of Dutch cheese; comparison shopping by American consumers makes the cross-elasticity positive, and price cuts by Dutch dairy farmers would probably cut into our Swiss cheese consumption. The sharp hikes in world-wide energy prices during the 1970s reflected, among other things, the low short-run supply elasticities in the energy-producing sectors of industrial countries. Yet in this model, we considered only a single product and only two countries, *without* regard to what is happening in the rest of the world or in other product markets—what is called a *partial-equilibrium* model.

SUMMARY

In this chapter we have tried to develop a commonsense, intuitive theory of international trade. The reason why nations trade is that it pays to do so.

On the supply side, the availabilities and costs of labor, capital, raw materials, and other inputs differ among countries, as do technology and the efficiency with which inputs are used; therefore, the costs of tradable products will differ. On the demand side, tastes and incomes tend to differ among countries. Supply and demand forces produce international price differences, which in turn create the profit opportunities that trigger international trade flows. Sellers can market their goods and services abroad at a higher price than they could obtain at home, and buyers can purchase goods and services from abroad at a lower price than at home. These possibilities can make individuals, groups, and countries more productive and better off. They create the gains from international trade.

Important Concepts

interregional (vs. international) trade	division of labor
factor intensity	elasticity
factor abundance	marginal cost
productivity	export supply
demand	import demand
supply	partial equilibrium

Questions

1. Having considered at an intuitive level the reasons for, and gains from, trade among nations, what role do you see for the *market* as an institution? Can you list some characteristics of *efficient* markets in allocating production and consumption globally?

2. Referring back to Figure 2-3, what would be the impact of an increase in demand for the product in country A? What would be the effect of an increase in supply of the product in country A?

3. Again referring to Figure 2-3, suppose you were a consumer in country A. How would you feel about an increase in demand for the product in country B? How would you go about assessing the impact of such a change on your own welfare?

4. The results in Figure 2-3 are based on *partial-equilibrium* analysis. Suppose we took into account the effects of trade in this product on all producers and consumers of all goods and services in countries A and B, and the feedback of these effects on the market for the single product with which we began. Would our original results necessarily hold? Why or why not? How would you go about evaluating this feedback?

Further Readings

Baldwin, R. E., and J. D. Richardson, *International Trade and Finance* (Boston: Little Brown, 1974). An excellent policy-oriented book of readings that applies some of the concepts we shall discuss.

Ingram, James C., *International Economic Problems* (New York: Wiley, 1978).

Kindleberger, C. P., *Foreign Trade and the National Economy* (New Haven: Yale University Press, 1962).

Mansfield, Edwin, *Principles of Economics*, 3rd edition (New York: W. W. Norton, 1980). A first-level textbook recommended for students requiring a basic review of microeconomic theory.

3

INTRODUCTION
TO TRADE
THEORY

Among other things, international trade theory helps to explain the direction and composition of commerce among nations, and its effects on the structure of national economies. In the real world, there are some 150 countries, each of which could conceivably export to—and import from—each of the others. And there are several thousand "products" that could enter into international trade—the exact number depends on how narrowly the term is defined.

If we combine the countries and the products, we end up with the three-dimensional matrix depicted in Figure 3-1A—for example, the United States sells $3 million worth of cows to France and $18 million worth to Japan, whereas France sells $1 million worth of cows to the United States and $2 million worth to Japan in a given year. Each cell or "cube" in the box contains a number—the money value (or physical amount) of one particular product that is exported from one country to another. If there are indeed 150 countries in the world and 2000 clearly identifiable traded products, then our trade matrix would contain 45 million cells! The cells along the diagonal between the upper-left and the lower-right corners of the front of the box have no entries because they represent *intra*national trade. The entries in many of the cells are zero—for example, it is not likely that Upper Volta exports mainframe computers to Paraguay. One of the principal tasks of trade theory is to explain why the many cells in our matrix contain the entries they do. These entries, which can be looked up in trade statistics published by the United Nations and other organizations, give us the *volume, direction,* and *composition* of international trade—*who* trades *what* with *whom.*

The linkage between a country's international trade and its domestic economy can be depicted as in Figure 3-1B, which represents a simple "input-output" table that defines the transactions among the various sectors of a single national economy. For example, the first row of the matrix tells us how

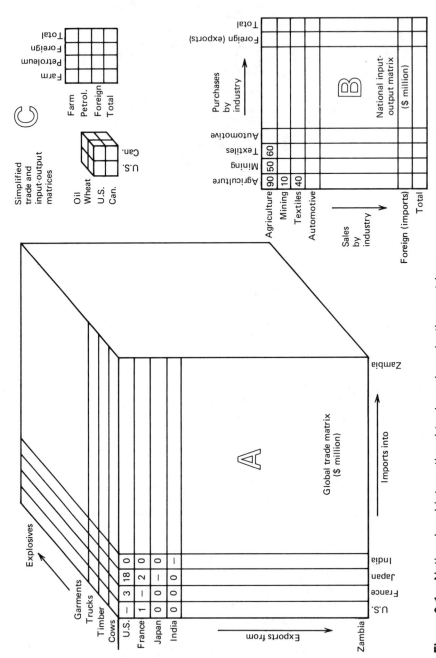

Figure 3-1. National and international trade and production matrices.

much the agricultural sector sells to itself ($90 million), to the mining sector ($50 million), to the textile sector ($60 million), and so on, including how much it sells to the foreign sector—its exports. Similarly, the first column tells us how much the agricultural sector buys from itself ($90 million), from mining ($10 million), from the textile sector ($40 million), and so on, and from the foreign sector—its imports. The bottom right-hand cell totals all purchases, or all sales, in the economy, and is a gross measure of national economic transactions. If there are some 300 industries in an economy, this matrix will have 90,000 cells—many of which again will be empty, depending on how large, diverse, and highly developed the country is.

Clearly, matrices A and B in Figure 3-1 are interrelated. A shift either in exports (a horizontal slice) or in imports (a vertical slice) in the trade matrix (A) will represent a shift in the foreign sector of the input-output matrix (B). A shift in a country's exports or imports will have implications both for the industries directly involved and for the industries supplying them, or buying from them. Similarly, a significant change in demand or supply in the B matrix may, through the trade linkage, produce a shift in trade flows in the A matrix.

We thus can visualize something like a 45-million-cell trade matrix, with each country's horizontal slice hooked into the export side of its input-output matrix, and each country's vertical slice hooked into the import side of its input-output table, with each input-output matrix containing some 90,000 cells. This incredibly complex set of matrices is ultimately what the theory of international trade tries to explain and predict. To simplify the problem and make it amenable to geometrical and algebraic analysis, economists have traditionally limited themselves to the so-called 2 × 2 × 2 model—two countries, two products, and two factors of production. Figure 3-1C shows the 2 × 2 trade matrix and input-output table that correspond to the matrices in Figures 3-1A and 3-1B. As we shall see, the principles that allow us to analyze the behavior of the simple model also tell us a great deal about the real world.

The discussion in Chapter 2 was intended to provide an intuitive "feel" for the circumstances determining international trade flows. The simple partial-equilibrium model presented at the end of that chapter was included to provide a similar "feel" for the usefulness of abstract models in depicting real-world behavior. That model considered trade between two countries in a single product. What happens when we add a second product and move closer to describing an entire (albeit simple) national economy?

ABSOLUTE ADVANTAGE

Suppose we look at a hypothetical world composed of only two countries, Canada and the United States. Both countries produce significant quantities of wheat and corn for domestic consumption, and there are, at first, absolutely

no trade relations, factor movements, or other economic ties between them—
each is assumed to be operating in a state of *isolation*. Also assume for the moment that the entire cost or value of the two products is the amount of labor
used in their production; ignore the costs of land and capital inputs. Now suppose, further, that one hour of labor can produce the following quantities of
wheat and corn in the two countries:

| | *Output of One Hour of Labor* | |
Product	United States	Canada
Wheat (bu.)	2	5
Corn (bu.)	20	10

In the time it takes a person to produce one bushel of wheat in the United
States (one-half hour), he or she can produce 10 bushels of corn. So a bushel of
wheat in the United States is ten times as costly and valuable as a bushel of
corn. Things are a little different in Canada. There it takes a person only one-
fifth hour to produce a bushel of wheat, yet he or she can turn out only 2
bushels of corn in that period of time. Therefore, a bushel of wheat in Canada
has only twice the value of a bushel of corn. Furthermore, the productivity of
labor in wheat growing is $2\frac{1}{2}$ times as high in Canada as it is in the United
States. Conversely, in corn production U.S. productivity is twice what it is in
Canada. Apparently the United States has an *absolute advantage* in the production of corn, and Canada has an *absolute advantage* in the production of
wheat.

Would it not pay, under such conditions, for the two countries to trade with
one another? The *direction* that trade would take can be determined immediately. Canada would export wheat to the United States, in return for
which the United States would export corn to Canada. Referring to Figure
3-2, it is clear that an enterprising American could take 20 bushels of U.S.
corn to Canada, exchange them there for 10 bushels of Canadian wheat, and
transport the wheat back to the United States. His 20 bushels of corn would
have brought him only 2 bushels of wheat if he had exchanged them domestically in the United States. His profit from trade, measured in wheat and
assuming no transport costs: 8 bushels. If trade were opened up under these
conditions, we would expect a large volume of such transactions, with both
countries gaining access to additional goods in the process. Relative prices of
the two products would ultimately be equalized between the two countries.
The United States would specialize increasingly in corn production, and
Canada in wheat production.

This simple method of absolute advantage illustrates what classical economists such as Adam Smith (1723-1790) believed governs international trade.

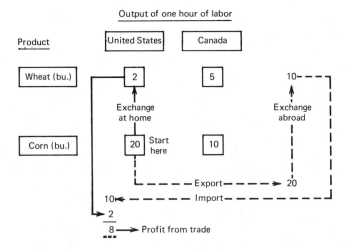

Figure 3-2. Barter trade under absolute advantage.

Based on the "labor theory of value," this model assumes that labor is completely free to move interregionally within a single country, yet is entirely immobile internationally. By contrast, if labor were free to move between nations, then differences in wage rates—and hence product prices—could be equalized via labor migration, and there would be no need for international trade. It is also assumed that transportation costs are negligible and that there are no other barriers to trade, such as protectionist tariffs and quotas.

Under these assumptions, absolute advantage might seem to be a good representation of the forces governing global commerce. But what if one country has an absolute advantage in the production of *all* products? According to the absolute advantage concept, there then could be no trade, since the country having the absolute advantage would have nothing to gain from exchanging its exports for imports.

COMPARATIVE ADVANTAGE

It remained for David Ricardo (1772-1823) and, later, John Stuart Mill (1806-1873) to develop a *general theory* of international trade that could explain the apparent existence of intercountry trade even in the absence of absolute advantage. In order to make explicit Ricardo's contribution—the theory of *comparative advantage*—let us change slightly the corn-wheat example, as follows:

| | *Output of One Hour of Labor* | |
Product	United States	Canada
Wheat (bu.)	10	8
Corn (bu.)	20	12

Note the difference. The United States now has an *absolute* advantage in the production of *both* wheat and corn, whereas in the earlier example it had an absolute advantage only in corn. Canada now has an absolute advantage in neither. We still apply the labor theory of value, along with the other assumptions made earlier. Under these conditions, will there be any trade between the two countries? The theory of absolute advantage would clearly deny this. Yet the theory of comparative advantage shows that there can be just as strong a basis for trade under these conditions.

Note that one hour of labor yields twice as much corn as wheat in the United States; hence, wheat will exchange for corn at a ratio of 1:2. In Canada, an hour of labor yields only 1½ times as much corn as wheat, for a Canadian domestic exchange ratio, wheat for corn, of 1:1½. In the United States, labor is twice as good at producing corn as it is at producing wheat, whereas in Canada it is only 1½ times as good at it. Conclusion: The United States has an *absolute* advantage in producing both, but it has a *comparative* advantage in producing corn; Canada has an *absolute* advantage in producing neither, but it does possess a *comparative* advantage in the production of wheat.

This situation is illustrated clearly in Figure 3-3. An American trader wishing to exchange corn for wheat within the United States could get only 10 bushels for 20 bushels of corn. But if, instead, he were to take his 20 bushels of U.S. corn to Canada, he could exchange it there for 13⅓ bushels of wheat, because the ratio of exchange in Canada is 1½:1 at the prevailing Canadian costs and prices. Taking his 13⅓ bushels of wheat back home, he finds that he has realized a trading profit, measured in wheat, of 3½ bushels. A Canadian trader could profit similarly by dealing in the opposite direction. Domestically he receives 12 bushels of corn for 8 bushels of wheat. But if he shipped the wheat across the U.S. border, he would receive 16 bushels of corn for it there. After returning the corn to Canada, he finds that he has realized a trading profit, in terms of corn, of 4 bushels.

The direction of trade in this simple model of comparative advantage is again easy to determine. Canada would export wheat to the United States in return for American exports of corn to Canada. Each country would begin to specialize in the production of that good in which it has a comparative advantage and import that good in which it has a comparative disadvantage. Trade between the two countries would flourish, and apparently both would be better off as a result; both would realize gains from international trade attributable to the difference in the prevailing corn:wheat exchange ratios. The United States is anxious for trade with Canada even though it can produce *both* pro-

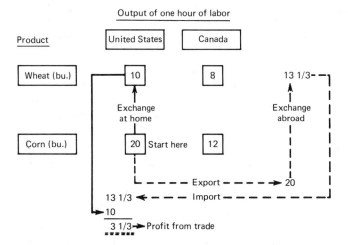

Figure 3-3. Barter trade under comparative advantage.

ducts more efficiently. In fact, it will be willing to trade corn for wheat—and will gain by doing so—as long as the Canadian corn-wheat exchange ratio is lower than the 2:1 figure that prevails within the United States. Should the Canadian ratio rise to 2:1, corn for wheat, neither country would possess even a comparative advantage. There would no longer be any reason for U.S.-Canadian trade to grow; since all prospects for further gain would have disappeared, trade would level off. Trade would remain at the level that led to the equalization of wheat:corn exchange ratios between the two countries. If they were equal to begin with, trade would be zero.

COMPARATIVE ADVANTAGE WITH MONEY

The principle of comparative advantage can be made a little clearer by repeating the example just presented in monetary terms. This enables us to show that *real* cost differences in comparative advantage actually translate into the monetary price differences to which we intuitively attributed international trade in the last chapter.

Suppose the prevailing wage rate in Canada is ten Canadian dollars (C$10) per hour, and the American wage rate is ten U.S. dollars (US$10) per hour. Translating Figure 3-3 into money costs, we would be left with the following:

	Cost of One Unit	
	United States	Canada
Wheat (bu.)	US$1.00	C$1.25
Corn (bu.)	US$0.50	C$0.83

We assume that the total labor cost equals the selling price in each case. Since one hour of labor produces twice as much corn as wheat in the United States, the price of a bushel of corn is half that of a bushel of wheat. In Canada, one hour of labor produces only 1½ times as much corn as wheat, and hence the price of a bushel of corn is two-thirds that of a bushel of wheat. Clearly, *relative prices* of the two products differ between the two countries.

But what about *absolute* prices? American traders know little about the price of Canadian wheat or corn in terms of their own currency—U.S. dollars—until they know the U.S. dollar value of one Canadian dollar—the *exchange rate*. Similarly, without knowing the exchange rate, Canadian traders have no information about the price of U.S. wheat and corn in their own currency.

Suppose the prevailing rate of exchange of the two currencies is C$1.00 = US$0.75 or, what is the same thing, US$1.00 = C$1.33. At the outset of trade, American corn exporters would realize about US$0.62 (C$0.83 × 0.75 = US$0.62) from every bushel of corn they sell to Canada, for a profit of US$0.12 per bushel. Canadian wheat exporters will receive C$1.33 (US$1.00 × 1.33 = C$1.33) for every bushel of wheat they sell in the United States, yielding a profit of C$0.08 per bushel. At that exchange rate, trade will occur in the same way as in the *barter* example given above. Because of increased demand, the price of corn will rise in the United States, and because of diminished demand for Canadian corn output, its price will fall in Canada. At the same time, the price of wheat will rise in Canada and fall in the United States. Eventually, the prices of the two products will be equalized in the two countries.

Suppose, on the other hand, the exchange rate of the two countries were C$1.00 = US$0.58, or US$1.00 = C$1.73. The U.S. corn exporter would not realize any profit in selling his product in Canada (C$0.83 × 0.58 = US$0.48), whereas Canadian wheat exporters would make enormous profits by selling in the United States (US$1.00 × 1.73 = C$1.73); and Canadian corn producers could also make small profits by exporting to Americans (at a price US$0.50 × 1.73 = C$0.86). Canadians would be more than willing to sell their wheat in the United States at that exchange rate, but Americans would not be willing to sell anything in Canada; hence there can be no two-way trade at that exchange rate. Conversely, the reader can easily work out that at an exchange rate of C$1.00 = US$1.25 (which equals US$1.00 = C$0.80) the positions would be reversed. American corn exporters would receive large gains in exporting to Canada, but Canadians would gain nothing in exporting wheat to the United States—and again there could be no two-way trade.

If we assume for the moment that economic relations between the two countries are completely limited to trade in wheat and corn, then the U.S. dollar value of American corn exports *must* equal the U.S. dollar value of American wheat imports, and the value of trade must be balanced. This can only occur at some exchange rate, *between* the limits of C$1.00 = US$0.58 and

C$1.00 = US$1.25, at which traders in *both* countries find it profitable to do business. Whatever this exchange rate turns out to be, the money value of trade between the two countries must be balanced at that particular rate of exchange of Canadian dollars for U.S. dollars. If it is not, then the exchange rate will shift to a point at which balance is restored. Later on, we shall have a great deal more to say about exchange-rate determination. We only need emphasize here that the rate of exchange between two national currencies may be essential to the direction and volume of trade basically predicted by the law of comparative advantage.

These examples should fix the concepts of absolute and comparative advantage clearly in the mind of the reader. Of the two, comparative advantage is the less restrictive and more general. Actually, the concept of comparative advantage is not limited to international transactions. It can be used to explain exchange between any two economic entities, even between individuals. The example of the manager and typist is often used to illustrate comparative advantage to beginning students of economics. The manager is both an excellent executive and a world-champion typist, whereas the typist cannot manage at all but can type reasonably well. Clearly, the manager has an *absolute* advantage in both managing and typing, whereas the typist has an *absolute* advantage in neither. Yet it obviously pays for the executive to hire the typist and concentrate his or her energies on managing, since this is where his or her *comparative* advantage lies, whereas the secretary indeed possesses a strong *comparative* advantage in typing.

In continuing the search for a general theory of international trade, we will extend our discussion of comparative advantage, trying to make it more detailed and a little less restrictive, and therefore more useful as a general analytical framework.

SPECIALIZATION

As a first step in this direction, we leave behind the labor theory of value, which we have adopted up to this point. The production of goods and services involves the use of land and capital as well as labor—that is, all of a nation's productive resources. Products are therefore valued according to the amount of land, labor, and capital that they embody. In addition, the assumption— implicit so far—that labor can legitimately be treated as a uniform factor of production clearly conflicts with reality. Labor varies widely in quality and enters the process of production in a variety of different ways. There is a way to abandon the labor theory of value, and yet retain the theory of comparative advantage as a principle of international trade.

Every beginning student of economics learns that a nation's economy possesses a certain maximum productive capacity, which is determined by the quantity of productive resources it has at its disposal—land, labor, natural resources, and capital—and that efficiency in resource use is in turn contingent on the level of technology, or useful knowledge. The student also learns that the nation may use this productive capacity in a variety of ways, and that it must make a number of choices regarding its priorities in output. The elementary "guns or butter" example offers a good illustration, in the simplest possible way, of the choices that must be made.

If we assume that a nation's production possibilities are limited to two types of goods, we can derive a so-called *transformation function*. The nation may choose, for instance, between private goods and public goods, war goods and peace goods, investment goods and consumption goods. In our example, we shall be a little more abstract, and from now on simply call the two types of outputs (like corn and wheat in our earlier examples) *A*-goods and *B*-goods.

In Figure 3-4, a typical transformation function (also known as the *production possibilities frontier*) is represented by line *ba*. If all of the nation's productive resources were used to produce *A*-goods, then quantity *Oa* of *A* would be produced. Conversely, if all resources were applied to the production of *B*-goods, then *Ob* of *B* would be produced. Given the transformation function *ba*, various combinations of *A* and *B* along it could be produced. Production at a point inside the area bounded by curve *ba* would mean that the nation is not using its output capability to its fullest extent. That is, it would be operating with less than full employment of its various resources, or not using them as efficiently as possible with existing technology. On the other hand, it would be impossible to produce at a point outside the production possibilities frontier *ba*, because the latter is *defined* by the total productive capacity under conditions of full employment. Hence, if the nation fully used all of its productive capabilities, it would be producing somewhere along line *ba*.

Now suppose there is a technological advance in the production of *A*-goods. By again fully employing its resources, the nation could produce *Oa'* of *A*-goods instead of *Oa*. This would result in a new transformation curve, *ba'*, somewhere along which there would be a new production point. Obviously, curve *ba'* lies outside line *ba*, and the nation can now raise its total output, while using the same quantity of resources, because of the advance in technology used in the production of *A*-goods. Something similar would be true if, instead, technology used in the production of *B*-goods became more advanced (*b'a*), if the technology level rose in the production of both goods (for example, *b'a'*), or if additional productive resources became available.

Under any transformation function, the economy must give up some quantity of one good in order to increase output of the other. For example, if (under the transformation function *ba'*) in order to get one additional unit of the *B*-good, the economy had to give up two units of the *A*-good, the marginal rate of transformation of *A*-goods for *B*-goods would be 2. When these production shifts are small, the rate at which they occur is defined by the *marginal rate of transformation*. Graphically, the marginal rate of trans-

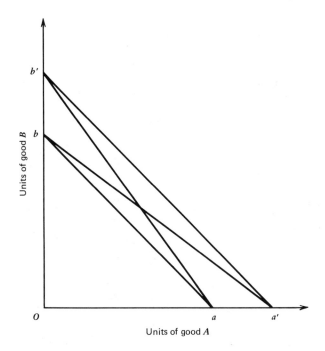

Figure 3-4. Transformation functions.

formation is shown by the slope of the transformation function at each point along the curve.

The transformation functions that we have described here are *linear*. This means that the marginal rate of transformation is constant throughout their respective lengths. We must give up a certain number of units of *A*-goods to be able to produce one extra unit of *B*-goods, no matter which point along these curves we are talking about.

Figure 3-5 illustrates one of the highly simplified straight-line transformation functions delineating the hypothetical capacity to supply two products, *A*-goods and *B*-goods, by the United States and the United Kingdom. If the United States uses all of the factors of production at its disposal in the most efficient possible way, it can produce either 50 units of *B* or 30 units of *A*, or any combination of the two along transformation curve *WX*. By the same token, the United Kingdom can produce either 15 units of *B* or 30 units of *A*, or any combination thereof along transformation curve *YZ*.

Note that the transformation functions here are linear, meaning that *constant opportunity costs* prevail. If it is decided to produce one additional unit of *B* in the United States, the economy must *always* sacrifice 0.6 units of *A* to do so. This is true no matter whether a great deal of *B* and little *A* is

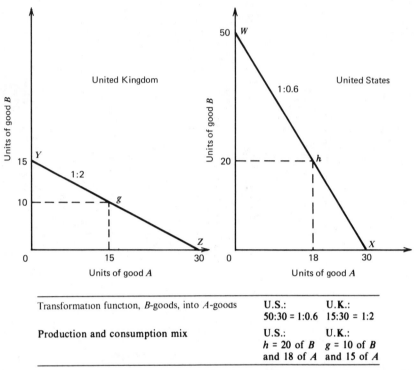

Transformation function, B-goods, into A-goods	U.S.:	U.K.:
	50:30 = 1:0.6	15:30 = 1:2
Production and consumption mix	U.S.:	U.K.:
	h = 20 of B	g = 10 of B
	and 18 of A	and 15 of A

Figure 3-5. Production and consumption in isolation: constant opportunity costs.

produced, or vice versa. Constant opportunity costs also prevail in the United Kingdom, except that there, the addition to output of one unit of B always calls for the reduction in A output by 2 units. In short, the *marginal rate of transformation* of B into A is 1:0.6 in the United States and 1:2 in the United Kingdom.

In the hypothetical isolated state, the consumption alternatives of the two countries are entirely defined by their respective production possibilities frontiers. Americans can consume anywhere along curve WX, and the British can consume anywhere along curve YZ. The precise consumption point in each case will be determined by the relative tastes and preferences in the two countries; for example, at points g and h in Figure 3-5.

The marginal rate of transformation, as we noted, reflects the relative prices of goods B and A. In the United States, one unit of B "costs" 0.6 units of A, and in the United Kingdom the same unit of B "costs" 2 units of A. It would appear that good B is in a real sense cheaper in the former country, whereas good A is cheaper in the latter. The United States has a comparative advantage in the production of good B, whereas the United Kingdom has a comparative advantage in the production of good A.

According to the theory of comparative advantage, the two nations would do well to trade, with the United States exporting good B to the United Kingdom in return for good A. Both should be able to enhance their economic well-being by so doing. In order to show this, let us simply place both the U.S. and the U.K. transformation curves on the same diagram, as in Figure 3-6, so that they touch at point X (or Z). Note that the British $B:A$ exchange ratio of 1:2, the slope of the line, has not been changed in the process.

GAINS FROM TRADE

Without trade, in our hypothetical situation, let us say that the United Kingdom is producing and consuming 15 units of good A and 10 units of good B at point b on its transformation curve YX. Let us assume, further, that the United States is consuming and producing at point e on its transformation curve WX. Now trade opens, and in response to the new opportunities for profits through exports, producers in the United Kingdom will tend to *specialize* completely in the making of good A. The United Kingdom thus produces 30 units of good A, yet may decide to continue consuming only 15 units of this, and to export the rest (15 units) to the United States. If it were possible to trade at the American $B:A$ exchange ratio of 0.6, the British exports of 15 units of good A would yield 25 units of imports of B. Britain can now consume the same amount of good A as before, but a great deal more of good B (25 units versus 10 units before trade, a gain of 15 units). Clearly, trade has enabled the United Kingdom to move from consumption point b to point c, which represents a much higher level of economic well-being, and which it could never have achieved in isolation.

What happens is that the British *production* possibilities frontier remains YX, but its *consumption* possibilities frontier becomes WX, which lies above YX no matter how much of good B or good A the United Kingdom decides to consume. For its part, the United States is neither better nor worse off than without trade. It simply produces less of good A and more of good B than before—it moves *along* its transformation curve from e to some other point on it. It is the United Kingdom that receives all of the gains from trade, equal to the quantity bc (15 units) of good B or, more generally, the vertical difference between WX and YX.

The example could easily be reversed, with the United States specializing in production of the B-good and exporting its B surplus to the United Kingdom for exchange into A-goods at Britain's prevailing 1:2 exchange ratio of B-goods for A-goods. In this case, the United States would be able to attain a substantially higher welfare level than that permitted by its own transformation curve and its own domestic exchange ratio, and would thus obtain most of the gains. But from the information given here, we cannot yet determine the

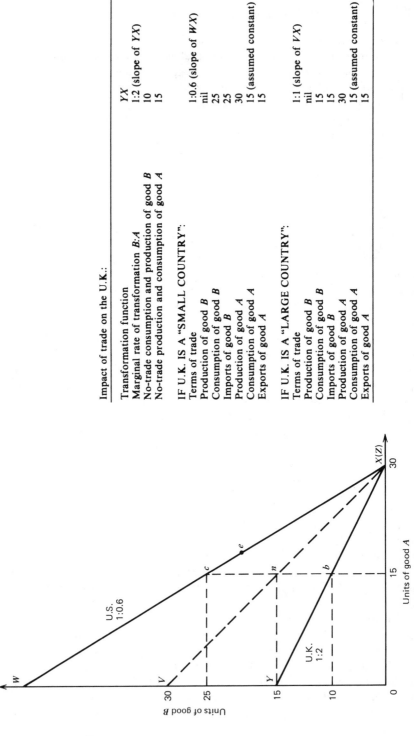

Figure 3-6. Production and consumption with trade: constant opportunity costs.

Impact of trade on the U.K.:

Transformation function	YX
Marginal rate of transformation B:A	1:2 (slope of YX)
No-trade consumption and production of good B	10
No-trade production and consumption of good A	15

IF U.K. IS A "SMALL COUNTRY":

Terms of trade	1:0.6 (slope of WX)
Production of good B	nil
Consumption of good B	25
Imports of good B	25
Production of good A	30
Consumption of good A	15 (assumed constant)
Exports of good A	15

IF U.K. IS A "LARGE COUNTRY":

Terms of trade	1:1 (slope of VX)
Production of good B	nil
Consumption of good B	15
Imports of good B	15
Production of good A	30
Consumption of good A	15 (assumed constant)
Exports of good A	15

position of the international exchange ratio (the *commodity terms of trade*) VX, except to say that it will always lie somewhere between WX and YX, so that both countries have something to gain from trade.

In short, if both countries are indeed to gain from international trade, the total *combined* output of both goods by the two countries, after trade is opened up, must exceed combined output of the two products before trade. These global output gains attributable to specialization in production are then divided between the two countries according to the final position of the international exchange ratio (VX) of the two products.

BIG COUNTRIES AND LITTLE COUNTRIES

Referring once again to Figure 3-5, recall that the absolute productive capacity for goods B and A was much more limited in Britain than in the United States, as Britain's transformation curve lies well within that of the larger country. What does this mean for the conclusions just presented?

First, if the British economy is much smaller than the American, the limited British supply capability effectively limits the volume of trade that can develop between the two countries. Even with complete U.K. specialization in good A, the difference between this level of output and domestic consumption is all that can be exported at the prevailing international exchange ratio for a certain amount of imported good B. Hence the size of the small country tends to determine the *upper limit* of the realizable volume of trade.

Second, chances are that the small country can achieve very favorable conditions of exchange for itself. A very small nation cannot significantly affect prices in a very big country, no matter how much it buys or sells in the latter's market, simply because it is not a large enough factor in the market to matter very much. For example, Costa Rica is unlikely to be able to sell enough sugar in the United States, or buy enough airplanes, to affect the U.S. price of either product. This means that the small country is likely to be able to trade at or near the *domestic* exchange ratio obtaining in the large country and hence—as we have seen—capture for itself the lion's share of the net gains from trade. This has been called "the significance of being insignificant," and, as we shall see, can often be quite important from a policy point of view.

TERMS OF TRADE

The international exchange ratio just mentioned is generally known as the *terms of trade* or, more accurately, the *commodity terms of trade*. The quantity of good B that exchanges for good A is the same as the ratio of the price of good A relative to the price of good B. If the ratio at which a country can acquire import goods in exchange for its export goods rises, we say that its commodity terms of trade *improve* or become *more favorable*.

To refer once more to Figure 3-6, the closer the commodity terms of trade (VX) settle to the U.S. domestic $B:A$ exchange ratio, the more favorable they will be to the United Kingdom, and the greater will be the latter's relative gain from international trade. At the same time, the American commodity terms of trade will be less favorable, and its gain from trade smaller. In the examples discussed so far, using a two-country, two-product model with constant opportunity costs, the *limits* to the commodity terms of trade are set by the initial domestic exchange ratios in the two countries, and the *actual* commodity terms of trade are determined by the forces of international demand.

The commodity terms of trade, as we have used them here, are relatively easy to compute. If the United States exports 1 unit of B and receives in return 2 units of A, its commodity terms of trade would be substantially more favorable than if it received only 1 unit of A for that unit of B. And the United Kingdom would consider its commodity terms of trade much more advantageous if it received 1 unit of B for 1 unit of A than if it had to export 2 units of A to get that unit of B. Commodity terms of trade that are relatively favorable for the United States signify relatively unfavorable commodity terms of trade for the United Kingdom, and vice versa. Similarly, *deteriorating* commodity terms of trade for one country must mean *improving* commodity terms of trade for the other in a two-country world.

The terms of trade can also be expressed on a monetary basis. For example, suppose the prevailing international price of good A is \$5.00, and the price of good B is \$2.50, with free international trade between the United States and the United Kingdom. The British commodity terms of trade are thus \$5.00/\$2.50, which equals 2. Now suppose American demand for good A suddenly expands, so that its price rises to \$6.00. We thus find the British commodity terms of trade improving (\$6.00/\$2.50 = 2.4) as the price of its export good (A) has risen while the price of its import good (B) has remained the same. It will receive more B-goods in return for each unit of exported A-goods than before the price of A rose. Simultaneously, the U.S. commodity terms of trade have deteriorated to the same degree. One word of warning: A deterioration in a country's commodity terms of trade doesn't necessarily mean that it is absolutely worse off. Even though its *share* of the gains from trade may have declined, the absolute *size* of those gains may have increased more than enough to offset this. The country may get a smaller slice of a significantly larger pie, and actually end up with more goods than before.

SUMMARY

We have discussed the principle of comparative advantage as an explanation of international trade by means of a simple two-country, two-product model. Trade is found to stem from differing production functions, or product-exchange ratios, between countries. Under constant opportunity costs, trade can result in the complete specialization of one or both countries in the production of a single product, with a resulting growth in the combined production of all goods. Gains from international trade may accrue to one or both countries involved, depending upon the relative strength of demand in them. The global use of resources will be more efficient, and this is the source of the gains from trade that are divided between the two countries according to the final commodity terms of trade.

Important Concepts

volume of trade	specialization
direction of trade	transformation function
composition of trade	marginal rate of transformation
2×2×2 model	gains from trade
absolute advantage	terms of trade
labor theory of value	small-country case
comparative advantage	large-country case

Questions

1. Suppose we had a two-country world composed of the United States and Denmark. In trade between the two countries, who would obtain the lion's share of the gains from trade? Why?

2. Suppose the two countries in the previous question were Germany and France. How would your answer change? Why?

3. Why, in our analysis of two countries' trade in Figure 3-6, do we end up with *complete* specialization by at least one country in one particular product? Can you think of a case where complete specialization actually occurs in the real world? What kinds of conditions might prevent it?

4. How does trade equalize the price of a product among countries? What kinds of circumstances might prevent such price equalization? Once prices are equalized, what happens to trade?

Further Readings

Bhagwati, J., "The Pure Theory of International Trade: A Survey," *Economic Journal*, March 1964.

Chipman, J. S., "A Survey of the Theory of International Trade," *Econometrica*, July 1965.

Krauss, Melvyn B., *A Geometric Approach to International Trade* (New York: Halsted-Wiley, 1979). An outstanding, modern geometric treatment of trade theory.

Marshall, A., *The Pure Theory of Foreign Trade* (London: London School of Economics and Political Science, 1930).

Meade, J. E., *A Geometry of International Trade* (London: Allen & Unwin, 1952).

Meade, J. E., *Trade and Welfare* (London: Allen & Unwin, 1952).

4

SUPPLY-SIDE ANALYSIS

The theory of international trade has evolved historically with an almost exclusive focus on the supply elements: How much of what products and at what relative prices can individual nations produce and exchange among each other? Continuing on this track for a while, we will identify as many supply-related factors as possible before introducing the demand side of the picture. We shall start with the same basic trade model used in the last chapter, and retain some of the assumptions of that model, namely: (1) free mobility of productive factors within a country; (2) complete factor immobility between countries; (3) given, unchanging tastes; (4) no transportation costs; (5) unchanging technology and factor endowments; (6) no barriers to trade, such as tariffs and quotas; (7) pure competition in all markets, with no government intervention in these markets; and (8) full employment of productive resources. We will, however, relax the assumption of constant opportunity costs as a first step toward increased realism.

INCREASING OPPORTUNITY COSTS

The straight line AB in Figure 4-1a is a transformation curve depicting constant opportunity costs. At each point along AB, a fixed quantity of wheat must be sacrificed if one additional yard of cloth is to be produced, even though a great deal of cloth and very little wheat may actually be produced, or vice versa. We say that the marginal rate of transformation of wheat into cloth is constant—that is, there are constant opportunity costs—as assumed in the last chapter.

Suppose a country was faced instead with transformation curve CDE in Figure 4-1b. This implies that each of the factors of production is *uniquely* suited to the production of *either* wheat or cloth, and that labor, capital, or other resources cannot be reallocated from wheat to cloth (or vice versa) in order to produce more of one and less of the other. Given available resources and productivity, production could occur at *C* (wheat only), *E* (cloth only) or *D* (both wheat and cloth)—or at any intermediate points. Only point *D* would seem to make sense—unless the country has some pretty strange preferences—since obviously *C* + *E* is better than either *C* or *E* alone.

Now assume that, to the contrary, it is possible to transfer resources between wheat and cloth production at constant opportunity costs between specific production points, as in Figure 4-1c; that is, it is relatively cheap in terms of lost wheat output to increase production of cloth in moving from *F* (wheat only) to *G* (lots of wheat, some cloth). But in moving from *G* to *H*, the amount of wheat sacrificed for a given increase in cloth output is a good deal higher, because the marginal product (defined as the change in output resulting from a given change in a factor input) of labor or capital now transferred from farms to factories has risen in wheat and fallen in cloth. This shift in relative productivities continues, step by step, as we go from *H* to *I* and from *I* to *J*. Thus, the *I-J* move would result in a massive loss in wheat output in return for a fairly small gain in cloth output. With such constant opportunity costs *between* these alternative production points, we thus end up with transformation curve *FGHIJ* in Figure 4-1c.

In other situations, successively greater amounts of wheat may have to be sacrificed for the sake of each additional yard of cloth. Why? Common sense would suggest that a country that undertakes substantial specialization in one particular good would find it rather costly to specialize even further. Particularly, as the degree of specialization increases, factor prices may tend to change as well, and this can explain the gradual increase in opportunity costs. Such a condition is represented by the curvilinear transformation function *KL* in Figure 4-1d. No longer is the marginal rate of transformation, wheat into cloth, constant. Rather, the curve is characterized by a *diminishing* marginal rate of transformation of wheat into cloth throughout the length of the curve; hence, it is drawn concave to the origin.

Under constant opportunity costs, the cloth-wheat cost and price ratio is constant. This is true no matter how much wheat or cloth is being produced. Under increasing opportunity costs, however, the relative price of the two products changes throughout the transformation function. If a great deal of wheat and little cloth is being produced, the price of wheat is high relative to the price of cloth. Conversely, the production of large amounts of cloth and little wheat signifies a high price of cloth relative to that of wheat. Graphically, rates of exchange between the two commodities are given by the slope of a line drawn *tangent* to the transformation curve at the particular point at which production is actually carried out.

For instance, in Figure 4-1e, suppose it is decided to produce 12 million bushels of wheat and 10 million yards of cloth at point *T* on the increasing-

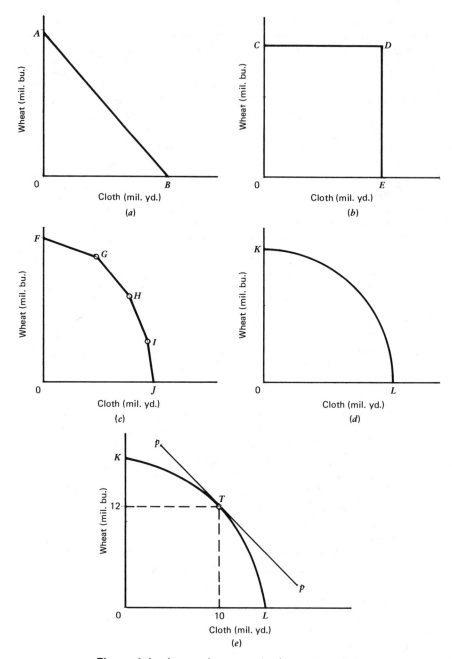

Figure 4-1. Increasing opportunity cost model.

opportunity-cost curve KL. At point T, the ratio at which wheat exchanges for cloth is given by the slope of the transformation curve at that point, and this is identical to the slope of a line pp drawn tangent to the transformation curve at T. It also indicates the relative price of wheat and cloth required to induce product markets to deliver the desired output mix, and to induce factor markets to distribute productive resources accordingly. In short, production and consumption of wheat (12 million bushels) and cloth (10 million yards) at point T means that the ratio of exchange of the two products will be the slope of pp. Note that if it is decided to produce more cloth and less wheat (i.e., move from T toward L), the slope of pp will increase—the relative price of cloth has to increase to induce cloth makers to produce more and to induce resources to shift from farms to textile factories. Similarly, a decision to increase wheat output (moving from T toward K) will mean a decline in the slope of pp.

TRADE UNDER INCREASING OPPORTUNITY COSTS: ONE COUNTRY

Now let us apply the notion of increasing opportunity costs to the model of international trade that we used earlier under the assumption of constant costs. In so doing, we will be adding a substantial degree of realism to even such a simple model, as increasing opportunity costs would seem to be a far better description of a nation's production alternatives which normally would seem to exist.

In Figure 4-2, suppose the United Kingdom is producing and consuming at point T (10 units of product B and 5 units of product A) in the absence of international trade. The prevailing domestic exchange ratio of product B to product A is given by the slope of line pp as 0.5:1, tangent to the U.K. transformation curve AB at point T. Suppose further that in the United States the prevailing domestic $B:A$ exchange ratio is 2:1, with product B being considerably less expensive relative to A than in the United Kingdom. Would it not pay for Britain to export some of product A in exchange for good B at the higher U.S. exchange ratio, given by the 2:1 slope of line p_ip_i? Yes. Britain could now move to point R on its transformation curve, specializing more in the production of product A by increasing its output of that commodity from 5 to 10 units and cutting back on B production from 10 to 5 units. If it chooses to continue to consume 5 units of A, it would have 5 units of A to export to the United States. In return for this, it would receive 10 units of product B at the indicated U.S. domestic exchange ratio.

As a result of international trade, therefore, Britain is able to consume 5 units more of B-goods, without consuming any fewer A-goods. It is clearly better off at consumption point S than at point T, and its gain from trade,

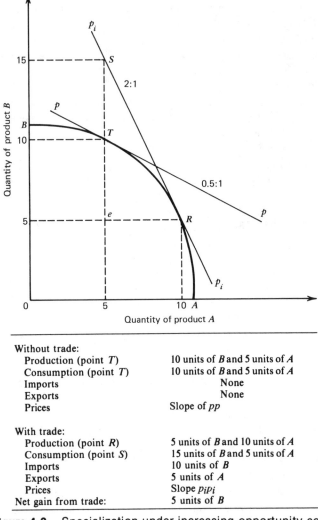

Figure 4-2. Specialization under increasing opportunity costs.

Without trade:	
Production (point *T*)	10 units of *B* and 5 units of *A*
Consumption (point *T*)	10 units of *B* and 5 units of *A*
Imports	None
Exports	None
Prices	Slope of *pp*

With trade:	
Production (point *R*)	5 units of *B* and 10 units of *A*
Consumption (point *S*)	15 units of *B* and 5 units of *A*
Imports	10 units of *B*
Exports	5 units of *A*
Prices	Slope $p_i p_i$
Net gain from trade:	5 units of *B*

measured in terms of *B*-goods, is 5 units. Of course, Britain could decide to consume more of *A*-goods, as well as *B*-goods, which would place the consumption point after trade somewhere between *S* and *R* on line $p_i p_i$. There would still be a gain from trade, since any such point would lie outside the U.K. transformation curve, and line $p_i p_i$ in effect becomes the country's consumption possibilities curve.

As long as the foreign exchange ratio between two products differs from the one at home, this model tells us that it pays for a country to trade internationally, and that it will gain in material well-being by doing so. The alert reader will immediately recognize this as nothing more than a restatement of the familiar principle of comparative advantage.

In the constant-opportunity-cost case, with a linear transformation curve, we found that one or both countries will specialize production entirely in one product. Under increasing opportunity costs, however, complete specialization is improbable, though not impossible. In Figure 4-2, the slope of line $p_i p_i$ would have to be very steep indeed in order to induce Britain to produce at, or close to, A, the point of complete specialization. Product B would have to be virtually worthless in terms of product A in order for this condition to occur. Britain would have to give up enormous amounts of good B as it approaches specialization in A-good production; this, again, is the principle of increasing opportunity costs.

If the international exchange ratio of B for A (the commodity terms of trade) turns out to be near that prevailing in the United States without trade, as in Figure 4-2, the United Kingdom will garner most of the gains from trade. The United States, on the other hand, will stand to gain very little. The reverse holds if the post-trade $B:A$ exchange ratio approximates the preexisting U.K. ratio. Much more likely, of course, is that the commodity terms of trade will settle somewhere between these two extremes, thus dividing the gains from trade between the two countries. Again, the exact position of the terms of trade will hinge on the relative strength of demand for products B and A in the two countries and on the relative sizes of the two countries.

TRADE UNDER INCREASING OPPORTUNITY COSTS: TWO COUNTRIES

Figure 4-3 depicts the two countries in more detail. In the absence of international trade, the United Kingdom is consuming and producing at point T (12 units of good B and 10 units of good A), and the domestic $B:A$ exchange ratio is given by the slope of line pp at 0.7:1. Similarly, in isolation the United States is operating at point V on its transformation curve, consuming and producing 10 units of B and 12 units of good A, the slope of line $p'p'$ being the domestic $B:A$ exchange ratio of 1:0.6. Now suppose that with international trade, the terms of trade—the international exchange ratio of B for A—settle at $p_i p_i$, or 1:1, which is now common to Britain and the United States. Given the terms of trade $p_i p_i$, the United States moves from the no-trade production point V (10 units of B and 12 units of A) along its transformation curve CD to point W (16 units of B and 8 units of A), thus expanding its production of good B. Assuming that it decides to hold constant its consumption of good B at 10 units, it can move its consumption of the imported good A to 14 units, exporting 6 units of good B to Britain in return for an equal quantity of good A. It gains from international trade in the amount of 2 units of imported A-goods.

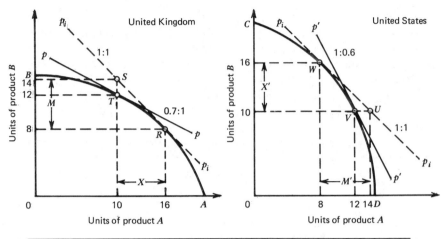

Figure 4-3. Trade under increasing opportunity costs.

	United Kingdom		United States	
	Good *B*	Good *A*	Good *B*	Good *A*
Without trade:				
Production	12	10	10	12
Consumption	12	10	10	12
Imports	none		none	
Exports	none		none	
Prices	Slope of *pp* (0.7:1)		Slope of *p′p′* (1:0.6)	
With trade:				
Production	8	16	16	8
Consumption	14	10	10	14
Imports	6	—	—	6
Exports	—	6	6	—
Prices	Slope of p_ip_i (1:1)		Slope of p_ip_i (1:1)	
Net gain from trade	2 units of good *B*		2 units of good *A*	

Meanwhile, Britain moves from its no-trade production and consumption point *T* (12 units of *B* and 10 units of *A*) on its transformation curve *BA*, to production point *R* (8 units of *B* and 16 units of *A*) at the international *B:A* exchange ratio p_ip_i (1:1). It expands its production of good *A* and cuts production of good *B*. If we assume that Britain will hold constant its consumption of good *A*, it will consume 10 units and export 6 units. In return, it will receive 6 units of good *B* from the United States, which permits consumption of 14 units of *B* at point *S*. The British gain from trade, measured in terms of its imported *B*-goods, is 2 units.

The total volume of trade in this example is 6 units of good *A* shipped from Britain to the United States, and 6 units of good *B* shipped from the United States to the United Kingdom. Each country increasingly produces that product in which it has a comparative advantage, thus moving toward greater specialization in it. Again, both nations gain.

FACTOR ENDOWMENTS

The theory of trade we have just developed is based on international differences in "conditions of production." Certain things seem to be produced better in some countries than in others, and this fact can apparently be exploited for everyone's benefit through trade. Technically, this has been expressed as differences between countries in transformation functions, or via production possibilities curves. But what is behind these differences? One traditional theory of comparative advantage, as we have seen, suggests international variations of *factor productivity*, or *efficiency*, as a basic reason.

A second fundamental cause of international differences in the conditions of production are variations in the *availability*, or endowments, of the factors of production—land, labor, and capital. This would attribute international (and interregional) differences in comparative costs to (*a*) different prevailing *endowments* of productive factors, and (*b*) the fact that the production of various commodities requires that the factors of production be used with different degrees of *intensity*. The quality of one unit of each factor of production is considered to be identical in both countries. Note the important difference between this approach and the earlier theory, which rested fundamentally on differing production characteristics and factor productivities as between countries.

Even at first glance, the factor endowment approach is appealing. It predicts that commodities requiring substantial amounts of labor should be produced in countries where labor is abundant relative to other factors of production, since wage costs will therefore be low relative to the cost of other inputs. These countries then export *labor-intensive* products to other nations where labor is relatively scarce and wage rates relatively high. Analogous rules should apply to products using the other factors of production intensively in their manufacture. Offhand, then, it would seem that Taiwan or Hong Kong should be specializing in labor-intensive goods and exporting them to Western Europe and the United States, and that Canada, Australia, and Argentina should be concentrating on the production of such *land-intensive* products as cereal grains, sheep, and cattle and be exporting them to Japan and Western Europe. The United States should specialize in the production of various types of machinery and other mass-produced items requiring plentiful capital and export them to various capital-poor areas of the world.

Figure 4-4 is an illustration of the pattern of world trade that accordingly might be expected to ensue. We are now using natural resources, labor, land, and capital as four distinct factors of production. If a certain good can be produced equally well by using either a lot of capital or a lot of labor, it may be difficult to characterize it as being either capital intensive or labor intensive. Obviously, a great many goods fall into this category, and it is necessary to know a good deal more about production techniques and costs before they can be fit into the overall scheme of trade theory.

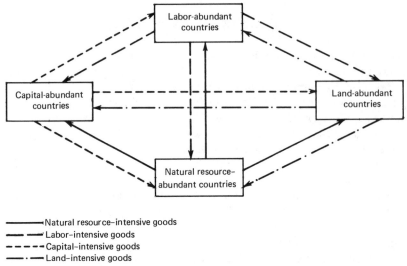

Figure 4-4. Factor endowments and the pattern of trade.

TRADE AND FACTOR PRICES

In labor-abundant countries, wages are likely to be low relative to the prices of other factors of production. Cheap, abundant labor used in the production of labor-intensive goods would seem to justify exports of labor-intensive products to other countries where this factor of production is scarce and wages are correspondingly higher. Similar principles ought to hold for other factors of production.

What, then, are the effects of international trade on the prices of productive factors? Suppose we take two countries, one (country L) labor abundant and the other (country K) capital abundant. Labor-intensive products begin to flow from country L to country K, whereas capital-intensive goods flow in the opposite direction. As more and more labor is demanded in country L for production of labor-intensive goods for export, wages begin to rise. Simultaneously, country L is importing capital-intensive goods from country K. This displaces domestic production of capital-intensive products, releasing large amounts of capital and thus lowering the cost of capital. In effect, net demand for the abundant factor (labor) increases and its price rises, while net demand for the scarce factor (capital) is reduced and its price falls, all as a result of international trade. Exactly the reverse happens in the capital-abundant country K.

As net demand for labor rises in country L and falls in country K, and net demand for capital rises in country K and falls in country L, will there not be a *tendency* for wages and the cost of capital, respectively, to equalize in the two countries? We have just seen that the answer to this question must be affirmative. Trade tends to equalize prices of the factors of production internationally. In fact, it may equalize relative factor prices just as effectively as if the productive factors themselves migrated from countries in which they are in relatively abundant supply to countries in which they are relatively scarce.

This can be nicely illustrated through a flow diagram such as that in Figure 4-5. In the top part of the diagram the export of labor-intensive goods from the labor-abundant country rises because of trade, causing output in that industry to expand. Being labor-intensive, that output growth absorbs a lot of labor and relatively little capital. Meanwhile, imports of capital-intensive goods into that economy rise as well, causing the domestic industry that competes with these imports to cut back production. Being capital-intensive, it releases a lot of capital and relatively little labor. What happens? Assuming fixed overall labor and capital supplies, the demand for labor rises relative to its supply, and the labor market tightens. At the same time, the demand for capital falls relative to its supply, and the capital market softens. So the price of labor rises relative to the price of capital.

Precisely the reverse happens in the capital-abundant country, when the price of labor *falls* relative to the price of capital. In both cases, the price of the abundant factor (which becomes relatively less abundant) rises relative to the price of the scarce factor (which becomes relatively less scarce). And when we compare the relative price of labor (or of capital) in the two countries, we note a clear tendency toward convergence. Under certain conditions, it can be shown that relative factor prices will be *completely* equalized—this is discussed in the Advanced Material section at the end of this chapter.

This overall concept is called the Heckscher-Ohlin theory of international trade, in honor of the two Scandinavian economists who developed it in the 1930s. It is clearly quite different from the classical Smith-Ricardo-Mill concept with which we started, developed more than a century earlier; in that concept, comparative advantage is based not on international differences in factor endowments but rather on differences in factor productivities.

SUMMARY

Unlike trade under constant opportunity costs, trade under increasing opportunity costs is unlikely to lead to complete specialization. The reason is that the opportunity cost, in terms of lost production of alternative types of goods, rises as more and more resources are pulled into the export sector. Nevertheless, trade permits a country to move to a higher consumption level than it could have achieved without trade.

Given that one of the principal sources of comparative advantage is differences in factor endowments, trade affects not only product prices and

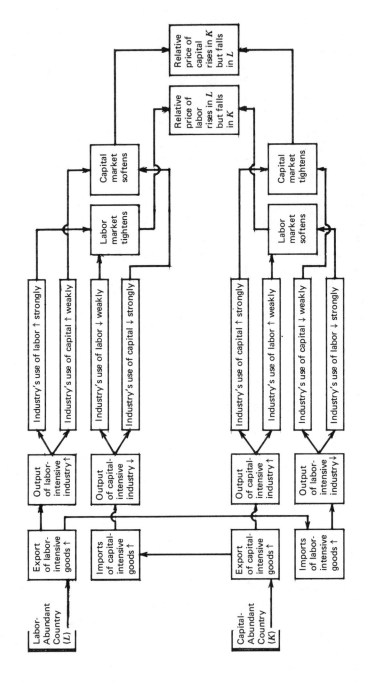

Figure 4-5. International trade and relative factor prices.

the output mix in the various participating economies, but also relative factor prices. Countries that have abundant capital and scarce labor are predicted to export capital-intensive goods and import labor-intensive goods. The reverse will happen in countries that have abundant labor and scarce capital. Moreover, trade will tend to cause the price of the abundant productive factor to rise in relation to the price of the scarce factor. Under certain conditions, we can also show that relative factor prices will equalize among trading countries. Our simple general-equilibrium trade model, taking account of increasing opportunity costs, can therefore tell us a great deal about the volume, direction, and product composition of trade, as well as its effect on the distribution of income via factor prices.

ADVANCED MATERIAL: Factor-Price Equalization?

It is easy to see how international trade leads to an equalization of *product* prices between countries. As long as price differences exist, it pays to expand trade, and this will remain true until all price differences are eliminated— assuming no transport costs, and so on. It is also easy to show, as we have just done, how trade results in a *tendency* for relative *factor* prices to equalize between countries. But it is much more difficult to believe that a *complete* equalization of relative factor prices will occur more or less automatically. Without barriers to international trade, and assuming factor qualities are the same everywhere, this would mean that U.S. wages, relative to the prices of other productive factors, would equal those prevailing in Japan; that the cost of capital in Germany would in relative terms equal that existing in Brazil, and so forth. After taking a look at the conditions under which such equalization might occur, we will discuss possible departures from them.

First, assume the following initial conditions: (1) two goods are produced in the two countries both with and without trade; (2) identical production functions, with constant returns to scale, prevail in both nations; (3) one product is always relatively labor-intensive; (4) both factors of production are qualitatively identical in all respects in the two countries; (5) both factors are used in the production of both goods; (6) no change occurs in the available supplies of productive factors; (7) there are no artificial restrictions to trade, and economic distances (transportation costs) are assumed to be zero; (8) per-

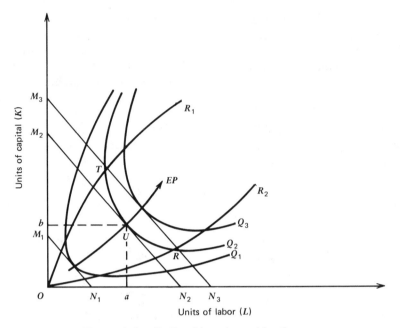

Figure 4-6. Optimal input combinations.

fect competition prevails in all markets; and (9) productive factors cannot move internationally.

Let us then describe our model, step by step. Try to recall the *isoquant* and *isocost* curves from intermediate economics courses. In order to produce a particular good, we assume that only two types of resources, labor (L) and capital (K), are needed. We also assume that inputs L and K are to some degree technically substitutable for each other, so that we can produce 1 unit of output by using either a great deal of L and very little of K, or a large amount of K and a small quantity of L, or a certain combination of L and K between these extremes. The different combinations of inputs L and K that may be used in the production of a set number of units of output can be represented graphically in the form of a curve such as Q_2 in Figure 4-6; this is called an *isoquant*, meaning simply that a fixed quantity of output may be produced using the various different combinations of inputs represented by the curve. The curve is convex toward the origin because as more and more of one input is used, it becomes increasingly difficult to substitute it for the other input. This involves a decreasing *marginal rate of substitution* of inputs in production.

Suppose now that the desired output level in Figure 4-6 is Q_2. Given two possible inputs, L and K, into its production, how much of L should be used and how much of K? We know that we would logically not use more of L than the quantity defined by point R, and that no more of K should be used than the quantity corresponding to point T. Beyond these points, more of *both* inputs would be used to produce an identical output of Q_2. Within these limits, how does the producer combine resources L and K to optimally produce quantity Q_2 of output.

Necessarily, the answer depends on the relative price of L and K. If L is more expensive than K, then relatively more of input K should be used, and vice versa. The ratio of the price of input L to the price of input K is given by the slope of the *isocost* function, shown in Figure 4-6 by line $M_2 N_2$, and representing a given level of expenditure on the two inputs. If the price of a unit of input L were \$2 and the price of a unit of input K were \$4, then the ratio of the prices of the two inputs would be 1:2 and the slope of the isocost line would be drawn accordingly. In order for Q_2 to be produced using an optimum input combination, quantity Oa of L and amount Ob of K should be employed. This combination of inputs L and K occurs where isoquant Q_2 is *tangent* to isocost curve $M_2 N_2$ at point U.

Why would not the production point instead lie somewhere between U and T? Because at any such point the marginal rate of substitution of K for L is greater than the ratio of the price of L to K, and it would thus pay the producer to substitute L for K until point U is reached; this would result in lower total production costs. Similarly, a production point anywhere on Q_2 beween U and R is suboptimal, because the marginal rate of substitution of K for L is less than the ratio of the factor prices, and total input costs could be reduced by substituting K for L until the factor combination represented by point U is again attained. Tangency of the isoquant with the isocost curve minimizes total expenditures on L and K needed to produce Q_2 of output.

Clearly, given the intention to produce quantity Q_2 of this particular commodity, the factor combinations resulting in lowest input cost can occur only where the isoquant is tangent to the isocost line—where the ratio of input prices exactly equals the marginal rate of factor substitution. Each conceivable output level, represented in Figure 4-6 by successively higher or lower isoquants (Q-curves), will possess an optimum production point; the line (EP) connecting all of these optimum points is called the *expansion path* of the firm. Assuming that a firm continues to optimize its use of factor inputs as its output grows and that the relative prices of the two factors of production do not change, then the expansion path traces the optimal use of the two inputs through successively higher levels of output.

What about the *shape* of the isocost and isoquant functions, on which this analysis is based? Isocost functions will always be linear so long as the factor-price ratio remains constant no matter how much of a given input is used, so they pose no problems in this regard. Isoquants, on the other hand, are not quite so simple. If two inputs are nearly perfect *substitutes* for each other, the isoquant will be only slightly convex, and the marginal rate of factor substitution in production will be nearly constant. Conversely, if two factors of production are perfect *complements* to each other, so that one cannot be used without a given quantity of the other, then the isoquant takes the form of a right angle. The optimum production point is then uniquely determined by the required, fixed factor combinations, regardless of the isocost function, given the quantity of output to be produced.

Most factor-input relations probably lie somewhere between these two extremes with respect to their substitutability, at least in the short run. We can be virtually certain that an isoquant will possess some degree of convexity. For instance, it is not easy, given the present state of the art, to envisage the use of only capital in production of a particular good without at least some labor, just as it is virtually impossible to employ only labor with no capital at all. Rather, it is clear that labor is substitutable for capital, and vice versa, to a considerable degree. Whether labor or capital is used more extensively depends on their relative prices—which, in the final analysis, depends significantly on the relative abundance of these two factors.

To expand this analysis to include output of *two different goods*, both using two factor inputs, take an economy that possesses only two productive factors, capital and labor, and produces only two types of goods, A-goods and B-goods. The endowments of labor and capital must of course be fully employed in the production of the two types of goods in order for the country to reach its output potential and thereby maximize its economic well-being. This is true no matter whether the emphasis is to be on the production of A-goods or on B-goods.

In Figure 4-7a, generally known as an Edgeworth box diagram, the total capital endowment of the economy is given by the height of the box, the distance AG or BH. Similarly, the length of the box (AH or BG) represents the nation's total endowment of labor. In order for both resources to be employed fully, the total labor force AH and capital stock AG must be entirely employed.

The use of labor and capital in the production of the A-good is represented by a series of isoquants, A_1, A_2, A_3, and so on, signifying successively higher output levels of that particular commodity. Similarly, factor use and production of the B-good is pictured by a series of isoquants, B_1, B_2, B_3, and so on, beginning at the B origin and expanding toward the lower left corner of the box. Any output combination of A-goods and B-goods where an A isoquant crosses, or is tangent to, a B isoquant will use up all of the available capital and labor. The reader can easily verify that production of the A-good at one point in the box and production of the B-good at another point represents an underutilization of resources—that is, less than full employment of all available capital and labor. Furthermore, the use of labor and capital will be optimized only where an A isoquant is tangent to a B isoquant.

This can be easily demonstrated. Suppose it is decided to produce at point S. Output of the A-good is A_3 and output of the B-good is B_3. At this point, BC of capital is used in the production of B-goods, and the remainder of the capital stock (CH or AE) is employed in producing the A-good. Amount BD

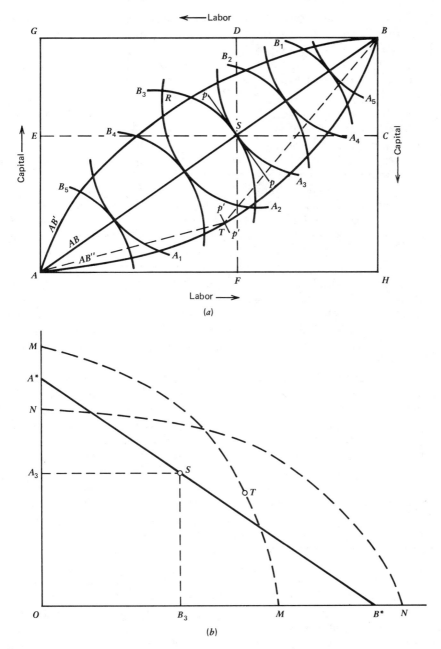

Figure 4-7. Two-factor, two-product analysis and derivation of a transformation function.

of the available labor force is used in producing the B-good, and AF (or DG) in producing the A-good. It is impossible to produce more of one good without thereby simultaneously decreasing the production of the other.

But why would not A-goods be produced at some point along isoquant B_3 other than point S? Because at any other point along B_3 (like R), it would be possible to increase production of the A-good (from A_2 to A_3) without simultaneously reducing output of the B-good—by simply moving along isoquant B_3 toward point S. Hence, in general, the use of available inputs of labor and capital will be optimal only when an A isoquant is tangent to a B isoquant. This, of course, holds true not only for the tangency of A_3 and B_3 at point S, but also for the respective tangencies of A_2 and B_4, A_1 and B_5, and so forth. At each individual tangency, different quantities of A and B will be produced, but efficiency in factor use will nevertheless be maintained.

The diagonal in Figure 4-7a, connecting all possible tangencies of A and B isoquants, is called an *efficiency locus*, or a factor-market "contract curve." At each point along the efficiency locus, labor and capital are being employed so as to most efficiently produce different quantities of A- and B-goods. This diagonal is the counterpart to the production possibilities frontier in Figure 4-7b. Notice that the linear efficiency locus AB produces the linear transformation function $A*B*$, indicating possible combinations of A and B that can be produced by this economy. Each point on the transformation function $A*B*$, such as S, also represents a point on the efficiency locus from which it is derived.

At point S in Figure 4-7a, AE of capital and AF of labor are used in the production of the A-good. The capital-labor ratio in the production of that good is therefore AE/AF. In the production of B-goods, the corresponding capital-labor ratio at point S is BC/BD. In general, the intensity with which factors are employed in the production of a given good is given by the slope of a straight line drawn from the origin, assigned to that commodity, to the production point. We noted in the previous discussion that with optimal factor combinations in the production of any good, the marginal rate of substitution of one factor for the other will equal the inverse of the ratio of the two factor prices. The price of labor relative to the price of capital at point S in Figure 4-7a is given by the slope of the common tangent pp. Note that these prices will be the same no matter how much A or B is produced, whenever, as along $A*B*$, the marginal rate of transformation is constant.

Now suppose that instead of yielding a linear efficiency locus such as line AB, the various tangencies had fallen along a curved path, so that the lower curve AB'' in Figure 4-7a turned out to represent the locus of all efficient points of factor utilization. Relatively more labor will then, at any such point, be used in the production of the A-good, and relatively more capital in the production of the B-good. Product A would be considered labor intensive, and product B capital intensive. Exactly the opposite would hold true if the upper curve AB' turned out to be the efficiency locus: the A-good would then be deemed capital intensive and the B-good, labor intensive. These relationships would also be reflected in the shape of the corresponding transformation functions in Figure 4-7b, in as much as these would be curvilinear (such as MM or NN).

Again, the proportions of productive factors used in the output of each of the two goods are given by the slope of a line drawn from the relevant origin to the production point. For example, if the efficiency locus is AB'', and it is decided to produce a certain combination of the A- and B-goods given by point T, then the slope of the dashed line AT indicates the proportions of capital to labor used in the production of the A-good. With the same output combination at point T, the slope of the dashed line BT represents the proportions of capital to labor used in the production of the B-good. The relative prevailing marginal products of the two factors under these circumstances—and hence their relative returns—are given by the slope of the common tangent to the two isoquants at the production point (in this case line $p'p'$, a common tangent to the A and B isoquants, not drawn, at point T).

Note that the relative marginal products and returns of the two factors, as given by the slope of this common tangent, will change as production is shifted along either of the curved efficiency loci. Thus, only if the efficiency locus is linear will the ratio of the marginal product of labor to the marginal product of capital be constant no matter how much of either good is produced.

We can now use this tool to show how international trade tends to bring about both product and factor price equalization simply by superimposing, in Figure 4-8, two box diagrams, representing the prevailing factor endowments in two trading nations. One of the two countries is labor abundant and has factor endowments given by the box $ACB'D$, and the other is capital abundant and has factor endowments given by the box $AEBF$. Both produce capital-intensive (B) goods and labor-intensive (A) goods. Their efficiency loci are, respectively, AB' and AB in Figure 4-8.

In the absence of international trade, let us assume that the labor-abundant country produces at some point, R, consistent with domestic demand conditions, whereas the capital-abundant nation similarly produces at point T. Comparing the labor-abundant to the capital-abundant country, we find that the returns to labor are lower relative to the returns to capital in the former, as indicated by the slopes of pp and $p_1 p_1$.

With international trade, the labor-abundant country begins to specialize increasingly in the labor-intensive A-good, moving along its efficiency locus toward B'. At the same time, the capital-abundant nation moves from point T in the direction of increased production of the capital-intensive good B. Trade will grow along the lines indicated earlier, until the prices of the two commodities are precisely equal in the two countries at points V and S, respectively. Both countries will then be employing exactly the same production methods, and the proportions of labor and capital used in the production of the two commodites will be equal for both countries. The prevailing ratios of the returns on capital to the returns on labor (the slopes of common tangents p_2p_2 and p_3p_3) must therefore also be equal.

In short, output in each country has shifted in the direction of increased specialization in the production of that commodity using relatively more of the abundant factor. Simultaneously, the returns to the abundant factor have increased as compared to returns to the scarce factor in each country. This has led to an equalization of the ratios of factor returns in the two economies, and the factor proportions (factor intensities) used in the production of both commodities have become identical for both economies.

Is it at all realistic, however, to assume, as we have done, that the production functions are identical (for each good) between the two countries?

One can argue that as economies grow, the technologies available in the productive process generally seem to reach some degree of uniformity among nations. The relative freedom of technology transfers promotes this. However, there is no certainty that technologies will be the same in every country. There is always a lag between invention and innovation, on the one hand, and the general, worldwide dissemination of the new knowledge, on the other. Also, the fact that the advanced technology is available is no guarantee that it will be put to use in the most effective manner possible. From a technological standpoint alone, then, nations may very well continue to differ, particularly given the international leads and lags in technology that we know exist.

What about other conditions that may influence the production functions—the character of the people, the climate, topographical conditions, the role of the government, and so forth? All of these can be expected to differ in varying degrees among nations. And what about the productive factors themselves? Are they in fact "qualitatively identical"? Is an Indian worker equally productive, given identical tools and techniques, as his American counterpart? Here again, differences in nutrition, education, discipline, and work habits might make one worker qualitatively quite different from his counterpart in another country, although such differences can easily be exaggerated.

The absence of such factor homogeneity is not always essential for factor-price equalization to occur in each and every circumstance. But in the main, the restrictiveness of the assumptions underlying the notion of complete factor-price equalization is sufficient to make it nonoperational for most practical purposes. This hardly deprives it of all significance, however. There is surely a pronounced *tendency* for trade to equalize factor prices internationally, and from a casual survey of real-world examples, the reader will find this a credible proposition. But complete equalization of the prices of factors of production internationally hinges upon the free mobility of the factors themselves. In actuality, free trade is only a partial substitute for factor mobility.

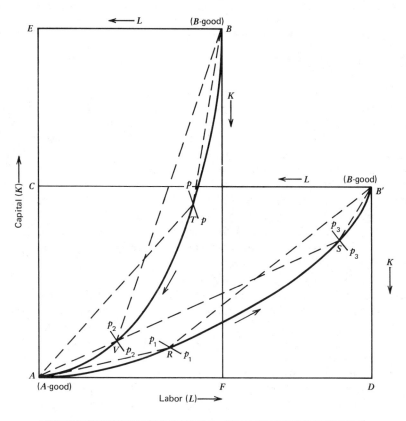

	Slope of:
Labor-abundant country, without trade (point R):	
Proportions of labor and capital used in A-good	AR
Proportions of labor and capital used in B-good	$B'R$
Ratio of return on labor to return on capital	p_1p_1
Capital-abundant country, without trade (point T):	
Proportions of labor and capital used in A-good	AT
Proportions of labor and capital used in B-good	BT
Ratio of return on labor to return on capital	pp
Labor-abundant country, with trade (point S):	
Proportions of labor and capital used in A-good	AS
Proportions of labor and capital used in B-good	$B'S$
Ratio of return on labor to return on capital	p_3p_3
Capital-abundant country, with trade (point V):	
Proportions of labor and capital used in A-good	AV ($= AS$)
Proportions of labor and capital used in B-good	BV ($= B'S$)
Ratio of return on labor to return on capital	p_2p_2 ($= p_3p_3$)

Figure 4-8. Trade, production, and factor prices: two countries, two commodities, and two productive factors.

Trade and The Distribution of Income

The factor-endowments approach to international trade theory yields a number of important insights into the effects of trade on the various structural relationships within national economies. From our simple model, we know what happens to (*a*) product prices, (*b*) factor-use intensities, (*c*) the composition of output, and (*d*) the relative returns paid to the factors of production—all as a result of international trade. We know, for instance, that trade increases the relative degree of scarcity of the productive factor domestically in abundant supply and brings about an increase in the relative returns paid to this factor, while lowering those paid to the scarce factor. Now suppose we look at a country where capital is abundant and labor is scarce. By the same token, will not international trade result in a reduction of wages relative to the cost of capital? If so, would it not be advisable from labor's standpoint to impede trade in some way and thereby keep relative wages at their high pretrade level?

Figure 4-9 depicts an efficiency locus for production in a relatively capital-abundant, labor-scarce economy producing a capital-intensive commodity, *B*, and a labor-intensive commodity, *A*. Without trade, let us assume production occurs at point *T*, with the slope of the common tangent, p_1p_1, to the two isoquants, A_2 and B_1, representing the ratio of the returns on labor to the returns on capital.

It is assumed that with international trade, the country naturally begins to specialize in the capital-intensive *B*-good in which its factor endowments give it a comparative advantage. Production thus shifts from point *T* to some new equilibrium—say, at *R*—representing greater specialization in the capital-intensive commodity. In the process, the shrinking import-competing industry (*A*), being labor intensive, releases relatively small amounts of capital and relatively large amounts of labor. The capital thus released is immediately absorbed in the expanding production of the capital-intensive (*B*) good, but there is, initially, less of an increase in demand for the released labor.

But the shortage of capital and the surplus of labor will put pressure on the respective factor prices, so that, in the end, the factor markets will be cleared. And both industries will adjust their relative factor inputs to these cost pressures. As a result, the *relative* amount of capital used decreases in both countries, and the *relative* amount of labor used increases in both industries. That is, the capital-labor ratio in the production of both goods is lower with trade at point *R* than without trade at point *T*. Hence the marginal productivity of labor declines, and that of capital rises, in both industries. If factor prices are an accurate reflection of marginal productivities, it follows that real wages will fall and that the real returns to capital will rise under these conditions, as a result of international trade. This is indicated by the slopes of the common tangents p_1p_1 and p_2p_2 in Figure 4-9.

In brief, when a country has a comparative advantage in the capital-intensive product, international trade has under these conditions adversely

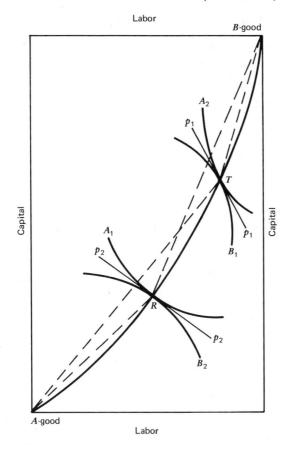

	Without trade	With trade
Production point	T	R
Factor intensities in B	slope of BT	slope of BR
Factor intensities in A	slope of AT	slope of AR
Relative factor prices	slope of p_1p_1	slope of p_2p_2

Figure 4-9. International trade and factor prices.

affected the relative position of labor. It alters domestic income distribution in favor of the owners of capital. Here, then, is a readymade argument for protection against imports and restriction of international trade. If production can be moved in the opposite direction, from free trade back toward the pretrade position at point T in Figure 4-9, then the whole process we described earlier will be reversed; this would illustrate the imposition of trade barriers on a situation of initially free trade.

Important Concepts

increasing opportunity costs

marginal rate of substitution

marginal rate of transformation

factor endowments

factor efficiency

factor intensity

factor price equalization

isoquant*

isocost function*

expansion path*

efficiency locus*

trade and income distribution

*Used only in Advanced Material section.

Questions

1. What would the factor endowments theory of international trade suggest about the position of organized labor in a labor-scarce economy as trade expands?

2. It is sometimes said that international trade and international movements of factors of production are substitutes for one another. Do you agree or disagree with this statement? Why?

3. Referring to Figure 4-3, suppose there occurred a transfer of technology from the United States to the United Kingdom, which significantly enhanced U.K. productivity in the supply of product B. What would be the impact on trade between the two countries?

4. It is often stated that small countries are "price takers" and that large countries are "price makers" in international trade. Explain the difference, from the point of view of trade theory.

Further Readings

Corden, W. M., *Recent Developments in the Theory of International Trade* (Princeton: International Finance Section, Princeton University, 1961).

Haberler, G., *A Survey of International Trade Theory* (Princeton: International Finance Section, Princeton University, 1961).

Johnson, H. G., "Factor Endowments, International Trade and Factor Prices," *Manchester School of Economic and Social Studies*, September 1957.

Robinson, R., "Factor Proportions and Comparative Advantage," *Quarterly Journal of Economics*, May 1956.

Samuelson, P. A., "International Factor Price Equalization Once Again," *Economic Journal*, June 1947.

Stolper, W., and P. Samuelson, "Protection and Real Wages," *Review of Economic Studies*, November 1941.

5

DEMAND-SIDE ANALYSIS

We have said a great deal about the conditions affecting international trade on the *supply* side. But nothing has yet been mentioned about the role of *demand* in determining the direction, composition, and terms of trade between nations. Yet it would be inconceivable to make a general statement about "who trades what with whom and at what prices" while completely ignoring the demand side of the economic equation.

Every reader knows that information about both supply and demand is necessary to arrive at an equilibrium price. This is no less true in international trade, in which the prices at which products are exchanged for one another are called the *terms of trade*. Very early in our study of comparative costs we found that the terms of trade determine how the gains derived from international specialization and trade are distributed among the countries of the world. At that point we set the terms of trade more or less arbitrarily and went on from there. We no longer need to do that once it is clear precisely how the terms of trade themselves are derived.

COMMUNITY INDIFFERENCE CURVES

We introduce the role of demand by posing a small problem. Suppose two countries possess identical production functions as a result of identical available technologies. Suppose they also have identical endowments of productive factors. The two countries therefore exhibit identical transformation functions. Is trade possible? According to the analysis presented in the preceding chapters, the answer would have to be no. Trade is based either on differences in factor productivities or in factor endowments between nations, and without such differences there seems to be no reason for international trade and no gains to be derived therefrom.

71

But once again turning to the real world, we find that trade does, in fact, flourish among countries that appear to have rather similar factor endowments and technologies: Germany and Great Britain, Belgium and the Netherlands, France and Italy, and so on. So there must be some other explanations for international trade besides the supply factors already enumerated. We thus have to consider demand as well.

An individual's demand for goods and services largely depends on two things: (a) personal tastes and preferences, and (b) disposable income. Tastes, or relative preferences, for two products can be represented through an *indifference curve*. Income may be depicted in the form of a *consumption-possibilities line*, drawn in a two-commodity space—that is, by the maximum amounts of the two goods that can be bought with an individual's limited income. Maximum satisfaction will be attained by consuming a combination of the two goods such that the consumption-possibilities line is tangent to one of the indifference curves. This represents the highest welfare level the individual can attain with a given level of income. Let us briefly review these concepts.

Presumably, the extra satisfaction that a person derives from obtaining one additional unit of a particular good declines as the number of units of that product in his or her possession increases. The satisfaction derived by obtaining the first automobile is generally considered to be greater than the additional utility derived from the second car, for instance. This illustrates the classic notion of *diminishing marginal utility*, which helps interpret the actions of consumers or users, as well as to explain the generally downward-sloping shape of consumer demand curves. Since the consumer derives less and less extra satisfaction from each additional unit of a good, he or she is willing to buy additional units only at successively lower prices. Moreover, if the consumer at all times seeks to maximize personal material welfare, then utility theory tells us that the consumer is, in fact, maximizing welfare only when the utility derived from the expenditure of one extra unit of money is equal for each and every product under consideration.

The principle of diminishing marginal utility appeals to common sense, and many students of economics consider it to be intuitively obvious. Although it also turns out to be highly useful in analyzing economic behavior, it is not readily quantifiable. An *indifference curve* is defined as depicting all possible combinations of two products that will yield a given, uniform level of satisfaction for the individual consumer. Curve *IC* in Figure 5-1 represents a certain level of satisfaction attained by consuming different combinations of products *A* and *B*. The same satisfaction level can be maintained by consuming large quantities of *B* and very little of *A* (in the upper segment of the curve), or by consuming a great deal of *A* and very little of *B* (toward the lower right extremity of the curve), or at any point in between. Indifference curves are almost always convex to the origin, because as consumers obtain more and more of *A*, they

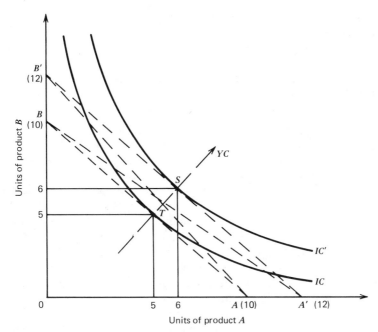

Figure 5-1. Indifference analysis.

are willing to give up less and less of *B* in order to get one additional unit of *A*. We say that the marginal rate of substitution of one good for the other—the amount of *B* an individual is willing to give up in order to obtain one additional unit of *A*, without incurring a loss of overall satisfaction as a result—diminishes throughout the extent of the curve.

A little thought will quickly make clear that a diminishing marginal rate of substitution of good *A* for good *B* in Figure 5-1 reflects the relative utilities of the two goods. In fact, the slope of the indifference curve equals the ratio of the marginal utility of good *A* to the marginal utility of good *B*. The indifference curve becomes vertical when the consumer's demand is saturated with *B*; it becomes horizontal when the individual's demand is saturated with *A* . These are unlikely but not inconceivable situations. The degree of convexity reflects the substitutability of the two products for each other. If *A* and *B* are perfect substitutes (e.g., two brands of flour), the curve might be a straight line and the marginal rate of substitution would be constant (one for one) throughout. On the other hand, if *A* and *B* are completely different (e.g., ice cream and bolts), the indifference curve would be sharply convex.

In order to maintain a given welfare level, the consumer must substitute one good for another according to the ratios specified by his or her particular indifference curve. In Figure 5-1, the individual's precise consumption point can be determined only if we know his or her income and the relative prices of the two goods. Suppose the consumer's budget of $100 suffices to buy 10 units of *A* or 10 units of *B*, or any combination of *A* and *B* along the *line of attainable combinations*, or *budget line, AB*. If the consumer maximizes his or her own welfare, consumption will be at point *T*, where the line of attainable combinations with an income of $100 is tangent to one of the indifference curves (here, curve *IC*), and 5 units of both *A* and *B* are purchased. The individual cannot consume at any other point on *IC* or at any point outside of the area bounded by line *AB*, because the budget of $100 and product prices of $10 each for both *A* and *B* would not suffice for it. On the other hand, the consumer would not want to consume at a point inside line *AB* or at another point on line *AB*, because this either would not use up the entire $100 budget or would misallocate his spending, and would result in attainment of a lower indifference curve and, hence, a correspondingly lower welfare level. All this means simply that consumers can maximize welfare only if they spend their money on *A* and *B* in such a way that they attain the highest possible indifference level consistent with their available budget. This is the tangency solution *T* in Figure 5-1, consuming 5 units of each of products *A* and *B*.

How can the consumer move to a higher level of welfare—above that represented by indifference curve *IC*? This must involve a move to a curve such as *IC'*. One way this would be attainable is through a rise in spendable funds, or real income, say from $100 to $120. Consumption will then be 6 units of each of products *A* and *B* at point *S*, where *IC'* is tangent to *A'B'*, assuming that prices haven't changed. It should be equally clear that successively higher incomes will lead to successively higher levels of welfare along *YC*, which connects the tangencies of all the indifference curves with all possible lines of attainable consumption combinations.

This permits us to define what is called the *income-consumption curve*. Of course, a rise in real income may take the form of decreases in the money prices of products as well as increases in money incomes. If the price of good *A* fell and the price of good *B* remained the same, the *AB* line would be less steep and the *YC* curve would normally be more nearly horizontal; conversely, the *YC* curve would usually assume a more nearly vertical shape if the money price of *B* fell and that of *A* remained constant. The new consumption-possibilities lines would then be parallel to line *A'B* in the former case, to line *AB'* in the latter case.

So far we have talked about indifference analysis only with reference to an individual consumer, and we have justified the construction of indifference curves on the assumption that the consumer is always able to judge which combinations of the two commodities yield equivalent satisfaction. Conceptually, this is not an unreasonable assumption. But what about the construction of indifference curves—*community indifference curves*—for the entire nation?

This proves to be much more troublesome, because of the great difficulty of making interpersonal comparisons of welfare levels. Suppose we assert that a nation would be just as well off consuming 8 million cars and 100 million books as it is consuming 4 million cars and 200 million books. Obviously, car lovers will be much better off under the former alternative, but book lovers will be far worse off. The two sets of individuals possess consumption indifference curves with very different shapes, and it is difficult to compare and to aggregate them. We cannot say for sure that community welfare would be unchanged by shifting the patterns of consumption from one combination of products to another. Therefore it is conceptually problematical to draw a single indifference curve for the entire community.

In the light of such strong objections, it is surprising that the community indifference curve has become the prime technique for dealing with demand in international trade theory. Several of the early writers used indifference curves to reflect community, or national, demand—without coming to grips with the problem of interpersonal welfare comparisons—by simply assuming that they had the same characteristics as individual consumer-indifference curves. Later on, it was thought that if in national shift in a consumption patterns, the gainers were to compensate the losers in such a way that all would be equally well off, the construction of community indifference curves would indeed be justified. Alternatively, one might simply assume that all inhabitants of a nation possess fundamentally identical and unchanging tastes.

Despite these and other rationalizations for the aggregate community indifference curve, it remains a tenuous concept. Yet because of its value in portraying the impact of demand on the patterns of international trade, we cannot avoid employing it as a tool of analysis. But keep in mind its limitations and shortcomings.

Figure 5-2 once again portrays a nation not participating in international trade. It is endowed with factors of production and technology that generate transformation function AB, with increasing opportunity costs. With the community indifference map composed of the CIC curves, optimum consumption and production occurs at point T, the point of maximum economic welfare. At this point the marginal rate of substitution in consumption precisely equals the marginal rate of transformation in production, and the prevailing domestic exchange ratio of product B for product A (which is identical to the ratio of the price of A to the price of B) is given by the slope of the common tangent pp. No other consumption or production point yields so high an economic welfare level. Only if transformation function AB can somehow be expanded outward—as by increasing the endowments of productive factors or by enhancing their productivity—can the national welfare level be raised in the absence of international trade.

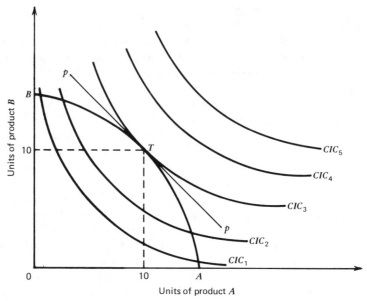

Figure 5-2. Community welfare maximization in isolation.

DEMAND AND INTERNATIONAL TRADE

Suppose, now, that there are two countries, *I* and *II*, with identical factor endowments and technologies but different tastes and preferences—that is, differently shaped community indifference curves. As Figure 5-3 shows, trade will occur, and both countries will be better off as a result.

Initially, in spite of the identical transformation curves, *A B*, the exchange ratio between the *A*-good and the *B*-good differs as between the two countries; this can be seen from the slope of line *pp* in country *I* and *p"p"* in country *II*. Country *I* prefers to consume larger quantities of good *B*(30 units) at point *S* than does country *II* (20 units) at point *S'* in Figure 5-3. The obvious reason for this price variance is not different supply conditions, but different tastes, as represented by the differently-shaped community indifference curves.

The existence of a pretrade price difference attributable to demand differences creates a new basis for trade. With international trade, the relative price of *A*- and *B*-goods will soon be equalized in the two countries— say, at the ratio represented by the inverse of the slope of line p_ip_i. At this price and exchange ratio, production in country *I* moves from point *S* to point *T*, and the level of consumption can move to a higher indifference level (numbered 2) at point *R*. Ten units of *A*-goods are now exported in return for 10 units of *B*-goods. Similarly, at the new

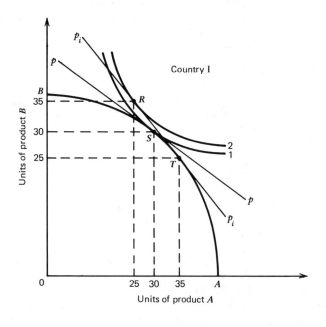

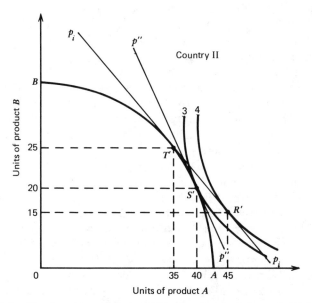

Figure 5-3. Trade and production with identical supply and differing demand conditions. (Refer to caption on the following page.)

	Country I	Country II
Consumption:		
Without trade	S(30 of A and 30 of B)	S'(40 of A and 20 of B)
With trade	R(25 of A and 35 of B)	R'(45 of A and 15 of B)
Production:		
Without trade	S(30 of A and 30 of B)	S'(40 of A and 20 of B)
With trade	T (35 of A and 25 B	T'(35 of A and 25 of B)
Prices (A vs. B):		
Without trade	slope of pp	slope of p''p''
With trade	slope of $p_i p_i$	slope of $p_i p_i$
Volume of trade:		
Exports	10 of A	10 of B
Imports	10 of B	10 of A

exchange ratio $p_i p_i$, country *II* shifts production from *S'* to *T'*, exporting 10 units of good *B* in return for 10 units of imports of good *A*, and advances to a higher indifference level (numbered 4) by consuming at point *R'*. Both countries gain in economic welfare as a result of international trade solely because of differences in national consumption preferences. Each has undergone a transformation of its output structure, with country *I* producing more of the *A*-good and country *II* producing more of the *B*-good. The gains from trade in this case, again, derive from the fact that each country is able to use its resources more efficiently than before.

What would have happened, on the other hand, if the demand patterns, and therefore the community indifference curves, in the two countries had been identical, but if their transformation functions had not been the same? Figure 4-3 (p. 54) provides the answer. Trade occurs, and gains are realized in accordance with the now familiar comparative cost model. In such a case, supply conditions alone are of determining importance. The addition of community indifference curves to that diagram would simply substantiate that the consumption point with free international trade lies on a higher indifference level than that attainable in isolation, and hence that there are welfare gains to be derived from international trade.

Finally, what happens, under constant or increasing opportunity cost conditions, when two countries possess identical technologies, identical factor endowments, and identical demand patterns? There will be no trade and no gains to be derived therefrom. Tastes, income, and supply conditions are everywhere the same, so that essentially no justification exists—either from the supply or from the demand side—for trade to occur. But there is one exception, which we shall discuss in Chapter 7: Economies of scale might still make trade worthwhile.

SUMMARY

Demand conditions can play an important role in determining the volume and direction of international trade. In pure trade theory, demand is usually expressed via community indifference curves, whose shape indicates relative preferences and whose level indicates the degree of welfare attained. There are serious questions about the use of community indifference curves, because of the great difficulty of interpersonal welfare comparisons. Nevertheless, international demand differences can, in themselves, give rise to trade— and trade, in this case as well, will create gains in national welfare levels. Both supply and demand factors must be incorporated in any comprehensive analysis of international trade.

Important Concepts

indifference curve	income-consumption curve
consumption possibilities line	community indifference curve
diminishing marginal utility	interpersonal welfare comparisons

Questions

1. French automobiles sell briskly in Germany, and German cars are bit sellers in France. Why?
2. Referring to Figure 5-3, suppose tastes in country *II* shifted in favor of product *A*. What would happen to the results of our analysis of international trade?
3. Can you explain where the gains from international trade come from in cases where trade is purely demand-determined?

Further Readings

Baldwin, R., "The New Welfare Economics and Gains in International Trade," *Quarterly Journal of Economics*, February 1952.

Caves, Richard E., *Trade and Economic Structure* (Cambridge: Harvard University Press, 1960).

Findlay, Ronald, *Trade and Specialization* (Baltimore: Penguin Books, 1970).

Haberler, G., "Some Problems in the Pure Theory of International Trade," *Economic Journal,* June 1950.

Lerner, A. P., "Diagrammatical Representation of Demand Conditions in International Trade," *Economica*, August 1934.

6

INTEGRATING SUPPLY AND DEMAND

At this point, we have acquired a fundamental, working knowledge of the respective roles played by supply and demand in international trade. But as yet we have failed to integrate the two aspects into a cohesive, general model. This we can now accomplish through the concept of *reciprocal demand*, and alternatively by so-called *offer curves*.

Suppose the domestic price ratios (determined by production costs) of two products, A and B, are 1:2 in country X and 1:3 in country Y. If the international terms of trade of A for B were 1:4, neither country would be willing to sell product A internationally; it could do better by exchanging A for B at home. Similarly, if the international A:B price ratio was 1:1, neither would be willing to sell B abroad. So the prevailing domestic price ratios (here, 1:2 and 1:3) set the limits within which the international price ratio (terms of trade) must settle. Only within this range will *both* countries be willing to trade. And we noted earlier that the closer to the domestic price ratio prevailing in country X the terms of trade come to rest, the larger will be the gains from trade garnered by country Y, and vice versa.

Precisely where, between these two domestic price ratios, will the terms of trade eventually settle? The answer is suggested by the law of reciprocal demand, first stated by John Stuart Mill, which shows that it is necessary to know the demand by both countries for both products before the terms of trade can be precisely determined. In this case, if country X, which has a comparative advantage in the production of good B, expresses a large demand for good A at almost any relative price, the terms of trade will tend to settle close to its own initial domestic A:B price ratio, and its trading partner, country Y, will then derive most of the gains from international trade. This is because country X, to get all of the A-goods it so badly wants, must offer its own export, good B, at a continued low price, whereas country Y can raise its

80

supply price of good A sharply. The equilibrium terms of trade will thus be close to the domestic, no-trade price ratio in country X.

Therefore, reciprocal demand conditions determine the international terms of trade at which all commodity markets will be in equilibrium. Supply equals demand both *within* each country and *between* them. The law of reciprocal demand is, however, meaningful only as long as demand in each of the countries is powerful enough to affect commodity prices in both of them. Consider trade in goods A and B between the United States and Mali. No matter what is Mali's demand for A and B, it alone will be too weak to affect relative prices of the two products in the United States. Hence, for all practical purposes, trade in A and B between the United States and Mali will occur at prevailing American domestic prices. Mali will derive virtually all of the gains that result from such trade, assuming there are no monopoly or monopsony elements at work in the various markets.

Small and—from a demand standpoint—insignificant countries thus appear to be in one sense in a favorable position in the international economy. Of course, this is not an unmixed blessing, since it places their economies at the mercy of the vagaries of demand and supply in the larger nations. A significant change in tastes, incomes, or technology in the large countries could easily wipe out highly specialized, export-oriented industries in the very same countries that previously reaped large gains from trade.

OFFER ANALYSIS

There is another way to express the role of demand in international trade, one that is somewhat more amenable to use in our analysis later on—via *offer curves*. In Figure 6-1, quadrant 2 contains the familiar community indifference curve, C_1, and transformation curve ab. Without trade, the economy can reach the welfare level represented by community indifference curve C_1, given the production alternatives possible under its existing resource endowments and technology. It produces and consumes 5 units each of good B and good A at point T.

Suppose, now, that we simply take the nation's "production block" Oab and slide it up along community indifference curve C_1 to a new hypothetical equilibrium point at T'. Consumption at T' is now 10 units of good B and 1 unit of good A. Production at T' is 2 units of good B and 7 units of good A. Six units of good A must now be exported in return for 8 units of imported good B.

Note that point T' is still on community indifference curve C_1, so that the country would in this case be no better and no worse off as a result of international trade—that is, it is indifferent whether it trades or not. The same thing happens when we slide production block Oab down along the community indifference curve to a new equilibrium, T''. Here again, although consumption and production patterns have changed drastically, the country is

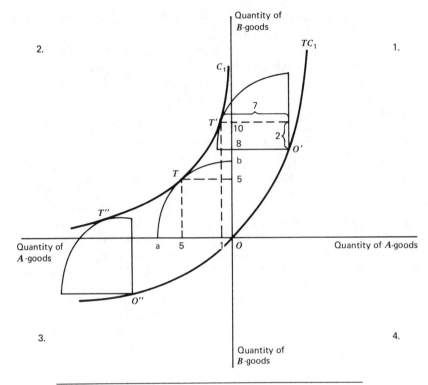

Figure 6-1. Derivation of the trade-indifference curve.

	Good B	Good A
Without trade (equilibrium at T):		
Production	5	5
Consumption	5	5
With trade (equilibrium at T'):		
Production	2	7
Consumption	10	1
Trade:		
Exports	—	6
Imports	8	—

equally well off at T'' as it is at T' or, without any trade at all, at point T. All T points lie on the same community indifference curve.

As we slide the production block Oab up and down along community indifference curve C_1 to represent different production and consumption combinations along the same indifference level, the corner of the production block, O, traces out the curve TC_1; this is called the *trade indifference curve*.

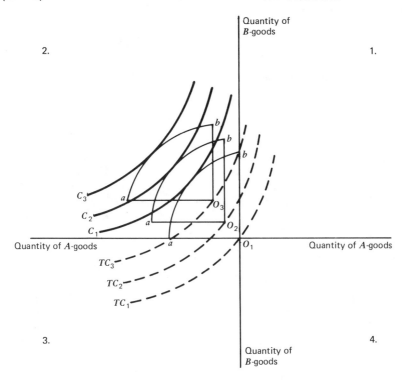

Figure 6-2. Derivation of the trade-indifference map from the consumption-indifference map.

At any point along curve TC_1, the country is indifferent as to whether or not it engages in international trade. Why? Since curve TC_1 is directly derived from the community indifference curve, together with the constant supply conditions represented by the unchanging production block, each point along TC_1 will pertain to one and the same level of welfare.

We can now derive a series or "family" of trade indifference curves corresponding to an equal number of community indifference curves, representing higher and lower levels of economic welfare (always leaving the size and shape of the production block completely unchanged). This is done in Figure 6-2. Trade indifference curves TC_1, TC_2, and TC_3 are thus derived from community indifference curves C_1, C_2, and C_3, respectively, and traced by the corner of the production block Oab. There is consequently one trade indifference curve for each community indifference curve. The higher the trade indifference curve, the higher the level of welfare that has been attained.

Keeping in mind the manner in which trade indifference curves are derived (i.e., what lies behind them), we can now use them to construct an *offer curve*. Suppose that, in the absence of trade, the relative domestic exchange ratio of

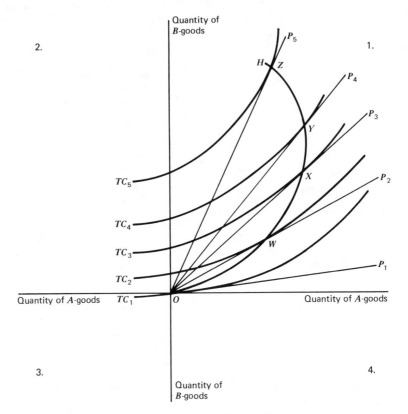

Figure 6-3. Derivation of the offer curve.

the B- and A-goods is given by the slope of line OP^1 in Figure 6-3. At or below this ratio we, as a country, would certainly be unwilling to offer any of our A-goods in return for imports of B-goods, since it is possible to get B-goods as cheaply, or even more so, at home.

If the international exchange ratio rose to OP_2, however, we would be willing to offer some A-goods in return for imports of B-goods. The higher prices received for our exports, relative to those we have to pay for our imports—the improved terms of trade—permit us to move to a higher trade indifference curve. In this case, we can reach point W, where OP_2 is tangent to TC_2. Hence, we are willing to offer substantially more of our A-goods for export at the price ratio OP_2 than at a ratio closer to OP_1.

In fact, as our terms of trade continue to improve and we keep getting more B-goods per unit of the A-goods that we export, we are willing to offer more and more of our A-goods for sale abroad (for example, at terms of trade P_3 and P_4, we will trade up to points X and Y, respectively). After a while, however, we are exporting so much of our A-good that it becomes very costly to produce and its domestic availability becomes very limited; it therefore will be more valuable. Similarly, we are importing so much of the B-good that our desire for even more of it is correspondingly diminished; and our costs of producing it ourselves have dropped sharply. At some point, we are willing to offer no more A-goods for B-goods. Beyond that point we will take on more B-goods only if we have to give up fewer A-goods as a result. Hence, at terms of trade between P_3 and P_4, our offer of A-goods in return for additional B-goods has passed zero and become negative (compare points Y and Z).

Curve OH, the succession of tangencies of all possible terms of trade lines with all possible trade indifference curves, is the home country's offer curve. It shows how much of its exports that country is willing to offer in return for imports at each and every international exchange ratio, or terms of trade. The offer curve is a graphical representation of what we have referred to as reciprocal demand. It subsumes domestic supply as well as domestic demand conditions for internationally tradable goods.

GENERAL EQUILIBRIUM

In the same way that an offer curve is derived for the "home" country (H), a second offer curve can be drawn for its trading partner, the "foreign" country (F). We simply construct the latter's transformation function and community indifference curves in the fourth quadrant of the coordinate plane, draw a second set of corresponding trade indifference curves, and construct an offer curve (OF) for the second country as well.

All of this is done in Figure 6-4, which presents the transformation curves and community indifference curves for two countries (H and F) and two products (A and B). The two countries' respective trade-indifference curves (not drawn) are derived as in Figure 6-2 above, and their respective offer curves drawn from the tangencies of the trade indifference curves with the various terms-of-trade lines.

Figure 6-4 shows the two countries' respective offer curves crossing at point R, with the resulting terms of trade given by the slope of the line OT. Only at this point does general equilibrium exist. The terms of trade OT exactly balance supply and demand for both products, A and B, in both countries, H and F, and clear all markets, domestic and international. Let us see how this occurs.

At terms of trade OT, country H is willing to offer 10 units of its A-goods in return for 8 units of B-goods. Simultaneously, country F offers 8 units of its exportable B-goods for 10 units of imports of the A-good. At those terms of trade, one country wants to supply precisely what the other country demands. Ten units of product A are thus exported to country H and

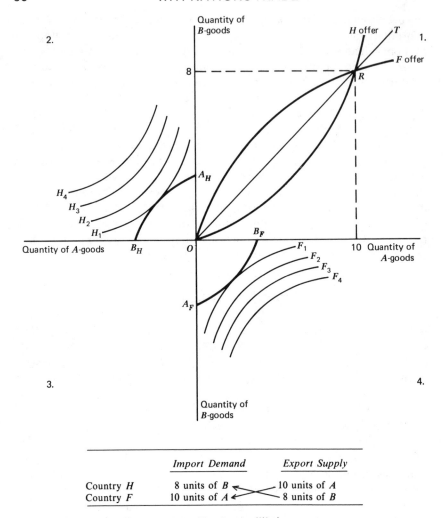

Figure 6-4. Trade equilibrium.

	Import Demand	Export Supply
Country H	8 units of B	10 units of A
Country F	10 units of A	8 units of B

imported by country F, whereas 8 units of good B are exported by country F and imported by country H.

From the way we have derived the offer curves, it is clear that the price ratio given by the terms-of-trade line OT now prevails domestically in both countries, as well as internationally, and that the supply of each product equals the demand in each nation. In home country H, domestic production of the A-good minus exports equals the domestic demand for it, and domestic production of the B-good plus imports equals the domestic demand for that product. The opposite is true in the foreign country *F*. All markets are cleared, supply equals demand domestically and internationally, and product prices have no further tendency to change. The system is in equilibrium.

SUMMARY

In this chapter we have devised a comprehensive analytical framework that draws together all of the salient demand and supply forces in international trade. It shows in a simple general equilibrium model virtually all of the aspects of trade that we are interested in: (1) the volume of trade; (2) the direction of trade; (3) the terms of trade; (4) the impact of international trade on the nation's production mix; and (5) its effect on the pattern of consumption within each of the trading countries. If we apply the results to the factor-price analysis developed in Figure 4-5, we can even say something about relative income distribution. One conclusion is that demand forces can overtake supply forces and that in such circumstances, supply conditions by themselves are misleading predictors of trade flows.

How realistic is it? Does a simple two-country, two-factor, two-product model such as this, possess significant predictive value in a world where there are many products, many countries, and additional factors of production? What about the usefulness of community indifference curves? What about transportation costs and other complications? These are some of the questions the skeptical reader will immediately raise; yet we shall soon show that our model is remarkably robust.

ADVANCED MATERIAL:
Equilibrium in Product and Factor Markets

From the discussion in this chapter, it is clear that the volume of trade can readily be predicted from the information given by the offer analysis and general equilibrium. The direction of trade can be just as easily foretold. Once we have two intersecting offer curves, we are in a position to predict "who exports what to whom," the composition and direction of trade, and also the terms of trade. And by simply tracing the trade point, *R*, backwards through the same analysis, we arrive at a tangency of a country's production block (the corner of which rests at *R*) and one of its indifference curves. It is thus possible simultaneously to determine the impact of trade on production patterns and on consumption combinations.

This is done graphically in Figure 6-5*a*. The two countries' respective offer curves intersect at point *R*, at terms of trade *OT*. Country *H* exports 10 units

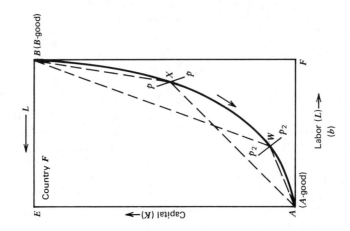

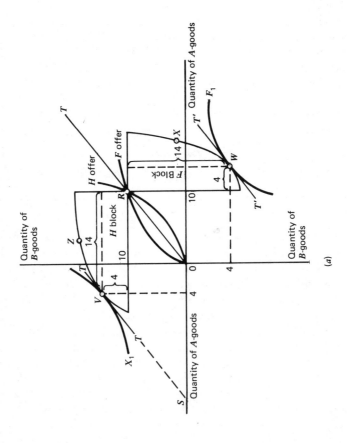

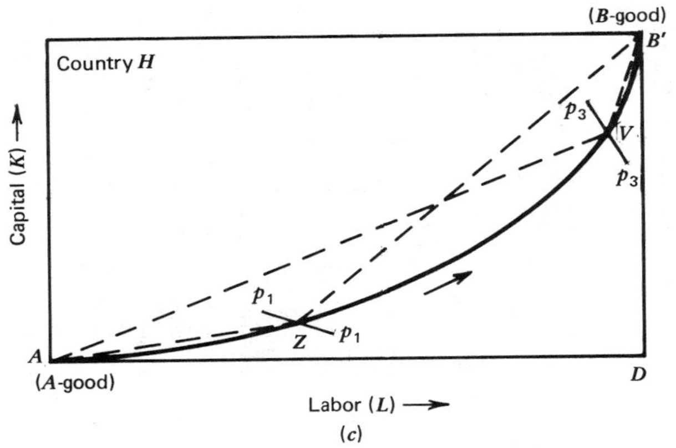

General Equilibrium With Trade:

	Country H	Country F
Trade:		
Exports	10 of A-good	10 of B-good
Imports	10 of B-good	10 of A-good
Production:		
Good A	14	4
Good B	4	14
Consumption:		
Good A	4	14
Good B	14	4
Prices:		
Domestic	TT	T'T'
Terms of trade	OT	OT
Factor prices	p_3p_3	p_2p_2

Figure 6-5.   General equilibrium.

of product A to country F, which in return ships 10 units of product B to country H. In country H, production and consumption take place at point V: 14 units of the A-good are produced, of which 4 units are consumed at home and 10 units are exported. Fourteen units of the B-good are consumed, of which 4 units are produced at home and 10 units are imported. In country F, on the other hand, production and consumption occur at point W. The A-good is consumed in the amount of 14 units, 4 of which are produced domestically and the remainder, 10 units, imported. The B-good is produced in the amount of 14 units, of which 4 units are consumed at home and the rest, 10 units, exported.

The exchange ratios (and prices) of the two products are the same in both countries, and they are given by the slope of a common tangent to the relevant community-indifference and transformation curves at points V and W. The slopes of both of these common tangents must be the same as the slope of the terms-of-trade line OT.

The transformation functions that produce the result we have just derived depend, of course, on the underlying availabilities of productive factors and the efficiency with which they are used. Suppose, as in Figure 6-5, product A is labor intensive and product B is capital intensive. The shape of the two countries' respective transformation curves—the H block and the F block— tells us that, assuming identical production functions, country H must be labor abundant. It can produce relatively more of the labor-intensive good A than the capital-intensive good B, as reflected in its box diagram in Figure 6-5c. Similarly, country F must be capital abundant, since it is able to produce relatively more of the B-good than the A-good, as illustrated in the box diagram in Figure 6-5b.

In moving to its general equilibrium trade position, country H shifts its production mix from point Z to point V and in the process, the factor prices and the intensity with which capital and labor are used in production shift as well. Labor, the abundant factor, gets more expensive, while capital, the scarce factor, gets cheaper, as reflected by the slopes of p_1p_1 and p_3p_3 in country H's box diagram—the marginal product of labor relative to the marginal product of capital. Similarly, the abundant factor in country F (capital) gets more expensive and the scarce factor (labor) gets cheaper as the production mix is shifted from point X toward greater specialization in good B at point W, again reflected in the slopes of pp and p_2p_2 and in the corresponding shifts in factor intensities: For the home country, if we extend line TT to the A axis at point S, then the distance OS measures the home country's national income in terms of the A good. Extension of line TT to the B axis would give us the home country's national income as measured in the B-good.

Important Concepts

reciprocal demand
offer curve
general equilibrium

Questions

1. Referring to Figure 6-4, what might be the effect of a shift in preferences towards the *B*-good in the home country on its terms of trade? What would be the effect of an increase in its ability to supply the *B*-good?

2. In a particular year Brazil finds that it is the victim of adverse weather conditions that destroy a third of its coffee crop. A year later there is the feeling that the catastrophe has actually left the country better off than before. Why might this happen?

Further Readings

Heller, H. Robert, *International Trade* (Englewood Cliffs: Prentice-Hall, 1973).
Krauss, Melvyn B., *A Geometric Approach to International Trade* (New York: Halsted-Wiley, 1979).
Meade, James E., *A Geometry of International Trade* (London: Allen & Unwin, 1952).

7

APPLYING
TRADE THEORY

The previous five chapters, which outlined the rudiments of the theory of international trade, concluded with a comprehensive analytical framework that not only encompasses supply and demand elements in the international economy, but also ties them back directly to the corresponding aspects of two national economies. Using this model, we can trace through a shift in demand or supply conditions in one or both countries, indicating its impact on the terms of trade, the volume and composition of trade, output structure, and factor returns both at home and abroad.

Up to now our discussion essentially has been static in nature, and very little has been said about the effects of changing factor supplies and technology on the volume, geographic pattern, product composition, and terms of trade among nations—that is, on the *dynamics* of international trade. Yet this matter is of great theoretical and practical significance, if only because we live in a world of change. Let us now try to find some ways in which our model of international trade may be amplified in these directions, and at the same time identify some of its limitations.

TERMS OF TRADE

Before continuing, we need to develop more precisely what we mean by the "terms of trade," so far defined as the price of a country's export goods relative to the price of the goods it imports—or the rate at which the two internationally traded products are exchanged for one another in the international marketplace. Simply stated, the terms of trade, TT, equal the index of export prices, P_x, divided by the price index for imports, P_m:

$$TT = \frac{P_x}{P_m} \times 100$$

If we take 1978 as the base year (= 100), and we find that in 1980 Australia's export prices rose 10 percent (to 110) and its import prices fell 5 percent (to 95), then its terms of trade improved by about 15.8 percent ($110 \div 95 \times 100 = 115.8$) over those two years.

If a country's terms of trade have improved, the prices of its exports must have risen relative to the prices of its imports. Conversely, a deterioration in the terms of trade means an increase in a country's import prices relative to its export prices. An improvement in the terms of trade means that a smaller quantity of export goods can be sold abroad to obtain a given quantity of imports. Similarly, a deterioration in the terms of trade means that a greater sacrifice—in terms of goods exported—is necessary to obtain a given amount of imports. Generally, imports are regarded as the ultimate objective or goal of international trade, and exports as the means of obtaining that objective—hence the origin of the terms "improvement" and "deterioration" in this connection.

When we are dealing with only two products bartered for each other, the terms of trade we have defined here represent a precise analytical concept, properly referred to as the *net barter terms of trade*. If the price of each internationally-traded product is precisely equal to the value of all the factors of production incorporated therein and input requirements do not change, then the terms under which products are exchanged for one another internationally are also the terms under which *productive factors* are, indirectly, exchanged for each other. Hence the terms of trade as defined here could equally be called the *factoral terms of trade*, whether they refer to a single factor of production (such as labor) or to a combination of such factors. In practice, however, the factoral terms of trade are extremely difficult to calculate, because inputs are constantly changing, both in composition and in quality, and one cannot then precisely attribute each product price to an equivalent sum of input values.

Now suppose prices of imports remain constant while prices of a country's exports rise by 20 percent from 1978 to 1980. The net barter terms of trade obviously would show a 20 percent improvement:

$$\frac{120 - 100}{100} = 0.20$$

At the same time, however, suppose productivity in the use of a particular factor of production (output per unit of input), such as labor (hours), rises by 10 percent. To find the factoral terms of trade, we have to take into account the increased productivity, since each unit of exports now contains a smaller amount of labor. Hence the factoral terms of trade show an improvement of 32 percent:

$$\frac{120 \times 1.10 - 100}{100} = \frac{132 - 100}{100} = 0.32$$

The result: One unit of exports now buys 20 percent more imports, but one unit of labor employed in the creation of these exports now buys 32 percent more imports. This is called the *single factoral terms of trade*. This measure could also be computed for capital or any other factor of production, alone or in combination with other factors.

If instead we want to find out how many more foreign units of productive factors (e.g., labor) a single exported unit of the domestic productive factor will buy—the *double factoral terms of trade*—we must adjust the import price index by the amount of foreign productivity gain. Thus, if in this particular example, productivity overseas of the factor in question has simultaneously risen by, say, 5 percent, the gain in the double factoral terms of trade would be about 26 percent:

$$\frac{120 \times 1.10 - 100}{100 \times 1.05} = \frac{132 - 100}{105} = 0.26$$

Although there are a number of advantages in using factoral terms of trade, the net barter terms of trade remains the favored concept. Another adaptation of the terms-of-trade concept is the *capacity-to-import index*, defined as the quantity of exports multiplied by the ratio of export prices to import prices:

$$Q_x \times \frac{P_x}{P_m}$$

This index measures a country's ability to buy imports, given its export capacity. It is used especially for analyzing the ability of developing countries to finance their import requirements.

SUPPLY AND DEMAND SHIFTS

Via the offer-curve analysis developed in the preceding chapter, we can portray the impact of shifts in supply and demand relationships on the volume and terms of international trade. For example, what will be the effect of a change in factor endowments or productivity?

An increase in the endowment of the abundant factor, or an increase in factor productivity in the export sector, expands a nation's transformation curve so that more of the export good can be produced. From the offer-curve derivation presented in the last chapter, it is easy to see that this shows up as a change in the level and shape of a country's transformation curve. Demand patterns being constant, the result will be an outward shift of the offer curve. The increase in the country's export capability tends to reduce the world price of its export good, forcing the country to export more, per unit of import, than before.

This is shown in Figure 7-1. Beginning with the equilibrium trade point R, country H experiences an increase in its ability to produce export commodity A. Efforts to export more reduce the price of A in the international market, thus shifting its terms of trade from OT to OT' (country F's offer curve remaining unchanged) and its offer curve from OH to OH', with a new equilibrium at R'. At the new terms of trade, it must export 8 units of good A more than the initial exports of 10 units in order to get only slightly more imports—12 units of B instead of 10—in return. Its terms of trade have deteriorated, while the overall volume of trade has grown to 18 units of A plus 12 units of B instead of 10 of A and 10 of B. As we shall see later on, however, a terms-of-trade deterioration does not *necessarily* mean a lower level of welfare.

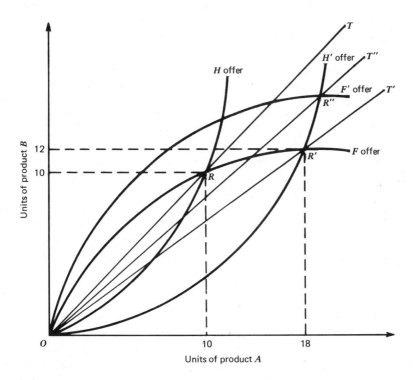

Figure 7-1. Effects of changed supply and demand conditions upon the volume and terms of trade.

If country F simultaneously undergoes an expansion of its export supply, both countries' respective offer curves will shift outward, and a new equilibrium, such as R'', might result. Whether in this case the terms of trade OT'' ultimately favor one country or the other, as compared with the original terms of trade OT, depends on the relative size of the export supply changes occurring in each country. Assuming demand conditions to be unchanged, that country undergoing the greatest export-supply expansion will normally find its terms of trade deteriorating. In any case, the volume of trade expands.

Suppose the supply of import-competing goods expands instead. The reason for this might be an increase in the supply of the scarce productive factor, or a rise in factor productivity in the import-competing sector. This will tend to result in a backward shift in the country's offer curve and (everything else being equal) an improvement in its terms of trade. The nation will then import only at the reduced prices charged by its own import-competing producers, and the drop in import prices will imply that its terms of trade improve.

Given two countries, H and F, the net effect on the terms of trade of a rise in the supply of import-competing goods in both countries depends similarly on the relative strength of the respective supply shifts. If the import-competing supply increase is greater in country H, then its terms of trade will typically improve, and those of country F will deteriorate (and vice versa). The reader can trace this out by using intersection R'' in Figure 7-1 as a starting point and working back to the intersection at R. The result here is a substantial decline in the volume of international trade.

Suppose, finally, that country H undergoes a significant expansion of output in the export sector, and country F simultaneously expands production in its import-competing sector, both because of shifts in factor supplies or technology. Country H would find export prices falling for two mutually reinforcing reasons. Naturally, everything else being equal, the terms of trade of country H will deteriorate as H's offer of its export good (A) increases and F's "reciprocal demand" for it is reduced.

Figure 7-1 can also help explain the impact of changes in demand on the volume and terms of trade. Let's go back to the original case, in which the two countries' respective offer curves intersect at point R and the terms of trade are given by the slope of line OT. Country H, for some reason, now undergoes a large increase in its demand for imports. In expanding its purchases of imported good B, there is an outward shift in country H's offer curve, since H is willing to offer a great deal more of its export good (8 units of A) for only slightly more imports (2 units of B). Hence a new equilibrium is reached at R', the price of imports rises, and its terms of trade deteriorate from OT to OT'.

Finally, if both countries undergo an increase in the demand for imports, both offer curves will expand outward, and a new equilibrium, such as R'', will be reached. Assuming supply conditions to be constant, that country with the greatest expansion of demand for import goods will normally find that its terms of trade have deteriorated.

As a general proposition, any domestic economic shift that results in an increased domestic supply of export goods, a reduced domestic demand for export goods, a reduced domestic supply of import-competing goods, or an increased relative domestic demand for import goods will tend to lead to an increase in the volume of trade and a deterioration in the country's terms of trade. Conversely, developments leading to a reduced supply of export goods, increased domestic demand for export goods, reduced demand for import goods, and an increased supply of import-competing goods tend to result in a reduction in the volume of trade and an improvement in a country's terms of trade.

In actuality, the impact of a change in domestic or foreign supply or demand conditions on a nation's terms of trade depends largely on the shape of the offer curve of its trading partner. From Figure 7-1, it is easy to see that no shift in country H's offer curve will result in a change in its terms of trade if country F's offer curve is a straight line, for the latter country is then, implicitly, willing to offer unlimited amounts of the A-goods and accept unlimited amounts of the B-goods at the terms of trade OT. In reality, this suggests that H is a *small country*, an insignificant factor in country F's markets. In general, the more nearly linear the trading partner's offer curve, the less will be the impact of domestic supply or demand changes on a country's terms of trade.

The kind of supply and demand shifts, and their international consequences, discussed here may indeed occur in a short-run context—for example, as a result of crop failures. They may also occur in the longer-run context of economic growth, reflecting gradual changes in relative factor supplies and factor productivities—and hence in international comparative advantages and terms of trade.

TECHNOLOGICAL CHANGE

What happens when we introduce changes in technology into our model of international trade? We know that international differences in technology are one reason for international trade, since they contribute to intercountry differences in production costs and prices, upon which the theory is founded. The United States is well advanced in the technology of agriculture. Japan has acquired the technology needed to mass-produce high-quality, fuel-efficient automobiles at low cost. Such examples suggest ways in which technical change may affect the direction and volume of trade, as well as the respective output structures of the trading nations.

Now suppose a particular technical innovation results in a substantial saving of labor—that is, less labor is needed to produce a given amount of output. Is not such *labor-saving* technical progress analogous in its effects to an actual increase in labor supplies? Similarly, would not a *capital-saving* advance be comparable to an increase in capital supplies (that is, investment)?

In fact, an innovation that influences the productivity of capital and labor in an identical (neutral) manner ought to leave the capital-labor ratio unchanged but have an effect on production and trade similar to an expansion of the supplies of both productive factors.

Referring to Figure 7-2, suppose a country is producing 25 units of labor-intensive good A and 10 units of capital-intensive good B at point W on the (labor-abundant) transformation curve A_1B_1. At the terms of trade TT, the country is exporting good A and importing good B, as it specializes in the production of the labor-intensive product (in which it has a comparative advantage).

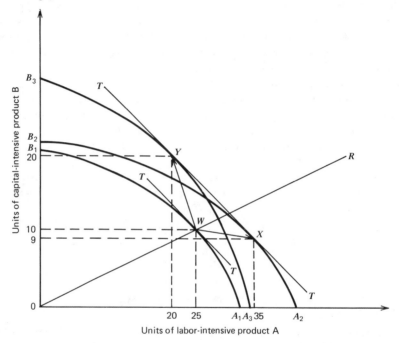

Figure 7-2. Labor-saving and capital-saving technological change.

Now suppose a labor-saving innovation occurs. This makes possible a substantial expansion of output in the labor-intensive industry (A) but only a moderate increase of production in the capital-intensive industry (B), as represented by the new transformation curve A_2B_2. If the terms of trade remain the same, TT, production will shift from point W to some point X. Output of the export good A is expanded by 5 units while production of the import-competing good B is reduced by 1 unit. A labor-saving innovation equally applicable to all industries in a labor-abundant nation could thus result in an expansion of exports.

Suppose, alternatively, that a capital-saving innovation occurs that allows significant output expansion in the capital-intensive, import-competing industry B and much less of a production increase in the labor-intensive export industry. The corresponding transformation curve is A_3B_3 in Figure 7-2. Again assuming that the terms of trade remain unchanged at TT, production shifts from point W to point Y. This time, output of the labor-intensive export good A is reduced by 5 units, and production of the capital-intensive, import-competing good B is expanded by 10 units. This type of innovation could reduce the overall volume of trade.

Our assumption of constant terms of trade in these examples is rather unrealistic, except for small countries whose behavior has no impact abroad. Our conclusions must therefore be modified somewhat in the case of large countries or certain small countries with unusual market power. Innovations that occur in the import-competing sector will tend to raise the price of the export good relative to the import-competing good and thus improve the terms of trade. Innovation in the export sector will tend to have the opposite effect, resulting in a deterioration of a country's terms of trade. These changes in relative product prices will mitigate the trade and production bias of any given innovation. Students can work this out for themselves by assessing the relevant shifts in the innovating country's offer curve and imposing the new terms of trade onto its transformation curve.

FACTOR SUPPLIES AND TRADE

We have seen how changes in relative supplies of productive factors and technology can affect the output structure of a nation, as well as the volume and pattern of its international trade. Is it not also likely that international trade may itself influence the supplies of productive factors?

We know from factor-endowments theory that trade seems to increase the relative scarcity of the abundant factor, as evidenced by the accompanying factor-price shift. If factor supplies are at all sensitive to the returns they generate, increases in factor returns will result in a growth of the available factor supplies. For instance, in a labor-abundant country, trade will tend to raise the relative wage rate and to increase the labor-force participation rate and the average number of hours worked per person, thus effectively enhancing the supply of labor; this implies that the labor-supply curve slopes upward. The reverse happens in regard to the scarce factor of production: Trade tends to lower the relative return paid to that factor and thus make it seem less scarce. This may lead to a partial withdrawal of that factor from the market and a commensurate reduction in available supplies.

In the absence of any international factor movement, we can conclude that international trade tends to encourage additions to existing supplies of abundant factors and reductions in available supplies of scarce factors. Trade itself may thereby enhance the comparative advantage created by differences in relative factor endowments.

REVERSAL OF FACTOR INTENSITIES

The fact that changes over time in factor supplies and efficiencies can influence—and even reverse—international trade patterns is clear. We have seen that this might result from growth in factor supplies, so that the scarce factor eventually might become the abundant factor, and vice versa. Applying the traditional factor-endowments analysis, the product composition of trade might shift as well, with exportables becoming importables, and importables becoming exportables. The second way in which this reversal can occur involves changes in production functions—for example, a labor-intensive good becomes capital intensive as a result of technical change. This would tend to reverse the product composition of trade, even in the absence of any change in relative factor supplies.

We have also seen that the factor-endowments theory requires production functions to be decidedly "biased." The production of one good must utilize one particular factor more intensively than production of the other. For example, wheat is best produced relatively land-intensively, many consumer durables capital-intensively, and so forth, so that a given product will always be characterized by "intensity" in some factor of production both at home and abroad. However, is it not possible that production functions need not be biased at all, or that their biases change, as with changing technologies?

Whenever production functions are similar among industries, relative factor endowments *do not necessarily determine* which products a country will export or import. This idea raises doubts about the validity of the factor-endowments theory, at least in the case of certain products—most probably, products with weak, varying or "symmetrical" factor intensities. For some products, therefore, the factor-endowments theory might be a reliable predictor, whereas for others it might not. And production functions tend to be altered over time as a result of changing technology. Labor-biased production functions may become capital-biased, or labor- and capital-biased production functions may become symmetrical, and vice versa, causing shifts in international competitive relationships and trade.

DECREASING OPPORTUNITY COSTS

Up to now we have assumed that perfect competition prevails in all markets, and that the cost structures of the producing firms must be consistent with this form of market structure. Decreasing costs, or increasing returns, have been ignored, since the definition of pure competition precludes internal economies of large-scale production. In the long run, all firms are presumed to be operating at optimal plant size, and further large-scale economies within firms are not possible. Moreover, external economies, such as those achieved through shared transport and communications facilities, have been ignored because they are usually more important under market structures other than pure competition.

But the highly complex industrial processes that characterize modern economic activity require a high degree of automation, possible only within large, highly integrated firms, and, usually, product differentiation. Technological differences may then be substantial, and the firms may realize internal and external economies of scale. Trade in manufactured goods between such highly industrialized countries as Germany and the Netherlands, or the United States and Japan, would seem to be attributable, at least in part, to such factors, rather than to differences in basic resource endowments.

Perhaps even more important is the fact that pure competition is not a very realistic picture of market structures in today's developed economies. Few industries, if any, come close to the purely competitive model. So the possibilities for decreasing costs are many and varied, and they may be just as characteristic of the real world as constant or increasing costs. Indeed, if an entire economy encountered decreasing opportunity costs, that could mean that its production possibilities curve would be *convex* (instead of *concave*) to the origin over a particular segment of the curve. By drawing such a curve, the reader can easily figure out that with international trade, production would never occur in the convex part. We leave it to the reader to figure out why.

TRANSPORT COSTS

We can now relax still another assumption by taking international transport costs into account and integrating them into the analysis. Transport costs can be thought of as the difference between the value of a product as it leaves the production point and its value as it arrives at its destination. Defined in this way, they include such items as freight charges, insurance premiums, and interest cost for the time the goods are in transit, as well as loading and unloading costs.

Suppose the price of wheat is $2 per bushel in Canada and $3 per bushel in the United States. Ignoring transportation charges, the Canadian price is $1 less than the U.S. price. But this isn't the relevant comparison. We need to know precisely how much both Canadian and U.S. wheat sell for in a single, given market. By the time the Canadian wheat reaches Houston, Texas, for instance, its price might actually be equal to that of the competing U.S. commodity, thereby eliminating any competitive edge. More generally, transport costs cause international price relationships to differ from what they otherwise would have been. As such, transport costs reduce the volume of trade, limit the gains to be derived from trade, change the trading nations' respective output structures and factor returns, and possibly even change the direction of trade. In short, transport costs affect international competitive relationships and everything connected with them. Just how transport cost, or, to use a better term, *economic distance*, bears on international trade flows is demonstrated in Figure 7-3.

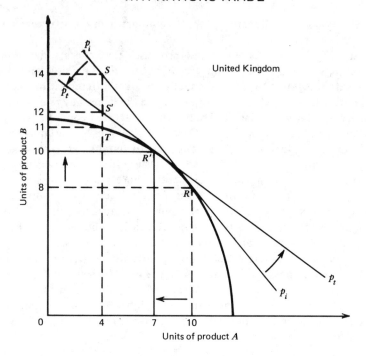

United Kingdom

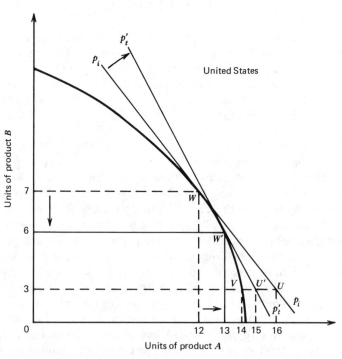

United States

	United Kingdom	United States
Production:		
In isolation	T (4 of A, 11 of B)	V (14 of A, 3 of B)
With trade	R (10 of A, 8 of B)	W (12 of A, 7 of B)
With trade and transport costs	R' (7 of A, 10 of B)	W'' (13 of A, 6 of B)
Consumption:		
In isolation	T (4 of A, 11 of B)	V (14 of A, 3 of B)
With trade	S (4 of A, 14 of B)	U (16 of A, 3 of B)
With trade and transport costs	S' (4 of A, 12 of B)	U' (15 of A, 3 of B)
Terms of trade:		
Without transport costs	$p_i p_i$	$p_i' p_i'$
With transport costs	$p_t p_t$	$p_t' p_t'$
Gains from trade:		
Without transport costs	3 of B	2 of A
With transport costs	1 of B	1 of A

Figure 7-3. Impact of transportation costs.

Suppose the terms of trade of product B for product A in the absence of transport costs in trade between the United States and the United Kingdom came to rest at $p_i p_i$. With an assumed demand pattern, Britain is producing at point R and consuming at S, whereas the United States produces at point W and consumes at U. Both consumption points, of course, are located on the terms of trade line. The introduction of transport costs results both in an increase in the price of imported A-goods for the United States and an increase the imported B-good price for the United Kingdom. Which party nominally pays the transport charges, of course, does not matter. In any case, the terms of trade move against *both* countries, from $p_i p_i$ to $p_t p_t$ for the United Kingdom, and from $p_i p_i$ to $p_t' p_t'$ for the United States. Britain is now forced to consume along line $p_t p_t$, and the United States along line $p_t' p_t'$. Britain moves from consumption point S to S', and the United States shifts its consumption from point U to U', if both countries leave their consumption of the respective export products unchanged. The loss of consumption, as compared with an absence of transport costs, clearly involve 2 units of product B for the United Kingdom and 1 unit of product A for the United States.

Production shifts from point R to R' in Britain, and from W to W'' in the United States. Each country simultaneously reduces the degree of its specialization in the product in which it has a comparative advantage, and each is less well off as a result of the imposition of transport costs. Transport charges, measured in terms of the two traded products, are 2 units of product B for U.K. imports and 1 unit of good A for U.S. imports.

Transport costs reduce differences in pre-trade prices of delivered products. In so doing, they limit the gains derived from trade, as well as the overall volume of trade. In the absence of transport costs, the ratios of internationally-traded product prices are identical in all countries, but with transport costs they are not. If the international terms of trade in the absence of transport costs are already close enough to the pretrade domestic price ratio prevailing in one of the countries, transport costs can cause trade to cease altogether. Finally, although such costs normally do not affect the direction of trade, they influence the degree of national specialization in production, and therefore the output structure.

TRANSPORT AND LOCATION

The discussion of transport costs underscores the importance of this factor in international trade, in spite of the fact that most of our trade models neglect it. Think of a steel mill, an auto assembly plant, a machine-tool factory, or any other industrial facility. Why is each of them located where it is? From a demand standpoint, it is clearly desirable that the site be close to the major markets for its output. From a supply standpoint, it must have sufficient access to labor, raw materials, and other inputs; hence it should be close to the sources of supply. Both sets of considerations affect potential profits, and some sort of optimal balance must be struck among the interests of demand, supply, and economic distance. This is the task of *location theory*.

Just as the economics of location affects the geographic structure of a national economy, so is it important to the international pattern of economic activity and to international trade. Transport costs affect different products in different ways. Frozen strawberries require an entirely different type of shipment than cement. It costs more to transport a small private aircraft weighing 2000 pounds than an automobile weighing 4000 pounds. It is more expensive to ship some products a few hundred miles from Santos, Brazil, to a village in the Brazilian interior than from Santos to Rotterdam. Such examples convey an idea of the complexity of transportation and location considerations for international trade. We also have to take into account the economics of the various transportation industries, which may be competitive or monopolistic, and land, labor, or capital intensive.

We can classify traded products according to their relative dependence on supply and demand conditions. If a product, for reasons of cost, must be produced in close proximity to the source of inputs, we say it is *supply-oriented*. If, on the other hand, the cost of transporting inputs is a minor consideration relative to the benefits derived from having final production located close to the ultimate market, we can say that a good is *demand-oriented*. Finally, if a good falls into neither category, it is called *neutral* with respect to its location orientation.

In aluminum smelting, for instance, we find major plants near their sources of electric power even when the major raw material, bauxite, is accessible only through water transportation. Plants must be located close to the source of the electric power because the electricity required to convert the bauxite to alumina has very high transmission costs. Similarly, fruit and vegetable processing is generally located close to the sources of raw-material supply in the farm areas. For instance, many agricultural commodities lose weight in the manufacturing process and are cheaper to transport in the processed state; peas lose their pods, corn its husks and cobs, coconut its shell, and so forth. If production locates internationally in accordance with supply characteristics, largely dictated by transports costs, it follows that changes in transport conditions may result in shifts in the location of output and, hence, in international trade. The development of modern, large-capacity cargo aircraft, for instance, has not only expanded the market of existing producers of goods ranging from orchids to transistors to cattle, but has affected the location of their production as well. Containerization of cargo, the Panama Canal, and the interstate highway system in the United States have had equally far-reaching effects on production and trade.

Demand-oriented goods are primarily attracted to the major origins of market demand. Automobile assembly in large countries generally occurs close to the primary markets, with components shipped in from supplier plants all over the country and even internationally. The bulk of an automobile is substantially greater than all of its parts shipped individually, and the transport cost of the final product tends to exceed that of its raw-material or component inputs; this explains in part the location of automobile production.

The manufacture of *neutral* products are pulled neither to the sources of input supply nor to their own markets. In such instances, production tends to occur at either the supply or the demand point, rarely at some point in between. In the petroleum industry, for example, it does not make much difference from a transport-cost standpoint whether the crude oil is refined before it is pumped aboard tankers in the oil-producing areas or after it is discharged at its destination.

The classification of products into supply-oriented, demand-oriented, and neutral groupings is not meant to discount the many other factors that affect the location of production. A given product may be basically supply- or demand-oriented, but processing may still take place at some intermediate point because the required supply of skilled labor is not available elsewhere. Or location may be the result of tradition, inertia, local entrepreneurship, benefits realized from agglomeration, or a host of other factors, some of which may well outweigh transport costs as a determinant of the location of production.

SUMMARY

In this chapter we have extended our basic model of international trade and production in several ways. First, we defined more carefully what is meant by the "terms" of trade, discovering that they can be calculated in a variety of ways to suit specific purposes. Second, we found that our basic model could predict the trade effects of domestic or foreign supply and demand shifts, in particular, connected with factor supplies and technical progress. International technology transfers can thus also be accounted for. We can also show how the basic model could help identify the effects of a diversion of resources into "public good" activities such as pollution control, as is done in the Advanced Material at the end of this chapter: Essentially, resources are diverted from the production of tradable to nontradable products, which negatively affects a country's ability to produce the former and, under certain conditions, may affect its international comparative advantage as well.

We have also discussed some situations that differ from the standard cases—for example, what happens if factor intensities reverse themselves; what happens when particular sectors are subject to decreasing instead of increasing opportunity costs; and how transport costs and location theory can be incorporated into our analysis. In each case, the theory has shown itself to be remarkably adaptable to a broad variety of real-world situations.

ADVANCED MATERIAL:
Nontraded Goods and Services

One of the features of traditional trade theory is that all goods and services produced by a national economy are assumed to be internationally tradable. As a result, it is easy to figure out how given changes in trade flows will affect a country's output structure, and vice versa. But some goods and services are simply not traded internationally. To varying degrees this is true of construction, haircuts, health care, and similar services, as well as goods such as gravel and ice cream. It is certainly true of intangibles such as environmental quality.

What happens, for example, to comparative advantage and trade when a society decides to improve its environment? Environmental damage that does not enter into the private costs of production creates nonmarket *social* costs, which need to be forced back into the market sector if rational decisions are to be made concerning the use of the environment. Pollution control aims at *internalizing environmental externalities*. In so doing, pollution control draws off resources from other sectors of the economy. This, in turn, is bound to affect a country's comparative advantage and international trade.

Consider Figure 7-4. Here we have a country that produces and consumes export good X and import good M, as in all of our earlier models; we have simply added environmental damage-avoidance (or environmental quality, E)

as a third possible "output" of society. Using a three-dimensional space, we can draw an *XME* transformation surface with the standard transformation function for tradable goods and services lying in the *XM* plane.

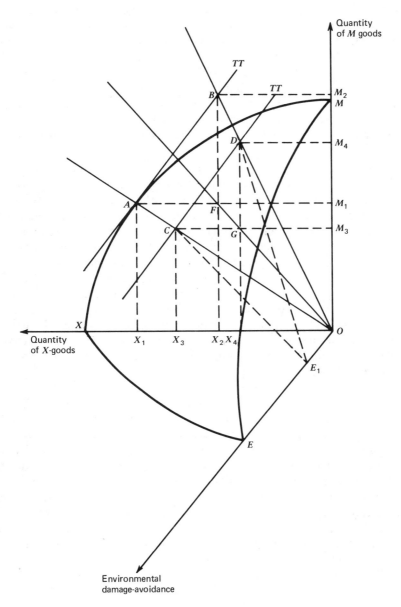

Figure 7-4.   Trade effects of pollution control.

Assume that the terms of trade are given by the slope of TT and that the XM price ratio is equal to the marginal rate of transformation at A. As in our other models, the production mix is OX_1 (of which X_2X_1 is exported) and OM_1, whereas the consumption mix is OM_2 (of which M_1M_2 is imported) and OX_2. If social preferences now shift in the direction of environmental control, the implicit price attached by society to environmental quality rises. Less of goods X and M can be produced as resources are increasingly devoted to pollution control. The XM transformation curve "shrinks" inward, and a new production equilibrium such as C would produce an improvement in environmental quality (E_1). But with unchanged terms of trade the tradable production mix may now be OX_3 (of which X_4X_3 is exported) and OM_3, in which case the consumption mix is now OX_4 and OM_4 (of which M_3M_4 is imported), along with OE_1 of (nontraded) environmental quality improvements.

Resource diversion into nontradable environmental quality has in this example (*a*) reduced output of tradables by $X_3X_1 + M_3M_1$, (*b*) reduced consumption of tradables by $M_4M_2 + X_4X_2$ (this is the real cost of pollution control to society), (*c*) reduced exports by $X_2X_1 - X_4X_3$, (*d*) reduced imports by $M_1M_2 - M_3M_4$, and (*e*) increased production and consumption of environmental quality of OE_1. Yet social welfare at consumption point D is presumably higher than it was at point B was at this point. Further shifts in social preferences in this direction will produce a further inward shift of the XM consumption point and the XM consumption point. Increased pollution control thus reduces the volume of both imports and exports. If the terms of trade, as well as the XM transformation function and community indifference curve, remain the same while successively larger amounts of productive re-sources are siphoned off into pollution control, the volume of exports and imports will decline accordingly.

We have assumed here that the international terms of trade remain unchanged as resources are shifted from the production of traded goods to pollution control; this is, of course, the "small country" case discussed earlier. Yet since pollution control means that we can produce less of *both* the exported and imported goods, the terms of trade can either improve or deteriorate, depending on which effect is stronger. If pollution control hits X more strongly than M, the country's offer curve will shift to the left and the terms of trade of the "large country" will improve, and vice versa. In the case of terms-of-trade improvement, the student can easily figure out that pollution control will entail a smaller drop in consumption levels of the X and M goods, and some of the costs of the environmental cleanup will, in effect, be borne by other countries.

Suppose, finally, that our export good X is capital intensive and our import good M is labor intensive, and that pollution control activities in the form of increased E are also capital intensive. Then the inward shift of the equilibrium X and M production levels in Figure 7-4 will likewise not be symmetrical; the country's comparative advantage will be undermined—the productive factor that gives rise to its comparative advantage is being disproportionately drained off into pollution control—even though the terms of trade are then likely to improve. Our point is, of course, to show that the basic trade model we have used is adaptable to the analysis of nontraded goods and services—even something as complex as pollution control.

Important Concepts

net barter terms of trade	transport costs
single factoral terms of trade	economic distance
double factoral terms of trade	location theory
capacity-to-import index	supply-oriented goods
technological change	demand-oriented goods
labor-saving innovation	neutral goods
capital-saving innovation	nontraded goods
factor-intensity reversal	externalities
decreasing opportunity costs	

Questions

1. The developing countries have long argued that "economic distance" presents them with a major disadvantage in international trade. Can you make a plausible case in support of this argument?

2. Cite some real-world examples where technological change has had a significant impact on the pattern of international trade.

3. Suppose the United States decides to invest a substantially larger amount of resources in occupational safety and health measures. How might this influence the pattern of U.S. international trade?

4. Can you cite some examples of factor-intensity reversal? How might it have influenced the flow of trade?

Further Readings

Corden, W. M., "Economic Expansion and International Trade: A Geometrical Approach," *Oxford Economic Papers*, June 1956.

Isard, Walter, *Location and Space Economy* (New York: John Wiley, 1956).

Isard, Walter, and Merton J. Peck, "Transport Costs and Location Theory in Interregional and International Trade Theory," *Quarterly Journal of Economics*, February 1954.

MacDougall, G. D. A., "Some Practical Illustrations and Applications of the Theory of Comparative Advantage," *Economic Journal*, December 1951.

Meier, Gerald M., *International Economics of Development* (New York: Harper & Row, 1968).

Walter, Ingo, *International Economics of Pollution* (London: Macmillan, 1975).

Walter, Ingo, (ed.), *Studies in International Environmental Economics* (New York: John Wiley, 1976).

8

EXTENDING
TRADE THEORY

Now comes the critical question: Is our trade theory any good? Good for forecasting the patterns of trade and its effects on other national and international economic variables? In this chapter we shall attempt to answer this question, and we shall present some recent modifications of the basic model—the so-called *neoclassical theory of trade*—designed to improve its actual predictive ability. Should we attribute international comparative-cost differences in the real world primarily to varying levels of factor productivity or to different factor endowments? Would it not be best, in a complex, multiproduct, multicountry world, to take the eclectic view that in reality almost everything matters?

MANY GOODS AND MANY COUNTRIES

So far, we have relied on a simple two-country, two-product, two-factor framework. In reality, of course, trade is carried on *multilaterally*, rather than bilaterally. In fact, the United States may ship good X to Britain and receive nothing directly in return. Rather, the United Kingdom may ship good Y to Brazil, which in turn sells good W to the United States. The United States has exported good X, for which it has received good W in an indirect way.

To illustrate how comparative advantage operates in a multilateral world, let us take four countries—France, Britain, Germany, and the United States—each of which produces two products, automobiles and corn. Assume demand is identical in each. In the absence of trade, the relative prices of the two products in the various countries (denominated in their respective domestic currencies) might be as follows:

111

Country	Standard Automobile (unit price)	Corn (price per bushel)	Price Ratio
France	20,000	80	250
United Kingdom	1000	10	100
Germany	8000	40	200
United States	10,000	20	500

By comparing the domestic pretrade price *ratios* of the two products among the various countries, a ranking of comparative advantage can be calculated, and some predictions can be made as to the general direction international trade might take. The United States has the greatest comparative advantage in corn production, whereas the United Kingdom has the greatest comparative advantage in the manufacture of automobiles. The rankings, in order of greatest to smallest comparative advantage, would appear like this:

Country	Standard Automobile	Corn
France	3	2
United Kingdom	1	4
Germany	2	3
United States	4	1

So we can be reasonably certain, from a supply standpoint, that in trade among these countries the United Kingdom will export automobiles for corn and that the United States will export corn in return for automobiles. Each of the two exports its products to all of the other three countries, since it has a comparative advantage over all of them. But what about France and Germany? In automobile production, France has a comparative edge only over the United States, whereas in corn production it has a comparative advantage over both Germany and the United Kingdom. We can predict that, in all likelihood, it too will turn out to be a corn exporter and automobile importer. The reverse holds for Germany, which has a comparative advantage in corn only over the United Kingdom and in automobiles over both France and the United States, and is likely to develop into an automobile exporter and corn importer.

It is also possible to gauge the probable *composition* of a single country's trade with another country (or the rest of the world). We only need to rank again the various tradable products by their comparative advantage. If we consider only two countries, Germany and Holland, the product in which Germany has the greatest comparative advantage must, by definition, be the one in which Holland has the greatest comparative disadvantage, and vice versa. And so we can simply rank a series of tradable goods, based on some assumed values, in order of comparative advantage, something like this:

Germany (rank)	Product	Holland (rank)
1	Machine tools	10
2	Automobiles	9
3	Chemicals	8
4	Pharmaceuticals	7
5	Optical equipment	6
6	Household appliances	5
7	Fluorescent lamps	4
8	Transport aircraft	3
9	Green vegetables	2
10	Tulip bulbs	1

With free trade, it is fairly certain that the direction of trade in the first few products would be from Germany and Holland, and in the last several categories from Holland and Germany. But what about the others? The precise identification the two countries' mutual exports and imports depends on the role of demand and the exchange rate between the German and Dutch currencies. For instance, if the German demand for Dutch goods expands relative to the Dutch demand for German goods, the number of product categories Holland exports will tend to grow; in turn, Germany may export more to third countries. Here again, comparative advantage in production gives us only a rough idea of the composition of trade.

THE LEONTIEF PARADOX

The next question is whether in looking at the actual flows of trade in many products among many countries, the traditional factor- and supply-based neoclassical theory of international trade indeed holds up. If it does not, what alternative explanations falling outside of our basic model may be necessary to describe what is going on in the real world? Certainly the most famous and controversial test of the factor-endowments theory of comparative advantage is that by the Nobel Prize-winning economist Wassily Leontief.

Recall that according to the factor-endowments theory, a given country should be importing products requiring large amounts of factors in scarce supply domestically, and exporting goods that intensively use factors in abundant supply. The United States, which apparently has relatively abundant capital and scarce labor—a high overall capital-labor ratio— would therefore tend to export capital-intensive goods and import labor-intensive goods. Using data for the year 1947, Leontief in 1953 came to the surprising conclusion that American exports actually appeared to be labor intensive and American imports capital intensive—exactly the reverse of what the factor-endowments theory would lead us to believe.

In the years since Leontief's discovery, there has been a virtual epidemic of studies attempting to put some further clothes on the pure theory of international trade, with the intention of explaining convincingly why the results turned out the way they did. For example, is it not possible that American imports happen to be natural-resource intensive? Since natural-resource industries also happen to be capital intensive, U.S. imports may appear capital intensive as well, but the embodied capital may in fact be American investment in resource dependent facilities abroad. A few of the studies we shall discuss depart entirely from conventional trade theory, with some rather original approaches. We shall presently summarize the debate.

HUMAN SKILLS

One possible reason for the Leontief paradox is that the quality of labor may not be everywhere the same—that labor in some countries may be more efficient than in others. Why and how would labor quality in reality vary? There may be differences in the skill levels of workers, which in turn may be the product of investments in education, training, and health—that is, in *human capital.* The U.S. labor force is generally better trained than, and as healthy as, those of other industrial countries, not to mention those of developing countries. More precisely, it is highly *skilled-labor abundant*, with the skills being largely the product of U.S. capital investment in human beings.

If this is correct, then skill intensity ought to show up in employment patterns of various kinds of labor, and differences in these patterns ought to be related in some significant way to international trade flows. Wage differences among groups of varying skill levels might be used to indicate relative productivity, which in turn ought to determine in part a nation's comparative advantage. Studies that have focused on this issue show that U.S. exports are in fact more labor-skill intensive than U.S. imports—hence they are more human-capital intensive—which is what one would expect. Others have succeeded in generalizing the importance of this factor as a determinant of trade patterns in a variety of countries, indicating that the incorporation of human capital can possibly undo the Leontief paradox.

TECHNOLOGICAL GAPS

Another possible explanation for the real-world behavior of trade is that innovation—whether related to management know-how, production processes, or products themselves—occurs in different countries at a different pace. A country that leads in innovation may enjoy an important comparative advantage in trade in technology-intensive products. A new product or process is developed. The technology does not yet exist abroad, so exports naturally take place. Then the technology becomes available abroad, and with the technological gap eliminated, other factors, such as labor costs, again become the primary determinants of comparative advantage. A prolonged technological gap between one country and the rest of the world can serve as an important underpinning of its trade position. One way to examine this issue is to look at specific high-technology products and examine where they were first developed, and how their production spread internationally over time.

Furthermore, it turns out that U.S. industries making a strong research effort also tend to be highly export-oriented. This fits well into conventional factor-endowments theory, since technological gaps are created by *investment* in research and development, and high-technology exports would be expected of capital-abundant countries. In any case, whatever gaps exist can easily narrow as technology diffusion becomes easier via international licensing, consulting contracts, construction of "turnkey" plants and intrafirm technology transfers by multinational corporations.

THE PRODUCT CYCLE

A more elaborate version of the technology-gap argument is the so-called *product-cycle theory*. According to the scenario depicted in Figure 8-1, a new product is developed, and it starts out being produced in small quantities by different firms in the home country, almost experimentally, with wide differences in techniques among firms. Markets develop and production becomes more homogeneous, with the national and international diffusion of know-how and less-efficient techniques being weeded out. The techniques that remain become widely accepted and standardized, and the products themselves become part of the firms' basic manufacturing lines. High-technology firms in advanced countries tend to export goods that fall into the early stages of the product cycle, and at the later stages production diffuses internationally as standardization, mass-production, and mass-marketing occurs. The advanced nations gradually lose their competitive advantage as relative labor costs and other factors again become more important.

The product-cycle theory concentrates on the sequential transition from differentiation to standardization, which occurs according to different time patterns for different products. In Figure 8-1, the "technology leader" begins exporting a new product, after its domestic infancy stage in Phase I, to the "technology followers" in Phase II, to whom it gradually loses its

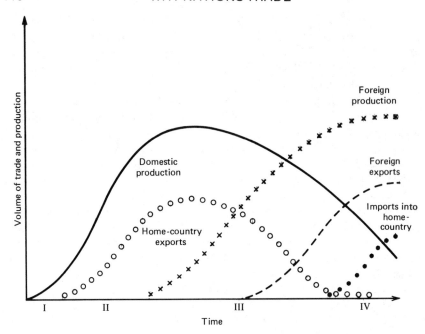

Figure 8-1. Possible trade and production patterns in the product cycle.

competitive advantage in Phase III and ultimately becomes a net importer in Phase IV. The "technology follower," in turn, eventually loses its competitive advantage to "third level" suppliers (e.g., developing countries) during successive periods of time. Statistically, there appears to be a high correlation between product differentiation and labor-skill inputs in U.S. trade, and a strong indication that American exports tend to concentrate relatively heavily on the "front end" of the product cycle. So the product-cycle theory also conforms rather well with the basic factor-endowments proposition, since it stresses investment in human skills and in research and development.

STAGES OF GROWTH

Alternatively, the causes of international trade may be directly related to the economic growth process. In the early stages of its growth, a country may produce many of its own consumer goods, such as textiles, and will even export some of them in large volume. Later on, having reached an advanced stage of development, it may export capital goods and sophisticated consumer goods and to import simple manufactures. Such economies, as they grow, tend to "integrate backwards" from goods closer to the final consumer to goods successively further removed from him. This time profile of production will then influence the product composition of traded manufactures.

SCALE ECONOMIES

Yet another possible explanation of trade patterns lies in the cost advantages that can be attained either in large diversified firms or in long production runs in specialized firms. In either case, economies of large-scale production can reduce unit costs and convey an international competitive advantage. The large size of the internal U.S. market, for example, may permit American producers of tradable products to operate at higher levels of efficiency than, say, Australian producers faced with a much smaller internal market. Production runs are longer, and product differentation is less pronounced. Hence scale economies in certain sectors may represent an important determinant of comparative advantage. The only way producers in small countries can achieve the same advantages is through easy access to—and a high degree of familiarity with—export markets.

There may well be a relationship between the large-scale production of exports and the size of the domestic economy, or the volume of industrial output. However, this relationship is probably rather tenuous, since large but poor countries such as India and small but rich countries such as Denmark and the Netherlands behave quite differently in this regard. Nevertheless, for a significant range of product groups and trading countries the attainment of scale economies seems to be an important determinant of trade.

PREFERENCE SIMILARITY

We have from the beginning emphasized the coequal importance of supply and demand in international trade. Although international differences in factor endowments may well govern trade in primary products, this may not necessarily be as true for manufactured goods. For them, the similarity or dissimilarity of *demand patterns* between coutries may be more important. Since by far the greatest share of overall international trade is today composed of manufactures, demand patterns would then play an important role in the overall global trade picture.

Demand patterns may influence the development of trade in the following way. In order for a country to export a certain manufactured product, it may first need an intensive *internal* demand for that good, so that the potential export industry is permitted to grow to viable proportions and efficiency. Domestic demand thus enables an industry to reach a large enough production scale to allow it to become competitive in the international marketplace. Moreover, a country may discover that its most promising foreign markets are countries at stages of economic development similar to its own—where demand for that type of manufactured goods has grown to a roughly equal point. Trade should then be most intense between nations showing rather similar demand characteristics.

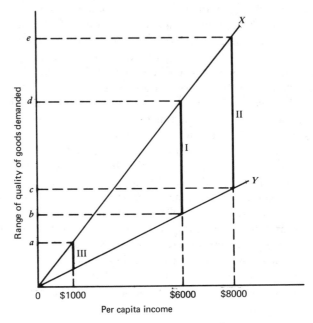

Figure 8-2. Demand patterns as determinants of international trade.

Figure 8-2 illustrates this relationship. The vertical axis denotes the general quality level, or degree of sophistication, based on some assumed values, that characterizes the national demand for manufactured goods, whereas the horizontal axis represents per capita income. Logically, one would expect growth in a nation's per capita income to call forth an increase in the average quality of the goods demanded. This is represented by the vertical distance between lines OX and OY, which expands and shifts upward with increasing income in Figure 8-2.

Now suppose two countries, I and II, have per capita incomes of $6000 and $8000 respectively. Note the relevant demand patterns. Country I demands goods in the quality range bd, whereas the demand pattern in the higher-income country II extends over quality range ce.

In country I, there is no demand for goods of a quality *higher* than d, and in country II the demand for commodities of a quality *lower* than c is zero. Only the quality range cd is common to both countries. Since there is no demand in I for country II's goods of quality range *de*, and no demand in *II* for country *I*'s goods of a quality range *bc*, trade between the two countries must fall in the range of goods *cd*. By the same reasoning, trade in manufactured goods between a highly developed country such as *I* and a relatively poor country such as *III*, should be relatively small and entirely determined by factor endowments, since there is no overlapping of demand patterns at all.

If we were to apply this theory to the real world, we would expect to see a large volume of trade in manufactures between such countries as Germany and the United States, Great Britain and France, and Sweden and Japan, but relatively little trade between the United States and Nicaragua, Germany and Upper Volta, and Great Britain and Haiti.

Essentially, this view says that trade in manufactures should be most intense between economically *similar* countries, whereas the factor-endowments approach implies that trade should be most pronounced between countries whose economic structures are fundamentally *different*. This possibly gives us one more alternative for looking at the factors governing international trade, one that is at least in part related to the product-cycle and scale-economy theories.

SUMMARY

What do we end up with, after all these amplifications and modifications? Clearly, the conventional theory of trade contains important insights. Relative factor endowments and relative factor efficiencies indeed help to determine trade in a broad range of products. Probably its predictive power is greater in regard to trade involving developing economies and highly standardized products.

At the same time, the traditional definition of "capital" must be broadened so as to include investment in knowledge (via research and development) and human resources (via education and training), along with the quantity and quality of physical production facilities. Such a definition of capital makes the traditional theory even more credible and promises to enhance greatly its predictive power, as does the incorporation of scale economies as a separate cost determinant.

Similar theoretical and empirical extensions have been made on the demand side—especially where supply and demand are interactive—so that a country's domestic demand begets an industry that eventually grows to be competitive in export markets. The preference-similarity and product-cycle theories are two cases in point, and they may help us understand why the United States both exports *and* imports cameras in large volume, or why Germany does the same with automobiles.

We are left, then, with a rather broad formulation of the pure theory of international trade, but one that seems to get encouragingly close to the truth. We can in fact explain many of the trade flows in a multiproduct, multicountry world, as depicted back in Figure 3-1. Yet how do we combine all of this into the kind of neat, conceptual, general model with which we began? Economists are still working on it.

Important Concepts

bilateral trade   product cycle

multilateral trade   stages of growth

Leontief paradox   economies of scale

human capital   preference similarily

technological gaps

Questions

1. Define the Leontief paradox, and describe its importance in the modern theory of international trade.
2. In your view, is the "product cycle" theory of trade in the tradition of pure trade theory as you have learned it so far? Why or why not? How would you reconcile the two?
3. Some people think the United States in the years ahead will develop into a "service economy." What would that imply for the structure of U.S. international trade?
4. The United States used to be a major net exporter of automobiles. Now it is a major net importer. Why? What is your prognosis for computers? For wheat?

Further Readings

Baldwin, R. E., "Determinants of the Commodity Structure of U.S. Trade," *American Economic Review*, March 1971.

Burenstam Linder, S., *An Essay on Trade and Transformation* (Stockholm: Almqvist & Wicksell, 1961).

Keesing, Donald B., "Labor Skills and Comparative Advantage," *American Economic Review*, May 1966.

Kenen, Peter B., "Nature, Capital and Trade," *Journal of Political Economy*, October 1965.

Leontief, W., "Domestic Production and Foreign Trade: The American Position Reexamined," *Proceedings of the American Philosophical Society*, September 1953.

Leontief, W., "Factor Proportions and the Structure of American Trade," *Review of Economics and Statistics*, November 1956.

Stern, R. M., "Testing Trade Theories in International Trade and Finance," in P. B. Kenen (ed). *International Trade and Finance: Frontiers for Research* (Cambridge: Cambridge University Press, 1975).

Vernon, R., "International Investment and International Trade in the Product Cycle," *Quarterly Journal of Economics*, May 1966.

II

Trade, Protection, and Factor Movements

9
INTRODUCTION TO TRADE POLICY

The theory of international trade teaches us that world output of goods and services can be maximized only under conditions of free trade and international specialization. Given the imperfect international mobility of the factors of production, trade between national economies must be unrestricted if productive resources are to be allocated in the most efficient way possible. The simple economic models we have used uncontestably show that this must be the case under reasonably plausible assumptions. And yet essentially free intercountry trade in goods and services has never been fully realized. Impressive movements toward trade liberalization have taken place from time to time, but they have often been followed by dramatic shifts in the opposite direction.

If economic theory is correct, why do the economic, social, and political interests that determine international trade policy fail to express such a basic proposition and to promote consistent and far-reaching efforts toward trade liberalization? This is the topic of the present chapter. We focus on why countries sometimes find it in their national interest to impose restrictions on international trade, why trade restrictions favor some factors of production over others (remember the factor-endowments theory discussed in Chapter 4), and why certain groups in society tend to fight for or against trade. We shall include an examination of the political as well as conventional economic dimensions of the problem.

TRADE POLICY AND THE NATIONAL INTEREST

We can begin with an examination of reasons why trade restrictions *might* be in the interest of the nation as a whole, as opposed to the interests of groups within that nation or of the entire world. Sometimes the national interest will favor trade restrictions, sometimes not. We shall therefore call these arguments *nonbiased* with respect to the specific choice of the desired policies.

Terms of Trade

A nation may under certain conditions be able to improve its material well-being by imposing restrictions on its exports or imports, if such action results in an improvement in its international terms of trade—that is, in a decline in the prices of products it buys from abroad and/or a rise in the prices of products it sells abroad. Such gains can only be achieved at the expense of the economic welfare of trading partners, who in turn may try to attain similar gains at the expense of the home country; such trade restrictions therefore invite retaliation. Hence, as we shall see later on, the terms-of-trade basis for barriers to free international commerce reduces to a matter of intercountry bargaining. In fact, a country's barriers around its market in part determine its bargaining power with trading partners, and its trade barriers also influence its ability to secure trade concessions in return for liberalization steps of its own. And institutions such as the Organization of Petroleum Exporting Countries (OPEC) can be viewed as vehicles for manipulating the commodity terms of trade in contravention of the free-trade principle.

Balance of Payments

International financial conditions may exert an important influence on a nation's trade policy. Later chapters will make clear that balance-of-payments deficits (roughly, excess foreign outlays over foreign receipts) tend to bring political pressures for trade restrictions, designed to cut expenditures on imports or to raise export earnings.

Meanwhile, trade restrictions, in that they affect prices inside the domestic economy in relation to those abroad, can have domestic financial consequences; briefly put, they alter the real value of a nation's currency. Conversely, changes in the value of the national currency may have implications for national commercial policy. Thus, questions of *international trade policy* and *international financial policy* are closely linked.

Clearly, balance-of-payments deficits or severe international pressures on its currency are more likely to move a country toward increased protectionism in its commercial policy and less likely to promote agreement on trade liberalization than the opposite circumstances. At the same time, using trade barriers for balance-of-payments reasons may well trigger retaliation on the part of countries whose payments situations suffer from such measures. These issues will be discussed in the second half of the book.

Distortions of Competition

Trade policy can be used for alleviating distortions within the national economy—for example, to offset market control in the hands of monopolistically organized industries or labor groups. To the extent that trade barriers help to reallocate production from areas where such distortions are serious to areas where they are not so troublesome, a benefit may be obtained by the nation as a whole. This issue is discussed more formally later on under the heading of the "theory of second best" (see Chapter 13).

Unemployed Resources

If a national economy is operating at unacceptably low levels of employment and capacity utilization, a government may seek to alleviate these conditions by means of trade policy. Import restrictions and export incentives tend to "switch" domestic expenditure from goods and services produced abroad to those produced at home, thereby strengthening aggregate demand and helping to reemploy idle resources. But on the other side of the fence, the foreign trade partners will then be selling less and buying more from abroad. If these economies likewise suffer from unused productive capacity and idle resources, such trade policy measures will be adverse to their interests, and countermoves may be expected. In other circumstances, a country suffering from inflationary pressures might want to liberalize its imports, since the increased expenditures on foreign-made products may reduce the effective demand for home-produced goods and force domestic suppliers to moderate their price increases.

Growth

Under certain conditions a country may be willing to forgo some of the gains attributable to unhindered international trade if this sacrifice promises even greater long-range benefits in terms of economic growth. The development of important new industries, or the economic survival of a regional development program, may seem to justify increased restriction of imports. A developing country, for instance, may wish to protect an emerging industry from low-cost foreign imports until such a time as the industry becomes internationally competitive. Or it may decide to protect certain sectors so as to promote diversification and the development of home-produced substitutes for imports. An assessment that the longer-term *gains from growth* outweigh the immediate *gains from trade* in any given instance may underlie the creation of obstacles to international trade.

Revenue

Certain kinds of restrictions on internatioal trade produce substantial fiscal revenues: tariffs, import levies and surcharges, license fees, and export taxes are some examples. Governments—particularly those with unreliable or poorly developed fiscal systems—frequently find it convenient to levy charges on international transactions, which then become an important substitute for ordinary income and sales taxes. They may do this despite their realization that the allocation of resources may be distorted and some of the potential gains from trade will remain unrealized.

Social Arguments

On occasion, purely social or moral arguments are raised in defense of trade restrictions. They are typically intended to ensure the attainment of politically accepted goals relating to life-styles, physical or mental health, or the environment. For example, heavy tariffs may be applied to imports of alcoholic beverages or tobacco products in order to reduce consumption levels. Export controls may be imposed on certain raw materials for ecological reasons or to conserve natural resources. Generally, trade policy is only one of many paths to the realization of such social-political goals, and it frequently represents a decidedly inefficient and inferior alternative.

Political-Military Arguments

Trade policy is a major component of a nation's foreign economic policy and hence is frequently employed in the pursuit of general foreign-policy goals. Trade concessions, as in the form of reduced tariffs, may be accorded to certain foreign countries for political reasons, and the withholding or withdrawal of such concessions may be a similar policy weapon. On the export side as well, a government may use trade controls to deny access by foreign countries to certain products. Existing or past trade sanctions against Rhodesia, South Africa, Uganda, Cuba, the U.S.S.R., the People's Republic of China, Iran, and most of the Soviet bloc (especially on defense-related products) are examples that may be cited. In spite of its frequent ineffectiveness in obtaining a major political objective, trade policy as a tool of "economic warfare" is still in widespread use.

Trade restrictions may also be employed to protect certain domestic industries against import competition when their output is ostensibly critical for national defense. The importance of such industries in a national emergency is deemed sufficient at least to offset the annual costs incurred—in terms of the induced inefficiencies and the trade gains forgone—in ensuring their survival. Such costs and forgone gains are in the nature of an insurance premium that is an integral part of the cost of national defense. National security considerations usually show up on the trade-restrictive side of the trade-policy debate, although they may on occasion support freer trade.

All of the foregoing reasons for barriers to (or, occasionally, subsidies for) international trade have a single underlying theme: the pursuit of national economic, political, and social goals. The arguments presented do not necessarily favor specific groups within a nation. They may, in fact, militate either in favor of or against freer trade, as none of them is inherently or consistently biased for or against free trade. They weigh into the trade-policy decision process as nonbiased elements in terms of Figure 9-1 on p. 137, discussed below. Their weight may shift in one direction or the other in accordance with shifts in the underlying economic, political, or social conditions.

TRADE AND INCOME DISTRIBUTION

Without trade, imagine that different groups of individuals are making various products for domestic consumption. Their real incomes are determined by the laws of supply and demand operating freely both in the market for goods and in the market for productive factors.

Now let us assume free international trade. Prices facing consumers fall as imports make competitive inroads on domestic suppliers. Production of those goods in which the country has a comparative advantage expands to meet the export demand. Meanwhile, output of goods in which the country has a comparative disadvantage contracts under pressure from import competition. The real incomes of industry-specific factors of production engaged in the export sector will tend to rise, whereas the real incomes of those still engaged in import-competing employment will tend to fall. Income will be redistributed from one group to another, and some will be better off and some worse off as a result of international trade.

True, some of those employed in the import-competing industries will be released and absorbed by the export industries, thus shifting them from one group to the other. But it is still not possible to make valid generalizations about the impact of international trade on general social welfare. Who knows whether the loss of the losers is greater than the gain of the gainers, or vice versa? This would involve drawing interpersonal comparisons—which, as we have already said, is strictly impossible.

Suppose, however, that some of the welfare gains of those engaged in the export industries are somehow taxed away, without affecting aggregate national income, and given to those experiencing welfare losses. Income is redistributed in such a way that while some gain, at least others do not suffer a reduction in welfare as a result of trade. We can then say that overall welfare has indeed increased. No one would lose, but some would gain. This is possible because, as we know, trade expands the overall "consumption set" of a country.

By assuming that income is redistributed in this fashion, we are in a position to make a positive statement about the welfare effects of free trade, even without being able to make interpersonal welfare comparisons. Unrestricted international trade will always *make possible* an increase in community welfare over and above that which prevails in isolation. Free international trade is a *necessary* but not *sufficient* condition for the maximization of social welfare when compared with no trade at all. Whether or not this overall welfare gain is actually realized depends entirely upon the degree to which real income is "equitably" redistributed from those who gain to those who lose as a result of international trade. On an even broader scale, world production of goods and services *will* gain from the specialization and resource reallocation that free trade makes possible, whereas world economic welfare *may* gain as a result. This is again contingent upon the redistribution of real income that occurs.

It may be useful to consider the income-distributional aspects of commercial policy from the perspective of two basic interest groups. The first of these—which might be called the *protection-biased sector*—advocates high levels of trade restriction in order to shield itself from foreign competition. The second group—the *trade-biased sector*—for equally compelling reasons of self-interest demands low trade barriers. It strives to obtain for its own use low-cost imports, or to ensure maximum access to foreign markets. The political process serves to resolve this conflict, and the existing national trade-policy position reflects this internal resolution, set against the essentially *nonbiased* considerations based on the national interest and outlined above. The final mix of commercial policies that results represents the bilateral and multilateral conciliation of differing national trade-policy positions on an international level. As the product of the internal and external conflict resolution and constantly shifting economic-political conditions, the resultant trade policy naturally cannot satisfy *both* the protection-biased and the trade-biased groups at home (or abroad), and this gives rise to constant pressure for change in that policy.

The general arguments for freer trade, which are based on static economic theory, assume effective competition in markets for goods, services, and productive factors, and commensurate flexibility in prices and costs. They do not take into account the existence of relatively inefficient and internationally uncompetitive domestic producers. Any move toward more liberal trade may affect the vital economic interests of such producers, their employees, managements, dependent municipalities and regions, suppliers, and other groups. These groups will naturally resist freer trade as it affects their industry and use whatever political power they have to prevent it. But since international trade theory assures us that the benefits of freer trade will *on balance* outweigh the damage free trade does to import-competing interests, obviously those groups in society that gain from liberalized trade could in theory somehow compensate those groups suffering damage from it—and still be ahead.

Two problems arise, however. First, the damaged groups may be hurt to such a degree that the harm is viewed as irreparable—a firm may cease to exist, a job or skill category may be eliminated, a town may lose all of its industry. As a result, those damaged may feel that no amount of adjustment assistance or compensation is sufficient to offset their losses. Whether or not just compensation would in fact be impossible, it is the *attitude* that is important and renders political resistance to freer trade extremely vociferous.

Second, even if it were possible to compensate the injured, there generally are no effective economic or political mechanisms to capture from the benefiting groups just enough real income to effect equitable reparations to those who lose. Both comprise highly diverse groups, with the benefits and costs attributable to freer trade distributed unevenly within these groups. In addition, the benefits of trade liberalization do not necessarily accrue to the economy during the same time period as the damages that must be absorbed. Besides, those benefited by freer trade will be expected to resist a removal of some of their gains for compensation purposes.

In short, the impossibility of intergroup and interpersonal comparisons of trade-induced gains and losses makes it difficult to render effective compensation on a national scale, as by setting up a network of compensatory taxes and subsidies. Therefore, the conflict between the gainers and losers from freer trade will be harder to resolve. Figure 9-1 on p. 137 presents a political-economic model of trade-policy decision making focusing on group interests within a national economy, and it can be used to diagnose and forecast group behavior in the trade-policy arena. The two principal protagonists are the *trade-biased* and *protection-biased* sectors just identified, with the *nonbiased* national-interest factors, presumably expressed by the national government, throwing their weight in one direction or the other on different issues.

Finally, one could argue that from a national-interest point of view, changing trade patterns and comparative advantages shift a country's production mix, not always smoothly, but in a shocklike manner, creating unemployed resources. In other words, the production point moves *inside* the country's transformation function for a time, while the unemployed resources are being reallocated by the factor market. This could be used as an argument for temporary trade restrictions to *slow down* the adjustment process and reduce its overall cost to society.

COMPOSITION OF THE PROTECTION-BIASED AND TRADE-BIASED SECTORS

Domestic business firms actually or potentially in competition with foreign firms for sales in the home market form the core of the protection-biased sector and generally stand in opposition to a more liberal trade policy. They prefer to see tariffs and other trade barriers become more restrictive as regards those products that they themselves supply. Around this core are grouped the labor unions and the owners of productive factors employed by these firms, domestic enterprises supplying them with raw materials and components, and businesses producing complementary products, as well as the political representatives of the regions and communities affected. All tend to support increased trade restrictions. Only to the extent that any of the suppliers are dependent on imported raw materials or components would the pervasive interest in more restrictive trade policies be mitigated. If the various political representatives of this protection-biased sector acted in a manner other than to oppose trade liberalization, they would be neglecting their responsibilities to their constituencies. Those who support a more restrictive national trade policy constitute an important political power bloc, based on the logical expression of their self-interest.

The opposing force—the trade-biased sector—is primarily concerned with access to foreign markets for exports, with the domestic availability and price of imported goods and services, and with foreign reactions to domestic trade-policy moves. Suppliers of exports realize that increased protectionism at home may result in the imposition of more restrictive trade barriers abroad, and in a narrowing of their markets. At the same time, they tend to be aware that they cannot widen their access to foreign markets—secured by reduced foreign trade restrictions—without domestic concessions to liberalize imports. This places the export suppliers squarely on the side of trade liberalization. Again, the owners of the factors of production used in the export-oriented industries, associated labor groups, firms supplying those industries with raw materials and intermediate inputs, and the representatives of export-dependent local and regional political jurisdictions join in opposing protection and in favoring generally freer trade. These interest groups are aided in their efforts by importers, distributors, retailers, and final consumers of imported goods and services, who likewise support trade liberalization. Not least important are business firms, financial institutions, and individuals with substantial investments abroad, who may realize that foreign retaliation against national trade-policy measures may manifest itself as investment controls detrimental to their interests. For instance, multinational business firms are concerned with free access to their foreign subsidiaries for raw materials, components, and capital goods; as we shall see in Chapter 16, multinational production networks function best under liberal trade and investment conditions. Together, these domestic interest groups make up a large but heterogeneous bloc diametrically opposed to the protectionist sector.

Of course, the alliance of forces for and against freer trade is not quite so simple as this, nor are the groupings so discrete. For example, most individuals are both consumers and producers, and this poses a conflict of interest for someone employed in an import-competing industry. Business firms, especially multiproduct diversified companies, may have among their operating divisions some that are decidedly export-oriented and others that fall into the import-competing group, while labor unions may have individual locals on different sides of the fence. Trade and industry associations, political representatives, and others may therefore face severe internal decision problems in reaching a coherent and defensible position on national trade policy.

To summarize, it appears that the interests of the *nonbiased, protection-biased*, and *trade-biased* segments of the modern economy, expressed through the political mechanism, determine the national trade-policy position. Their respective economic interests are mirrored, however imperfectly, in the national debate on trade policy and in the final national trade-policy stance. Shifts in the salient variables—such as a change in relative prices at home or abroad, a change in domestic or foreign technology or productive efficiency, or a shift in demand patterns—will produce corresponding changes in the positions of the various groups on the proper course of national trade policy, and the political dynamics will eventually bring about changes in that policy itself.

BEHAVIOR OF THE PROTECTION-BIASED SECTOR

Changes in trade policy will also change the actual involvement of certain firms and industries in the production of import substitutes. Should stronger trade restrictions be introduced: (*a*) established producers will find that they are earning increased profits on larger volumes of output and higher prices on such goods; (*b*) marginal producers will find that they are now operating at a profit and are in a position to expand; and (*c*) some inefficient producers who formerly had been excluded from the production of the import-competing items because of excessive costs will now find that the new, higher price permits them to undertake profitable production. Even if such "infant" industries in time become efficient enough not to need protection, they will have a built-in tendency to push for continued shielding from imports, since that provides security for extra output and profits.

At the other end of the scale, declining, "senile" industries tend to be even more active in their efforts to obtain protection. Dated management techniques, obsolete technology and capital facilities, and labor restrictions may have reduced productivity to such an extent that the enterprise is no longer able to compete effectively against similar industries established more recently in other countries. Hence, they feel a special need for protection.

As national economies develop, the very new "front-edge" industries and those at the "back edge" of the industrial spectrum will thus form the vanguard of protectionist interest. The former have not yet attained a competitive advantage in international trade, and the latter are gradually losing it. Major protectionist strength may be attained if the front-edge and, especially, back-edge industrial groups comprise a large part of the national economy.

In general, a liberal trade policy can be relied upon to "clean out" lagging and increasingly noncompetitive producing units and sectors through import competition, thereby freeing productive factors for more efficient use in other parts of the economy. This "scavenging effect" of international trade tends to have a broad positive impact on economic growth. Economic development is always an uneven process, and one of the major symptoms of this unevenness is the continual emergence of front-edge and back-edge industries of the kinds just described. Imports serve an important role in the growth process by efficiently wiping out back-edge industries—supplanting their production with that of foreign suppliers possessing an international comparative advantage—and releasing productive resources for use in front-edge, perhaps exporting industries. To the extent that imports are impeded through tariffs or other trade restrictions, of course, their scavenging function is likewise impeded, with a corresponding negative effect on growth.

The economic health of many communities is closely linked to the prosperity of a domestic firm or industry engaged in import competition. Since national legislatures are normally elected on a local basis, their members are influenced by community pressures emanating from the economic prospects of producers operating in their constituencies. Even in countries in which the national legislature does not specifically determine trade policy, it is often able to influence the executive authority, or pressures may be brought to bear in other ways.

The protection-biased sector is usually in an inherently strong political position because the possibilities of gain or loss attributable to trade-policy shifts are *immediate* and *direct*. For them, increased trade barriers would seem to result in an obvious output expansion, increased employment and higher profits, regional prosperity, and a general gain in real income of all concerned. They need only point out that if imports were not present, the domestic market would be served by the domestic producers. They can also argue that a reduction in trade barriers will result in a direct loss to them, a cut in their "fair share" of the market, a reduction in output and employment, idle capacity, and generally harmful effects upon their region. These are the kinds of short-run pressure that representatives in the national government respond to. After all, it is their business to look after the economic interests of their constituents and, whenever possible, to mitigate any government actions that are harmful to these parties.

BEHAVIOR OF THE TRADE-BIASED SECTOR

Consumer groups, insofar as they can organize for political action, tend to promote a more liberal national trade policy. Trade barriers impose losses on consumers, who will thereby have less choice in their purchases and have to pay higher prices for protected items. Those who would purchase a given product only at a lower price are squeezed out of the market as a result of trade barriers. Those remaining in the market pay a higher price for the product, thus effectively losing real incomes and ability to purchase other products.

Consumers have tended to be the least-effectual members of the trade-biased sector. This should not be taken to mean that the loss or gain in consumer satisfaction resulting from a trade-policy shift is not very substantial, even though the consumer movement in recent years has enhanced its political clout in many countries. Part of the difficulty derives from the fact, noted earlier, that consumers are normally producers, employees, and investors as well, and their interests in these capacities may well be damaged by a vigorous promotion of their concerns as consumers. In addition, the loss in consumer welfare because of trade barriers is difficult to identify in practice. They may represent only a small portion of the price of the final imported product. Under conditions of rapid economic growth and high employment, consumers simply refuse to get agitated about the marginal losses in real income attributed to trade barriers, and inflation may overwhelm the price effects of any specific trade barrier.

Closely allied to the consumers in matters of trade policy are the importers, distributors, and retailers of foreign-made goods, whose welfare is very directly linked to the flow of these products into the national market. Large retail chains, discount houses, and mail-order concerns tend to draw a major share of their low-priced consumer durables, textile products, footwear, toys, and various other items from foreign sources, and generally they actively oppose trade restrictions and support trade liberalization.

Support for a liberal trade policy may also be expected from domestic firms who buy inputs from abroad. But import-using firms often belong to the import-competing sector, which can make their stand on trade policy equivocal. If generally higher trade barriers are applied, their own output will be protected; at the same time, prices of imported inputs will rise, with a negative impact on output and profits.

Consumers, importer-distributors, and import-using firms are joined by exporters, who are anxious to promote minimum import barriers so that foreigners will be able to finance the purchase of their export goods and so that foreign reciprocal trade concessions can be secured, or retaliatory trade restrictions avoided. Business firms investing in foreign production facilities also generally support freer trade. They may wish to supply foreign affiliates with raw material inputs from the home country, to serve the markets of other countries from their foreign bases, or to maintain a favorable investment climate abroad.

Export interests often experience difficulty in translating their economic interests into effective political action. Since these interests generally represent vigorous, growing sectors of the national economy, the direct or indirect damage they suffer from domestic import restrictions will constitute only a forgone gain, rather than outright layoffs, cuts in output, or reduced profits. Also, they often fail to see the relationship between the freedom of imports and the volume of their exports.

THE POLITICAL TRANSFORMATION

We have attempted to sort out the basic economic forces that determine the national trade-policy position, in particular, those emanating from the trade-biased and the protection-biased sectors. Essentially nonbiased forces may swing the political balance in one direction or the other, and they may be enlisted by either side on behalf of its own position. These forces must operate within an overall domestic political structure that is essentially neutral with respect to trade policy and ideally is geared to mediating conflicting group interests in the name of national collective objectives. Unfortunately, the process of translating the economic interests into political influence over policy making is subtle, unstable, and not amenable to conventional economic analysis. The political results may not necessarily reflect the economic balance of power, in part also because the national executive, responsible for *implementing* trade policy, may choose policy techniques that have economic effects other than those desired by the dominant economic-political groups.

Changes in structural and competitive conditions at home and abroad induce the economic groups affected by international trade to reevaluate their positions. A group that has favored a liberal trade policy in the past may find that a more restrictive commercial policy is now better suited to its needs. New political alignments may be successful in changing trade-policy legislation, and a change in national commercial policy may thus result from a change in economic structure. These forces, evident throughout the history of international trade policy, drive the trade-policy decision-making process outlined in Figure 9-1.

National trade policy may also change because of a change in the very process of policy making. Such changes can occur through (*a*) increasing or decreasing political influence of a given interest group, (*b*) a revised interpretation by such a group of its best interests, (*c*) a new general attitude about what constitutes the national interest in international economic and political matters, (*d*) new trade-policy techniques, (*e*) *logrolling* by politicians trading votes on unrelated policy matters, and so forth.

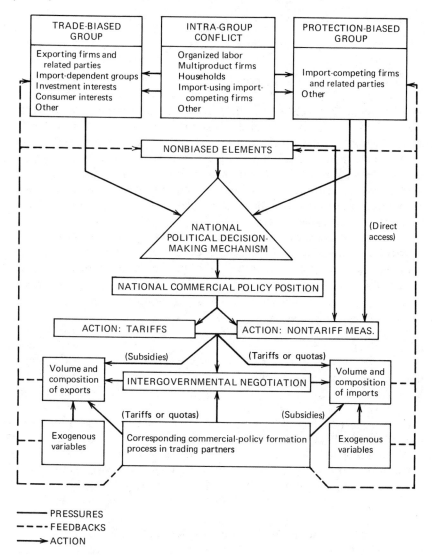

Figure 9-1. Development of the national trade-policy position.

ACCESS TO THE INSTRUMENTS OF TRADE POLICY

Once a national trade-policy position has been established, along the lines indicated in Figure 9-1, it must of course be implemented. In part, the techniques chosen depend on the pressures brought to bear during the course of the decision-making process just described. A particular protective device may be specified by elements of the protection-biased sector and be accepted in the course of the political transformation. Or other trade-policy devices may be substituted in the bargaining process, either because they are less onerous than the former or because the danger of foreign repercussions is thought to be less serious.

The output of the national decision-making process will be either to raise or to lower restrictions to trade, or to leave them unchanged. If the political balance weighs in favor of liberalization, a mandate is normally created for international negotiations to bring this about—under the proviso that the bargaining outcome be as favorable as possible to the interests of the trade-biased sector and do as little damage as possible to the protection-biased sector. When damage to import competitors is unavoidable, provision may be made for tax-financed financial assistance to the injured industries and related economic groups—a case of compensation by the gainers (the general public) from freer trade to the losers.

But suppose the political balance weighs in favor of increased trade restrictions. The policy mix chosen will then reflect the specific demands of the protection-biased sector, as modified in the political decision-making process by the influence of opposing and nonbiased sectors. Account will be taken of the likely foreign reactions and of damage to import-using groups.

The availability of access to the instruments of trade policy may not be symmetrical between the two interest groups. Whereas the trade-biased interests may have to expose themselves to the entire policy-making mechanism to get their way, it is sometimes possible for the protection-biased interests to short-circuit this process by resorting to certain "nontariff barriers." These are restrictions on imports applied by a variety of governmental units, often with little apparent coordination, central direction, or even awareness on the part of national decision makers; we shall discuss these barriers in detail in Chapter 11. And so it is possible for individual protection-seeking forces to avail themselves of such measures and translate their interests into policy action without themselves being subject to public debate and scrutiny, or to the opposing forces in the political arena.

INTERNATIONAL CONCILIATION

Once a national trade-policy position has been established, it must confront similar forces in other national economies. The latter will often influence the domestic decision-making process. If foreign political forces are moving an important trading partner to apply trade restrictions, this fact weighs in favor of the protection-biased sector in the domestic decision process. In some instances retaliation may even be mandatory, as a result of existing provisions in the trade laws. Conversely, moves abroad toward freer trade will influence the national debate on the side of the trade-biased sector. In short, the national trade-policy position is not formed in an international vacuum.

The national trade-policy position, once established, may be subjected to conciliation efforts either bilaterally or under the auspices of established international institutions, particularly the General Agreement on Tariffs and Trade (GATT), which we shall discuss in Chapter 13. A protection-biased trade-policy position may be implemented "legally" or "illegally" under accepted international rules. In the former case, the consultative process will tend to determine policy responses abroad, if any. In the latter case, there is greater risk of hostile conflict and, possibly, specific retaliatory sanctions. On the other hand, a trade-biased policy move by a major nation may produce international consultation that leads to a more general reduction of international trade barriers. The degree of such liberalization will depend upon the relative international clout of the trade-biased forces in the participating countries, as reflected in their national commercial-policy positions and in the mandates accorded their representatives in the international negotiations.

SUMMARY

Although trade theory teaches us that free international exchanges of goods and services generate maximum global welfare, what is best for the world is not necessarily best for individual countries or, especially, for groups within those countries. Since policy with respect to international trade is formulated largely at the national level, it is important to understand the national political and economic forces that produce movements toward or away from free trade. Some groups in society identify fundamentally with liberal trade, whereas others see their interests as being closely linked to protection. The former groups typically include actual or potential exporters, workers employed by them, most multinational businesses, and consumers. The latter groups comprise mostly inefficient or declining import-competing industries, their workers, and their communities. The two sides periodically battle it out in the national political arena, and the results largely determine the direction of national trade policy. This, in turn, has to be played off against corresponding political-economic forces in other countries, with consequences for the general global climate of international trade.

Important Concepts

national-interest arguments for protection

group-interest arguments for protection

gains from trade vs. gains from growth

protection-biased sector

trade-biased sector

infant industries

trade liberalization

Questions

1. Suppose you were looking at two large manufacturing firms, one highly diversified across industrial product groups and the other not. Everything else being equal, which one do you think would tend to be more protectionist in trade policy matters? Why?

2. It is claimed that a politician's votes on matters of trade policy can be forecast on the basis of the economic makeup of his or her constituency. Why?

3. One important argument for protecting a nation's steel industry is its role in national defense. If you were asked to make this case intellectually defensible, how would you account for the economic costs involved, and how would you justify them?

4. Some criteria in assessing the efficacy of a nation's trade policy are *efficiency, equity,* and *reciprocity.* Define each of these terms, and indicate its importance in the trade-policy context.

Further Readings

Amacher, R. C., G. Haberler, and T. D. Willett, eds., *Challenges to a Liberal International Economic Order* (Washington, D.C.: American Enterprise Institute, 1979).

Baldwin, R. E., *The Political Economy of Postwar Trade Policy* (New York: New York University Graduate School of Business Administration, 1976).

Blackhurst, R., R. Marian, and J. Tumlir, *Trade Liberalization, Protection and Interdependence* (New York: Unipub, 1978).

Krauss, Melvyn B., *The New Protectionism* (New York: New York University Press, 1978).

Yeager, L. B., and D. G. Tuerck, *Foreign Trade and U.S. Policy* (New York: Praeger, 1976).

10

TARIFFS

We shall now discuss the instruments, or tools, of trade policy. The most widely employed restriction on international trade is the *tariff*. A tariff is a charge levied on goods as they cross the national customs frontier. There are two types of tariffs. An *ad valorem* tariff on imports is usually calculated as a percentage of the total value of the product as it enters the country, including its cost and all transportation charges—its *c.i.f.* (*cost, insurance,* and *freight*) value. A *specific* tariff, on the other hand, involves a fixed monetary duty per unit of the imported product (e.g., $500 per automobile, $5 per ton of a certain chemical, and so on). Of the two types of tariffs, the *ad valorem* duty is by far the more common.

Whereas both of these types of levies apply to imports, there are also *export duties*, which are placed on goods leaving a country, and *transit duties*, which are placed on goods crossing a country on the way to a destination elsewhere. Neither of these levies is very important (export duties are unconstitutional in the United States); but they do raise some relevant questions, especially in developing countries.

In most cases, tariffs are applied with the sole intention of reducing the volume of imports. Naturally, tariffs may also raise government revenues, and sometimes are applied for this purpose alone; these levies on international trade are called *revenue tariffs*.

How do tariffs affect trade? To take the simplest possible illustration, suppose there are two countries, *I* and *II*. Five pounds of sugar sells for $0.60 in *I* and for $0.40 in *II* without international trade. Naturally, if free trade prevailed, manufacturers in *II* would export sugar to *I*, thus driving down the price of sugar in that country. If it wants to prevent this, all country *I* has to do is levy a 50 percent *ad valorem* tariff on sugar imports from country *II*. Assuming no transport costs, with the tariff the sugar produced in country *II*

141

would sell in country *I* for exactly the same price as the domestic product ($0.40 + 50 percent tariff = $0.60). In the absence of quality differences, there would no longer be any reason for consumers in country *I* to buy sugar from country *II*, and sugar imports would cease.

This can be illustrated more generally by means of a partial equilibrium supply-and-demand analysis, shown in Figure 10-1. Without trade, equilibrium in country *I* is at point *R*, with 15 units of the product being produced and consumed (at a price of $20). Meanwhile, in country *II*, 23 units are being produced and consumed at a price of $14. With trade, at equilibrium, a price of $16 prevails in both countries. At that price, country *II* produces a surplus of 10 units, which it exports to country *I*, where it exactly equals the 10-unit shortage prevailing there at the new price. The volume of trade thus is 10 units.

If country *I* wishes to prevent these imports, it need simply impose a tariff of $6. This will raise the minimum price of any potential imports to $20, domestic supply will expand by 5 units from *U* to *R*, domestic quantity demanded will contract by 5 units from *T* to *R*, and all imports will be shut out. For country *II* the demand for its export is eliminated, price falls by $2, and output contracts by 7 units from *N* to *M* while domestic quantity demanded expands by 3 units from *L* to *M*. Hence, in the absence of transport costs, a tariff equal to the difference between the domestic and foreign pretrade prices has the effect of eliminating trade between the two countries.

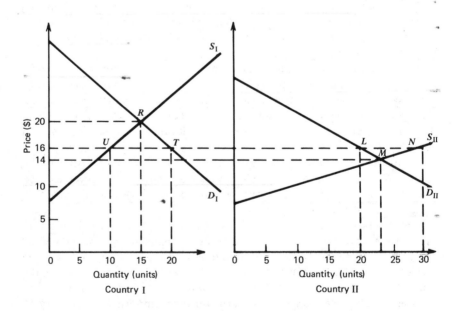

Figure 10-1. Tariffs and the volume of trade.

With transport costs, a somewhat lower tariff will have the same effect. The reader can easily see that a less restrictive tariff—less than $6—will reduce the volume of trade by a smaller amount, and not eliminate it entirely.

TARIFFS, PRODUCTION, AND CONSUMPTION

Let us look next at the impact of a tariff on production and consumption. Figure 10-1 demonstrates that any tariff will tend to raise the domestic price of a product above its free-trade level, and thereby stimulate its domestic production and reduce its domestic consumption.

This is shown more clearly, again in terms of partial equilibrium analysis, in Figure 10-2. Curves D_d and S_d are the domestic demand and supply curves for the particular good under consideration. Without trade, production, consumption, and price are determined at point E (15 units at a price of $20). Under free-trade conditions, however, the foreign supply—here assumed to be perfectly elastic—must be added to the domestic supply, resulting in the overall supply curve $S_d S_f$. Equilibrium is now at point F, with 25 units being consumed at $10, of which 5 units are produced at home and the rest (20 units) are imported. Now a tariff of $6 is applied, which raises the horizontal portion of the supply curve (assuming foreign prices remain unchanged) by the amount of the tariff to $S_f + T$. Equilibrium now shifts to point G. As a result of the tariff, the domestic price has gone up to $16, causing a reduction in consumption to 20 units. At the same time, the higher prices have encouraged domestic producers to expand output to 10 units, so that imports are reduced from 20 units to 10 units.

Without the tariff, the total *consumer surplus* is represented as the area NFL. Consumer surplus is defined as the difference between what the purchased goods are worth to the consumers and what they actually pay according to the market price—that is, the area under the demand curve above the prevailing price. With the tariff, it is reduced from NFL to NGM, for an overall consumer-surplus loss of $MGFL$.

This loss to consumers is reflected in several other economic changes. First, the tariff makes it possible for the government to collect revenues from the import duty. Tariff revenues always equal the amount of the duty times the quantity of goods actually imported. Here, the revenue collected equals $6 × 10 units = $60, or the area t in Figure 10-2. This represents that part of the loss in consumer surplus that is transferred to the government in the form of money—the *revenue effect* of a tariff.

A second part of the loss of consumer surplus is transferred, again in monetary terms, to domestic producers. At the higher tariff-imposed price, producers receive additional income ("rent") in the amount r ($45) in Figure 10-2. Since this consumer-surplus loss is matched by an equivalent increase in the *producer surplus*, it is tantamount to a redistribution of real income from

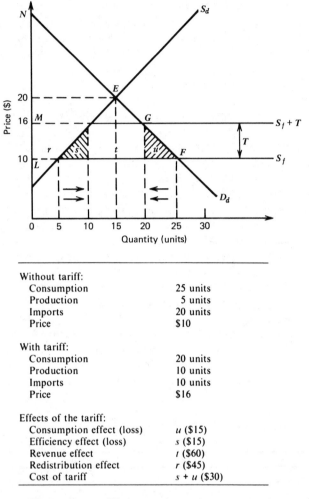

Figure 10-2. Effect of a tariff on consumption, production, government, revenues, and income distribution.

Without tariff:	
Consumption	25 units
Production	5 units
Imports	20 units
Price	$10

With tariff:	
Consumption	20 units
Production	10 units
Imports	10 units
Price	$16

Effects of the tariff:	
Consumption effect (loss)	u ($15)
Efficiency effect (loss)	s ($15)
Revenue effect	t ($60)
Redistribution effect	r ($45)
Cost of tariff	$s + u$ ($30)

consumers to producers—a *redistribution effect* of the tariff. A producer surplus is defined as the difference between what suppliers actually receive for their products at market prices and the lowest amount they would have been willing to sell those products for (their total variable production costs).

With areas r and t of the overall loss of consumer surplus $MGFL$ accounted for ($45 + $60 = $105), we need now explain the remaining areas, s and u. By increasing output by 5 units as a result of the tariff, producers find that they must operate at successively higher unit costs as they receive diminishing returns to the variable inputs and progress upward along their supply (marginal cost) curve. In addition, they may have to pay some factors of production higher and higher prices—factors that naturally are withdrawn from other sectors of the economy. So area s ($15) of the consumer-surplus loss is matched by the value of the extra resources being drawn into the protected sector from other sectors because of the reduction in their productive efficiency. It represents a real loss to the economy, which is often called the *efficiency effect* of a tariff. The amount by which domestic output rises on account of the tariff—from 5 units to 10 units in Figure 10-2—is usually called the *protective effect* of a tariff.

We have now accounted for almost all of the loss of consumer surplus $MGFL$ ($135) attributed to the tariff: r ($45) is transferred to producers, t ($60) is transferred to the government, and s ($15) is a net loss to the economy resulting from the tariff-induced expansion of domestic output. The remainder, area u ($15), is the residual loss of consumer satisfaction not accounted for in any of the above ways—the *consumption effect* of the tariff. It, too, represents a real loss to the economy. Some consumers are squeezed out of the market by higher prices, and the effective range of choice is narrowed for all consumers. The total net cost imposed by the tariff on the economy is thus the sum of the efficiency effect and the consumption effect, areas $s + u$ ($30) in Figure 10-2; this sum is sometimes called the *deadweight loss* associated with a tariff.

Suppose the tariff were raised to a level ($10) that blocked out all imports. Imposition of such a prohibitive tariff would place equilibrium at point E in Figure 10-2. The "cost" of the tariff—the combined consumption and efficiency effects—would increase greatly, as would the redistribution effect. The revenues collected under the tariff would be zero, however, since no goods are imported upon which duties can be collected. A similar effect could be obtained by sealing the national frontiers to the particular good in question and thus banning all imports of it.

Note also that the more inelastic the domestic supply curve, the smaller will be the efficiency effect of a tariff, and the smaller the "cost" of the tariff to the economy. Fewer productive resources will be diverted into the protected sector, and the forgone output in other sectors will be smaller. Similarly, the more inelastic the domestic demand for the product, the smaller will be the consumption effect and the associated "cost" of the tariff. In either case, the tariff will achieve a smaller reduction in imports, and the burden it imposes on the economy will be correspondingly smaller.

TARIFFS AND THE TERMS OF TRADE

Aside from the various tariff effects just illustrated by simple supply-and-demand analysis, customs duties also can improve the terms of trade of the country imposing them. (Note that we are dropping the assumption that world prices are constant.) Since the terms of trade determine the relative gains from international trade accruing to a country, an improvement in its terms of trade represents an increase in its share of the global gains from trade. If the terms of trade for one country improve, they must simultaneously deteriorate for one or more other countries. By thus increasing the size of its "slice of the pie"—the "pie" being the gains from trade—a country automatically reduces the gains obtained by its trading partners.

Perhaps the best way of illustrating the impact of tariffs on the terms of trade is through the use of offer curves. In Figure 10-3, offer curve OH is drawn for the home country, exporting A-goods and importing B-goods, and offer curve OF is drawn for the foreign country (or the rest of the world), which exports B-goods and imports A-goods.

Under free trade, intersection of the two countries' offer curves occurs at point R, with the terms of trade being given by the slope of the line OT_1. At the free-trade equilibrium point, the two countries' respective trade-indifference curves (f_1 and h_1) are tangent, meaning that neither of the two countries can gain further from international trade without the other one losing. A shift in the trade point to the left means a higher trade-indifference level for country H but a lower level for country F, and vice versa.

Now suppose the home country imposes a tariff on imports, or a tax on its exports. Either of these steps implies a reduced desire for international trade, and in a two-commodity barter model, they are in fact equivalent. In doing so, it in effect demands that the foreign nation give up a larger quantity of its own export good in order to receive a given quantity of imports—the home country's export good. Or, putting it another way, the home country is willing to offer less of its export good in return for a certain quantity of imports from abroad. In the international marketplace, the result is a shift in the home country's offer curve to the left—say, from OH to OH_t. The fact that the foreign offer curve, OF, is indeed curved means that the home country has some degree of monopoly or monopsony power, and can influence international prices by its own actions—that is, the home country is a *price maker*. This is a precondition for manipulating the terms of trade in this way. We shall assume, for the moment, that the foreign country does not retaliate, so that the new intersection of the foreign offer curve, OF, and the domestic tariff-distorted offer curve, OH_t, occurs at point S. As a result of the tariff, the volume of trade declines from 30 units of A and 30 units of B to 10 units of A and 20 units of B at point S in Figure 10-3.

Note that the new terms of trade (OT_2) are more favorable to the home country; it must now export fewer A-goods to get a given quantity of B-goods in return—10 units of A for 20 units of B (1:2) instead of 30 units of A for 30 units of B (1:1). Note also that the home country has reached a higher trade-indifference level (h_2) by imposing the tariff, but that the foreign country's new trade-indifference level (f_2) is substantially inferior to that prevailing under free-trade conditions.

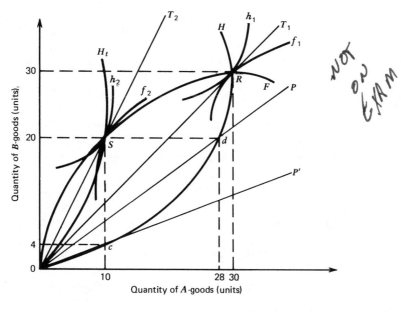

Free trade:	
Equilibrium	R
Exports by H	30 units
Exports by F	30 units
Indifference level of H	h_1
Indifference level of F	f_1
Terms of trade	OT_1
Domestic price ratio	OT_1
With tariff:	
Equilibrium	S
Exports by H	28 units
Exports by F	20 units
Indifference level of H	h_2
Indifference level of F	f_2
Domestic price ratio	OP or OP'
Terms of trade	OT_2
Tariff revenue:	
Expressed in A-goods	S_d = 18 units
Expressed in B-goods	cS = 16 units

Figure 10-3. Effect of a tariff on the terms of trade.

By definition, the distance between the tariff-distorted and the free-trade offer curves is the tariff revenue collected by the home-country government. Collection may be made in either of the two goods, since neither has a unique status as a means of payment and no money exists. If the government decides to take tariff payments in A-goods, the tariff revenue connected with trading at point S will amount to the distance Sd, or 18 units of A-goods. The tariff *rate*, measured against the amount of actually exported A-goods, will then be 18:10, or 180 percent. If, instead, the tariff is payable in B-goods—the traders having to hand over part of their imports to the customs officials—the tariff revenue will amount to cS, or 16 units of B-goods. The *rate* of this tariff, measured against the gross amount of imported B-goods, will then be 16:20, or 80 percent. The reason the two alternative tariff rates will be numerically different is that they are calculated on different bases. Also, each method of tariff collection will have its distinct effect on the relative scarcity of the two goods in private domestic markets, and hence on the relative domestic price. If the tariff is levied in A-goods, the domestic price ratio will be the slope of OP in Figure 10-3. If it is levied in B-goods, the corresponding ratio will be OP'. Naturally, the relative private scarcity of A-goods will be greater under the former system; therefore, OP is steeper than OP'.

The effect of the tariff itself can be viewed in terms of either of the two traded products. Without the tariff, country H was willing to offer 28 units of its A-goods in exchange for 20 units of B-goods under its free-trade offer curve, OH, at point d. With the imposition of the tariff, the new tariff-distorted offer curve shows that country H is willing to offer only 10 units of A-goods in return for the same 20 units of B-goods at point S. Hence, the amount of its exports that it was willing to offer in the absence of the tariff is greater than what it is willing to offer with the tariff in return for an identical amount of imports. Alternatively, the tariff's effect can also be viewed in terms of B-goods. Without the tariff, in return for 10 units of its exports, country H was willing to accept 4 units of imports at point c, but now it can acquire 20 units of imports for the same amount of its exports at point S. Hence the tariff is depicted as an increase in the quantity of imports demanded in return for a set amount of exports.

The extent of the improvement that one country can expect in (*a*) its terms of trade and (*b*) its trade-indifference level, by imposing a tariff, depends on the shape of the other country's offer curve. Moreover, whereas the tariff may result in a substantial improvement in the terms of trade of the country imposing it, this need not happen. The other country may retaliate by imposing its own tariff. Let's briefly examine these two matters.

PRICE TAKERS AND PRICE MAKERS

The shape of the *foreign country's* offer curve will largely determine the degree to which a country will improve its terms of trade by imposing a tariff. Specifically, is the home country a *price maker* or a *price taker*? In Figure 10-4 there are a number of foreign offer curves of different shapes: OF_1, OF_2, OF_3, and OF_4. The home country imposes a tariff that shifts its offer curve from OH to OH_t. Note what happens to its terms of trade given the variously shaped for-

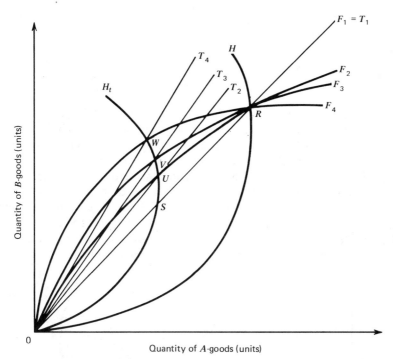

Figure 10-4. Tariffs and the elasticity of offer curves.

eign offer curves. If the foreign offer curve is a straight line (OF_1), it must be identical to the free-trade terms-of-trade line. Such an offer curve means that a country is willing to offer its exports in return for imports at a certain fixed ratio of exchange, which never changes no matter how much it imports or exports. In this case, it is impossible for the home country to change its terms of trade no matter how it changes its tariff. The terms of trade at S are the same as they were at R. The home country is a price taker; it has absolutely no power to affect international prices by its own actions.

The more curved the foreign country's offer curve (the more monopoly or monopsony power the home country has), the more a given tariff change will improve the home country's terms of trade—it is a price maker. Note that the same tariff-induced shift in the home country's offer curve $(OH$ to $OH_t)$ produces equilibria (S, U, V, W) that show increasingly favorable terms of trade (OT_1, OT_2, OT_3, OT_4) the more curved the offer curve of the trading partner. Here again we can talk in terms of "small" versus "big" countries. For all intents and purposes, the offer curve of the rest of the world facing Guatemala or Upper Volta is a straight line, since these small countries are economically insignificant relative to their overall trading partner, the rest of the world. They possess no monopoly or monopsony power at all. Internationally, they are price takers, since the terms of trade are dictated to them by the world market.

RETALIATION

Figure 10-5 illustrates the impact of retaliation, counter-retaliation, and tariff "wars" on the terms and volume of international trade. We begin once more with point R, where the two countries' offer curves cross under free-trade conditions. The terms of trade are given by the slope of line OT_1. Again, the home country imposes a tariff, shifting its offer curve to OH_t, hoping to attain a new equilibrium at S and the improved terms of trade OT_2.

This time, however, the foreign country retaliates and imposes its own tariff, thus shifting its offer curve to OF_t. Equilibrium of the two tariff-distorted offer curves is now V, where the terms of trade (slope of OT_3) may well be much below what the home country had originally intended to achieve,

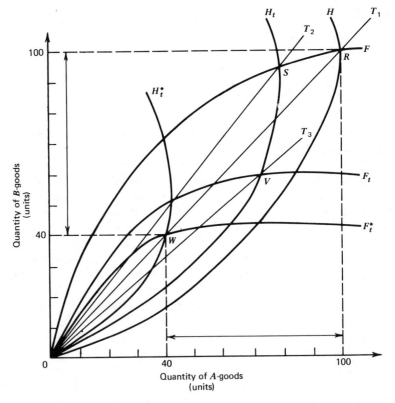

Figure 10-5.   Tariff retaliation and the terms of trade.

and which may actually be more favorable to the retaliating country than were the free-trade terms of trade. The result, of course, is that the initial tariff has backfired.

The home country may now counter-retaliate by again raising the tariff on its imports of B-goods, and the foreign country may meet this new challenge with yet a higher tariff of its own. This cycle of retaliation and counter-retaliation may repeat itself over and over until some point such as W is reached, where the ultimate, tariff-distorted offer curves of both countries (H_t^* and F_t^*) might intersect in such a way that neither country has noticeably improved its terms of trade.

But look what has happened to the volume of trade. It has fallen from 100 units of the A-good plus 100 units of the B-good to 40 units of the A-good plus 40 units of the B-good. The prices of import goods in both countries must have risen dramatically as a result of the successive increases in import duties, and consumption of them has been cut down commensurately. In short, if one country imposes a tariff that is not subject to retaliation, it may gain at the expense of its trading partner. If the other country retaliates, and especially if this leads to counter-retaliation, both countries are likely to lose output and income as a result.

THE OPTIMUM TARIFF

From the analysis presented here, it would seem that in the absence of retaliation, a country should be able to levy an import tariff that yields optimal terms of trade and, hence, a maximum level of community welfare. Beginning at the free-trade position (or any tariff-distorted trade position), as a country raises its tariffs unilaterally, the terms of trade improve and the volume of trade declines. The improvement in the terms of trade initially tends to more than offset the effect of the accompanying reduction in the volume of trade, so that a higher trade-indifference curve is reached and community welfare is enhanced. Beyond some point, however, it is likely that the detrimental effect of the successive reductions in trade volume (and forgone gains from trade) will begin to outweigh the positive effect of further improvements in the terms of trade; community welfare then begins to fall. Somewhere in between there must be a tariff that will maximize a country's welfare level.

Figure 10-6 illustrates the existence of such an optimum tariff level. Free-trade equilibrium again is at point R, where the home and foreign countries' offer curves intersect. At that point, the volume of trade is 100 units of the A-good and 100 units of the B-good, and the terms of trade are given by the slope of line OT. The home country (H) now wishes to impose a tariff that will maximize its community welfare—that is, place it on the highest possible trade-indifference curve, assuming no retaliation by the foreign country.

Under free-trade conditions at R, country H attains the trade-indifference level h_1, which crosses the foreign offer curve (OF) at R and at some other point T. Any tariff that distorts the home country's offer curve between points T and R will lead to a higher trade-indifference level. (If the new tariff-distorted trade point is at T, of course, the trade-indifference level will be unchanged.)

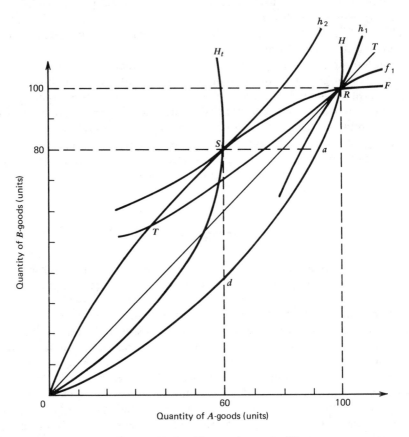

Figure 10-6.   The optimum tariff.

The highest possible trade-indifference curve that the home country can reach is one that is tangent to the foreign offer curve. This is trade-indifference curve h_2, tangent to foreign offer curve OF at point S. If the home country can impose a tariff of such a size that the tariff-distorted offer curve (OH_t) intersects the foreign offer curve (OF) at point S, this is the optimum tariff. Given the foreign offer curve OF, there is no tariff the home country can impose that will yield a higher level of community welfare. Here, the home country now exports only 60 units of the *A*-good in return for 80 units of the *B*-good, as opposed to 100 *A* for 100 *B* under conditions of free trade.

Once again, the magnitude of the optimum tariff depends upon the shape of the foreign offer curve in the vicinity of the free-trade equilibrium point. If the foreign offer curve there happens to be horizontal or negatively sloped, the rate of the optimum tariff will be very high. The reader can easily verify this rather special case by redrawing Figure 10-6 accordingly and then imposing successive increases in home country tariffs by shifting *OH* to the left. An example might be trade between the OPEC countries and the rest of the world in the 1970s. With everyone "hooked" on oil and very few substitutes available in the short term, OPEC could dramatically shift its offer curve,to the left (through export taxes and production cutbacks), resulting in enormous improvements in its terms of trade and permitting much larger imports of other goods, services, and financial assets per barrel of oil exported.

In actuality, the probability is that the foreign country will retaliate against the home country's imposition of an optimum tariff, since it will otherwise be placed on a lower trade-indifference curve. So the foreign country may levy an optimum retaliatory tariff of its own that crosses the home-country's tariff-distorted offer curve at a point that yields the foreign nation a maximum trade-indifference level. Then the home country may counter-retaliate with another optimum tariff and the tariff-war process outlined in Figure 10-5 runs its course. Note the danger to free trade implied by this scenario—as long as the other country's offer curve is not a straight line (such as OT), each country will always be tempted to improve its welfare through tariffs or other trade distortions.

SUMMARY

Customs duties represent the most commonly used type of import restriction and have effects on domestic and foreign prices, output, consumer welfare, government revenues, the income of protected suppliers, and economic efficiency. They effectively drive a "wedge" between the domestic market and the rest of the world—they push relative prices at home away from relative prices abroad. Under certain conditions, tariffs can be used by countries to improve their terms of trade, and there may exist an optimum tariff that will lead to maximum community welfare. However, because other countries might retaliate, the imposition of tariffs for terms-of-trade or other reasons may in the end not achieve the desired results.

The tariffs we have been dealing with in this chapter are called *nominal tariffs,* and our examples have mainly pertained to finished goods. If a country applies tariffs to both finished goods and imported inputs (parts, components, raw materials) into those goods, one can compute *effective tariffs*, which take both kinds of duties into account. The notion of an effective tariff is explained in the Advanced Material section that follows.

ADVANCED MATERIAL:
Effective Tariff Protection

Do tariff rates really measure what they seem to measure, namely, the degree of protection of the domestic industry in competition with imports? Recall that the *protective effect* of a tariff can be identified as the increase in output by the import-competing industry that would not have been possible without protection—the move from 5 units to 10 units of domestic output in Figure 10-2. In this case, the tariff rate indeed seems to provide a rough measure of the degree of protection accorded the producer. But instead of increased final output, perhaps what really should be measured in this regard is the increased *value added* (the value of final sales minus the value of all raw materials and intermediate inputs) in the import-competing industry that results from protection. Value added measures the value of primary factor inputs—land, labor, and capital—used in a firm or an industry, and it reflects the level of activity better than does the value of final output, or sales. The theory of effective protection points out that it is not only protection of final products that is important, but also protection of all the inputs used in the production of those final products.

To cite a very simple example, suppose country *I* imposes a 20 percent *ad valorem* duty on imports of poultry. Given some knowledge of domestic and foreign demand and supply conditions, we would feel qualified to make a statement concerning the degree of protection for domestic poultry suppliers under the 20 percent tariff, and we would predict that poultry imports will drop. Suppose, now, that we are given the additional information that country *I* has at the same time lowered its tariff on imports of feed grains from 20 percent to zero. Clearly, domestic poultry producers' costs will fall, their competitive position will improve, and the volume of poultry imports will drop even further.

The point is that a given duty on any finished product will have a substantially greater protective effect if it is combined with low tariffs on the imported inputs of the protected industry than if the tariffs on these inputs are high. Conversely, it will have a somewhat lesser protective effect if the national customs duties on imported raw material and other inputs are high rather than low. In short, a given protective tariff on a finished good may either overstate or understate the real, or *effective*, rate of protection accorded domestic suppliers, depending on the level of the tariffs imposed on inputs.

Under these conditions, the analysis of individual tariff rates is clearly insufficient and must be combined with an analysis of the overall national tariff structure. To calculate the effective rate of protection (ERP), we simply deduct from the nominal tariff on a given product the weighted average of the tariffs imposed on all inputs—each weight being the proportionate contribution of each input to the value of the final product.

It is not difficult to compute the effective rate of protection given to suppliers of a particular finished good. The total value of any finished good reflects the value added by the manufacturer, plus the total value of all of the material inputs used. Per dollar of output, therefore, the total value is the value added in that industry (v_j) plus the sum of the values of each input (i) contributed to that product (a_{ij}). With n inputs, this may be written as

$$v_j + \sum_{i=1}^{n} a_{ij} = 1. \tag{1}$$

If a tariff is placed on the competing imported product, the domestic selling price of good j will rise by the amount of the tariff, t_j. Assuming a perfectly elastic supply of inputs, all of this will be reflected in a higher value added by the domestic suppliers (v'_j). With the tariff, the above equation thus becomes

$$v'_j + \sum_{i=1}^{n} a_{ij} = 1 + t_j. \tag{2}$$

But tariffs may also be imposed on the inputs themselves, so that the value of each input becomes $1 + t_i$. Equation (2) then becomes

$$v'_j + \sum_{i=1}^{n} a_{ij}(1 + t_i) = 1 + t_j. \tag{3}$$

The *effective rate of protection* (ERP) is defined as the increase in the value added per dollar of domestic output as a result of tariffs—that is, the difference between v_j and v'_j, expressed as a percentage of free-trade value added per output dollar, or

$$ERP_j = \frac{v'_j - v_j}{v_j}. \tag{4}$$

Rewriting equations (1) and (3), we get, under free trade,

$$v_j = 1 - \sum_{i=1}^{n} a_{ij} \tag{5}$$

and, with tariffs,

$$v_j' = 1 + t_j - \sum_{i=1}^{n} a_{ij}(1 + t_i). \tag{6}$$

Substituting in the numerator of equation (4) gives us

$$ERP_j = \frac{[1 + t_j - \sum_{i=1}^{n} a_{ij}(1 + t_i)] - [1 - \sum_{i=1}^{n} a_{ij}]}{v_j} \tag{7}$$

which simplifies to

$$ERP_j = \frac{t_j - \sum_{i=1}^{n} a_{ij} t_i}{v_j}. \tag{8}$$

So the effective rate of protection on a given finished good will be higher, the lower are tariffs on raw material and component inputs, relative to the tariff on the product itself—that is, the lower are the various values of t_i relative to the value of the tariff on the finished good (t_j). Note that the formula presupposes fixed input proportions (fixed a_{ij} values); if they could vary, estimating effective protection becomes even more difficult.

Since all international discussions of tariffs and their effects involve estimates of the degree of protection embodied in them, this particular addition to tariff theory is of substantial importance. It points out the limitations inherent in direct comparisons of nominal rates of duty, just as it is misleading simply to employ a mean tariff level to characterize the overall tariff barriers of a country.

Important Concepts

tariff	deadweight loss
consumer surplus	cost of a tariff
consumption effect	small-country case
efficiency effect	large-country case
revenue effect	retaliation
redistribution effect	optimum tariff
protective effect	effective protection

Questions

1. Suppose the United States is considering an increase of 50 percent in its tariff on color television sets. If you knew the delivered cost of imported TVs, the existing tariff, and the existing quantity of imports, could you figure out the effect of the proposed tariff hike on domestic consumers and producers? What else would you need to know? How would you go about the task?

2. Once imposed, a tariff creates a vested interest for its retention. Explain the economic basis of this vested interest.

3. Sometimes it may pay a country to reduce its import duties unilaterally. Even though this may cause a deterioration in its terms of trade, the tariff cuts raise the level of welfare attained. Using the theory you have learned, explain how this may occur.

4. A country raises the level of import duties on automotive glass by 100 percent. Explain how this will tend to affect value added in the domestic automobile industry.

Further Readings

Corden, W. M., *The Theory of Protection* (Oxford: The Clarendon Press, 1974).

Corden, W. M., "The Structure of a Tariff System and Effective Protective Rates," *Journal of Political Economy*, June 1966.

Corden, W. M., "The Calculation of the Cost of Protection," *Economic Record*, April 1957.

Krauss, Melvyn B., *A Geometric Approach to International Trade* (New York: Halsted-Wiley, 1979).

Johnson, H. G., *Aspects of the Theory of Tariffs* (London: George Allen & Unwin, 1971).

Johnson, H. G., "The Cost of Protection and the Scientific Tariff," *Journal of Political Economy*, June 1960.

Vanek, J., *General Equilibrium of International Discrimination* (Cambridge: Harvard University Press, 1965).

11

NONTARIFF BARRIERS

Quantitative trade restrictions limit trade by permitting only specified amounts of particular goods or services to cross the national customs frontier. This type of trade barrier differs fundamentally from tariffs, which permit unlimited quantities to enter the country as long as the duties are paid. The effects of these two types of trade barriers are, however, not totally dissimilar, as will soon be evident. After examining quantitative trade restrictions, we shall go on to survey other types of trade impediments that fit into neither of the two major categories (tariffs and quantitative restrictions), but that are by no means trivial.

QUOTAS

The most important quantitative restriction on international trade is the *quota*. A quota is an absolute limit on the physical quantity or value of goods or services that may be traded over a set period of time. Quotas may be applied to either imports or exports. For example, Japan might rule that to assist its beleaguered growers of low-quality oranges, only 900 tons of the fruit may be imported in a given year; this is called an *import quota*. Or the Swedish government might declare that, to ensure the future health of the Swedish economy, it is necessary to limit exports of iron ore in a particular year to 100,000 tons; this is called an *export quota*. Quotas such as these are called *global*, or *nondiscriminatory*, because they simply set a limit on the total trade in a certain good or service vis-à-vis the rest of the world as a whole. Once that limit is reached, all further trade is prohibited.

Global import quotas contrast with so-called *selective* or *discriminatory* quotas, which differentiate according to the countries from which the goods originate. Country *I* might impose an overall quota of 20 million oranges per year, of which 4 million must come from country *II*, 3 million from country *III*, 3 million from country *IV*, 6 million from country *V*, and 4 million from country *VI*. This is a selective quota, and the import limits for each country are generally subject to bilateral negotiations. In many cases, selective quotas may also be connected to long-standing commercial or political treaties, or to ongoing international conflicts. Among the special kinds of selective quotas are the *voluntary export restraint* (VER) and the *orderly marketing arrangement* (OMA), negotiated bilaterally with exporting countries under the threat of mandatory import quotas.

A final type of quota is the *tariff quota*, which sets a limit on the amount or value of merchandise that may be imported under a given tariff rate, with any imports in excess of that limit subject to a higher duty. For instance, Mexico might place an *ad valorem* tariff of 20 percent on the first 10,000 automobiles imported in a particular year, 25 percent on the next 5000 cars, and so forth.

Figure 11-1 is a partial-equilibrium, supply-and-demand representation of quota effects on a single product. Under free trade, assuming zero transport costs and an elastic world supply, imports (100 units) make up the difference between domestic supply (20 units) and demand (120 units) at the equilibrium price of $100.

The government now decides to limit imports of this particular product to a fixed quantity of 60 units by imposing a quota in that amount. The supply curve thus becomes $S_d + Q_M$. The reduction in imports from 100 to 60 units raises the equilibrium price to $120, increases the domestic quantity supplied from 20 to 40 units, and reduces the quantity demanded from 120 to 100 units. The quota has had *protective* and *consumption* effects similar to those of a tariff. In fact, either a tariff or a quota may be used with similar effect to increase domestic output and reduce domestic quantity demanded. The total loss of consumer surplus is represented as the area $r + s + t + u$. Of this total, areas s and u in Figure 11-1 may again be considered the cost of the quota in terms of decreased productive efficiency and the residual loss of consumer satisfaction. Part of the consumer surplus is similarly transferred to producers via the *income-redistribution* effect, as represented by area r.

But what about the revenue effect of a quota? By imposing a quota, the government does not collect any customs duties on imports, yet the lost consumer surplus represented by area t must go to someone. If the foreign supply curve is perfectly elastic, as assumed here, and if the government does not interfere in the import process other than by imposing the quota, these revenues will go to the importers; their markups on imported merchandise will be correspondingly higher. If, on the other hand, the government decides to *sell* permission to import (in the form of *import licenses*) under the quota to the highest bidders, then the government will collect revenues identical to those accruing to it under a tariff of an equivalent import-restrictive effect. A third, perhaps less likely, possibility is that these revenues will be collected by the foreign exporters—assuming that they are able to raise delivered prices sufficiently to take away most or all of the revenue (t) otherwise accruing to the importers or the government. The question of how such revenues would be divided hinges on the competitive relationships between the exporters and importers concerned.

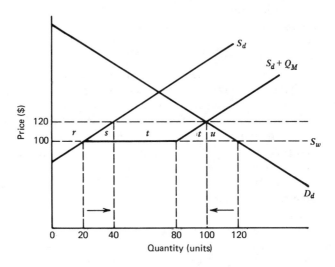

Figure 11-1. Partial-equilibrium analysis of the effects of import quotas.

This analysis shows the primary effects of quotas to be very similar to those of tariffs. They (*a*) raise the prevailing domestic price of the product, (*b*) reduce the quantity of imports, (*c*) reduce the quantity demanded, (*d*) increase the domestic quantity supplied, (*e*) redistribute real income from consumers to producers, (*f*) yield revenues that may go to the government or be divided among domestic importers and foreign exporters, and (*g*) result in a deadweight loss to the economy.

Note that once the import quota has been filled, the domestic price of the product under consideration will be entirely divorced from the foreign price. If there should be a rise in domestic demand, prices at home will increase, but this will have no impact on prices or output abroad or on the volume of trade. The quota will permit no further imports. A similar rise in domestic demand under a tariff (except for a prohibitive or confiscatory tariff), by contrast, would raise imports and put pressure on production (and perhaps prices) abroad. With a tariff, the connection between foreign and domestic prices and output is always maintained. Under a quota, this relationship is severed once the quota is filled.

TERMS-OF-TRADE EFFECTS

Like tariffs, quotas may also be used by a country trying to improve its terms of trade vis-à-vis its trading partners. The mechanisms and the results, however, are quite different, as shown in Figure 11-2.

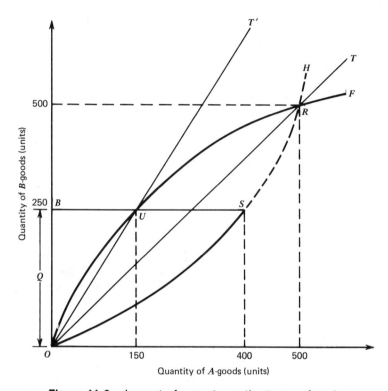

Figure 11-2.   Impact of a quota on the terms of trade.

The free-trade offer curves for the home and foreign countries are, respectively, OH and OF. The free-trade terms of trade are given by the slope of line OT, and the home country exports quantity 500 units of the A-good in return for quantity 500 units of the B-good. Now the home country imposes a 250-unit quota on imports of the B-good; the home country's imports of B-goods cannot exceed this quantity. So the home country's quota-distorted offer curve becomes OSB, and it intersects the foreign country's offer curve, OF, at point U. The new terms of trade will be OT'. For the home country, there is a substantial improvement over the free-trade terms of trade—as is also true when a tariff is imposed—and, depending on the shape of the home country's trade-indifference curve, this should make possible an improvement in economic welfare. But exactly how?

Assume that the quota is administered through a system of import (or export) licenses auctioned off by the government in exchange for *A*-goods. Initially, the gains will then accrue to the government, via a budget surplus. But this surplus can of course be disposed of through spending for the public's benefit or through tax cuts—in either case, raising real incomes. If, by contrast, licenses are distributed on a first-come, first-served basis, the welfare gains will be concentrated in the hands of the favored importers, perhaps to be redistributed through domestic policy measures.

If, however, there is monopolistic collusion among exporters in the foreign country while domestic importers compete freely with one another, this added income may instead go to the foreign exporters, and the nation's terms of trade may, in fact, deteriorate; but this cannot be shown by offer curves, which assume perfect competition. The reverse would be true if the exporters competed freely and there was monopsonistic collusion among the importers— whereupon the importers would capture the revenues. Lastly, if there is rivalry among both importers and exporters, the distribution of the quota-induced revenues will be indeterminate unless the precise bargaining strengths of the two sides are known.

Again, the *potential* for improvement in the terms of trade through the imposition of a quota—or any other import-limiting restriction—hinges upon the shape of the foreign country's offer curve and the retaliatory action, if any, that the latter decides to take. In this respect, too, the terms-of-trade effects of quotas are similar to those of tariffs.

QUOTAS VERSUS TARIFFS

Suppose a government decides to protect a particular import-competing industry. Why might it choose to use quotas rather than tariffs, and what are the welfare implications of each strategy? First of all, quotas are much more precise and, in their effect, much more certain. If an *ad valorem* tariff of 10 percent is imposed on imports of wheat, no one knows how much wheat will be imported or at what prices it will be sold. This naturally depends on supply conditions abroad, over which a government has no control. A bumper crop abroad and falling world prices of wheat could lead to a surge of imports despite the 10 percent tariff—and prove disastrous for domestic farmers. The quota avoids this difficulty. The government simply sets a price for wheat that will yield farmers a "fair" return, estimates demand at that price and the quantity that domestic farmers will be able to supply, and sets an import quota for the remainder. Uncertainty with regard to foreign supply conditions is thus a strong reason for the use of quotas as opposed to tariffs.

Second, if domestic demand for a particular imported product is particularly *inelastic*, a case may also be made for quotas. For instance, suppose a large quantity of automobiles is imported even after tariffs have been successively raised. If a government still wants to reduce automobile imports, a quota offers an alternative to raising the tariff still further. Imports of cars are limited to a set number, and buyers and sellers then bid for them, with the market price being established in the usual way. Similarly, a highly inelastic foreign supply may also point to the use of quotas. If foreign producers must sell the goods they have on hand at virtually any price, they can and will hurdle just about any tariff to compete on the domestic market. Here again, if domestic producers are to be protected, an import quota is likely to be more effective than a tariff.

Third, quotas tend to be more flexible, more easily imposed, and more easily removed than tariffs, which are often regarded as permanent measures and rapidly build vested interests that fight their removal. Quotas have many characteristics of a more temporary measure, are often designed to deal only with a current "emergency" problem, and may be administratively removable as soon as circumstances warrant. Also, other countries may be less apt to view quotas as permanent threats to their exports, and thus be less likely to retaliate.

Finally, quotas may also be used as a way of preventing foreign recessions from spreading into the home country. A country undergoing a recession may attempt to alleviate it by stimulating its exports in a variety of ways; and if the recession is accompanied by a general slowdown in inflation, the export stimulus will indeed be automatic. The home country—its trading partner— will then experience a rise in imports, and any recessionary pressure in its economy will be aggravated. So, to avoid worsening the domestic economic situation and partly insulate itself from the economic misfortunes of other countries, a country may invoke quotas as the most feasible way of cutting back the damaging wave of imports. Such temporary maladjustments in economic activity may be no reflection of the underlying comparative cost relationships, and the gain in achieving fuller employment may well outweigh the costs of the market distortions associated with the quotas.

As these arguments show, there are *some* conditions under which quotas may be superior to tariffs as an instrument of trade policy. But, on the other hand, quotas can seriously damage the international trade mechanism by *removing* it from the operation of the price system and market forces. There is a danger that trade-policy administrators, operating without the guidance of relatively freely determined prices, will make grossly inappropriate judgments about the associated costs. This danger is even more serious if quotas are granted on a discriminatory basis, with political, military, and social considerations interfering with their calculations.

Second, we have seen that quotas tend to support collaboration among importers and exporters. The administrative allocation of quotas to importers reduces competition and fosters the monopolization of imports. Similarly, among foreign exporters, quotas tend to promote such anticompetitive cooperation as may be needed to bargain effectively with the home country's importers. If it is agreed that import and export monopolies are a decided liability—as we shall argue in the next chapter—then quotas may be an inferior policy instrument.

Third, in a period of inflationary pressure, quotas (like tariffs) tend to feed inflation by keeping out import competition, just as they help control further downward price pressure in times of recession by reducing the supply of imports.

Given a decision to protect a particular industry, a country must reach a decision on the type of trade barriers to use. Apart from obligations under international agreements that may *fix* the level of tariffs or commit countries to abstain from quotas, there are considerable differences in the economic effects of the two types of trade restrictions.

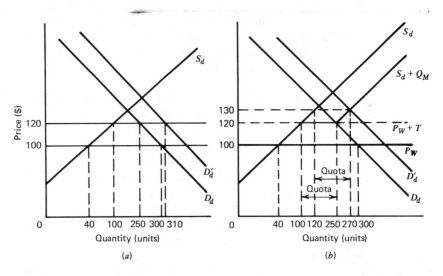

Figure 11-3. Tariffs versus quotas in partial equilibrium. (*a*) Tariff. (*b*) Quota.

Consider, for example, Figure 11-3. Figure 11-3*a* shows a nominal protective effect of 60 units being secured by import-competing producers via a tariff that raises the price from $100 to $120. Figure 11-3*b* shows the same nominal protection of 60 units resulting from a comparable quota of 150 units, raising domestic price by the same amount ($20). Apparently, a tariff and a quota have the same impact, except for possible differences in the revenue effects.

But suppose domestic demand for the product now expands. With the tariff, the price remains at $120 and imports expand from 150 to 210 units. With the quota, quantity imported remains constant at 150 units, and price rises to $130. In effect, the quota results in a new supply function, $S_d + Q_M$, as opposed to the perfectly-elastic world supply at $P_w + T$ in the case of the tariff. Hence expanding domestic demand—or contracting domestic supply (not shown)—means a relatively greater degree of trade restriction and negative welfare implications in the case of quotas as opposed to comparable tariffs. The reader can work out for himself what happens when domestic demand *declines* relative to domestic supply, and quotas turn out to be superior to tariffs in terms of welfare.

VARIABLE LEVIES

An effect very similar to that of quotas can be achieved by means of *variable levies*, used to protect an import-competing industry. Consider Figure 11-4. Suppose a government wants to guarantee its wheat farmers a price of $80 per unit. Clearly, this price could not be maintained if imports were free to enter at a lower world market price, such as $70. So the government will impose an import levy of $10 per unit, which initially guarantees that 200 units are sold by domestic farmers and imports are restricted to 200 units. Now, if the world market price drops to $60, the government simply increases the variable levy (VL) from $10 to $20, which leaves prices and imports where they were and prevents the shock from being transmitted to the domestic farm sector. Similarly, if there is a domestic crop failure (so that S_d shifts to the left), the variable levy can be adjusted so that the price facing consumers does not rise above $80.

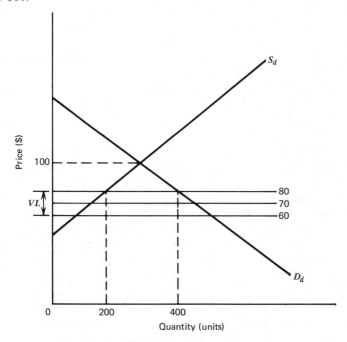

Figure 11-4. Variable levies.

Variable levies can thus ensure that imports merely serve as a "plug" between domestic demand and domestic supply at the target price of $80. Perhaps the best examples of variable levies are those imposed by the European Economic Community (EEC) as part of its Common Agricultural Program (CAP). These levies are adjusted so as continuously to equalize farm-good import prices to the politically determined EEC price levels, regardless of shifts in world market prices. Its relatively inefficient farmers are given such high levels of protection that internal prices are actually often set above the hypothetical $80 in Figure 11-4, resulting in a massive oversupply of farm produce—"butter mountains" and "milk lakes" that then must be destroyed, converted into cattle feed or other noncompetitive products, or dumped on world markets at distress prices and encroaching on the markets of more competitive foreign suppliers. The EEC variable-levy system is surely one of the most costly forms of protection in existence today.

SUBSIDIES

Besides quotas and variable levies, still another way to protect the domestic industry from imports is to subsidize it. Consider Figure 11-5. Suppose the government decides to protect the import-competing industry in such a way as to raise its production from 250 to 500 units. We have seen that this could be done by means of a tariff, quota, or variable levy that would raise domestic prices from $100 to $120, for example. The welfare effects of such a step are already known, and include a consumer surplus loss of hcdg.

Instead, the government could leave the price at $100 and subsidize the import-competing industry to get it to increase its output from 250 to 500 units. Ideally, this could be accomplished by just paying for the incremental costs of the added production above the initial unit-cost level, in which case the cost of the subsidy would be the area abe in Figure 11-5, for a total cost to the taxpayer of $2500. Realistically, however, the government may have to pay the full subsidy for the entire incremental range of output of 250 units, in which case the amount of subsidy is the area afbe, or $5000; of this, $2500 (abe) covers the added production costs and the other $2500 (afb) goes to the producers as a pure profit. Finally, the government may not be able to identify and separately subsidize the incremental output of 250 units, but may in practice have to subsidize the entire output of the product, 500 units. In this case the amount of the subsidy will be $10,000, of which $2500 goes to cover increental production costs and $7500 goes to domestic producers as extra profit.

Note that consumers, as consumers, may be better off under all of these three forms of subsidy than they would have been with an "equivalent" tariff, quota, or variable levy. Why? Because the price they have to pay remains at $100, and their welfare losses are limited to whatever share of the subsidy they have to pay through their taxes. The efficiency cost of a subsidy to society is

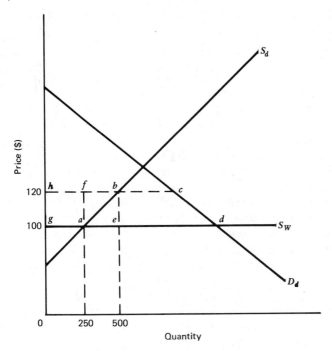

Figure 11-5. Subsidies.

limited to the triangle *abe* in Figure 11-5 (as opposed to triangles *s* + *u* in Figure 10-2, for example), and therefore economists tend to favor subsidies if an industry must be protected. So why aren't subsidies used much more widely? Part of the reason may be that they make protection of an internationally uncompetitive industry much more obvious than other types of barriers and, as a result, tend to be resisted politically even by those who stand to benefit from them. Another reason is that they cost the government money (whereas tariffs actually *raise* government revenues); this makes subsidies unpopular among legislators, and politically vulnerable.

OTHER NONTARIFF BARRIERS

There exist a variety of other nontariff distortions of international trade, usually referred to, somewhat imprecisely, as *nontariff barriers* (NTBs). *Import-directed* NTBs tend to result in higher prices of imports and import-competing goods for domestic purchasers, or to reduce the supply of goods available, by (*a*) imposing significant extra costs on foreign exporters or domestic importers; (*b*) limiting the volume of imports permitted; (*c*) imposing conditions of high uncertainty and risk on domestic importers or foreign exporters (to which they respond by limiting the volume of trade); or (d) a combination of the above. *Export-directed* NTBs may artificially stimulate sales abroad by lowering or removing costs that would otherwise have to be borne by exporters. This permits lower export prices and enhances the domestic suppliers' competitiveness in world markets. For foreign consumers and users, such measures will—if successful—bring about lower prices and increased supplies of the commodities in question. Export-directed nontariff barriers may also be aimed at *impeding* sales abroad, particularly of primary commodities, when the aim is to increase supplies at home, raise export prices, or avoid resource depletion.

Unlike tariffs, nontariff barriers can be subject to substantial uncertainty, which imposes an increased risk on exporters and importers alike. They may be varied unexpectedly—even when import-destined goods are already in transit—and are often subject to wide administrative discretion. To the extent that importers and foreign exporters are risk averse, the impact of NTBs on the volume of trade may in fact be many times that implied by the associated actual costs. Foreign exporters may shift sales to their own domestic markets or to export markets in countries that do not impose NTBs, even in the face of lower prices. Wholesalers and retailers in the home country may shift their purchases to domestic suppliers—in spite of higher domestic prices—rather than face substantial uncertainty about the final prices or availability of imports.

Nontariff barriers, then, tend to operate primarily through (a) subsidies to import-competing producers, (b) indirect costs imposed on imports, (c) quantitative restrictions on imports, (d) subsidies to export suppliers, and (e) quantitative restrictions on exports. A wide variety of NTBs may be identified, all of which work in one or more of these ways. There are also a large number of policy measures that are applied without the specific purpose of impeding imports or artificially stimulating exports, but that nevertheless distort trade volumes or prices of traded goods. Such "trade distortions" (trade-distortive policies) can be added to the list of NTBs.

The following typology of NTBs is useful for analytical purposes. *Type I*: measures designed primarily to protect domestic industry from import competition, to restrict exports, or to strengthen domestic industry in competing with imports or competing for export markets; these are sub-classified into import-directed and export-directed groups. *Type II*: trade-distorting policies and practices that are imposed primarily with the intent of dealing with nontrade-related problems but that are periodically and purposely employed for trade-restrictive reasons. *Type III*: policies and practices applied exclusively for nontrade-related reasons, but that un-avoidably serve to distort international competitive conditions and hence affect trade. A comprehensive inventory of NTBs according to this typology is given in Table 11-1. We shall focus here on a few categories that have received special attention.

IMPORT LICENSING

As an administrative device, licensing may serve as a source of trade distortions by raising costs, increasing uncertainty, or both. Several distinct types of licensing may be identified. First, licensing may enforce quantitative import restrictions, such as quotas, on a global or selective basis, temporarily or permanently. For example, *import calendars* (or seasonal quotas) are sometimes used in the agricultural sector, limiting imports to periods when there is no domestic harvest or when the harvest is inadequate to meet domestic demand at acceptable prices. *Conditional imports* may be permitted in case of domestic agricultural supply shortfalls. *Discretionary imports* in the nonagricultural sector sometimes leave decisions on permissible imports to the public authorities that are supposed to assess the state of the domestic market.

Import licensing may be an adjunct to *exchange controls*, whereunder an import permit will be available only when and if authorization for payment in foreign exchange has been granted by the monetary authorities. And *statistical licensing* may be used to keep track of imports or exports for a variety of information purposes, ranging from collection of trade statistics to monitoring the volume of trade in "sensitive" products. Whereas statistical licensing does not exist to administer particular trade barriers, it may generate significant incremental costs and uncertainties that can have a trade-restrictive effect.

Licensing procedures affect trade in two principal ways—via costs and uncertainty—and they tend to be especially troublesome for firms in developing countries. This is particularly true in the case of "discretionary licensing" with no published quota, where import licenses are issued in an *ad hoc* manner and the degree of uncertainty involved is especially high. Even "automatic" or statistical licensing may involve costs and delays in the securing of licenses. For example, licenses may be issued only at a specific location, which may not be the normal place of business of the importer. The period of validity of the license may be very short, making orderly compliance with technical or health formalities or conclusion of import contracts difficult. Issuance of licenses may be conditional on the imported goods being further processed or reexported from the importing country. Or the end user of the imported product may have to be identified on the license application, permitting authorities to apply pressure on him directly.

GOVERNMENT PROCUREMENT

Virtually all national governments discriminate in favor of domestic suppliers in their own purchasing decisions. Such discrimination against imports has become increasingly important with the expanding role of government

Table 11-1

Classification of Nontariff Measures According to Intent and Manner of Operation

Type I Measures (Primary Distortive Intent)	*Type II Measures* (Secondary Restrictive Intent)	*Type III Measures* (No Apparent Trade-Distortive Intent)

A. Import-Directed Measures
1. Quantitatively-operating
  a. Import quotas, globally administered.
  b. Import quotas, selectively administered.
  c. Licensing, discretionary/restrictive.
  d. Licensing, liberal.
  e. "Voluntary" export restrictions.
  f. Embargoes.
  g. Domestic-procurement practices by national governments or other public units.
  h. State-trading practices.
  i. Domestic-content and mixing regulations.
2. Operating through costs and prices
  a. Variable levies and supplementary import charges.
  b. Advance-deposit requirements.
  c. Antidumping and countervailing charges.
	1. Quantitatively-operating
	  a. Communications-media restrictions.
	  b. Quantitative advertising and marketing restrictions.
	2. Operating through costs and prices
	  a. Packaging/labeling regulations.
	  b. Health, sanitary, and quality standards.
	  c. Safety and industrial standards and regulations.
	  d. Border-tax adjustments.
	  e. Use taxes and excises.
	  f. Customs clearance procedures, consular formalities, and related practices.
	  g. Customs classification procedures and related practices.
	  h. Customs valuation procedures and related practices.
	  i. Exchange restrictions.
		a. Government manufacturing, sales, and distribution monopolies covering individual products or groups of products.
		b. Government structural and regional development policies affecting trade.
		c. *Ad hoc* government balance-of-payments policy measures.
		d. Differences in tax systems.
		e. Differences in national social-insurance systems.
		f. Differences in allowable depreciation systems.
		g. Spillovers from government-financed defense, aerospace, and nonmilitary procurement.
		h. Scale effects induced by government procurement.
		i. Variations in national standards, regulations, and practices.

d. Direct subsidies to import competitors.
e. Credit restrictions on importers.
f. Tax benefits and other indirect subsidies to import competitors, including credit concessions.
g. Discriminatory internal transport charges.
h. International commodity agreements and orderly marketing arrangements.
j. Disclosure regulations and "administrative guidance."
k. Government-provided entrepreneurship, research and development financing, and related aids for the import-competing and export sectors.
j. External transport charges and government-sanctioned international transport agreements.
k. Port transfer costs.

B. Export-Directed Measures
  1. Quantitatively-operating
    a. State trading practices.
    b. Export quotas and licensing.
  2. Operating through costs and prices
    a. Direct subsidies to exporters.
    b. Indirect subsidies to exporters, including tax and credit measures.
    c. Government-supported dumping practices.
    d. Export charges.
    e. International commodity agreements and orderly marketing arrangements.

activities in national economies. Private or joint public-private enterprises may also be heavily influenced by government practices in their procurement patterns, particularly if they themselves depend on the government for a major share of their business. And foreign aid is generally tied to procurement in the donor country. For all of these reasons, government procurement decisions that are not based purely on price and quality considerations have aroused growing international concern.

Examples include the "Buy American" Act, initiated in 1933, whereby United States government agencies gave domestic suppliers a 6 percent price advantage—or 12 percent if the supplier is a small business or situated in a depressed region. In 1959 the U.S. Defense Department for balance-of-payments reasons, instituted a 50 percent price margin in favor of domestic suppliers that is still in force. The United Kingdom has given preference to its domestic suppliers of military equipment, post-office equipment, and computers. France has favored its domestic airframe and computer industry. But in the Federal Republic of Germany, a 1960 government decree forbids discriminatory procurement for government account. Japan has no legal provisions favoring domestic procurement, but in fact most goods are bought only from national sources if domestic suppliers exist. Such practices appear to be ubiquitous.

Discriminatory government procurement can result in more indirect market distortions as well. For example, the existence of a favored home market may induce domestic suppliers to raise prices and profit margins well above internationally competitive levels, and this in turn may allow export sales at prices that do not cover full costs. The resulting price discrimination permitted by an artificial market segmentation may thus injure competitive foreign suppliers both in the home market and in markets abroad. Such behavior has historically been a problem in the electrical equipment industry. The intent behind discriminatory government procurement may be to maintain employment in a depressed industry, to develop technology-intensive industries such as aircraft or computers, or to aid disadvantaged socioeconomic groups associated with import-competing lines of economic activity. Finally, discriminatory government procurement may be related to considerations of national security.

Too often, the "buy national" philosophy involves pure protectionism that has permeated the economy by direct or indirect government involvement in purchasing decisions. Except where justified by special national-security requirements, it is difficult to rationalize the negative impact of these procurement practices. They raise the cost of providing government services above what it would otherwise be, lower the quality of those services, and contribute to economic inefficiency and a misallocation of resources. By keeping foreign suppliers from the market, they invite retaliation and the spread of similar policies abroad, so as to narrow export opportunities for domestic suppliers.

TECHNICAL BARRIERS TO TRADE

Technical standards are generally intended to ensure the proper functioning of a machine or tool, interchangeability of parts or other inputs, or quality control—particularly as related to health, sanitary, and safety issues. These standards may be voluntary or mandatory, or a combination of the two. They are often accompanied by test methods designed to ensure that these objectives are in fact achieved. By their very nature, standards and testing requirements are generally thought to favor domestic over foreign suppliers, because compliance tends to be relatively easier for local firms. Foreign manufacturers first have to ascertain precisely what the product standards are, and especially in a relatively uncoordinated, decentralized, and heterogeneous system such as that in the United States, this may involve substantial search costs, delays, and uncertainties.

Second, products must be certified, as through submission of samples to a certifying body in the importing country. In the process, fees may be assessed, and costly delays incurred. The certification process lends itself to protectionist abuse. Information necessary for certification may purposely not be made available. The certifying body may refuse to accept foreign-made products or impose prohibitive fees for certification and testing. It may refuse to send inspectors abroad for certification purposes, or to accept foreign certification procedures, and so on.

Nevertheless, one of the legitimate purposes of industrial standards is to *broaden* access to markets for the products covered. The narrower the market, the more pronounced are the adverse trade effects likely to be, and extending standards from local to regional, national, and international coverage is itself tantamount to trade liberalization. Yet many countries have extremely diverse and unsystematic arrangements for standards formulation and certification. The potential for disrupting access to markets, intentionally or not, is obviously enormous.

CUSTOMS VALUATION

Another source of nontariff barriers to market access lies in the clearance of internationally traded products through customs. Officials may delay clearance, impose various costs, or otherwise inhibit import transactions and increase the degree of uncertainty associated with international trade.

A rather serious problem is that of *customs valuation*, the valuation of imported products for purposes of duty collection. Clearly, an *ad valorem* tariff on an imported product will be higher if the customs officer values it at $120 than at $100. So rules are needed to prevent the customs valuation process itself from becoming a further impediment to trade. Currently the most common system of valuation is the Brussels Definition of Value (BDV), used by over 100 countries. Although the BDV is based upon a "notional" or "normal" value, in practice the invoice price of the imported good is usually accepted as the relevant value if the importer is independent of the exporter. Many developing countries, however, establish their own minimum, average, or official prices as the "normal" product values, so as to reduce customs fraud.

The principal countries that have not adopted the BDV are the United States, Canada, and New Zealand. The U.S. valuation system is complex. Valuation is generally based on the invoice price of the imported good. Most of the remaining valuation decisions are made through a "constructed cost of production" estimate. A small fraction of total imports are valued at the higher of the invoice price and the domestic price in the country of export, at the U.S. domestic price of the imported good, or at the U.S. price of similar, domestically produced goods. The last method, called the American Selling Price (ASP) method, has now been scrapped.

There are several genuine concerns about such valuation practices. First, the alternative valuation methods are often invoked with respect to goods exchanged between related parties (rather than in "arm's-length" transactions) and are therefore suspect. Second, if the invoice price is used as the basis for valuation, most countries make adjustments for such items as advertising expenses and royalties not reflected in the invoice price; these adjustments can appear arbitrary. Third, the use of domestic prices in the country of export may result in overvaluation, since those prices are often artificially high because of input tariffs or internal taxes. Lastly, valuation based on prices of domestically produced goods in the importing country ignores comparative cost advantages and disfavors producers in the lowest-cost supplier countries.

SUBSIDIES AND COUNTERVAILING DUTIES

Recently, the effects of export subsidies on the pattern and volume of international trade have drawn increasing attention. So has the proper use of "*countervailing*," or offsetting, actions undertaken by the governments of importing countries to reduce the effects of such subsidies. Pressure to impose countervailing duties has grown, especially in the United States. The export subsidies in question sometimes involve outright grants or tax credits, sometimes low-cost provisions or guarantees of credits for export sales, or subsidies on the cost of transportation of exported goods.

The forms of *domestic* subsidies to industry that affect exports are more numerous and complex. Three general types of domestic subsidies can be identified. First, subsidies are offered to specific industries in order to help them overcome economic difficulties, assure production for national defense purposes, or accelerate overall industrial development. Clearly, domestic subsidies that impede the phase-out of declining industries in importing countries also impede the growth of production in the exporting countries. Second, subsidies can play a part in regional development plans. Third, certain subsidies are designed to promote capital formation, research and development, labor retraining programs, or other particular economic functions.

Subsidies may be economically justified if they increase economic efficiency by correcting market distortions or externalities. In fact, economic theory generally dictates a preference for the use of a policy that acts directly on the objective—usually, as we saw earlier, a subsidy rather than a tariff. Distortions may arise in factor as well as product markets. Distortions in labor markets occur through minimum or artificially maintained wages, the existence of monopolistic unions, laws governing the firing of employees, and in many other ways. Distortions in capital markets can be traced to credit controls, or to taxes, or to inflation-related risks.

Positive externalities in exporting may occur if the start-up costs to one firm produce spillover benefits to other, follower firms—say, through the development of a pool of trained labor or through the development of knowledge about lower-cost production methods. In these situations, compensatory subsidies can actually enhance the prospects for competitive trade relationships by exposing the true social comparative advantages and disadvantages.

Yet the effects of subsidies on international trade depend on how they are applied. Most *domestic subsidies* are based on the "origin principle," according to which the subsidy is given to domestic production regardless of whether the output eventually is sold on the home or the export market. *Export subsidies*, on the other hand, are applied only to goods sold abroad. *Countervailing duties* are devices through which importing countries protect themselves against the impact on their import-competing industries of incoming goods whose production or sale is subsidized abroad; they usually require computation of the degree of subsidy, and the setting of an import charge that is supposed to "neutralize" that subsidy. Obviously there is plenty of scope for overcompensating for the subsidy, so countervailing duties can easily become trade restrictions in their own right.

ACCESS TO SUPPLY SOURCES: EXPORT CONTROLS

Events in the 1970s and 1980s have added a new dimension to international trade policy, traditionally concerned almost exclusively with protecting domestic producers and their access to markets. There is a new concern about assuring access to sources of supply, particularly of fuels, industrial raw materials, and food products—that is, about buyers and users, rather than producers. The energy crises of the 1970s highlighted the importance of stable import supplies to all major crude-oil importers. Figure 11-6, which describes

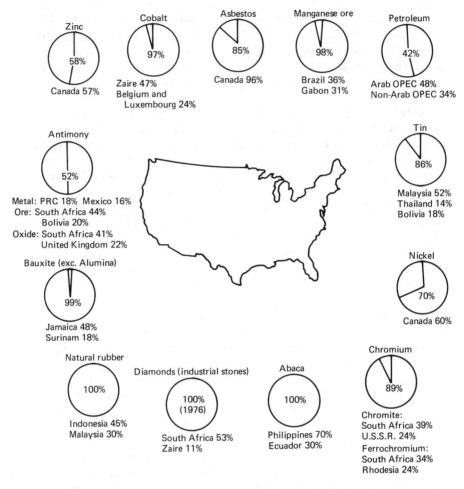

Figure 11-6. U.S. import dependence and import sources (1977 estimates except where noted).

Note: Figures within the circles represent the share of total U.S. imports in estimated domestic consumption. Figures outside the circles indicate principal foreign suppliers and the percentage they comprise. For example, the U.S. imports 85 percent of its asbestos; 96 percent of that comes from Canada and 4 percent comes from other foreign sources.

Source: U.S. Department of State.

the degree of U.S. import dependence on various minerals and fuels, provides a dramatic illustration of the same general point. The problems of assured demand outlets and assured supply sources, of course, are not independent, and liberal policies in the latter area generally, over time, will help to reduce periodic problems in the former.

Overall, two types of export controls may be analyzed: (*a*) those imposed at the request of the importing country on the exports of its trading partners, and (*b*) those imposed on the home country's own exports.

The effects of export quotas, imposed by foreign countries (the potential importers), are similar to those of equally restrictive import quotas imposed by these countries themselves. Prices in the latter rise, their output of similar product groups increases, and their consumption of them is reduced. Their terms of trade tend to deteriorate as import prices rise relative to export prices—in terms of Figure 11-2, p. 161, the exporting country's (country *F*'s) offer curve becomes horizontal once the quota has been filled. Whatever additional revenues arise out of this country's export quota are virtually certain to be captured by the exporters themselves, who would appear to possess all of the monopoly power in this case.

In some instances, the imposition of quotas on the exports of foreign countries may be a direct extension of the trade policy of the home country. An example of this situation is the imposition of textile export quotas by Japan at the behest of the United States during the mid-1960s. The United States was able to force Japan to impose these quotas on its own exports largely as a result of a very strong American bargaining position. Thus, it was able to protect its own textile suppliers without itself bearing the onus of imposing protective measures. These measures, already discussed briefly in Chapter 9, take the form of voluntary export restraints (VERs) and orderly marketing arrangements (OMAs).

The second category, the imposition of export quotas by the home country, deserves some additional analysis. Figure 11-7 is a partial-equilibrium representation of the impact of such export quotas. Figure 11-2 (see p. 161) can be used to draw very similar conclusions from a general-equilibrium point of view.

In Figure 11-7, D_d represents domestic demand for the product in question, D_f is the foreign demand, ΣD is the sum of the domestic and foreign demand, and S_d is the domestic supply. By assumption there is no foreign supply. Under free-trade conditions, a price of $60 prevails, with equilibrium at E—250 units are produced, of which 80 units are used at home (point G) and the rest (170 units) are exported. Total export receipts are $10,200 ($60 × 170), and domestic receipts are $4800 ($60 × 80).

Now suppose the country imposes an export quota of 100 units. The quantity sold domestically rises from 80 to 100 units, with a fall in the domestic price to $50. Quantity exported is reduced to the quota level of 100 units, represented by perfectly inelastic supply S_q, with a rise in the export price to $75. Total export receipts are now $7500 ($75 × 100). As a result of the quota, the net change in export receipts is –$2700 ($7500 – $10,200). This reflects the effect of higher export prices combined with lower export volume. The net change in domestic sales is $200 ($5000 – $4800), the combined effect of a lower domestic price and higher sales volume.

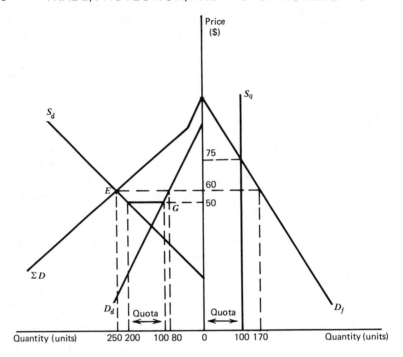

Figure 11-7. Effects of export quotas: partial equilibrium.

It is not difficult to see that the effect on total product sales (domestic and foreign) of a given export quota will be more expansionary (*a*) the less elastic the foreign demand for the product, (*b*) the more elastic the domestic demand for the product, and (*c*) the less elastic the domestic supply of the product. Each of these conditions will tend to increase those areas in Figure 11-7 that represent higher sales revenues relative to those areas representing reduced revenues. Also, the more inelastic the foreign demand, the more likely it is that export quotas will result in improved terms of trade, since this will ensure a substantial rise in export prices. It will also ensure that export receipts rise—that is, that the fall in quantity exported has a lesser bearing on foreign sales revenues than the rise in export prices.

In this particular example, exports alone are restricted. The result, from the standpoint of domestic consumers, is a reduction in price. But the same *international* effect can be brought about in other ways, although with quite different ramifications for domestic consumers. Suppose that the country, instead of imposing an export quota, simply limits total production of the export commodity or destroys some of this output. Under appropriate elasticity conditions, producers will still benefit, because of increased receipts. Domestic consumers will now lose as prices at home are forced to rise *along with* export prices (the domestic supply curve in Figure 11-7 shifts to the right).

SUMMARY

In this chapter we have considered the effects on international trade and production of trade restrictions other than tariffs. Import quotas can reduce trade volumes and distort production patterns just like tariffs. But they are often administered differently, and their longer-term consequences in practice tend to be more restrictive; of course, in themselves they produce no government revenue. Variable levies, which are particularly prevalent in agricultural trade, are similar to quotas and equally distortive in their trade effects. Subsidies to import-competing firms can likewise protect and distort industrial development. They are usually preferable to tariffs or quotas, however, particularly from the standpoint of domestic consumers. We also examined a variety of other nontariff barriers, including those classified under import licensing, government procurement, technical barriers to trade, customs valuation procedures, subsidies, countervailing duties, and export controls. Many of these pose complex and difficult challenges for trade liberalization, as we shall see in Chapter 13.

Important Concepts

import quota	subsidies
export quota	nontariff barriers
global quota	import licensing
selective quota	government procurement
voluntary export restraint	technical barriers to trade
orderly marketing arrangement	customs valuation
tariff quota	countervailing duties
variable levies	export controls

Questions

1. It has frequently been said that that the liberalization of nontariff barriers is extraordinarily difficult to negotiate. Give some reasons why this may be so.

2. Suppose you were a domestic manufacturer of wooden clothespins beset by import competition. Can you think of some NTBs you might wish to plead for? How would they help you? How would your answers change if you were a tomato grower? A manufacturer of automobiles? A maker of lighting fixtures?

3. An argument often raised by the developing countries is that NTBs affect them more seriously than their industrialized competitors. Can you think of some arguments to support or refute this assertion?

4. Recent concerns with consumer, environmental, and safety issues are said to have multiplied the incidence of NTBs. Explain this statement.

Further Readings

Baldwin, Robert E., *Nontariff Distortions of International Trade* (Washington, D.C.: The Brookings Institution, 1970).

Corden, W. M., *The Theory of Protection* (London: Oxford University Press, 1971).

Dam, K. W., *The GATT: Law and International Economic Organization* (Chicago: University of Chicago Press, 1970).

Hawkins, Robert G., and Ingo Walter (eds.), *The United States and International Markets* (Lexington, Mass.: D. C. Heath, 1972).

Walter, Ingo, "Non-Tariff Measures and the Export Performance of Developing Countries," *American Economic Review*, May 1971.

12

TRADE
AND MARKET
STRUCTURE

In discussing the theory of trade policy, we have surveyed a variety of circumstances that determine whether producers *are allowed to* compete freely in international markets. Here we shall focus on the question of whether producers in fact *do* compete with one another, and whether the market environment within which firms operate internationally is conducive to the maximization of the conventional gains from international trade.

Our discussion of the theory of trade policy concerned itself with the impact of governmental distortions on the volume and direction of international trade, national output structure, income distribution, and world and national economic welfare. It attempted to reconcile the obvious existence of barriers to trade with the powerful arguments in favor of freer trade. Yet even the arguments for free trade have one basic weakness: They generally rest on a price system that freely and automatically responds to changes in supply and demand conditions, both in the markets for goods and services and in the markets for productive factors. This condition, of course, often does not hold in the real world. We shall now examine a variety of market conditions that may distort international competition and indicate their typical effects on international trade patterns.

ELEMENTS OF PERFECT COMPETITION

In the main, the theory of trade and trade policy centers on the optimal allocation of productive resources, domestically and internationally, via free trade and perfect competition, and on the misallocation of resources because of impediments to trade. Yet every student of economics learns that market structure in the real world seldom corresponds to the pure-competition model. This is true of both the markets for products and the markets for productive factors. Under pure competition the seller has no control over the price of his product, which is determined by the market forces of supply and demand and is dictated to him; he is a price taker. At that market price he can sell all he can produce, but at a higher price he can sell nothing. Perfect competition can prevail only if (a) the product of the various competing suppliers is homogeneous in quality; (b) there are a large number of competing firms, each one of which holds only a small share of the market; (c) there is free entry into and exit out of the industry; and (d) there is perfect knowledge about all relevant market conditions.

Although the perfect competitor finds that his selling price is beyond his control, he can still freely vary the quantity he produces. He will, therefore, continue to increase output as long as one extra unit sold yields additional revenues that exceed the additional costs involved in producing that one extra unit. That is, as long as *marginal revenue* exceeds *marginal cost*, it pays for him to expand output. Profits will attain a maximum when marginal cost equals marginal revenue. Since, for the perfect competitor, the price of the extra unit sold is the same regardless of how many units he sells, marginal revenue and price are identical. He will therefore produce a quantity sufficient to ensure that the marginal cost of the last unit sold just equals the selling price.

This situation is presented diagrammatically in Figure 12-1. The price of the product ($100) and the total quantity purchased (10,000 units) are determined by the interaction of supply and demand in the market. Since the firm can sell all it can produce at that price, its demand curve, D_F, is horizontal. At the same time, each additional unit sold yields the additional revenue of $100 so the marginal revenue curve, MR, is identical with the demand curve. The perfectly competitive firm produces 200 units, where marginal cost (MC) equals marginal revenue (MR). With free entry and exit, there can be no long-run monopoly profits, so that the average-total-cost curve (ATC) will be tangent to the demand or average revenue curve. Since the average-total-cost curve is always intersected by the marginal-cost curve at its minimum point, this tangency ($MC = MR = ATC$) must occur at minimum average total cost.

If perfect competition prevails in all markets, resource allocation and output will be highly responsive to demand changes. Since production always occurs at minimum average total cost, resources in the industry are employed with maximum efficiency. Because there can be no long-run pure profits, price always equals the sum of the individual resource costs. Finally, if perfect competition prevails in the market for productive resources as well, the cost of each factor must be identical with what it could have earned in alternative employment in any other industry. All of this occurs automatically via the price mechanism.

This is the market structure assumed to exist in the theory of international trade. It may not be an entirely realistic assumption. Before the Industrial

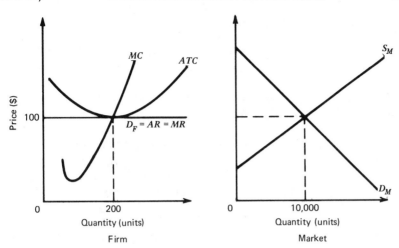

Figure 12-1. Price and output determination under perfect competition.

Revolution, it may well have been true that international trade involved goods produced under highly competitive conditions—mainly primary commodities—so monopolistic elements in such markets could possibly be discounted. This is certainly not true today. Many traded goods are produced and distributed under decidedly monopolistic conditions, as are internationally traded services and technological knowledge.

ELEMENTS OF MONOPOLY

Many goods entering international trade today are not very homogeneous. Rather, they are differentiated from one another in a variety of ways. Entry into industries is rarely free, with all the patents, technical know-how, heavy capital requirements, and other obstacles that must be overcome. Knowledge is not perfect; it is seldom possible to know what is going on in all parts of the market for a given good simultaneously. Firms are not small relative to the total market size, nor should they be, when significant economies of scale can be realized. Meanwhile, the markets for productive factors may contain similar monopolistic elements on the supply side (e.g., powerful unions), and localized monopsonistic influences sometimes exist on the factor-demand side.

A firm operating in an industry characterized by a monopolistic market structure has at least some control over price. Since its product is more or less differentiated from that of its competitors, it may raise its price without losing all of its customers; to this extent, it is a *price maker*. Increased sales are possible only at lower prices, and so the demand curve facing the imperfectly-competitive firm is downward sloping. Its marginal revenue curve falls below the demand curve; since it must lower the price of *all* units to sell one additional unit, marginal revenue is always less than average revenue.

Figure 12-2 reflects how imperfect competition differs from perfect competition. The demand (average revenue) curve is downward sloping and the marginal revenue curve falls somewhere below it. With cost curves similar to those presented above in connection with perfect competition, the firm in monopolistic competition will also maximize profits or minimize losses where marginal cost equals marginal revenue—that is, at point S. It will therefore sell 200 units at $50. Its average total cost is $30, and with an average revenue of $50, its profit per unit is $20. Total revenues are $10,000 ($50 × 200), total costs are $6000 ($30 × 200), and total profits are $4000.

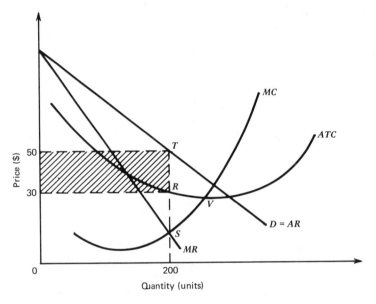

Figure 12-2. Price and output determination of an imperfectly competitive firm.

Note that the firm operates at a cost level (R) that is higher than the minimum attainable with a given plant size (V). This means that resources are being employed with less than maximum efficiency. Note also that the output level at which $MR = MC$ is less than that at which $MC = ATC$. Since the perfectly competitive firm in the long run always produces where $MR = MC = ATC$, it follows that output levels under imperfect competition tend to be lower than the corresponding perfectly competitive levels. Finally, pure profits are possible under this limited form of competition—because of the absence of free entry into the industry, even in the long run.

We have designated as imperfectly competitive all firms facing a downward-sloping demand curve. Taken in the broadest sense, this includes both pure monopoly (one supplier), oligopoly (few suppliers), and monopolistic competition. Economists usually claim that under such conditions output will be lower, prices higher, and resources utilized less efficiently than under perfect competition. Imperfect competition in the productive factor markets has a similar effect (e.g., monopoly labor unions). The economy is not nearly so free to adjust to changing demand pressure, either domestic or international, and this rigidity can influence the ability of comparative advantage to govern international trading relationships. On the other hand, we have seen that economies of scale—which are possible only under imperfect competition—can be an important force in influencing comparative costs internationally.

The specific impact of imperfect competition on international trade is extremely difficult to assess. The outputs of suppliers located in various parts of the world indeed are *not* perfect substitutes for one another, and it would seem that the volume of trade will be below what it would have been if they were perfectly substitutable; yet demand forces operating internationally thrive on product differentiation. The cross-trading of commodities is enormous: automobiles from Germany to France and France to Germany, machine tools from Belgium to Great Britain and vice versa, and so on. The stimulus that product differentiation brings to international trade through demand variation and economies of scale also helps to reduce the potential negative impact of imperfect competition on international trade. It does, however, suggest that we employ the classical analytical tools of international trade with some caution.

INTERNATIONAL CARTELS AND PRICE DISCRIMINATION

Suppose only two firms in the world produce a certain type of chemical, one located in the United States and the other in Germany. The demand for this chemical is presumed to be widespread throughout the world, and both firms compete actively in each and every market. The German firm even competes for a share of the U.S. market, and vice versa. Given this situation, would it not be profitable for the two firms to *agree not to compete*, either explicitly or implicitly? The world market for this type of chemical might be divided by agreement between the two firms, with neither invading the territory of the other. Each would have a monopoly position in its own market, setting prices at whatever level maximizes its own profits—a level presumably above the competitive price. Such an agreement would be called an *international cartel*.

Any formal agreement between firms or supplier countries to share the market or otherwise restrict competition may be classified as a cartel. When such agreements cross international frontiers, they become of direct concern to us in studying the behavior of international trade. The purpose of cartels is simple: to secure profits for each participant in excess of what the participant could have earned under conditions of unrestricted competition. We shall see a little later that the problem of mutual distrust in cartels fosters internal tensions that often lead to their demise. For this reason, an international cartel will often be very formally structured by some sort of association that has the power to hold it together.

International cartels among private businesses probably had their heyday between the two world wars. Pharmaceuticals, chemicals, electrical machinery, and machine tools head a long list of goods in which international trade was subject to the influence or control of cartels. Of the total volume of world trade during the interwar period, it appears that around one third came under the direct influence of cartels. This certainly takes us far from the perfectly competitive ideal. As late as 1964 in Europe, there was considerable discussion of a grand cartel in the production of automobiles among Volkswagen, Fiat, and Renault that would divide the European market either geographically or by type of vehicle for the collective benefit of the three giant manufacturers. And in the 1970s there were cartel-like actions, usually with government support, to "organize" markets in industries as diverse as steel, synthetic fibers, uranium, and shipbuilding, not to mention the international OPEC oil cartel.

The general goal of a cartel is to maximize profits for its members by suppressing competition among them. In effect, a cartel creates a monopoly in a market where at least some degree of competition, most probably an oligopoly, existed beforehand. One method is to split up the overall market geographically, or by product category, so that each member firm has an effective monopoly in its own particular segment of the market. Resale from one market to another is prevented. Each firm sets prices to maximize profits, given demand conditions in its particular designated market.

Alternatively, the cartel may supply the entire market by allocating output quotas to its members and jointly marketing the product. Or the cartel may simply fix the price of the good or service in question, and the members compete for the market on the basis of quality alone. These are only a few of the forms cartels may take.

Only a monopoly or a cartel has the ability to *discriminate* between markets in regard to prices charged for a relatively uniform good or service. If resale is prevented in some way, one price could be charged for a certain product in Germany, another in France, and still another in Italy, in accordance with demand conditions in the three markets. Total profits of the cartel as a whole would be maximized if *each individual buyer* could be induced to pay the maximum amount he or she is willing to pay rather than go without it. This form of price discrimination is clearly impossible to realize fully. Much more likely is the division of the market into broad *segments* according to their demand characteristics, and then charging each segment a different price. The chief criterion for such price discrimination is the elasticity of demand in each market segment.

Suppose we take a hypothetical international wine cartel, selling in France and Great Britain. Frenchmen being habitual wine-drinkers, their price elasticity of demand is likely to be low—an increase in the price of wine is likely to cause a relatively small reduction in consumption. For the British, on the other hand, beer and ale may serve as good substitutes for wine, so they are likely to possess a substantially higher price elasticity of demand for wine. The cartel would be wise to charge higher prices for a given type of wine in France than in Great Britain, thereby maximizing overall revenues and profits.

This can be shown graphically in Figure 12-3, which presents the average and marginal revenue curves for two national markets, characterized by different price elasticities of demand—AR_1 and MR_1, versus AR_2 and MR_2, respectively. By simply adding the marginal revenue curves for the two markets, the combined marginal revenue curve (ΣMR) facing the cartel can be derived. The marginal cost curve (MC) and the average total cost curve (ATC) for the entire cartel have also been drawn.

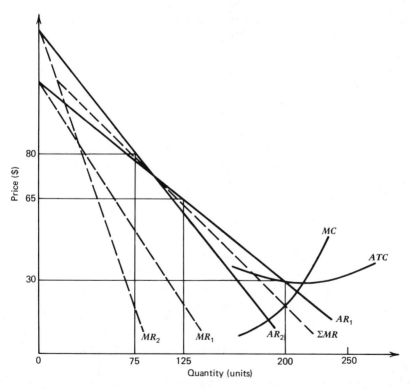

Figure 12-3. Market segmentation and price discrimination.

In order to maximize profits, the cartel will operate where its marginal cost equals its combined marginal revenue, at point T, producing a total of 200 units. Of this total, it sells 125 units in the first market (where $MC = MR_1$) and 75 units in the second (where $MC = MR_2$). The first market is willing to take 125 units at $65, whereas the second market is willing to absorb 75 units at $80. Marginal cost has thus been equated with marginal revenue in each of the two markets. Total costs are $6000 ($30 × 200) and total revenue is $14,125 [($65 × 125) + ($80 × 75)], leaving profits of $8,125. Maximum profits are attained for each market, the total of which substantially exceeds the profits that would have been attained if a uniform price had been set for *both* markets. By preventing the establishment of a uniform price through free competition, therefore, the international cartel assures that the profits of each of its members are enhanced. This highlights the aforementioned importance of governments as handmaidens of, or active participants in, cartel-like activities. Governments can, by means of trade policy, prevent the international resale of cartelized products and thus make possible the segmentation of markets.

All cartels possess a basic inner tension that can easily lead to their demise. For example, a cartel member, allocated a certain area, may be unable to resist invading its neighbor's territory whenever it appears safe to do so. Hence, the cartel may degenerate into some form of noncollusive oligopoly—which can indeed benefit the consumer, but which is detrimental to the profits of the producers. Again, the role of government in preventing such a course of events may be criticized.

How are international cartels controlled and prevented from regaining the importance they enjoyed during the interwar period? Many countries, led by the United States, Germany, and Great Britain, have adopted legal and other types of restrictions that hinder or prevent the operation of private cartels. Where cartels are thought to be unavoidable, government control and participation in cartel negotiations have been imposed. Not least important, the European Economic Community has taken steps that discourage and attempt to control international agreements that restrict competition within it.

DUMPING

A special case of international price discrimination is the practice of *dumping*, or selling goods abroad at prices lower than those charged at home or below the full unit costs of production. The generally accepted definition of dumping focuses on selling abroad at lower prices than at home. The United States, on the other hand, has adopted the norm of *full-cost recovery*, including normal profit, because of its concern with the growing subsidization of firms abroad by their governments; these subsidies result from direct government ownership or the practice of offsetting losses of private firms with public funds.

A monopolist who finds that the elasticity of demand for his output abroad is higher than at home is being perfectly rational if he charges higher prices at home than he does in the export market. He is simply maximizing his total profits by practicing price discrimination of the type discussed above. This is true as long as the export price still exceeds the average incremental costs of the exported units, so that it contributes something to his fixed charges. Furthermore, if he is operating in the area of increasing marginal costs, it is likely that the practice of dumping will raise his domestic selling price, thus further increasing the spread between the home and the export price.

In fact, if the monopolist is in a position to sell in several foreign markets characterized by varying degrees of price elasticity of demand, each of which is greater than that prevailing at home, it pays for him to dump in each of these markets at a different price. It would seem, then, that the possibilities for dumping are virtually unlimited in international trade. But remember that price discrimination is possible only if *resale* from one market to another is somehow prevented, by law or by virtue of transportation costs. Such a condition is not often fulfilled in the international economy.

Suppose, for instance, a firm is selling matches at home for $0.20 a pack and dumping them abroad for $0.10 a pack. If there are no restrictions on trade and if transport costs are minimal, what is to prevent enterprising individuals from buying matches abroad at $0.10 and reimporting them for sale at home for something less than $0.20, and earning a tidy profit in the process? Under such conditions, international *arbitrage* will see to it that the domestic and foreign price of matches is quickly equalized and that the dumping practice ceases.

Although this example may be somewhat extreme, it is nonetheless true that the *maximum* difference between the home price and the dumping price abroad is always determined by the possibility and cost of resale in the domestic market. For some products, arbitrage may be very effective and virtually costless, so that the scope for dumping may be narrow indeed.

At first glance, the practice of dumping would seem to bring about a volume of trade that tends to be somewhat higher than if this practice did not occur— and a potentially significant benefit for the importing country's consumers. In addition, it would appear to result in expanded production on the part of the dumping firm. Of course, the importing country is likely to possess its own import-competing suppliers (and factors of production), whose output will be reduced commensurately as a result of the increased volume of dumped imports. It may not take long under such conditions for the importing country to levy its own import duty or to otherwise restrict imports—through *antidumping measures*—thereby wholly or partially eliminating the practice of dumping. A version of this measure was introduced by the United States in the late 1970s under the so-called *trigger price mechanism* applied to imported steel. Imports priced below the calculated Japanese delivered cost of steel, presumed to be the most competitive, trigger a "fast-track" antidumping investigation to provide quick relief to the domestic industry. Selling abroad below full-cost recovery attributable to government subsidies can be similarly offset by so-called *countervailing duties* that neutralize the subsidy element.

The word "dumping" may seem like a misnomer, since it connotes the elimination of some sort of surplus. This hardly describes a permanent, profit-motivated practice of selling more cheaply (or more expensively) abroad. There are, however, some forms of dumping that more closely fit the connotations of the word itself. *Sporadic* dumping may be temporarily engaged in by firms with excess inventories. A dress manufacturer may find that the domestic demand for a certain style is rapidly fading, and it may want to sell its inventory on foreign markets for anything it can get. Or the domestic demand for a given good may be slack, and this situation may also call for sales abroad at prices that cover all variable costs and in addition make some contribution toward fixed costs. Such practices can transfer part of the burden of adjusting to seasonal or cyclical variations in demand to competing industries abroad. When this happens, a good case can be made for strong countervailing action on the part of the importing country.

Predatory dumping can be condemned on the same grounds as predatory domestic pricing policies. A firm may be said to pursue a predatory pricing policy if it reduces the price of a given product to such an extent that its competitors are driven out of business. It then raises prices again to cash in on its new monopoly position. Predatory dumping is the same thing, only on an international scale. Once its foreign competitors are ruined, the firm again raises prices in accordance with the new demand conditions in the foreign market. In fact, if foreign demand is sufficiently inelastic, the subsequent price abroad may actually be *higher* than the domestic price. By contrast, temporary dumping as a means of *establishing* a product in a foreign market is nothing more than an accepted form of sales promotion. The trick for policy makers, of course, is to distinguish among different forms of dumping, so that sensible policies can be designed.

COMMODITY AGREEMENTS AND COMMODITY PRICES

For many products—especially, agricultural commodities and raw materials—the elasticity of demand and the elasticity of supply are both very low. Small variations in demand or supply can cause very large fluctuations in price. Figure 12-4 presents short-run demand and supply functions for a certain commodity—say, coffee—pertaining to the individual supplier and to the market as a whole. If we assume that the market for coffee is perfectly competitive, then the demand curve facing each producer is horizontal.

In the first case (Figure 12-4a), a decline in foreign incomes or a change in tastes abroad causes the market demand curve for coffee to shift slightly to the left, resulting in a substantial drop in market price, from \$100 to \$90. The

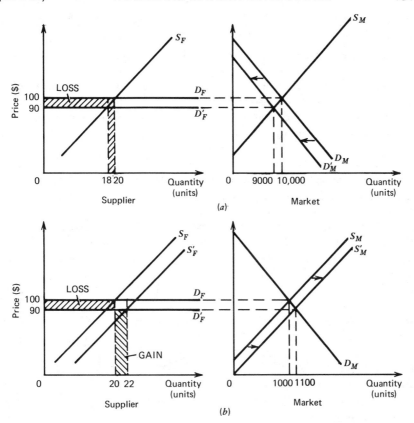

Figure 12-4. Changing market conditions and commodity price. (a) Demand shift. (b) Supply shift.

producer feels this as a fall in his horizontal demand curve and, with supply unchanged, the reduction in his sales quantity is 2 units and his revenues fall by $380 [($100 × 2) + ($10 × 18)]. Part of this amount represents a reduction of his profit.

In the second case (Figure 12-4b), favorable weather conditions cause a rightward shift in the market supply curve, which, with demand constant, similarly results in a substantial price decline. For the individual producer this again means a drop in his horizontal demand curve, sales thus being reduced by $200 ($10 × 20). This time, however, his loss is not so great, since he partakes of the general supply increase with a rightward shift in his own short-run supply curve—in this case, by 2 units or $180 ($90 × 2). The loss induced by the price decline may or may not outweigh the gain caused by the increase in quantity sold. In this example it does, by $20.

There is only one way that commodity producers operating in this sort of market structure can protect themselves from price reductions: by restricting supply. In Figure 12-4, the original price could have been maintained and the producers' losses minimized if all suppliers had simply agreed to reduce the amount of coffee they place on the market—and if the resultant drop in quantity sold was less than the proportionate drop in price that would otherwise have occurred. This is the task of *commodity agreements*, which can benefit suppliers whether the market structure is perfectly competitive (as in this case) or monopolistic. Agreements controlling the worldwide supply of commodities in these circumstances may be either private or intergovernmental.

Private commodity agreements are essentially cartels and involve the creation of a central association that allocates production quotas to each supplier. This is done in such a way that the world price is maintained at the desired level. Excess supplies, if they occur, must either be stored or destroyed. This is the weakness inherent in private commodity agreements, since each individual supplier is understandably anxious to dispose of his surplus in a way that still yields at least some revenues, however minimal. Any significant undercutting of a private commodity agreement in this manner can lead to its demise.

One result is the evolution of *intergovernmental* commodity agreements, which elevate the question of controlling supply to a level of national importance. This is particularly true in the case of developing countries that are highly dependent on exports of one or two commodities. How can fluctuations in their export prices and receipts be stabilized so that the contribution of the export sector to economic growth can be enhanced? Individual developing countries normally are powerless to bring about such stability by regulating the volume of their own exports and output, and individual importing countries generally also can do little in this regard. Whatever stability is achieved must involve either bilateral agreements, between exporting and importing nations, or multilateral schemes, either among the supplying nations or among the importing nations or both.

Developing countries almost always view commodity agreements as a desirable solution to export instability. However, is it possible for such stabilization schemes to avoid pegging prices at unrealistic or market-distortive levels and seriously missing long-run price trends? The answers—and opinions on the importance of the question itself—are almost always couched in emotional terms. It is clear that any disequilibrium system, such as a commodity agreement, will usually involve production quotas, disagreements among suppliers, stockpiling problems, and financing difficulties. In addition, if the agreed-upon price is set at a sufficiently high level, substitutes may be developed and the affected commodity may be shut out of the market entirely.

Analytically, the operation of commodity agreements is quite simple. In Figure 12-5, curve *DD* represents the demand for a developing nation's exports of a given primary commodity. Curve *SS*, which is relatively inelastic, represents that country's supply of the commodity for export. Suppose equilibrium price and quantity are initially $100 and 900 units, respectively. A fall in export demand to *D'D'* would reduce the price to $80, quantity exported to 800 units, and export receipts from the original $90,000 ($100 × 900) to $64,000 ($80 × 800). By establishing a *minimum price* of $90, the commodity agreement prevents export prices from falling below that level. Given an identical demand reduction, export receipts fall to $67,500 (90 × 750), which is more than under free-market conditions.

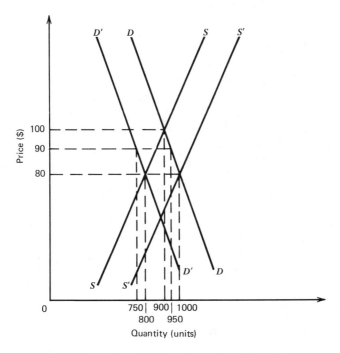

Figure 12-5. Commodity price stabilization.

In a similar manner, commodity agreements may prevent a drastic price reduction resulting from an inordinate expansion of export supply. Suppose supply grew, perhaps because of unusually favorable crop conditions, from *SS* to *S'S'*. With constant foreign demand (*DD*), price would fall to $80, and export receipts would be reduced from $90,000 ($100 × 90) to $80,000 ($80 × 1000). By limiting the price reduction to $90, the commodity agreement assures that export receipts fall to only $85,500 ($90 × 950). It is not difficult to see that commodity agreements will be more effective in preventing a fall in export receipts in response to supply and demand shifts (*a*) the more inelastic is the foreign demand and (*b*) the more inelastic is the domestic export supply. Naturally, the agreements also have to have the financing necessary to buy up the excess supply at a price of $90.

Commodity agreements are subject to the same problems of enforcement, stockpiling, administrative complexity, and financial costs as other cartel arrangements. Still, many development economists regard them as helpful in reducing price instability and in promoting a stabler climate for long-term growth. Whether or not commodity agreements provide the solution is, however, open to question, as the analogous experience with farm-support programs in developed nations amply testifies.

Long-Term Price Movements

Besides stabilizing commodity prices to help developing countries, arguments have been advanced that commodity agreements should also be used to rig markets to provide "fair" prices for the poor countries' exports—that is, to improve their terms of trade. What has been the long-range performance of the terms of trade of developing nations? Have they fallen "unfairly"? One set of arguments centers on the notion that over the past century prices of primary goods have fallen substantially relative to prices of manufactures. Since the developing countries mainly import manufactured goods and export primary commodities, this movement must have resulted in a long-term deterioration of their collective terms of trade. This means that the developing countries have had to export increasing amounts of their products in order to get given quantities of imports. This loss to the underdeveloped world was the developed countries' gain, since there occurred a simultaneous, secular improvement in their collective terms of trade. This is often referred to as the *Prebisch-Singer thesis*, after its two main proponents.

The alleged long-term deterioration of the developing countries' terms of trade is attributed to a variety of factors: (1) The income elasticity of demand for primary products is claimed to be a good deal less than that for manufactured goods; combined with raw-material saving innovations, this has led to an overall reduction in the demand for primary goods relative to the demand for manufactures. (2) The markets for manufactured goods are alleged to be much more monopolistic than those for primary commodities. The market power of manufactures has made the prices of industrial goods "sticky" and prevented them, in contrast to primary commodity prices, from falling in recessions. Over successive business cycles, the ratchet-type behavior of industrial prices has made them rise relative to those of primary commodities. (3) Technological change has had a differential price impact. In the production of primary goods, productivity has risen markedly, and the fruits of this productivity increase have been passed on to purchasers in the form of lower commodity prices. Productivity in industrial activity has grown even more rapidly, but the gains from it have been distributed to the owners of productive factors in the form of higher real wages, interest, rent, and profits, with very little of the productivity increase being reflected in lower prices of industrial goods.

The Prebisch-Singer thesis maintains that these three sets of factors have been responsible for the apparent secular deterioration in the terms of trade of the primary-goods-producing areas. Since these happen to include most of the developing areas of the world, there has, allegedly, been a transfer of real income from the poorest to the least poor countries.

The thesis is open to serious question. In the first place, the allegations are based largely on movements in the British terms of trade from the late 1800s to the end of the 1930s. During this time, the British net barter terms of trade actually did improve substantially, and its developing-country trading partners must have experienced a corresponding decline. But the British import and export composition undoubtedly was unique and not suited as an inverse proxy of that facing the developing areas of the world today.

Moreover, there is always the question of *quality* change. The quality of primary products tends to remain relatively constant—with some rare exceptions, such as seedless grapes or navel oranges—simply because they do not lend themselves to quality improvement. Meanwhile, the quality of manufactures has risen substantially—a 1920 automobile is not the same as a current model. If quality changes were taken into account, then, the improved character of the developing areas' imports, combined with the relatively unchanging quality of their exports, would render any indicated deterioration of their terms of trade much smaller and perhaps negate it entirely.

Also, the income elasticity of demand for primary goods—especially for foodstuffs—may well be low, but this does not constitute the sole determinant of the terms of trade. Rather, changes in supply conditions are equally important. So, although the *demand* for industrial goods may have grown more rapidly than the demand for primary commodities, so has the *supply* of industrial products during the process of industrialization.

Furthermore, there is some question whether the net barter terms of trade are really what we want to look at. Should we not, instead, examine the changes in the amount of imports that a given quantum of productive factors in the primary-goods-producing areas have been able to buy? Clearly, this must have risen as productivity grew in the primary-producing regions.

Finally, the alleged "ratchet effect" of prices in developed countries over the business cycle has not been well established. Prices in the *international* marketplace respond to competitive conditions prevailing not in one country, but in many countries. This reduces even further the role of market imperfections in bringing about upward pressure on the developing countries' import prices. In the light of all of these considerations, then, the idea of a secular deterioration in the terms of trade of developing nations loses most of its persuasiveness.

In recent years the prices of both renewable and nonrenewable raw materials have shown a marked tendency to rise, in part because of unprecedented prosperity among the industrial countries and in part because of increasing supply limitations in certain raw-material industries. Moreover, in the petroleum field the exporting countries have been spectacularly successful in cartelization and in driving up prices. For the developing countries as a whole, therefore, a significant improvement in the terms of trade is already under way, and this is resulting in a major transfer of income *from* the developed countries—as well as some income redistribution *among* the developing countries themselves. These developments have undermined the case for broad-scale commodity agreements specifically favoring raw-material producers in the developing world.

CONTROL OVER EXPORT INDUSTRIES

The control of exports on the part of a single country is, at least in part, analogous to intergovernmental commodity agreements. The objective is to limit the supply of the commodity on the world market, increase its price, and thus improve the country's terms of trade. What a commodity agreement attempts to do multilaterally, export control seeks to achieve unilaterally. The basic prerequisite for the success of such export control is that the nation be an important world-market supplier of the product in question. Whether an improvement in the terms of trade actually comes about as a result of export-control schemes depends on the nature of the demand for the export and how dominant, relative to others, the country is as a supplier.

If the demand for an exported product facing a country is less than perfectly elastic, unilateral restriction of that export will increase its price. Import prices remaining constant, its terms of trade will tend to improve. The question is whether or not the improvement in the terms of trade will, from a revenue standpoint, be more than offset by the resultant decline in the volume of exports. This depends on the elasticity of foreign demand. The lower the elasticity, the more likely it is that the country will benefit from restricting exports unilaterally. Similarly, the lower the domestic elasticity of supply, the more effective will be the restriction of exports, since the ensuing drop in the home-market price will then not depress output very much.

Suppose, for example, Chile were the sole producer of copper in the world. The demand for copper is relatively inelastic, since there are few good substitutes in the short run. By simply reducing its exports, Chile would be able to drive the world price of copper upward. The consequent improvement in its terms of trade, import prices remaining unchanged, would more than offset the relatively small reductions in the volume of exports required to achieve it. Chile would simply be acting rationally, as any good monopolist, supplying copper to the rest of the world up to a point where its marginal export receipts equal its marginal cost of production.

There are two ways in which exports can be restricted—by limiting the exports themselves and by reducing output. The first interferes only with the supplies reaching buyers abroad, whereas the second limits quantities available to both domestic and foreign consumers. The *export quota* limits the amount of goods that can be sold abroad. Domestic prices may fall drastically while export prices rise or remain stable. The glut on the domestic market under such conditions may be eliminated by means of stockpiling or destruction. Domestic consumers and producers both can benefit in real terms at the expense of foreign consumers. Alternatively, an *export duty* may be imposed. This causes suppliers' receipts from exports to be lower than those from domestic sales at identical prices, and thereby discourages exports. This will have an effect similar to that of export quotas. In order to be successful, both export quotas and export duties require accurate knowledge of the foreign elasticity of demand, which is not always readily available.

Similar terms-of-trade effects provided by interference with exports themselves can be achieved by limiting production, although the impact on the domestic economy will be different. A government may (*a*) dictate that suppliers limit output, (*b*) purchase part of the output and destroy it, or (*c*) purchase all of the output, destroy or stockpile part of it, and sell the rest. All of these measures will limit the supplies available to *both* foreign and domestic purchasers, and increase the prices paid by both. The terms-of-trade effects of the measures, everything else being equal, will be approximately the same as in the case of pure export restriction. But the price to domestic consumers will rise, and there is likely to be a redistribution of real income from consumers to producers. In this case, domestic producers will tend to benefit at the expense of both foreign and domestic consumers.

Export restrictions thus depend for their success in improving the terms of trade on the partial or complete absence of good substitutes or competing suppliers in other countries. Like commodity agreements, they can possibly be justified to the extent that they reduce severe price fluctuations. In addition, they may serve to achieve a long-term improvement in a country's terms of trade. The latter effect will be limited, however, if new substitute products develop. Steel, silver, and aluminum can substitute for copper, for example, just as nuclear, hydroelectric, and solar power, natural gas, and coal can substitute for oil in virtually all its uses. In the long run, there is always the likelihood of substitution as technology adjusts to the new market conditions.

STATE TRADING

Up to now, we have generally assumed that international trade is carried out by profit-maximizing private firms, responding solely to actual or potential international price differences. In this framework, the government interferes only by imposing sanctions and controls that bear on all firms engaged in international trade, and it does not directly assume control of trade itself. These conditions, where *all* international transactions are handled privately, are almost never met today.

In some countries, notably the Soviet Union, the People's Republic of

China, and other centrally planned economies, the state handles almost *all* international transactions. In others, such as India, international trade is conducted partly by the state and partly by private firms. Still other countries, such as the United States, West Germany, and Switzerland, conduct their international trade predominantly on a private-enterprise basis, although the government does enter directly into certain international trade transactions.

Whenever the national government or any of its agencies directly engages in imports or exports of goods and services, it is said to be involved in *state trading*. There is no apparent reason why state trading need differ from international commerce via private markets. In fact, if the government agencies simply limit themselves to buying in the cheapest market and selling in the dearest market, with the objective of maximizing profits, there is no difference. But they do not. In actuality, the pattern of state-controlled foreign trade differs markedly from that which exists under private trade. State trading very rarely conforms to the patterns of comparative advantage, because it is influenced by a large number of considerations other than relative prices and costs.

Political considerations play an important role in state trading. Why would Czechoslovakia, which traded predominantly with the countries of Western Europe during the period between World War I and World War II, suddenly shift its trade almost exclusively toward the Soviet Union in the late 1940s and the 1950s? The answer is obvious, and it has nothing at all to do with comparative advantage. Exports must at times be strictly controlled so that strategic materials reach friendly nations on favorable terms and fail to reach actual or potential adversaries. And imports may be manipulated so that they bolster the economies of friendly countries or harm the economies of unfriendly nations.

Complete state trading imposes both an import and an export monopoly on a country's foreign trade. It can therefore be used as a tool to improve the national terms of trade and to increase a country's share of the gains from trade. Similarly, it can be employed to protect certain segments of the domestic economy from import competition, or to artificially support other industries by directly or indirectly subsidizing the sale of their products on world markets.

State trading typically operates through *bilateral trade agreements*, which may be expressed in physical (barter) or monetary terms. In most instances, the bilateral trade agreement will specify the quantitative rates of exchange at which the goods will be traded. For example, the Soviet Union agrees to sell Cuba X number of tractors in return for Y tons of sugar. Or, the price may be set in monetary terms, using some generally acceptable currency. Sometimes price may be left open, subject to negotiation at the time the goods are actually traded.

Bulk purchase is another favorite state-trading device, periodically used in non-centrally planned economies. The importing government agrees to buy annually a certain quantity of a commodity from a chosen supplier country, or it may even agree to purchase all of a country's exportable surpluses for a set number of years. It is sometimes argued that bulk-purchase agreements contribute to economic efficiency by making future product supplies and prices less uncertain for domestic consumers and users, and future market possibilities and prices less uncertain for the foreign suppliers. However, this must be weighed against the costs connected with forgoing the efficiency gains from relying on comparative advantage. Bulk-purchase agreements tie the buyer to the seller, and vice versa, over an extended period of time, regardless of what happens to relative world supply-and-demand conditions in the interim (unless the contracts embody provisions for renegotiation of the terms).

SUMMARY

Departures from free competition in international markets are not exclusively attributable to government trade restrictions. They may also be caused by the way industry is organized. In this chapter, we have examined a number of different alternative market conditions, beginning with a review of the essential differences between perfectly and imperfectly competitive markets. In the international arena, competition can be restricted through cartels, designed to segment markets and drive prices above their competitive levels by means of restricted supplies and other collusive supplier actions. Individual producers can also price-discriminate by dumping in foreign markets below home prices and thereby raise profits, provided resale among national markets can be somehow prevented. Particularly when such dumping is predatory, or when it transfers cyclical or sectoral adjustment problems to other nations, it may inspire countervailing actions by the target country. Moreover, governments themselves frequently distort international competition (e.g., through export restraints or subsidies) and join together in commodity agreements designed to dampen price fluctuations or to peg commodity prices. These practices are often justified by developing countries as a means of improving their terms of trade. Finally, state trading, which monopolizes some or all international transactions in the hands of the government, may also serve to offset or circumvent the pressure of competitive markets, or to redirect trade so that it will suit purely political purposes. Inevitably, such practices will have negative implications for the efficiency of the global system of trade and resource allocation.

Important Concepts

perfect competition	arbitrage
marginal revenue	antidumping measures
marginal cost	predatory dumping
monopoly	commodity agreements
imperfect competition	Prebisch-Singer thesis
price discrimination	export control
international cartel	state trading
dumping	bilateral trade agreements

Questions

1. The theory of international cartels suggests that they have a pronounced tendency to fall apart. Why?

2. Explain OPEC as a form of international cartelization. What factors have made it a success, where other cartels have failed? Explain how OPEC has resulted in a transfer of real income and wealth in the world economy.

3. You are an executive flying New York to London round-trip economy class, having paid $980 for the privilege. The passenger next to you is a college student who has paid $360 for the same thing. How can this happen? What makes such pricing rational for the airline?

4. Differentiate between "predatory" and other forms of dumping in international trade. What policies would you suggest should be used to discourage such practices? Can you think of practical ways to distinguish "predatory" dumping?

Further Readings

Helleiner, G. K., *International Trade and Economic Development* (London: Penguin Books, 1972).

Johnson, Harry G., *Economic Policies Toward Less Developed Countries* (Washington, D.C.: The Brookings Institution, 1967).

Kostecki, M. M. (ed.), *State Trading in Market Economies* (London: Macmillan, 1981).

MacBean, A. I., *Export Instability and Economic Development* (London: Allen & Unwin, 1966).

Pryor, F. L., "Foreign Trade Theory in the Communist Bloc," *Soviet Studies*, July 1962.

Viner, Jacob, *Dumping* (Chicago: University of Chicago Press, 1923).

13

TRADE LIBERALIZATION

Thus far, our discussion of trade policy has focused almost exclusively on *departures* from the free international exchange of goods and services. We have found that there are many reasons—all having to do with national or group interests—why distortions of international competitive conditions exist, despite the evident gains from freer trade. In this chapter we will presuppose that trade is suppressed by tariff and nontariff barriers, and examine the conditions under which it may make sense to move toward freer international exchange on a *nondiscriminatory*, or *global*, basis.

TRADE LIBERALIZATION IN THEORY

Suppose a variety of restrictions have reduced a nation's trade substantially below what it would otherwise have been. Will the country be better or worse off by *unilaterally* removing part of all of its national import and export barriers, thereby stimulating trade and realizing more of its potential for international specialization and gains from trade? Or is it advisable to remove import restrictions only if the country's trading partners *reciprocate* by removing their barriers to its exports? Let us pursue these questions by using the analytical tools developed in connection with the theory of protection in Chapters 10 and 11.

Figure 13-1 presents a case in which only one country has imposed a tariff—for example, it has an import duty without facing any retaliatory tariff abroad. Offer curves OH and OF represent the home and foreign countries, respectively, with the free-trade point being R. Under free trade, the home country would have reached a welfare level represented by the trade indifference curve h_1, which crosses the foreign offer curve a second time at some point S.

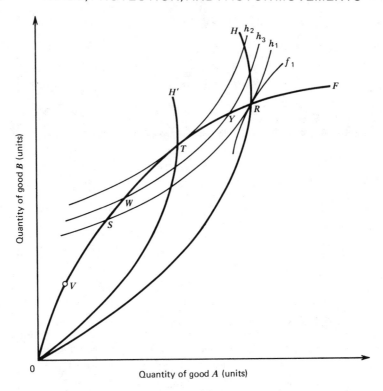

Figure 13-1. Unilateral tariff reduction with only one tariff.

If the home country has imposed the *optimum* tariff or one lower than the optimum tariff, so that its tariff-distorted offer curve OH' intersects the foreign offer curve OF at or to the right of the point of tangency (T) with one of its own trade indifference curves (h_2), there is no way it can reduce its own tariff and thereby improve its welfare level. Any reduction in the optimum tariff (or in a tariff lower than the optimum), including the complete elimination of the tariff, will cause the gains stemming from its increased trade *volume* to be more than offset by the deterioration in its *terms of trade*, placing it on a lower trade-indifference level.

If, on the other hand, the levy imposed is *higher* than the optimum tariff, so that the trade point lies between S and T (e.g., at point W), a unilateral partial reduction in the import duty, bringing it *closer* to the optimum tariff (between W and T, or Y and T) will result in a welfare gain. However, a tariff reduction leading to a trade point between Y and R will leave the country worse off. Finally, if the trade point with the tariff falls to the left of S on the foreign offer curve (for example, point V). then *complete* elimination of the tariff will also lead to a higher welfare level.

Taking a more realistic situation, suppose both countries maintain import duties. This means that the point at which the two countries' respective tariff-distorted offer curves intersect must lie *within* the area bounded by the two free-trade offer curves. Referring again to Figure 13-1, the trade point will fall somewhere inside the boundaries *OH* and *OF*. Its precise location, of course, depends on the levels of the two countries' import duties. In this case, too, it would pay for a country to reduce its tariffs unilaterally *only* if the resultant shift of the trade point along the foreign country's tariff-distorted offer curve leads to a higher trade-indifference level.

Instead of a unilateral tariff reduction, a *bilateral* relaxation of trade restrictions through negotiation promises greater success in raising the national welfare level. Take two cases: in one it is agreed to abolish completely all tariffs between the two countries, and in the other the agreement states merely that the tariff barriers of both nations should be reduced. Let's take a look at both situations from the point of view of the home country.

In Figure 13-2 we again have the two free-trade offer curves, *OH* and *OF*, intersecting at point *T* and placing the home country on the trade-indifference curve h_1. As suggested above, if both countries levy a tariff the new trade point—where the two tariff-distorted offer curves intersect—must lie somewhere within the area bounded by *OH* and *OF*. In order to be beneficial for the home country, the movement from the tariff-distorted trade point back to the free-trade point *T* must involve a movement to a higher trade-indifference level. Should the tariff-distorted offer curves be *OH'* and *OF'* in Figure 13-2, for example (with the trade point at *S*), it is clear that the removal of all tariffs by both countries and a return to the free-trade point *T* represents a higher trade-indifference level for the home country and is therefore desirable.

However, what if the trade point with tariffs falls somewhere in the area *M*? Bilateral removal of all import duties and a return to the free-trade point *T* will then represent a *decline* in welfare for the home country, and therefore would be undesirable from its point of view. So we can say that if the tariff-distorted trade point falls within the area bounded by the foreign free-trade offer curve (*OF*) and the home country's free-trade indifference curve (h_1)—the area *M* in Figure 13-2—it is not advisable for the home country to engage in a negotiated tariff removal. It will be better off leaving both its own and the foreign country's respective tariffs as they are. If, on the other hand, the tariff-distorted trade point falls *anywhere else* in the area bounded by *OH* and *OF*—that is, anywhere *except* in the area *M*—the home country will gain from a removal of all tariffs by both nations.

It is much more likely that both countries will agree not to remove tariffs between themselves completely, but simply to lower them somewhat—to *liberalize* trade but not free it entirely. In geometrical terms, this means a shift from the tariff-distorted trade point, *not* to the free-trade point *T* but to some *other* point within the area bounded by *OF* and *OH*. Under what conditions will it then pay for the home country to engage in bilateral, negotiated tariff reductions?

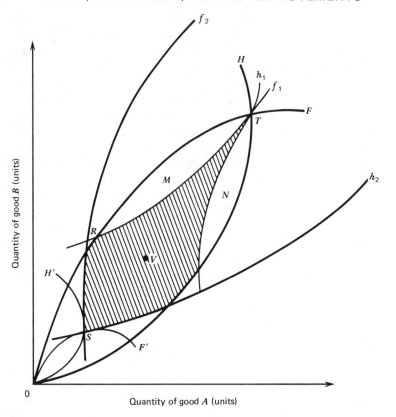

Figure 13-2. Mutual tariff reduction by negotiation.

In Figure 13-2, suppose the tariff-distorted offer curves OH' and OF' intersect at point S. The home country attains the trade-indifference level h_2, while the foreign country reaches f_2 under these conditions. Both countries will gain from negotiated tariff reduction only if the new trade point lies inside these two curves—within the shaded area or areas M or N, at a new point such as point V. Since neither country is likely to accept a negotiating outcome that renders it worse off than before, only trade points that represent higher welfare levels for both countries can be considered as likely outcomes.

Once a new trade point such as V is reached (which represents reduced tariffs on the part of both countries), negotiations for further tariff reductions can begin anew. This time point V would be the corner of a second "area of mutual gain" (not drawn), within which the new trade point would lie. Successive tariff negotiations could ultimately reduce all tariffs to zero and herald a return to free trade at point T. In the process, all of the adverse resource-allocation effects of the tariff would have been destroyed and neither country need have undergone a decline in welfare in the process. As noted earlier, only if the trade point falls within the areas marked M or N in Figure 13-2 during the course of the negotiations would it not be in the interest of one or the other country to pursue tariff reductions to their ultimate free-trade conclusions.

The analysis presented here rests on the assumptions built into offer curves and community indifference curves, the weaknesses of which were recognized earlier. So we can talk only in terms of "tendencies" and "likelihoods" when we discuss the impact of trade liberalization on the economic well-being of the countries involved. Nonetheless, such theoretical models do help us understand what goes on in the real world and to render reasonably sound judgments on the probable effects of actual or proposed trade-policy measures. What happens when free trade is impossible to achieve in actuality, or when free trade may not in fact lead to optimum collective welfare, is discussed in the Advanced Material section on the "theory of second best," at the end of this chapter.

GLOBAL TRADE LIBERALIZATION IN PRACTICE

To appreciate the real-world relevance of the theory of international economic policy, one also needs to be familiar with the institutions that have been set up to deal with actual policy issues. This brief section discusses how different nations—the United States, in particular—have formulated their trade policies, and have striven to achieve a liberalization of international trade, over the years.

The Great Depression of the 1930s was a time of international economic disintegration and fragmentation. Impediments to trade were so severe that they virtually precluded meaningful international specialization. Instead, nations strove to bolster national economic independence and self-sufficiency. Each nation fought to insulate itself from the worldwide economic collapse that was occurring and, in so doing, ensured that the international depression reached the depths that it did. For the United States, the famed Smoot-Hawley tariff of 1930 marked the high point of protection. Some 25,000 products, about 53 percent of all imports, were subject to a tariff at that time. The Smoot-Hawley tariff did much to accelerate the upward movement of tariffs on the part of other countries as well, and it sabotaged efforts by the League of Nations to reverse the dangerous trend toward economic disintegration.

Not long thereafter, however, an era of trade liberalization began—one that has continued until today. Marked by repeated successes and failures, this period has succeeded in instilling a widely held feeling that increases in trade restrictions constitute setbacks to world economic progress. The results, as evidenced by U.S. tariff levels, are depicted in Figure 13-3.

The Reciprocal Trade Agreements Act

Only a few years after the Smoot-Hawley tariff, the United States instituted the Reciprocal Trade Agreements Act, which allowed the President, without the permission of the Senate, to negotiate tariff reductions (or increases) with other countries by up to 50 percent, contingent upon full reciprocity on the part of the other country concerned. (Previously, tariff reductions had been accomplished by treaty, requiring Senate approval.) The new legislation greatly increased American flexibility in trade negotiations, but it was still premised on commodity-by-commodity haggling and applied only to bilateral discussions between the United States and its individual trading partners.

The Reciprocal Trade Agreements Act, which originally was to be in force for three years, was subsequently extended periodically until 1962. It embodied, as part of U.S. trade policy, *unconditional most-favored-nation* (MFN) treatment. This implies that any tariff concessions granted to a single foreign country would automatically be extended to all other countries granted such treatment as well—in return for which the foreign country had to agree to grant similar most-favored-nation treatment to the United States. This effort to make essentially bilateral trade agreements multilateral was partially offset by a *chief supplier clause*, which permitted tariff reductions to be applied exclusively to imports from a country that was, or had the potential of becoming, the principal supplier of U.S. imports of a particular commodity; this clause effectively circumvented MFN treatment at the time.

After the end of World War II, the movement toward trade liberalization gained momentum, yet progress continued to be slow, partially because of the overriding problems of a reconstruction of the war-torn European economies. Nonetheless, 1948 saw the drafting of the Havana Charter, designed to create the International Trade Organization (ITO), which was intended to effect a worldwide reduction of trade barriers and to promote economic growth and stability. For the first time, there was hope of establishing a central, multinational coordinating agency that promised to help implement trade liberalization on a broad scale. The hope dimmed when strong political opposition caused the United States to refuse to ratify the Havana Charter. Since the United States at that time remained the single most important trading nation, the ITO was doomed to failure.

Not all was lost, however. While the ITO charter was being drafted, the General Agreement on Tariffs and Trade (GATT) was established as a temporary measure to help bring about mutual tariff reductions while the ITO was being set up. GATT, which still exists today as the single most effective mechanism for worldwide trade liberalization, constitutes a basic set of rules under which trade negotiations take place, and a forum for overseeing the implementation of these rules. Unconditional most-favored-nation-treatment, for instance, is incorporated as a clause in GATT, as are other provisions for

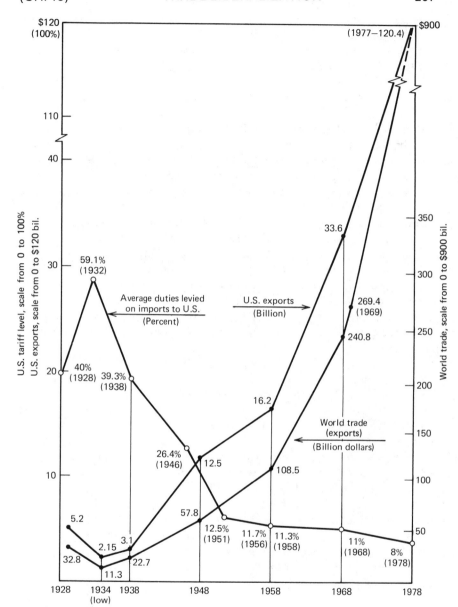

Figure 13-3. Trends in trade and tariffs, 1928-78.

Note: U.S. export totals include military grant-aid.
Source: U.S. Department of State.

nondiscrimination. Uniform *escape clause* arrangements permit signatories to modify trade agreements if serious injury occurs to domestic producers. The record of GATT is an enviable one, encompassing seven separate rounds of tariff negotiations since its inception.

The Trade Expansion Act

The U.S. Trade Expansion Act of 1962 granted the President substantially greater authority than the previous trade legislation had embodied. It allowed him to make far more significant tariff concessions and to facilitate domestic economic adjustment to the new import competition through federal assistance. This represented a new departure in U.S. trade legislation. It clearly recognized that trade liberalization carries with it relocation costs as labor and capital move out of import-competing industries and into other, more viable pursuits. In the course of normal economic activity on the national level, such relocation costs are an accepted fact of life: A firm scores a cost-reducing or product-differentiating breakthrough, and thereby drives competitors out of business or captures a larger share of the market. The factors employed by the lagging firms must make the costly move to new pursuits. Such costs are generally recognized as being a necessary part of the economic growth process. For the economy as a whole, they are repaid many times over through increased real incomes.

In trade liberalization, this process of dislocation and reallocation is not very different. Yet the fact that institutionalized restraints on foreign competition have slowed or prevented it makes it potentially more noticeable—and often more severe—than when it occurs in the normal course of competitive market shifts in the national economy. Since the economy as a whole will normally benefit from trade liberalization, why should not the economy as a whole also bear some of the costs involved in relocating the productive factors displaced by the reduction of long-standing trade barriers? This is the rationale employed in the *adjustment assistance* provisions of the Trade Expansion Act, which were aimed at increasing the mobility of productive resources by providing firms with technical assistance, tax relief, and financial aid that would facilitate any necessary changes in the operations of the affected firms. Similarly, the act proposed to cover the cost of labor retraining and relocation, as well as income assistance to displaced workers during the adjustment period.

The Kennedy Round

The Trade Expansion Act of 1962 served as the basis for the so-called Kennedy Round of trade negotiations under the auspices of GATT—a reciprocal bargaining process that extended from 1963 to 1967. Major tariff reductions were agreed upon, averaging almost 40 percent and spread over a wide variety of manufactured and semimanufactured products. These reductions were implemented according to a predetermined schedule, ending in 1972.

As tariff rates were negotiated downward on a reciprocal product-by-product basis, the relative importance of nontariff barriers grew. An initial attempt was made to reduce certain NTBs under the Kennedy Round; it failed because the United States had no prior negotiating authority in this area under the Trade Expansion Act, and agreements reached in Geneva failed subsequently to be ratified by the Congress. Consequently, the early 1970s saw a sudden interest in identifying, classifying, and examining the possible impact of nontariff distortions, both within GATT and in other organizations, such as the United Nations Conference on Trade and Development (UNCTAD) and the Organization for Economic Cooperation and Development (OECD). Apart from the relative growth in the importance of NTBs, there was a fear that such devices would be used to offset the trade expansion expected to occur through tariff reductions. Very little progress was made, however, not least because of the difficulty of developing viable negotiating strategies for dealing with the entire complex of NTBs.

The Tokyo Round

Meantime, new trade-liberalization proposals began to surface, in part motivated by a feeling that a policy vacuum following the successful Kennedy Round might lead to a backsliding into protectionism. Again the United States took the initiative, advocating a further freeing of trade in industrial products and steps to relax restraints on agricultural trade. Yet these proposals were tied to "safeguard" arrangements that would facilitate import restrictions in the event severe import pressure were to involve politically unacceptable adjustment costs. The proposals were contained in the Trade Act of 1974, upon which a new round of *multilateral trade negotiations* (MTN) generally called the *Tokyo Round*, got underway in Geneva in 1975, lasting until 1979. The outcomes were ratified by the U.S. Congress in the fall of 1979. In addition to a further staged cut in tariffs by about one third (cf. Table 13-1), the new agreements focus mainly on efforts to liberalize the bewildering array of NTBs.

The approach used in the Tokyo Round concentrated on five specific NTB problem areas: industrial standards, government procurement, subsidies and countervailing duties, licensing, and customs valuation. For each, a code of conduct was designed that countries may subscribe to and that tries to ensure that the respective NTBs conform to international agreements.

The *Agreement on Technical Barriers to Trade*, generally called the Standards Code, negotiated in the MTN provides that industrial standards should not result in unnecessary obstacles to trade, and that imports should be treated no differently from domestically produced goods. National treatment should apply, and regional, state, and local regulations are to be brought into compliance with the code on a best-efforts basis. Signatories to the code will provide foreign suppliers, especially developing countries, with assistance in institutional and legal efforts to comply with technical standards, and help them to establish standards, regulatory bodies, and certification schemes of their own.

Table 13-1

Average Percentage Cuts in Tariffs on Industrial Products by the Major Industrialized Countries in the MTN

Country	*Percentage Tariff Cut*	
	Actual Offer	Swiss Formula[a]
Australia[c]	2.8%	b
Austria	21.5	54.4%
Canada[c]	29.1	33.1
European Community		
Belgium-Luxembourg	28.3	41.1
Denmark	25.8	40.7
France	27.8	40.2
Germany	27.1	41.5
Ireland	26.7	41.2
Italy	27.0	39.9
Netherlands	26.7	41.5
United Kingdom	27.7	40.3
Finland	25.2	51.1
Japan[c]	25.3	40.7
New Zealand	11.8	b
Norway	24.8	45.7
Sweden	23.0	35.5
Switzerland	21.2	38.3
United States	34.1	34.9
ALL COUNTRIES	26.4	37.6

[a] The Swiss formula was the actual basis of negotiations.
[b] Not a formula country.
[c] Based on prevailing rates, which include unilateral reductions in the post-Kennedy Round tariffs.

Source: United States Senate, Committee on Finance, Subcommittee on International Trade, *An Economic Analysis of the Effects of the Tokyo Round of Multilateral Trade Negotiations on the United States and Other Major Industrialized Countries* (Washington, D.C., GPO, 1979).

The *Agreement on Government Procurement* is an attempt to attack competitive distortions caused by government procurement practices, by setting standards for the procurement process itself. It embodies detailed rules on how tenders for government contracts should be invited, and how successful bidders should be chosen. Perhaps even more important, it attempts to make "transparent" the procurement process itself and the laws, regulations, procedures, and practices that govern it. "National treatment," or nondiscrimination, is guaranteed foreign suppliers for most large contracts.

Negotiations on the issue of subsidies and countervailing duties were also concluded. The United States pressed for the prohibition of all export subsidies, but was willing to consider differential treatment for the developing countries if they, in turn, were willing to phase out their subsidies as each develops or becomes internationally competitive in particular subsidized products. The other developed countries pressed the United States to adopt injury criteria that involve *proof* of injury before countervailing duties could be imposed; they argued that strong injury criteria would also improve the position of the developing countries. On their part, the developing countries pushed their right to use both export and domestic subsidies, while arguing against the use of countervailing duties against their subsidized exports.

The *Code on Subsidies and Countervailing Duties* eventually agreed upon in the MTN recognizes domestic subsidies as legitimate policy instruments whose use nonetheless should avoid adversely affecting other countries. Export subsidies are prohibited except on agricultural products. An illustrative list of prohibited export subsidies is appended to the code. Procedures are specified in the code regarding the permissibility of countervailing actions if a country believes its interests are adversely affected by another country's subsidy. They require factual proof of both the existence of a subsidy *and* adverse effects from the subsidy.

The *Agreement on Import Licensing Procedures*, or Licensing Code, commits signatory governments to a far-reaching simplification of licensing procedures and to neutrality and fairness in their administration. This includes provisions to prohibit discrimination among suppliers and to ensure the availability of foreign exchange, publication of procedural information and quota sizes, the right to appeal adverse licensing decisions, adequate periods of validity, minimum license quantity, and liberalized compliance with licensing requirements. It applies both to "statistical" licensing and to administer import restrictions, and incorporates administrative machinery similar to those in the other codes.

The *Customs Valuation Code* was negotiated in the MTN so as to define, and require adoption of, acceptable alternative valuation methods for imports. It permits either f.o.b. or c.i.f. valuation. But the following valuation methods are specifically banned: (1) the selling price of goods produced in the country of importation; (2) any system that requires use of the higher of two values; (3) the price of goods on the domestic market in the exporting country; (4) any production cost method not the same as the one defined in the agreement; (5) the price of goods produced in the exporting country for sale to another country of importation; and (6) minimum, arbitrary, or fictitious values.

The five codes agreed upon in the Tokyo Round should do a great deal to help liberalize the broad range of NTBs covered by them—or at least contain their spread. Certainly the major failure of the MTN was the inability, at least so far, to successfully conclude a code governing the application of temporary "safeguards" against severe domestic disruptions caused by expanding imports. GATT allows safeguard measures that can reverse the injurious effects of increases in imports that, in turn, result from trade liberalization moves. The injured country may revoke a negotiated liberalization step as long as necessary to prevent injury. Consultations among all affected countries are required, and the exporting countries are permitted to retaliate selectively.

In practice, few "safeguards" have been imposed under these GATT provisions. Rather, "safeguards" have been imposed bilaterally, and they have increasingly been applied (or "voluntarily" negotiated) against the exports of developing countries, especially South Korea, Taiwan, Brazil, Mexico, and Hong Kong, in "import-sensitive" sectors such as footwear, consumer electronics, and steel. As more developing countries emphasize export-led growth based on nonprimary products, selectively applied "safeguards" are likely to increase in severity.

Increasingly, countries have negotiated "safeguards" to prevent import increases stemming not from trade liberalization, but from shifts in comparative advantage. We have seen that economic efficiency and growth require structural adjustments to these shifts. In the absence of adjustment, many "safeguards" become permanent protection devices. This is why the failure to agree on "safeguards" in the MTN is so dangerous. At this writing, the safeguards issue remains unresolved, and the imposition of VERs and OMAs remains unrestrained by international rules of conduct.

TRADE, PREFERENCES, AND ECONOMIC DEVELOPMENT

Traditionally, the developing countries have not played very powerful roles in international negotiations to liberalize trade. For one thing, most of them have been too weak to have a strong voice in bargaining. For another, their economic conditions often, in the view of their governments, have not permitted reciprocity in the reduction of tariffs, elimination of subsidies, nondiscrimination in government procurement, and the like. Instead, the developing countries have pressed for *preferential* and *nonreciprocal* access to the major industrial markets for manufactured and semimanufactured goods, while at the same time pushing for cartel-like commodity agreements to cover their major exports.

In the area of tariffs, the developing countries began agitating for preferential treatment in the late 1960s. A twofold beneficial effect was expected: (1) the terms of trade of the developing nations would improve as duties were preferentially reduced, resulting in a transfer of income (initially customs revenues) from the importing to the developing exporting countries; and (2) the volume of developing-country exports would rise as demand for their products shifted to them from suppliers in developed countries not receiving preferential market access.

Trade preferences for developing countries are not a new idea, having been embodied in such schemes as the British Commonwealth Preference System, the EEC preferential trading relationships with former colonies of its members and other developing countries, and the U.S. Laurel-Langley Agreement with the Philippines, among others. A breakthrough in this area came in 1971 when the Generalized System of Preferences (GSP) was implemented by the EEC, Japan, and several other industrial countries. The preferences were negotiated in UNCTAD. The *horizontal equity* (each supplier nation treated equally) embodied in MFN treatment was thus recognized as being inherently unfair to the developing countries, which can hardly be considered "equal" in competitive terms. By according special trade concessions to the developing countries, the GSP attempts to provide an element of *vertical equity* (unequals treated unequally) intended specifically to benefit them.

By accepting the GSP, the developed countries committed themselves to admit a variety of manufactures from developing countries on a tariff-free or reduced-tariff basis, without demanding reciprocity on the part of the beneficiaries. Generally excluded are agricultural commodities and a range of "sensitive" goods—which, unfortunately, encompasses many of the products in which the developing countries may have an immediate or near-term comparative advantage. On top of this, most of the preferences incorporated tight "ceilings" on the volume of permissible preferential imports into each developed country. If a developing country actually succeeds in taking advantage of the preferences by rapid export expansion, the preference is likely to be withdrawn. And when the exporting industries are competitively structured, the bulk of the gains may in fact go to the importers in the developed countries, and not to the nominal beneficiary countries. For its part, the United States did not implement its own preferences scheme until four years after the original GSP implementation date.

The preference arguments were repeated once again during the course of the Tokyo Round, when the developing countries demanded, without much success, "special and differential" treatment with respect to the nontariff barrier codes being negotiated. Many developing countries also felt that the general MFN tariff cuts would undermine their hard-won tariff preferences under the GSP. In the end, virtually all developing countries refused to sign the act marking the close of the Tokyo Round.

The Tokyo Round came at a time of continued debate in developing countries over the role liberal trade ought to play in the growth process of the poor countries. The idea of "balanced" versus "unbalanced" economic growth is often discussed in this connection. Those advocating "balanced" growth contend that a variety of industries should be simultaneously established by the developing nation in a parallel manner. Advocates of "unbalanced" growth disagree. They believe, instead, that the intensive development of a few, selected, export-oriented industries will pull with them a wide variety of supplier and satellite industries and that this will ensure more rapid growth.

In either case, arguments are likely to be heard for protection as a way of speeding the balanced or selective—as the case may be—development of industries. Those advocating unbalanced growth may call for "infant-industry" protection for the "lead" industries on the grounds that they will eventually attain economic viability. On the other hand, proponents of balanced growth may call for import barriers on a much wider set of products, since many of the industries slated for expansion will indeed have to be import-competing. Some economists have carried this thesis to the point where protection is demanded on "infant economy" grounds. But there is little reason why balanced growth should have to concentrate on import-competing industries, and the wisdom of extensively protecting these industries is open to question. The cost in economic inefficiency and distortion of resource allocation may well outweigh whatever sectoral benefits are derived.

The arguments against free trade under conditions of economic backwardness are largely based on the premise that growth must be inward-oriented—that is, it is based on the domestic market, and dependence on foreign markets is something of a liability. Yet we find countries such as Japan, New Zealand, Norway, and Denmark, all of which have attained respectable growth rates, that are largely dependent on foreign trade and apparently thriving under it. And countries such as South Korea, Singapore, Taiwan, and Malaysia, among the "miracle" economies in the developing world, have all followed trade-oriented growth strategies. Not only may a country better its static welfare by specializing according to the dictates of comparative advantage, and thus reaping the gains from international trade, but by so doing, it may simultaneously share in the longer-run growth of the entire world economy.

On the other hand, export industries easily become vulnerable to market developments in other parts of the world. This can militate against the export sector's effectiveness in leading economic growth, even if all other factors are favorable, and introduce a significant element of risk. Growth rates in the export sector may fluctuate erratically. Variations in export revenues may then be transferred back to the remainder of the economy and adversely affect incomes, employment, capital formation, and entrepreneurial activity. So there is no guarantee that the export sector will be a reliable engine of growth, if only because of the vagaries of the international marketplace. And export-led growth strategies can be thwarted by protectionism abroad, particularly since many of the products ideally suited for developing-country exports—textiles, clothing, leather goods, consumer electrical equipment, and various other light manufactures—are precisely the ones considered most "sensitive" in the advanced countries. This is one reason why the developing countries have placed so much stress on trade liberalization and improved market access.

SUMMARY

Depending on the nature of existing trade restrictions, conventional general-equilibrium trade models tell us that it may or may not make sense for a nation to liberalize its trade unilaterally. They also tell us that negotiated, reciprocal liberalization may be the way to recoup the potential gains from trade that have been forfeited because of tariffs or other impediments to market access. In practice, trade liberalization has been carried out on a reciprocal, multilateral basis under the auspices of GATT, and has succeeded in dismantling most of the tariffs that were imposed during the Great Depression years. The latest of these exercises was the Tokyo Round in the late 1970s, which cut tariffs still further and for the first time attempted to set comprehensive rules of conduct with respect to NTBs. The developing countries achieved preferential liberalization of market access through the GSP, but have been concerned that they have not been accorded special, differential treatment in regard to NTBs. Their concern has been amplified by a continuing debate about the role of trade in the economic development process.

ADVANCED MATERIAL: The Theory of Second Best

What is the "best" trade policy that a country can follow to maximize the material well-being of its people? As we discussed at the beginning of Chapter 9, maximum overall efficiency is not necessarily the same thing as maximum welfare, if we accept the fact that we cannot make interpersonal welfare comparisons and that changes in trade do indeed affect income distribution. But if we did discover a theoretically optimal commercial policy, would conditions in the real world then approximate those we have assumed to exist in determining this policy? Suppose they do not, or suppose the optimal trade policy is otherwise blocked as a realistic alternative. What would be the next-best solution?

However we decide to deal with the distribution problem, welfare maximization requires a comparison of social benefits and social costs. Logically, social welfare can be maximized only when marginal social benefit equals marginal social cost in all economic activities. If any transaction produces a marginal benefit to the recipient that is greater than the marginal cost to the producer or seller, overall social welfare improves. In reality, marginal cost to the seller indeed often diverges from marginal value to the buyer. This is because the classical theoretical assumptions do not hold true:

(*a*) there rarely exists perfect competition, either in the markets for goods and services or in the markets for the factors of production; (*b*) governments intervene with all sorts of subsidies, taxes, and controls; and (*c*) there do exist external economies and diseconomies in production and consumption. Under such conditions, it is *not* a foregone conclusion that trade liberalization, for instance, improves social welfare and economic efficiency, and that increased trade restrictions are harmful. In fact, the welfare impact of *any* commercial-policy measure under such conditions is uncertain.

All we can say is that any commercial policy which, at the margin, reduces the divergence between social value and social cost in the economy—whether it involves increased or decreased trade restrictions—will improve social welfare; this is, in fact, a truism. For example, suppose the United States lowers its tariffs on imports of automobiles. The divergence between the marginal social cost and marginal social value of cars may thus be narrowed, and social welfare rises as a result. But the resultant increase in American automobile purchases will simultaneously cause a rise in U.S. consumption of automotive services, insurance, gasoline, oil, and so forth—in which the divergence between marginal social benefit and marginal social cost may very well be large. The result of this divergence may be a social welfare loss in these aspects of the economy. Moreover, the added U.S. automobile purchases may additionally bring a decline in purchases of television sets, in the production and sale of which there may initially be very little divergence between marginal social value and marginal social cost. So, if (*a*) the *increased* cost-benefit divergence connected with the new sales of automotive supplies, or with the new spending on other goods, outweighs (*b*) the *reduced* cost-benefit divergence in automobile production, social welfare will indeed decline because of the tariff reduction.

Such arguments can be used to justify the existence of trade restrictions—for instance, in cases where there is a franchised import-competing monopoly, where the imports consist of alcohol and drugs, and where the restriction is part of an accepted agricultural support program.

Many other examples of this nature could be cited, some of which would also account for the effects of trade policies on the exporting country, and perhaps on third countries as well. The conclusion: If real-world conditions are such that the classical assumptions underlying the free-trade ideal are seriously violated, or if universal free trade is practically unattainable, a "second-best" solution has to be found, and this solution may involve decreased or increased trade restrictions. In each instance, the impact of a specific commercial-policy step on all affected divergences between social value and social cost must be weighed. Only if the *net result* is a decreased overall divergence can the policy be judged beneficial from the standpoint of social welfare. This makes the net social impact of any trade policy very difficult to measure or foresee. Even completely unrestricted international trade may not always be the best policy.

Important Concepts

reciprocity

Smoot-Hawley tariff

Reciprocal Trade Agreements Act

unconditional most-favored-nation
   clause

chief supplier clause

General Agreement on Tariffs and
   Trade

adjustment assistance

Kennedy Round

Tokyo Round

NTB codes

trade preferences

theory of second best

Trade Expansion Act

Questions

1. How would you go about trying to estimate the impact of the GSP on developing countries' exports? How about the impact of the Tokyo Round on the effectiveness of the GSP?

2. Developing countries have argued that they should be given "special and differential" treatment in the liberalization of nontariff barriers. How can this be justified? Can you think of some ways this could be done?

3. Now that the Tokyo Round has been concluded, where do you think international trade negotiations ought to proceed next? What dangers lie ahead that have not been adequately dealt with in the Tokyo Round?

4. Three issues that have not been extensively covered in trade negotiations are trade in agricultural commodities, access to energy and raw materials, and international trade in services. Can you think of some ways each of these might be tackled?

Further Readings

Amacher, Ryan C., Gottfried Haberler, and Thomas D. Willett (eds.), *Challenges to a Liberal International Economic Order* (Washington, D.C.: American Enterprise Institute, 1979).

Baldwin, Robert E., *The Multilateral Trade Negotiations* (Washington, D.C.: American Enterprise Institute, 1979).

Blackhurst, Richard, Nicholas Marian and Jan Tumlir, *Adjustment, Trade and Growth in Developed and Developing Countries* (Geneva: GATT, 1978).

Blackhurst, Richard, Nicholas Marian, and Jan Tumlir, *Trade Liberalization, Protectionism and Interdependence* (Geneva: GATT, 1977).

Cline, William R., *et al., Trade Negotiations in the Tokyo Round* (Washington, D.C.: The Brookings Institution, 1978).

McCulloch, Rachel, *Economic and Political Issues in the New International Economic Order* (Los Angeles: International Institute for Economic Research, 1979).

Murray, Tracy, *Trade Preferences for Developing Countries* (London: Macmillan, 1977).

Nowzad, Bahram, *The Rise in Protectionism* (Washington, D.C.: International Monetary Fund, 1978).

14

REGIONAL ECONOMIC INTEGRATION

Between the extremes of multilaterally free trade and full-blown protectionism lie a number of possible compromises. One of the most prominent is regional trade liberalization, with trade barriers remaining between the region and the rest of the world, as best exemplified by the European Economic Community (Common Market). We can identify several distinct forms of regional trade liberalization, ranging from a simple relaxation of intraregional trade restrictions to a complete economic unification of the nations of the region.

The *free-trade area* is perhaps the most elementary form, and it is concerned almost exclusively with the elimination of restrictions on trade among the participating countries. Each nation abolishes its tariffs on imports from member countries, generally on a gradual basis over a five- or ten-year adjustment period. This permits the industries in each country, faced with reduced protection and heightened competition from imports, to adapt progressively to the new competitive environment. Each participating country remains free to set its own tariffs on imports from nonmember countries, so there is the danger that goods originating in nonmember countries may be imported into a member country maintaining a high *external tariff* via another member imposing a low external tariff. This is called *trade deflection*, and may have to be prevented by means of relatively complex administrative procedures and *rules of origin* for traded goods. Moreover, in member countries imposing low external duties, there will be an incentive to establish *tariff factories*, which use imported raw materials and components in manufacture for subsequent export to partner countries with high external tariffs; and this practice may similarly have to be prevented.

In addition to eliminating internal tariffs—while maintaining individual national external tariffs—the free-trade area often works to reduce or eliminate certain internal nontariff restrictions on trade, including quantitative limits on imports and a variety of more subtle administrative trade barriers. The free-trade area must, however, maintain customs procedures between members, especially for the certification of origin for traded products.

The _customs union_ represents a somewhat higher level of regional market unification, or economic integration. Barriers to trade among the member countries are removed, just as in the free-trade area, but each nation in the customs union is no longer free to determine its own tariffs with respect to the outside world. Rather, a common external system of tariffs, and perhaps other trade restrictions, is established that embraces the entire customs union. Ultimately, each nation will maintain identical restrictions on imports from nonmember countries. Intraunion trade conditions will approximate those that prevail interregionally within any single nation.

The _common market,_ in addition to regional free trade, provides free mobility of labor and capital. Workers and professionals of all kinds are free to move anywhere within the integrated area in response to differences in prevailing wages and salaries, as well as in employment opportunities. Capital is free to seek out the highest obtainable yields anywhere within the area. The intent, of course, is to extend the unified market for the output of goods and services to productive factor inputs as well. Common markets usually also provide for the abolition of restrictions on the free mobility of proprietorships, partnerships, and corporate business enterprises, thereby helping to make entrepreneurship more responsive to changing market conditions.

The _economic union_ aims to go even further, and to deal with a number of economic policy matters that confront the common market. Suppose the intraunion movement of goods, services, labor, capital, and entrepreneurship were completely free. If there remained substantial differences among the member countries with regard to governmental economic and social policies, a significant distortion of intraunion trade and factor flows could still result. Particularly important in this respect are the monetary and fiscal policies that the member states implement for purposes of domestic economic control, as well as national direct and indirect taxation systems, agricultural support programs, social security programs, transport policies, regional planning, and government subsidies to selected industries. The economic union purports to alleviate the problems arising from such differences in national policies by coordinating or harmonizing these policies within the framework of the union.

Once regional economic integration approaches the more advanced stage of an economic union, with free internal trade and factor mobility being supported by substantial economic policy harmonization, the next logical step in the integration process may be the creation of a _monetary union_. This requires the eventual replacement of the individual members' national currencies by a single currency circulating in the entire integrated area. If indeed monetary union can be achieved, the member countries must be willing and able to transfer a substantial degree of national sovereignty to a supranational central bank that controls the issue of the common currency and the regulation of banks and other financial institutions. To complete the integration process, member states must give up their autonomy of action in virtually every other aspect of economic policy as well, and the relationship of the central authority and the individual member nations assumes a form not unlike federal-state economic relations in the United States. By this time, regional economic integration has run its full course, and several national economies have been welded into a larger, multinational economy that may truly be considered a unified whole.

STATICS AND DYNAMICS

It is convenient to discuss the effects of the free regional mobility of goods, services, and productive factors in terms of its static and dynamic effects on national economies inside and outside the region. Our analysis of the statics of integration refers to the once-and-for-all shifts in resources allocation, productive efficiency, and consumer welfare induced by the integration move. In any viable integration scheme these ought to be positive, so that they result in an increase in real income per capita within the region; otherwise the scheme will make little sense.

The dynamics of integration, on the other hand, have to do with the longer-term effects of an economic union on the rate of growth of the member economies. The creation of a single regional market composed of several national economies may, under favorable circumstances, increase the rate of capital formation and perhaps also the rates of labor-force growth, techno-logical innovation, and human-resource development; and it may permit further economies of large-scale production. Hence, the overall rate of economic progress in the member countries should be able to accelerate.

We can differentiate graphically between the static and the dynamic effects of economic integration through a hypothetical time-series graph such as that in Figure 14-1. Using the vertical axis to measure real income per capita under full-employment conditions (Y^*/N), assume that the combined, historical rate of growth of the member economies is represented by a time series M, which, in the absence of integration at time I, would continue more or less as before. Positive static benefits from integration in the amount X— which, in the absence of integration at time O, would continue more or less as before. Positive static benefits from integration in the amount x— does not, after the initial shock, represent any increase in the *rate* of growth. Alternatively, if we assume an absence of static benefits but considerable dynamic gains, series D will apply instead. Note that the enhanced rate of economic growth ensures that the level of Y^*/N eventually exceeds that attained earlier by static gains alone, which is one reason why some economists consider the dynamic effects of integration to be of potentially greater significance than the static ones. The relative importance of the two effects depends on their respective magnitudes and on how rapidly they appear; gains sooner are usually better than gains later. Optimally, of course, both static and dynamic effects would make themselves felt in a positive manner, as in the case of growth path $S + D$ in Figure 14-1. Let's first examine the static effects of regional free trade.

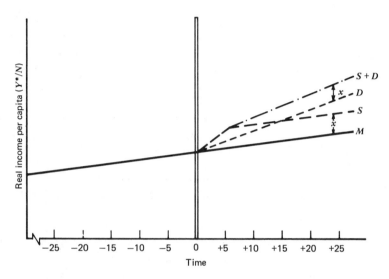

Figure 14-1. Static and dynamic effects of integration.

Consumption and Production Effects

The creation of a regional free-trade area signals a departure from the protected market in favor of limited free trade. The entire regional market is open to the lowest-cost, most efficient suppliers in any of the member countries. At the same time, the range of choice for consumers in each member country is broadened, and if they can now buy at lower prices, their real incomes will be raised. Whereas tariff and quota discrimination no longer exists inside the union, it still applies to suppliers located in nonmember countries, for these suppliers now must hurdle the individual or common external-trade restrictions of the region in order to compete in the new and larger protected market.

Within the union itself, consumers will tend to shift their purchases from high-cost, relatively inefficient domestic producers that have long enjoyed a protected national market, to low-cost suppliers located in partner countries. Production of each and every good theoretically will shift toward the lowest-cost supplier within the region, and ultimately approach some hypothetical regional least-cost position. Simultaneously, the volume of trade among member countries will increase as the intraunion reallocation of production proceeds. This is called the *positive production effect* of regional free trade. It is, of course, beneficial to overall productive efficiency.

Consumers, too, benefit in the process. They are no longer restricted to high-priced domestic products, but are free to search out the lowest prices obtainable within the entire union. To this extent, their real incomes are increased, and their expanded consumption choice tends to further increase their welfare. Such beneficial influences of regional free trade on consumers are called *positive consumption effects*.

The positive production and consumption effects thus involve a basic reallocation of production and consumption patterns within the free-trade zone and a stimulus to trade and specialization among the member economies. The overall process is called *trade creation*.

Before regional trade liberalization, the lowest-cost producer anywhere in the world may be able to surmount the existing national trade barriers. He will then be free to compete with domestic producers for a share of the national market. With the creation of regional free trade, however, the trade barriers facing producers in nonmember countries will no longer apply to competing potential suppliers in member nations; the barriers are discriminatory. It is then possible that production will be shifted from low-cost producers in nonmember nations to relatively high-cost producers in partner countries. To the extent that this occurs, production will be reallocated from low-cost to high-cost suppliers, and from a global standpoint, productive efficiency will suffer. The efficiency decline connected with such a "diversion" of trade is termed the *negative production effect* of regional free trade.

These shifts in trade patterns also make themselves felt directly in the area of consumer welfare. In the absence of regional free trade, consumers can buy goods at world-market prices plus any tariff that may be applied at the national level. These prices are essentially the selling prices of the most efficient of world suppliers. With regional free trade, however, the elimination of intraunion trade barriers, in the face of restrictions on imports from the rest of the world, may induce the consumer to shift his purchases from the low-price suppliers in nonmember countries to high-price suppliers in partner countries. To this extent, the consumer is prevented from communicating his preferences to the respective suppliers, and his range of choice among competitive suppliers may directly be reduced. We refer to this as the *negative consumption effect*. Like the negative production effect, it is also reflected in a shift of trade from nonmember to member countries.

Negative consumption and production effects of regional free trade thus tend to depress the volume of trade of the participating nations with nonmember countries by diverting it to other member nations. This process is termed *trade diversion*. Trade partly changes direction and becomes increasingly inward-oriented: that is, it becomes more "regionalized" within the confines of the free-trade zone.

A few qualifications need to be added. If, in the case of any one product, the union turns out to include the lowest-cost world producer, then it can only have a beneficial, or trade-creating, effect with regard to that particular good. There can be no negative static production or consumption effects and therefore no trade diversion. If, on the other hand, none of the member countries has produced a particular good before formation of the union, and all of them have imported it from nonmember countries, they may continue to do so after integration, and the union will then have no impact on trade patterns at all—no positive or negative consumption or production effects, and therefore no trade creation or trade diversion. Finally, suppose that before integration, all member countries produce a particular good, except at different costs. In this instance, the net effect of the union will in all probability be trade-creating, since the low-cost producers will displace the high-cost suppliers in the previously protected markets of the latter. In such a case, the losses incurred by third-country suppliers will be minimal.

Other Static Gains

Two other sources of static gains from the formation of customs unions deserve mention here: administrative economies resulting from the elimination of internal trade barriers, and induced shifts of the member-nations' collective terms of trade.

The existence of restrictions on trade obviously means that a costly administrative apparatus must be maintained in order to enforce the existing tariffs and quotas. Border-crossing points must be manned, customs offices staffed, boundaries patrolled to prevent smuggling, and so forth. Each nation must maintain its own tariff commission to set import restrictions and classify commodity groups for tariff purposes, hear appeals from domestic manufacturers, and change tariffs and quotas when necessary. In addition, administrative agencies dealing with health, product quality, advertising, and other standards also have a hand in controlling inflows of foreign goods.

With all internal tariffs eliminated, the cost saving to the national member governments resulting from total or partial liquidations of such agencies can be substantial in itself. Moreover, the creation of a common external tariff and the combination and centralization of all such tasks with regard to imports from nonmembers can result in further public-sector economies in customs unions. In addition, a great deal of time and effort is involved in crossing international customs frontiers, and if all the connected explicit and implicit costs to the private traders were added, their magnitude would undoubtedly be surprising.

Furthermore, a customs union may improve the collective terms of trade of its members. This is especially true if the union tends to be trade-diverting. If the elimination of internal trade restrictions and the imposition of common external trade barriers diverts imports from nonmember to member countries, it will tend to depress the union's import prices, and if export prices remain constant, the collective terms of trade of the members will improve. If the elasticity of demand for the union's imports is low, and if it is an important force in the world market, the terms-of-trade improvement may be quite substantial. At the same time, the rise in intraunion exports will tend to reduce export supplies to the rest of the world, thereby putting upward pressure on the union's collective export prices.

In terms of the offer-curve analysis presented in Chapter 10, the offer curve of the members may shift inward, thereby inducing an improvement in their terms of trade, just as effectively as if they had all raised their tariffs simultaneously against the outside world. The larger the economic size of a customs union, and the greater its trade-diverting impact, the more will the terms of trade of its members be likely to improve vis-à-vis the rest of the world.

Finally, a customs union acting in international trade negotiations (such as the Tokyo Round discussed in the last chapter) tends, especially if it is large, to have a great deal more bargaining power than any of its individual members. It might be able to exact tariff concessions on the part of nonmember countries that otherwise would have been unthinkable.

Customs Union versus Trade Liberalization

Suppose that, from a static point of view, a country's membership in a customs union (or free-trade area) is largely beneficial: the positive consumption and production effects outweigh the negative ones. Is this the best possible solution? Could the country not have done even better by taking an alternative course in its commercial policy, so that regional free trade is actually suboptimal from its own point of view? One alternative to a customs union, of course, involves simply reducing trade barriers unilaterally, on a nondiscriminatory basis: that is, lowering or eliminating tariffs and quotas on imports from all other countries, regardless of origin. It is possible to show that such a step would, under certain conditions, in fact lead to greater welfare gains than would membership in a customs union.

In Figure 14-2, curves D_d and S_d denote a certain country's domestic demand and supply curves for a given good, produced under conditions of increasing costs. In isolation—without international trade—equilibrium would be attained at point L, with 1600 units produced and consumed at a price of $400. Domestic output at that price exactly equals the quantity demanded.

Line S_n represents the supply conditions on the world market faced by this particular country. It is assumed that the country is not an important force in

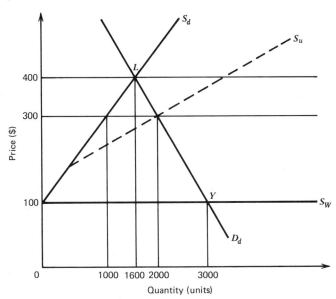

Figure 14-2. Customs union versus unilateral tariff reduction.

world market demand and therefore cannot affect the world price of the good by its purchases (i.e., it cannot influence its own terms of trade by varying its imports). Hence S_u is horizontal. With completely free trade, therefore, equilibrium of supply and demand would be reached at point Y, with 3000 units demanded at the world price of $100 and entirely satisfied by imports, with domestic production nonexistent.

Now suppose that the country does import this product but imposes a tariff of $200 on each unit imported. Consumers now demand 2000 units and are paying $300 for each unit. The demand is satisfied in the amount of 1000 units by domestic suppliers, the rest (1000 units) imported from the cheapest available source at the world market supply price of $100. If the country decides to enter into a customs union with one or more other nations, the customs-union supply function facing it will be S_u, comprising domestic supply plus that of the partner countries. The price to consumer will remain at $300 if the common external tariff is at least $200. There seem to be no significant negative consumption effects. A quantity of 2000 units will still be demanded, but it will be supplied exclusively by producers within the customs union. The original imports of 1000 units from the rest of the world will be eliminated, as will the tariff revenue ($200,000 = $200 × 1000 units) previously collected.

Whereas the customs union in this case involves no detrimental consumption effects, the production effects tell a different story. Clearly, the elimination of 100 units of imports at a world market price of $100, and their replacement by the output of producers in partner countries at a price of $300, constitutes a shift from lower- to higher-cost suppliers and is therefore harmful to overall productive efficiency; it represents trade diversion with negative production effects.

If, on the other hand, the initial tariff was set at $300, then total consumption before the customs union was satisfied by domestic production at a price of $400. There were then no imports from the rest of the world. Formation of a customs union under such circumstances results in the partial displacement of high-cost domestic production by the output of other member countries. At the same time, the cost to the consumer is reduced from $400 to $300, and his range of choice is broadened. We thus have positive production effects—shifts in production from high-cost domestic to low-cost union suppliers—plus positive consumption effects. The customs union in this instance is trade-creating and entirely beneficial from the standpoint of both consumption and production.

The effect of entry into a customs union is fairly clear-cut, then, if the preunion tariff level was above $300 or below $200. But what if the initial tariff lay between $200 and $300? A customs union benefits the consumers by lowering the price to $300. On balance, there would probably be a positive consumption effect. Without a customs union, demand was satisfied partly by domestic suppliers and partly by imports from the lowest-cost world suppliers. With the union, domestic output is reduced to less than 1000 units, but some of the low-cost world suppliers are displaced by producers in partner countries, thus raising the true cost of supply to the economy. The net production effect in this case is therefore partly positive and partly negative.

From the three cases discussed here, it appears that a customs union will always be detrimental if the nation's initial tariff in Figure 14-2 was below $200 (negative production and consumption effects), but beneficial if the initial tariff equaled or exceeded $300 (positive consumption and production effects). If the initial tariff was around $250, however, could the nation not have benefited more if instead of joining a customs union, it simply lowered its tariffs unilaterally and on a nondiscriminatory basis to $200? The positive consumption effect in either instance would be the same as in a customs union, yet the higher-cost suppliers in partner countries, along S_u, would in this case not displace any low-cost nonmember suppliers, along S_w. At the same time, the nation would be collecting customs revenues equal to $200,000 ($200 × 1000 units).

We are left, then, with a choice between a customs union and unilateral tariff reduction. Of the two, the second course may sometimes seem preferable. Yet by joining a customs union, other nations simultaneously reduce their own barriers to the exports of the home country, something not accounted for in our diagram. There occurs a general shift in the direction of optimum production and consumption conditions within the entire union—a beneficial consequence that does not apply to unilateral tariff reduction. The gains attainable through unilateral tariff reduction thus might not exceed those entailed by customs union. Moreover, the customs-union approach, even if it does appear inferior from the viewpoint of productive efficiency and consumer welfare, may well be by far the more feasible and practical solution from a policy standpoint.

REGIONAL FREE TRADE: DYNAMICS

With an understanding of the statics of economic integration, we can now proceed to examine the impact of regional free trade on the member nations' collective and individual rates of economic growth. The dynamic gains discussed here are associated with large markets—markets that may be achieved either via regional integration or in a broader context via trade liberalization.

Scale Economies and Competition

Freer trade is believed to have the capacity to yield significant growth dividends through the creation of a larger market out of several smaller national markets and associated reductions in costs. This is certainly true for economic integration among industrial economies. The effective size of the market governs the volume of output possible in various industries. This, in turn, determines the realization of scale economies in those industries.

Economies of scale are attributable to a variety of factors, each of which is influenced by effective market size. Certain types of capital equipment may be efficiently used only when the volume of production is comparatively large. The most advanced production methods, which are almost synonymous with the application of sophisticated capital equipment, may be feasible only when they are applied to large output quantities. High-volume production and consumption also yield per-unit cost savings as a result of smaller required inventories and bulk purchases. Labor, too, can be used more effectively in large-scale operations, and highly trained, specialized personnel can then be usefully employed. Not least important is the quality of management, which tends to be higher in large firms than in small ones. Overall, the introduction of freer trade will, via the higher output volumes of firms competing in a new, larger market, tend to yield significant scale economies. And even without considering increased plant size, freer trade may force existing plants to specialize in fewer products, thereby realizing similar economies of scale.

Aside from the efficiency gains attributable to large-scale production, the creation of a relatively free market for goods and services among a number of national economies can benefit long-run efficiency in other ways as well. The increase in competition among existing or newly entering firms forces each of them to intensify its efforts to retain an adequate share of the expanded market for its particular output, and preexisting oligopolies or near-monopolies may be destroyed by the economic integration. Yet the stimulative effect of regional trade liberalization on interfirm competition will materialize only if firms are not able or permitted to create monopolies or cartels on a broader, union-wide scale. A coordinated antitrust policy—either through cooperation among the participating nations' governments or via the creation of a supranational antimonopoly organization—may be needed to prevent regional monopoly formation.

Savings, Investment, and Risk

Regional economic integration may have effects on the levels of saving, and investment and on perceptions of risk. Now, it is not at all certain that regional economic integration by itself stimulates the rate of saving. Indeed, there is little evidence that internally generated capital formation has accelerated as a result of regional economic integration projects such as the European Common Market. Yet experience has shown that integration does indeed tend to attract substantial investment capital from nonmember countries. This has been particularly true with regard to U.S. investment in the EEC, which reached unprecedented proportions during the first half of the 1960s. This may be termed the *new-investment benefit* of economic union. Firms and individuals may be reluctant to invest heavily in production facilities in small, fragmented national markets. Yet they may consider a large, integrated market as an opportunity to send a substantial amount of capital into the area. In addition, the stimulus that freer trade is expected to exert on productive efficiency and on economic growth may enhance the long-term profit potential within that market.

The integration of national markets may also reduce the degree of risk associated with investment. A large market may decrease the likelihood that a specific investment undertaking will fail and make it easier to project the likely future profits. Intraunion trade is itself subject to far less uncertainty under conditions of regional free trade. No longer is there a possibility of administrative variation of tariffs and other trade restrictions within the union, and the eventuality of such explicit or implicit costs in foreign trade is eliminated. Firms are more willing to enter into extensive intraunion international transactions—transactions that they would have been reluctant to engage in if the chances of adverse administrative measures still existed. The reduction of risk and uncertainty makes provisions for cost-increasing "risk premiums" on intraunion trade unnecessary. This facilitates an equalization of prices throughout the region—a basic prerequisite for a more efficient resource allocation.

Labor, Resources, Technology, and Entrepreneurship

Regional economic integration may influence the contribution of labor to economic growth in three ways: (1) by instituting free labor mobility, thereby inducing workers to seek jobs abroad that better utilize their skills and permitting countries with scarce labor to expand output without encroaching very much on production in labor-surplus countries; (2) by attracting labor into the union from nonmember countries through the lure of wider employment opportunities; and, possibly (3) by fostering broad-based improvement of labor quality within the integrated area.

As economic integration proceeds from a unified market for goods and services to a unified market also for the factors of production, the barriers to international labor movements within the economic union are eliminated. Labor is free to move anywhere within the integrated area, exactly as within a single nation. The benefits derived from free international labor mobility will be greater, the more extensive is the wage disparity between the participating labor-surplus and labor-deficit countries, or between the workers' productivity in one country as against another. Suppose one or more countries possess substantial labor surpluses, and others suffer from a measure of labor scarcity. The combined output and the overall welfare of the nations involved will rise greatly because of the temporary or permanent migration of labor from the surplus to the deficit areas. If labor does in fact move in response to wage differentials, which are assumed to reflect relative productivity levels, then the transfer of workers from low- to high-productivity employment will also benefit all concerned.

Labor migration in these ways permits the recipient countries to expand output beyond what was possible before the infusion of new workers. The workers' home countries may in return receive wage and salary remittances and increased exports of home products to the expatriate labor force. Meanwhile, there will be a reduction in the number of unproductive individuals at home.

Even so, if the movement of labor results in a depletion of the labor supply of the heretofore labor-surplus areas, then the possibilities of future economic development in such areas will be further restricted. And if it is predominantly the skilled workers who migrate, the labor-surplus area may conceivably be worse off than before, and the standard of living of the people remaining behind may actually decline.

The contributions of natural resources to economic growth can vary enormously from one development stage to the next, and from one nation to another. If a nation is able to trade internationally, and if its other sources of growth are developing rapidly, a lack of this or that natural resource need not be an insurmountable obstacle to economic advance. Regional free trade and economic integration may reduce further the importance of natural resources.

By assuring access to raw-materials supplies, it can permit a country to freely import scarce raw materials produced by partner countries and assure it of a permanent intraunion market for export with which to pay for them. Similarly, if integration includes the freedom of business firms to establish themselves anywhere within the union, the absence within a single nation of resources such as land for industrial expansion, clean air and water, or inland waterways does not necessarily hinder the growth of industries requiring them.

Lastly, regional economic integration may foster technological change. For example, experience tells us that large firms can afford to engage in extensive research and development programs, whereas small firms are more limited in this regard. If freer trade does, in fact, result in increased firm size because of the extension of the market, these larger firms may then initiate ambitious research programs that they alone have the financial capabilities to undertake. This is especially pertinent as general technological advance makes research increasingly costly. Moreover, economies of scale often accrue to research and development activities, just as in the manufacturing process. As a firm extends the size and scope of its research activities, its productivity in research will be enhanced. Further growth benefits can be derived from changes in managerial practices, including streamlined business organizations and the application of advanced data-processing systems, and from infusions of managerial or technical talent from outside the integrated area. There is ample evidence, for example, that the much-publicized "managerial revolution" sweeping the EEC countries in the 1960s was in large measure triggered by U.S. firms enticed into the field by prospects of an integrated and rapidly growing market.

A related dynamic effect concerns the realization of additional external economies. Resource availabilities may encourage or necessitate a high degree of industrial concentration within specific areas. Interactions among firms located in such industrial centers—through flows of physical goods, labor, capital, entrepreneurship, and technology—may create a number of mutual benefits, as through new transportation systems, communications facilities, and other aspects of the economic infrastructure. These developments in themselves support economic growth. Still, anyone familiar with congested, urban areas of heavy industrialization will be quick to object that after a certain point, external diseconomies will set in as well, and these may neutralize some of the gains in physical productivity.

Finally, we should consider the role of entrepreneurship. We know that an economy must have individuals or organizations willing and able to assume risk—that is, willing to move in new, uncharted directions—in order to grow. For this reason, the mobility of entrepreneurship from one nation to another may be important from the standpoint of the recipient nation's economic development. Not only may the willingness to bear risk become more evenly distributed among the integrating countries, but the movement of direct investment capital may also, through fresh entrepreneurial initiatives, be encouraged. In addition, the probability that capital will be channeled into its most productive uses on a union-wide scale will be greater. To be sure, some harmful movements of entrepreneurship are certainly not excluded as a possible side effect of the institution of free enterpreneurial mobility. For instance, favorable treatment of business profits or capital gains in one country may attract entrepreneurs, even though this may be ultimately counterproductive for the region. Other differences in national policies, as they affect the climate of business operations, may similarly lead to unjustified movements of entrepreneurial activities. But ideally, such problems can be avoided through the harmonization of national economic policies.

WHEN DOES REGIONAL TRADE LIBERALIZATION MAKE SENSE?

What determines the success of regional free-trade schemes in bringing about the hoped-for static and dynamic benefits for the participating countries? Why has the European Common Market been considered such a rousing success, whereas most integration experiments in East Africa, Latin America, and elsewhere have ended in failure? Some important reasons have to do with (1) economic size, (2) economic distance, (3) output structure, and (4) the level of preexisting trade restrictions.

Economic Size

The greater the economic size of the area undergoing integration, the more likely will be the kinds of production and consumption changes identified with static gains. The probability that low-cost suppliers of tradable goods will be included in a given union is naturally higher, the larger the absolute size of that union and the more producing units it encompasses. To illustrate, suppose countries *I* and *II* both produce radios for their limited domestic markets and impose high protective tariffs to keep out imports. Country *III* also produces radios, but at a much lower cost than either *I* or *II*. It applies a negligible or zero tariff on imports of radios and competes actively on world markets for the product. Suppose, further, that integration between *I* and *II* is contemplated. Since both national radio industries produce at high cost relative to *III*—and if the existing cost differences between the two countries are slight—we would expect very little increase in radio trade between them after all barriers have been removed. Hence the potential static benefits of such a union, in both the production and the consumption of this particular product, are slight.

If, on the other hand, the union is extended to include country *III*, internal trade in radios will develop rapidly, and production shifts from the high-cost suppliers in *I* and *II* to the more-efficient producers in *III*. If most producers in

I and *II* turn out to be marginal, radio production in these two countries will probably be eliminated. Alternatively, they will be forced to step up efficiency in production to the point where they are competitive with suppliers in *III*. Total combined production of radios by all three countries in all probability will rise, and radio prices in *I* and *II* will drop. Increases in the size of integration projects are thus likely to raise both total output and productive efficiency. Possibly, substantial differences in national tastes and preferences might limit the size of the market for many products, and the extension of the size of a union would then do little to increase the market facing the suppliers of such goods. Yet this limiting factor may gradually be overcome as the integration process itself increases buyer awareness of alternative products and thereby reduces such demand differences.

Economic Distance

Naturally, there is little scope for trade creation if the passage of goods between member countries is obstructed by inefficient, high-cost transport systems. As a general proposition, prospects for increased trade and specialization within a customs union will be greater, the smaller the economic distance between member nations. "Economic distance," as a concept, is probably most useful when it is defined in terms of transport costs, or as a spatial element that affects the potential shifts in trade flows and production patterns. In regional free trade, the higher the transport costs within the union, the less will be its potential benefits. Needless to say, although geographic distances may be small, economic distances may, because of poor transport facilities, be large.

Output Structure

The degree of overlapping, or rivalry, between the output structures of two or more national economies is another important factor affecting the potential benefits of an economic union between them. *Competitiveness* and *complementarity* are perhaps best defined with reference to the existing range of tradable goods produced in countries contemplating integration. Two economies are said to be *competitive* if there exists a considerable overlap in the goods produced in the two countries, most typically by industries sheltered from import competition by protective tariffs. This holds whether or not the goods are exported and actually do compete in international markets. Conversely, *complementarity* characterizes two economies with a great deal of difference between their respective output structures. For example, the German and Canadian economies should be considered complementary: Canada to a large degree specializes in the production of agricultural commodities whereas German output is characterized predominantly by industrial goods. In contrast, the German and Japanese economies might be described as primarily competitive: Both are highly industrialized, and they produce a similar range of goods.

The more complementary the economies undergoing integration (that is, the less the degree of overlap between their respective outputs), the less will be the potential static benefits of regional free trade. Hence integration between a highly industrialized country and a predominantly agricultural one may yield relatively few benefits for either economy. Any increase in trade between complementary economies resulting from integration will tend to occur primarily at the expense of imports from nonmember countries. Conversely, the greater the structural competitiveness, or rivalry, between two such economies prior to integration, the greater will be the potential static benefits. Initial tariffs between such economies are likely to be relatively high, and their removal may easily lead to a shift from high-cost to low-cost production within the union. Marginal firms will be eliminated, and production will increasingly be concentrated within the most efficient firms in the union. Moreover, the larger the preunion differences in production costs, the greater will be the consequent increase in efficiency. Intraunion trade will increase sharply, and discrimination against outside suppliers in the form of decreased import demand may well turn out to be relatively minor. Even when cost differences are unimportant, integration of competitive economies will tend to increase the range of choice of consumers and thereby enhance their economic well-being.

Level of Trade Restrictions

A final consideration in estimating the potential impact of regional free trade is the nature of restrictions on trade prior to the union. In general, the more restrictive the preunion tariffs and quotas, the greater the anticipated benefit of a customs union, for two reasons. First, from an internal point of view, very restrictive preunion tariffs imply the existence of highly protected national markets, and their removal in all probability will lead to a rapid growth of intraunion trade. Positive production and consumption effects—via trade creation—are therefore likely to be quite substantial, while the danger of trade diversion is commensurately reduced. Second, the existence of high preunion national tariffs suggests that the volume of trade with nonmember countries before the union was small. To be sure, such trade may not grow very much as a result of the union, since suppliers in third countries must now hurdle the common external tariff, but neither will it be diverted in large volume from nonmember to member countries. High preunion tariffs therefore generally imply few negative production and consumption effects as a result of the union—that is, little trade diversion.

SUMMARY

Regional economic integration represents an alternative to the liberalization of barriers to international trade and factor movements on a broader multilateral basis. It can be carried out with various degrees of intensity, through simple free-trade areas, customs unions, or full-fledged economic unions. Under favorable circumstances, the potential benefits to the participating economies tend to follow the degree of integration achieved. Static gains stem from the reallocation of production from high-cost to low-cost member suppliers and lower prices to consumers, whereas possible losses involve production and purchase shifts from low-cost nonmembers to higher-cost members. The overall static effects of regional free trade may in fact not be as positive as those of nondiscriminatory trade liberalization. These gains will be achieved, in part, at the expense of the rest of the world, especially if nonmembers, because of the union, experience a deterioration in their terms of trade.

Regional integration may also convey dramatic growth benefits through higher rates of capital formation, technological change, scale economies and the like, all stemming from the expanded regional market. The overall benefits will tend to be higher when the member nations' economies are predominantly competitive. In the absence of worldwide free trade and factor movements, regional economic integration remains an important option.

Our efficiency and welfare analysis of economic integration schemes clearly also has implications for nonmember countries, which suffer from trade discrimination as a result. For this reason, such schemes are not viewed as favorably from the outside. We have seen that broad-based, nondiscriminatory trade liberalization is often the preferred solution, but sometimes not the most feasible one. For an examination of some of the recent experiments in economic integration, both from inside and outside perspectives, the student may wish to consult some of the readings cited at the end of this chapter.

Important Concepts

free-trade area	economic union
external tariff	monetary union
trade deflection	consumption effects of integration
rules of origin	production effects of integration
tariff factories	trade creation
customs union	trade diversion
common market	statics versus dynamics of integration

Questions

1. What circumstances do you think may account for the success of economic integration in Europe, compared with the much less favorable record in Central America, Africa, and elsewhere?

2. Suppose you were an automobile manufacturer in the EEC. What economic considerations would determine your views on the EEC's negotiating positions during the Tokyo Round?

3. The United States was highly supportive of the formation of the EEC and its early development, but far more skeptical about its special trading arrangements with the members' former colonies, the Mediterranean states, and other countries. Why?

4. Do you think a North American Free Trade Area comprising Canada, Mexico, and the United States would make sense? Why or why not?

Further Readings

Balassa, Bela, *Economic Integration* (Homewood, Ill.: Richard D. Irwin, 1961).

Jensen, Finn B., and Ingo Walter, *The Common Market* (Philadelphia: Lippicott, 1965).

Lipsey, R. G., "The Theory of Customs Unions," *Economic Journal*, September 1960.

Scitovsky, T., *Economic Theory and Western European Integration* (London: Allen & Unwin, 1958).

Sellekaerts, Willy, "How Meaningful are Empirical Estimates of Trade Creation and Diversion?," *Weltwirtschaftliches Archiv*, No. 4, 1973.

Swan, Dennis, *The Economics of the Common Market*, 3rd ed. (Baltimore: Penguin Books, 1975).

Vanek, J., *General Equilibrium of Economic Integration* (Cambridge, Mass.: Harvard University Press, 1965).

15

INTERNATIONAL FACTOR MOVEMENTS

We have stressed repeatedly that international trade and movements of productive factors can in a sense be regarded as substitutes for one another. A labor-scarce country, for example, can either import labor itself or import labor-intensive products from countries with plentiful labor supplies. The two options, of course, carry with them vastly different economic implications both for receiving and for supplying countries, and they raise different sets of policy issues. In this chapter we shall discuss the economics of international labor movements, foreign investment, and technology transfers within the framework of simple factor-transfer models and, in the next chapter, in the context of the multinational enterprise.

MIGRATION

Historically, the United States has certainly been one of the most favored targets of international migration. During the 100 years between 1830 and 1930, the American economic growth record as we know it could hardly have been possible without a massive population infusion from abroad. Not only did immigration provide the labor needed to bring the nation's plentiful, high-quality land into production, but it also introduced agricultural know-how that made the immigrants immediately useful as contributors to growth. Other immigrants brought with them knowledge that could be applied in nonagricultural pursuits. Moreover, immigration stimulated demand and hastened the process of specialization and industrialization that characterized U.S. growth during this era. At the same time, the withdrawal of this population from Europe probably did little to inhibit growth there; it almost certainly detracted from the European economic advance much less than it contributed to American growth.

The economics of migration may be illustrated via Figure 15-1. Given two countries in isolation, I and II, curve MVP_I depicts the marginal value product of labor in I, and MVP_{II} represents the marginal value product of labor in II. Assume the total labor supply in I is ON_2 and that in II is $O'N_2$. Total national output (which can be measured by the area under the marginal-value-product curve) in the first country will therefore be $OADN_2$, and in the second country $O'BEN_2$. The wage rate in I will, under factor-market competition, be OW_3, whereas in II it will be $O'W_2$.

Now suppose we permit labor to move freely between the two countries, and assume that migration is costless and occurs solely in response to wage differentials. Workers will move from I to II until the wage rates are equal at OW_1. A total of N_1N_2 workers will migrate. Total output in the country of emigration (I) shrinks from $OADN_2$ to $OACN_1'$, and in the country of immigration total output rises from $O'BEN_2$ to $O'BCN_1$. The total production gain in II (N_2ECN_1) outweighs the production loss in I (N_1CDN_2) by the amount CED, the overall increase in combined production as a result of migration. Wage rates for those who remain in I will rise from OW_3 to OW_1, whereas the wages of the original labor force in II will fall from $O'W_2$ to $O'W_1$.

Migration will be more beneficial (a) the lower the marginal value product of labor in the country of emigration and the more slowly it declines with employment; and (b) the higher the marginal value product of labor in the country of immigration and the more slowly it falls with employment. Each of these conditions will contribute to raising the gain in combined production (area DCE in Figure 15-1) from migration.

There will also be a redistribution of income from the owners of capital and land to labor in the country of emigration, and a reverse redistribution in the country of immigration. In country I, of the initial national product $OADN_2$, quantity OW_3DN_2 went to labor and quantity W_3AD to other productive factors. After the migration, of the total product $OACN_1$, quantity OW_1CN_1 goes to labor and the rest (W_1AC) to the cooperating factors. Labor's relative share of the national product is clearly increased. In country II, of the initial national product $O'BEN_2$, the shares of labor and other productive factors were $O'W_2EN_2$ and W_2BE, respectively. After the inflow of immigrants, the shares of the total product $O'BCN_1$ going to labor and other factors are $O'W_1CN_1'$ and $W_1'BC$, respectively. The point is that as a result of migration, labor becomes relatively more scarce in I and less scarce in II, with the result that relative income shares change in favor of the newly scarce factor in each country. Note again that the country of emigration loses output and income (N_1CDN_2), but that this loss is less than the gain (N_2ECN_1) of the country of immigration, for a net global output gain of CED. Some of this loss for the former can be recouped if the emigrants send remittances back home—which is very often the case.

Migration between nations is of course controlled by a great many noneconomic as well as economic variables. Religious, racial, and political oppression were reasons for large-scale international migration in the past,

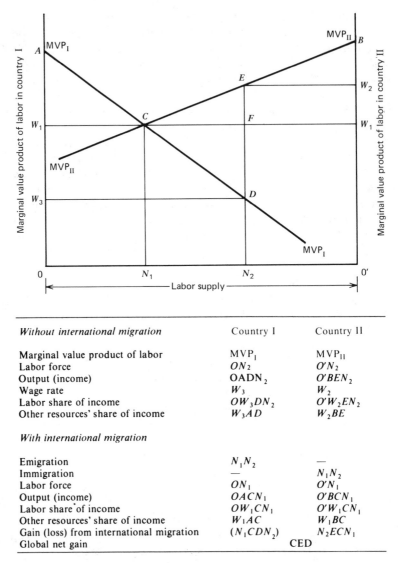

Without international migration	Country I	Country II
Marginal value product of labor	MVP_I	MVP_{II}
Labor force	ON_2	$O'N_2$
Output (income)	$OADN_2$	$O'BEN_2$
Wage rate	W_3	W_2
Labor share of income	OW_3DN_2	$O'W_2EN_2$
Other resources' share of income	W_3AD	W_2BE

With international migration		
Emigration	N_1N_2	—
Immigration	—	N_1N_2
Labor force	ON_1	$O'N_1$
Output (income)	$OACN_1$	$O'BCN_1$
Labor share of income	OW_1CN_1	$O'W_1CN_1$
Other resources' share of income	W_1AC	W_1BC
Gain (loss) from international migration	(N_1CDN_2)	N_2ECN_1
Global net gain		CED

Figure 15-1. Effects of international migration.

and there is no question but that such considerations have been of substantial importance. But what about the purely economic pressures on the international movement of people? This is basically a question of the costs and returns involved. Presumably, migrants envision higher real incomes and higher standards of living for themselves and their families when they move from one place to another. They leave one set of circumstances under which their productivity is relatively low and enter one where it is relatively high, perhaps because their services are combined with greater quantities of other inputs. This forms the basis for the benefits that can be derived from migration.

But migration also involves a cost. Obviously, it costs something to move yourself, your family, and your worldly possessions from one place to another in transport expenses alone. It also takes time, and no income is generally received in the interim. In addition, there are indirect costs both in the inconvenience of moving and in the social, cultural, and language adjustments that must be made. These may be impossible to measure, except in a very implicit way by the individual. The potential migrant, in making his or her choice, must compare all of the explicit and implicit costs of migration with the economic and noneconomic gains he or she expects, as described in Table 15-1. If the gains significantly exceed the costs, the decision clearly will be to migrate. If the individual's roots in his home environment are extremely strong, however, the gains may have to be so great as to virtually preclude him from taking this step.

Demographically, the most obvious effect of international migration is that it increases the population of the destination country and decreases the population of the country of origin. Moreover, the *human capital* embodied in a migrant represents an irrecoverable loss to the country of origin and a windfall gain to the country of destination. The term "brain drain," which gained popularity in Western Europe during the 1960s, refers to the migration of highly trained individuals, especially to the United States, in response to higher wage levels and better job opportunities. Unlike foreign investments in physical capital, a nation rarely earns a return on its exports of human capital unless the remittances of the emigrants assume very sizable proportions indeed. And the character of the migrants is relevant, as well. Are they young, adventurous, and energetic people, or are they merely outcasts who cannot find productive work at home? Thus, the quality of migrants, as well as the quantity, is significant for both economies.

Immigration policy varies widely from one country to the next. Some countries, already suffering from population pressure, discourage immigration altogether. Other countries, suffering from underpopulation, encourage immigration only on a selective basis, with the notion of attracting primarily high-quality additions to their labor forces. Still others encourage immigration on a temporary basis only, preferring to retain the right of expulsion should the labor shortage become less acute and unemployment threaten the indigenous work force. Such policies, regulated by labor permits, provide a kind of unemployment insurance for the home-country labor force, since the "guest workers" will be let go first in times of economic slack.

What about the relationship of international migration to trade? The factor-endowments theory taught us that unrestricted international trade under certain conditions tends to equalize factor prices between countries.

Table 15-1
Migration: Short-Term Costs and Benefits

	Benefits		Costs	
	Individual	Social	Individual	Social
Emigrant Countries	1. Increased earnings and employment for migrants	1. Increased human capital with return migrants	1. Transport costs	1. Loss of social investment in education
	2. Training (human capital) obtained abroad	2. Foreign exchange receipts via migrant remittances	2. Adjustment costs abroad	2. Loss of "cream" of domestic labor force
	3. Exposure to new culture, etc.	3. Increased output per head because of outflow of un-employed and under-employed labor	3. Separation from relatives and friends	3. Uncertainty of continued inflows of remittances may hinder development plans
		4. Reduced pressure on public sector		4. Social tensions caused by raised expectations of return migrants

5. Demonstration effects on consumption patterns worsen the balance of payments

6. Remittances generate inflation by easing pressure on financing public sector deficits

Immigrant Countries

1. Cultural exposure through migrants

1. Potential growth and lower inflation potential

2. Increased internal labor force mobility and lower unit-labor costs

1. Greater labor market competition in certain sectors

1. Dependence on foreign labor in particular occupations

2. Increased demands on the public sector (e.g., provision of more social services)

3. Social tension with concentration of migrants in urban areas

Source: OECD.

Clearly, any impediments to the free movement of goods internationally will ensure that such equalization does not and cannot occur in this way. Suppose trade were restricted by tariffs and quotas, yet all frontiers were opened to free international migration. Labor would then move in response to real wage differentials, everything else being equal, from low-wage to high-wage countries, with the effects indicated in Figure 15-1. This lowers real wages in the latter—the labor-scarce country—and raises them in the former, with the result that differences in relative factor costs diminish. In each instance, output of the import-competing goods rises, production of export goods falls, and trade dwindles. Carried to the limit, costless migration will continue until real wages, as well as returns to capital, are equalized internationally, and trade ceases altogether in this model. It is clear that migration can indeed serve as a substitute for trade inasmuch as it narrows differences in relative factor endowments.

In the real world, of course, there are other factors to be considered, particularly international differences in production functions and differences in demand patterns between countries, as well as the fact that labor is never entirely mobile internationally. Migration cannot, realistically, replace trade. But it can cooperate with trade in improving the allocation of productive resources and raising productive efficiency in the world economy.

CAPITAL TRANSFERS

Like labor, capital is a source of national economic growth, and it can be increased in two ways: through internal generation and through inflows from abroad. Unlike labor, however, financial capital is extremely mobile internationally and responds quickly to international differences in returns, at least when there are no government restrictions on it and the risks seem tolerable.

For the recipient countries, borrowing abroad or attracting foreign investments increases the resources available to them by making additional imports possible. It makes little difference whether the imports (ultimately financed through the capital inflow) consists of consumption or capital goods, as long as the incremental resources thus made available are eventually channeled into real capital formation. For instance, if the necessary capital goods can best be supplied internally, borrowing abroad may be used to import food and other consumer goods, which, in turn, liberate domestic resources that can then be channeled into the production of capital goods. If, on the other hand, the desired capital goods are more easily obtainable abroad, then the receipts from foreign borrowings or investments can be used directly to finance their importation. In either case, the additional resources have the potential for contributing to real capital formation.

Foreign capital will therefore be especially welcome if some types of equipment cannot be made available at home, at least not without a costly rechanneling of resources into lines of production for which they are ill-suited, or which are too short to be economically feasible. But even when the needed equipment must come from abroad, foreign capital is certainly not the only way to finance it. Instead, domestic resources could be channeled into export production, and the resulting foreign-exchange receipts used to secure the necessary imports.

From a financing standpoint, foreign borrowing can be considered a substitute for internally generated capital formation—that is, domestic saving. Yet there is a danger in letting foreign capital finance imports of foodstuffs and other consumer goods, while domestic resources continue to be employed in the production of similar commodities. This results merely in a temporary rise in domestic consumption levels, which, although perhaps desirable in and of itself, contributes nothing to capital formation and very little to economic growth—except, perhaps, by improving the quality of labor through higher levels of nutrition and health. Meanwhile, it commits the country to pay out interest and dividends, as well as to return the principal of the foreign funds, in the future.

When we speak of capital flows between countries, we are sometimes referring to their purely financial aspects, and sometimes to the accompanying changes in real capital formation and capital stocks. The two aspects need, of course, not always go perfectly hand in hand, as our example with foreign-financed consumer-good imports illustrates. But to demonstrate the effects of capital flows on production and income, let us for the moment pretend that foreign financial capital goes entirely into purchases of foreign capital goods. Let's also ignore all qualitative differences among such goods, as if real capital were homogeneous, both nationally and internationally.

ABSORPTIVE CAPACITY

We next need to determine the amount of borrowing that a country should logically undertake from foreign sources. Borrowing abroad necessarily involves a cost in the form of repayments of interest and dividends. These represent a portion of a nation's future output, to be used in servicing its external debt. If externally financed capital formation is to contribute to economic growth, its net contribution to output must at least exceed this amount.

Suppose for the moment that the labor force, technology, and other inputs remain unchanged. Diminishing returns will see to it that the yield on incremental additions to the stock of capital falls after some point, and once it has fallen to the level at which the cost of debt service is just being covered, there is no further justification for additional foreign borrowings. Under such conditions, which are likely to exist in the short run, we say that a nation's "absorptive capacity" with respect to external capital is limited. Even in the long run there may be limits to absorptive capacity if physical-capital formation outpaces the growth of cooperative factors such as labor.

Let us look at this question a little more closely. In Figure 15-2, curve AM depicts the marginal value product of capital (net of depreciation) corresponding to each and every level of the national capital stock. Suppose OH is

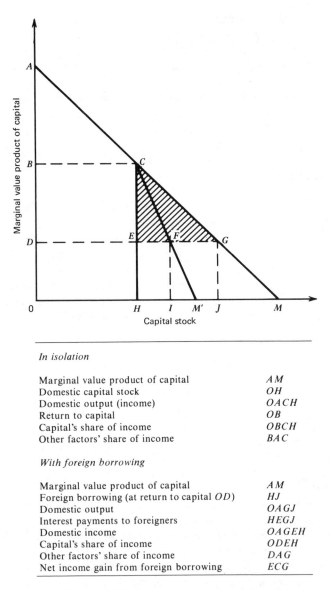

In isolation	
Marginal value product of capital	AM
Domestic capital stock	OH
Domestic output (income)	$OACH$
Return to capital	OB
Capital's share of income	$OBCH$
Other factors' share of income	BAC

With foreign borrowing	
Marginal value product of capital	AM
Foreign borrowing (at return to capital OD)	HJ
Domestic output	$OAGJ$
Interest payments to foreigners	$HEGJ$
Domestic income	$OAGEH$
Capital's share of income	$ODEH$
Other factors' share of income	DAG
Net income gain from foreign borrowing	ECG

Figure 15-2. Capacity to absorb capital.

the national stock of productive capital, all of which is owned by domestic residents. Total national output (also on a net basis) then comprises the area under the curve $OACH$, of which the area BAC represents the real wages paid to other productive factors and the area $OBCH$ represents the earnings of the invested capital at a yield OB.

Suppose, further, that foreign borrowing increases the national capital stock to OJ. Total output becomes $OAGJ$, for an increase of $HCGJ$, with real returns to other factors rising by $DBCG$ to DAG. Of the total capital stock OJ, only quantity OH is owned by domestic residents, as before, and hence their earnings fall from $OBCH$ to $ODEH$. The remaining earnings on the capital stock, $HEGJ$, is paid to foreign lenders.

The results of foreign borrowing? Earnings of domestic owners of capital have fallen by $DBCE$, all of which is transferred to the other factors of production whose relative productivity and employment have risen as a consequence. Total output has risen by $HCGJ$, of which ECG goes to noncapital productive factors, and the remainder, $HEGJ$, is paid to foreign lenders at a yield of OD. Foreign borrowing under conditions of diminishing marginal value product of capital thus tends to redistribute real income from the owners of capital to the owners of other productive factors in the capital-importing country. This assumes, of course, that the marginal-value-product-of-capital curve remains stable.

If foreign lenders require a yield of OD, the total absorptive capacity of this particular economy is HJ of foreign capital. Should the marginal-product-of-capital curve fall more rapidly, for example, along CM', absorptive capacity at that particular yield will be correspondingly reduced to HI. And if additions to the national capital stock over and above the amount OH are completely unproductive and therefore have a zero yield, the capacity of the country to absorb capital from abroad is clearly zero, regardless of how low a rate of return foreign lenders are seeking. In this sense, when we talk about capacity to absorb foreign capital, we are concerned with the slope of that segment of the borrowing country's marginal-product-of-capital curve corresponding to capital stock levels in *excess* of that available internally (i.e., to the right of point C in Figure 15-2).

It would seem logical that the absorptive capacity of some capital-poor economies is limited, with a "break" in the marginal-value-product curve at any given point in time. This can be attributed to a number of factors: (1) The noncapital agents of production, particularly entrepreneurship and labor possessing the skills and qualities needed, are often scarce or even nonexistent. Although entrepreneurial and technological skills can be imported along with the capital, and labor may be trained to meet the needs of the capital infusion, this may not be possible in the short run. (2) It takes time to organize a variety of different complementary facilities to render any substantial new investment productive. This particularly involves the creation of efficient transportation, communication, power, and port facilities. If few or none of these already exist or cannot be supplied concurrently, the productivity of foreign capital infusions will be limited indeed. Again, these facilities can be created, but perhaps not in the short run.

TWO-COUNTRY CAPITAL TRANSFER

We can now look at the economics of foreign lending from both the borrower's and the lender's viewpoints. In Figure 15-3, we assume a two-country world composed of two different economies and a total capital stock of OO'. Of this total capital endowment, assume that OC belongs to a developed country, I, and $O'C$ to a developing economy, II. The two curves MVP_I and MVP_{II} represent the marginal value products of capital at different investment levels for the advanced and the developing economy, respectively. Remember that under competition, the returns to factors are equivalent to their respective marginal value products.

In isolation, the advanced country will invest its entire capital stock OC at home, at a yield of OK. Total product is $OXGC$, with $OKGC$ going to the owners of capital and KXG going to cooperating factors of production (such as labor and land). Similarly, the developing country invests all of its capital $O'C$ at home at a yield of $O'J$, with its total product being $O'YIC$, of which $O'JIC$ goes to the owners of capital, and the remainder (JYI) to the cooperating productive factors.

Now suppose we open up the system to free international capital flows. The advanced country, under *ceteris paribus* conditions, will now invest OD of its capital at home, and the rest, DC, will be lent to the developing economy, in both countries at a rate of return of OE. Total domestic product in the former is now $OXFD$, to which must be added earnings on the foreign loans in the amount $DFHC$, for a national income of $OXFHC$. Its income with free capital transfers has obviously increased by the amount FHG ($OXFHC - OXGC = FHG$), so the lending country has gained accordingly. Internally, returns to noncapital productive factors are reduced from KXG to EXF, and returns to capital are increased from $OKGC$ to $OEHC$.

For the borrowing country, the inflow of foreign capital in the amount CD causes a drop in yield from $O'J$ to $O'L$. Domestic output grows from $O'YIC$ to $O'YFD$, or by the amount $CIFD$. ($O'YFD - O'YIC = CIFD$.) Of this increase in output, the amount $CHFD$ must be paid to the foreign lenders, so that the net gain in national income accruing to the domestic economy is HIF ($CIFD - CHFD = HIF$). Returns to domestic owners of capital fall from $O'JIC$ to $O'LHC$, whereas returns to the owners of noncapital productive factors rise from JYI to LYF. From a world standpoint, total production has risen from $OXGC + O'YIC$ to $OXFD + O'YFD$, or by an amount $FHG + HIF$ (the shaded area in Figure 15-3). The more slowly the marginal value product of capital falls with investment in both countries, the larger will be the gains that can be derived through international lending.

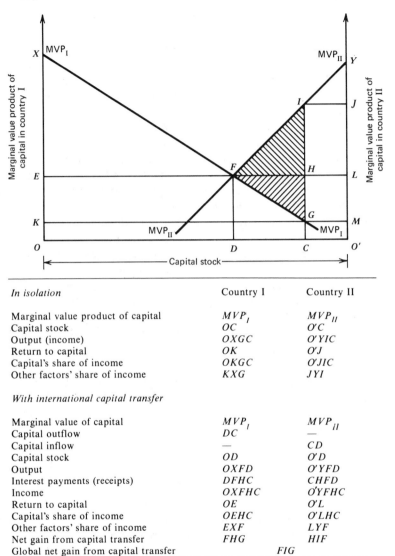

In isolation	Country I	Country II
Marginal value product of capital	MVP_I	MVP_{II}
Capital stock	OC	$O'C$
Output (income)	$OXGC$	$O'YIC$
Return to capital	OK	$O'J$
Capital's share of income	$OKGC$	$O'JIC$
Other factors' share of income	KXG	JYI

With international capital transfer		
Marginal value of capital	MVP_I	MVP_{II}
Capital outflow	DC	—
Capital inflow	—	CD
Capital stock	OD	$O'D$
Output	$OXFD$	$O'YFD$
Interest payments (receipts)	$DFHC$	$CHFD$
Income	$OXFHC$	$O'YFHC$
Return to capital	OE	$O'L$
Capital's share of income	$OEHC$	$O'LHC$
Other factors' share of income	EXF	LYF
Net gain from capital transfer	FHG	HIF
Global net gain from capital transfer		FIG

Figure 15-3. International capital transfers, yields, and income distribution.

What about the output provided by foreign-financed capital facilities? There are two possibilities: (*a*) that it will be exported and (*b*) that it will be absorbed domestically. If the export market is of sole or overriding importance, as is true for oil wells in Libya, iron ore mines in Venezuela, or copper production in Zambia, this consideration does not constitute a major obstacle. If, on the other hand, the output is designated for domestic consumption, a market for the products involved must be provided. This market may not exist or may be in the early formative stages, and a further limitation will thus be imposed on the marginal value product of capital and the absorptive capacity of the borrowing country.

All of these considerations would seem to indicate that at least initially, the marginal productivity of imported capital in some developing countries probably falls rapidly. If so, their capacity to absorb foreign capital will be strictly limited. In the intermediate or long run, of course, each of these limitations can and probably will be overcome, with consequent increases in their absorptive capacity. This process may be hastened through (*a*) infusions of technical assistance; (*b*) educational and training programs aided by foreign countries or international agencies; (*c*) temporary importation of key personnel; (*d*) development of social and economic overhead facilities; and (*e*) concentration on capital projects promising substantial export potential, or for which a viable internal market already exists.

But what happens if national planners *think* the marginal value product of capital is defined by curve *ACM* in Figure 15-2, but actually it is *ACM'*? That is, suppose it falls steeply with increments to the existing capital stock. The country would be wrong to borrow *HJ* of capital, obligating itself to *EGJH* in interest payments to foreigners, when real output of the economy will only rise by *HCM'*. Whether these payments exceed the incremental output depends on whether area *FGJM'* exceeds area *ECF*. If they do, then the difference will have to be taken from the preexisting output *OACH* and the country will be poorer in an absolute sense. And if the difference cannot easily be extracted from this preexisting output, the country will encounter a *debt-service problem* that could pose future difficulties for its ability to borrow from abroad.

SUMMARY

In this short chapter we have shown by means of a simple model how gains to the world economy can be achieved by the international transfer of productive factors—labor and capital—and how these gains in many ways parallel the traditional gains from trade. A labor-scarce country can import labor-intensive goods or it can import the workers themselves. Either way, it will gain. A capital-abundant country can either sell capital-intensive goods abroad at a high price or it can export capital and reap the returns. Either way, it will gain. And world output grows as factors of production are reallocated from low to high marginal-value-product pursuits, either through product trade or through actual factor transfers. As in the case of trade, factor movements also affect income distribution in the countries involved, and cause a tendency toward factor-price equalization.

Under certain conditions, the marginal value product of the imported factor (particularly capital) may drop sharply. Unless accurately assessed, this may lead to debt-servicing problems for the capital-importing country. This problem may be alleviated in a number of ways, one of which is by attracting *foreign direct investment* in lieu of foreign borrowing. This brings us to the topic of the multinational corporation, which is the subject of the next chapter.

Important Concepts

migration	capital transfers
marginal value product of capital	absorptive capacity
marginal value product of labor	brain drain
debt-service problem	

Questions

1. International factor transfers and international trade are substitutes for one another. In terms of static gains from improved resource allocation, explain this statement.

2. Using Figure 15-3, explain the factors that determine the size of the gains from international capital transfers and their distribution between countries and between groups within those countries.

3. Referring to Figure 15-2, suppose planners in a particular developing country think the marginal-value-product-of-capital function is ACM, but actually it is ACM'. They then go out and borrow HJ of capital at a rate of interest OD. Explain the problems the country will have in servicing its external debt.

4. A $1 billion copper mine in Zambia built with borrowed funds at 12 percent interest may be less productive than an identical mine built with a $1 billion investment by a foreign copper company. Explain why this may be so, using Figure 15-2 for guidance.

Further Readings

Caves, R. E., and G. L. Reuber, *Canadian Economic Policy and the Impact of International Capital Flows* (Toronto: Toronto University Press, 1969).

MacDougall, D., "The Benefits and Costs of Private Investment from Abroad: A Theoretical Approach," *Economic Record*, March 1960.

Metzler, L. A., "The Transfer Problem Reconsidered," *Journal of Political Economy*, June 1942.

Papanek, G., "The Effect of Aid and Other Resource Transfers on Savings and Growth in Less Developed Countries," *Economic Journal*, September 1972.

16

THE MULTINATIONAL ENTERPRISE

Perhaps the most important international economic institution in existence today is the multinational corporation (MNC), which combines within a single corporate entity many of the elements we have discussed thus far—international trade, factor movements, and technology transfers—and many more that we shall discuss in the remainder of this book. It is perhaps fitting, therefore, that this pivotal chapter, in which we begin to connect trade and factor transfers to money and finance, should be devoted to the MNC.

Any company that manages, owns, or controls production facilities in several foreign locations qualifies as an MNC. During the postwar period, international direct investment and production activities by such firms have increased rapidly—compared both with world output and with the volume of international trade. The growth has been facilitated by concrete steps to liberalize controls over international direct investment by most of the major industrial countries. Yet the major reasons for it lie in the organizational and financial advantages of global networks of production and distribution, not accruing to purely national firms. These advantages include greater bargaining power both in the marketplace and vis-à-vis national governments.

It has been estimated that the production of MNCs accounted for as much as 20 percent of world output in the mid-1970s, and that the *intrafirm* trade of these firms now represents almost 25 percent of all international trade in manufactures. As the importance of foreign production and foreign markets has grown, many MNCs have found it essential to plan their operations and logistics on a worldwide basis. International shifts in product and factor markets, political trends, changes in tax rates, and balance-of-payments and exchange-rate developments have become crucial influences on the MNC's planning and decision-making processes. And with their expansion of production, processing, and distribution facilities in multiple markets, their role in international trade has increased correspondingly.

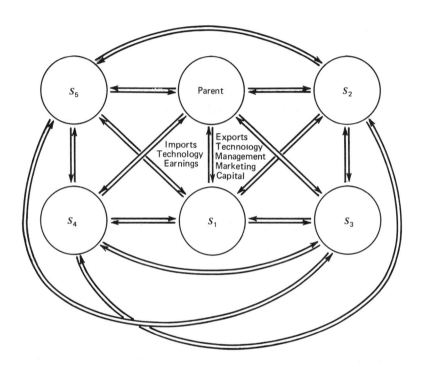

Figure 16-1. Schematic diagram of a hypothetical multinational firm.

Figure 16-1 presents a schematic picture of a multinational enterprise. The parent firm provides one of its affiliates (S_1)—which may wholly or partially owned—with capital, management, technology, parts, marketing networks, and skilled labor. In return, some of the affiliate's output may be exported back to the parent, along with earnings remittances and (sometimes) technology developed at the affiliate level. Similar linkages exist between the parent and each of its other affiliates, and there are linkages among the affiliates themselves as well. Imagine the complexity of the MNC network of a firm such as Exxon, General Motors, ITT, or Nestlé, with affiliates of various types in scores of countries! A small sampling of some of the largest MNCs is given in Table 16-1.

Table 16-1

Foreign Content of Major Industrial Corporations (with sales of over $1000 million, 1976)

Rank	Company	Nationality	Major industry	Government ownership (percentage)	Total consolidated sales (millions of dollars)	Foreign sales as percentage of total consolidated sales — Exports from home country	Sales of overseas affiliates to third parties	Foreign assets (as percentage of total assets)	Foreign earnings (as percentage of total earnings)	Foreign employment (as percentage of total employment)
1	Exxon	United States	Petroleum	—	48,631	72		54	—	—
2	General Motors	United States	Motor vehicles and parts	—	47,181	24		12	18	—
3	Royal Dutch/Shell group	Netherlands-United Kingdom	Petroleum	—	36,087		62	50	64	49
4	Ford Motor	United States	Motor vehicles and parts	—	28,840		31	40	45	51
5	Texaco	United States	Petroleum	—	26,452		—	54	45	—
6	Mobil	United States	Petroleum	—	26,063		—	49	38	—
7	National Iranian Oil	Iran	Petroleum	100	19,671		—	—	—	—

	Enterprise	Home country	Industry		Sales					
8	Standard Oil of California	United States	Petroleum	—	19,434	59 ⎫	43	48	—
9	British Petroleum	United Kingdom	Petroleum	68	19,103	5 ⎬ 78	—	—	52
10	Gulf Oil	United States	Petroleum	—	16,451	55	43	46	—
11	IBM	United States	Office equipment	—	16,304	50 ⎫	36	55	—
12	Unilever	United Kingdom-Netherlands	Food	—	15,762	8 ⎬ 40	36	51	44
13	General Electric	United States	Electrical	—	15,697	12 ⎫	27	37	30
14	Chrysler	United States	Motor vehicles and parts	—	15,538	28 ⎬ 26	33	22	47
15	ITT	United States	Electrical	—	11,764	49	36	39	—
16	Standard Oil (Indiana)	United States	Petroleum	—	11,532	25	34	22	13
17	Philips	Netherlands	Electrical	—	11,522	37	26	—	78
18	ENI	Italy	Petroleum	100	9983	54	—	—	17
19	Française des Pétroles	France	Petroleum	35	9928		65	—	—
20	Renault	France	Motor vehicles and parts	100	9353	45	—	—	—

Source: United Nations Center on Transnational Corporations.

SOURCES OF COMPETITIVE STRENGTH

The phenomenon of the multinational enterprise has been analyzed in great detail in recent years. Its development into the preeminent form of private international economic organization in existence today is based on competitive power—power that derives from an ability to organize and coordinate systematically a wide variety of international transactions. As a result, MNCs can often provide consumers with better and cheaper products or services, react faster to changing economic conditions, and more adroitly overcome or capitalize on market distortions created by governments, as compared with national firms. And they can often generate larger and stabler profits, to the benefit of their owners—their stockholders—and tax-collecting governments.

A number of different explanations have been offered for the multinational's competitive strength. First, the MNC is viewed as a superior type of enterprise at a time when the classical requirements for efficient markets seem to be increasingly violated. The pattern of international transactions has evolved from one of many buyers and sellers, relatively homogeneous products, and low transaction costs to one of sophisticated, highly differentiated product groups, especially involving complex, semi-finished goods and technical know-how usable within a small number of large-scale firms. Under such circumstances, it is argued, intrafirm transactions may be more efficient than contracts between independent buyers and sellers, and this may help explain the "institutional comparative advantage" of the MNC.

Second, the MNC is viewed as possessing a significant degree of monopoly power deriving from the "appropriability" of technology. The firm absorbs useful knowledge from its home and host environments—product, process, management, and marketing know-how—and generates additional knowledge itself through internal research-and-development (R & D) efforts. Shielded by industrial property rules, corporate secrecy, and the sheer difficulty of replicating complex technologies, the firm develops market advantages that competitors find difficult to match and that become real proprietary assets of the firm. Third, the multinational enterprise can be considered an "information factory" that systematically gathers and organizes information about market developments, comparative costs, and technologies through its global affiliate network. The information is continuously funneled to corporate headquarters to be screened, evaluated, and ultimately fed back into the various operating units of the firm.

The fourth advantage is the availability to the MNC of scale economies that may not be accessible to national firms. In subdividing the production process internationally to achieve lower input costs, the firm may be able to reap scale economies by concentrating entire plant operations on certain parts of the overall production process. In much the same way, MNCs can achieve scale economies in management and R & D by increasing their staffs sufficiently to generate a cross-fertilization of ideas and a supportive infrastructure of technical and managerial talent. Fifth, scale advantages may also be derived from the sheer financial size of multinational firms. The capital commitments for large, efficient projects may be beyond the capabilities of smaller national firms. And the combination of size and geographic breadth implies access to international sources of equity and debt capital not so easily tapped by national firms.

A sixth explanation is the multinational firm's alleged ability to monopolize markets. In order to widen price-cost margins, the firm may engage in "horizontal" and "vertical" acquisitions that reduce the level of competition. MNC affiliates, furthermore, can engage in predatory competitive practices if there is cross-subsidization among operating units of the international corporate structure. Once the local competition has been destroyed, output prices can be raised and permanent monopoly gains can accrue to the multinational enterprise.

Perhaps the most widely accepted general explanation of the MNC's competitive strength is its "packaging" function. The firm's involvement in a particular national market often entails a wide variety of transactions. It typically provides the local affiliate with financial capital, intermediate goods, raw materials, capital equipment, specialized manpower, product technology, process know-how, management and marketing know-how, and access to export markets through the firm's own distribution channels. The links thus encompass trade, international factor flows, and technology transfers, all at the same time. It is this package of tangible and intangible goods, services, and capital, as distinct from its constituent parts, that is credited with much of the contribution of the MNC to national economies and with its power in the marketplace.

By its very nature, the MNC will also have a great deal of flexibility in escaping artificial barriers to international trade and payments. Tariffs and quotas can be avoided by shifting production inside the protected area. Exchange restrictions can similarly be avoided through intracompany "transfer pricing," through which the parent may repatriate blocked profits by importing from other company units at less than full value or by exporting to them at inflated prices. Finally, similar invoicing techniques can help reduce the overall tax burden of the MNC by shifting profits into low-tax countries.

THE EFFECTS OF MULTINATIONAL FIRMS: A GLOBAL VIEW

We must first pose the question of whether MNC activities on the whole enhance or reduce world economic welfare in comparison with a situation in which MNCs did not exist. Clearly, both positive and negative effects may be involved.

The Volume of World Investment

MNCs certainly affect the international allocation of real investment, and most likely its overall volume as well. The volume of global real-capital formation may be enhanced by the presence of MNCs if investment in *host* countries rises more than investment falls in *home* countries as a result of the initiation or expansion of MNC activity. It would seem probable that MNCs have indeed promoted capital formation on a world wide basis. MNCs tend to have access to more sources of financial capital and superior information systems and can apply their funds in activities with higher expected yields and/or lower risk than strictly national companies. Several empirical studies have examined the evidence on whether foreign investment by MNCs supplements or substitutes for indigenous investment in *host* countries. They generally conclude that some MNC investment supplements domestic investment in these countries, whereas some serves to substitute for it. On the other side of the investment flow, the evidence on whether MNC investment reduces or leaves unaffected *home*-country capital formation is even less convincing. So the net effect on global capital formation is still open to question.

International Allocational Efficiency in Production

Efficiency can be treated in two related dimensions: allocational efficiency and operational efficiency. The first, international allocational efficiency, deals with the implications for world output of those MNC activities that cross national boundaries, while absorbing local inputs in the production process.

One way of characterizing the international allocative effects of MNCs is the following. Its production process is broken down into relatively small steps that are allocated to affiliates in various host countries on the basis of relative factor input costs, differential transport costs, international trade barriers, and the like. The MNCs' advantages in information, decision-making, and risk reduction imply that their production activities are likely to be subject to a finer, more economical division in these dimensions, so as to promote further international specialization, whether because of differing factor endowments, factor qualities, production functions, or other aspects of comparative advantage. If the underlying economic forces in any case tend to guide the international economy toward a similar allocation of production, the existence of the MNC network surely accelerates the international (partly intrafirm) specialization of production and increases the gains from international trade.

An additional point involves the "portfolio effect" of diversified national locations on the overall risk of the MNC as a business enterprise and a vehicle for stock holdings. In itself, each foreign affiliate may not, after all, prove to be economically viable, and earnings from it may turn out to be inadequate or even negative, whether because of commercial failure or because of nationalization without appropriate compensation. But the variance through time of the total earnings of the MNC may be reduced by investment in projects or countries in which earnings are not correlated with the earnings of its other projects. Such diversification reduces the net risk borne by its owners and tends to increase the value of the firm on the stock markets.

This favorable effect of MNC activity will materialize only if the firm diversifies internationally via a portfolio of projects that the individual investor could not himself acquire by investing in the securities of national companies in several countries. This will generally be the case only if capital-market *segmentation* is more pronounced for *indirect* (portfolio-type) investment than for *direct* investment (within MNCs, in particular). Not only do national securities laws and disclosure requirements differ; there is also a strong likelihood that MNCs have more information about their own foreign projects than individual stockmarket investors could ever have about the foreign companies they might invest in. To the extent that this is true, MNCs may make a special net contribution to world welfare by reducing investor risks and increasing investor wealth.

Operational Efficiency

The MNC may, in addition, achieve greater efficiency in its own operations than a single-nation firm. There is, first, the matter of competition in host-country markets. If the national industry is competitively lethargic, the injection by an MNC affiliate of a new competitive force into the local market may shock it into increased operational efficiency. This was, in the view of some observers, an important outcome of the influx of U.S. companies (including banks) into Europe during the 1950s and 1960s. Moreover, the evidence suggests that the competitive overlap in products supplied by local and foreign-owned firms in that market has increased significantly since 1960. So there is some presumptive evidence that MNC activity may strengthen competition and reduce monopolistic influences. But, as we have already noted, MNCs may sometimes, by strategic predatory pricing, reduce competition and increase the degree of monopoly in their industries. In addition, they may influence government policy or the terms of their collaborative arrangements with host governments so as to secure exclusive or competitively sheltered market access in host countries. These negative, anticompetitive implications must be balanced against the positive influences, and the overall evidence is contradictory.

A second aspect of MNCs that we have associated with their competitive strength are *economies of scale* arising from the size of individual plants or the centralization of certain system-wide activities such as R & D, foreign-exchange management, or corporate planning. The evidence on plant size is ambiguous, but the realization of economies of scale through centralization of specific nonmanufacturing activities is more apparent. R & D, in particular, is normally tightly centralized in countries that have the most ample engineering and scientific resources, which normally means the United States, the United Kingdom, France, Germany, and Japan. To the extent that MNCs are able to achieve such economies of scale, global economic efficiency may of course be strengthened.

Negative Effects on the World Economy

Despite the efficiency gains achieved by MNCs, their activities seem to have certain negative implications for the affected economies. First, as noted, economic activity by MNCs may in part turn out to be anticompetitive, and thereby harm either allocational or operational efficiency in their host or home countries. For example, in selecting the various components of its "package" of inputs and production techniques, the MNC may actually combine resources for which alternative, cheaper sources of supply are available on the outside. Such "tie-ins" may be designed to maximize the economic rent accruing to the MNC, and they may distort the allocation of resources so that high-cost MNC-related suppliers substitute for lower-cost alternative suppliers. The "bundling" of the MNC package then carries with it the possibility of an anticompetitive resource allocation.

In addition, the market power of multinationals may serve as an effective barrier to the entry of competitors lacking the input-, product-, or financial-market advantages of the MNC. This could lead to growing concentration and monopolization in world markets, as the multinationals further exploit their superior competitive positions. So far, however, the evidence suggests that markets have in fact become *less* concentrated through time.

Also, MNCs generally have a direct interest in the establishment or preservation of particular governmental policy measures relating to trade, taxes, foreign investment, and overall economic policy that favor their own interests. Given their size and weight, they are sometimes in a position to wield substantial policy-making influence in host as well as home countries. Perhaps more often than not, these efforts have led to anticompetitive policy steps and to a reduction in the efficiency and output potentials of these economies.

Finally, from a global point of view, the very flexibility of MNCs may allow them to impose external costs on the world economy that purely national firms might not. For example, MNCs may find it easier to move plants to "pollution havens" where environmental control requirements are absent or lax. And when there are environmental effects spilling over national borders (for example, in water or air pollution), the world as a whole may suffer higher social costs of these kinds.

To summarize, the MNC carries both positive and negative implications for global welfare. Given its capacity to mobilize resources and its flexibility in using them, it may not only improve allocational and operational efficiency in the use of world resources, but also may raise the level of investment and the pace of technological change. Yet there are also some negative aspects. Whether MNCs are, on balance, positive or negative contributors to the world economy, remains uncertain. And in a rapidly changing world of complex technologies and giant production scales, the feasible alternatives are very difficult to envision. The global welfare effects of MNCs constitute an immensely important issue that needs to be considered carefully in weighing the pros and cons of public policies that challenge free international investment and/or attempt to regulate MNC operations. But policies are made by nations, according to perceived national interests, and there is as yet no effective political mechanism for reconciling these interests and subordinating them to the collective interests of the world economy.

BENEFITS TO THE HOME COUNTRY

In a general-equilibrium context, the benefits of MNCs' foreign activities arise in one of two forms. The returns to the factors of production employed in them will tend to be either higher or less risky than would be the case in the absence of foreign activities. These higher rewards may be distributed to stockholders in the form of dividends, to management and technical employees through higher salaries, or to the labor force through higher wages. Following the predictions of neoclassical trade theory, the abundant factors in the home country will tend to benefit from MNC foreign operations, whereas scarce factors may be harmed. Overall, the gains of the gainers are likely to exceed the losses of the losers.

A second source of benefit is the access to lower-cost products made abroad by the MNC. In dividing the production process more finely, some activities are transferred to lower-cost foreign facilities producing for export back to the home country. The resulting gains go partly, via price reductions, to the purchasers of the final products. For foreign investments in the extractive sector, this particular source of benefit is obvious.

HOME-COUNTRY CONFLICTS

Opposition to foreign direct investment and technology transfers by MNCs stem predominately from their short-term effects on particular sectors, regions, or income groups. The principal pressures for regulation and control of foreign operations thus address specific *domestic* economic ills or alleged injustices, rather than their effects on foreign nations. Among the more important charges against MNCs in the United States and other major MNC home countries is that they lead to a domestic job displacement, an erosion of national competitive advantages, an avoidance of tax liabilities, the suppression of competition, and the undermining of domestic economic policy.

Job Displacement

The most controversial issue relating to the home-country effects of foreign direct investment is the impact of overseas production by MNCs on the domestic labor market. Despite the fact that multinationals span the spectrum of industries, from services to extractive products, this issue is focused almost exclusively on manufacturing. The jobs controversy underlies the steps taken by several European nations to reverse their traditionally liberal policies toward foreign investment by corporations based in their own countries.

The evidence on labor-market effects of foreign investment is now plentiful. There is no doubt that some home-country jobs are eliminated by foreign production by MNCs. Production that could have been carried out at home may be transferred abroad, making some workers redundant. There is offsetting job creation as well, however. It has been shown that positive causal relationships often exist between U.S. exports to particular foreign markets and production by U.S. firms within these markets. Hence some jobs in fact owe their existence to MNC facilities abroad.

The net impact of MNCs on home-country labor demand depends on the relative size of the job-elimination effect and the job-creation effect. The former, in turn, depends on the international competitive situation faced by the MNC in the various markets it supplies. If it would have lost the markets to a foreign competitor anyway had it not invested abroad, no loss in jobs can be attributed to the foreign production decision, and the foreign activity is "defensive." If it could have retained these markets and still supplied them from the home country in the absence of foreign investment, but instead engaged in overseas production to raise profits or reduce risk, then some home-country jobs will clearly be destroyed; the foreign activity can then be deemed "aggressive."

Although there is a wide range of estimates on the net number of U.S. jobs destroyed (up to 2 million) or created (up to 600,000) in this way, all estimates suggest relatively small *net* impacts on domestic jobs, as compared with the effects of other fluctuations in total labor demand. The macro-adjustment required for the labor market to absorb such foreign-investment-induced shocks thus seems quite small.

But the skill, location, and industry characteristics of the jobs created are not the same as those of the jobs eliminated. The microadjustment burdens placed on particular segments or members of the labor market can indeed be significant. The jobs eliminated—both directly, in the affected industry, and indirectly, in supplier industries—tend to have higher proportions of semiskilled and unskilled (predominantly unionized) operatives, whereas the jobs created have higher proportions of managerial, professional, technical, and clerical workers. Like the domestic conflicts created through international trade, the MNC jobs issue is basically an adjustment problem for factors that are internationally less competitive.

Erosion of Capital and Technological Advantages

Along with jobs, MNCs are alleged to export capital and technology, to be combined with cheaper labor in host countries. In the process, it is claimed, (a) the capital and technological advantage of the United States is eroded; (b) the international competitiveness of its manufacturing base is compromised; (c) manufacturing activity (and the associated jobs) shrinks, thus robbing the economy of high-productivity, dynamic industries; and (d) the rising share of national income coming from abroad in the form of MNC earnings increases the vulnerability of the economy to foreign economic and political change. In short, the U.S. economy could follow the path of the United Kingdom, ultimately becoming a *rentier*-like, services-oriented economy with low growth and massive displacement of output and manual workers in the manufacturing sector.

There is no effective way to substantiate or disprove the general validity of this sort of selective, one-sided analysis. Suffice it to say that there is a good deal of distrust of the liberal international investment policies of the leading MNC home countries in the past two decades and that the adversaries of the MNCs have produced a long litany of complaints.

Inequitable and Inefficient Taxation

MNCs, through the sophisticated use of tax havens abroad, transfer pricing; and tax holidays and incentives offered by host countries, are said to be able to escape their "fair" share of home-country fiscal burdens. This point applies specificlly to U.S. MNCs as a result of the U.S. provisions for a deferral of income taxes on reinvested foreign earnings and the foreign income tax credit against corporate income taxes payable at home. There has also been considerable debate over whether these provisions constitute an implicit subsidization of foreign investment. To this extent, they may artifically stimulate the expansion of foreign operations of American MNCs and accelerate the domestic production/job displacements described above.

Complication of Domestic Economic Policies

The existence of MNC networks of foreign affiliates may frustrate the implementation of certain economic policies in the home country. The home country's antitrust policy objectives may be made four difficult to achieve; income-maintenance and minority-employment policies may be compromised by expansion of overseras operations; and efforts to limit the supply of certain strategic products to specific foreign countries may be thwarted by the foreign affiliates of the nation's MNCs. Other examples exist, showing how MNCs add layers of implementation difficulties in several areas of microeconomic policy.

At the macro level, the greater access of MNCs to foreign sources of financial capital may provide an avenue of escape from restrictive domestic monetary policies, thus complicating domestic stabilization measures. In addition, balance-of-payments or exchange-rate objectives may be rendered more difficult to achieve with the additional trade and financial interconnections among MNC headquarters and affiliates. Although these macro issues may not be a major concern for large countries such as the United States, for smaller home countries with large MNCs, such as Switzerland or Sweden, the problems appear less trivial.

Policy Reponses in Home Countries

Home-country political pressures against MNCs have been directed especially toward unemployment and balance-of-payments issues. Although most OECD countries maintain a relatively liberal stance toward the foreign investment activities of their international firms, almost all have imposed some limits or conditions on the expansion of such activities. In the earlier postwar period, these rules were mainly for balance-of-payments purposes. In the 1970s, limiting adverse effects on domestic production and employment became a more urgent objective.

From 1965 to 1974, the United States maintained capital-outflow restrictions for portfolio investments, bank lending and new foreign direct investments by U.S. MNCs, all for the purpose of improving the balance of payments in the short run. Other countries, including the United Kingdom, France, Japan and Italy, have also limited or discriminated against foreign expansion by their MNCs for similar purposes.

In the more recent past, organized labor has in several countries pushed for limitations on the expansion abroad of MNCs. Worker participation laws in West Germany and Sweden bring representatives of home-country workers directly into the managerial decision-making process, and job protection of home-country employees has in some cases been guaranteed as a price for expansion of foreign production by MNCs based in these countries. In the United States, the same type of pressure has led to a stance of firmer and firmer protectionism by the AFL-CIO and various individual unions. The most serious attempt to screen and regulate MNC activities was the Burke-Hartke bill of the early 1970s, which would have subjected foreign-investment and techonology-transfer decisions by American MNCs to a test of their U.S. employment effects before they could be carried out. This legislation failed to gain approval, although similar legislative programs have been urged by the AFL-CIO in every Congressional session since that time.

A HOST-COUNTRY VIEW

Conflict between the MNC and its home-country detractors is mirrored in a magnified form in its relations with its host countries. Its conflicts with the latter frequently produce policies that restrict trade, capital flows, and technology transfers. Through these policies, host countries try to capture a greater share of the output and income gains brought about by MNCs, or to reduce what they regard as negative economic or social effects of MNC activities.

Sources of Gain

The potential gains to host countries from foreign direct investment include enhanced capital formation, increased income and employment, technological advancement, and a net contribution to the balance of payments. The social value attached to these effects is of course a matter of preferences. It may be, for example, that the employment objective overrides all of the others, so that job creation will be viewed positively even if MNC contributions in other areas are only marginally positive, or even negative. And what is considered a favorable economic contribution in one country may be regarded quite differently, and give rise to restrictive policies, in another.

With respect to capital formation, the questions is whether or not foreign direct investment in fact enlarges the national capital stock. The answer depends, of course, on what would have happened if the MNC investment had not been made. Would a rival MNC have undertaken the investment? Would local entrepreneurs have done so? If so, then there may be no net increase in capital formation. If not, then the MNC can be credited with the full amount of the gain. This is true whether there are actual flows of financial capital from abroad, or whether part or all of it is raised locally. In many cases it seems plausible that if local entrepreneurs or rival MNCs could have undertaken a particular investment, they presumably would have done so. If they in fact did not, then one can point to a gain in capital formation.

The argument about balance-of-payments gains or losses (see Chapter 20) runs along similar lines. Such gains or losses depend on the initial inflows and the induced imports of capital equipment, intermediate goods, and raw materials, induced exports, and the repatriation of earnings over time. What would have happened if the investment had not been made? Again, there can be no definitive answers, and restrictive assumptions will be necessary when the net balance-of-payments effects are to be assessed and policies to deal with them are to be formulated.

The same is true of the income and employment effects. There may not only be a reduced level of unemployment and underemployment, but formal training programs and on-the-job training routinely carried out by MNC affiliates may benefit labor-force efficiency and add to the overall stock of human capital.

There have been fewer controversies about the gains stemming from technology infusions via the MNC. At least in the short run, no technologies comparable to those supplied by the MNC may be available locally, so that the technology components of the MNC "package" make available new or better products or boost the efficiency of productive factors in the host country. Managerial know-how, especially, represents a form of technology that is difficult to develop with the local resources of a small or less-developed country. Another critical MNC element is entrepreneurship and risk taking. As an institution, the MNC is geared to an entrepreneurial role, as it scans the international environment for profit opportunities. Having found one, it assesses the economic and political risks in relation to the expected returns. It may be able to engage in ventures in host countries that local entrepreneurs are unable to undertake because of the MNC's diversification across many projects in many countries. By assuming such extra risks, the MNC performs an additional entrepreneurial service for its host country.

Unless national policy measures interfere, MNC involvement can in these ways create "static" gains through more efficient production and better labor-force utilization at the national host-country level. The "dynamic" benefits are more difficult to predict, since the host country over the longer haul may have greater opportunities for restructuring its economy along similar lines without relying on MNCs.

Sources of Conflict

Each of the benefits ascribed to MNC involvement in host countries has its reverse side. There are potential costs and conflicts associated either with the international financial effects of the foreign direct investment or with the distribution of the real gains between the firm and the host country.

For example, at the outset of an MNC-related project, host countries like to see a maximum inflow of capital from abroad, whereas MNCs prefer to limit their net capital commitment by financing locally as much of the project as possible. Although host governments may recognize the need to import capital equipment, they are interested in minimizing the import bill associated with material inputs, and they may try to pursue this objective through trade restrictions, exchange controls, or "local content" regulations. The policy measures applied by the host country to achieve that result may conflict with the MNC objectives of minimizing costs, achieving product-quality targets, and remitting profits. At the same time, the host-country government may try to pressure the MNC into expanding exports, which in turn may conflict with the firm's plans for efficiently serving different national markets from specific production points.

Perhaps an even more controversial subject is technology. MNCs are regularly accused of bringing into host countries "inappropriate" technologies not well suited to local factor conditions—for example, by using advanced labor-saving technology in highly labor-abundant host countries with chronic unemployment. Such projects may not only fail to absorb very much unemployed labor, but also drive out of business local competitiors who operate more labor-intensively. Such allegations are made despite the fact that standard technologies often cause MNCs to be "locked into" capital-intensive production, with little scope for technological substitution.

MNCs are accused of failing to do research and development in host countries, which leads to underemployment or emigration of skilled research-oriented individuals and contributes to a permanent national dependence on imported technology. The fact that multinational firms spend only about 6 percent of their R & D budgets outside their home countries (less than 1 percent in developing countries) raises their vulnerability to such criticism. Host countries have tried, with mixed success, to encourage local research and development, but the existence of economies of scale in R & D and the need to maintain close managerial oversight over it have limited the international spread of R & D within the MNC networks.

Host-country fiscal and financial policies can be at cross-purposes with MNC activities. Tax avoidance and circumvention of exchange controls through intracompany transfer pricing are two areas in which the objectives of the host government and MNC management often clash. There is also the possibility that multinationals will escape the dictates of domestic monetary policies. Whereas local firms must cut back on investment spending during periods of national monetary restraint, affiliates of MNCs may be in a position to resist this policy via intracompany loans and access to international financial markets. Besides causing a slippage in the effectiveness of monetary policy, MNC affiliates can gain a competitive advantage over domestic competitors that are forced to toe the line.

And there is the problem that MNCs may introduce greater economic instability into the host economy. Especially in highly labor-intensive, export-oriented activities such as assembly of electronic components, abrupt withdrawal by MNCs as economic or political conditions change could have serious destabilizing consequences, and this has to be taken into account by host-country governments. A different risk of instability is associated with a heavy concentration on export production of income-elastic products, demand for which drops off dramatically in times of recession in major markets. This can lead to wholesale plant shutdowns within foreign subsidiaries.

Another area of potential conflict is competition policy. The question is whether the presence of MNC affiliates increases or reduces the degree of competition in host-country markets. The evidence is ambiguous. Examples of heightened competition attributable to foreign investment abound, but so do examples of predatory behavior to drive out local firms and negotiation for monopoly positions in local markets as a condition for entry. MNCs have also been accused of causing "excessive" competition, as a large number of different MNC affiliates, in a bandwagon effect, enter a small market and start producing at uneconomical levels of production.

Another "cost" perceived to be connected with foreign ownership of business is the loss of control over local economic decisions. Extraterritorial management is the issue here, with fundamental decisions affecting local operations being made at MNC headquarters by individuals who, allegedly, know or care very little about local conditions or the effects of their actions on the host-country economy. There is a similar question of economic-political extraterritoriality, pertaining to the application of MNC home-country laws in such areas as antitrust, trade boycotts, and business conduct in the host countries. A local MNC affiliate may even seem to act as an agent for the home-country government.

National Control of MNCs

The distinct conflicts between MNC and host-country objectives have naturally led to attempts at national political control of MNC operations. Only in a few highly industrialized countries is such control relatively minimal. There are essentially five ways a host country can seek to control MNC operations within its borders during the life of a foreign investment project.

First, it can apply "entry controls." This involves an *ex ante* assessment of the prospective impact of each project on the national economy and on politically significant domestic interest groups. A registration and screening procedure may be set up to administer the entry controls. Entry may be denied if the prospective effects of the foreign investment proposed are considered harmful. Second, it might restrict the permissible types of organizational and financial corporate structure, or particular industries may be considered off limits to foreign investment altogether. This can involve prohibition of majority-owned affiliates, which will in effect mandate local joint ventures. Or ownership positions in fixed assets may be banned completely, with participation in the host-country economy limited to "turnkey" plants, management contracts, and the like. The intent is generally to limit foreign equity ownership so as to permit an effective local voice in the management of the enterprise.

Third, the host country can apply operating controls of various types once the foreign investment has been made. These may or may not be different from rules governing domestic enterprise. They can include domestic-content rules limiting the maximum share of imported inputs, price and wage controls, credit controls, local-ownership requirements, and environmental regulations. Operating controls will normally reduce the profitability of the local MNC affiliate and influence future investment behavior—and at the limit, they may cause the firm to pull out. For the host country, the effectiveness of operating controls depends on understanding their effects on MNC behavior. Fourth, the host country can apply financial controls on the remission of profits by MNC affiliates, perhaps via a maximum rate of remittances as a proportion of invested capital. Finally, the host country can nationalize or expropriate the entire MNC investment, or purposely make controls on it so onerous that the firm is induced to sell off its assets to local interests and depart.

There are numerous actual examples of the five control techniques outlined here. The Philippines relies primarily on entry controls, and Canada has attempted to move in this direction in recent years. Various countries ban banking, mining, and telecommunications from foreign ownership. Japan generally tolerates only joint ventures. India is particularly notable for its myriad operating controls. Brazil offers comparatively free entry and a relatively free operating environment for foreign investment, but nevertheless applies controls on earnings remissions. Cuba and Chile have gone through periods of extensive terminal controls.

JOINING THE ISSUE

The bottom line in evaluating international investment and MNCs should be their actual effects on the global allocation of resources, ideally achieved in accordance with the dictates of free, competitive markets for goods, services, and factors of production. Yet national markets are not free or always competitive, but subject to innumerable policy-inflicted distortions. Nor are the international markets free. This means that the international allocation of capital through foreign investment does not conform to the ideal of the market, but is likewise distorted. At the same time, the distortions existing in goods-and-services markets, or in national factor markets, can in part be overcome by international capital flows. As traditional trade theory teaches, trade and factor flows tend to substitute for one another, and when trade is blocked, capital flows can, at least in part, restore the missing gains in resource allocation.

As in regard to international trade, we are interested both in the magnitude of these gains and in their distribution. In international investment, the principal protagonists are the capital-exporting and capital-importing nations. Yet, there is a third actor, the multinational firm, whose actions can influence the allocation of gains between home and host countries, or possibly direct some of the benefits to third countries. There is of course the additional question of the amount that the MNC can appropriate unto itself for the exclusive benefit of its shareholders or employees. No credible estimates of how this three-way split of gains (or losses) is actually carried out exist.

Obviously, the multinational firm maximizes its objectives globally, whereas countries are forced to maximize their objectives nationally. For this reason there has been increasing pressure for rules governing international investment so as to reconcile the divergent interests and secure greater global benefits from MNCs. There seems to be a strategic advantage for the MNC in its battles with home- and host-country governments. Recent initiatives include regional arrangements such as the EEC's competition policy, as well as the broader approaches taken through the proposed UNCTAD code of conduct on transfer of technology, the OECD code on MNC behavior, and a similar code now under development by the Commission on Transnational Corporations of the U.N. Economic and Social Council. None of these severely restrict international corporate investment or production.

The main problem with such international efforts to regulate international investment is that they assume a broad coincidence of interest among the regulators—whereas in reality, most of the conflicts surrounding the MNC simply reflect the contrary interests of host and home countries, or groups in these countries. It will therefore be difficult to get agreement on the outlines of a general international MNC control system, let alone assure its effectiveness once promulgated. This means that control of international investment and multinational corporate behavior—at least outside cohesive regional economic groupings—will ultimately boil down to a matter of national policy. Home and host countries will separately try to assess the effects of foreign direct investment against their respective economic and social objectives.

SUMMARY

This chapter concludes our discussion of international trade and international movements of productive factors, and the policy issues surrounding them.

We have examined the multinational enterprise and its particular "institutional comparative advantages" that have driven it to a dominant position in the international economy. We have discussed its salient characteristics—its sources of competitive strength, its impact on global resource allocation, and its impact on home and host countries or groups within them. MNCs inevitably produce both costs and benefits—which are, however, nearly impossible to measure in practice. The multinationals remain at the center of international economic controversy. Supranational efforts to regulate them are under way, but may be frustrated by the lack of shared national objectives or a lack of efficient enforcement powers. Besides, it is not clear that in regulating MNCs, many of their contributions to allocative efficiency and growth in the international economy would not be sacrificed.

Important Concepts

foreign direct investment

multinational corporation

institutional comparative advantage

appropriability of technology

MNC "package"

"portfolio effect" of MNCs

operational efficiency

home-country benefits

home-country costs

host-country benefits

host-country costs

control of multinationals

Questions

1. Multinational firms have been accused of "worsening" global income distribution, both within countries and between countries. Can you develop some arguments supporting and refuting this charge?

2. Using the pure theory of trade, identify ways in which MNCs may enhance the global gains from international trade and specialization in production.

3. Multinationals are said to be able to neutralize some of the welfare losses associated with barriers to international trade and factor flows. Explain this statement.

4. Heavy involvement of multinationals in a nation's economy is alleged to undermine its economic sovereignty. Why? Can you think of ways to defuse this problem without sacrificing the benefits that MNCs provide?

Further Readings

Areskoug, Kaj, "Private Foreign Investment and Capital Formation in Developing Countries," *Economic Development and Cultural Change*, April 1976.

Barnet, Richard J., and Ronald Müller, *Global Reach* (New York: Simon & Schuster, 1974).

Bergsten, C. Fred, Thomas Horst, and Theodore H. Moran, *American Multinationals and American Interests* (Washington, D.C.: The Brookings Institution, 1978).

Buckley, Peter J., and Mark Casson, *The Future of Multinational Enterprise* (New York: Holmes & Meier, 1976).

Dunning, John H. (ed.)., *Economic Analysis and the Multinational Enterprise* (London: George Allen & Unwin, 1974).

Gladwin, Thomas N., and Ingo Walter, *Multinationals under Fire: Lessons in the Management of Conflict* (New York: John Wiley, 1980).

Hawkins, Robert G. (ed.), *The Economic Effects of Multinational Corporations* (Greenwich, Conn.: JAI Press, 1979).

Hood, Neil, and Stephen Young, *The Economics of Multinational Enterprise* (London: Longman, 1979).

Moran, Theodore H., *Multinational Corporations and the Politics of Dependence* (Princeton: Princeton University Press, 1974).

Vernon, Raymond, *Storm over the Multinationals* (Cambridge, Mass.: Harvard University Press, 1977).

Vernon, Raymond, *Sovereignty at Bay* (New York: Basic Books, 1971).

III

International Financial Transactions and Markets

17

PURPOSES AND METHODS OF INTERNATIONAL FINANCE

We have now completed our treatment of the real aspects—that is, the goods-and-services side—of international economic relations. We will devote our attention from now on to their financial aspects, which we have ignored almost entirely thus far. Although this will at first seem like a sharp break in the flow of the discussion, it will soon become evident that there are strong parallels between goods-and-services trade and financial transactions, and that international finance can in fact be regarded as a special type of international trade. Later on, we will also see how real and financial international economic problems are interconnected, especially in the broad relationships among national economies. The subjects of trade and finance will then converge.

This introductory chapter presents the basic terms and principles used in international financial analysis. It draws some illuminating parallels between financial transactions and ordinary trade, in particular with regard to their causes and effects. It briefly describes the major categories and characteristics of financial transactions among nations. The chapter is designed to lay the groundwork for the following discussion of more specific and technical international financial issues, from the analysis of particular financial markets (in Chapters 18 and 19) to the methods of international financial accounting (Chapter 20), the problems of macroeconomic interdependence (Chapters 21-23), and finally, the development of the global financial system (Chapters 24 and 25).

DOMESTIC AND INTERNATIONAL FINANCE

All financial activity revolves around money or claims to money—and ultimately around the goods and services that money can buy. Sometimes these claims take the form of legally binding promises of future payments. In other cases they represent part ownership of corporations and, as such, entitle their holders to share in the future incomes of these enterprises, primarily through dividend distributions. This is, of course, how we distinguish between *debt* and *equity*. All borrowers and equity-issuing corporations are sellers of financial claims of one kind or another, whereas the lenders and equity buyers are purchasers of such claims. In addition, already-issued claims can, if they are negotiable, circulate among the public through repeated resales. This describes the *secondary market*, through which ownership of financial claims is transferred from one party to another, without involvement by the original issuers. Whether we are speaking of the new-issue market or the secondary market, the two transacting parties may or may not reside in the same country. If they do not, the transaction is clearly international.

But let us be a little more precise. "Finance" can technically be defined as the *procurement or allocation of loanable funds*. "Funds" here means immediate purchasing power, whether obtained in the form of cash or credit. The term "loanable" simple indicates that the funds are meant to be returned in some form at some date in the future; funds obtained through sales of goods and services are naturally not loanable. Accordingly, international finance implies the procurement of loanable funds by a resident of one country from a resident of another. From the latter's standpoint, this is an allocation of funds to a foreign party.

Funds can be procured, domestically or internationally, through issues of stocks, bonds, notes, bills, and other marketable financial instruments, or through loans from financial institutions or commercial suppliers. They can also be procured through resales of marketable financial instruments previously bought. Funds can be allocated through lending, deposits with financial institutions, purchases of marketable financial instruments, and repayments of previously incurred debts.

In practice, almost all financial claims are substantiated by some kind of written documents, such as loan contracts, bond or stock certificates, or passbooks. For our purposes, we shall refer to all these documents as *securities*. Accordingly, borrowers are sellers of securities that they themselves issue. When they make their final repayments, they effectively become repurchasers of these securities. Conversely, lenders are securities buyers—as are those who supply loanable funds through the secondary markets. A similar perspective can be applied to corporations issuing equity securities and occasionally repurchasing their own stock certificates.

Since all modern forms of *money* (currency and demand deposit balances) technically consist of debts issued by either government agencies or private banks, money should also be regarded as a type of security. The money holder is a creditor to the money-issuing organization, and by adding to his money balances, he is effectively supplying loanable funds to that organization in return for a debt instrument. Plain currency will normally never be repaid—

although historically it has often been redeemable in precious metals—but this does not truly negate its debt nature. Withdrawals of bank deposits, by contrast, are equivalent to repayments by the debtor, the bank, at the request of the depositor. Money buildups are a way of allocating funds so that they will be readily available whenever they are needed. They are therefore perfectly *liquid*. This view of money may at first seem odd or artificial, but it is the only one that can accurately explain the nature and consequences of national or international monetary relationships.

INTERNATIONAL ILLUSTRATIONS

If an American buys a newly-issued British corporate bond, he becomes a supplier of loanable funds to the British corporation, and hence to the British economy at large. He might be regarded either as an exporter of loanable funds or as an importer of a British bond. Funds will gradually dribble back to him through interest payments and amortization of principal, and the final redemption of the bond upon maturity can be construed as an American reexportation of this security. If the bond had been outstanding for some time, it might instead have been bought from a financial investor in, say, France. In this case, the American bond buyer would have supplied loanable funds to France, rather than to Britain, and France would have become the security exporter. Analogous descriptions can be made for trade in equity funds, or for financial transactions between sellers and buyers of goods and services. For instance, international accounts receivable are in actuality imported securities of a special kind and, as such, evidence that loanable funds have temporarily been exported.

Foreign governments and banks supply the American economy with additional funds whenever they purchase U.S. government treasury bills or add to their deposits with banks in the United States. In the latter case, the funds will almost certainly be used for relending to the public or, possibly, the government. This is what happens when banks pass on the funds, obtained through deposits, by making loans to businesses or consumers, or by buying government securities.

Banks, as well as other financial institutions, are engaged in financial *intermediation*. In our terminology, this activity can be described as the simultaneous sales and purchases of different kinds of securities, with different maturities and catering to different segments of the economy. Intermediation through banks and other depository institutions has the further consequence of changing the overall maturities of the financial instruments available to the saving and investing public. Because of this intermediation, the maturities will tend to be shorter, since bank deposits effectively take the place of medium- or long-term bank loans. Imagine having to place your surplus funds in business loans, maturing at specific dates, and not having the convenience of checking accounts! Such intermediation leads to a *maturity transformation* in the direction of a more liquid economy. This concept, too, will help us later on to understand the financial relationships between the United States and the rest of the world.

INTERNATIONAL CAPITAL FLOWS

Especially in the context of aggregate international financial relations, flows of loanable funds are often called *capital flows*. The term can refer either to debt transactions or to equity transactions, or to return flows of the funds that originally were lent or invested, as shown by the diagram in Figure 17-1. By contrast, payments of interest, dividends and other types of net returns are, conventionally, not included under this concept. Instead, these particular

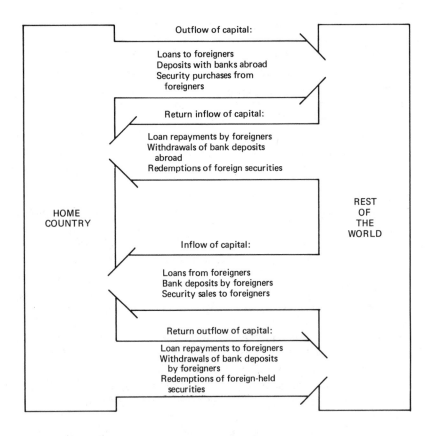

Figure 17-1. Main categories of capital outflows and inflows.

flows are considered to be a kind of income paid for a special "service"—access to somebody else's capital. This is a fine distinction, but it has been generally accepted both in domestic corporate accounting and in the official accounting of aggregate international economic transactions (as we shall see in Chapter 20).

When touching on certain kinds of capital flows in Chapters 15 and 16, we focused primarily on the associated flows of goods and services—in particular, on the effects on real capital. At one point, we even made the facile assumption that capital transfers are synonomous with transfers of physical capital goods—an assumption usually made in the traditional theory of international trade and factor movements. We are now in a position to clarify and elaborate on this distinction.

Capital exports represent international supplies of loanable funds, while *capital imports* represent the corresponding demands. These flows transfer purchasing power from one nation to another—but they do not in themselves indicate how that purchasing power will be used. Some capital inflows may actually lead to immediate capital outflows through other channels or markets. For an internationally active bank, this will be a rather normal occurrence. Other capital inflows may lead to purchases of foreign consumer goods, just as if the capital-importing country had been receiving a kind of international consumer credit. Yet some capital inflows may indeed lead to imports of capital goods, so that these flows actually will perform the function of investment finance. How the capital-exporting nation generates its excess of loanable funds is another question, and the empirical answer to it will vary from situation to situation. It would therefore be a serious mistake to flatly equate capital flows with equivalent losses of physical capital for the capital-exporting countries and equivalent gains of physical capital for the capital importers.

There is one additional, important category of funds flows among nations—*unilateral transfers*, as through intergovernmental aid and private international donations. Such gifts and grants definitely transfer purchasing power from payers to payees, yet they are not strictly "loanable." Some writers and statisticians regard them as capital flows, whereas others treat them as a third category of international economic transactions, apart from goods-and-services trade and bilateral capital transactions. This is merely a semantic issue; yet to avoid confusion, we have to be sensitive to it.

PRICE CONCEPTS

In each domestic or international trade transaction, there is always an explicit or implicit price. We know what constitutes "price" in an ordinary cash purchase—the amount of money payable for one unit of the purchased good. We also know from our examples of international barter trade that "price" can be a ratio between the quantities of traded products. Thus, the price of wheat in cloth is the number of yards of cloth that have to be paid for a bushel of wheat, and the price of cloth is the inverse of that ratio. Since financial transactions also constitute trade, there ought to be similar price relationships in them as well. Indeed there are.

To an extent, financial transactions resemble cash purchases of commodities. Making a loan, for instance, can be regarded as a sale of credit—as if credit, or the use of funds for a specified length of time, were a special kind of commodity. The rate of interest is then the unit price of the credit, payable by the debtor to the creditor.

Alternatively, one can look upon a financial transaction as a "bartering" of funds available at different points in time. The deliveries of the funds occur, of course, when the loan is made and when it is repaid, or when the security changes hands from seller to buyer and, later, back to the seller upon its redemption. The loanable funds that are bartered can thus be said to be "dated" in accordance with the timing of their respective availabilities, and there will be an implicit barterlike price relationship between them. Technically, the price of future-dated funds in current-dated funds is the ratio of the amount of funds payable today for the right to claim a certain amount of funds at a particular time in the future. Similarly, the inverse ratio defines the price of current-dated funds in terms of future-dated funds.

Consider a simple $100 loan, to be fully repaid in a lump sum in one year. (If we were dealing with another maturity, such as six months, we could easily convert the figures to per-annum equivalents, in accord with common practice.) The annual interest rate is 15 percent. Today's *price of future funds*,

$$P_{FF} = \frac{\$100}{\$100\,(1 + 0.15)} = 0.87$$

This is, in effect, the relative price today of funds available in one year, per unit of such funds (i.e., per dollar). It is also the relative price of a security entitling the bearer to claim funds one year later, provided the security carries an effective yield of 15 percent. The difference between this relative price and unity—13 percent—is today's "discount" on future funds. It reflects what is often called the "time value of money"—or, better, the value of the uses to which funds could be put during this time interval.

Conversely, it might be said that the *price of current funds*, measured in future funds,

$$P_{CF} = \frac{\$100\,(1 + 0.15)}{\$100} = 1.15$$

This is nothing more than a $1 principal plus interest ($0.15), and it is equally well described by the interest rate itself—the conventional net measure of the price of credit. Clearly, there is an inverse relationship between the interest rate and the implicit security price: The higher the interest rate, the lower the P_{FF}.

However, we are generally concerned not just with nominal (money-valued) funds, but with the *purchasing power* over goods and services. What "real" price did people have to pay in January 1976 for funds advanced in January 1975, if the general price level, P, rose by 8 percent and the interest rate was 15 percent? Suppose we let i' stand for the implicit *real* (inflation-corrected) interest rate. The nominal interest rate, i, can then be broken up into an inflation component and a real component:

$$1 + i = (1 + \frac{\Delta P}{P}) \ (1 + i')$$

so that

$$1 + i' = \frac{(1 + i)}{1 + \frac{\Delta P}{P}} = \frac{1.15}{1.08} = 1.06$$

and

$$i' = 6\%$$

The 6 percent figure measures the net real sacrifice made by the borrower for his advance use of funds—for spending above and beyond what he financed through his own income or by using up his assets. It also measures the net real return to the lender for his postponed use of funds—for curbing his own spending and making available his excess funds to others.

Analogous price relationships can be developed for multiperiod transactions in which loans are repaid in installments; the per-annum interest rate will then be a special kind of average annual credit price. There is, of course, no such stipulated price in the case of equities. But the investors will count on a long-term stream of dividends, or a combination of dividends and capital gains upon the resale of the shares on the stock market. These are the components of their investment returns.

Since, when equity securities are purchased, their future returns cannot be exactly known, they have to be estimated. For the investors the relevant price variable will then be the *anticipated* relative returns, as evaluated on the basis of the expected magnitudes and timing of potential dividends and capital gains and the degrees of risk perceived to be connected with them. Because of the subjective aspects of all such evaluations, no uniform market rate of return can be observed on any one stock. Nor can one precisely identify the implicit price that an equity-issuing corporation has to pay through successive dividend distributions, if it wants to induce investors to buy its stock. When looking ahead, one also cannot precisely adjust for an inflation rate that is still unknown.

If the transaction is international, there may be an additional complication. The returns, or the debt service (i.e., the interest and amortization payments), may be contractually payable in a *foreign currency*. From the international lender-investor's standpoint, the home-currency rate of return will depend on the rates at which he can convert this currency into the foreign currency and, later, reconvert foreign currency into his home currency. For an international borrower, his home-currency price of foreign-currency credit will similarly reflect the rates of currency conversion when he receives and repays funds. This is a matter of the relative *exchange rates*, a subject that we will explore much more fully in Chapters 18 and 19. For now, we only need to realize that international financial prices can have an exchange-rate dimension, which sometimes increases and sometimes reduces the apparent price of, or return on, an international financial transaction.

WHY NATIONS TRADE FINANCIAL ASSETS

As in goods-and-services trade, the main economic motives for international financial transactions lie in *international price differences*. Financial transactors turn to foreign markets whenever prices there are more attractive than those at home. The existing price differences can reflect intercountry differences in the financial prices we have just identified—interest rates, rates of return, or security prices, prevailing in the respective national financial markets; or they can reflect perceptions of changing exchange rates.

Let us concentrate on the first of these sources of price differences. The logic of international financial behavior then becomes straightforward: Borrowers tend to go abroad when foreign interest rates are below domestic interest rates, because their demand for funds can then be met more cheaply. Conversely, lenders and investors will generally consider supplying funds to foreigners only if they thereby earn larger returns than they would in the home market. Expressed in terms of security prices, this means that potential security issuers and sellers will try to become exporters of securities (borrowers) when security prices abroad are higher than those at home (which is the implication of lower foreign rates of interest or return). And the incentive for security imports (lending) will of course lie in lower security prices abroad (i.e., in higher foreign rates of interest or return).

The opportunity to engage in international finance will normally increase the income and wealth of both parties. Or it will at least improve their income and wealth prospects at the time the transactions are concluded. Low-interest borrowings abroad will tend to increase the net after-interest income derived through the employment of the borrowed funds, compared with the income the borrower could earn if he obtained financing domestically. Conversely, the interest earnings or stock returns on foreign securities can obviously add to the income and wealth of the investors, and so can the proceeds from high-price security sales on foreign money or capital markets. The analogies with the profits made by the American wheat exporters, or by the British wheat importers, in our commodity-trade illustrations are transparent. We can therefore say that there are *gains from financial trade*, just as there are gains from goods-and-services trade.

But financial trade itself is likely to affect the prevailing international and national financial prices. And the price shifts will help determine the distribution of the gains between the borrowing (or security-exporting) and the lending (or security-importing) nation. We sense intuitively that the magnitude of the gains will depend on whether and by how much foreign financial prices, because of financial trade, will shift in the direction of those initially prevailing at home. The bigger the shift, the smaller the gains from trade.

A couple of illustrations may help: If American investors on a massive scale were to turn to the German stock market in the hope of capitalizing on rising earnings by German corporations, this would quickly lead to an increase in German stock prices—and to a decline in the relative returns on these assets, for both American and German investors. The American capital outflow would then be cut short. On the other hand, if Belgian business firms started to take out bank loans in New York rather than in Brussels, chances are that the New York banks would charge the same rates as before, because the Belgian borrowers would still not be a very large factor on the demand side of the New York market. The Belgian firms would then be able to continue these low-cost borrowings as long as they had sufficiently profitable uses for the funds.

The issue is which party, or which country, will have the greater influence on the equilibrium price of funds that will tend to be established between them. This price will constitute the international *financial terms of trade*. The large country, financially speaking, will generally have less to gain because of the offsetting price influence of its own transactions. It will, to some extent, be an international *price maker*. The small country, by contrast, will capture a bigger share of the overall gains—and it may be a *price taker*, inasmuch as its own rates of interest and return will shift so as to approximate those already prevailing abroad. This simplified analysis assumes that there are no significant government restrictions or subsidies on either international or national financial transactions—an assumption that is violated, in varying degrees, by virtually all countries. Even so, there are clear tendencies for markets to adjust in the directions predicted by our simple theory.

To define more precisely the gains from financial trade, we actually need a two-period model that shows how international lending or borrowing interacts with domestic investment and consumption, somewhat like the one we used in analyzing two-commodity trade and production. Such a model is presented in an Advanced Material section at the end of this chapter.

RISK AND DIVERSIFICATION

The reasons for international financial transactions can be more complex than we have implied so far. They can involve different risk attitudes or risk perceptions, or different opportunities for coping with risks. This is a highly sophisticated theoretical topic, and we shall only summarize the most important points in it.

In comparing the prospective returns or repayments on different securities, the potential security buyer may find that there is more uncertainty about the returns on one type of security than on another. The former thus seems riskier. To almost all investors, risk is a negative feature; investors are *risk averse*, and to accept risk, they have to be compensated through additional returns. Yet the extent of risk aversion is a subjective matter—a matter of taste. So is, to some extent, the evaluation of the riskiness of each security. Particular home-country investors may find foreign securities that better accommodate their own attitudes toward risk. At the same time, certain foreign investors may find securities in the home country that, for reasons of relative risks, especially suit them.

For instance, moderately risk averse Americans may want to buy high-risk securities from more risk averse foreigners, whereas the latter may be happy to shift into lower-risk securities available in the United States. In this case, the desired *risk-return trade-offs* will differ internationally. Or Americans may subjectively attribute less risk to a particular foreign security than do the foreigners themselves, and they may therefore be willing to offer a higher price for it; the different risk estimates may be caused by differences in available financial forecasting expertise, or simply a case of native American optimism.

But the demand for financial assets must be put in the context of the investors' entire security *portfolios*. Modern portfolio theory shows how investors examine not only the risk characteristics of each available security, but also the interrelationships among these risks. The potential returns on a certain security may be highly covariant, or not covariant at all, with those on other securities: that is, the same factors that cause the returns on one security to change may or may not cause the returns on other securities to change as well. By combining, in the same portfolio, securities with low (or even negative) covariances in returns, the investor can reduce the riskiness of his entire portfolio. This is the benefit of *diversification*.

Frequently these covariances will differ for international security combinations, as compared with exclusively domestic security combinations. An American investor might then restructure his portfolio by obtaining foreign securities that have low covariances with his domestic securities. If the expected returns, despite the associated risks, are adequate, his diversified portfolio will become more "efficient"; it will be worth more to him and very likely to many other American investors. Meanwhile, foreign investors may, for portfolio reasons of their own, want certain American securities.

Regardless of the precise international return relationships, there may then result a two-way trade in securities, motivated by different diversification requirements at home and abroad. In the process, investors in both countries can make additional gains in real wealth via financial trade. But remember that these gains are in the nature of anticipations—they will not always be borne out by actual future events, certainly not for parties with contradictory anticipations.

ACTUAL FINANCIAL METHODS

The financial requirements and capabilities of different economic units (households, firms, governments) depend on their individual economic objectives and resources. Some units generally are suppliers of loanable funds, and their main financial objective is to find high-return, low-risk outlets for their *surplus* funds, at home or abroad. Most households belong to this category, yet the "retail" nature of their financial transactions preclude them from directly entering foreign financial markets on a significant scale. A business firm, by contrast, may have financial needs, connected with capital expenditures, in excess of its own retained earnings. It is then in financial *deficit*, even though it might be accumulating particular types of financial assets (such as working capital). If the firm is large and engages in exports or imports, or is somehow affiliated with foreign firms, it is likely to want to avail itself of foreign financial markets.

Financial institutions, by their very nature, specialize in intermediating between surplus and deficit units. The larger ones tend to engage in various forms of borrowing, lending, or security trade with foreign-based parties on a routine basis. At times, they will be net funds demanders, at times net funds suppliers, vis-à-vis the rest of the world. The fourth sector in the national economy, government, is nowadays almost always in financial deficit and therefore has huge borrowing needs. Some governments are lucky enough to be able to fill some of these needs outside their national boundaries.

Table 17-1 contains a brief inventory of the chief debt and equity instruments that, somehow, cross national borders. Some of them are short-term, others are long-term; some are marketable (negotiable), whereas others establish debtor-creditor relationships for the entire terms of the financial contracts. These instruments may be denominated and payable in the debtor's home currency, in the lender's home currency, or in a third, internationally acceptable currency. All of these circumstances depend on the preferences of the market participants and on the practices that have evolved for particular market situations.

Table 17-1
Main Instruments in International Finance

Issuer (Borrower)	Instruments
Nonfinancial corporations	Trade credits (from foreign suppliers) Bank loans and credits (especially for trade finance) Commercial paper Notes and bonds Loans from foreign affiliates Shares
Private financial institutions	Deposits (on behalf of foreigners) Acceptances (of export-import drafts) Commercial paper Notes and bonds Loans from branches and affiliates Shares
Government agencies	Treasury bills, notes, and bonds Intergovernmental loans (including aid loans received) Credit from international financial institutions (e.g., IMF, IBRD)

Manufacturers and other nonfinancial firms incur international debts to each other and to banks, in particular in the financing of imports. These debts—mostly short-term—take the form of accounts payable and trade credit from banks. Such firms also issue short-term commercial paper, medium- and long-term notes, and long-term bonds, which can be purchased by foreign corporations. Most of these instruments have historically been dominated in the issuers' home currencies, simply because they have been tailored primarily to domestic investors. Some of the outstanding shares of large corporations often end up in the portfolios of foreign financial institutions (or individuals). Also, there are large internal financial transfers within multinational corporations. For instance, U.S. affiliates of foreign firms routinely obtain financing in this way, just as U.S.-based MNCs help supply the financial needs of their affiliates abroad. In fact, MNCs have become major extramarket vehicles for international capital flows.

Banks and other financial institutions attract foreign funds in somewhat different ways—by accepting deposits from foreign businesses and governments, through interbank arrangements for export-import finance, and through loans from their foreign branches and affiliates. The majority of these items are short-term and hence add liquidity to the creditors' portfolios.

The governments of large industrial countries, especially the United States, indirectly obtain foreign finance when foreigners purchase their bills, notes, or bonds on the secondary markets. (We shall later examine how foreign governments use such instruments as stores of liquid international purchasing power and as tools for exchange-rate management.) Moreover, governments at times enter into mutual credit deals—for example, to help one country overcome an international financial crisis, or as part of a foreign aid program. Lastly, governments can obtain short- or long-term credit from international institutions such as the International Monetary Fund and the International Bank for Reconstruction and Development. Whatever the maturity, interest-rate,, or currency characteristics of these debts, they produce inflows of loanable funds and enhance the current purchasing power of the borrowing nations.

SUMMARY

This chapter has introduced the standard concepts used in financial theory and practice and has applied them to international debt and equity transactions. We have demonstrated how such transactions can be viewed either as security trade or as trade in loanable funds, and how the prices of securities inversely reflect the prices of loanable funds. Just like ordinary commodity trade, financial trade tends to create gains for the trading parties. These gains stem in part from interest-rate and return differentials, in part from wider opportunities for risk-reducing portfolio diversification. We concluded with an inventory of the main financial instruments issued by corporations, financial institutions, and governments to foreign parties, and thereby becoming vehicles for international capital flows.

We have thus paved the way for an analysis of the main topics in international finance: international financial markets, international financial accounting techniques, and the problems of global economic-financial interdependence, financial policy, and financial cooperation. In dealing with each of these topics in the following chapters, we shall build on the principles established in this chapter.

ADVANCED MATERIAL:
Finance and Intertemporal Consumption Choice

We have stressed that financial transactions are exchanges of funds and purchasing power, available at different points in time. The main purpose of such transactions, whether domestic or international, is to change the potential levels of spending over time. This can be shown more clearly through a formal geometric model.

Such a model can demonstrate why, and in what amount, economic units such as firms, companies, or governments will want to supply or demand funds on the financial markets. It can be applied to a single unit, facing either a domestic or a foreign financial market, or to the sum of all such units in one nation, confronted with various international markets. The model we will use is an extension of the traditional two-commodity trade model that we covered in detail in Part I of this text; yet the focus is on total consumption, rather than the consumption of particular commodities. It captures the basic character of saving, investment, and the associated financial-market transactions.

Each individual is assumed to pursue a goal of consumption maximization. But he plans ahead. He wants to provide for both his current and his future needs, and perhaps also for those of his dependents. He knows what he wants to achieve in this regard. That is, he has certain definite *intertemporal preferences*, much like his relative preferences among various consumption goods.

These preferences define the lifetime welfare, or utility, that he would obtain through different hypothetical combinations of consumption levels in the present and in future time periods. In particular, they define how much additional consumption he would require in one period in exchange for a cutback in consumption in another, if he is to maintain a given level of lifetime welfare. Normally, the lower his consumption in a given period, the more reluctant he will be to reduce it further, since to him the relative marginal value of consumption in this period will then be high. Conversely, if his consumption in one period was unusually high, a cutback would generally not be very painful to him, since its marginal value would be relatively low.

Pretend that the consumer's initial income and wealth are predetermined. The one way in which he can then improve his intertemporal consumption path is by saving or dissaving. Saving implies a postponement of consumption opportunities—a deliberate delaying of consumption. Dissaving occurs through a decumulation (running down) of past savings or through net borrowing, and it implies that consumption opportunities are shifted forward in time. Saving is hence his vehicle for an *intertemporal transformation* of his consumption. The crucial variables affecting his transformation opportunities are his returns on saving and his costs of borrowing. These returns and costs will indicate how he can select those transformation opportunities that best match his intertemporal preferences.

Savings can, of course, be placed either in real assets such as plant and equipment, inventories, or "human capital," or in financial assets such as loans, securities, and money. If the consumer channels his saving directly into real assets (as by buying a house), he is actually performing the task of a producing enterprise. An extreme example of this is the self-sufficient family farm; it is a closed economic unit. Decisions about saving are then also decisions about investment, and they will reflect the productivity of its real assets. If, by contrast, the consumer has limited direct investment opportunities of his own, he will have to channel some of his saving, his funds surpluses, to the financial markets. His saving decision will then reflect the returns offered by these markets. A dissaving consumer may conceivably be liquidating some of his real assets and paying for his added consumption through the sales proceeds. Or he may be going into debt. These decisions, too, will hinge on his real-asset productivity or the prices prevailing in the financial markets.

The Case of the Individual Consumer

Figure 17-2 illustrates the pure consumer case, in which he or she happens to be a saver in the current period. For simplicity, only two periods are covered, the "current" one (say, the coming year) and a "future" one (say, the following year). We are thus ignoring the possibility that the consumer could choose between short- and longer-term saving and consumption changes (just as we shall later ignore longer-term investment projects). The loss in realism will easily be outweighed by the gain in the clarity of the argument.

In this picture, the individual consumer initially has no tangible real or financial assets and derives his entire income from work, as represented by point T. His current wages amount to 80 units of the standard consumption good (or a basket of food, clothing, etc., the size of which corresponds to an index number of 80). In the future period, his work will produce only 25 such units—perhaps he is partially retiring. If he did not have the chance to save or dissave in any form, he would have to consume his entire income in each period, and he would be stuck at point T. His intertemporal welfare would then be indicated by the indifference curve IC, which passes through T.

But he can, in fact, enter the financial markets. The going real one-year interest rate (corrected for the effects of inflation) is, we assume, 20 percent. As a consumer, he will then be better off by saving a portion of his current income, placing the saved funds in the financial market, reclaiming these funds (inclusive of returns) in the future period and shifting consumption accordingly.

How can one tell? By drawing a financial (intertemporal) price line, ii, with a slope of $1 + i$ (i.e., 1.20) and locating its point of tangency with the indifference map. The tangency occurs at point S, which is the highest possible level of welfare for this consumer—higher than that at T. To reach S, he will have to save 50 units out of his current income (or its monetary equivalent), which leaves only 30 units for current consumption, and purchase financial claims with them. His real return on them will be 20 percent of the base amount, or 10 units, so that in total he will receive repayments equivalent to 60 units. His future consumption will then be expanded to 85 units—the sum of his wages (25), his net return on saving (10), and the principal of his past

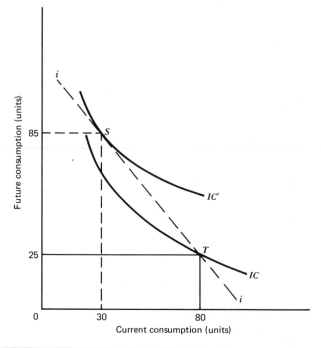

Figure 17-2. Intertemporal consumption choice through financial saving.

	Current period	Future period
Without saving (income and consumption at *T*):		
Consumption	80 units	25 units
With saving (income from work at *T*, consumption at *S*):		
Rate of interest		*i* (= 20%)
Saving	50 units	-50 units
Interest income	—	10 units
Consumption	30 units	85 units

saving (50). His tangible wealth—not counting his wage-producing human capital—will return to zero.

This consumer has clearly reaped intertemporal consumption gains from financial trade. The magnitude of these gains depends on (1) the level and time structure of his basic income, (2) the rates of interest or return at which these income receipts can be intertemporally transformed into various combinations of consumption levels, and (3) his intertemporal preferences. Since this individual is a price taker, his transformation function is linear, for he can count on the going rate of interest, regardless of the magnitude of his saving. This enhances his gains.

We could easily construct other examples. We could consider a consumer with similar preferences but with much lower current income and much higher future income. He would most likely end up being a dissaver-borrower, "mortgaging" his future wages and shifting consumption into the present. So might a consumer whose preferences are skewed much more in favor of current consumption. Finally, the results would be otherwise if market rates were different from the 20 percent rate we have assumed. The reader should be able to handle these cases by himself, both graphically and verbally.

The Case of the Open Economy

In dealing with a whole nation, we have to pretend that we can somehow sum up the intertemporal preferences of all its citizens, without worrying about how to make interpersonal welfare comparisons. We are familiar with this problem from our discussion of trade theory, so we will proceed as if the *IC* curves in Figure 17-3 correctly depicted the aggregate national preferences as between current and future consumption.

We can then turn to the matter of the nation's intertemporal transformation opportunities. To define them, we need to make some simplifying assumptions about the nation's resources and their productivity, and about the types of goods produced. The capital stock consists entirely of machines of a standardized type. Add the special assumption that they have only a one-year life, so that we do not have to deal with the varying output effects of machines acquired during different periods in the past. In other respects, we retain the assumptions of standard trade theory: fixed labor supply, free competition, flexible prices, and full employment.

Two kinds of goods can be produced, consumption goods and capital goods (machinery). Existing resources can equally well be used for producing either type of goods, and we disregard any costs or delays incurred when switching from one production process to the other. Note the implication that existing machines can become inputs into the production of identical (although brand-new) machines—with the cooperation of labor, of course. Consumption goods cannot be stored from one period to another; they are perishable.

Conceivably, production could be entirely geared to making consumption goods for immediate use. We have drawn the diagram so that if this were done, output would reach a level of about 100 million units of the consumption good—that is, the distance *OA*. This would measure the gross domestic product in the current period. And if there are no initial foreign assets or liabilities, and no capital flows in the current period, this would also define the potential level of current consumption. But nothing would be set aside for future consumption, and starvation would loom around the corner.

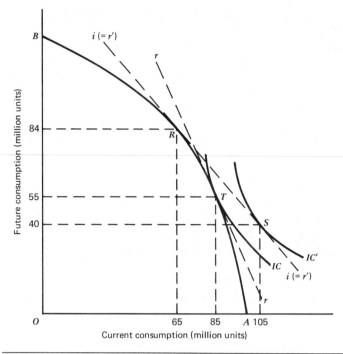

	Current period	Future period
Closed economy (production and consumption at *T*):		
Rate of return		*r*
Consumption	85 units	55 units
Open economy (production at *R*, consumption at *S*):		
International rate of interest		*i* (= 10%)
International borrowing	40 units	—
International repayment	—	44 units
Domestic rate of return		*r'* (= 10%)
Consumption	105 units	40 units

Figure 17-3. Intertemporal resource allocation through investment and international borrowing.

At the other extreme, the nation could conceivably concentrate entirely on providing future consumption goods. It might do so through exports of consumption goods in exchange for imports of capital goods—a simple case of barter. If the international commodity terms of trade were given (because the nation we are describing is small and insignificant in the world market), each unit of consumption good could then, via trade, be transformed into a given number or fraction of capital goods. If foreign and domestic production costs are identical, you may realize that the outcome would be the same as if the capital goods had been produced at home, rather than imported; so we need not differentiate between these two cases. In both cases, the added capital goods will create an identical amount of future consumption goods. We have, rather arbitrarily, set this amount at about 130 million units—that is, the distance OB. But that would imply a current consumption level of zero—also a bit absurd.

Rather, the nation will, of course, seek to provide both current and future consumption goods, in some feasible and desirable combination. What combinations are possible? That depends on the productivity of capital at each level of capital available—a productivity that can best be measured in units of future consumption goods produced per unit of current consumption goods forgone. The gross marginal productivity of capital will then be synonymous with the marginal *rate of intertemporal transformation*. If r denotes the corresponding net productivity of capital—which is here equivalent to the net return—the marginal transformation rate will be $1 + r$. This indicates the possible trade-off between future and current consumption through shifts in output (or commodity trade). Just as suggested by the "law of diminishing returns," the transformation rate declines with higher investment, and higher future consumption levels. As a consequence, the nation's own consumption possibility frontier will be curvilinear and concave to the origin, as shown by curve AB in Figure 17-3.

The term "financial autarky" suggests an absence of all international financial transactions. In this state of affairs, the nation would choose position T, with current consumption at 85 units and future consumption at 55 units. Indifference curve IC is at point T tangent to the transformation curve, and the slope of the domestic intertemporal price line, rr, is $1 + r$. At T, the marginal rate of intertemporal transformation equals the marginal *rate of intertemporal substitution*—a precondition for optimal choice between current and future consumption. Note the similarities between this solution and that shown in Chapters 4 through 6 for the two-industry economy that has not yet entered into any international commodity trade.

Now introduce the possibility of one-year international borrowing or lending (or security trade). The important consideration is then the relative domestic and foreign rates of return or interest (i.e., the relative rates of intertemporal transformation of purchasing power). Here, the illustration pertains to a situation in which the world-market interest rate, i, is lower than the initial domestic rate of return; we assume the former to be 10 percent, and to remain at this level. So apparently there is an incentive for international borrowing. The rest of the world has a *comparative advantage* in producing current consumption goods, the home country having one in future consumption goods. It will pay to trade financially, for the home country can thereby "buy" lower-priced current funds in exchange for higher-priced future funds in the world market.

But how do we link the capital inflow to consumption? We ignore the problems of inflation and exchange rates by assuming that the borrowing is denominated in real terms—that is, in consumption goods. We assume that there are no transport costs or government restrictions. Unless the borrowed funds were immediately reinvested abroad, they will have to be used for international purchases, since no other alternative exists. These purchases will take the form of commodity imports not paid for through exports—they will represent the nation's net imports in the current period (or, as we shall later call them, a trade deficit). These net imports will translate directly into equivalent amounts of additional consumption opportunities.

Meanwhile, the added availability of current consumption goods will make future consumption goods seem relatively more scarce and "expensive." This acts as a stimulus to domestic capital accumulation—as does the foreign claim on future consumption goods, to be supplied in repayment of the loan. The analogy is obvious: When trade in goods opens up, exporters get a chance to sell at higher prices in the world market, and the export industry grows at the expense of the import-substitute industry (instead of "exports," read "future consumption goods"). Or we can put it this way: Lower-cost finance obtainable abroad stimulates domestic investment. In equilibrium, investment will have been pushed just far enough to make the domestic rate of return equal to the world interest rate: $r' = i$.

Graphically, the new production equilibrium will be at R, the point where the international financial price line, ii, is tangent to the domestic transformation curve. Its slope is $1 + r'$, or $1 + i$. At R, the amount of current consumption goods obtainable through domestic production (or export-financed imports) equals 65 units, whereas the corresponding amount of future consumption goods is 84. Borrowing, and borrowing-financed imports, equals 40 units. Through them, current consumption can be expanded to 105 units, as shown at point S. Repayment of principal and accrued interest for one year will absorb an amount of goods equivalent to $40(1 + 0.10) = 44$ units of consumption goods. Repayment will therefore require a net export of goods such that the feasible level of future consumption will be reduced to 40 units of consumption goods. At S, the common line representing both the international and the domestic rates of return, labeled ii or $r'r'$, is tangent to indifference curve IC', and its slope is identical to the marginal rate of intertemporal substitution. This parallels the result of free commodity trade in the two-industry case, with partial specialization in the commodity—read "future consumption goods"—in which the home country has a comparative advantage. The attainment of IC', as compared to IC, is the gain from international financial trade, a gain in intertemporal welfare.

One can easily adapt this model to the situation of an international lender. Its initial domestic rate of return will then have to be shown to be lower than that in the international market. Its foreign financial investment will in effect become a partial substitute for domestic real-asset accumulation. The relative positions of T and R will be reversed. Future consumption will be higher than under financial autarky. This country, too, will be able to reach a higher intertemporal indifference curve. Lastly, by combining a borrower and a lender, one could show a general international equilibrium, with each nation having an influence on the final international terms of trade and the gains from trade being shared accordingly.

Important Concepts

loanable funds	real interest rate
liquidity	diversification
intermediation	capital flow
secondary market	gains from financial trade
intertemporal preferences*	intertemporal comparative
rate of intertemporal	advantage*
transformation*	rate of intertemporal
	substitution*

*Used only in the Advanced Material section.

Questions

1. Describe the various ways in which you, as an individual, could engage in international financial transactions. What instruments would you be dealing in? Who would the foreign parties be? Would you be generating capital inflows or outflows?

2. "Future-dated" funds are usually cheaper than "present-dated" funds. Why is this so?

3. A naive, popular view holds that a person should avoid getting into debt, whenever possible. How would you, as an economist, answer somebody who applied this rule to an entire nation? What is the basic rationale for international borrowing?

4. An American stockholder wants to expand his portfolio by purchasing a selection of high-yield Western European stocks. But he hesitates because the risk on each individual stock in most cases seems disproportionately high. Try to advise him. Especially, should he consistently stay away from high-risk European stocks? Or can you suggest a more efficient strategy?

Further Readings

Areskoug, Kaj, "Intertemporal Resource Allocation in Developing Countries: The Role of Foreign Capital," *Review of Economics and Statistics*, November 1976.

Hirshleifer, Jack, *Investment, Interest and Capital* (Englewood Cliffs, N.J.: Prentice-Hall, 1970).

Miller, Norman, "A General Equilibrium Theory of International Capital Flows," *Economic Journal*, June 1968.

Moore, Basil, *An Introduction to the Theory of Finance* (New York: The Free Press, 1968), Chapters 1-3.

Polakoff, Murray, *et al.*, *Financial Institutions and Markets*, second edition (Boston: Houghton Mifflin, 1981), Chapter 18 ("Foreign Investment").

18

INTERNATIONAL MONEY AND CREDIT MARKETS

The introductory material in Chapter 17 suggested that international financial transactions are carried out in many different ways and through the use of many different instruments. Some transactions are bilateral in that they involve two private or governmental parties making a deal directly with each other. Other transactions occur within organized financial markets, with many security buyers and sellers competing with one another on a regular basis and perhaps being assisted by brokers and intermediaries. These markets may, like the New York money and capital markets, be primarily domestic, even though a substantial minority of the participants tend to be foreign. This is true of all markets for short-term government securities, and of equity markets. And for this reason, we will not explicitly deal with them in this text.

On the other hand, there are a limited number of financial markets that lack that kind of national identity. Their geographic locations are more diffuse, and more often than not, the parties to each transaction are of different nationalities. These markets deserve the label "international." The three types of markets that fit this description are the Eurocurrency markets, the international bond markets, and the foreign exchange markets. The Eurocurrency and international bond markets both deal in credit—the former primarily short-term; the latter, long-term. They are the main focus of this chapter. We will particularly stress the special opportunities that these markets create for lenders or borrowers residing in different countries and that are reflected in relative returns and costs. Yet our main points will also illustrate the situations of lenders or borrowers who wish to enter the national financial market of a foreign country. To them, the distinction between "foreign" and "international" markets may be trivial. The third set of truly international markets, the foreign exchange markets, requires a separate, more technical analysis, found in Chapter 19.

GENERAL CHARACTERISTICS

Each financial contract must have a *unit of account*—a unit of value in which the rights and obligations of the parties are specified. Within each nation, the commonly accepted unit of account is, of course, the national currency—that is, one unit of the designated legal tender (in the United States, a dollar issued by the monetary authorities). With the increased rate of inflation, however, some types of contracts, especially wage and pension contracts, frequently have cost-of-living clauses, and the actual unit of account will then be not a plain dollar, but a price-adjusted dollar. In international transactions, there is generally no common currency to rely on, and the possible options in the choice of unit of account will be broader.

In regard to financing commodity trade, practice varies sharply. Invoices can be made out in the exporter's home currency, in the importer's home currency, or in a third country's currency; and the currency in which the invoice specifies that payment be made will constitute the unit of account contained in their mutual sales-purchase contract. Before the goods have been paid for, at least one of the parties (or his commercial bank, which may take over the obligation for the interim) will have a claim or obligation in foreign currency—the exporter as a creditor, or the importer as a debtor.

Currently, it is much more customary to denominate such commodity contracts in the exporter's, rather than the importer's, currency. At the same time, the currencies of the largest trading nations, such as the United States, West Germany, and Britain, are used more often than those of smaller countries, or countries with very unstable currencies. The leading internationally used currencies, especially the dollar, also serve as *vehicle currencies* in transactions among non-U.S. organizations—in particular, among European, Canadian, and Japanese multinationals.

Similar unit-of-account practices and options exist in international lending and borrowing. Multinational firms conducting business in many separate countries will often routinely enter the local financial markets of the countries where they operate, as well as the broader international markets. To them, the distinction between home and foreign currencies will be blurred, and the problem of appropriate units of account will not be so serious. For firms with more limited international involvements, however, the currency aspects of all potential lending or borrowing will be more critical. On the one hand, they will normally have a built-in preference for their home currencies—these are the ones they use for the vast majority of their purchases, receipts, and financial-market transactions. On the other hand, the international financial markets may offer additional, attractive opportunities for lending or borrowing, and current market practice may require the use of foreign currencies. The primary distinguishing characteristic of international financial markets will then be the availability of foreign-currency credit, or of money and credit instruments denominated in foreign currencies.

The currency aspect of international finance depends greatly on the political and institutional arrangements for the entire international monetary system and for money and banking in individual nations. It especially reflects the rules and practices in regard to the trading and valuation of national currencies. These issues will be taken up in due course. At this point, we should be aware that alternative systems of currencies and exchange-rate determination could call for a drastically revised analysis of international lending and borrowing.

Another feature of the international financial markets is a general absence of government regulation and control. No single government can claim jurisdiction over them, and intergovernmental efforts to establish international controls have not been effectively pursued. To be sure, each national government can try to restrict or subsidize the financial activities of its own residents, and of organizations operating on its territory. But by so doing, it may simply put its own residents at a disadvantage in the international marketplace, and this therefore may not be a good strategy. Also, multinational corporations typically have a great deal of international flexibility in the choice of financial markets, so that they can easily circumvent national attempts to control them. They are hard to police.

How one evaluates this market freedom is partly a matter of economic ideology, partly a matter of identifying and interpreting the relevant data. To some observers, the lack of effective controls over international financial markets poses a threat to national financial policies, and perhaps to the stable functioning of the global financial-economic system. To others, it is a blessing in disguise, in that it permits an escape from unwarranted national economic restrictions and promotes a healthy state of free competition.

RETURNS AND COSTS

Those who wish to engage in foreign-currency lending or borrowing will usually have to enter the foreign exchange markets, as well as a foreign or international credit market. Thus, the foreign-currency lender will have to purchase the foreign currency needed to make his loan. He does this by instructing his bank to execute that purchase in the foreign exchange markets. To be sure, he might already be holding foreign-currency balances with foreign banks, but even if he does, he may not want to draw down these balances at the time of the loan. So let us assume he will need currency in the same amount as the loan he is about to make.

Regardless of how he obtains this currency, he will most likely be keenly concerned about its cost and value. He will be looking for good *home-currency* returns, and these returns will depend on the cost and future value of the foreign currency. The American lender thinks in dollars. Mentally, as well as in executing the deal, he will have to convert currency back and forth.

Take an American one-year loan to Italy, denominated in lire. Assume that the Italian borrower is perfectly creditworthy, so that there will be no question of his ability or willingness to make prompt repayment. And ignore any other possible complications, such as an Italian withholding tax on the interest or possible government restrictions on the funds flows.

The interest rate on the loan is i_f, with interest and principal fully repayable at the end of the 12-month period just beginning. Use R to denote the rate of exchange between the dollar and the lira, so that R in effect becomes the dollar price of the Italian currency. (We could have defined it in the opposite way, as lire per dollar; but we adopt the former, more customary approach, and will stick to it throughout the text.) Let subscript o indicate the date the loan is made and subscript 1 the date it will be repaid. As in Chapter 17, we will put the whole calculation on a \$1 starting basis.

Going step by step, we find that the initial dollar converts into $1/R_o$ lire, available for allocation toward the lira loan. At the end of the year, the lira funds will have grown to $1/R_o (1 + i_f)$. To reconvert this amount into dollars we have to multiply it by the dollar value (dollar price) of the lira at that time—that is, the exchange rate one year later, or R_1. The dollar proceeds of the repaid loan will thus be $1/R_o (1 + i_f)R_1$. But we are probably more concerned about the net return, in dollars but calculated as a percent of the dollar originally lent out, on the entire transaction. Using i^* to denote this return, we find that, by our own definition,

$$1 + i^* = R_1/R_o (1 + i_f)$$

so that

$$i^* = R_1/R_o (1 + i_f) - 1$$

or, with Δ indicating change over time,

$$i^* = \frac{R + \Delta R}{R}(1 + i_f) - 1$$

If the values of i_f and $\Delta R/R$ are reasonably small (as they would be in our case), this expression simplifies to approximately

$$i^* = i_f + \frac{\Delta R}{R}$$

This equality tells us that the dollar returns on foreign-currency loans consist of two parts, the foreign interest rate and the relative (percentage) change in the exchange rate over the time of the loan. But this change may be positive or negative, so that i^* may accordingly be larger or smaller than i_f. A lender who correctly foresees that the dollar value of the lira will drop by 3 percent over the year will thus be able to calculate his dollar return on a 17 percent lira loan as 14 percent. At the outset, he may, however, feel uncertain about the exchange rate pertaining to his reconversion of lire into dollars, so his calculation will describe only an anticipated return, and a risky one at that. (The foreign exchange aspect of this loan is actually more complex, and the lender could in fact arrange beforehand to sell the lira loan proceeds at a predetermined exchange rate—the so-called *forward* or *futures* rate. We will explore these alternative strategies in the next chapter.)

Consider, instead, a case of foreign-currency borrowing. Again, let us regard the U.S. dollar as the home currency of the potential borrower. He is contemplating taking out a loan from a French-owned bank, the loan being denominated in French francs. We may use the same symbols as before, as long as we realize that i_f now stands for the interest rate payable in francs to the foreign lender and that R now refers to the dollar price of French currency. Each franc borrowed will convert into R_o dollars, and the dollar equivalent of the repayment obligation a year hence will be $(1 + i_f) R_1$ per franc borrowed. The gross dollar cost of servicing this loan, as a percent of the funds obtained, will then be

$$1 + i^* = R_1 / R_o \ (1 + i_f)$$

where i^* now stands for the net percentage home-currency cost of such borrowing. Again, this expression will give us the approximate definition

$$i^* = i_f + \frac{\triangle R}{R}$$

If the franc increases by 5 percent in price over the year, a 7 percent franc loan will therefore cost roughly the equivalent of a 12 percent dollar loan obtained directly from a bank at home. But not knowing the future, the American borrower may have under- or overestimated this cost. Unless he is very well diversified, he will have had to weigh the risk of just such miscalculations.

EUROCURRENCY MARKETS

Among the international financial markets, the most remarkable, and the most puzzling, are the Eurocurrency markets. They have become a vital part of the global financial system. They have led to major innovations in multinational corporate financial behavior—and they have created a lot of headaches for policymakers.

What is a "Eurocurrency"? It sounds like a unit of money circulating throughout Europe or issued by a cooperative, integrated European banking system. This is definitely *not* the case. Rather, the term essentially denotes bank deposits placed with European commercial banks but denominated in currencies other than the home currencies of the respective banks. These deposits are thus foreign, or external, from the standpoint of each of these banks. They are time deposits, not "currency" in the ordinary domestic sense of the word. Nor are Eurocurrencies identified with all of Europe, or even exclusively with Europe.

The prefix "Euro" simply refers to the fact that the market has been concentrated in Europe insofar as the location of the deposit-receiving banks—often called "Eurobanks"—is concerned. Yet similar practices have developed elsewhere, especially in Asia (Hong Kong, Singapore, and Tokyo) and Canada (and, at least for bookkeeping purposes, in special offshore tax havens such as the Bahamas and the Cayman Islands). The term "Eurocurrency" is often used also for these non-European bank deposits, despite the obvious misnomer, but the term "Asiadollar" is sometimes preferred in describing U.S. dollars placed with banks in that part of the world. Eurocurrency deposits can be denominated either in U.S. dollars or in other leading currencies. Eurodollars may thus be placed in any European or any non-U.S. country, whereas Eurosterling, Eurodeutschemarks, or Euroyen can technically appear on the books of banks anywhere outside of the United Kingdom, West Germany, or Japan, respectively.

Origin, Size, and Composition

It is impossible to pinpoint the precise origin of the Eurocurrency markets. Even before World War I, some non-American banks, especially Canadian and Swiss banks, accepted U.S. dollar deposits for subsequent investment in the U.S. money market. The practice gradually spread, and after World War II foreign banks started to relend dollars, deposited with them, to their European customers or to other non-American banks. The reasons for placing these deposits outside the United States seem to have varied: more favorable interest rates abroad payable to the depositors; stricter regulatory controls over banks in the United States, which gave foreign banks a competitive edge in the bidding for funds; and the sheer convenience for European businesses in concentrating their banking affairs closer to home. A number of Eastern European countries also started to make Eurodollar deposits. They seem to have feared that in a political crisis, their deposits in the United States might be frozen or otherwise jeopardized.

Certain international developments in the 1950s and 1960s gave further impetus to the growth of the markets. By that time, the interest rates that banks in the United States were permitted to pay on deposits—in accordance with the so-called Regulation Q—were significantly below those offered in

Europe. European exchange controls (restrictions on currency conversions) had been lifted or liberalized, and this allowed European firms to own dollar assets that previously had to be turned over to the national monetary authorities. There were increasing capital outflows from the United States to Europe, and the dollar deposits that Americans offered in payment for European assets were absorbed by European banks and governments, who in turn reinvested some of these dollars in Europe. And American business firms in Europe wanted additional Eurodollar loans, so as to finance their expanding activities there. There were thus strong expansionary forces both on the supply and on the demand side of these funds flows.

Measuring the growing size of the markets has proven difficult. Since there is no central supervisory, data-collecting agency, statistics have to be gathered from many diverse sources. A special statistical problem is how to treat the large amount of *interbank* deposits, which reflect the repeated relending, from bank to bank, of the same original dollar deposits fed into the markets. It is now agreed that for most analytical purposes, these deposits should not be counted.

Available estimates indicate that the overall Eurocurrency market, exclusive of interbank deposits, grew from a modest volume of less than the equivalent of $10 billion in the early 1960s to $400-$600 billion in the late 1970s. Of this amount, the overwhelming portion consisted of Eurodollars, followed by Eurodeutschemarks (see Figure 18-1). Meanwhile, the Asiadollar market has grown to a deposit or loan volume of $10-$15 billion. To get a U.S. perspective on these data, one might point out that total demand and time deposits with all U.S. commercial banks amounted to about $1 trillion toward the end of 1979, whereas the U.S. money supply, as conventionally defined, then stood at $375 billion. Eurocurrency deposits therefore represent a significant addition to total bank deposits in the Western world. More important, the dollar segment of the market adds greatly to the global supply of short-term dollar assets. But it would be misleading to consider it part of the U.S. money supply (or money stock), for these dollar deposits are not really supplied by banks in the United States, nor are they owned primarily by U.S. residents.

The Chain of Transactions

Consider the following typical situation, illustrated in Figure 18-2. A multinational firm—U.S.- or foreign-based—has sold goods out of its inventory. In payment for these goods it has acquired additional demand deposits, kept with a U.S. commercial bank, labeled A. When this bank collected the newly deposited funds, D/D_1, its reserves increased dollar for dollar. But the multinational firm now decides, because of prevailing interest rates, to shift these balances to a Eurobank (numbered I), perhaps located in Frankfurt. By so doing, it acquires a Eurodollar time deposit, T/D_1^e, and the

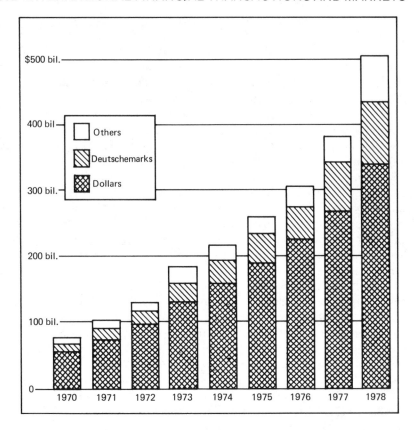

Figure 18-1. Size and composition of the Eurocurrency market.

Eurobank gains ownership of a deposit of equal size, D/D_2, which it places with its correspondent American bank, labeled B.

Quite possibly, Eurobank I does not at present have any requests among its customers for dollar loans, at least not at the going international interest rate. Eurobank II, located in London, is, however, actively bidding for dollars on behalf of its customers. Eurobank I therefore relends the acquired funds by transferring them to Eurobank II in return for an interbank Eurodollar deposit, T/D_1^e, issued by the latter. After Eurobank II in London has placed the funds with its correspondent U.S. bank (C), thereby acquiring the deposits D/D_3, it makes a Eurodollar loan to a multinational firm, which may be in the process of purchasing supplies needed in its planned production. Most likely, this firm temporarily places the loan proceeds in its U.S. bank (D), so that it will be able to pay its suppliers through withdrawals from its deposit account

Multinational Firm (Seller)

- Inventory	
$+ D/D_1$	
$- D/D_1$	
$+ T/D_1^e$	

U.S. Bank A

+ Reserves	$+ D/D_1$
- Reserves	$- D/D_1$

Eurobank I (in Frankfurt)

$+ D/D_2$	$+ T/D_1^e$
$- D/D_2$	
$+ T/D_2^e$	

U.S. Bank B

+ Reserves	$+ D/D_2$
- Reserves	$- D/D_2$

Eurobank II (in London)

$+ D/D_3$	$+ T/D_2^e$
$- D/D_3$	
$+ \text{Loan}^e$	

U.S. Bank C

+ Reserves	$+ D/D_3$
- Reserves	$- D/D_3$

Multinational Firm (Buyer)

$+ D/D_4$	$+ \text{Loan}^e$
$- D/D_4$	
+ Inventory	

U.S. Bank D

+ Reserves	$+ D/D_4$
- Reserves	$- D/D_4$

U.S. Firm (Seller)

- Inventory	
$+ D/D_5$	

U.S. Bank E

+ Reserves	$+ D/D_5$

Figure 18-2. Creation and relending of Eurodollars.

(which has been credited by D/D_4) with this latter bank. If these suppliers are American firms, they will simply place their sales proceeds with their own banks (E), thus acquiring deposits D/D_5.

In this example, the original multinational seller firm has supplied spendable funds, via the intermediation of two Eurobanks, to the multinational buyer firm. But on a net basis, no funds have really left the United States, for the total amount of U.S. bank liabilities has remained unchanged throughout the whole process. There has only occurred a *redistribution* of deposit liabilities, and the reserves that accompany them, among different U.S. banks. Globally speaking, the nonbank public now holds an additional short-term asset, T/D_1^e, and has incurred a new loan liability in the same amount (Loan^e). Since the deposit is almost always of shorter maturity than the loan, the public as a whole is now more liquid. The whole process thus entails a liquidity-creating maturity transformation, as does the analogous depositing and relending within each national system of bank or nonbank financial intermediation.

The example might be modified in several ways so as to suggest alternative situations. The original depositor might have been a foreign government—especially, an agency of an oil-exporting nation—that wishes to alter the composition of its international short-term assets, or it might have been a wealthy individual who just has sold American bonds or stocks. The Eurobanks might have been located elsewhere, even in Singapore or Montreal; and they might have been branches or affiliates of U.S. banks. Moreover, the chain of banks might have been longer, so that the repeated relending of the funds might have resulted in a "pyramiding" of interbank deposits, each bank marking up the interest rate along the route. In other cases, the last Eurobank in this chain may convert the dollars received into other currencies on the foreign exchange markets, because these currencies are the ones its borrowing customers want. Or the final borrower of the Eurodollars may have sought these funds for purposes other than financing his dollar imports—to purchase dollar-denominated securities in New York, in particular.

Further potential complications can arise. When another party receives the dollars from the Eurodollar borrower, he might not deposit them in the United States but in another Eurobank. If this is the case, he will enable this bank to make further Euroloans, either directly or through its correspondent banks in the Eurosystem. The funds will then make another "loop" before completing the "round trip" back to the United States, and the overall amount of intermediation will increase.

This process should be faintly recognizable to those who recall what they learned in their first money-and-banking course: It is a special *multiplier* process, similar in principle to that in the Federal Reserve system. In this system, reserve assets can be injected, or withdrawn, through open-market operations and changes in the public's holdings of plain currency. As reserves are passed on from bank to bank via loans to the public, these reserves can generate multiples of new credit and deposits. Analogously, deposits with U.S. banks are a kind of reserve asset in the hands of Eurobanks, capable of generating additional credit via these latter institutions. When the proceeds of Euroloans are redeposited in Eurobanks, they too create a multiplier phenomenon.

The size of the Eurodollar multiplier is, however, in dispute. On the one hand, the absence of reserve requirements in the Eurodollar market could in theory make it very large; on the other, most borrowed Eurodollars are returned to American parties and leak out of the Eurobank system after their first or second "round trip." This distinguishes them from the reserves held by Federal Reserve member banks, for these reserves cannot so easily, except through deliberate open-market sales, leave this system. The consensus is that the Eurodollar—and Eurocurrency—multiplier is generally quite small, yet it must be highly susceptible to changing global financial-market conditions.

Private Opportunities

The Eurocurrency market adds an important dimension to corporate financial strategy and management. Multinational companies look upon it as a convenient short-term outlet for surplus funds, often with better return prospects than those in U.S. or foreign local markets. Eurocurrency deposits can be vehicles for *arbitrage* among different domestic and international markets. This general concept refers to the simultaneous buying and selling of the same commodity in different markets and at different prices. Here, the "commodity" is credit, or securities, of a particular nature, and the aim is to take advantage of differentials in money-market yields. Borrowers, conversely, have in the Eurocurrency market an additional source of medium- or long-term loanable funds, obtainable at costs that may compare favorably with those in alternative markets. They, too, may use it for arbitrage-type purposes: A decline in the interest costs of Euroloans may induce them to restructure their liabilities, as these fall due, in favor of larger Euroloan commitments or to build up their overall asset portfolios through credit from Eurobanks.

From the perspective of the Eurobanks, the market enables them to diversify their "products" with respect to both lending and deposit creation. By entering the Euroloan business, a bank might better accommodate customers engaged in exports and imports or in the expansion of their worldwide production and distribution networks. Such loans may well carry currency risks connected with unforeseen future depreciations of the currencies in which they are denominated. Yet loan diversification can usually reduce the overall riskiness of the banks' entire loan portfolios. By broadening their deposit facilities, the Eurobanks may similarly gain a competitive edge over those banks that are limiting themselves to transactions in local currency.

Large American banks can let their foreign branches bid aggressively for Eurodollars and thereby enlarge their Federal Reserve deposits at the expense of other American banks. For them, the Eurodollar market is a supplementary source of short-term funds, sometimes with a cost advantage over ordinary domestic sources of funds. The Federal Reserve has regarded this as inequitable and has imposed special reserve requirements on Eurodollar borrowings, effectively raising the costs of these funds.

Policy Implications

Because it intermediates such a huge volume of funds, the Eurocurrency market inevitably will affect macroeconomic conditions in various national economies. These effects will be relatively large for those countries whose domestic financial systems are small relative to the volume of their Eurocurrency transactions; in particular, their interest rates will be more vulnerable to Euromarket pressures. (This parallels the observation that international commodity trade plays a relatively bigger role in the economies of small countries and that their domestic prices readily adjust to those in the world market.)

The added short-term capital mobility created by the Eurocurrency market helps channel funds, and command over real resources, from less-productive to more-productive funds uses. If this occurs, the real incomes and wealth of both the suppliers and the recipients of these funds will normally be increased. This is the traditional free-trade argument, applied to the services of a special type of productive factor, credit.

But the freedom of financial trade is in reality neither complete nor entirely multilateral, for many financial restrictions (i.e., trade barriers) still remain among the national markets linked to the Eurocurrency market. Had the U.S. and European economies been completely open financially, the flow-of-funds pattern would surely have looked quite different. To the extent that Eurocurrency activity is an escape from national financial regulations, it may actually lead to anticompetitive distortions in the flows of funds. Its resource-allocative effects may then in some cases be counterproductive.

One concern is that the market, through its generation of huge amounts of moneylike assets (so-called near-monies), is inherently inflationary. But the Euroloan liabilities incurred by the public along with its Eurocurrency deposits greatly reduce the net liquidity creation attributable to the market, and this lessens the public's propensity toward increased spending. The ultimate source of the global inflation in the 1970s and 1980s surely lies elsewhere—in expansionary national financial policies.

Yet for individual European countries, sudden shifts of funds between the national and the Eurocurrency markets can cause serious financial instability and complicate their efforts to pursue independent money and credit policies. For one thing, Eurocurrency borrowings can weaken the authorities' chances of restricting credit-financed business expenditure. Also, if these borrowings are done in foreign currencies, the proceeds may be sold on the foreign exchange market and cause undesired instability in currency values. To neutralize this effect, the authorities could consider purchasing these currencies on their own behalf. But they would then inject fresh reserve assets— normally, central-bank deposit liabilities—into the domestic financial systems, with further expansionary monetary consequences. In other circumstances, sudden outflows of funds into foreign-currency deposits can put unwelcome upward pressure on interest rates. Such flows can also destabilize currency values.

But what are the market's implications for money, spending, and inflation in the United States? Haven't U.S. dollars been drained off the U.S. economy? And hasn't the new abundance of foreign-held dollars meant that the dollar's international value must have been lowered?

There is no such drainage. Since Eurodollar flows do not generally change the amount of credit and deposit liabilities on the books of U.S. banks, the funds, as noted, do not actually leave the U.S. financial system. Unless the deposits are redistributed among banks with different lending opportunities or credit policies, there can be no significant impact on the total U.S. money and credit supply. From the U.S. standpoint, the Eurodollar market supplements, rather than supplants, the domestic financial market.

As for the value of the dollar, recall that the added international supply of U.S. bank deposits (by depositors in the Eurodollar market) is by and large matched by an added international U.S. bank deposit demand (by the Eurodollar borrowers). Therefore, the net impact on the relative international availability of U.S. bank deposits is ambiguous; yet it is this availability that determines the strength of the currency.

Another way of expressing this situation is to point out that the market produces both capital outflows and capital inflows from and into the United States. Shifts of dollar deposits to foreign banks indicate outflows of funds from the United States, whereas their return to this country indicates inflows; the typical Eurodollar "round trip" involves just such a combination of flows. If these flows at times induce shifts in currency values, there is no fundamental reason why these shifts should be mostly downward—or upward, for that matter. Moreover, Eurodollar transactions may often substitute for capital flows that would have occurred had the market not existed. It would be impossible to forecast the net outcome of all these potential flows in the hypothetical absence of the market.

In a broader context, the Eurodollar market may well have enhanced the international use and usefulness of dollar-denominated assets, even though it may sometimes have made the dollar more unstable. It has widened the dollar's acceptance both as a unit of account and as a medium of international transactions, making it more nearly a global currency. In this respect, the dollar is filling a need on the part of the world economy, connected with the gradual integration of national economies and reflecting the absence of a unified global system of banking and money.

THE INTERNATIONAL BOND MARKETS

Another link in the global credit markets are the international bond markets. These are the markets created through the issuing of bonds—that is, long-term instruments of private or government debt—outside the country in which the issuer-borrower resides and through the secondary-market trading of such bonds. They are international, first, because the securities are issued in nondomestic markets and, second, because borrowers and lenders typically are of different nationalities.

In regard to marketing technique, one can distinguish between two types of international bonds. One is the bond issued in what, from the issuer's standpoint, is a single national foreign capital market. Examples are the European corporate bonds frequently issued on the American capital market. Another one, in 1979, was the issue by Sears, Roebuck of "samurai" bonds — bonds denominated in yen and placed on the Japanese capital market. Such bonds are often referred to as *traditional foreign bonds*. The other type consists of bonds issued simultaneously in several national markets, or in what practically is a multinational market. Typically, this is done through international syndicates of brokerage houses or investment bankers who act as underwriters—temporary, intermediating buyers of the bond issues. The national markets involved in these multicountry issues have mainly been in Western Europe, although Japan, Canada, and, lately, the United States have sometimes also been represented. This type of bond is therefore called a *Eurobond*, even though the geographic prefix of this term is actually too restrictive.

It is tempting to regard Eurobonds as a long-term counterpart to Eurodollars. Yet the parallel is misleading. Eurobonds, unlike Eurocurrency deposits, are generally not the debts of financial intermediaries, since they are in most cases issued by manufacturing corporations or non-American government agencies; and the funds raised through their issue are typically used for financing spending rather than relending. Also, the prefix "Euro" in Eurobond is not meant to indicate the typical residence of the debtor; he may be based in the Western hemisphere or in the Far East.

Yet both the Eurobond and the Eurocurrency market provide outlets for surplus funds for varying lengths of time. They are alternative sources of investible funds. And like Eurocurrencies, Eurobonds are issued in a variety of currency denominations, and herein lies much of their appeal. Consider a habitual deficit unit such as the government of Finland. It has no large domestic capital market that it can easily tap without sending financial shockwaves throughout the domestic economy. By going to the international market and issuing bonds in U.S. dollars, or Deutschemarks, or Swiss francs, it can more easily attract investible surplus funds, especially from those who prefer well-known international currencies over the less-familiar, less-acceptable Finnish markka. Alternatively, the Finnish government could go to a large foreign capital market with a minimum of restrictive controls, such as that of the United States, placing bonds denominated in that country's currency on that market; this would exemplify the traditional foreign bond technique.

On the other side of the market, many financial investors wish to diversify or take advantage of apparent international return differentials, without the cost of the withholding taxes, exchange controls, or impaired liquidity often associated with national capital markets. To them, the Eurobond market can offer attractive securities denominated in acceptable currencies, backed by the prestige of well-known organizations and easily resold in the secondary market.

Choice of Currency

Both issuers and buyers of international bonds have to consider the possibility that relative currency values will change during the life or holding period of the bonds. Normally, each issuer or buyer has an identifiable home currency in which he calculates his costs, revenues, or profits. For the bond issuer, and the owners of the issuing organization, the home-currency cost of servicing a bond denominated in a foreign currency must be calculated on the basis of the expected future rate of exchange between the home currency and the denomination currency. A depreciation of the latter relative to the former will make debt service cheaper, for less domestic currency will then be required to discharge the debt-service obligations embodied in the bond. Conversely, a relative appreciation of the denomination currency would add to the domestic cost of repayments. For the bond holder, such potential exchange-rate changes will have the opposite effects. He would benefit from the prospect and realization of an appreciation of the foreign currency in which his bonds are denominated; its depreciation would conversely entail a capital loss. Naturally, both issuers and buyers will weigh these possibilities, along with the nominal interest rate and other features of the bond transaction. The cost and return formulas we used earlier in this chapter can be applied.

But currency choice also reflects perceptions of risk. Bond issuers and holders alike generally attribute special cost or return uncertainties to bonds denominated in foreign currencies. Since they can never be perfectly sure that their future exchange-rate projections will be accurate, they will always face the possibility that actual exchange rates may turn out to be either higher or lower. Some bond issuers and holders might be able to diversify away most of these currency risks. Or they might be able to *hedge* their asset-liability positions by acquiring both assets and liabilities in the same foreign currencies, so that most of the currency risks will cancel out. But more typically, such risks cannot be avoided, and the risk-averse financial manager will require a special "risk premium" on the return on a high-risk bond purchase.

The difficulty in matching the currency preferences of bond issuers and bond buyers has led to the introduction of other units of account, based on combinations of currencies. One variant of such *multicurrency issues* permits the bond holder to be repaid in any one of two or several currencies in accordance with the initial exchange rates among them. This means, in effect, that he will seek repayment in that currency that has appreciated, or appreciated the most, relative to the others, since his return will then be the largest. For instance, assume that the relative value of the French franc and the British pound is believed, by a particular investor, to be subject to significant variations—a very realistic belief in the 1960s and 1970s. The right to be repaid in either currency will tend to make his expected return higher than that on plain franc or plain pound bonds. It could also lessen the possible instability of that return. But what about the issuer? He would be stuck with potentially higher repayment obligations, although possibly also benefiting from a reduction in the sheer uncertainty about these costs.

Several other types of multicurrency provisions have been adopted. The original *European Unit of Account* (EUA), made to equal one U.S. dollar, was to be redefined in value if a certain minimum number of the Western European currencies were to appreciate or depreciate; but since exchange rates in actuality moved erratically in both directions, it kept its original par value. The *Eurco*, introduced in 1973, was defined so as to equal a trade-weighted average of the values of the currencies of the members of the European Economic Community. Within that average, the ups of some currencies could be offset by the downs of others. In the food-and-drink jargon of finance, these units of account have been referred to as "currency cocktails"; yet the investing public has not, so far, shown much appetite for these items on the international asset menu.

The multicurrency units of account should be seen as forerunners of a common currency for the entire EEC. Currency unification is one of the goals of the Community. When the European Monetary System (EMS) was officially launched in the spring of 1979, it was announced that the future EEC currency will be labeled ECU (European Currency Unit). It, too, is defined as a weighted average of the existing national currencies, and it may in the future become a standard intra-European unit of account. These various steps toward monetary unification are intended to tie the national money and capital markets more closely together, especially by increasing the stability of financial returns and costs and by facilitating intercountry lending and borrowing.

Trends and Prospects

The geographic makeup of the international bond market changed dramatically during the 1960s. New York had long been the preferred source of funds for foreign bond issuers desiring to go outside their own national capital markets. The reasons for New York's attractiveness had to do with its size, stability, and liquidity—or, according to the old cliché, its "depth, breadth, and resiliency." These characteristics greatly facilitated the marketing of both American and non-American issues at predictable interest rates and low transaction costs. And the international status and credibility of the U.S. dollar made it the preferred investment currency.

But things changed rapidly in 1963. Along with other measures to shore up the nation's external financial position, the Kennedy administration imposed a special tax on American purchases of foreign securities, the so-called *Interest Equalization Tax* (IET), which was aimed at restricting U.S. capital outflows by reducing the net after-tax yield on such investments. In a technical sense, the measure succeeded, for it practically prevented most potential foreign borrowers from entering the New York market, and this type of capital outflow almost came to a halt. Beginning at the same time, U.S. corporations were discouraged from expanding their investments in plant and equipment abroad through the use of domestic funds or foreign earnings. The U.S. government imposed, first, a set of guidelines, and later, a system of mandatory controls on such capital outflows. All told, these *capital-outflow restrictions* led both U.S. multinationals and foreign corporations (and government agencies) to turn to alternative capital markets, in particular to those in Europe. The result was a sudden growth of Euromarket activity and the emergence of Eurobonds.

Until the mid-1970s, more than half of the volume of Eurobond issues were accounted for by American multinationals, which in this way managed to raise the funds they needed to maintain and increase their productive facilities abroad. Rather naturally, they usually denominated these bonds in U.S. dollars. Meanwhile, many large foreign multinationals and governments also started to avail themselves of this developing market. They issued bonds either in dollars or in European currencies, or occasionally in multicurrency units. Issuers belonging to the major European countries seemed to prefer to offer bonds either in dollars or in their own respective currencies, especially Deutschemarks, Swiss francs, and Dutch guilders.

The Nixon Administration in 1974 eliminated the entire program of capital-outflow controls, but the Eurobond market continued its steady growth. Apparently it had developed sufficient momentum to withstand the renewed competition from the reinternationalized U.S. bond market. As Table 18-1 indicates, the Eurobond market—still dominated by dollar issues—and the foreign segment of the New York bond market now coexist side by side. Even so, these international markets remain small relative to the aggregate volumes of U.S. and other industrial-country bond and capital markets. Compared with the hugely inflated Eurocurrency market, the international bond markets are minuscule.

Yield comparisons among different issues are complicated by the fact that there are differences in maturities and amortization schedules, as well as in the

Table 18-1
International Bond Issues (in billions of U.S. dollar equivalents)

	1973	1977	1978	1979
Eurobonds				
By issuer:				
U.S. corporations	$ 0.9	$ 1.1	$ 1.1	$ 2.9
Foreign corporations	1.3	7.3	4.5	7.2
Government entities	1.6	7.6	6.9	7.0
International organizations	0.4	1.7	1.5	1.7
By currency:				
U.S. dollar	2.4	11.6	7.3	12.6
(Average yield)	(8.3%)	(8.0%)	(8.6%)	(9.1%)
Deutschemark	1.0	4.1	5.3	3.6
(Average yield)	(9.3%)	(6.4%)	(6.6%)	n.a.
Other	.8	2.0	1.6	2.5
Total	4.2	17.7	14.1	18.7
Foreign bonds in the U.S.	1.0	7.4	5.8	4.5
Foreign bonds outside the U.S.	2.6	8.8	14.4	17.7
Total international bonds	7.8	34.0	34.3	41.0

Note: The average yields (per annum) are for long-term "straight" (nonconvertible) debt issues by U.S. corporations.

Source: Morgan Guaranty Trust Company of New York, *World Financial Markets,* various issues.

relative credit standings of different borrowers. Also, some bonds are convertible into corporate stock at predetermined share-per-bond conversion rates, whereas others are "straight" debt issues. In short, the "commodities" traded are not quite homogeneous.

Still, the approximate nominal yields cited in Table 18-1 are representative. The higher yield on dollar issues, as compared with Deutschemark issues, in 1977-78 might be interpreted as reflecting a "premium" for the ongoing depreciation of the dollar against the stronger Continental currencies. This may suggest a tendency toward an equalization of international long-term credit prices, as estimated in any one currency. On the other hand, in 1973 the nominal yields on Deutschemark issues were relatively higher, possibly because the 1971 and 1973 devaluations of the dollar had made it appear to have greater near-term strength.

The growing international financial markets are an important aspect of the gradual financial-economic *integration* of the leading industrial economies. The geographic segmentation of both commodity and financial markets is weakening, and national markets are exposed to greater and greater external competition. The main forces behind this trend are the expansion of multinational business, the strengthened competitive positions of Western Europe and Japan, and the relaxation of many government barriers to international transactions. International economic theory strongly suggests that these developments are beneficial to global resource allocation and world economic growth. Yet they can entail severe transitional adjustment problems and costs to individual nations, industries, and firms.

SUMMARY

We have in this chapter tried to characterize the main international financial markets and the facilities they offer to lenders and borrowers. They are linked to national financial markets, especially through arbitrage flows. They permit lending or borrowing in various foreign currencies, and the values or costs of these alternatives depend on anticipated or realized changes in exchange rates. Lenders clearly prefer appreciating currencies; borrowers, depreciating currencies. But uncertainty about exchange rates can also produce indirect costs that can discourage many less-diversified firms from entering particular international markets. The Eurocurrency markets serve as outlets for short-term funds and as sources of credit for multinational corporations and foreign governments; but their critics view them as destabilizing and as a threat to national money and credit control. On a much smaller scale, the international bond markets complement the national markets for long-term debt instruments.

In analyzing these markets, we have repeatedly referred to the importance of exchange rates, and of an understanding of the exchange markets. This is the topic that we will now take up.

Important Concepts

Eurodollar	deposit multiplier
Eurocurrency	Eurobond
vehicle currency	multicurrency bond
near-money	ECU
hedging	IET
arbitrage	traditional foreign bond

Questions

1. What is the difference, if any, between a Eurodollar and an "ordinary" dollar? If you were a large corporation, which would you rather hold? Does the Eurodollar have its own exchange rates against nondollar currencies?

2. The OPEC governments have placed a large part of their "petrodollars" in the Eurocurrency market, thereby permitting them to be "recycled"

to oil-importing nations. Construct a plausible example of such recycling by setting up the appropriate "T-accounts" (partial balance sheets) for a depositing OPEC government, a Eurobank, and a Eurodollar borrower (say, the government of Italy).

3. To some observers, the spectacular growth of the Eurodollar market is an alarming sign of excessive, inflationary money creation by the U.S. authorities. To others, it is a vote of confidence by the international financial community in the continued soundness and stability of the American currency. Which is closer to the truth? Can one really tell?

4. Imagine that a German pension fund manager is contemplating the purchase of either Eurodollar bonds with a 12 percent coupon or domestic German bonds with a 9 percent coupon. The maturities are the same. He estimates that the U.S. dollar will depreciate, on average, by about 2 percent per annum against the Deutschemark over the life of the bond. Which bonds should he purchase? What if the expected dollar depreciation had been 4 percent? What if, in addition, he requires a one percent risk premium on the dollar?

Further Readings

Aliber, Robert, *The International Money Game*, 2nd ed. (New York: Basic Books, 1976).

Areskoug, Kaj, "Exchange Rates and the Currency Denominations of International Bonds," *Economica*, May 1980.

Bank for International Settlements, *Annual Reports*. (Regularly contain surveys of developments in the Euromarkets.)

Bell, Geoffrey, *The Euro-Dollar Market and the International Financial System* (New York: Wiley, 1973).

Dufey, G., and I. Giddy, *The International Money Market* (Englewood Cliffs, New Jersey: Prentice-Hall, 1978).

McKenzie, George, *Economics of the Eurodollar Market* (London: Macmillan, 1976).

19

THE FOREIGN EXCHANGE MARKETS

When the parties to an international transaction settle their accounts, one of them usually has to arrange for a conversion of currency. Rarely do they have foreign cash to spare for their foreign payments, and rarely do they wish to collect their receipts in that form. There is therefore an obvious need for facilities through which different currencies can be exchanged for one another—that is, for foreign exchange markets. The term "foreign exchange" thus indicates the process of settling obligations denominated in foreign currency. It has also come to describe the financial instruments through which such settlements are made—that is, demand deposits with foreign commercial or central banks, or comparable claims in foreign currency.

For private firms interested in doing business abroad, the foreign exchange markets are an indispensable facility—a central way-station for the traffic of international commerce and finance. For governments, they are a barometer that, with great sensitivity, registers economic-financial developments at home and abroad. They are thus a chief concern of international economic policy. Not surprisingly, the topic of foreign exchange is at the core of all international economic analysis.

This chapter stresses two things—the nature of contemporary foreign-exchange facilities and transactions, and the purposes they have in different facets of international business and finance. After a short description of how the markets are organized and how contracts are made, we will go on to analyze how these markets can accommodate the needs of international commodity traders, lenders, investors, and borrowers, and also of government authorities. In dealing with private firms, we will show how exchange market conditions fit into their profit and return calculus. In dealing briefly with governments, we will note how they might lend their weight to one side or other of the market; but we will defer our detailed discussion of this macrofinancial policy topic until Chapter 23. For the most part, the issues in this chapter belong in the area of private microfinance.

ORGANIZATION

The foreign exchange markets have no distinct geographic locations. Rather, they consist mainly of a network of commercial banks located in large cities in the biggest trading nations, with correspondents in smaller nations and cities and with tie-ins to other financial markets. Through the aid of brokers, these banks execute transactions both on behalf of their customers and for their own account. The currencies of almost all market-based, noncommunist nations are traded on a routine basis, in accordance with telephone and telex instructions to the banks to debit or credit the accounts of the parties involved. Since all large private commercial banks take part in the daily trading of almost all currencies, one can even say that there is, in effect, one huge international exchange market—an international supermarket for national monies.

The foreign exchange market has many of the textbook characteristics of a highly competitive market. Each of the "commodities" traded—the various currencies—is just about perfectly homogeneous, since, say, a check drawn on one British bank is almost perfectly equivalent to one drawn on another. Information about market developments, especially in the form of new price signals, are transmitted rapidly and freely, and transaction costs are very small when measured against the volume of a typical, large transaction. Also, the volume of daily trading is so big that most private exporters, importers, and financial managers can disregard the possibility of any price effects of their own planned currency transactions—so they are clearly price takers. If, however, the majority of them changed their market behavior in a similar fashion, there would of course be price effects, but this is a different situation. Big governments are in a category of their own.

Estimates by U.S. banks indicate that in the world as a whole, the volume of foreign exchange trading is about $100 billion per day, or around $30 trillion per year—a truly staggering amount. Technically, this estimate is based only on the market turnover of U.S. dollars. But when other currencies are exchanged for each other, the trading is very often done in two steps via the dollar (e.g., lire to dollars and dollars to pesetas, instead of lire directly into pesetas). Therefore, the figure on the dollar turnover can serve as a rough measure of the total volume of transactions in almost all pairs of currencies.

SPOT AND FORWARD TRADING

Every foreign exchange contract specifies not only the quantities of the two currencies to be exchanged but also the time of their delivery. Some contracts call for delivery within one or two days after the contract has been drawn up; these involve *spot* transactions. Others call for delivery at a specified later date. Under present practice, banks arrange currency contracts for delivery at the end of a specified number of days. These are called *forward* contracts, concluded in the interbank forward market. The most common maturities are 30, 60, 90, and 180 days. But when interested parties (perhaps including the banks themselves) can be matched up, maturities exceeding one year are also feasible. In addition, the International Monetary Market (associated with the commodity exchanges in Chicago) has since 1972 been trading in currency *futures*. These are contracts in relatively small, standardized amounts of foreign currency, to be delivered at one of four alternative annual dates (on the third Wednesday of March, June, September, or December). These contracts are very similar to the futures contracts that are available in a broad range of agricultural commodities and metals, from pork bellies to gold. A futures market is now also being established in New York City.

In regard to both forward and futures contracts, the currency amounts to be exchanged are defined at the time the contract is made. The parties are thus bound to deliver these amounts, regardless of any changes that in the meantime might occur in market conditions, or in their own economic circumstances. Every such contract represents a combination of an asset (a right to receive) and a liability (an obligation to pay) in a pair of currencies. For instance, a person who contracts to sell Swiss francs forward for dollars (or issues a Swiss franc futures contract in dollars) will have a Swiss franc liability as well as a dollar asset, as he will be obligated to deliver Swiss francs in exchange for dollars. Yet there will be no net transfer of either currency until the delivery date, except to the extent that the bank or the exchange broker requires a "margin"—a security deposit that helps ensure ultimate payment.

In each foreign exchange transaction, the amounts of the two currencies that change hands in themselves define their price relationship. And knowing the price, we can easily calculate how much a given quantity of one currency will trade for in the other. If, say, $500,000 is exchanged for £250,000 (i.e., 250,000 British pounds, or pounds "sterling"), the price, or *exchange rate*, is obviously $2.00 per pound, or £0.50 per dollar. The former can be thought of as the dollar price of sterling, and we will denote the dollar-per-pound exchange rate by $R_{\$/£}$. Then, if the currency quantities traded are denoted by $Q_\$$ and $Q_£$, we realize, especially through our understanding of barter, that $Q_\$ = Q_£ \times R_{\$/£}$. It is equally true that $Q_£ = Q_\$ \times R_{£/\$}$, since £250,000 is the product of $500,000 and £0.50.

In the United States, exchange rates are now usually defined in terms of dollars and cents per unit of foreign currency—that is, as the domestic price of that currency. Yet converting such a rate into the equivalent rate of foreign-currency units per dollar is a simple mechanical matter, since you only have to invert the former. This can be verified through a study of the recent spot-rate quotations listed in Table 19-1.

Table 19-1
Spot Exchange Rates, March 27, 1980

	U.S. Dollar	British Pound	Canadian Dollar	Deutschemark	Swiss Franc	Japanese Yen
U.S. dollar	1.000	0.460	1.188	1.924	1.832	250.1
British pound	2.176	1.000	2.584	4.185	3.985	544.0
Canadian dollar	0.842	0.387	1.000	1.620	1.542	210.6
Deutschemark	0.520	0.239	0.617	1.000	0.952	130.0
Swiss franc	0.546	0.251	0.648	1.050	1.000	136.5
Japanese yen (×1000)	3.999	1.838	4.749	7.693	7.325	1000

Note: To find the exchange rate of currency X in terms of currency Y, identify the row pertaining to X and the column pertaining to Y, and find their intersection.

Source: World Business Weekly, April 7, 1980.

European banks are often asked to quote the exchange rates of various non-American currencies in terms of their own currencies—for example, the rate of Swiss francs per Deutschemark, or vice versa. This applies to forward as well as spot quotations. From the American standpoint, these are the *cross rates* of the two European currencies. They can be derived from the dollar rates of the respective currencies, whether or not the actual currency exchange takes place via two offsetting transactions in dollars.

This is so because any discrepancy between the currency amounts obtainable one way as against another would lead to *arbitrage* transactions among the three currencies, and the arbitrage would bring the rates into line with each other. As in other markets, competition leads to consistency among prices. Therefore, the quoted $R_{SwFr/DM}$ cannot, except for fleeting moments, differ from the corresponding rate obtainable through a conversion first into and then out of dollars. A stepwise transaction of this kind would result in an effective $R_{SwFr/DM} = R_{SwFr/\$} \times R_{\$/DM}$. Assume, as in Table 19-1, that $R_{SwFr/\$} = 1.83$ and $R_{\$/DM} = 0.52$, so that, mathematically, $R_{SwFr/DM}$ ought to equal 0.95. If some banks actually quoted a higher cross rate, it would be profitable to sell marks to them and buy back the marks by first selling francs for dollars and then selling these dollars for marks. This fortunate situation could not be sustained. Arbitrage possibilities of this kind also prevent any significant differences in the rates established in different geographic centers, say, among New York, Frankfurt, London, Zurich, and Tokyo. They help create an integrated worldwide foreign exchange market.

No such mechanical consistency prevails between spot and forward (or futures) rates. Nor does it exist among forward (futures) rates for contracts with different maturities. In essence, it is a matter of "product" quality, of which delivery date is an important aspect. Just as a machine delivered today is not, in regard to its usefulness, equivalent to an "identical" machine delivered at a later date, so are currencies payable at different times also not economically equivalent. Therefore, there is no necessary equality among their market prices (exchange rates).

The difference between the currently quoted spot rate, denoted by SR, and the corresponding forward rate, denoted by FR, for a particular maturity can be of special interest. To indicate, say, a maturity 90 days from the current date, we use the subscript "90." For the sake of comparability among different currency pairs, this difference is usually expressed as an annualized percentage of the quoted spot rate. For instance, if 90-day sterling is currently traded at an $FR_{90} = \$2.02$, and the current $SR = \$2.00$, one can calculate the relative difference, in percent per annum, as follows:

$$\frac{FR_{90} - SR}{SR \times \dfrac{90}{365}} = \frac{\$2.02 - \$2.00}{\$2.00 \times \dfrac{90}{365}} = 0.04, \text{ or } 4\%$$

The fraction 90/365 here is a maturity factor that converts a 90-day rate into its annual equivalent. The 4 percent is the *forward premium* on sterling, as measured against the dollar.

A British bank might prefer to express this rate relationship in terms of sterling per dollar, and it would then be looking at the inverse of each of the rates just quoted. It would find that the 90-day forward premium on the dollar would be negative; and it would rather describe it as a 90-day *forward discount* on this currency. With asterisks indicating sterling-per-dollar equivalents of the dollar-per-sterling rates quoted above, it would calculate this forward discount in the following manner:

$$\frac{FR^*_{90} - SR^*}{SR^* \times \dfrac{90}{365}} = \frac{£.4950 - £.5000}{£.5000 \times \dfrac{90}{365}} = -0.04, \text{ or } -4\%$$

Measuring how these rates change over time can, at first, be rather confusing. What is "up" to one observer may look like "down" to somebody with a different (upside-down) perspective. But those who remember the trade-theory examples will recall that as the wheat-to-cloth price increases, so will the cloth-to-wine price decline. Describing relative exchange-rate movements is not much more complicated, at least not in a two-country framework.

To simplify the mathematics, consider the following exaggerated swings in spot or forward exchange rates. If the rate for the British pound over a certain time interval has changed from $2.00 to $3.00, this clearly represents a 50 percent *appreciation* of the pound, as measured in dollars. Conversely, this could be described as a change in the dollar value, as calculated in British currency, from £0.50 to £0.33—that is, a 33 percent dollar *depreciation*. That the percentages differ may seem peculiar, but it is only a matter of simple algebra. As it turns out, the rate of depreciation will always be lower than the corresponding rate of appreciation calculated from the same data.

Let us take this example one step farther. Assume that, meanwhile, the Deutschemark has appreciated from $0.50 to $0.60 and that cross rates are perfectly consistent. Then ask yourself, How much has the pound appreciated in terms of the Deutschemark? (Hint: $R_{DM/£} = R_{\$/£} \div R_{\$/DM}$). If you have hopes of becoming a foreign exchange trader, you will quickly realize that the answer is 25 percent.

The problem of evaluating exchange-rate movements becomes more complex when one wants to consider many exchange-rate shifts at one and the same time. For instance, one may want to describe the overall change in the international value of the dollar, or possibly compare the respective changes in the international "strengths" of the dollar and the Deutschemark. How has the dollar fared, globally speaking, and how does the dollar's performance compare with that of the mark? If the dollar declined by 16.7 percent vis-à-vis the mark (as in the previous example), does that mean that in the whole international context, the dollar's performance was also 16.7 percent "worse" than that of the mark? Not quite, since this figure does not tell us how the two currencies performed against third currencies.

Mathematically, this involves the problem of how to average the many exchange rates that pertain to each individual currency. As yardsticks, all foreign currencies are not equally important, and it is necessary somehow to weight them. But how? The most sensible answer might be to look at the volume of total international transactions conducted with each trading partner and weight the trading partners' currencies accordingly. But reliable country-by-country records exist only for merchandise trade, and the current practice is to construct the weights from these data. The resulting averages are referred to as *effective exchange rates*. Figure 19-1 shows estimated changes in the effective exchange rates of six leading currencies since the early 1970s. By this reckoning, the U.S. dollar value was virtually unchanged, while the Swiss franc and the Deutschemark had gained sharply.

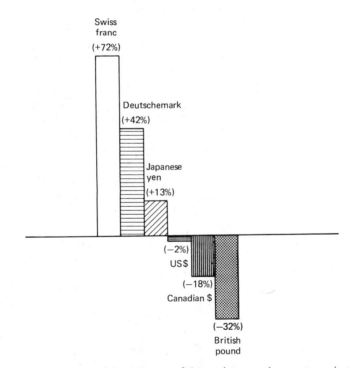

Note: The data are trade-weighted averages of changes in spot exchange rates against all major currencies, measured from the official exchange rates established on December 18, 1971.

Source: World Business Weekly, April 14, 1980 (based on calculations by Morgan Guaranty Trust Company).

Figure 19-1. Changes in effective exchange rates, 1971-80 (as of March 27, 1980).

EXPORT AND IMPORT COVER

What explains the need for forward—or futures—exchange markets? Aren't the spot markets adequate for exchanging currencies when these are actually needed? The answer, in very general terms: Most economic units want to minimize the uncertainties about their potential future income and expenditures, so long as this does not unduly reduce their profit prospects. Forward exchange contracts (and currency futures contracts) can help them do so by locking in some of the price and cost factors affecting them in the future.

Specifically, many international buyers and sellers share a common interest in reducing the uncertainties that would result from their reliance on the spot exchange market. Both parties may find forward contracts more advantageous to them than the prospect of having to undertake spot transactions later on at unpredictable exchange rates. Indeed, either party may be willing, if necessary, to pay a price for the reduction of uncertainty by paying a forward rate in excess of what he anticipates will be the future spot rate. This is something like insurance—which most people perceive to be worthwhile, even though, on average, it will in the end be a losing proposition.

Take an exporter who customarily demands payment within 90 days after the signing of his sales contracts with a foreign buyer. If he invoices the buyer in the latter's home currency, the sales contract is effectively an added foreign-exchange claim, as well as a source of revenue. (See Table 19-2, which introduces a standard flow-of-funds framework, with funds sources listed as credits and funds uses as debits.) The exporter then will be *exposed* in the foreign currency: His future home-currency proceeds from the export sale are subject to the risk that the future spot rate between the two currencies may be less favorable to him than he expects. If he wants to estimate the domestic-currency equivalent of this revenue, he has to make a spot rate forecast. Yet he will realize that his forecast is subject to error, and hence a source of risk.

To remove this risk, the exporter may enter into a contract to sell the foreign currency forward 90 days. The forward contract should be tailored exactly to the sales contract in regard both to the quantity of currency to be sold and to the timing of its delivery. Through such a contract, his foreign-currency asset will be matched by a foreign-currency liability, making the net change in his currency exposure, stemming from his export deal, zero. His flow-of-funds statement will then, as shown in Table 19-2, show a new forward exchange liability that exactly offsets his initial foreign exchange claim, as well as a new domestic-currency claim. He has *hedged*—or, in the more common terminology, *covered*—his export contract, and the forward exchange contract constitutes that cover.

In another situation, the exporter may invoice the buyer in his own—the exporter's—home currency. It will then be up to the importer to secure the amount of this currency that is required for fulfilling the contract. The importer may be content to sit it out and take his chances in regard to the spot

Table 19-2
Currency Exposure and Cover for Exports and Imports

<table>
<tr><td colspan="2" align="center">*Exporter*
(Invoicing in foreign currency)</td></tr>
<tr><td>Uses of Funds (Debits)</td><td>Sources of Funds (Credits)</td></tr>
<tr><td colspan="2" align="center">Export contract</td></tr>
<tr><td>+ Foreign-currency claim,
  payable in 90 days</td><td>+ Revenue (from goods sold)</td></tr>
<tr><td colspan="2" align="center">Forward exchange contract</td></tr>
<tr><td>+ Domestic-currency claim,
  payable in 90 days</td><td>+ Foreign-currency debt,
  payable in 90 days</td></tr>
<tr><td colspan="2" align="center">*Importer*
(Invoiced in foreign currency)</td></tr>
<tr><td>Uses of Funds (Debits)</td><td>Sources of Funds (Credits)</td></tr>
<tr><td colspan="2" align="center">Import contract</td></tr>
<tr><td>+ Expenditure (on goods
  bought)</td><td>+ Foreign-currency debt,
  payable in 90 days</td></tr>
<tr><td colspan="2" align="center">Forward exchange contract</td></tr>
<tr><td>+ Foreign-currency claim,
  payable in 90 days</td><td>+ Domestic-currency debt,
  payable in 90 days</td></tr>
</table>

rate at the time he has to pay up. Or he may play it safe, buying the exporter's currency at the going 90-day forward rate in exchange for his own currency. Through such a cover, he will eliminate the added foreign-exchange exposure and risk that is associated with his import transaction. Table 19-2 shows how he will match his commercial foreign-currency debt by a contract to buy the requisite amount of foreign currency forward in the appropriate maturity. His import expenditure will then indirectly produce domestic-currency debt, very much as if he had actually been invoiced in domestic currency.

Exporting and importing firms thus have a choice as to the handling of their commercial contracts. When should they cover? This question involves weighing their expected earnings, costs, and risks against their overall objectives and financial situations. The alternative strategies are outlined in Table 19-3. An exporter may find that the pertinent forward rate, measured in domestic currency units per unit of foreign currency, is higher than his estimate of the spot rate for the same currency and time of delivery. By covering, his prospective earnings will then actually improve. In another case, an importer may find that the pertinent forward rate is lower than the rate he estimates to have to pay in the spot market later on for the same currency. It seems like a bargain. In either case, there is no reason to hesitate, since forward cover seems profitable. The insurance analogy will then not be appropriate, since insurance always carries a positive cost.

In other situations, forward rates may look unattractive compared with the anticipated future spot rates. Some exporters may regard forward rates on the currencies they are invoicing in to be comparatively "low." Some importers, dealing in other markets or simply having different views of future spot-rate changes, may consider the forward rates relevant to them to be comparatively "high." All these commodity traders must evaluate the likely magnitude of the forward-spot rate differential and the degree of risk connected with it.

If they are trading continuously in several foreign markets, the commodity traders' overall financial positions will probably be well diversified in regard to the currency composition of their cash flows. Paying the apparent cost of forward cover may then seem unnecessary. On the other hand, firms with only occasional sales or purchases abroad might opt for the relative safety of being covered, despite the apparent cost. Their forward cover will thus be a kind of insurance policy. It is true that once their commercial and foreign-exchange contracts have been fulfilled, they may find that their forward cover actually reduced their profits. But this is a normal possibility in any risk-avoiding business strategy. Financial managers do not have the benefit of hindsight, and the occasional failure to realize a chancy profit does not indicate imprudent or inefficient management.

Table 19-3
Exchange Market Strategies for Commodity Traders

Category of Trader	Strategy	Motive for Strategy
Exporter	Cover, via forward sale of contracted future foreign-exchange proceeds	Offset risky foreign-currency asset (account receivable); maximize anticipated home-currency earnings (if $FR_n > E(SR)_n$)
	Spot sale of foreign-exchange proceeds upon their receipt	Maximize anticipated home-currency earnings (if $E(SR)_n > FR_n$)
Importer	Cover, via forward purchase of the foreign exchange needed for contracted future payment	Offset risky foreign-currency debt (account payable); minimize anticipated home-currency costs (if $FR_n < E(SR)_n$)
	Spot purchase of needed foreign exchange at the time of payment	Minimize anticipated home-currency costs (if $E(SR)_n < FR_n$)

Definitions of symbols: FR_n = currently quoted forward exchange rate, in domestic currency units per unit of foreign currency, for delivery in n days (when foreign-exchange receipt or payment is to take place. $E(SR)_n$ = spot exchange rate, in domestic currency units per unit of foreign currency, expected, on the basis of current estimates, to prevail at a time n days into the future.

INTEREST ARBITRAGE

The foreign exchange activities of lenders, investors, and borrowers are more complex than those of commodity traders, and also more crucial to their profits and incomes. These parties usually have to enter the foreign exchange markets twice—in connection both with their initial transactions and with the associated repayments or returns. The influence of their foreign exchange strategies on their profits and incomes is especially strong because their profit margins, relative to the volume of their activities, tend to be thin. Therefore, a miscalculation of an exchange-rate movement could, for them, easily turn a large expected profit into a large actual loss.

Let us first consider outflows of funds, via lending or purchases of securities and with the contracts defined in foreign currency. Lenders and investors try to take advantage of interest and return differences between different national money markets (or between them and the Euromarkets). They are said to be engaged in *interest arbitrage*, in these cases via the medium of the exchange markets. They continuously renew or readjust their asset portfolios by reinvesting the proceeds of the redemption or sales of securities that they previously had purchased. If funds of this kind flow from the domestic market to a foreign market, this will, from the domestic standpoint, represent *outward* arbitrage. From the standpoint of the country receiving the funds, it will be a matter of *inward* arbitrage. The ultimate purpose of such transactions is to generate home-currency returns to the arbitrageurs. These returns will depend on exchange rates, as well as on nominal interest rates, yields, or returns payable in foreign currency.

The lender, in particular, has two distinct options—to cover his newly acquired foreign-currency asset or to leave it uncovered. What will his return calculation look like? If he does cover, it means that he will acquire two foreign exchange contracts: one spot purchase contract and one forward sales contract. As shown in Table 19-4, he will then end up with a net new claim in domestic currency, in lieu of the foreign-currency asset, so that he will avoid incurring any foreign exchange exposure. Such combinations of matching spot and forward contracts—one a sale, the other a purchase—are called *swaps*.

The foreign-currency lender who follows this strategy will be able to count on a definite rate of home-currency return, i^*, that consists of two components—the foreign currency yield, i_f, and the gain or loss on the swap. The latter is equal to the forward premium or discount, as the case may be, on the foreign currency, measured in percent per annum. Using our previous approximate formula,

$$i^* = i_f + \frac{FR_n - SR}{SR \times \dfrac{n}{365}}$$

Table 19-4
Currency Exposure and Cover for International Financial Transactions

Lender (foreign-currency security buyer)	
Uses of Funds (Debits)	Sources of Funds (Credits)

Loan contract (security purchase)	
+ Foreign-currency asset, maturing in 90 days	
− Domestic-currency deposit	

Forward-exchange sales contract	
+ Domestic-currency claim, payable in 90 days	+ Foreign-currency debt, payable in 90 days

Borrower (issuer of foreign-currency debt)	
Uses of Funds (Debits)	Sources of Funds (Credits)

Loan contract	
+ Domestic-currency deposit	+ Foreign-currency debt, payable in 90 days

Forward-exchange purchase contract	
+ Foreign-currency claim, payable in 90 days	+ Domestic-currency debt, payable in 90 days

where n is the number of days to maturity, both in the loan contract (or security purchases) and in the forward exchange contract.

For example, an American firm has an opportunity to place funds in Switzerland at a local, Swiss franc yield of 10 percent per annum for 180 days. The firm checks the going spot and forward rates for this currency and finds that there is a 6 percent per annum forward premium on it (i.e., the 180-day forward rate exceeds the spot rate by 3 percent, which converts into a 6 percent rate per annum). Its total home-currency yield, i^*, on such an investment would then be $10\% + 6\% = 16\%$. Is this a "high" or "low" return? The most immediate comparison is with domestic 180-day investment, and the yield in this case, i, is assumed to be 15 percent. We sense that Switzerland has a 1 percent edge and that the Swiss option thus is preferable. To conceptualize the comparison, we can calculate the *covered interest differential*, CID, as the difference between the home-currency yield on foreign investment and the domestic yield, so that

$$CID = i^* - i$$
$$= i_f + \text{forward premium (or, − forward discount)} - i$$
$$= 10\% + 6\% - 15\% = 1\%$$

Naturally, the positive CID suggests that, unless even better investment possibilities exist elsewhere, funds should be shifted toward Switzerland.

But what about the option of remaining uncovered? This is one of the strategies listed in Table 19-5. It would involve a spot purchase of Swiss francs, the investment of these francs in the Swiss money market, and the intention to reconvert the franc proceeds of this investment (principal plus interest) when the funds are repaid. The precise home-currency return cannot be calculated, since the future spot rate for the Swiss franc cannot be known beforehand. The firm's research department may, however, make a forecast, perhaps indicating an annualized anticipated rate of Swiss franc appreciation amounting to 4 percent (i.e., an anticipated increase of 2 percent over the 180 days). The expected uncovered home-currency return will therefore be 10% +

Table 19-5
Exchange Market Strategies for Lenders and Borrowers

Category of Transactor	Strategy	Motive for Strategy
	Spot purchase of foreign exchange, and a simultaneous forward sale of the forthcoming foreign-exchange proceeds from repayment	Offset risky foreign-currency claim (loan); maximize home-currency returns (if $FR > E(SR)_n$)
Foreign-currency lender		
	Spot purchase of foreign exchange, and spot sale of foreign-exchange proceeds from repayment upon their receipt.	Maximize anticipated home-currency return (if $E(SR)_n > FR_n$)
	Spot sale of the foreign exchange just obtained, and a simultaneous forward purchase of the foreign exchange needed for the subsequent repayment	Offset risky foreign-currency debt (loan liability); minimize home-currency cost of debt service (if $FR_n < E(SR)_n$)
Foreign-currency borrower		
	Spot sale of the foreign exchange just obtained, and a spot purchase of the needed foreign exchange at the time of repayment	Minimize anticipated home-currency cost of debt service (if $E(SR)_n < FR_n$)

Definitions of symbols: see Table 19-3.

4% = 14%. This option is undoubtedly less attractive than domestic investment: Its expected yield is lower; and in addition, it is risky.

At other times, the choice may not be so clear-cut. Assume that new data, say on price trends in the Swiss economy, call for a sudden revision of the estimated Swiss franc appreciation to a rate of 8 percent per annum. If money market yields are unchanged, the expected dollar yield on investment in Switzerland will be 10% + 8% = 18%—a rather impressive rate, it would seem.

Yet if this were to become an isolated instance of foreign investment, and if there are no offsetting accounts payable in Swiss francs, it would be a risky proposition. But if the firm has developed a set of required foreign-exchange "risk premiums," it should still be able to reach a rational decision. Perhaps it has set its current required Swiss-franc premium at 3 percent. In this case, the uncovered Swiss-franc alternative just breaks even with domestic investment, and covered Swiss-franc investment again becomes the preferred employment of the available funds.

Comparable opportunities for interest arbitrage exist also for borrowers, whenever they can adjust their maturing liabilities. Borrowers with access to different national or international credit markets can, through the arbitrage technique, shift their sources of loanable funds. In this way, they can try to minimize their home-currency borrowing costs, either on a covered or on an uncovered basis. See Tables 19-4 and 19-5 for alternative strategies. A low foreign interest rate on, say, short-term bank loans might make foreign-currency borrowing seem attractive, but uncertainty about the future spot rate may introduce an extra implicit cost. Yet the borrower can eliminate this exchange risk by simultaneously buying the amount of foreign currency forward that he will later need for his repayment. This will constitute his cover. By so doing, he may increase, or decrease, his estimated home-currency borrowing cost, depending on the relationship between the forward rate and the expected future spot rate. Alternatively, if the price of forward exchange looks too high to him, he may indeed, depending on his overall portfolio situation, take his chances by leaving himself uncovered.

The formulas we used for investors can then be reinterpreted so as to pertain to borrowers as well, with interest rates indicating their nominal local costs of funds in the two money markets. Of course, to borrowers the lower-cost markets will be viewed as the more favorable, and they may decide to tap foreign markets with negative CIDs. Or they may take the uncovered, riskier route—borrowing relatively cheaply abroad while hoping that the foreign currency will not appreciate so much as to wipe out the negative foreign-interest differential. But by using the same formulas, we do not mean to suggest that the relevant interest rates will normally be the same for investors and borrowers. In reality, markets are segmented, and not all parties will have access to the same funds sources or outlets, at least not at the same rates. Transaction costs can also vary. One foreign money market may then at the same time serve as a source of funds to certain borrowers and as an outlet for funds to certain investors residing in the same country.

INTEREST PARITY

As interest arbitrageurs try to take advantage of day-to-day or week-to-week interest-rate and exchange-rate changes, their actions will alter demand and supply conditions in money and exchange markets. This may put pressure on spot and forward rates, and possibly also on interest rates. In particular, outward arbitrage will tend to raise spot exchange demand and therefore put upward pressure on the spot rate (as before, defined as the domestic price of foreign currency). If most arbitrageurs cover, they will at the same time increase their supplies of forward exchange and thus put downward pressure on the forward rate. Conversely, when there is an incentive for funds to flow in the opposite direction—that is, inward—there will be a tendency for the spot rate to drop and the forward rate to rise.

Consequently, once a new arbitrage incentive has emerged, forces will be set in motion which will start to reduce or eliminate this incentive. This is but another application of the general rule that arbitrage activity will tend to wipe out price differentials, and unless the markets are artificially segmented, arbitrage will help to integrate them into a larger whole. Any financial development affecting either national interest rates or spot and forward exchange rates will produce counteracting pressures that tend to restore the preexisting net return and cost relationships.

In regard to covered short-term funds, such international return and cost equality—under which $i^* = i$—is called *interest parity*. When parity prevails, there is, by definition, a zero covered interest differential—i.e., CID = 0—and no incentive for further arbitrage flows. But if parity is actually observed on a particular day, this does not mean that no arbitrage transactions have occurred or are occurring. On the contrary, the existence of parity suggests that large arbitrage movements might have occurred prior to the moment parity was achieved. And the continuation of approximate parity may require continued funds movements.

The interrelationship between interest and exchange rates, and between these rates and covered arbitrage flows, is illustrated in Figure 19-2. The vertical axis measures the yield differential for comparable securities between the domestic and a foreign money market. The differential may, of course, sometimes be in favor of the foreign market, sometimes the domestic market. The horizontal axis measures the forward premium or discount on the foreign currency. The diagonal is the interest-parity line. It depicts all possible combinations of interest differentials and forward premiums, or discounts, that mathematically would produce interest parity.

It is obvious, both intuitively and from the interest-parity formula, that large positive foreign interest differentials—or "margins"—will, in theory, be associated with large forward discounts. Simply put, relative gains from interest differentials will then be offset by losses on the foreign exchange swaps. Conversely, if there were gains to be made through foreign exchange swaps, parity would imply that these gains were compensated for by

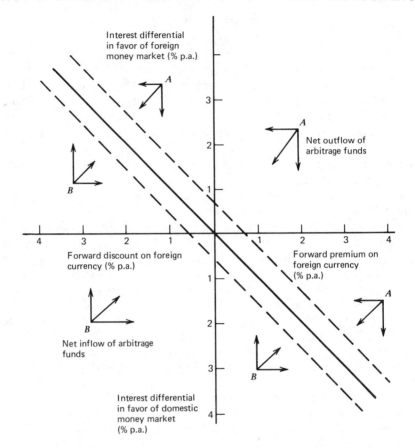

Figure 19-2. Interest parity and flows of covered arbitrage funds.

comparable losses of interest income caused by the switching of money markets.

Figure 19-2 also shows the direction of the capital flows that will tend to occur if the interest differential and the forward premium (discount) are temporarily inconsistent with parity conditions. If an interest differential in favor of the foreign money market is combined with a forward premium, or only a relatively small forward discount, there will be a net incentive to move arbitrage funds abroad, and thus a tendency for a capital outflow. The same holds if a small interest differential in favor of the domestic market is combined with a large forward premium on the foreign currency. Graphically, such situations lie above and to the right of the parity line, as indicated by the points labeled *A*. As these funds move out of the domestic money market, through the exchange market and into the foreign money market, the forward premium may start to shrink, or the foreign interest-rate margin may start to decline, or there will be a combination of these two effects. The arrows drawn from points *A* suggest these various possibilities.

The converse situation is illustrated by points *B*. Here there are net gains to be made through a substitution of domestic for foreign securities. The market correction of this deviation from parity, carried out through capital inflows, may entail exchange-rate shifts, or interest-rate shifts, or both. These possibilities are suggested by the arrows drawn from points *B*.

But since perfect interest parity will not normally be attained, there will typically be a *band* of possible combinations of interest rates and forward premiums (and discounts). The broken lines on each side of the parity line in Figure 19-2 are meant to suggest such a parity band. As the edges of this band are approached from the outside, the corrective capital flows are likely to diminish. Yet the width of the band cannot be precisely defined. It will vary among different pairs of money markets and will be subject to changes over time. Generally, the larger and "deeper" the two money markets, and the larger the volume of overall exchange market activity in the two currencies, the smaller the likely departures from parity and the narrower the band. Whether parity is achieved ultimately depends on all the forces in both the spot and the forward markets, and especially on how a joint equilibrium is established for them. This is a highly technical problem, discussed in the Advanced Material section at the end of this chapter.

Looking at daily rate quotations on national money-market instruments (e.g., treasury bills in New York, London, Frankfurt, Montreal, Zurich, and Tokyo), one frequently finds covered arbitrage margins of up to 1 or 1.5 percent in favor of one center over another. This is not really so surprising, since there are many types of spot and forward transactions not related to interest arbitrage, and since not all arbitrage transactions are covered—that is, covered interest arbitrage apparently does not dominate market conditions.

Table 19-6
Covered Arbitrage Yields in Eurocurrency Market
(Average quotations on July 26, 1979)

Currency	90-Day Interest Rate (in % p.a.)	Spot Rate (in U.S. cents)	90-Day Forward Rate (in U.S. cents)	90-Day Forward Premium (P) or Discount (D) (in % p.a.)	Covered Yield to U.S. Investors (in % p.a.)
U.S. dollar	11.0	—	—	—	—
British pound	14.0	232.9	231.3	2.9D	11.1
Canadian dollar	11.3	85.59	85.50	0.4D	10.9
Deutschemark	6.4	54.98	55.62	4.7P	11.1
Swiss franc	1.3	60.75	62.26	9.7P	11.0
Japanese yen	5.6	0.4653	0.4717	5.4P	11.1

The Eurocurrency market, however, approaches closely a single integrated money market, and interest rates in it interreact very easily and quickly with exchange rates. This is even more true for the daily loan and deposit transactions among the Eurobanks themselves—the hypercompetitive core of the market. Table 19-6 shows a set of recent interest rates payable on 90-day interbank Eurocurrency deposits denominated in different currencies, along with the spot and forward exchange rates for these currencies. The data have been interpreted from the perspective of a U.S. financial investor—or somebody who thinks in terms of U.S. dollars. The table thus shows the covered U.S. dollar yields obtainable through Eurocurrency deposits in nondollar currencies, as well as on deposits in Eurodollars. The yields were virtually identical The three low-interest currencies—the Swiss franc, the Japanese yen and the Deutschemark—all had the compensating advantages of forward premiums. Conversely, the high-interest-bearing British pound was subject to a large forward discount. And by comparing any one pair of currencies, one can quickly verify that each interest differential was matched by a forward premium on the lower-interest currency of roughly the same percentage magnitude.

SPECULATION

Forward exchange contracts can serve purposes other than that of providing cover for commodity or security transactions. Some market participants try to take advantage of apparent differences between the quoted forward rates and the rates they foresee will prevail in the future spot market. If an American firm finds that the 60-day forward rate for pound sterling is below the level at which it expects the sterling spot rate to be in 60 days, there will appear to be a chance for it to profit from this price differential. To do so, it will have to enter into a contract to buy sterling 60 days forward, with the intention of selling the same amount of sterling in the spot market 60 days into the future. It can then expect to make a profit equal to the apparent percentage difference between these two rates, multiplied by the amount of its forward commitment. Hence if the forward rate was $2.11 and the *expected* future spot rate were $2.13, a £100,000 contract would produce a *potential* profit equal to $2000.

Meanwhile, other Americans may have other spot-rate expectations. They may regard forward sterling to be overpriced relative to these expectations and will therefore believe they can profit from a forward sale of this currency. When the forward contract matures, they instruct their banks to purchase the amount of sterling they owe in the spot market and to credit them with any dollar profits resulting from these two transactions.

Forward purchase or sales contracts of these kinds produce foreign-exchange risk. As indicated in Table 19-7, if sterling, contrary to expectations, appreciates, those who have sold this currency forward will suffer losses. On the other hand, for forward buyers this turn of events may create profits in excess of what they had anticipated. This is the name of the game of chance.

Table 19-7
Exchange Market Strategies for Speculators

Expected Spot-Rate Change	Strategy	Profit or Loss Outcome
Increase so that $E(SR)_n > FR_n$	Forward purchase of foreign exchange, for resale in the spot market upon maturity	If expectation is borne out, a margin of realized profit = $SR_n - FR_n$ If expectation is not borne out, a margin of realized loss = $FR_n - SR_n$
Decrease so that $E(SR)_n < FR_n$	Forward sale of foreign exchange, with settlement through spot foreign-exchange purchase upon maturity	If expectation is borne out, a margin of realized profit = $FR_n - SR_n$ If expectation is not borne out, a margin of realized loss = $SR_n - FR_n$

Definitions of symbols: $E(SR)_n$ and FR_n: see Table 19-3; SR_n = actual spot rate emerging n days into the future.

Such forward transactions, not linked to any specific commodity or security transactions, are described as forward-exchange *speculation*, or "pure" speculation. The term unfortunately has undertones of immoral, antisocial behavior, and multinational firms take pains to persuade the public and their stockholders that they do not themselves speculate. In their interpretation, they only take prudent steps to protect their profits against unfavorable exchange-rate movements. But these steps do entail forward-market speculation, which at times turns out to be an extra source of profits, at times a drain on profits. Regardless of the actual outcomes, it seems absurd to apply other moral standards to foreign exchange transactions than to other risky steps in the ordinary course of business—for example, routine adjustments of inventories along with shifting anticipations about future product prices.

In fact, speculators of all kinds can perform a useful social service. They help reduce the segmentation of markets and bring yields and costs into closer accord with social opportunity costs, for the benefit of a more efficient resource allocation. Thus, forward speculators who correctly foresee future spot-rate trends can help bring forward rates into line with the emerging spot rates and lessen the distortive effects of "unrealistic" forward rates. Surely, speculators may miscalculate and occasionally generate perverse price, return, and cost pressures. Yet the successful profit makers stand a better chance of surviving in the market. They are likely to dominate the picture over the long haul.

Pure foreign-exchange speculation does not in itself involve a commitment of funds, apart from required "margins" payable in advance. And typically, the speculator does not want to use up any foreign currency that he may hold in meeting his obligation to deliver, nor does he care to take delivery of the foreign currency due him. That is why he just instructs his bank to liquidate his forward contract, on his behalf, in the spot market when it is due.

There is a speculative element also in uncovered exports and imports and in uncovered interest arbitrage. These transactions are risky, too. This may be a crucial part of the profit calculus. Especially the uncovered arbitrageur will wear two hats, one of which is that of the pure speculator, the other being that of the money market investor. The common feature of all exchange market speculation in this broad sense is exposure to unforeseeable spot-rate movements in the future.

GOVERNMENT TRANSACTIONS

In addition to these private commercial and financial transactions, there are several types of government transactions in the exchange markets. All governments undertake some foreign expenditures that may require currency conversions, either by the spending agencies themselves or by the foreign recipients of the funds. Governments also receive funds from abroad, especially from other governments with which they have trade, aid, or credit agreements, or military relations. Unless the foreign-currency funds received are used for immediate expenditure outside the recipient country, they may have to be exchanged for local funds in the spot market. And unless payments abroad can be financed out of existing government holdings of foreign currency, the required currency may have to be purchased in the spot market.

Governments also enter the spot markets for a more special reason—for the sake of *intervention*. This term denotes spot sales or purchases undertaken by government treasury departments, special government currency boards, or central banks for the specific purpose of putting pressure on the spot rate. The intention may be to increase the spot rate, or to lessen its ongoing decline—or to decrease it, or to modify its upward trend. According to official pronouncements, the authorities usually intervene so as to "stabilize" the spot rate, either at a steady level or at what may look like a longer-run trend. Yet "stability" becomes an elusive goal when the basic private market forces are changing in an unforeseeable fashion, perhaps in response to intervention itself. So it is an open question whether intervention in fact does make spot rates more stable than they otherwise would have been. The international rules and practices that govern intervention policies will be examined in detail in Chapters 24 and 25, but their immediate consequences, and their interconnections with other market forces, belong in this chapter.

Of course, standard demand and supply analysis is applicable. U.S. intervention *sales* of foreign currency, such as pound sterling, will place downward pressure on the dollar-per-pound spot rate, at least as long as other market forces do not respond so violently as to fully compensate for these sales. U.S. intervention *purchases*, conversely, will tend to raise the spot rate above the level which it would otherwise reach. Such sales or purchases are of course settled in U.S. dollars—that is, deposit balances with Federal Reserve banks. From the British perspective, the former action will look like purchases of dollars, paid for in pounds. It shifts the relative availability of the two currencies toward more pounds and fewer dollars. The latter action—U.S. purchases of pounds—will to the British look like additional dollar supplies, offered in payment for these purchases. This can be viewed as a step to reduce the relative availability of pounds, and hence to support the pound's price in the market. The same applies if the U.K. authorities are intervening through purchases or sales of U.S. dollars (against British pounds), for the private market does not really know or care where the new government demands or supplies are coming from.

Table 19-8
Strategies of Government Exchange-Market Intervention

Exchange-Rate Objective	Type of Intervention	Effect on Private Demand and Supply
Reduce (possibly, stabilize) the spot rate (SR)	Spot sales of foreign exchange	Induce an offsetting excess private demand, especially stemming from outward arbitrage
Increase (possibly, stabilize) the spot rate (SR)	Spot purchases of foreign exchange	Induce an offsetting excess private supply, especially stemming from inward arbitrage
Reduce the forward rate (FR_n)	Forward sales of foreign exchange	Induce an offsetting excess private demand, especially stemming from the return of covered inward arbitrage funds
Increase the forward rate (FR_n)	Forward purchases of foreign exchange	Induce an offsetting excess private supply, especially stemming from the return of covered outward arbitrage funds

Definitions of symbols: SR: current spot rate, in domestic currency units per unit of foreign currency; FR_n: see Table 19-3.

The spot intervention strategies associated with different spot rate objectives on the part of the authorities are outlined in Table 19-8. The last column in this table indicates the typical effect of each type of intervention on the private supply-demand balance in the market, and the reader will find the same effects illustrated graphically in Figure 19-3. Think of it this way: Government intervention upsets the private market balance that otherwise would have been achieved, and it forces private parties to generate the extra demand or supply required to restore balance in face of government intervention. Government spot sales—an added supply force in the market for foreign currency—requires, for the sake of balance, a matching addition to private purchases—added private demand. Conversely, spot intervention purchases would push the private market participants to supply the added amount of foreign currency that the authorities are absorbing. What motivates these private demand or supply shifts? A change in the spot rate, induced by these intervention moves.

The diagram in Figure 19-3 pertains to the market for pound sterling, and we ignore all complications connected with the existence of other currencies. Left to its own devices, the private market would be cleared at a spot rate, SR, equal to $2.15 per pound. This is where the private demand curve, $D_\text{£} D_\text{£}$,

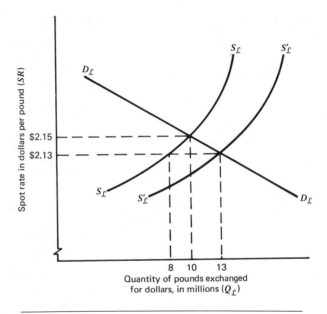

	Without intervention	With intervention
Private demand	£10 mil.	£13 mil.
Private supply	10	8
Net government supply	—	5
Spot rate	$2.15	$2.13

Figure 19-3. Intervention and spot-market equilibrium.

intersects the private supply curve, $S_{\pounds}S_{\pounds}$. On this day, described by the diagram, the volume of pounds traded, $Q_{\pounds}$, would be £10 million. And the volume of U.S. dollars exchanged for spot pounds would be $SR \times Q_{\pounds} = \$2.15 \times$ 10 million, or \$21.5 million. But the U.S. or U.K. authorities intervene, supplying £5 million and creating an aggregate private-government supply schedule, $S_{\pounds'}S_{\pounds'}$, lying at a distance of £5 million to the right of $S_{\pounds}S_{\pounds}$. The new market balance requires an SR equal to \$2.13. Intervention has thus lowered the spot rate by \$0.02. At this rate, there is an excess private spot demand for pounds exactly equal to the government intervention supply.

The reality behind this result is, most likely, that American interest arbitrageurs have jumped at the opportunity to purchase the government-supplied pounds at what they perceive as a new bargain rate. Or, put it differently: The reduced spot rate has produced an added covered or uncovered yield advantage on investment in London, as compared to New York. This advantage induces American and British investors to shift additional funds to the British money market. Also, both American and British borrowers might now borrow additional amounts in New York, rather than in London. Why? Americans will have less incentive to borrow in London, since at the new, reduced spot rate, the dollar proceeds from such loans will be smaller and their percentage borrowing costs higher. Britons, however, will receive more pounds per dollar borrowed in New York, since each dollar now converts into £1/2.13, or £0.469, instead of £1/2.15, or £0.465. The spot-rate change may seem insignificant, but seemingly small spot-rate shifts, via their effects on yield differentials, can be of great consequence for short-term international lending and borrowing.

This means that private demands and supplies will be highly elastic and that even large amounts of intervention can quickly generate offsetting private demand or supply shifts. A further consequence is that the authorities will be limited in their ability to manipulate spot rates. The more elastic is private demand and supply, the larger the volume of intervention necessary to achieve a desired spot-rate adjustment. This is nothing more than elementary microeconomic market analysis. To review this subject, the reader might redraw Figure 19-3 with steeper, less elastic $D_{\pounds}D_{\pounds}$ and $S_{\pounds}S_{\pounds}$ curves; in this case, the amount of intervention sales required to push the spot rate down by \$0.02 per pound will be smaller.

Governments and central banks occasionally intervene in the forward exchange markets as well. The main purpose of forward intervention is to change the forward premium or discount on foreign currency so as to alter the direction or amount of short-term capital flows into or out of the country (see Table 19-8). For instance, the British authorities have on many occasions sold dollars forward (i.e., purchased pounds forward) in times of crisis for the British currency. Their intention has been to increase the dollar-per-pound forward rate—the forward pound price—and thereby reduce the forward discount on the pound. In this way, they have tried to create a covered interest differential in favor of Britain, with the consequence that short-term funds would return to it.

The problem with this strategy is that when their forward contracts are to be liquidated, the U.K. authorities may have to draw on their dwindling holdings of dollars. The forward intervention will then only have postponed inevitable British losses of dollar assets. Alternatively, the British authorities may have to purchase the needed dollars in the spot market and allow the pound to depreciate after all, contrary to their intentions. Under more favorable circumstances, the intervention may be a useful stopgap during a temporary market disturbance that has ceased by the time the forward intervention contracts mature. Or it may buy time for the implementation of economic policy reforms that help correct the problems that produced the original capital outflows. If such reforms are in progress, the authorities may choose to renew their forward contracts as they mature and thus postpone the day of reckoning. But their reform program may then gradually lose credibility and invite speculative attacks on the currency. In itself, neither spot nor forward intervention can permanently conceal or thwart basic market forces.

SUMMARY

Foreign exchange transactions involve bank deposits denominated in different currencies. The foreign exchange markets provide a mechanism for settling international debts arising from commodity trade, lending, borrowing, and security transactions among parties residing in different countries. Along with spot contracts, the markets offer forward and futures contracts in a variety of short-term maturities. Forward and futures contracts are used as a means of reducing foreign exchange risks. They can provide cover for exports, imports, and interest arbitrage positions. They can also serve as instruments for pure speculation.

Spot and forward markets are linked to each other via covered arbitrage flows. The stronger this link, the more likely it is that interest arbitrage will produce interest parity among the leading national money markets. But the tendency toward parity is sometimes undermined by speculative pressure in forward markets. Governments, acting alone or in cooperation with each other, try to manipulate and stabilize exchange rates through market intervention, especially in the spot market. The purpose and methods of intervention are matters of macroeconomic policy and international policy cooperation—the subjects of Chapters 23 through 25.

ADVANCED MATERIAL:
Determination of Spot and Forward Rates

We have analyzed how different participants in the exchange markets can enter into spot or forward contracts, and how spot and forward rates will affect their return, profit, and cost calculations. From this analysis, it is obvious that any given change in the spot or forward rate will act as an incentive for the market participants to change the extent of their foreign exchange supplies or demands. After all, these rates are a kind of prices, and price changes affect the quantities demanded and supplied. We have, however, failed to explain how the totality of demand and supply forces in the spot and forward markets determine these rates, and we have not shown how different market participants interact with one another through their influence on these rates. We will try to fill these gaps in this section, which attempts to pull together the main market elements and present a broader, more integrated view of the foreign exchange markets.

Table 19-9
Main Components of Foreign-Exchange Demand and Supply

Demand	*Supply*
Spot Market	
Uncovered imports (currently payable)	Uncovered exports (currently payable)
Outward interest arbitrage	Inward interest arbitrage
Liquidations of speculative forward contracts (contracts to sell foreign currency)	Liquidations of speculative forward contracts (contracts to purchase foreign currency)
Official intervention in support of foreign currency	Official intervention in support of the domestic currency
Forward Markets	
Covered imports (currently contracted, payable later)	Covered exports (currently contracted, payable later)
Covered inward interest arbitrage (return flow of funds)	Covered outward interest arbitrage (return flow of funds)
Pure speculation in favor of foreign currency	Pure speculation in favor of the domestic currency
Official intervention (to encourage capital outflows)	Official intervention (to encourage capital inflows)

As a first step, the main components of demand and supply in spot and forward markets are summarized in Table 19-9. In addition to commodity traders and interest arbitrageurs, two special categories of spot transactions deserve to be noted. On the demand side, there may be speculators who are now liquidating their previously concluded contracts for the forward sale of foreign currency. Speculators who had sold, say, sterling forward, will currently have to purchase the same amounts of sterling spot so as to be able to deliver under these contracts. In addition, the domestic or foreign authorities may be purchasing foreign currency, presumably to strengthen its international value—that is, to raise SR. On the spot-supply side, we have listed the converse types of transactions—spot sales stemming from liquidations of speculative contracts to purchase foreign currency forward, and possible government intervention in support of the domestic currency—that is, aimed at reducing SR. The columns for the forward markets list the familiar categories—covered commodity trade, covered interest arbitrage, pure forward speculation, and possible government intervention on either side of the market.

Deriving Demands and Supplies

In accordance with conventional demand-and-supply analysis, we must account for the interdependence between the quantities demanded and supplied, on the one hand, and the exchange rates on the other. Although the individual transactors will normally regard the rates as given, their aggregate responses to changes in these rates will in turn influence these rates. Market equilibrium will require two conditions to be met: (1) all transactors have adjusted themselves to the going rates, and (2) their behavior is mutually consistent, so that the markets will clear.

It seems almost a foregone conclusion that demand will respond negatively to exchange rates, whereas supply will respond positively. Our analogies with commodity markets reinforce this presumption. But we have to make sure that this is truly so. One special reason why the conventional demand-and-supply analysis might have to be amended is that what looks like a demand from one currency's standpoint will be a supply from another currency's standpoint. The way we describe demand for foreign currency must therefore also be a plausible description of the supply of the home currency.

Commodity Trade

We shall concentrate most of our discussion on commodity trade, taking it as a prototype for all private exchange-market transactions. We shall ignore multilateral complications, as if Britain were actually synonymous with the entire rest of the world. And we will, for now, focus on the spot market. In so doing, we are making a leap in time, pretending that commodity traders react to the current spot rate even though they probably made their commercial commitments some time ago. To rationalize this procedure, let us pretend that they had accurately foreseen the spot rate and geared their behavior to it, rather than merely to subjective anticipations. Had they in actuality taken out forward cover, the same analysis could anyhow have been applied to the forward market instead.

Two technical issues need to be resolved. Do the American and British exporters invoice in pounds or dollars? This, we ought to realize, is actually a nonissue. In either case, one party will have to enter the exchange market, either as a seller or as a buyer of pounds; neither the Americans nor the British are assumed to be willing to accumulate or decumulate the currency of the other country. The second problem is more critical. Are the prices of the traded goods affected by changes in the spot rates? And if so, how? This is a matter of how the exchange market is linked to particular commodity markets, and it will have a bearing on the quantities of pounds passing through the spot market. Rather than introduce a full-scale analysis of the interconnected commodity markets, we will make a couple of alternative, black-and-white assumptions. There will naturally be intermediate cases, too.

In our illustration, the U.S. demand for pounds will of course be connected with the U.S. demand for British products. This demand will depend on the dollar prices of the imported products in the United States; what pound prices the British pay for them is, in and of itself, immaterial to the American buyers. Suppose American purchases account for only a small fraction of the total British supply of the traded products. The amount of American purchases then has no significant effect on their pound price. We might then say that the product price is *rigid in pounds*. A higher dollar-per-pound rate, SR, will in this case automatically make the dollar price in the United States proportionately higher, with a doubling of the spot rate for the pound resulting in a doubling of the U.S. price of, say, Scotch. This will inevitably cause a drop in the quantity of this product that Americans demand. The demand for pounds will then be directly proportional to the demand for the imported commodity, at all spot rates, and have the *same elasticity*.

Suppose, alternatively, that American purchases account for a large portion of total British sales of a particular product group—say, sweaters. American demand will then influence its pound price, both in Britain and to non-British buyers. Especially in the short run, larger American purchases may then induce an expansion of production and hence higher prices in pounds, with reduced purchases having the opposite effect. If, at the same time, this product competes with very similar American products (e.g., American-made sweaters), the price of the imported good may effectively be *rigid in dollars*, independently of spot-rate gyrations.

An increase in the spot rate, SR, taken by itself, will still make this product somewhat more expensive to the American buyers, but the accompanying tendency for Americans to cut back these purchases will induce a reduction in its price in pounds. It is as if the British producers in effect were willing to compromise with the U.S. buyers so as not to lose too much of the U.S. market. This will lessen the reduction in the American demand for the British product. The import-related demand for pounds will then reflect not just the demand for this product, but also the extent of the British price response. The pound demand schedule will have a different elasticity than the schedule for the underlying product demand.

Consider now the supply side of the spot exchange market, illustrated through U.S. exports to Britain. Naturally, the American export supply will translate into a pound supply as well. American exporters to Britain expecting payment from their British customers will look upon a rising spot rate as a growing inducement to expand these export sales and the production required to sustain them. This will be especially true when prices are *rigid in pounds*, for spot-rate increases will then lead to proportional increases in their dollar revenue. These conditions indicate that there is a large competitive market dominated by British producers, whereas the U.S. market for these or substitutable products is either small or noncompetitive. American exports of such products will then, because of the spot-rate increase, expand until their rising marginal dollar costs of production have exactly caught up with their increased prices as expressd in dollars (i.e., the marginal dollar revenue). The pound supply resulting from such exports will have an elasticity that mirrors that of the exporter's marginal cost curve—upward sloping, and normally more elastic in the long than in the short run.

If, instead, the U.S. home market for U.S. exportables and their substitutes is highly competitive, it will usually dominate the pricing of these products, and the prices of such exports will be *rigid in dollars*. A higher spot rate will then imply a lower price in Britain for these exported products, since each dollar will translate into fewer pounds than before. The reduction in the British price ought to create greater demand and sales opportunities in Britain, as measured in volume terms, and there will surely be an increase in *dollar* export revenue. But what matters here is the exporters' *pound* revenue—that is, the amount of foreign currency they will supply to the exchange market. In this respect, the outcome is ambiguous. If the British demand for these American products is *inelastic*, the added volume of sales will be insufficient to make up for the drop in the pound price connected with the increase in *SR*. Hence the pound revenues generated by the U.S. exporters, and the quantity of pounds they supply to the spot market, will also decline, contrary to what might seem intuitively plausible. The slope of the pound supply curve will then be *backward bending*—a "perverse" case not usually encountered in ordinary microeconomics. On the other hand, if the British demand for the American products is *elastic*, the increase in quantity sold will more than offset the drop in the British price, and pound—as well as dollar—export revenue will expand. In this case, the pound supply curve will have a normal positive slope, even though its elasticity may be low.

One simple way to understand these seemingly odd results is to examine the case in Figure 19-4 and the accompanying data. The U.S. supply price is given at \$4 (column 1). Assume that the British import demand function, D_{uk}^{m}, with respect to the British price, P_{uk}, is a straight downward-sloping line (like

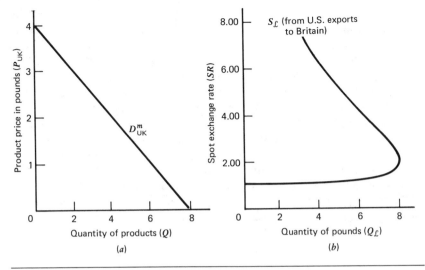

(1) Supply price (P_{US})	(2) Spot rate (SR)	(3) Purchase price (P_{UK})	(4) Quantity demanded (Q)	(5) Pound revenue ($P_{UK}Q$)	(6) Dollar revenue ($P_{US}Q = P_{UK}Q \times SR$)
$4	$1.00	£4.00	0 unit(s)	£0.00	$0.00
$4	1.14	3.50	1	3.50	4.00
$4	1.33	3.00	2	6.00	8.00
$4	1.60	2.50	3	7.50	12.00
$4	2.00	2.00	4	8.00	16.00
$4	2.67	1.50	5	7.50	20.00
$4	4.00	1.00	6	6.00	24.00
$4	8.00	0.50	7	3.50	28.00
$4		0.00	8	0.00	—

Figure 19-4. The case of a backward-bending foreign-exchange supply schedule. (a) U.K. import demand (for U.S. export product). (b) Supply of pounds.

those in elementary economics textbooks), as suggested by the data in columns 3 and 4. What happens to the pound revenue of the U.S. sellers if the British price, in this case because of an exchange-rate change, should fall? As long as the import demand is elastic (that is, within the upper half of the demand schedule), sales revenue in pounds will increase, reaching a maximum of £8 at an SR equal to $2.00. But when import demand turns inelastic (below the midpoint of the schedule), sales revenue in pounds will decrease, as, of course, will the amount of pounds supplied by U.S. exporters to the exchange market. As shown via the data in column 5, the corresponding pound-supply function, $S_£$, with respect to the exchange rate, will at first have a positive slope and then start to bend backwards.

There has been a great deal of academic concern that with a possibly backward-bending supply curve, exchange rate shifts would not lead to any predictable changes in export earnings; and perhaps the whole exchange market would, for this reason, be very unstable and erratic. Yet there is little real-world evidence that foreign-currency revenue from the total exports of a country declines with increasing spot rates, or increases with declining spot rates. The exporters' supply of foreign currency thus generally appears to have some positive elasticity. This may primarily reflect the fact that almost all countries face strong competition in their export markets, including competition from exporters in third countries (which we have not considered). Exporters in any one country will then typically be *price takers*. The expansion of their market shares abroad that follows a depreciation of their own currencies—that is, an increase in SR—will then generate larger foreign-currency revenues. And the overall behavior of the market will of course not depend exclusively on commodity trade.

Interest Arbitrage

In regard to interest arbitrage, demand and supply schedules can be derived in comparable ways, except for the need to distinguish between spot and forward transactions. The easiest way to see the parallels between product trade and interest arbitrage is to replace the word "product" with "security." One can then specify security demands and supplies as, partly, a matter of local security prices in each money market and, partly, a matter of exchange rates.

From the U.S. standpoint, an increase in the current spot rate in dollars per pound will in itself make purchases of British securities, payable in pounds, more expensive. In proceeding, let us assume there is no change in forward rates, or in expected future spot rates. The current spot-rate change will then reduce the American investors' returns, as calculated from contractual interest payments or expected dividends. On the other hand, such a spot-rate change will make borrowings in Britain more profitable. These transactions will then create larger immediate dollar proceeds, and the interest cost of borrowing in Britain, as measured in dollars, will decrease. Such a spot-rate shift will therefore be a disincentive for Americans to buy British-held securities—or to lend to the British. And it will be an incentive for Americans to sell securities to the British—or to borrow from them. As lenders, Americans will want fewer pounds than before, so their demand for pounds will go down. And as borrowers, they will most likely have additional pounds to sell, so their pound supply will go up.

These examples demonstrate that the interest arbitrageurs' demand for spot exchange is negatively dependent on the spot rate, whereas their supply of spot exchange is positively related to it. And comparable generalizations apply to their responses to forward rates. There is, in fact, strong evidence that the elasticities of the arbitrage demand and supply schedules are, by comparison with product trader schedules, highly elastic. For one thing, most of the internationally traded securities issued by any one country have close substitutes among the securities available elsewhere. In particular, treasury bills issued by different industrial-country governments are quite similar, apart from their currency denominations; and so are the standard types of credit extended by commercial banks for the financing of trade. On both the lender and the borrower sides, a high substitutability makes for a high sensitivity of demand and supply to small exchange-rate changes. The curious case of a backward-bending supply curve therefore is not worth considering in this context. If interest parity had always held, the elasticity of arbitrage flows would, by implication, have had to be infinite. In reality, there are limits on the amounts of funds that arbitrageurs control or want to absorb, even if the rates should suggest further unrealized profit opportunities. And differential information and transaction costs may prevent particular arbitrageur groups from fully capturing all the return or cost advantages that otherwise would exist.

Speculation

In the forward markets, we need to consider pure speculators as well. Their demands and supplies are predicated on expectations of future gains in the spot market, and therefore on particular spot-rate expectations. But they are sensitive also to forward rates—the prices at which they initiate their quests for profit. Lower forward rates make it cheaper for them to acquire speculative purchase contracts, whereas higher forward rates make the contracts seem more expensive. The converse applies to sales of forward currency: Higher rates are incentives to sell, lower rates not to sell. For each given set of future spot-rate expectations, speculators' demand for forward exchange is therefore likely to be negatively related to forward rates, whereas speculators' supply will be positively related to forward rates. Here, too, the conventional demand-and-supply framework seems to be approximately applicable.

Joint Spot-Forward Equilibrium

Our supply-and-demand analysis for the spot and forward markets should permit us to demonstrate how the equilibrium exchange rate is established in each of them. But spot and forward equilibriums are not mutually independent; they are linked to each other, mainly via covered arbitrage. This means that if, for whatever reason, there should occur a shift in one of the demand or supply elements in the spot market, there will result not only a change in the spot rate, but also a shift in various forward demand or supply schedules and a change in forward rates. Similarly, a change in one of the demand or supply elements in one of the forward markets will produce a reaction in the spot market, and hence a new spot rate. In fact, an initial shift in one spot or forward schedule will create a series of mutual readjustments of the covered arbitrage schedules. These readjustments will continue until the equilibrium rates in all spot and forward markets are consistent with one another. It therefore makes little sense to speak of equilibrium in only one of these markets, for market prices will come to rest only when there is a *joint* equilibrium in the entire range of spot and forward markets.

Let us illustrate the interdependence between the spot market and one forward market—the one for 180-day maturities—again, with reference to the British pound. In Figure 19-5 the quantities of pounds demanded and supplied have been summed up horizontally into the aggregate schedules $D_£ D_£$ and $S_£ S_£$ in each of the two markets. As indicated by Table 19-9, the spot schedules chiefly comprise uncovered commodity trade, interest arbitrage flows, and possibly, intervention support for either the pound or the dollar. The forward schedules include covered exports and imports, covered arbitrage flows (which entail forward cover on funds to be repatriated), pure speculative sales or purchases, and possibly, some official intervention. The intersections of the schedules show the equilibrium spot and forward rates, at which both markets are cleared. In this illustration, the 180-day forward rate for the pound is $2.03, versus a spot rate of $2.00. The forward premium on the pound is thus 3 percent per annum.

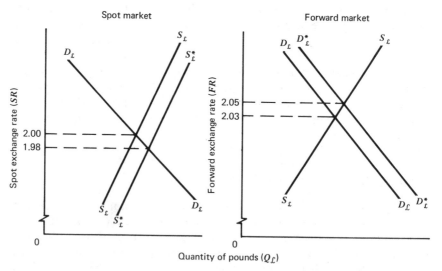

Note: The shift in the spot supply schedule to $S^*_£ S^*_£$ and in the forward demand schedule to $D^*_£ D^*_£$ results from inward covered arbitrage, following an increase in the domestic interest rate.

Figure 19-5.   Joint equilibrium in spot and forward-exchange markets.

A couple of examples will show the jointness of spot and forward markets. An increase in U.S. interest rates would increase the spot supply of pounds (in search of better returns in the United States) and, if investors cover, increase the forward demand for this currency. The new spot supply would be $S^*_{£}S^*_{£}$, the new forward demand $D^*_{£}D^*_{£}$, in Figure 19-5. The direction of the pressures created in the forward market is thus the opposite of that in the spot market. By tracing through these demand and supply changes in the two diagrams, one discovers that there will be an enlarged forward premium on the pound. With the new spot rate at $1.98 and the new forward rate at $2.05, the new premium will be about 7 percent.

Does this make sense? Indeed it does, for the new covered arbitrage flows will continue until the change in the interest differential has been approximately matched by a change in the forward premium or discount. Competitive arbitrage will see to it that the added interest-rate margin in favor of New York is pretty much offset by an added forward premium on the pound.

In another example, pretend that the British authorities have just announced a new anti-inflationary program. The market believes they will have some success in reducing the gradual decline of the pound in the spot market, especially vis-à-vis the dollar. The newly formed expectations will then make it potentially less profitable for international speculators to hold forward sales contracts in pounds (and more profitable to hold forward purchase contracts in pounds), considering the likely higher costs of (or gains from) the liquidation of such contracts. The forward $D_{£}D_{£}$ schedule will then move rightward to $D'_{£}D'_{£}$ as speculators try to build up their net forward positions in pounds (see Figure 19-6). The same tendency could have been shown through a leftward shift of $S_{£}S_{£}$, with the same effect on the forward rate. Speculation will thereby push the forward rate in the same direction as the change in the expected future spot rate 180 days into the future, which we can denote by $E(SR)_{180}$.

Yet this result would indicate a larger forward premium on the pound. There will therefore be an immediate new arbitrage flow into Britain, with consequent upward pressure also on the current spot rate. In the spot market, demand will expand to $D''_{£}D''_{£}$. As the arbitrageurs take out cover, they will at the same time push the forward market supply to $S''_{£}D''_{£}$. Since in this case interest rates are assumed to be unchanged, the spot- and forward-rate changes might be of similar magnitudes, at least if covered arbitrage plays a dominant role in the entire exchange market. Speculation will in this way, via the arbitrage connection, produce the same type of rate changes in the spot and forward markets.

On the other hand, covered interest arbitrage does not always have such a dominant influence over exchange rates. Speculation is sometimes a stronger market force. Also, the more international investors learn to diversify their portfolios, the less need they will have for forward cover, and the weaker the pressure, from this source, on the forward rate to conform with parity conditions. Changes in speculative pressure can hence push the forward rate

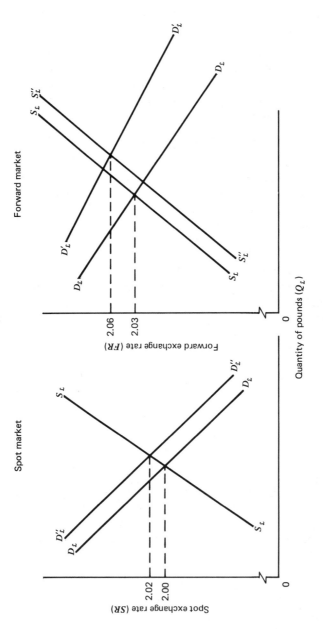

Spot market

Forward market

Quantity of pounds $(Q_£)$

Note: The shift in the forward demand schedule to $D'_£ D'_£$ is due to speculation in favor of the British pound, connected with an increase in the expected future spot rate. The subsequent shifts in the spot demand schedule to $D''_£ D''_£$ and in the forward supply schedule to $S''_£ S''_£$ are due to outward interest arbitrage, triggered by the speculation-induced increase in the forward rate.

Figure 19-6. Speculation and joint exchange market equilibrium.

away from its parity level with interest rates and the going spot rate. In our example, this could produce a positive covered interest differential in favor of London. To suggest this possibility, the revised demand and supply schedules in Figure 19-6 have been drawn so as to widen the forward premium on the pound from an initial 3 percent to a final 4 percent per annum.

Generally, arbitrage and speculation are in the short run the most potent and volatile market elements. The former tends to link the current spot market with the various forward markets, thereby creating pressure toward interest parity. The latter tends to link forward markets to future spot markets—or rather, to the market's perceptions of these markets, thereby aligning forward rates with anticipated future spot rates. Very often, the pressures of arbitrage and speculation are operating at cross-purposes. Official intervention constitutes an additional market force, which is not amenable to the kind of analysis we have applied in this chapter. It further adds to the unpredictability of exchange rates, in particular by altering the relative incentives for private speculation.

Important Concepts

spot rate	interest arbitrage
forward rate	covered interest differential
cross rate	swap
forward premium (discount)	"pure" speculation
currency exposure	intervention
export (import) cover	effective exchange rate

Questions

1. If you, as an American business executive, know that you will need half a million Canadian dollars in six months, how would you go about acquiring them? What type of currency contract would you enter into, now or later? Does it matter if you have the funds (in U.S. dollars) available right away, or only in six months?

2. Assume that the dollar spot rate for the Swiss franc fell by 5 percent while, over the same period, the dollar spot rate for the Italian lira rose by 7 percent. Calculate the resulting change in the franc spot rate for the lira, or in the lira spot rate for the franc.

3. Assume the dollar-pound spot rate is $2.20. The 90-day interest rate is 8 percent in the United States and 11 percent in Britain. Somebody informs you that the forward rate is at its parity level. What is the forward rate?

4. You are a well-diversified American currency speculator, and your crystal ball tells you that, contrary to prevailing market opinion, German interest rates will shortly go up. You feel pretty sure that the authorities will do nothing to counteract the resulting capital flow to Germany or the associated exchange-rate pressures. What will be your next speculative move?

Further Readings

Eiteman, D., and A. Stonehill, *Multinational Business Finance*, 2nd ed. (Reading, Massachusetts: Addison-Wesley, 1979), Chapters 3 and 4.

Grubel, Herbert, *International Economics* (Homewood, Illinois: Irwin, 1977), Chapters 10-12.

Kubarych, Roger, *Foreign Exchange Markets in the United States*, Federal Reserve Bank of New York, 1978.

Lessard, Donald, ed., *International Financial Management* (Boston: Warren, Gorham & Lamont, 1979), Chapters 13-26.

Tsiang, S. C., "The Theory of Forward Exchange and Effects of Government Intervention on the Forward Exchange Market," *IMF Staff Papers*, April 1959.

Wihlborg, Clas, *Currency Risks in International Financial Markets*, Princeton Studies in International Finance No. 44 (Princeton: Princeton University, 1978).

IV

Balance-of-Payments Analysis

20

THE BALANCE OF PAYMENTS

All applied economic analysis requires input of statistical data, and the validity of research will always depend on the methods through which the supporting data have been assembled and interpreted. This naturally applies to international, as well as domestic, economic problems. For macroeconomic and macrofinancial purposes, both government policy makers and private forecasters need to be able to inform themselves of the changes that are taking place in the overall relations between the home country and the rest of the world. The conventional way of summarizing such data is by compiling a *balance of payments*—that is, an annual record of outward and inward payments between the residents of one country and those of other nations. This chapter explains the principles that are commonly followed in the compilation of this record. The following three chapters discuss how it can be used for analyzing international economic relations and devising an appropriate macroeonomic policy for an open economy.

The balance-of-payments account summarizes data collected from many different private and public sources. It essentially shows the overall changes in the nation's international financial situation during the year. It tells us how well we, as a nation, have fared in our changing asset-liability relationships with other nations, and it catalogs shifts in our international liquidity. It is an important macroeconomic analytical tool that can help us identify the results of changes in domestic spending and output or in domestic money and credit conditions. To government officials and central bankers, it can reveal the international consequences of their policies and practices, good or bad.

But what, really, is a "good" balance of payments? To answer such a question, we must first acquaint ourselves with the types of data that are available and the terminology used in their presentation. We will do this by, first, establishing the basic principles of all *flow-of-funds* accounting. After that, we will examine each component of the balance-of-payments account and explain how the different components fit into the overall picture. Finally, we will show briefly how this statistical information can be squared with a different type of international economic data—data on the levels of the nation's foreign assets and liabilities.

FUNDS FLOWS AND PAYMENTS ACCOUNTING

The easiest way to catalog economic transactions between one economic unit and the units it is dealing with, is by listing the resulting inflows and outflows of funds. This method is used in corporate financial analysis, and it can equally well be applied to the international transactions of an entire nation. As a prelude to our discussion of balance-of-payments accounting, we will therefore look at the major funds flows occurring through a typical manufacturing corporation. This should enable us later to think of the nation as one single unit within the world economy—perhaps called America, Inc.

Funds *inflows* are conventionally classified by the nature of their various sources—that is, by the types of transactions creating these inflows. Inflows are recorded as *credits*. Funds *outflows* are similarly classified by their various destinations, or uses—that is, by the type of transactions through which they are disposed of. Outflows are recorded as *debits*.

A fundamental distinction is drawn between transactions involving income or expenditure and transactions involving changes in assets, liabilities, or equity. The former category mainly concerns sales and purchases of various outputs and inputs—that is, transactions in goods and services. This part of a flow-of-funds statement can be called the *current account*. The second category of funds flows concerns lending, borrowing, changes in cash balances, and other security transactions, and also purchases of fixed real assets. This part of the statement is usually called the *capital account*. Over time, each completed financial transaction will of course show up twice, if not more times, as the original flow produces a return flow of interest or dividends, along with amortization of principal or proceeds from security sales. As we shall see shortly, the former return flows are conventionally placed in the current account, whereas the latter return flows—repatriation of capital—appear in the capital account.

The funds flowing through our hypothetical manufacturer during the accounting year are indicated by the simplified sources-and-uses-of-funds statement in Table 20-1. Its principal source of funds on current account (the upper part of the ledger) is of course its sales revenue, with the addition of net income from security holdings. Its main current-account debits are its expenditures on labor, raw materials, fuel, and other current inputs. It also normally pays taxes to various levels of government. In calculating these taxes, it will make special allowances for the depreciation of its real assets and

Table 20-1
Corporate Sources and Uses of Funds

Uses of Funds (Debits)	Sources of Funds (Credits)
Current account	
Current expenditure	Income
Wages and salaries	Sales revenue
Raw materials, parts, and fuel	Interest and dividends
Interest	
Taxes	
Dividends	
Capital account	
Real-asset acquisition	Net borrowing
Plant and equipment	Net issues of bonds
Land	Net trade credit received
	Net borrowings from banks
Net financial-asset acquisition	Other borrowing
Net security purchases	
Net trade credit extended	Net issue of stock
Other net lending	
Changes in bank deposits	

for changes in its inventories, but these adjustments do not represent actual funds flows and therefore do not belong in this statement. Some of the remaining funds typically are paid out as dividends, at least if the firm generates a normal amount of profits.

On capital account, many funds sources can be grouped under the general heading of borrowing, or increases in liabilities. This item includes new bond issues, bank loans received, issues of commercial paper, trade credit obtained (i.e., increases in accounts payable), and other, less important items. All these items should be net of transactions that wipe out existing liabilities—payments for previously purchased goods, redemptions of outstanding bonds or commercial paper, and other forms of repayments. The corporation may occasionally issue additional stock, or repurchase already outstanding stock. The net issue of additional stock—or external equity—thus becomes another, though less regular, source of funds on capital account.

The funds obtained in these various ways must all somehow be used. This is because funds, in the abstract sense of purchasing power, do not exist in any pure, storable form. The funds available for capital-account purposes are of two kinds: any excess of funds obtained on current account, and net inflows through borrowings and equity issues. They can be used for two types of asset acquisitions, real and financial. Real-asset acquisitions consist of purchases of plant, machinery, and land (fixed assets), often referred to as capital expenditure. Net acquisitions of financial assets include purchases of marketable securities, trade credit extended (new accounts receivable), and buildups of bank deposits and plain currency holdings—all net of security sales, repayments received, and deposit withdrawals. The sum of all inflows (credits) will then equal the sum of all outflows (debits), as it must under the double-entry bookkeeping method.

This framework is general enough to be approximately applicable also to other types of economic units—private financial institutions, households, and governments. Of course, some of the financial instruments will differ, and so will the relative magnitudes of the flows. For all types of units, some of the transactions may involve foreign parties, so that some funds sources or uses will also be foreign. If we then aggregate all economic units in the home country, transactions among themselves will cancel out and only those with foreigners will remain.

These remaining accounting items will make up the balance of international payments. The reader should now sense that the items pertaining to sales revenues from foreigners actually describe exports, whereas those pertaining to expenditures on foreign goods and services entail imports. That capital-account items can describe international flows of loanable funds should also be apparent. We will now describe international payments step by step, while keeping in mind our analogy with the manufacturer and other smaller economic units.

CURRENT ACCOUNT

Recall how in our corporate flow-of-funds statement we first listed all transactions in goods and services and separated them from capital transactions. International payments accounting follows a similar, but not quite identical, practice. The *current account* of the balance of payments records all product transactions, even if the products are in the nature of machinery or other capital goods. Thus, what for a domestic firm is a noncurrent capital expenditure will for a nation be listed as a current-account import. This terminological divergence reflects differences in practical purposes: The focus of international payments accounting is the shifts in the nation's financial assets and liabilities, not—as for corporations—the shifts in its total-asset or net-worth position.

The current-account items that strictly pertain to international product sales or product purchases can be referred to as the *goods and services* account. Table 20-2 contains a generalized analytical format of this account. It includes both tangible physical items—ordinary merchandise—and a number of intangible items, such as insurance, tourism, and shipping. The former are sometimes called "visible" trade, the latter—essentially service items—"invisible" trade (although our vision should be good enough to observe the latter, too).

Table 20-2
Current Account of the Balance of Payments

Uses of Funds (Debits)	Sources of Funds (Credits)
Goods and Services	
Imports (purchases) of merchandise	Exports (sales) of merchandise
Imports (purchases) of services	Exports (sales) of services
Transport services purchased	Transport services sold
abroad	abroad
Insurance services purchased	Insurance services sold
abroad	abroad
Tourist expenditure abroad	Tourist expenditure by
Other services purchased abroad	foreigners in the home country
Investment income payments	Other services sold abroad
on home-country assets owned	Investment income receipts on
by foreigners	foreign assets owned
Goods-and-services balance ($\gtrless 0$)	by domestic residents
Transfers	
Transfers to foreigners	Transfers from foreigners
Remittances abroad by	Remittances received from
foreign workers	workers abroad
Pensions paid to foreigners	Pensions received from abroad
Other private donations	Other private donations
Government grants to	Grants to government from
foreigners	foreigners
Transfer balance ($\gtrless 0$)	
Current-account balance =	
Goods-and-services balance +	
Transfer balance ($\gtrless 0$)	

An example of an import of goods: A U.S. merchant decides to purchase 100 tons of coffee from a Brazilian exporter. The goods arrive in New York and are paid for through a check drawn by the buyer on his bank in favor of the Brazilian firm. The coffee import is recorded as a goods-and-services debit for the United States (whereas, at this point, Brazil's new dollar claim represents a credit in the American capital account). An example of an export of services: A Frenchman buys a ticket for Miami on a U.S. airline, but pays for it in French francs. There will be a U.S. goods-and-services credit (matched by a capital-account debit in the form of the new U.S. franc claim). Other service transactions show up as royalties, consulting fees, and government military expenditures abroad.

A bit of reflection should reveal that the treatment of international transport charges will vary with the way in which exports and imports are valued and with the ownership of the transportation vehicle. When traded goods are valued inclusive of "cost, insurance, and freight" (c.i.f.), shipping charges are hidden in the merchandise items. But if the exported or imported goods are valued on an f.o.b. ("free on board") or f.a.s. ("free alongside ship") basis, freight is obviously not included in their valuation. The U.S. government has long valued U.S. exports on the f.a.s. basis and in 1980 started to calculate imports through the c.i.f. method. This means that when U.S. exports are carried on U.S.-owned ships or airplanes, there will be a transport credit in the U.S. payments account, since shipping will produce revenue from abroad. When U.S. imports are carried on U.S. vessels, a transport credit will also be entered, in this case as an offset to the "overcharging" for imported goods.

One special "service" category is *investment income*, which consists of inpayments and outpayments of interest, dividends, and other forms of profits on internationally held assets. Such income accruing to U.S. residents on their assets abroad—bank balances, loans, securities, real estate, or whole enterprises—naturally is recorded as a credit, whereas comparable income to foreigners on their assets in the United States is recorded as a debit. (Incidentally, investment income corresponds to what is called "net factor income from abroad" in national-income accounting; this represents the difference between the gross *national* product and the gross *domestic* product.)

There is, however, a definitional problem: how to treat investment income that is actually not remitted but retained—that is, plowed back into the host-country economy. One alternative is to include both the remitted and the retained earnings in the current account. But the reemployment of the retained portion in the host country will then have to be entered as an offset on capital account (as a flow from the home country to the host country). If, by contrast, we record only the remitted portion, no such offset will be needed. Under the first alternative, now used by the U.S. government, one gets a more complete picture of the income relationship with the host country. Under the second, used by most other countries, one gets a better picture of the actual transfer of funds.

Let us now glance at the U.S. balance-of-payments record, as presented through the format adopted by the U.S. Department of Commerce. Table 20-3 shows a summary of that record for certain years within the 1970-79 period, with credits and debits listed consecutively in one column, and with minus signs for debits. Included among U.S. goods-and-services exports are reinvested, as well as repatriated, corporate U.S. earnings abroad; similarly, the retained American earnings of foreign-owned corporations are treated as U.S. goods-and-services imports. Note the rapid growth of total exports and imports; in nominal (current-price) terms, U.S. foreign trade more than quadrupled over the decade.

The International Monetary Fund (IMF) uses a somewhat different format, as seen in the 1977 data in Table 20-4 for four selected countries. The U.S. government data are naturally in U.S. dollars, but the IMF has started to rely on its own unit-of-account invention, the Special Drawing Right (SDR),

Table 20-3
The U.S. Balance of Payments, 1970-79
(As reported by U.S. government)
(Credits: + ; debits: – ; in billions of dollars)

	1970	*1977*	*1978*	*1979*
Exports of goods and services	65.7	184.6	220.8	286.3
Merchandise	42.5	120.8	141.9	182.1
Travel and transportation	6.0	14.8	17.0	19.8
Receipts of investment income	11.8	32.6	43.5	65.9
Remitted direct-investment				
income	5.0	12.8	13.6	19.6
Reinvested corporate earnings	3.2	7.3	12.1	18.2
Other	3.6	12.5	17.8	28.1
Other	5.5	16.4	18.5	18.6
Imports of goods and services	–60.0	–194.0	–229.7	–281.0
Merchandise	–39.9	–151.7	–176.1	–211.5
Defense expenditures	–4.9	–5.8	–7.3	–8.4
Travel and transportation	–8.0	–18.0	–20.0	–22.5
Payments of investment income	–5.4	–14.6	–21.8	–33.5
Remitted direct-investment				
income	–0.4	–1.2	–1.6	–2.2
Reinvested corporate earnings	–0.4	–1.6	–2.3	–3.8
Other	–4.6	–11.8	–17.9	–27.5
Other	–1.8	–4.0	–4.6	–5.0
Unilateral transfers, net	–3.3	–4.7	–5.1	–5.6
U.S. government grants	–1.7	–2.8	–3.2	–3.5
Other	–1.6	–1.9	–1.9	–2.2
Changes in U.S. assets abroad	–9.3	–35.8	–61.0	–63.4
Official reserves	2.5	–0.4	0.7	–1.1
Gold	0.8	–0.1	–0.1	–0.1
SDRs	–0.9	–0.1	1.2	–1.1
Reserve position in the IMF	0.4	–0.3	4.2	–0.2
Foreign currencies	2.2	0.2	–4.7	0.3
Other government assets	–1.6	–3.7	–4.7	–3.8
Private assets	–10.2	–31.7	–57.0	–58.5
Direct investment	–7.6	–12.9	–16.7	–24.8
Foreign securities	–1.1	–5.5	–3.5	–5.0
Bank claims	–1.0	–11.4	–33.0	–26.1
Other	–0.6	–1.9	–3.9	–2.7
Changes in foreign assets in the U.S.	6.4	50.8	63.7	33.9
Official assets	6.9	36.7	33.8	–15.2
Private assets	–0.6	14.2	30.0	49.1
Direct investment	1.5	3.7	6.3	7.7
Other	–2.2	10.4	23.7	41.4
Allocations of SDRs	0.9	—	—	1.1
Statistical discrepancy	–0.2	–0.9	11.1	28.7
Memoranda				
Balance on merchandise trade	2.6	–30.9	–34.2	–29.5
Balance on goods and services	5.6	–9.4	–8.8	5.3
Balance on current account	2.3	–14.1	–13.9	–0.3
Transactions in U.S. official reserve				
assets and foreign official assets				
in the U.S., net	9.8	35.0	31.7	–15.5

Source: U.S. Department of Commerce, *Survey of Current Business*, March 1980.

Table 20-4

Selected Balances of Payments, 1977 (as reported by the IMF);
(credits: +; debits: –; in billions of SDRs)

		West Germany	Japan	Brazil	United States
A.	*Goods, services, and transfers*	3.2	9.3	–4.1	–13.1
	Merchandise exports, f.o.b.	97.5	67.9	10.3	103.3
	Merchandise imports, f.o.b.	–80.9	–53.1	–10.3	–129.9
	Trade balance	16.6	14.8	0.0	–26.6
	Services: credit	24.0	13.9	1.3	53.6
	Services: debit	–30.7	–19.1	–5.5	–35.7
	Private transfers	–3.0	–0.2	0.0	–0.8
	Government transfers	–3.6	–0.2	0.0	–3.6
B.	*Long-term capital*	–4.7	–2.3	5.0	–10.7
	Private assets and liabilities	–4.5	n.a.	3.5	n.a.
	Official assets and liabilities	–0.3	n.a.	1.5	n.a.
	Total, *A plus B* (basic balance)	–1.5	7.0	0.9	–23.8
C.	*Short-term capital*, incl. errors and omissions	5.5	–1.5	–0.3	–6.3
D.	*Counterpart items* [(de)monetization of gold, SDR allocations]	—	—	—	—
	Total, *A through D* (official settlements balance)	4.0	5.5	0.6	–30.1
E.	*Reserves and related items*	–4.0	–5.5	–0.6	30.1
	Monetary gold	0.0	0.0	0.0	–0.1
	SDRs	0.6	0.0	0.0	–0.1
	Reserve position in the IMF	–0.1	–0.2	0.0	–0.3
	Foreign exchange	–4.2	–5.3	–0.4	0.3
	Liabilities	–0.3	—	–0.1	30.3

Note: The average value of the SDR (at which the original data were converted) was $1.17.
Source: International Monetary Fund, *Balance of Payments Yearbook*, 1978.

whose value is calculated as a weighted average of 5 leading national currencies. (For more on SDRs, see Chapters 24 and 25.) The use of different data formats is unfortunate for the balance-of-payments student in a hurry, but it helps to make us aware of some important problems of interpretation. In regard to the goods-and-services record, the two approaches are, however, quite similar, and the two sets of data on U.S. merchandise and service trade could rather easily be reconciled.

Although their "current" status may not be obvious, unilateral *transfers* are usually also placed in the current balance-of-payments account. These are basically gifts—donations—between residents (individuals, businesses, or governments) of different nations. Typical examples, listed in Table 20-2, are emigrant remittances by "guest workers" from their host countries to their home countries; pensions (which, as payments for past labor services, might better have been regarded as investment income on human capital), and government-to-government grants, mostly in the form of aid from developed to developing countries. When such transfers involve outpayments, they are recorded as debits; when they involve inpayments (receipts), they are recorded as credits.

It is easy to imagine where the matching entries to transfers will appear. For instance, foreign aid in the form of commodity shipments (say, food or machinery) will be represented by a credit under exports for the donor country, and by a debit under imports for the recipient. Cash transfers by workers, insurance companies, or governments will normally lead to asset reductions or liability increases on the books of banks or government agencies in the payers' home country. These are credits that match the corresponding transfer debits.

That even unilateral transactions require double entries might seem paradoxical, but should be understandable to those who appreciate the logic of flow-of-funds analysis. Each act of giving is a use of funds by the donor (transferor), while the delivery of the transferred products or cash can in itself be construed as a source of funds; after all, they could have been exchanged for other assets. The transferee, conversely, uses the funds he acquires through the gift (a source to him) by taking possession of these products or this cash (as it were, buying these assets). Metaphysical, perhaps—yet a way of rationalizing the accepted double-entry method.

INTERPRETING THE CURRENT-ACCOUNT BALANCE

When all these debits and credits have been recorded, calculating the net result, or balance, is a simple, mechanical matter. (Note how we are suddenly using the word "balance" in a different sense.) One might first tabulate a goods-and-services balance, as suggested by Table 20-2 (and actually done by the U.S. government in a special "memorandum" at the bottom of Table 20-3). If this balance is positive, by definition there will be an excess of receipts (credits) over payments (debits). If it is negative, there is, conversely, an excess of payments over receipts. A positive balance (such as that of Japan or West Germany in 1977) implies essentially a *trade surplus* (trade measured inclusive of services), whereas a negative balance (such as that of the United States in most recent years) similarly implies a *trade deficit*. Alternatively, the former situation is sometimes described as an *export surplus*, the latter as an *import surplus*. However, in some sources the terms "trade," "exports," and "imports" refer only to goods (i.e., merchandise), and the concepts of "balance," "surplus," and "deficit" will then have to be reinterpreted accordingly.

One can also show a separate transfer-account balance (perhaps to get a measure of the flow of charity, or the demand for good-will "investment"). Or one can add transfer items to the goods-and-services items, so as to derive the balance on total current account. Since this balance is also defined as the excess of credits over debits, it is shown in Table 20-2 as an offsetting entry in the debit column. But it may of course be either positive or negative.

The current-account balance is of special interest. A *current-account surplus* implies that the total transactions in this account have produced a net leftover of funds that can be applied to other, purely financial purposes. The nation will then, by necessity, be an international *supplier of loanable funds*, a role that permits it to build up its assets, or to reduce its liabilities, vis-à-vis the rest of the world. Conversely, a *current-account deficit* implies a shortfall of funds stemming from transactions on this account, a gap that has to be made up for through other, foreign-obtained funds. The nation will then be a net *demander of loanable funds* in the international economy, the demand being met through foreign-asset liquidations or through borrowings from (or security sales to) other nations. Whether positive or negative, the current-account balance is said to measure the nation's *net foreign investment, I_f*:

$$I_f = X - M$$

This term helps bridge the analytical gap between the balance-of-payments and the national-income accounts. We are all familiar with the national income, or product, definition (whether gross or net):

$$Y = C_p + I_p + G + X - M$$

where C_p stands for private consumption, I_p for private investment, G for government purchases, and X and M for exports and imports of goods and services. The equation shows the various sources of national income—three types of domestic spending (which create income receipts), plus the net spending by the rest of the world, via international trade, on the home-country's product. This net rest-of-the-world spending is $X - M$.

Let us separately look at domestic and rest-of-the-world spending. If $X - M$ is a positive number (indicating a goods-and-services surplus), total domestic spending—$C_p + I_p + G$—obviously, according to this equation, has to be less than the total national product. The implication is that the remaining product is being sold to foreigners in exchange for new net financial claims or liability reductions against them. If $X - M$, by contrast, is negative (a goods-and-services deficit), home-country spending exceeds the national product. The spending excess is then effectively paid for through foreign-asset reductions or foreign-liability increases.

Yet the astute student will realize that to accurately measure net foreign investment, X and M should here include the retained portion of investment income in both directions. Earnings plowbacks are indeed an important form of investment and asset growth, internationally as well as domestically. He may also sense that when there is a nonzero transfer balance, the situation becomes a little messier. Consider a net donor nation. Its outward transfers, if carried out through product exports, will reduce the portion of national product available for domestic spending, while, in the standard definition, leaving national income unchanged. Yet these particular exports do not result in any actual improvement in the donor nation's net foreign-asset position. If effected through cash donations, such transfers lead to a worsening in the donor country's net foreign-asset position, without permitting any additional domestic spending. For such a country, its actual net foreign investment (I_f) will in either case be correspondingly smaller than its goods-and-services balance. For a country receiving net transfers, the converse conclusions apply.

CAPITAL ACCOUNT

A major differentiation within the balance-of-payments account must be made between goods-and-services entries and strictly financial entries. But the origins and implications of these latter entries vary greatly. For some purposes it is appropriate to set aside changes in government short-term foreign assets—that is, in what is called official foreign *reserves*, or international monetary reserves—and deal with them separately. The *capital account* will then include only nonreserve financial items. This distinction, though a bit artificial, can be justified by the fact that changes in reserve accounts are directly a matter of government policy, and in turn subject to the rules of the international monetary system, whereas other capital flows primarily reflect market forces. The IMF has adopted this practice (see Table 20-4). By contrast, the U.S. government at present does not subdivide the financial entries in this fashion, but instead differentiates between changes in U.S. foreign assets, including reserves, and changes in the assets that foreigners hold in the United States (see Table 20-3).

As before, funds inflows can be identified by their sources, outflows by their uses. And these sources and uses describe the types of transactions, instruments, or parties involved. Table 20-5 accordingly shows a condensed listing of the broad categories of capital-account flows. A separation is made between long- and short-term flows, with the cutoff point for the former placed at a remaining maturity of one year. Note that "long-term" in this context thus includes debt that in domestic financial analysis is usually called "medium-term." There is also a possibility that long-term securities might be sold within the calendar year of their purchase, and both parties to a short-term loan transaction might count on rolling it over into the long term. The nominal classification of maturities can in these cases be misleading.

Table 20-5
Capital Account of the Balance of Payments

Uses of Funds (Debits)	Sources of Funds (Credits)
Long-term Capital	
Direct investment abroad, net of repatriation	Direct foreign investment in the home country, net of repatriation
Private portfolio investment abroad, net of repayments and resales of securities	Private foreign portfolio investment in the home country, net of repayments and resales of securities
Government lending abroad, net of repayments	Government borrowing abroad, net of repayments
Short-term Capital	
Private trade credit extended to foreigners, net of repayments	Private trade credit received from abroad, net of repayments
Private deposits placed in foreign banks, net of withdrawals	Bank deposits received from private foreigners, net of withdrawals
Private purchases of foreign money-market instruments, net of redemptions and resales	Sales of private money-market instruments to private foreigners, net of redemptions and resales
Other private lending abroad, net of repayments	Other private borrowing abroad, net of repayments
Government lending abroad (other than through reserve asset accumulation), net of repayments	Government borrowing abroad (other than through issues of liquid liabilities to foreign authorities), net of repayments

Capital-account balance ($\gtrless 0$)

At the extreme long end of the maturity spectrum are inflows and outflows of *direct* private investment funds. These are defined so as to describe acquisitions, or extensions of control, of entire enterprises—in most cases, requiring at least 50 percent ownership. Typically, these funds are offered in exchange for equity, as through stock sales and purchases. But multinational firms often arrange loans among their own divisions or affiliates in different countries—yet there can hardly exist any effective repayment obligations within a group of enterprises under common ownership. Therefore, such *intracompany* lending is also treated as direct investment, equivalent to outright equity transactions. The first item in the credit column of Table 20-5 thus, for the United States, will include loans by Volkswagen headquarters in West Germany to its U.S. subsidiaries, along with any Arab takeovers of American hotel chains and the establishment of newly incorporated U.S. affiliates of Japanese banks. The corresponding items on the credit side pertain to similar funds uses abroad by American firms (or, rarely, wealthy individuals).

Repatriations of previously made investments are treated as negative items that are offset against the new outflows or inflows of such funds. For instance, should there, in a particular year, be a net return outflow of direct investment funds from the United States to the foreign investor nations, there would be a negative net U.S. direct-investment credit in the sources-of-funds column (equivalent to a positive *debit*—i.e., an actual *use* of funds).

The second capital-account item is long-term private *portfolio* investment. In the sources-of-funds column, this category, as in Table 20-5, includes net sales of stocks, corporate bonds and other private long-term securities (including loan obligations) to foreigners—except when the latter have or gain control over the issuing or borrowing U.S. enterprises. In practice, the majority of the investing foreigners are financial institutions and individuals who, through these investments, acquire nondomestic assets for their portfolios. The left-hand column, conversely, records net private home-country purchases of similar foreign assets under similar circumstances. In Table 20-3 such outflows of U.S. capital are recorded in part as changes in foreign securities and in part as changes in bank claims. The remaining long-term items pertain to flows to and from the home-country government. In actuality, most of these flows involve intergovernmental loans (or loans to or from international agencies). Table 20-3 suggests that the U.S. government is only a small-scale international lender; its borrowings are a very different story.

The last category in the capital account refers to short-term nonreserve capital transactions, mostly private. Inflows, to be credited, stem from trade credits received by home-country importers, sales of treasury bills and commercial paper to private foreigners, and deposits made by private foreigners in home-country banks—all on a net basis. Outflows, which are of course debited, consists primarily of net trade credit extended (as via bankers' acceptances), private purchases of foreign money-market instruments, and private deposits in foreign banks (including foreign branches of U.S. banks). As government short-term capital flows are almost entirely of a reserve nature, they do not normally belong here. Exceptions occur when a government is engaged in trade credit or in intergovernment lending by acquiring nonliquid securities (which do not qualify as "reserves").

OFFICIAL RESERVE ACCOUNT

We now turn to those special financial entries that indicate changes in government-owned foreign monetary reserves. The *official reserve account* is something like a national record of international cash movements, carried out by governments. But the "cash" term has to be interpreted more broadly here than in the domestic context. And the governments in question are not only the national treasury departments, and any special government currency agencies, but also the central banks, however independent they may regard themselves.

The account shows changes both in the home-country government's foreign assets and in home-country liabilities to foreign governments or other official authorities, whenever these liabilities represent the foreign reserves of those foreign entities. Why do we include changes in such liabilities in this account? Because such shifts in foreign-owned claims on the home country are a matter of policy abroad, and the international monetary policies of foreign countries are closely intertwined with those of the home country. These liability changes result primarily from exchange market intervention, as do changes in the home country's official reserve assets. And recall that such intervention, whether done by the home country or by foreign countries, will help determine the exchange rates between the domestic and foreign currencies.

Table 20-6
Official Reserve Account

Uses of Funds (Debits)	Sources of Funds (Credits)
Change in:	Change in:
Official gold reserve	Liquid liabilities to foreign authorities
SDR holdings	Securities issued by home-country
Reserve position in the IMF	government
Official foreign exchange holdings	Balances with home-country banks
Foreign government securities	
Balances with foreign banks	
	Net official reserve-account change ($\gtrless 0$)

Table 20-6 lists the chief types of entries made in this account. Until the mid-1960s, governments still settled a substantial part of their mutual debts by transferring ownership of monetary gold (kept mostly in the vaults of the Federal Reserve Bank of New York) from debtors to creditors, but this practice has virtually disappeared. (More will be said in Chapters 24 and 25 about the past and present roles of gold and other reserve assets.) Today, the small gold-reserve entries that are made stem mostly from the resumption by several governments of gold sales on the private market. The U.S. Treasury has thus for some time held periodic gold auctions—and the official U.S. gold reserve has obviously shown a corresponding decline. Privately held gold is considered a commodity, not an international monetary asset, so it does not belong here at all.

The second reserve item listed on the debit side is described as changes in holding of Special Drawing Rights (SDRs) on the IMF. Such changes occur in two ways. First, upon their creation they are distributed—or "allocated"—to IMF member countries, which thereby gain additional foreign reserves of a particular kind. Secondly, already existing SDRs can be transferred among governments, as weak-currency (highly indebted) countries exchange some of their SDRs for the currencies of stronger-currency (reserve-accumulating) countries. The recorded net change in a country's SDRs in a particular year might reflect one or both of these occurrences, with additions as positive debits and reductions as negative debits.

Another rather obscure asset item follows: the change in the home country's "reserve position in the IMF." The technical background for this phenomenon will be provided in Chapter 24. Here we need to know that the IMF account of each IMF member reflects several kinds of transactions between the organization and its various members: (1) "subscriptions" of foreign currencies, which are the member's basic contributions to it (positive entries); (2) the member's borrowings, called "drawings," from it (negative entries); and (3) IMF lending of the particular member's own currency to other members (for which the former member earns a positive entry in its IMF account). These IMF transactions are thus part of the international settlements mechanism and are recorded along with other reserve-asset changes.

Quantitatively, the most important reserve item is normally foreign exchange holdings. They are mostly in the form of securities issued by foreign governments or bank balances abroad. Changes in these holdings originate mostly through spot market intervention, but also through inter-government lending and borrowing. A government that has sold foreign currencies—in order to support its own currency and prevent it from depreciating—will of course register reserve losses (negative debits) here. Conversely, a strong-currency government, intervening by foreign-currency purchases to prevent an appreciation of its currency, will register reserve gains (positive debits).

Our description of the liability entries in the official reserve account will be simpler. The foreign exchange reserves of one nation represent liquid monetary liabilities of the nations supplying these instruments. For example, buildups of foreign government holdings of U.S. dollars, through intervention purchases or otherwise, are recorded as positive credit entries in the U.S. reserve account. See Table 20-6 and, for an actual illustration, also see the U.S. data (a $30 billion credit in 1977) in Table 20-4. Such foreign dollar accumulations, and comparable decumulations, are also part of the international settlement mechanism, and they help measure changes in the net international liquidity of the United States. These liability items are significant only for countries that supply widely held *key currencies* to the rest of the world, since only such currencies actually enter government foreign reserves. At present the list includes also, but on much smaller scales, the United Kingdom, West Germany, France, and Switzerland.

Having accounted for all categories of reserve items, one can of course calculate the net reserve-account balance. A positive net change in reserve assets over liabilities—a net debit—would suggest that the official "cash" position has improved; and there must have been funds available for allocation to this purpose. On the other hand, a negative net would indicate a deterioration in this respect, with funds having had to be drawn from this source to meet the requirements of international settlements.

This completes our description of the various balance-of-payments entries. Every conceivable international economic transaction should, in principle, be allocable somewhere among these accounts (with double entries, one credit and one debit). Nevertheless, in practice there are inaccuracies in the reported data—because of incomplete collection procedures and accidental or deliberate misrepresentations. Many of these inaccuracies probably cancel out and remain hidden. But some do not, and therefore leave an unexplained gap between total credits and total debits. This missing residual is technically offset through a special entry called "errors and omissions" (or "statistical discrepancy"), usually entered either just before or after the official reserve account (as a net debit or credit). Yet the IMF recently decided to lump it with short-term capital flows, where most of the missing items in actuality might belong.

In this fashion, the various accounts will be formally reconciled. As before, let us describe each net balance, other than that on reserve account, as a net credit, regardless of its actual positive or negative sign. We can then write the following definitional identity:

Current-account balance (credit) + capital-account balance (credit) + errors and omissions (credit) – official reserve-account balance (debit) = 0.

THE TOTAL PICTURE

It is often unnecessary, or too time-consuming, to examine and reconcile all the detailed payments inflows and outflows. In general macroeconomic analysis and business forecasting, many of these details will be uninteresting. The right amount of information may just consist of a summary description of the main account relationships, or one crucial account balance. Yet there is no single perfect way of condensing all the available statistics.

The best way of illustrating how a given set of balance-of-payments statistics can be interpreted is by regrouping the data in different ways. Consider the hypothetical data in Table 20-7, measured in some hypothetical currency unit (either the home currency or a common international unit of account). This balance of payments is roughly in accord with the data setups we have previously been looking at, except in a few minor respects. Investment income has been listed separately from goods and nonfinancial services in the current account. Return flows of capital (repayments made and received, along with resales and repurchases of securities, across the borders) have not, as before, been netted out of the respective categories of gross capital flows, but instead have been entered on the opposite sides of the ledger. The grand total of recorded credits, or debits, has been made to equal 60 units.

As a first accounting exercise, let us sum up and net out all the current-account figures—imports, exports, investment income, and transfers. This gives us a net debit of 8—a current-account deficit. See summary version *A* in

Table 20- 7

A Hypothetical Balance of Payments (in a hypothetical currency unit)

Uses of Funds (Debits)		Sources of Funds (Credits)	
Imports (goods and nonfinancial services)	26	Exports (goods and nonfinancial services)	21
Transfers, net payment	6	Investment income, net receipt	3
Outflow of long-term capital	12	Inflow of long-term capital	10
Return outflow of long-term capital (repayments made and repurchases of securities from foreigners)	7	Return inflow of long-term capital (repayments received and resales of securities to foreigners)	8
Outflow of nonreserve short-term capital	4	Inflow of nonreserve short-term capital	5
Return outflow of nonreserve short-term capital (repayments made and repurchases of securities from foreigners)	2	Return inflow of nonreserve short-term capital (repayments received and resales of securities to foreigners)	3
Change in official reserve assets (increase)	3	Change in liquid liabilities to foreign authorities (increase)	10
Total debits	60	Total credits	60

Table 20-8 (which is entirely based on the hypothetical data in table 20-7). If we, then, tally all the items on capital and official reserve accounts (ten altogether), we derive, as we must, a matching net credit of 8. This is technically the funds surplus on total capital account (broadly interpreted)— or the capital import—that the current-account deficit in itself implies. And the latter is the real counterpart of the net funds inflow through financial transactions. In turn, the net capital-account credit can be thought of as an export of securities. The nation can therefore be said to have financed its current-account deficit through net security sales, or through a partial drawdown of its net foreign assets.

The print media would report this current-account balance as "unfavorable." From the narrow standpoint of the implicit net international-asset change, it is. From the broader perspective of how the nation wants to use its resources over time, it may quite possibly have been preferable to a current-account surplus. The data tell us only that the nation during the accounting year mortgaged some of its future opportunities for goods-and-services expenditure, for better or worse. In so doing, it added to its obligations for future international debt service—which would have to be discharged through the use of funds obtained via future current-account surpluses.

Under the next alternative data presentation (version *B*), transfers and investment income have been set apart from other current-account items. The 3 units of international purchasing power obtained through investment income must derive from past net buildups of assets abroad—at the time, a postponement of spending opportunities. Adding and subtracting all the inflow and outflow items pertaining to capital and reserve-account entries

Table 20-8
Four Summary Versions of a Balance of Payments (based on Table 20- 7)

Uses of Funds (Debits)		Sources of Funds (Credits)	
		A	
Current-account balance (deficit)	8	Capital- and reserve-account balance (inflow)	8
		B	
Net product imports (goods and nonfinancial services)	5	Investment income	3
Transfers, net payment	6	Net capital inflow, total	8
Total	11	Total	11
		C	
Current-account balance (deficit)	8	Net return inflow of nonreserve capital	2
New net outflow of nonreserve capital	1		
Total	9		
		Net change in official reserve accounts (loss)	7
		Total	9
		D	
Goods and services imports	26	Goods and services exports	24
Transfers	6	Inflow of long-term capital, net of return flow	3
Outflow of long-term capital, net of return flow	4	Subtotal	27
Total	36		
		Net inflow of short-term capital, incl. official settlements	9
		Total	36

A – D: a reconciliation of the various
balances (surplus: +; deficit: –)

Goods and services balance	–2
plus transfers (–6) equals	
Current account balance	–8
plus long-term capital flow (–1) equals	
Basic balance	–9
plus nonreserve short-term capital flows (2) equals	
Official settlements balance	–7
equals net reserve account change (–7)	

produces a net inflow of 8 units. Together with the 3 units of investment income receipts, a total of 11 units were available for current-account uses. Of this amount, 6 units were given away (perhaps "invested" in political alliances abroad). The remaining 5 were exchanged for net product imports, through which the nation augmented its current domestic product supply above and beyond its own production. Yet in its national-income equation, the figure corresponding to $X - M$ will only be -2 units (3-5).

Version C disaggregates the capital account so as to separate reserve-account items and net return flows of capital. These return flows amounted to $8 + 3 = 11$ units of inflows and $7 + 2 = 9$ units of outflows. The 2 units of net flows thus received, together with 7 units of net reserve-asset loss, were apparently allocated as follows: 8 units went into covering the current-account deficit, and 1 unit into financing a new net outflow of nonreserve capital.

In themselves, the added 3 units of reserve assets might just look like a cash leftover placed in the national kitty. But we know that it might reflect aggressive intervention purchases of foreign currencies. And it seems to have depended on the willingness of other nations to add to their reserve holdings of the nation's own currency (to the tune of 10 units)—otherwise, the 3-unit foreign reserve increase might not have been possible. No doubt, the home country is supplying a key currency. To a limited extent, it has acted like a bank, or some other financial intermediary: It has *borrowed short* (even if not necessarily through the taking of deposits), and it has used a portion of the borrowed funds—1 unit's worth, net—for *lending long*.

This balance-of-payments summary (C) has been divided into two main parts separated by a broken line. The purpose of this device is to illustrate the most popular contemporary way of summarily describing the overall payments result. According to the data, the total nonreserve items, placed "above the line," produced a funds deficit (a net debit) of 7 units. This figure is matched by an identical net credit on reserve-asset account—roughly, a reserve loss—recorded "below the line." On the one hand, this figure measures (above the line) the net amount of private and long-term government transactions that were not mutually settled through the matching of demands and supplies in the foreign exchange market. On the other, it measures (below the line) the net settlements that were in fact carried out by the home country's and foreign countries' governments and that thereby made up that demand-supply gap in the exchange market.

The above-the-line deficit (or, in another example, surplus), which thus has been officially settled, is usually called the *official settlements balance.* Sometimes it is called the "official reserve transactions balance," or simply the "overall" balance. Obviously, it can be measured either above or below the line. But since it is normally easier to gather the required data on the reserve account, one may in practice prefer to measure it below the line. On this basis, the United States incurred large deficits in almost every year during the 1970s.

The official balance captures the *change* in official international liquidity. By contrast, the *level* of such liquidity can be evaluated only through a look at the *stocks* of the relevant assets and liabilities. The official balance, moreover, gives an indication of potential exchange-rate movements: Had the actual official reserve changes not taken place, there could not have occurred any net exchange-market intervention involving the home country's currency, and additonal exchange-market pressure of one kind or another would have resulted. Barring other, compensating events, exchange rates would then have been different. In our example, the home country's currency must have benefited from net intervention support, by purchases of its currency by other governments (equaling 10 units). Without such support, the home currency would surely have depreciated—but by how much we cannot even guess without a detailed exchange-market model and without the additional data needed to apply that model.

U nder another approach, one separates those capital items that are believed to reflect more stable and fundamental changes in the nation's—and other nations'—economy. These items are then placed above the line, whereas the more volatile, transitory items are placed below the line. Long-term capital flows are thought to belong in the former category, even though many times, long-term securities may be resold on a short-term basis in response to transitory financial circumstances. Short-term capital flows of all kinds are placed below the line—despite the fact that short-term credits can often be rolled over into the longer term.

Version *D* shows this arrangement of our hypothetical data. There is an above-the-line deficit balance of 9 units, compensated for through a 9-unit net inflow of short-term capital, including the funds flows occurring via official reserve changes. Again, one may choose to measure this balance above or below the line. It is referred to as the *basic balance*. Needless to say, a country might be in basic surplus while in official deficit, or vice versa. How these various balances can be numerically reconciled with each other is shown at the bottom of Table 20-8.

The basic-balance concept is no longer used in U.S. government releases, but it still figures in the IMF format. It suffers from a certain arbitrariness and artificiality: How "basic" are tourist expenditures, and how "unbasic" are short-term trade credits among firms with long-term, continuing supplier-customer relationships? It seems more and more as if the search for one magic measure of a nation's international payments performance will be futile. Rather, we will have to decide exactly what we are looking for and evaluate those particular accounts that provide the pertinent information.

THE INTERNATIONAL INVESTMENT POSITION

Although the balance of payments records international economic events, it does not show the cumulative results of those events. Some of the transactions it records involve flows of inputs into current consumption or production. Others build up or reduce existing stocks of financial claims and liabilities. These characteristics, of course, separate current- and capital-account transactions. The former flows affect the nation's *stock* of physical assets and would be relevant in a complete recording of a nation's aggregate wealth. The latter flows—capital flows—affect the nation's financial balance sheet vis-à-vis the rest of the world. This account is usually summarized under the heading of the *international investment position*, alternatively labeled the "balance of international indebtedness."

The international investment position is derived from all existing known financial relationships with other nations. It covers both private and official items, summed up in an aggregate net figure. The word "investment" is here the stock counterpart of the flow concept "net foreign investment" in national-income accounting; both are broad, especially in that they include both debt and equity relations.

Table 20-9 contains a summary of recent data on the United States, collected by the U.S. government. The list of accumulated U.S. assets abroad differentiates, first, between government and private assets and, then, among

Table 20-9

The U.S. International Investment Position, 1974-78 (at year-end; in billions of dollars)

	1974	1977	1978
Net U.S. international investment position	58.8	72.4	76.7
U.S. assets abroad	255.7	383.0	450.1
Official reserve assets	15.9	19.3	18.7
Gold	11.7	11.7	11.7
SDRs	2.4	2.6	1.6
Reserve position in the IMF	1.9	4.9	1.0
Foreign currencies	0.0	0.0	4.4
Other government assets	38.4	49.6	54.2
Private assets	201.5	314.1	377.2
Direct investments	110.1	149.8	168.1
Foreign securities	28.2	49.4	53.4
Bank claims	46.2	92.6	129.6
Other	17.0	22.3	26.1
Foreign assets in the U.S.	196.9	310.6	373.3
Official assets	79.8	141.9	175.1
Private assets	117.1	168.7	198.2
Direct investments	25.1	34.6	40.8
Other	92.0	134.1	157.4

Note: The official U.S. gold reserve is here valued at the obsolete price of $42.20 per ounce. The values of other assets have been adjusted so as to reflect changes in their market prices and, if denominated in foreign currencies, in the dollar exchange rates of these currencies.

Source: U.S. Department of Commerce, *Survey of Current Business*, August 1979.

various asset types within these two categories. The official reserve data reveal a very low U.S. ratio between such assets and total U.S. assets abroad—a ratio of only 4 percent. Yet this figure would be several times higher if the American monetary gold stock were valued at the current market price of gold, rather than, as done here, at an official $42.20 price of no current consequence.

The bulk of American assets abroad, estimated at $450 billion in 1978, are in the form of direct investment, bank claims (a very volative item), and portfolio holdings of marketable securities. The main explanations for the size and growth of these assets are American takeovers of foreign firms; a physical expansion of existing American affiliates abroad, financed through equity or debt transfers from the United States, or through earnings retentions abroad; and a gradual upward revaluation of existing assets so that they will keep abreast of inflation (and of changes in exchange rates). In trying to reconcile annual changes in these stock data with the corresponding balance-of-payments data, one should remember that these latter revaluations, under current practice, are not generally registered in the balance of payments.

Comparing U.S. assets abroad with the comparable foreign assets in the United States, one detects some other glaring "imbalances." On the official side, foreign assets in the United States, at $175 billion in 1978 and overwhelmingly liquid, easily outstrip the American counterpart abroad. The implicit U.S. official "liquidity ratio" (reserve assets divided by liquid liabilities to foreign authorities) is just 10 percent (but might be around 100 percent at current gold prices). This relationship is a counterpart of the corresponding flow relationship in the recent U.S. balance of payments: The United States has supplied increasing amounts of short-term liabilities to the rest of the world, and foreign nations have absorbed these liquid dollar assets by running overall payments surpluses and undertaking intervention purchases in the exchange markets.

Put these observations in the context of the disproportionately large stock of U.S. foreign private capital, both short- and long-term, and you see a reinforced picture of the global banking function of the United States. It is in the business of banks to supply, rather than demand, liquidity; and the United States, similarly, has long had a strongly negative net position with respect to its foreign-exchange assets and liabilities. Banks and other financial intermediaries borrow short and lend long, thereby producing a transformation of available asset maturities for the public. So does the United States.

The U.S. role as a global superbank has expanded over the last decade. Whereas in the 1950s and 1960s the main customers were Europe and Japan, an entirely new customer group showed up in the 1970s: the oil-exporting countries. A large part of their payments surpluses have found their way into the United States—as "petrodollars" invested in U.S. government securities or, partly via the Eurodollar market, in claims on U.S. or U.S.-owned banks. Reliable data are not available, but there is no question that these nations, as short-term creditors, have played a big role in the intermediation of international loanable funds through the U.S. economy.

At the top of Table 20-9 is the *net U.S. international investment position*—or the difference between total U.S. assets abroad and total foreign assets in the United States. It has risen somewhat in recent years, at least in nominal (current-price) terms, reaching a recorded $77 billion in 1978. Clearly, this figure is subject to a wide margin of possible error, given the many difficulties in data collection and valuation. But the United States is most definitely a net international creditor. It has stored part of its national wealth abroad (the main part being stored at home in buildings, equipment, improved land, education, and possibly, healthier and more productive human bodies).

That wealth is apparently yielding a rather handsome return, judging from the net receipts of investment income in Table 20-3. The net recorded yield for 1979 was $32 billion ($66 billion – $34 billion = $32 billion), which suggests a pretty good "markup" between the cost of borrowings abroad and earnings on U.S. foreign lending and investment. But this net figure is a broad average and need not at all be indicative of the returns obtainable on recent, or potentially expanded, investments. Regardless, there may well come a time when it will seem desirable to liquidate part or all of that wealth, so as to take advantage of these postponed spending opportunities, via net imports of goods and services. This, surely, is part of the ongoing intertemporal bargain between the United States and the rest of the world.

SUMMARY

The balance-of-payments account records the flows of funds between one nation and the rest of the world on an annual basis. It is subdivided into a series of more narrowly defined accounts that list particular international sources and uses of funds, from trade in goods and services to unrequited transfers, private capital flows, and official reserve transactions. Double-entry bookkeeping ensures that total credits will always equal total debits, apart from purely statistical errors and omissions.

A goods-and-services surplus represents a net product supply to the rest of the world. Conversely, a goods-and-services deficit can fill a gap between the national product and total domestic spending. In the former situation, there is typically a buildup of foreign assets or a liquidation of foreign liabilities. In the latter, the nation's net indebtedness vis-à-vis other nations is increasing. The net stock of such assets and liabilities are measured by the international investment position, which is positive for creditor nations and negative for debtor nations.

Economists and statisticians have tried to devise one convenient measure of the overall balance-of-payments result, especially as a guide and target for economic policy. But these efforts have been inconclusive. Even so, the official reserve account is of particular concern, because it directly reflects ongoing exchange market intervention and may signal a need for changes in international or domestic economic policy. To make this judgment, we must first understand the macroeconomic interrelations between the home country and the rest of the world—a topic that will occupy us throughout the next three chapters.

Important Concepts

current account	loanable-funds demand (supply)
capital account	net foreign investment
double-entry bookkeeping	official foreign reserves
"invisible" trade	key currency
investment income	goods-and-services surplus (deficit)
emigrant remittance	official settlements balance

Questions

1. The daily press usually describes a trade (or current-account) surplus as "positive" and a corresponding deficit as "negative." Draft a one-paragraph "letter to the editor" in which you criticize the use of these adjectives and explain to the readers how deficits sometimes might be "good" and surpluses "bad" from a longer-run national standpoint.

2. Examine Table 20-3, and describe the apparent trends in U.S. exports, imports, investment income, transfers, capital outflows, and capital inflows during the 1970s.

3. Assume, half-seriously, that one could regard the U.S. economy as a huge corporation within the world economy, with other nations being its customers, suppliers, creditors, and debtors. Let's call it "America, Inc." Judging from Table 20-9, how would you then evaluate America's international balance sheet? Also indicate if and how you suspect that the published data might be partially inaccurate or misleading.

4. Country X, a non-reserve-currency country, in 1980 had a $6 billion current-account surplus, a $4 billion net capital outflow and a $2 billion official reserve increase. In 1981, its current-account position "deteriorated" by $4 billion, while net capital outflows increased by $1 billion. What must have happened to its official reserves (and what was its official settlements balance) in 1981?

Further Readings

Fieleke, Norman, *What is the Balance of Payments?* (Boston: Federal Reserve Bank of Boston, 1976).

Kemp, Donald, "Balance-of-Payments Concepts—What Do They Really Mean?", Federal Reserve Bank of St. Louis, *Review*, July 1975.

U.S. Department of Commerce, *Survey of Current Business* (quarterly and annual surveys of the U.S. balance of payments and international investment position).

21
MECHANISMS OF INTERNATIONAL ADJUSTMENT

In analyzing the balance-of-payments account in the previous chapter, we noticed how various inflows and outflows might be connected with each other. But we did not really explore these interconnections. In particular, we did not discuss how international transactions reflect ongoing changes in the domestic or foreign economies, nor did we explain how such transactions can affect the overall performance of an economy. This we will try to do presently, however. The topic might best be described as international or global macroeconomics. But the conventional description for it focuses on the mutual "adjustments" occurring in the trade and capital flows of each country, and, indirectly, in its entire economy. Hence the term "balance-of-payments adjustment."

In dealing with a subject of such a scope and complexity, we will have to think in broad aggregates. And we must remember that each sector, market, or economic function is an interdependent aspect of the entire national, or even global, economy. The perspective is lofty—yet the practical implications are far-reaching. How does a high U.S. rate of inflation affect the American balance of payments, the dollar, and the economies of other nations? How are business cycles and unemployment problems transmitted from one nation to another? We will summarize the prevailing theories about these matters, step by step, and apply them to a limited number of actual cases.

We will use the following strategy. First, we will summarize the main kinds of economic and financial linkages among nations. We will then introduce some theoretical notions of "balance" that define equilibrium conditions in particular markets and provide us with reference points in the analysis of change and adjustment. Subsequently, we will make a systematic description of the major channels of payments "disturbances" and ad-

378

justments, starting with purely monetary phenomena and proceeding to changes in income, spending, and output.

REAL AND FINANCIAL LINKAGES

Trade theory demonstrates how private markets can satisfy the mutual national requirements for physical products or, indirectly, factors. The study of capital movements and international financial management similarly indicates that it may be advantageous for different nations to compete and bargain with each other in the international or national financial markets. These interdependencies are at once competitive and cooperative. By and large, they expand the range of national economic opportunities and promote economic welfare, yet they can pose serious temporary difficulties in particular markets, sectors, and nations.

As we know, product trade creates a variety of *real* links between demand and supply conditions at home and abroad. Shifts in world-market prices can produce, via their effects on imports, changes in the product composition of home-country expenditure. If the country is sufficiently small, it will be a price taker. If not, it will, to some degree, be a price maker, and its responses to foreign supply changes will in turn modify the world-market price situation. Conversely, changes in home-country demand patterns, perhaps because of differential income elasticities of demand from product to product, will change the volume and composition of its purchases abroad, with potential consequences for real income and demand in other countries. Trade in productive factors (labor, physical capital, and technology) and in intermediate goods affects the productive capacity of the importing nations, and often also their export performance. Just think of the global economic changes wrought by the cutbacks in world crude oil supplies in the 1970s. These are examples of real linkages among nations. They are illustrated in Figure 21-1 (specifically, linkages #1 and #2).

Turning to examples of *financial* linkages, we can envision comparable connections between demands and supplies in the national and international markets for money, loanable funds, and securities. An increase in world-market interest rates tends to stimulate capital outflows from any given country with a reasonably open financial system, as suggested by link #4. If the country (as assumed in Figure 21-1) is small, it will normally adjust its own interest rates to those abroad. If it is large relative to total global financial markets, it is more likely to have a noticeable influence on world credit and security prices. The global banking function of the United States nicely illustrates this kind of back-and-forth financial linkage across the oceans.

However, we should not compartmentalize product and financial trade, but rather, acknowledge how they complement each other. Financial markets, within or among nations, would not exist without the prior existence of product markets. What use is credit if you cannot, ultimately, spend it on goods and services? The most obvious real financial linkage among nations is that between long-term international sales of stocks or bonds and concurrent imports of real assets that expand production capabilities (suggesting a combination of linkages #3 and #2). Similarly, as demonstrated in development economics, output and trade patterns to a large extent are formed by prior inflows of private and official capital. The list of real financial interconnections among nations is almost endless.

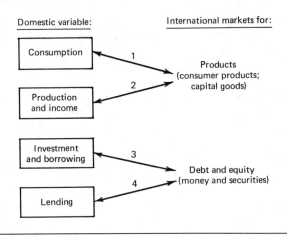

Description of main linkages

1. Changes in international product prices affect the level and composition of consumption (via import supply).
2. Changes in international product prices affect the level and composition of exports, and thereby the level of income (via export demand).
3. Changes in international rates of interest or return affect the cost and availability of of foreign financing for investment (via capital inflows).
4. Changes in international rates of interest or return affect purchases of foreign debt and and equity securities, and thereby portfolio income (via capital outflows).

Figure 21-1. Links between the domestic economy and international markets.

CONDITIONS FOR EXTERNAL AND INTERNAL BALANCE

In a world of truly free and open markets, national economies would quickly register and react to economic changes abroad. If competition were perfect and all prices flexible, there could exist no shortages or surpluses of any kind, even if there were sudden shifts in international demands or supplies. If, by contrast, there are market imperfections or government market interferences, the markets will be unable to correct such imbalances fully and quickly. Even so, market-dominated economies have at least a partial capacity for self-correction. The corrective mechanism lies in flexible prices. Price changes can induce adjustments of various kinds—in lending, borrowing, security sales, money accumulation, investment, employment, production, and consumption at home and abroad. Such adjustments help restore *equilibrium*—and they help ensure that the activities of different economic units are mutually compatible and that the allocation of resources among them will be relatively efficient. We will later take up the problem of how government policy might facilitate, or occasionally hinder, these processes.

Since a nation's balance of payments is a focus for all its international economic transactions, it is natural to tie the analysis of its international economic adjustments to the state of its balance of payments. The various payments accounts reflect how strongly and quickly a nation responds to changes in world market conditions. But international payments and receipts are closely reflected in the exchange markets, and these also provide readily observable indications of shifting international payments developments.

In particular, the exchange markets provide a rough measure of the extent of overall payments balance. Such *external payments balance* exists whenever the difference between all private—or, more precisely, nonreserve—foreign-exchange demands and supplies stands at zero. There may be various combinations of current-account surpluses (deficits) and capital outflows (inflows), but, by definition, they add up to zero. There is thus, by definition, no exchange-market intervention and no change in the official assets and liabilities on reserve account. The exchange rate will then be *freely floating*—that is, flexible and responsive to private demand and supply pressure—and this condition will guarantee external payments balance. If, however, this result is achieved only through severe government controls over private trade or capital flows, the term "balance" will be misleading. Rather, there will then be a concealed imbalance in the form of a market tendency toward an excess demand, or supply, in the exchange market.

In rare cases, payments balance may be achieved because private exchange demands and supplies happen to be equal at the preexisting exchange rate. Or, more typically, it may be achieved through the equilibrating effects of a change in this rate. The exchange rate will then effectively have carried the main burden of adjustment. The two situations should be differentiated. The former involves not only payments balance but also a kind of *external monetary balance*, for it preserves the price (exchange-rate) relationship between domestic money and foreign monies. The technical conditions required for such balance to be achieved are listed in the last column of Table 21-1.

Table 21-1
Conditions for Internal and External Balance

Internal Balance		External Balance	
Real Balance (full employment)	Monetary Balance (price stability)	Payments Balance (zero net official settlements)	Monetary Balance (exchange-rate stability)
Labor supply = labor demand; no unplanned inventory change; no unplanned underutilization of capital	Money supply = money demand; change in money supply = change in product and security supply	Foreign exchange supply = foreign exchange demand; current-account surplus (deficit) = capital outflow (inflow) on nonreserve account	Home-currency supply to foreigners = foreign demand for home currency; change in supply of tradable products and securities = change in demand for tradable products and securities

Imbalances can of course be positive or negative (in a purely algebraic sense). It is self-evident that overall external payments imbalances can consist of surpluses (which involve an excess private foreign-exchange supply) or of deficits (involving an excess private foreign-exchange demand). In regard to external monetary imbalances, there might be an appreciation, or a depreciation, of the domestic currency. Whenever there is net intervention but exchange rates are still not stable, external monetary imbalance may exist side by side with a payments imbalance. For instance, a country with a tendency toward a payments surplus may allow this surplus to be partly—but only partly—offset by currency appreciation. There will then be a residual payments surplus, absorbed through intervention purchases of foreign currencies.

Within a nation, one can also look at balance from two separate perspectives. If demands and supplies in all product and factor markets are in equilibrium—a very unlikely event in reality—complete *internal real balance* prevails. As explained in column one of Table 21-1, involuntary unemployment is then zero, and the markets for capital goods and intermediate goods see to it that no firm gets stuck with underutilized facilities or unwanted, unsold inventories. Sometimes this kind of balance is, a bit too simply, described as "full employment." It presumes a high degree of flexibility in both product and factor prices, in the downward as well as upward direction.

In the financial sphere, there is a question of whether, at the same time, there is balance among total loanable-funds demands and supplies, and between demands and supplies in individual markets for securities and money. If the answer is yes, one might refer to this situation as one of *internal monetary balance*, since money plays a key part in all financial markets. The change in the money supply will then, as indicated in Table 21-1, be no larger or smaller than the change in the product and security supply. With no excess money, there can be no upward or downward pressure on prices. "Price stability" is, of course, the conventional term for this situation—and we know it has become an elusive norm. Should either the real or the financial sector be unbalanced, equilibrating forces will be set in motion, easing unemployment, correcting inventory levels, and adjusting financial portfolios. These processes will be smoother and quicker if wage rates, product prices, and interest rates are highly flexible.

Internally, as well as externally, there are interconnections between the possibilities for internal and external balance. Adjustment of an imbalance in either the domestic or the foreign sector will upset any balance that may exist in the other sector. For example, a tightening of money and credit conditions may discourage private real investment and upset the market for capital goods. It may then reduce the demand for labor, thus aggravating unemployment, and produce changes both in private capital flows and in foreign trade. If we examine a particular nation's economy over time, we will find that these adjustments and readjustments are going on continuously. We would be hard put to find actual cases of complete internal balance, let alone combinations of internal and external balance.

These balance concepts can be regarded as analytical and normative benchmarks. They will help us describe vairous types of disturbances that affect a nation's international transactions and trigger pressures toward adjustment. The remainder of this chapter will take up a limited number of cases that describe some important mechanisms through which such disturbances and adjustments can occur. In each case, the picture we draw will abstract from many of the likely side complications and concentrate on a few crucial variables. By combining features of two or several cases, the reader can construct more plausible real-world scenarios, with multiple disturbances and simultaneous adjustment processes along different tracks.

THE ROLE OF MONEY AND PRICES

We shall first consider a disturbance in the form of a change in the quantity of money existing in the home country. If the country originally enjoyed price stability, the injection of new money implies a disturbance of the internal monetary balance. Our task is to trace out its consequences, internally and externally. What are the adjustment mechanisms? Will they restore balance? And if so, how?

But we should first explain how the monetary expansion has come about. The monetary authority (the central bank) might have "monetized" an additional portion of the outstanding government debt by purchasing publicly held treasury securities (i.e., via open-market purchases). Or the commercial banks may have offered the public additional demand-deposit balances through newly extended bank credit. Or the public may, on its own initiative, have shifted funds out of time deposits into demand deposits. But as these circumstances may be unimportant, we could resort to Milton Friedman's famous, half-serious analogy with a government helicopter: It suddenly drops an evenly distributed amount of paper currency over the entire nation, never mind why it would do such a crazy thing.

What will happen? Everybody finds himself with a sudden excess of money relative to his real income and wealth, and he actually feels wealthier from his own, myopic perspective. His portfolio balance—as between goods and money, in particular—is out of kilter. He starts adjusting by expanding his purchases, and there develops an overall excess demand for goods and services. If the domestic economy is in real balance, no additional output will or can come forth, and the demand pressure results in a compensating increase in the general price level. If, by contrast, there were an initial real imbalance in the form of unemployment and idle capacity, there might be a positive output response. But this result is likely to be very short-lived. Once real balance has been approximately attained, the impact of further money-supply expansion will fall entirely on the price level. And if producers and workers are already used to living with inflation, their price responses to such disturbances might be swift and direct, regardless of any slack in the economy.

This internal adjustment process should be familiar from standard macro-theory. It presents the simplified picture of the classical *quantity theory*. In this theory, money functions exclusively as a means of payments— the only means of payments. Its effect on the price level is illustrated via the *equation of exchange*, which shows the definitional identity between total expenditure and total receipts in a closed economy. This equation is conventionally written $M^s \times V = P \times Q$, with M^s standing for the money supply, V for the income velocity of money, P for the general price level (measured by a price index), and Q for the physical quantity of output (say, the gross national product per year at constant prices). V is here assumed to be constant and Q is determined by real factor supplies, not—except possibly in the short run—by M^s. Changes in M^s then will lead to parallel changes in P, and the rate of inflation will thus equal the rate of excess money creation. There is thus one dominant cause-and-effect relation:

$$M^s \uparrow \Longrightarrow P \uparrow$$

Now assume instead that this country has an open economy and that product exports and imports are freely permitted. The monetary expansion then leads to a demand both for importables (actual or potential imports) and for exportables, and possibly also for nontraded products. The new demand pressure thus spills over onto foreign transactions—and completely so, if there are no idle resources at home. Imports start to rise, whereas exports start to decline, so there will be a tendency toward a trade deficit and an external payments imbalance. If the country is small, it will exercise no influence on world market prices, and the import expansion and export contraction will consist of volume adjustments at the going foreign-currency prices of the traded products.

But can a trade deficit really emerge? Who is going to finance it—that is, provide the funds through which it can be paid for? We are still ignoring the possibility of private security markets and capital flows, so the only potential financier is the government. But in the classical world of the quantity theory, the government will not involve itself, either because it has no foreign reserves and no access to international credit suppliers, or because it has chosen a policy of exchange-market *laissez faire*. It will then be up to private traders to square their own foreign-currency demands and supplies—in other words, to bring about payments balance on their own.

This will have to be done through an increase in the price of foreign currency, which represents an exchange market depreciation of the domestic currency. The depreciation discourages the growth in imports by increasing the home-country prices of foreign goods, and it encourages exports by increasing the home-currency revenues from sales abroad. The new exchange rates will be such as to reequate export revenues and import expenditures, thereby leaving product trade and overall payments in balance—although at the expense of external monetary balance.

In this fashion, the old quantity theory can be extended to the international scene. Even then, money does not in any way affect real conditions, or the existence of internal real balance. In fact, the economy very much resembles a barter system, except for the mechanical way in which payments are settled (through transfers of money). Relative product prices will not change, either within the national economy or between it and the world market. For any given rate of monetary expansion in the trade-partner countries, the added expansion of home-country money will create a proportional increase in all product prices in the home country. A comparable increase will occur in exchange rates, R, measured in domestic currency per foreign currency:

$$M^s\!\uparrow \Longrightarrow P\!\uparrow \Longrightarrow R\!\uparrow$$

Exchange rates will then move exactly so as to equate the decline in the currency's international purchasing power with the decline in its purchasing power at home. This outcome is shown in the list of alternative adjustment scenarios in Table 21-2. For example, a doubling of the money supply will cut the currency's domestic purchasing power in half, and the accompanying 50 per cent exchange-market depreciation (implicit in a doubling of R) will have the same effect on its real value abroad. In the classical metaphor, money is only a superficial "veil" all around. These ideas also make up the core of the modern "monetarism" that has blossomed in the international economic literature in the last couple of decades; more on this school of thought later.

Table 21-2
Effects of Money Supply Expansion

Initial Domestic Situation	Effects on Internal Balance		Effects on External Balance	
	Under Floating Exchange Rate	Under Pegged Exchange Rate	Under Floating Exchange Rate	Under Pegged Exchange Rate
Full employment; trade and payments balance	Proportional inflation; continued full employment	Less-than-proportional inflation; continued full employment	Proportional exchange-rate increase	Trade and payments deficit; capital outflow
Unemployment; trade and payments balance	Less-than-proportional inflation; reduced unemployment	Less-than-proportional inflation; reduced unemployment	Less-than-proportional exchange-rate increase	Trade and payments deficit; capital outflow

The proposition that exchange-rate movements will fall in line with relative price movements in the trading countries is called the *purchasing-power-parity theorem*, which is based on the classical thinking outlined here. It does not deny the possibility of short-term departures from parity, especially when governments take drastic steps to influence exchange rates, through exchange-market intervention in particular. But it claims that over the longer run exchange rates and prices will have to converge around this parity and that government intervention cannot permanently stop this trend.

A related concept is that of *real exchange rates*. These are the ratios at which similar products can be exchanged across the borders through the necessary transactions in product and exchange markets. Consider a standardized, broadly available product such as wheat. Within a given nation, it can be sold for local currency, which can be converted into foreign currency at the going exchange rate, and the conversion proceeds can in turn be used for purchasing the same product in the foreign country. If you do this and end with the same quantity as you started with, the real exchange rate is unity. And this means that purchasing power parity prevails. If you end up with a bit more, or less, the real exchange rate deviates from unity, and at this moment, the exchange rate is out of step with its parity position.

A Complication: Intervention

We will now examine the case in which the domestic or foreign authorities intervene in the exchange market and the exchange rates thus do not float freely. Possibly the authorities are trying to stop or reduce an emerging domestic-currency depreciation and to this end sell foreign currency in exchange for domestic currency. They may, in effect, be *pegging* the exchange rate at its initial level.

If the home country intervenes on its own, its authorities will then draw down their foreign exchange reserves. In this way, they will fill the foreign exchange gap created through the shrinkage of net exports and place that foreign exchange in the hands of importers, for payment to the foreign sellers. A trade deficit, and a payments deficit, will then materialize, and it will effectively be financed by the drawdown of reserves. Should foreign authorities be doing the intervening, they will correspondingly add to their holdings of the home country's currency—in this case, undoubtedly a key currency—while issuing more currency of their own. Either situation will lead to a reduction in the home country's net foreign-reserve position. As indicated in Table 21-2, the domestic price pressure will lessen, and the new inflation will be less than proportional to the monetary expansion.

The monetary expansion will in the process trigger changes not only in exports, X, and imports, M, but also in domestic expenditure for private investment, I, and consumption, C:

$$M^s\uparrow \Longrightarrow \frac{X\downarrow}{M\uparrow} \Longrightarrow \frac{I\uparrow}{C\uparrow}$$

There are two complementary ways to envision the connection between the new trade deficit and the increase in domestic expenditure. The added money assets encourage people to add to their real assets as well—via investment. Meanwhile, they allocate part of their new monetary wealth to extra consumption. And the government-financed trade deficit will create a net supply of foreign products entering the country—most likely in some combination of consumption and capital goods—which somehow has to be absorbed. Note that the negative value of $X - M$ will represent negative "foreign investment" in the national-income sense of this term.

But the intervention just described will gradually destroy the newly created domestic money, as the authorities buy up domestic currency and take it out of circulation. If the monetary expansion is a one-shot affair, the demand pressure will gradually evaporate, and the trade account will return to its former balance. If the monetary expansion continues, the spillover of demand onto tradable products will go on. But the home country's foreign reserves will then gradually be depleted (or foreign countries will feel oversupplied with the home-country currency), and the process cannot go on indefinitely. Some other adjustment must set in, through market pressure or government policy changes.

In the interim, the domestic economy may move closer to real balance and employ whatever resources initially had been idle. As for internal monetary balance, it need not be seriously disturbed, for the intervention permits the new price pressure to be siphoned off onto the world market. Foreign countries may actually become dumping grounds for part of the home country's newly created money: Their intervention will expand their own money supplies, as their authorities try to maintain their exchange rates. In short, the home country will then have "exported" some of its monetary expansion to these foreign countries.

This scenario has a great deal in common with the actual interrelations between the United States and other parts of the industrial world in the 1960s and early 1970s. At that time, the relatively rapid and accelerating money-supply expansion in the United States lead to a deterioration of the U.S. trade balance and an improvement in the trade balances of less inflation-prone countries, especially West Germany and Japan. The mutual commitment not to change the existing exchange rates forced the latter countries to mop up, through intervention purchases, the excess U.S. dollars supplied to the international market in exchange for their own currencies. This, in turn, meant that the United States was, in effect, "exporting" part of its inflation, and this became a source of friction in their international economic-political relations. To be sure, many other factors were also contributing to these results, but relative rates of money-supply expansion indeed seem to have mattered a great deal. The financial dominance of the United States in the world economy permitted it to maintain a prolonged payments imbalance, as it escaped the burden of adjusting its payments situation to its self-inflicted monetary disturbances. Meanwhile, it imposed external disturbances, and also internal monetary disturbances, on the cooperating foreign nations.

When exchange rates are, as in this example, pegged, national money supplies will be closely linked to each other—almost as if the nations that peg their exchange rates were sharing the same currency. The individual country will then have great difficulty in determining the rate of growth of its money supply. It may, for reasons of domestic stabilization, prefer the growth to be moderate, but the intervention necessary to sustain its exchange-rate peg forces it—or other intervening nations—to pump out more and more of its currency. It could perhaps tighten its domestic monetary policy to offset the intervention, but such countermoves will typically, through their anti-inflationary effects, heighten the very need for intervention. So it may be a losing battle. If the country wants to retain its exchange rate peg, it will ultimately lose its ability to conduct an independent national monetary policy.

The floating of all major currencies in the early 1970s technically broke that intercountry money-supply link. This step was believed to restore national independence in monetary policy—in particular, by shielding foreign nations from changes in U.S. monetary conditions. But the large foreign holdings of dollar assets and the strong interconnections between U.S. and foreign financial markets still create a large measure of interdependence in matters of money and credit. And the authorities still intervene in the exchange market, although in a less systematic manner. The float is not free but *managed*. As a result, a partial international linkage of national money supplies still exists.

Securities and Interest Rates

So far, we have considered only one type of financial instrument— money. As the next step toward realism, let us allow for long-term interest-bearing securities as well. Assume that there is one standardized type of bond with negligible credit risk, issued either by the government or by private corporations and traded on the domestic capital market. A monetary expansion will then have an unsettling effect on this market, as it initially induces the money-rich public to attempt to adjust its portfolio by acquiring additional bonds. This will push up the market price of previously issued bonds, thereby lowering their yield, and newly issued bonds will now carry a lower coupon. The increased availability of money may also make the volume of new bond issues, and bond-financed expenditure, larger. Yet if the monetary expansion is short-lived, the volume of bonds will stabilize itself at a new, higher level proportionate to the new money and price levels. The real value of bonds will remain unchanged, and the interest rate will move back up again.

If the capital market is internationally open, part of the new bond demand is likely to direct itself abroad. There will then be a tendency toward a capital outflow, along with a trade deficit. But in the absence of any exchange market intervention, the domestic currency will depreciate so as to offset these tendencies and preserve external payments balance. The monetary shock will thus again be absorbed, internally and externally .

On the other hand, if the monetary expansion continues, lenders (bond buyers) will start demanding compensation for the apparent erosion of the purchasing power of these assets. They will require higher nominal yields, and bond issuers, sensing a growth in their nominal incomes, will feel they can afford to pay such yields. Once the rate of inflation has settled down to a steady trend, the capital market will establish an *inflation premium* on interest rates that converges with the rate of monetary expansion—or in a growing economy, with its excess over the growth in output, Q. Conceivably, the public will also demand interest to be paid on money balances. As a mathematical approximation, the nominal interest rate, i, will then gradually tend to exceed the real interest rate, i', by a margin equal to the rate of inflation:

$$i - i' \approx \frac{\Delta P}{P} \approx \frac{\Delta M^s}{M^s} - \frac{\Delta Q}{Q}$$

This result is illustrated in Figure 21-2. Three of the axes (joined at the origin) pertain, respectively, to the rates of monetary expansion, inflation, and increase in nominal income, Y (where $Y = PQ$). The fourth axis pertains to the nominal rate of interest. The three solid 45° lines show the relationships between the three pairs of variables: money versus prices; money versus nominal income, and prices versus the nominal interest rate. The money-price line (labeled I) starts at point B—a point at which, hypothetically, the money supply is unchanged. The point has been placed at a negative 4 percent rate of inflation, as this is the assumed rate of output growth—which can absorb a corresponding portion of the money supply. For prices to be stable, there would then have to be a 4 percent monetary growth, as shown by the intersection of the money-price line with the horizontal axis at point A. The money-income line (II) starts at the origin, because under a stable money supply, nominal income would also be stable. The price/interest-rate line (III) goes through point C on the horizontal axis. This point is at an interest rate of 2 percent—that is, the assumed underlying real interest rate upon which monetary expansion can place an inflation premium.

When real growth is exactly matched by money growth, the economy is on a noninflationary path. This situation corresponds to the inner, broken-line rectangle with a length of CA and a height of BO. Additional, inflationary money growth expands the rectangle equally in all four directions. This is suggested by the larger rectangle, which has a length of

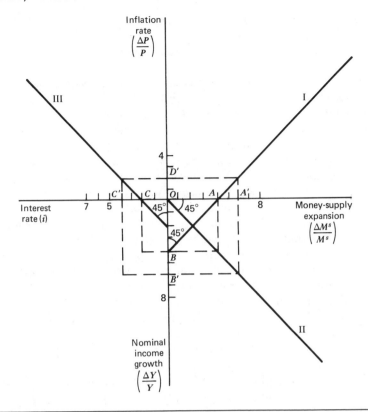

Line I shows the equivalence between changes in the rate of money supply growth and in the rate of inflation. A 4 percent money-supply growth is assumed to be noninflationary.

Line II shows the proportionality between changes in the money supply and in nominal income, based on the assumption that the velocity of money is constant.

Line III shows the equivalence between changes in the rate of inflation and in the nominal interest rate, based on the assumption that the current inflation rate is fully accounted for by lenders and borrowers. The underlying real interest rate is assumed to be 2 percent.

The *rectangle* with the length CA and the height BO pertains to a situation of price stability. The rectangle with the length $C'A'$ and the height $B'D'$ pertains to a situation of 2 percent inflation.

Figure 21-2. Effects of a prolonged monetary expansion (all variables are in percent per annum).

$C'A'$ and a height of $B'D'$. The distances OD', AA', BB', and CC' are all equal to the rate of excess money expansion and to the inflation premium. They show how the economy has monetarily swollen up around its inner, real core.

This is a picture of unchanged internal real balance, coupled with internal monetary imbalance (inflation). Externally, a flexible exchange rate ensures continued payments balance. Any differential between the rates of domestic and foreign inflation will require continuous exchange-rate correction. We do not, however, need to consider capital flows. The reason is as follows. Although a higher rate of monetary expansion at home than abroad will create a *nominal* interest differential in favor of the home country, both foreign and domestic financial managers will recognize that this differential is merely an inflation premium, and they will anticipate it to be offset by an accompanying depreciation of the home country's currency. The preexisting international *real*-yield relationship will therefore not have been altered, and there will be no incentive for capital flows in either direction.

This is a simple version of the monetarists' open-economy model. In it, all parties, at home and abroad, fully and correctly discount all nominal money values for future inflation; they have, through experience, acquired perfect foresight in this regard. Clearly, these conditions will frequently be violated in the transitional short run when the rate of money-supply growth has just started to increase, or, in a reverse example, to decline. But they seem much more realistic in the longer run.

In actuality, the authorities may not wish to see the domestic currency depreciate. Perhaps they want to facilitate imports through an "overvaluation" of the currency while the prices of domestically-produced import substitutes are going up. Or they might attach a special prestige value to the currency's international worth. Whatever the reasons, their refusal to permit the exchange rate to adjust will lead to a different external payments situation and to pressure for alternative adjustment processes. We already outlined the monetary and price effects of intervention in the context of a simple money-and-product model. (Refer also to Table 21-2.) We will now elaborate on those effects in an expanded financial context.

Money Creation and Banking

For a realistic description of how international payments disturbances affect a modern financial system, we have to account for the existence of banks and other private financial intermediaries. We also have to allow for different types of money within each economy. When we do so, we will find that some of the adjustment processes will be accelerated, while working in the same directions as previously indicated.

To start, we must recall that the public in all modern economies holds money in two forms. One consists of plain currency—that is, notes and coins issued by the monetary authorities (in the United States, by the Federal Reserve and the Treasury). The other consists of demand and other transaction deposits with private banks. For the individual, the distinction between currency and demand deposits is fairly trivial. But it is crucial to our analysis of monetary disturbances, monetary adjustments, and exchange-market intervention.

Since intervention purchases have to be paid for, they create monetary claims on the intervening authorities. These claims normally end up in the reserves of commercial banks, in compensation for the deposits issued by these banks to customers who have presented their foreign-currency earnings or proceeds to them. This is what happens when these customers—exporters and international borrowers—ask their banks to purchase their newly acquired foreign currency in exchange for additions to their deposit accounts. The banks then initially become the owners of additional foreign-currency balances. But if the central bank steps in and buys them, the commercial banks will acquire additional reserve balances on deposit with the central bank—that is, monetary claims on this authority. This is how the central bank makes its payments—by going deeper into debt.

The added bank reserves permit the banks to make additional loans to the public (or to buy additional government securities from it). Through these actions, even more bank deposit balances will be created. This process is called the *credit and money multiplier*, so named because the initial reserve injection will have a multiplicative effect on bank deposits and the overall money supply. How much larger this effect will be depends primarily on the magnitude of the banks' legal reserve requirements. Another helpful concept is that of *high-powered money*, defined so as to include all monetary claims on the authorities. When such money enters bank reserves, it can and normally will create multiples of another type of money—that is, certain kinds of bank deposits. The general public can hold high-powered money only in the form of currency, and its multiplicative power can be realized only if currency is deposited with banks and thus becomes part of bank reserves.

Returning now to our monetary payments disturbances, we can better appreciate the consequences of exchange-market intervention. Intervention purchases create high-powered domestic money, thereby greatly enlarging their monetary effects. Intervention sales do the opposite—destroying high-powered money. In turn, the price effects will also be larger. And the claim by surplus countries such as Western Germany, Japan, and Switzerland that they have in the past been forced to "import" inflation via intervention purchases of U.S. dollars becomes even more understandable. Conversely, the inflationary pressures in deficit countries have been partly offset through their intervention sales, depending on the relative magnitudes of these sales and the size of the money multiplier in each such country.

But what has then happened to monetary conditions in the United States? When the U.S. authorities intervene, the effects are just like those we have described for foreign countries. But when foreign authorities intervene by purchasing dollars, they usually place these dollars in U.S. Treasury securities, purchased on the open market, and thereby feed these dollars back into the hands of the U.S. public. If financed in this way, U.S. payments deficits will *not* absorb any part of the U.S. money supply. If financed through U.S. sales of, say, Deutschemarks and British pounds, they do, however. So key currency countries are in this respect special cases. In practice, however, this distinction will not matter very much, because the authorities in these countries can usually take offsetting policy actions at home and approximately establish the money supplies they deem appropriate.

The Essence of the "Monetary Approach"

The payments disturbances and adjustments discussed so far have all centered on changes in the money supply, with money being closely tied to prices and exchange rates. This perspective is identified with the so-called *monetary approach* to the balance of payments. This approach is an outgrowth of neoclassical quantity theory. In many respects, it parallels the monetarist analysis of domestic inflation and macroeconomic stabilization policy that has emerged in recent years, mostly from the Chicago school.

Internationally, its main thesis is that the payments balance is a "monetary phenomenon," rather than primarily a matter of conditions in the markets for tradable products, or of the levels of aggregate saving and expenditure. Money thus plays a pivotal role in both disturbances and adjustment. In the extreme, all disturbances will seem to have a monetary origin, and only a monetary correction will move them—through a change in the relative international price of monies (i.e., exchange rates) or through an elimination of the original money-supply change. Internal balance, in this view, requires an elimination of the excess growth of money at home, and exchange-rate stability is achievable only by maintaining a money growth rate comparable to those in the trading-partner countries.

It is generally acknowledged that the new international monetarists have made important contributions to the development of adjustment theory. Because of their insights and persuasiveness, interpretations of contemporary balance-of-payments problems now focus much more on monetary factors. In the early and mid-1960s, it was rarely suggested that the U.S. payments deficit had much to do with the U.S. money supply, or its relationship to money growth abroad. Fifteen years later there was a rather strong consensus that the poor performance of the dollar, especially against continental European currencies, to a large extent mirrored relative inflation rates and relative rates of money and credit creation. Yet there are those who oppose the monetarists and claim that especially in the short run, money plays only a small, subsidiary role in the typical real-world adjustment. And they believe that we need to focus more on variations in the *demand* for money, because such variations can counteract changes in the money supply and obscure the importance of the latter. The debate goes on.

Evidence on Purchasing-Power Parity

The purchasing-power-parity theorem easily lends itself to empirical testing. Actually, every international tourist does some testing through his own comparison shopping: He or she may make travel plans in part on the basis of the relative costs of hotel rooms, food, and entertainment; moreover, the tourist may be looking for souvenir bargains, duty-free liquor, or antiques suited for high-profit, low-risk smuggling. At least for these particular items, the tourist wants real exchange rates to depart from unity.

Table 21-3
Rates of Inflation and Changes in Exchange Rates
(averages, in per cent per annum, for 1968-1978)

Country	Change in Wholesale Prices	Actual Change in Exchange Rate	Theoretical "Parity" Change in Exchange Rate
Argentina	113%	75%	101%
Chile	109	132	97
Turkey	16	11	9
Portugal	13	5	7
Italy	11	3	5
Greece	10	2	4
U.K.	10	2	4
U.S.	6	—	—
Thailand	6	0	0
West Germany	5	- 8	- 1
Japan	3	- 6	- 3

Note: Exchange rates are in foreign-currency prices of the U.S. dollar. "Parity" = purchasing power parity. Parity exchange-rate changes have been calculated through the formula

$$\frac{R_{f/\$} + \triangle R_{f/\$}}{R_{f/\$}} = \frac{P_f + \triangle P_f}{P_f} \div \frac{P_{US} + \triangle P_{US}}{P_{US}}$$

where $R_{f/\$}$ is the exchange rate (in foreign currency per dollar), P_f the foreign price level, and P_{US} the U.S. price level; $\triangle$ denotes the average annual change in the particular variable.

Source: International Monetary Fund, *International Financial Statistics*, various issues.

Table 21-3 contains data on recent price changes and exchange-rate changes in a sample of 11 countries. The data span ten years, a period long enough to describe long-term trends, and are expressed in average annual percentages. The actual rates of depreciation or appreciation against the U.S. dollar (second column) can be compared with the hypothetical exchange-rate changes (third column) that would have occurred under perfect parity, given the reported price-level changes.

A glance at the table tells us that there were significant departures from the indicated parity rates for many of the countries, but that the overall correlation pattern between price and exchange-rate changes was nevertheless quite strong. The Latin American countries with extreme inflation rates thus suffered by far the greatest currency depreciation—or, technically, increases in their local-currency prices of the U.S. dollar. On the other hand, the two countries with less inflation than the United States—Japan and West Germany—experienced an appreciation of their currencies.

In interpreting these results, we should keep in mind several things. No price index can ever perfectly capture changes in general price levels, for it is practically impossible to devise a truly representative product sample. The price indexes we have used pertain to products that may or may not enter international trade. Had we confined the test to traded products, the chances that the data would fall precisely in line would have been greater. The observed discrepancies between parity and actual exchange-rate changes might reflect changing transportation costs or trade restrictions, temporary private capital flows that have strengthened or weakened particular currencies, or government intervention policies that have distorted the international price mechanism.

Table 21-4

Rates of Inflation and Interest (average rates of change in prices per annum; long-term government bond yields)

Country	Change in Wholesale Prices, 1976II-1979II	Change in Wholesale Prices, 1978II-1979II	Bond Yield, 1979II
Portugal	30%	40%	17%
U.K.	14	11	12
Italy	13	14	14
Australia	11	14	10
Sweden	9	11	10
U.S.	8	11	9
West Germany	3	4	8
Japan	2	4	8

Source: International Monetary Fund, *International Financial Statistics*, various issues.

We can also test the international monetarist proposition regarding interest rates—that inflation rates will be reflected in capital markets, as well as in exchange markets. Table 21-4 shows recent one-year and three-year inflation rates in a small group of countries, along with data on a set of roughly comparable interest rates, pertaining to long-term government bonds. The statistical fit is not terribly good; but again, there is a distinct pattern, with high inflation rates being associated with relatively high bond yields, and vice versa. This holds about equally for the three- and one-year inflation data.

These and similar published test by and large support the monetarist view, at least as far as the longer-term trends are concerned. There can be little doubt that monetary conditions have a pervasive influence in all financial markets and that even the developed countries have by now become very inflation-conscious. This learning experience must have reduced the public's "money illusion"—its failure to see the realities underneath inflation-distorted data. At the same time, many short-term payments disturbances and adjustment processes may be only remotely related to changes in money supplies and price levels, and the bold clarity of the monetarist scenario should not blind us to other channels of adjustment.

NONMONETARY DEMAND AND SUPPLY CHANGES

In each economy there are two sets of markets—goods-and-services markets and financial markets. There are three basic types of assets—real assets, securities, and money (or deposits with financial institutions)—exchanged for one another through cash or credit transactions. A balance-of-payments disturbance could originate in either set of markets. And it could involve a sudden supply-demand imbalance between any two of these asset types, not just—as the simple quantity theory would have it—in the supply of money relative to goods and services. All conceivable adjustment processes will involve all of these asset relations.

Our attention now turns to disturbances that initially manifest themselves as demand or supply shifts in goods-and-services markets. We are thus admitting that those markets need not always be in automatic balance. We will specifically look at the case in which there are ample unemployed resources of labor and physical capital—so ample that the economy may remain in a state of real imbalance throughout the adjustment. In other words, the initial slack is sufficient to accommodate any new demand for products or labor. It should then be inferred that neither product prices nor wage rates are very flexible downward, for if they had been, that slack would already have been eliminated. Our examples are in the tradition of the Keynesian theoretical model. They are particularly credible for the short run, when such slack can more easily exist. They tend to ignore or downplay price changes, because in this state of affairs most adjustments can be accomplished through changes in nonprice variables—especially in product quantities or in the level of employment and capacity utilization.

Real investment by business firms is a relatively unstable component of the aggregate product demand, as compared with consumption spending. Should business firms abruptly turn more optimistic in their profit expectations, they will likely try to expand their purchases of capital goods. To this end, they may undertake new borrowings (or, occasionally, equity issues) so as to procure the needed funds, or they may partly liquidate existing financial assets that they hold. Their new purchases will represent a new excess product demand, which will soon be met through an expanded production and supply of needed capital goods.

The new domestic capital-good purchases will create additional income for the capital-good producers, their employees, and their suppliers, who in turn will increase their spending and initiate further income increases within the economy. The size of the income increase induced through this chain of spending changes will be determined by the *investment multiplier*, which defines the relationship between an *autonomous* investment increase and the induced change in aggregate income.

The key variable is the *marginal propensity to consume*, MPC. It is defined as the amount of additional consumption per unit of additional income, or $\Delta C / \Delta Y$, and it measures the strength of the income recipients' tendency to respend the newly earned funds. The ordinary domestic investment multiplier can accordingly be written

$$\frac{\Delta Y}{\Delta I} = \frac{1}{1 - MPC}$$

from which one can verify that the larger the MPC, the larger will be the multiplier. Consider two absurd extremes: an MPC equaling one, and an MPC equaling zero, and calculate the value of the corresponding multipliers; this exercise will give you a feeling for the quantitative significance of the MPC. Figure 21-3a shows an expenditure-income diagram for a closed economy in which a rise in investment from I to I' creates a much larger income expansion, as indicated by Y' relative to Y.

In an open economy, part of the induced spending will normally consist of imports, or possibly of exportables diverted to the domestic market. This tendency is conventionally mesured by the *marginal propensity to import*, MPM=$\Delta M / \Delta Y$, and the open-economy multiplier incorporating this effect can be shown to equal

$$\frac{\Delta Y}{\Delta I} = \frac{1}{1 - MPC + MPM}$$

Thus, the higher the MPM, the smaller the open-economy income effects ultimately resulting from the initial investment expansion. There are hence two *leakages* out of the domestic income-expenditure stream—financial saving (captured by 1 - MPC, the unconsumed, unspent portion of the added income) and expenditure for imports; exports are here assumed to be at a fixed level.

Figure 21-3b is based on the same consumption and investment functions as those in Figure 21-3a, but makes an allowance for exports and imports as well. Since imports rise with income, they reduce the ongoing income expansion. Graphically, this is indicated by the slope of the total expenditure line, $C + I + X - M$, being smaller than the corresponding line for the closed economy in Figure 21-3a. A higher MPC, or a lower MPM, would have made the expenditure line steeper again, so that equilibrium income would also have been larger. More complex multipliers would be needed if we wanted to allow for secondary changes in investment, induced by changing income and profit expectations, or for changes in exports.

The size of emerging trade deficit will naturally depend on the investment multiplier. In addition, the increase in the investors' loanable funds demand might put upward pressure on interest rates and encourage an inflow of capital. In other words, there will be two mutually counteracting disturbances in the overall balance of payments. If prices are truly to be stable, the government will have to peg the exchange rate—or the prices of traded products would vary. But the overall payments picture may improve or worsen, and we cannot determine the type of intervention steps it will have to take. This greatly depends on the sensitivity of capital flows to the emerging interest differential. The implications for internal and external balance can be found in the bottom row of Table 21-4—which, for comparison, also shows the consequences of a flexible exchange rate under varying labor market conditions. Naturally, the income increase will be accompanied by reduced employment in our basic multiplier example.

Further complications arise if the home country is large. Its new purchases from other countries will produce additional income for them. As a consequence, they will increase their spending and their imports—some of which will represent the home country's exports. There will hence be feedbacks through both the trade accounts and the capital accounts. From the home-country standpoint, these *foreign repercussions* will constitute a kind of return leakage that reinforces the domestic income increase, while helping to tighten up international credit availability and push up interest rates. This could be a sketch of the United States insofar as U.S. spending and foreign trade strongly influence world demand and supply conditions in both product and financial markets.

In other situations, the initial disturbance may show up directly in the trade account. Perhaps there is an increase in the international demand for the home country's exports or a disproportionate productivity increase in the export sector.

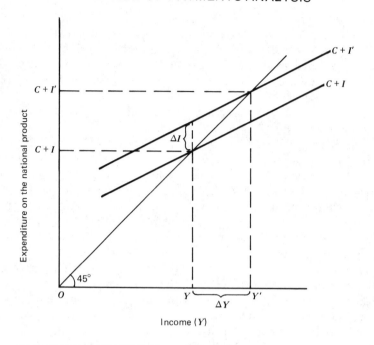

Variables	
C:	Consumption expenditure (dependent on Y).
I:	Initial investment expenditure (independent of Y).
I':	Changed (increased) investment expenditure (independent of Y).
Y:	National income (= total expenditure).
(Government purchases are assumed to be zero).	

Figure 21-3 (a). Investment change and income. (Closed economy.)

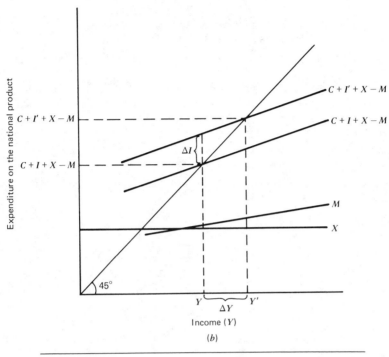

Variables

C I, I': See Figure 21-3*a*.
X: Exports of goods and services (independent of Y).
M: Imports of goods and services (dependent on Y).
Y: National income (= total expenditure on the national product).
(Government purchases are assumed to be zero.)

Figure 21-3 (*b*).   Investment change and income. (Open economy.)

Table 21-4
Effects of a Domestic Spending Increase
(increased demand for loanable funds)

Initial Domestic Situation	Effects on Internal Balance		Effects on External Balance	
	Under Flexible Exchange Rate	Under Pegged Exchange Rate	Under Flexible Exchange Rate	Under Pegged Exchange Rate
Full employment; trade and payments balance	Inflation; continued full employment	Inflation; continued full employment	Trade deficit; capital inflow; uncertain exchange-rate change	Trade deficit; capital inflow
Unemployment; trade and payments balance	Reduced unemployment	Reduced unemployment	Trade deficit; capital inflow; uncertain exchange-rate change	Trade deficit; capital inflow

Note: The spending increase might consist of an autonomous increase in private investment or consumption, or in government purchases.

There will then, typically, be a tendency toward a trade and payments surplus. If intervention is undertaken, this action will of course create additional money and income, thus initiating an expansionary process. Inflationary pressures will then increase, especially in full-employment economies. By contrast, if the domestic currency is allowed to appreciate freely, the cheapening of imported products will push prices downward, so as to lessen any ongoing inflation (see Table 21-5). It will then be harder for domestic producers of import substitutes to compete with the lower-priced imports. No wonder that large segments of German and Japanese industry have strongly opposed the upward revaluation of the Deutschemark and the yen, despite the impressive export records of these two countries.

EQUILIBRIUM IN FINANCIAL AND PRODUCT MARKETS

In discussing the case of an autonomous increase in investment, we hinted at some of the likely side effects on financial markets. The added need for investment finance might nudge interest rates upward and induce a capital inflow. These developments could have further monetary or financial consequences as a result of exchange-market intervention, changes in currency

Table 21-5
Effects of an Increase in Export Revenue

Initial Domestic Situation	Effects on Internal Balance		Effects on External Balance	
	Under Flexible Exchange Rate	Under Pegged Exchange Rate	Under Flexible Exchange Rate	Under Pegged Exchange Rate
Full employment; flexible prices; trade and payments balance	Deflation; continued full employment	Inflation; continued full employment	Exchange-rate decrease	Trade and payments surplus
Unemployment; trade and payments balance	Uncertain employment change	Reduced unemployment	Exchange-rate decrease	Trade and payments surplus

values, or adjustments of financial portfolios. Ideally, we should consider the likely interreactions among these various markets, but we would then run the risk of cluttering up our discussion with too many unimportant details. There exists, however, a convenient theoretical framework, derived from the Keynesian model, that can be adapted to our own particular problems; in its closed-economy versions, it is often used in intermediate macroeconomics. It is referred to as the *IS-LM* model. We will introduce it here, while deferring its policy applications to the next chapter.

This model relies heavily on the idea of "equilibrium." The term is almost synonymous with "balance"—except for its particular Keynesian connotations here. Even a "general equilibrium" in this model need not imply full employment, so the labor market may actually be unbalanced. Think of "general equilibrium" as any situation in which there is no further pressure toward change in overall spending, income, or financial activity, whether for domestic or for international reasons. For now, we ignore the government sector and changes in government policies.

Closed Economy

The equilibrium level of investment is that amount of private capital expenditure that has been perfectly adjusted to the cost of investment finance and the prospective investment return. The cost of finance is essentially the going rate of interest—specifically, the bond yield. As we just showed, the level of investment is closely tied, via the investment multiplier, also to the level of income.

The equilibrium level of income must therefore itself be a negative function of the rate of interest. In other words, successively lower rates of interest, causing correspondingly higher levels of investment spending, would result in successively higher equilibrium income levels, and vice versa.

At the same time, each income level produces its particular level of financial saving. Just as saving represents a leakage out of the income-spending stream, so does investment create an addition to this stream. Equilibrium requires that investment exactly make up for that leakage—by investment, I, being equal to saving, S. Aggregate domestic demand will then equal aggregate domestic product—i.e., income. The indicated combinations of possible interest-rate and income levels in a closed economy can be expressed as an IS function, which defines equilibrium, with $I = S$, in the *product* markets (for all capital and consumption goods and services, other than labor). See Figure 21-4a. Clearly, the IS function is negatively sloped.

In a similar manner, we can relate various income levels to the rate of interest, so as to ensure that these variables are *monetarily* consistent. Money is used for transaction (spending) purposes and for short-term investment (asset) purposes. The total demand for money (M^D), or "liquidity preference" (LP), is thus composed of a transaction demand—which is a function of the level of income—and an investment demand—a negative function of the rate of interest:

$$M^D = LP_y + LP_i$$

Since the total stock of money in existence, M^S, by definition must be held by the public in some form, it must in equilibrium equal total money demand:

$$M^S = M^D$$

Assume the supply of money remains constant. At successively higher levels of income, larger and larger amounts of money will be demanded to meet transaction requirements (LP_y), and this reduces the amounts left over for investment purposes (LP_i). In their futile efforts to fill this investment demand for money, financial investors will sell some of the bonds they have had in their portfolios, and this will cause bond prices to fall and the interest rate to rise. Higher income will therefore mean a higher interest rate, and vice versa. We can accordingly derive an LM function, which shows for each and every income level in a closed economy the associated equilibrium rate of interest (i.e., where $M^D = M^S$). At each point along the *LM* function, the money market is thus in equilibrium. It has a positive slope, as seen in Figure 21-4*a*.

It will now be clear that the only possible general equilibrium that can exist is one that satisfies equilibrium both in the product market and in the financial market. There is only one combination of interest rate and income where this can occur. At any other combination, corrective forces will be set in motion in one or both markets. This will eventually result in a return to the general equilibrium point, such as point *E* in Figure 21-4*a*. For example, points to the right of (or above) *IS* show situations in which income and/or the interest rate is unsustainably high, given the volume of spending; there will be a recessionary tendency. At points to the right of (or below) *LM*, income is too high, or the interest rate too low, to equate money demand and money supply; there is pressure toward tighter money and credit conditions and reduced economic activity.

Open Economy

For an open economy, we must also account for the effects of trade and capital flows. Trade is most immediately connected with income, especially via import demand and the *MPM*. Capital flows are primarily tied to financial markets, especially through short-term interest arbitrage. We can therefore assume that there is (1) a generally negative relation between the level of national income and the trade balance, and (2) a positive relation between the rate of interest and the net capital inflow. Overall payments balance can of course be achieved through trade surpluses, coupled with capital outflows, or through trade deficits, coupled with capital inflows. It therefore seems that equilibrium is this regard could be achieved either through low incomes and low interest rates, or through high incomes and high interest rates. In Figure 21-4*b*, curve *FE*—indicating equilibrium in foreign exchange—represents all possible pairs of interest rates and incomes consistent with these relationships, at a given exchange rate. Any interest-rate and income combination represented by a point to the left of *FE*, therefore, must denote a payments surplus, since income is there too low, or the interest rate is too high, for balance. Any point to the right of *FE*, conversely, must indicate a payments deficit.

The *IS* and *LM* curves, duplicated from Figure 21-4*a*, show the requirements for internal equilibrium, and as drawn here, the *IS*, *LM*, and *FE* functions intersect at one and the same point, *E*. Apparently, internal equilibrium can be attained simultaneously with external equilibrium at the going rate—a rather fortunate condition. Income should then equal Y_e and the interest should be i_e.

This general-equilibrium framework can be used as a means of illustrating various types of payments disturbances. A domestic money-supply expansion will shift the *LM* curve to the right (to *LM'*), reducing the rate of interest

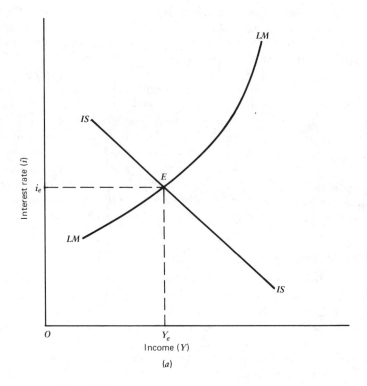

Figure 21-4 (a). Internal general equilibrium.

and, through additional investment, raising equilibrium income. The three schedules will then no longer intersect at the same point. Instead, there will be three intersection points—which suggests an absence of overall equilibrium. Judging from the fact that the *IS-LM* intersection now lies to the right of the two intersections involving *FE*, internal equilibrium would generate a payments deficit. And this would undermine that equilibrium. Something has got to give.

Perhaps *FE* could be shifted into a simultaneous equilibrium with *IS* and *LM*. How? Through a currency devaluation or depreciation, which would push *FE* rightward. This would plug the income leakage, especially through reduced imports, and pave the way for a sustained higher income level. If it is perfectly flexible, the exchange rate will, in effect, automatically

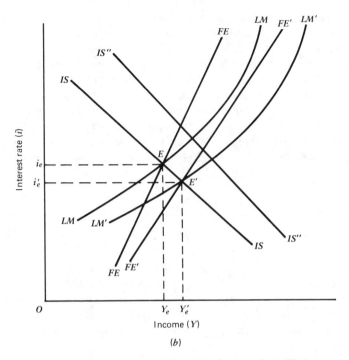

Figure 21-4 (b).   Internal-external general equilibrium.

move *FE* to *FE'* and produce a new overall equilibrium at *E'*. The alternative to an exchange-rate shift is, of course, intervention. This step would lead to an offsetting monetary contraction, such that the *LM* curve will start to pull back to the left. In time, the initial money-supply expansion might be completely wiped out and equilibrium at point *E* restored.

In other cases, an autonomous addition to investment demand, or a reduced propensity to save, could move *IS* to the right, as to *IS"*. This would upset the preexisting general equilibrium. Again, a currency depreciation could, in principle, restore overall equilibrium, one in which the interest rate is higher than it was initially (not shown in Figure 21-4). The interest rate increase will curb the expanding demands—especially investment demand—on product markets and help bring forth the domestic or international funds needed for their financing. It should not be difficult to examine other types of disturbances along the same lines.

The limitations of this simplified general-equilibrium framework must be pointed out. As mentioned, it does not allow for changes in the price level. The role of the *FE* schedule is a bit odd, as it assumes that each interest rate level will generate a continuous inflow or outflow of capital. In reality, there would be one-shot adjustments of investor portfolios, after which capital flows may cease. By contrast, the underlying domestic multiplier process consists of flows that may take considerable time. So the whole time perspective is unfocused. And if at least some categories of labor are fully employed, income changes are likely to result in changes in wages, costs, and prices as well. But then, no simple model can tell the whole story.

SUMMARY

National market economies are linked to one another via goods-and-services trade and capital flows. Through these channels, disturbances occurring in one nation's product or credit market can be transmitted to the markets of its trading partners. This holds for changes occurring in the supply of or demand for money, in the propensities to spend or save, in productivity, and in financial behavior.

Each major payments disturbance sooner or later requires some kind of international and external economic adjustment. As far as external payments are concerned, a floating exchange rate is an automatic adjustment mechanism. Although it ensures that the exchange market will be in balance, the domestic economy may still suffer short-term imbalances, especially in the labor market or in the utilization of real capital. This is especially the case when product and factor prices are relatively inflexible. If the exchange rate is pegged, the burden of adjustment will fall on domestic spending, income, lending, and borrowing. But if the domestic rate of money and credit expansion is seriously out of step with that abroad, the internal adjustment process will be continuously undermined by differential inflation rates and the resulting distortions in price and interest-rate relationships. As the new monetarists have demonstrated, exchange rates must in the long run be allowed to compensate for such differentials.

But governments are more concerned with the short run. For them, the problem of payments adjustment becomes one of economic policy, because policy can change both the extent of disturbances and the way the national economy adjusts to them. Consequently, we will now put the adjustment problem in the context of an economy subject to central guidance and manipulation.

Important Concepts

payments adjustment

internal balance

external balance

general equilibrium

quantity theory of money

purchasing power parity

real exchange rate

inflation premium

money multiplier

high-powered money

investment multiplier

monetary balance-of-payments
  approach

Questions

1. The Brazilian consulate has commissioned you to do a study of the main economic-financial linkages between Brazil and the United States. What types of linkages do you expect to find, and how will you go about finding information on them?

2. Countries X and Y are initially both in overall balance (with full employment and price stability); their exchange rate, although freely floating, is stable. Suddenly, the citizens of X speed up their private expenditure and thereby increase the velocity of money in this country. Trace out the most obvious consequences for prices, incomes, and interest rates in the two countries and for the exchange rate.

3. Consider an economy with fixed exchange rates and an initial internal-external equilibrium (in the Keynesian sense). There now occurs a shift in consumer tastes in favor of foreign, as opposed to domestic, products. What will happen to the trade and payments balance and to income? Apply the *IS-LM-FE* framework, and indicate how the various schedules will tend to move. (Don't forget to account for the monetary effect of exchange-market intervention.)

4. Assume that the U.S. economy was to experience a long-run inflation rate (say, over the next decade) of about 10 percent per annum. Meanwhile, assume that Argentina was to have an inflation rate of about 40 percent. Under these circumstances, what would your projection be for the average annual rate of depreciation of the Argentine peso against the dollar? Against the currencies of countries with price stability?

Further Readings

Frenkel, J., and H. Johnson, eds., *The Monetary Approach to the Balance of Payments* (London: Allen & Unwin, 1975).

Johnson, Harry, "Toward a General Theory of the Balance of Payments," in his *International Trade and Economic Growth* (Cambridge: Harvard University Press, 1961).

Meade, James, *The Balance of Payments* (London: Oxford University Press, 1951), Part II.

Officer, Lawrence, "The Purchasing-Power-Parity Theory of Exchange Rates: A Review Article," *IMF Staff Papers*, March 1976.

Stern, Robert, *The Balance of Payments: Theory and Economic Policy* (Chicago: Aldine, 1973).

22

MONETARY AND FISCAL ADJUSTMENT POLICIES

All contemporary governments try to exercise an influence over economic transactions with foreigners. They sometimes have clearly defined international economic goals. These might be related to the building of long-term economic-political alliances, changing the size or character of the export sector, or taking advantage of international credit markets. Even if a government does not have any such intentions, it will usually take into account the international implications of its overall economic policies. This is especially true of its policies for macroeconomic stabilization. Such policies tend to have international side effects, and their effectiveness depend on how international trade and capital flows react to them. And when the government wants to influence the process of international payments adjustment, these efforts become an integral part of the overall stabilization program.

Generally, the problems of macroeconomic policy in an open economy will be different from those in a closed economy. Access to international product and capital markets create added opportunities to fill the nation's product and credit demands and to compensate for temporary shortages at home. At the same time, reliance on international markets makes the nation vulnerable to adverse foreign influences, thereby creating new sources of instability and weakening the scope for national economic policy control. It is a two-way street.

In classifying economic policies with important international consequences, one can distinguish between two broad categories. The first category involves policies that effect the general level of spending, income, production, employment, prices, or other national aggregates and whose consequences spill over onto international transactions. The second category pertains to measures directly aimed at changing the level or composition of international trade or capital movements—as via changes in exchange rates or trade restrictions—while possibly also having side effects on purely domestic activity. The common adjectives used for describing these policy types are *expenditure-changing* and *expenditure-switching*. The terms emphasize their demand-management aspects, rather than their supply aspects, a legacy of the underlying Keynesian analytical approach. In this chapter, we will concentrate on the former, and in particular, on monetary and fiscal policies. We will hence be dealing with adjustment processes that do not depend on changes in exchange rates—that is, with policies that might permit these rates to remain stable, with or without intervention support.

To the makers of public policy, the merit of all potential policy strategies must be evaluated against their policy goals. And when they have multiple goals, there will often be a trade-off: As they are pushing the economy closer to one goal, they may be pulling it away from another. These trade-offs are in the nature of benefits and costs, although they are difficult to measure. We will therefore first try to sort out what these goals are, and indicate some of the principal costs and benefits of policy-induced shifts in international transactions. Our conclusions in these regards will help us to appreciate the advantages and disadvantages of different adjustment policies. On the practical plane, they will help us take a position on whether, say, British monetary policy should be aimed at keeping British payments in balance, or at stabilizing the domestic U.K. economy— perhaps with spillover effects on other economies.

POLICY GOALS IN OPEN ECONOMIES

A rational discussion of economic policy requires, first, a careful definition of the policy *goals*; second, an identification of available policy *instruments*; and third, an economic analysis of the *effectiveness* of these tools in achieving those goals. Defining policy goals—or other social objectives— is ultimately a matter of political or social ideology. In themselves, they are not subject to economic analysis. What economics can do is to analyze the economic implications of different goals that policy makers actually or potentially may try to pursue. In this way, economics helps to define the range of social choice, given the resources at our individual or collective disposal. That choice, of course, has international aspects.

We like to think that government policy, despite the inefficiencies of bureaucratic organizations, tends to be well coordinated, so that the left hand knows exactly what the right hand is doing. We need then not be terribly concerned about the possibility that different branches or agencies of the government try to achieve contrary economic results, or that those in charge of international affairs will have different objectives from their colleagues in domestic affairs. By and large, governments will then try to influence international transactions in such ways as to further the main goals of their overall national policies: rapid real economic growth, high levels of employment, reasonable price stability, and a modicum of income redistribution, subject to the preservation of a reasonable amount of individual economic and social freedom. Note that this list does not include any specifically international goals.

Among these policy goals, real income growth undoubtedly ranks first in the long run. But short-run considerations tend to dominate the public policy debate, whether or not they are consistent with longer-term growth. Also, the conflicting aspirations of different interest groups tend to divert public attention from more basic economic concerns. Achieving full employment, price stability, income redistribution, and various regulatory changes are popularly perceived as more urgent. International economic policy will therefore be directed primarily to inducing adjustment processes that make it easier to satisfy such interests. The longer-term goals of a more efficient resource allocation and freer trade and capital movements will frequently be set aside.

COSTS AND BENEFITS OF INTERNATIONAL TRANSACTIONS

Some of the broad connections between international economic policy measures and the objectives of income growth, high employment, and reasonable price stability are fairly obvious. They are suggested by the cost-benefit list in Table 22-1. The policies have been defined by the overall direction of their effects on goods-and-services trade or capital flows; what measures they involve will become obvious when we look at particular policy instruments.

It is almost self-evident that exports, and any policies that successfully promote exports, will normally strengthen both the nation's trade account and its overall payments position—in the sense of pushing these accounts in the direction of surpluses. Such policies will, moreover, tend to increase domestic employment opportunities, at least in the export sector. Expanded exports point toward a reduction of current opportunities to consume and invest, since they siphon off part of the available output to foreign buyers. Yet as they lead to foreign-reserve accumulation, they increase the nation's potential consumption and investment in the future. As suggested by Table 22-1, these are the main costs and benefits of export-promoting policies, whether the policy actions are of a monetary, fiscal, tariff, quota, or exchange-rate nature.

Of course, a policy to promote imports would generally do the opposite: decrease potential employment in import-substitute industries and enlarge current investment and consumption at the expense of similar opportunities

Table 22-1

Benefits and Costs of International Economic Policies

Direction of Policy	Main Benefits	Main Costs
Promotes exports of goods and services	Higher income and employment in export sector; reserve buildup and future opportunities for net imports	Loss of current consumption and investment opportunities; potential increase in inflation
Promotes imports of goods and services	Greater opportunities for current consumption and investment; potential decrease in inflation	Possible job losses in import-competing sector; reduction in reserves and in future opportunities to consume and invest
Promotes private capital outflows	Future return inflow of capital and future opportunities for net imports	Reserve loss, or a need to generate an offsetting trade surplus
Promotes private capital inflows	Reserve buildup, or greater opportunities for current net imports	Need to generate a future return outflow of capital (and a future trade surplus)

in the future. As far as domestic price stability goes, exports—via the associated reduction in domestic product supplies—tend to accelerate current inflation, whereas imports tend to lessen it.

Any policy that directly or indirectly paves the way for a greater capital outflow will have one of two consequences: Either it will require a balance-of-payments offset in the form of net exports—a trade surplus—or it will have to be financed through a drawdown of official foreign reserves. The effects of capital inflows will, as suggested in Table 22-1, be the reverse. In addition, any government steps to change capital flows may have implications for domestic financial markets, with further, indirect effects on resource allocation, productivity, and the inflation rate. The cost-benefit calculus will then be even more difficult.

It is apparent that each type of international economic-policy measure will normally have both positive and negative ramifications. There can be no question of either maximizing or minimizing the levels of trade or capital flows in either direction; rather, the right balance among these various effects must be found. Therefore, any coherent program of economic policy sophisticated enough to address these matters will seek to *optimize* these international variables so as to *maximize* their joint contribution to the achievement of more basic socioeconomic goals. And this requires a delicate cost-benefit comparison.

The mercantilists of the eighteenth century thought that trade and payments surpluses were inherently good, mainly because they strengthened the nation's international investment position and permitted an acquisition of monetary gold. But we now realize that there may be better ways to conduct international trade and finance and to store national wealth, especially in the form of more-productive domestic real assets. Nor should we fall into the trap of regarding payments balance, or trade balance, as in itself a worthwhile policy objective, without putting it in the context of overall national economic circumstances. At times, a payments deficit may be in the national interest; it may be a logical accompaniment to a short-term policy of mitigating inflationary pressure, relieving tightness in the labor market, or removing an unnecessary accumulation of foreign reserves. At other times, a trade or payments surplus may be more in tune with the nation's economic goals, or with the state of the domestic economy.

APPLICATIONS OF MONETARY AND FISCAL POLICY

Let us examine some situations that will normally call for a revision of general macroeconomic policies. Pretend that some kind of external or internal imbalance has suddenly emerged and come to the attention of the authorities. Needless to say, an external imbalance may consist of a payments deficit or a payments surplus, and it may show up via official reserve losses or gains (or comparable shifts in monetary liabilities to foreign governments). Alternatively, there may be an internal imbalance in the form of an unacceptable level of unemployment, or capacity underutilization. Or it may consist of overfull employment that leads to labor market inefficiencies, or excessively rapid inflation. It might also lie in what is called "stagflation"—a situation that, we would find, is much harder to rectify. What should the government do about these possible imbalances?

Monetary Policy: Case 1

Take the following example. There has been a reduction in world demand for the home country's exports, perhaps because the home country lags behind its main trade competitors in technological development, or because of a relative slowdown in economic activity abroad. This implies a deterioration in its terms of trade. As a result, its trade and payments balance has started to deteriorate. Foreign reserves are being depleted, and so are the opportunities for compensatory borrowing abroad. But the government has decided not to let the exchange rate float, and it is reluctant to devalue the current outright.

In the *IS-LM-FE* analysis, reintroduced in Figure 22-1, this means that the three schedules do not intersect at the same point. The domestic

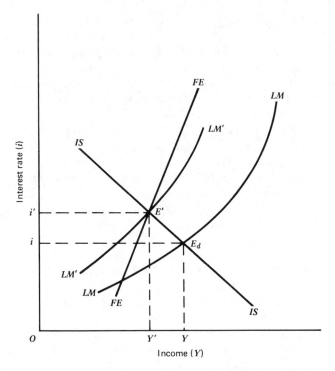

Figure 22-1. Monetary policy and internal-external equilibrium (case 1).

economy is in equilibrium at E_d, with income at Y and the interest rate at i. But there is a disequilibrium—a deficit—in international payments at that point, and the indicated combination of Y and i cannot, under current conditions, be sustained. In essence, a product-market equilibrium consistent with payments equilibrium would require a *lower* income, which would imply lower imports and put a stop to the external spending leakage through the trade account, and a *higher* interest rate, which would attract foreign capital and help curb spending at home. This is indicated by the intersection of *IS* and *FE*, relative to E_d.

But both the lower income and the higher interest rate would imply a reduced demand for money (and a higher demand for securities), and this would not permit money demand to equal the money supply. Therefore, from the standpoint of money-market and balance-of-payments equilibrium, the interest rate, as well as income, needs to be *lower* (see the intersection of *LM* and *FE*). If it were, the reduction in the transaction demand for money connected with reduced income could be offset by a larger investment demand for money. The latter would constitute added idle cash balances, to be held until the interest rate had moved back up to a more "normal" level.

The government, through a central bank that shares its policy concerns, may try to correct this situation through *monetary policy*. To close the external deficit, the central bank may use any of the traditional tools at its disposal: It may raise its discount rate, sell securities on the open market to soak up bank reserves, raise statutory bank-reserve requirements, or employ a combination of the three weapons. The reduction of the money supply and the tightening of general credit conditions will then cause the domestic interest rate to rise relative to those abroad. Investors and lenders at home will then have less incentive to place their funds abroad. Conversely, foreigners will have an incentive to shift their funds out of their own domestic money markets. The home country's balance of payments thus will tend to improve via the capital account.

To do the job, the money and credit contraction should be of such a magnitude that the *LM* schedule shifts leftward to the position *LM'* in Figure 22-1. In this position, the *LM'* schedule intersects with both *FE* and *IS* at *E'*. This is the overall equilibrium situation, combining internal balance—in product and money markets—with external payments balance. Income is then *Y'*; the interest rate, *i'*.

It should be noted that losses of international reserves on the part of the home country would automatically result in a gradual reduction of the domestic money supply, insofar as this tendency is not deliberately countered by an expansionary monetary policy on the part of the central bank. In this sense, there is an automatic correction mechanism that moves the *LM* schedule to the left, and it may seem that no deliberate monetary policy action will be required. But this process may be too slow, and the reserve losses incurred during it may be too severe—or reserves may be too low to make this type of adjustment possible.

Governments that do offset the money supply effects of reserve losses—or gains—are said to be *sterilizing* these reserve shifts. In our example, the government does *not* engage in such sterilization, because it prefers to let the money supply shrink. And it takes additional domestic monetary steps to speed up the monetary contraction.

What has happened in the domestic economy? With a rise in domestic interest rates and the cost of loanable funds, the likelihood is that aggregate home demand has been reduced. Borrowings by business firms and consumers, and perhaps also by state and local governments, have declined. The multiplier effect has operated in reverse so that income has declined from *Y* to *Y'*. So has, in all probability, employment. Via the marginal propensity to import, import expenditure has been reduced, and the balance of payments has improved by way of the current account, as well as the capital account.

Monetary Policy: Case 2

Internally, an imbalance can arise through a decline in private spending. Because of demographic changes, there may occur a decline in consumer purchases. Or investment expenditure may be reduced because of a more pessimistic longer-term profit outlook. As we recall, such an autonomous spending decline will move the *IS* curve to the .left, suggesting lower equilibrium income at any given interest-rate level. This will, meanwhile, produce domestic money-market pressure toward a lower interest rate—which will in itself help remove the shortfall in spending. Figure 22-2 shows the disequilibrium situation that now exists, with *IS* lying to the left of the point where it could intersect both *LM* and *FE*. At internal equilibrium, denoted by E_d, income is too low—or the interest rate too high—to produce external equilibrium. There is thus a payments surplus.

This imbalance, too, could be attacked through monetary policy—in this case, through a policy shift in the expansionary direction. The central bank might then engage in open-market purchases (which would inject new high-powered money into the banking system and start creating multiple

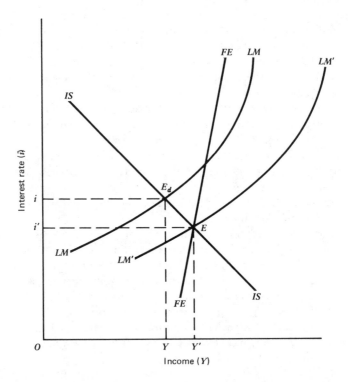

Figure 22-2. Monetary policy and internal-external equilibrium (case 2).

increases in bank credit and deposits). Alternatively, it could decrease bank reserve requirements, thereby making existing bank reserves even more high-powered, or it could encourage more bank borrowing at its discount window through a reduction of the discount rate. For the imbalance to be precisely corrected, the new interest rate should be i'. Spending will then be high enough to generate an equilibrium income corresponding to Y', according to Figure 22-2.

Fiscal Policy Cases

But there is an alternative policy strategy—one involving *fiscal policy*. Regardless of the source of this imbalance, the fiscal option should be evaluated along with a possible change in monetary policy. One or the other—or a combination of monetary and fiscal measures—may in the end be found to be preferable. Sometimes the two types of policy may complement each other; sometimes they may operate at cross-purposes.

The two main tools of fiscal policy are government expenditures and tax rates, especially those on personal and corporate income. In most countries, a large portion of government outlays consist of transfer payments—for example, poverty assistance, unemployment benefits, subsidies, and pensions. These expenditure items should be differentiated from government purchases of goods and services, because they do not in themselves represent demands on product markets. While these funds normally are spent by the transfer recipients, these expenditures are accounted for either through consumption or through private investment. In fact, transfer receipts by the public can be treated, for these purposes, as negative taxes.

Like autonomous changes in private spending, a change in government purchases of goods and services will have a *multiplier* effect on total income. Added government purchases create income for those who are selling goods or services to it, that is, for government contractors, suppliers, and employees. When these parties later spend their newly earned funds, they in turn create additional income, and additional spending, in other sectors of the economy, and so on. Yet part of the income increase leaks out of the private spending stream through the additional taxes that have to be paid on the added income. The net multiplier caused by government purchases therefore reflects both tax rates and the public's propensity to spend its after-tax income.

Naturally, changes in tax rates work in reverse. An increase in tax rates reduces the funds available for private spending, and the resulting spending decrease will send ripple effects through the entire economy. The aggregate spending decrease that will ultimately occur will be a multiple of the new tax collections. This will represent a negative tax multiplier, or a positive tax-reduction multiplier. Its magnitude will generally be lower than that for government purchases, as the initial tax bite may be softened by a reduction in taxpayer saving.

But changes in government purchases, transfers, or tax rates will also affect the overall government budget result. Since most governments are usually in deficit, it will be a matter of an increase or decrease in this deficit. In turn, the change in the deficit will affect the government's need to borrow on the domestic (or, occasionally, foreign) money and capital market. If the deficit grows, the added government demand for loanable funds will put upward pressure on interest rates. By contrast, if the deficit, because of fiscal restraint, should shrink, there will normally be an easing of interest-rate pressure from this particular source.

Fiscal policy can be a tool of balance-of-payments adjustment, as well as of restoring internal balance. Its effectiveness depends on the policy responses of the private sector, and—if the country is large—also on reactions in the international markets. We can immediately apply the *IS-LM-FE* framework.

There is, perhaps, a payments deficit, so that domestic equilibrium will be at point E_d in Figure 22-3. To maintain the exchange rate, the monetary authorities have to intervene in support of the home-country currency. In itself, the intervention has of course a contractionary monetary effect, with the consequence that the *LM* curve begins to shift leftward. Yet

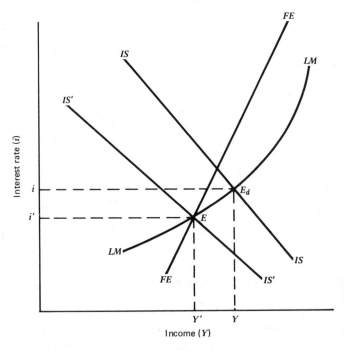

Figure 22-3. Internal-external balance and fiscal policy.

the authorities may have reasons to oppose the interest-rate increase that is now in prospect; it would hurt the housing sector too much. So the central bank insists on sterilizing the deficit by a compensatory money-supply expansion. In other words, the government is not permitting the indicated leftward shift of *LM* to run its course.

The government—the administration and the legislature—instead decides to embark on a policy of fiscal restraint. It believes that this step can establish an income level that eliminates the payments deficit without requiring a higher interest rate. In this case, it may devise a cleverly fine-tuned program of expenditure cuts and tax increases that pushes *IS* leftward to the position of *IS'*, so as to establish an overall equilibrium at *E*. Income will then have declined from *Y* to *Y'*, and the interest rate has actually dropped from *i* to *i'*. There is likely to be a capital outflow, but the newly emerging trade surplus is sufficient to offset it.

Special Situation: Elastic Capital Flows

It is conceivable that international capital flows are extremely sensitive to international interest-rate differentials—especially when they are predominantly short-term and can easily be hedged in the forward exchange market. Our analysis will then have to be modified. Small interest-rate changes will then create large additional capital flows, in one direction or the other. Relative to income changes, interest-rate movements will then be much more powerful in disturbing or restoring payments equilibrium.

Graphically, this means that the *FE* schedule will be flatter—perhaps even flatter than the *LM* schedule. In the extreme, the *FE* schedule might be a straight horizontal line—as if only an infinitesimally small interest-rate change would be needed for the correction of a payments deficit or surplus, regardless of the income level. Implicitly, the international flow-of-funds elasticity with respect to relative interest rates is then infinite.

Figure 22-4 has been constructed accordingly. It suggests that the interest rate is effectively, via the *FE* schedule, pegged at the world-market level, i_W. If the *IS* and *LM* schedules, as here, intersect above the *FE* schedule, the domestically determined interest rate, *i*, will be above the world market rate. There will then be an inflow of capital, and a payments surplus.

Internal economic conditions then indicate an equilibrium income level of *Y*. But this income level is not tenable. With the capital inflow occurring at the associated interest rate, *i*, there will be a continuous sale of foreign currency in exchange for domestic currency by international interest-rate arbitrageurs, based at home or abroad. This forces the central bank continuously to intervene and to issue additional high-powered domestic monetary liabilities—that is, to keep the printing press running full speed. Perhaps the payments surplus could be sterilized, but it will, in practice, be very difficult for the central bank to do so. Such action would normally

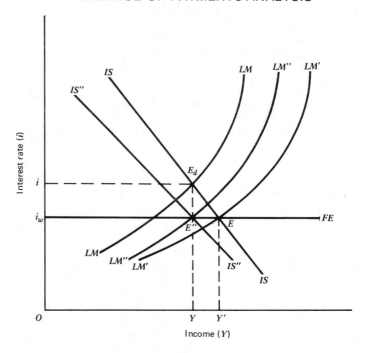

Figure 22-4.   Internal-external balance under perfect capital mobility.

require large, continuous open-market sales, and the central bank would ultimately exhaust its holdings of government securities. Sterilization may then no longer be feasible.

Therefore, the money supply will increase exactly until the domestic interest rate has fallen from its initial level, i, to the world-market level, i_w. This entails the money-market situation described by LM', which intersects the IS curve at E. Income will then be forced up to Y'—which might seem fortunate, but may gradually create inflationary pressure. In this case, monetary policy is entirely impotent in determining national income— a surprising and important conclusion. Monetary policy is effectively determined abroad, through the international financial linkage provided by the fixed exchange rate.

Is there an alternative in the form of fiscal policy? Yes, the government can undertake a fiscal restraint program that reduces the interest rate to the world-market level and eliminates the net capital inflow. If it wishes to keep income at Y, it can, at the same time, allow a moderate expansion of the money supply. The fiscal restraint, with the accompanying reduction in government borrowing on the domestic capital markets, will shift IS to IS'' in Figure 22-4. The capital inflow and the monetary expansion will proceed until LM'' intersects IS'' exactly at income Y and interest rate i_w—the one sustainable interest-rate level, associated with overall equilibrium at E''. In this case, fiscal policy can thus do what monetary policy cannot—determine income under a fixed exchange rate while capital is exceedingly mobile.

POLICY CONFLICTS AND THE POLICY MIX

In the IS-LM-FE model, internal equilibrium is of a special, Keynesian kind—one that might entail large unemployment and a real income level below the full-employment potential of the economy. In using this model, we have thus skirted the issue of whether the overall equilibrium is consistent with the goal of maximum real income. Perhaps an overall equilibrium could be established at a higher real-income level—unless the requirement for external balance makes this absolutely impossible.

To answer this question, we have to take a closer look at the relationship between internal economic conditions and the balance-of-payments situation. In addition, we have to consider whether better policy results could be achieved if *both* monetary *and* fiscal policy were adjusted at the same time. This is certainly conceivable. After all, these are two different instruments, with different capabilities for economic control. And we should relax the Keynesian price-level assumption and account for variations in the rate of inflation.

"Internal balance" will then, as in our original definitions, have both an employment and income aspect and a price-stability aspect. In reference to the actual policy debate in the 1970s and 1980s, this is obviously a much more relevant view. Internal imbalance can thus take the form of either an excessive or an inadequate growth of demand, given the nation's production possibilities. The former situation is one of rapid (or more rapid) inflation, possibly accompanied by declining unemployment rolls and real income gains in the short run. The latter situation is, conversely, one of relative slack and recession, and a moderation of inflation—or perhaps stagflation.

Each of these situations calls for a different policy response. The prospect of further inflation suggests some combination of a tax increase, reduced government spending, and monetary restraint—in short, restrictive monetary and fiscal policies. Recession, on the other hand, demands expansionary monetary and fiscal measures. How do these policy requirements of internal balance compare with those of external balance?

Assume, as before, that it is impossible or undesirable to employ restrictions on international trade and capital flows. Neither is it desirable to adopt a flexible exchange rate. Adjustment of a balance-of-payments deficit thus calls for restrictive economic policies that will reduce domestic incomes, and perhaps prices, and raise domestic interest rates. Imports will then be reduced, and it is possible that exports will rise; also, capital flows will shift in favor of the home country, so that the balance of payments improves. Whether monetary or fiscal policies should be used to restore external balance would at first glance seem to depend on (a) the marginal propensity to import, (b) the responsiveness of prices to decreasing aggregate demand, (c) the price elasticity of demand for imports, and (d) the responsiveness of capital flows to changes in domestic interest rates.

A payments surplus under the same circumstances would, by the same reasoning, appear to call for the opposite types of policy responses. Credit ease and/or expansionary fiscal measures could thus result in a restoration of balance through increased imports, reduced exports and a capital outflow.

But will a given monetary or fiscal policy program, designed to redress either an external or an internal imbalance, simultaneously serve to alleviate the other imbalance? Or will the correct policy remedy for an external imbalance prove to be precisely the wrong medicine for the internal imbalance, and vice versa? A schematic list of possible situations and their policy implications is provided in Table 22-2.

Table 22-2
Policy Requirements under Different Internal and External Conditions

Case	Internal Condition (involving prices, employment, and income)	Policy Require- ment	External Condition (involving trade and or capital flows)	Policy Require- ment
1	Inflation	Restraint	Deficit	Restraint
2	Recession	Expansion	Surplus	Expansion
3	Inflation	Restraint	Surplus	Expansion
4	Recession	Expansion	Deficit	Restraint
5	Balance	Neutrality	Deficit	Restraint
6	Balance	Neutrality	Surplus	Expansion
7	Inflation	Restraint	Balance	Neutrality
8	Recession	Expansion	Balance	Neutrality
9	Balance	Neutrality	Balance	Neutrality

Conflict Situations

Case 1—excess inflation accompanied by a balance-of-payments deficit— presents no problem. Monetary policies designed to reduce money supply growth, raise domestic interest rates, and thereby depress aggregate demand will simultaneously attract foreign capital and reduce the outflow of domestic capital. This will help restore payments balance. To the extent that restrictive monetary measures are indeed successful in depressing aggregate domestic demand and incomes, they will also benefit the balance of payments via reduced imports. Restrictive fiscal policies would have a similar effect on incomes and imports, and to the extent that prices are flexible in a downward direction, the balance of payments would benefit additionally through increased price competitiveness of exportables. Restrictive monetary and fiscal policies in case 1 thus help restore both internal and external balance under these conditions. Any policy that helps cure the payments deficit automatically aids in the restoration of internal balance (barring exceptional fiscal effects on interest rates).

Meanwhile, the payments deficit itself acts as a brake on domestic inflation, in that the import surplus helps satisfy the excess demand and acts as a depressing influence on domestic incomes; also, any net capital outflow tends to tighten domestic credit. Both of these results are desirable from the standpoint of internal balance, and if left alone, they might in and of themselves ultimately lead to a restoration of both internal and external balance. Yet the process might be much too slow, and politically too costly; an immediate belt-tightening might be preferable.

Case 2, domestic recession coupled with a payments surplus, tells a similar story. Again the payments surplus itself—in the form of an excess of exports over imports or a net capital inflow—acts as a stimulus to the domestic economy and, if economic policy remained neutral, might eventually restore overall balance. Whether or not monetary or fiscal measures are applied specifically to wipe out the payments surplus, any techniques intended to restore internal balance by stimulating domestic economic activity will automatically tend to have this effect. Expansionary monetary policies and the associated lower domestic interest rates will alleviate any net capital inflow. With or without expansionary government expenditure and tax measures, they will cause a rise in domestic incomes and prices, thereby reducing the trade surplus.

In both cases—excess inflation, with a deficit, and recession, with a surplus—internal and external policy requirements are consistent with each other. Policy moves to restore internal balance—real balance, in particular—automatically help restore external balance as well, and vice versa.

But what about case 3, excess inflation accompanied by a payments surplus? Any effort, via demand management, to combat the inflation at home will simultaneously aggravate the payments surplus. Monetary restraint at home will result in higher domestic interest rates and net capital inflows that, while increasing the payments surplus, will partly offset the domestic credit restriction. Restrictive tax and government-expenditure policies, by reducing imports and perhaps increasing exports, will also tend to increase the surplus—which, in turn, aggravates the inflationary pressure at home. Any attempt to restore internal balance under these circumstances thus aggravates the external imbalance.

Equally frustrating is an economic slump combined with a payments deficit (case 4). Externally, it is necessary for the nation to eliminate its deficit—or it will exhaust its international reserves, its ability to borrow abroad, or the willingness of foreigners to hold its currency. Meanwhile, it will be under powerful pressure to stimulate the domestic economy and return to reasonably full employment. A sharp conflict exists. Monetary restraint and restrictive fiscal and tax policies may benefit the balance of payments, but they will almost surely drive the domestic economy deeper into recession. Conversely, the monetary and fiscal ease needed as a cure for the domestic recession will only result in an increase in the payments deficit. Milder conflicts arise if the internal situation is one of balance while international payments are in deficit or surplus—and when payments balance coexists with recession or increasing inflation (see cases 5-9 in Table 22-2).

The Optimal Policy Mix

The solutions to these dilemmas lie in manipulating the tools of economic policy in such a way that the positive response to a given policy measure in one area exceeds the negative response in the other. To ilustrate: Suppose international capital flows are highly sensitive to changes in interest rates in the home country. Restrictive monetary policies resulting in higher interest rates would thus cause a significant improvement in the capital account of the balance of payments. The negative impact of this development on aggregate domestic demand could be offset by expansionary expenditure or tax measures. This could result in a net improvement in the balance of payments without an accompanying deterioration in the domestic situation. In particular, if the marginal propensity to import is low, the expansionary expenditure and tax measures could, in their domestic impact, more than offset the monetary restraint. There could then be an improvement both in the domestic economy and in the balance of payments. The newly induced imports, in other words, would not be large enough to offset the turnaround on private capital account.

One suggestion along these lines—involving a differentiation of policy goals and tools—emanates from Robert Mundell. He has proposed a "principle of effective market classification," under which each policy weapon ought to be aimed at that market on which it has the greatest relative influence. Hence, if monetary policy affects external balance (the foreign exchange market) more than it does internal balance, then it should be used for promoting external balance, and its undesired domestic effects should be neutralized by opposite fiscal policies. Mundell contends that the use of any other policy mix may actually promote external and internal imbalances.

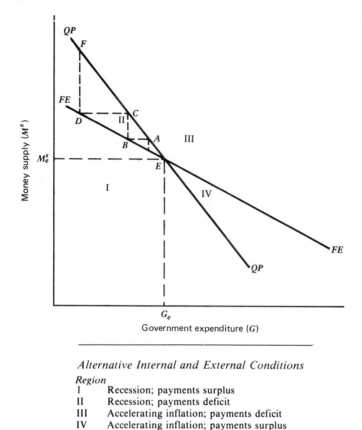

Alternative Internal and External Conditions

Region
I   Recession; payments surplus
II   Recession; payments deficit
III   Accelerating inflation; payments deficit
IV   Accelerating inflation; payments surplus

Figure 22-5.   Internal-external balance and the policy mix.

This is neatly demonstrated in Figure 22-5. There are only two policy variables: the money supply and government expenditure (or, possibly, tax rates). Both external and internal balance can be maintained by using different combinations of expenditure (or budget) policies and monetary policies. Curve *FE* shows all possible policy combinations that will maintain external balance: Payments balance can be assured by low levels of government expenditure combined with large money-supply growth (with a strong current-account balance offsetting a weak capital-account balance); or it can be assured through high expenditure levels combined with slow money growth (with a strong capital-account balance and a weak current-account balance). Any policy combinations along *FE* will thus ensure external balance.

Similarly, curve QP (defined by output quantities and price levels) shows the policy combinations that will ensure internal balance. Low-inflation full employment can be maintained by monetary restraint combined with budgetary ease, or by restrictive budgetary measures accompanied by monetary ease. Both FE and QP thus slope downward.

But their slopes need not be identical, and we are illustrating the case in which QP is steeper than FE—for reasons that we will explain shortly. Because their slopes here differ, FE and QP are bound to intersect, as at point E. This point indicates the one and only combination of policies that will assure both internal and external balance. That combination of money supply and government expenditure is defined by M_e^s and G_e.

Any combination of budgetary and monetary measures represented by a point to the left of FE represents a payments surplus, whereas any point to the right of it signifies a payments deficit. Similarly, any point to the left of QP represents a domestic recession, whereas any point to the right of it signifies rapid inflation. Hence any point in the region labeled I represents a recession-surplus combination, and any point in region III an inflation-deficit combination. Points in regions II and IV illustrate recession-deficit and inflation-surplus combinations, respectively.

As stated earlier, there is no problem with inflation-deficit and recession-surplus situations, since the restoration of both internal and external balance calls for the same policy responses. Any measure designed to promote balance in one area will automatically promote balance in the other and drive the economy closer to overall equilibrium. Rather, it is under conditions of inflation-surplus and recession-deficit that the policy conflict arises, for each measure designed to promote balance in one area will work against balance in the other. The job of the policy makers will thus be particularly challenging when the economy is in region II or IV.

Suppose we pick point C in Figure 22-5 as our analytical starting point. The domestic economy is in balance but there is a payments deficit, because C is on QP but to the right of FE. We now attempt to restore external balance by increasing the budget surplus via a cutback in government expenditure, and we thereby move to point D on FE. Although external balance has been attained, a recession has been brought about at the same time. Internal balance can be restored by simply expanding the money supply and moving to point F on QP, but this results in a renewal of the payments deficit—most likely, a larger deficit than at C. By applying fiscal policy for external balance and monetary policy for internal balance, we find ourselves moving farther and farther from overall equilibrium via a series of alternating external and internal imbalances.

What if we reverse the policy mix and employ monetary policy for external balance and fiscal policy for internal balance? Returning to the initial point, C—which combines internal balance with a payments deficit— we now reduce the money supply until external balance is secured at point

B on *FE*. This represents a domestic recession. But we can offset it by an expansionary fiscal policy. A restoration of internal balance will then occur at point *A*, which is closer to the overall equilibrium than the point preceding it. Additional alternate policy moves will bring us closer and closer to that ultimate goal—point *E*. Hence, a policy mix stipulating monetary policy for external balance and fiscal policy for internal balance will eventually permit both objectives to be attained simultaneously.

Why is it that this particular policy mix works, whereas the opposite mix does not? The answer lies in the way *QP* and *FE* are drawn, the line for the external balance being flatter than that for the internal balance. Drawing *QP* and *FE* in this way was not an arbitrary decision but a way to depict a basic assumption in Mundell's model. Since capital is assumed to be free to move internationally, monetary policy will tend to have a relatively stronger effect on the balance of payments than on national income. Hence only a minor money-supply change is needed to compensate for any given shift in budget policies—and the low slope of *FE* captures this trade-off. One should add, however, that this conclusion can only make sense in the short run. In particular, a tight monetary policy may not lead to a continuous capital inflow, and a further tightening may be needed to sustain this inflow after the initial portfolio adjustments. The positions of both *QP* and *FE* may be unstable, if there are changes in the domestic or foreign price level. And finding their actual positions would, in any case, be a superhuman task.

Our conclusion, qualified as it is, can be expressed more generally: In cases of policy conflict, internal and external balance can be simultaneously maintained if there are two policy tools available and they do not have exactly the same relative effects internally and externally. It is a matter of their comparative internal and external efficiencies being different. A certain amount of specialization in their application will then produce the best overall result. The trick is to assign each policy weapon to that particular task which it can handle better. Accordingly, this is often called the "assignment problem" of international economic policy.

SUMMARY

All broad-based government economic policies affect the process of international payments adjustment in some way or other. Sometimes policies are deliberately formulated so as to speed up this process, or to minimize the degree to which it interferes with the pursuit of domestic economic policy goals. The more open the economy is, the greater, usually, is the weight that the policy makers will give to problems of payments adjustment. Countries such as Britain and West Germany have often tried to use monetary policy to correct imbalances in their external payments, and especially to influence interest rates and capital flows. But monetary policy invariably has consequences also for private investment, income, and employment, and these consequences may be detrimental. This poses a dilemma for the policy makers. It was an especially painful one for the British in much of the 1960s and early 1970s, with their sluggish industrial performance and frequent balance-of-payments crises.

In theory, when two or several policy instruments are available, the chances of satisfying both internal and external policy objectives will generally be improved. If the effects of each instrument are reasonably distinct and predictable, the authorities in most cases ought to assign monetary policy the task of external balance and fiscal policy that of internal balance. This has been a standard short-term prescription for the optimal mix of expenditure-changing, demand-oriented policies. But in applying this rule, one must also consider whether the relevant authorities—the central bank, the national administration, and the national legislature—actually share and pursue the same economic goals. Their policy priorities may differ, and so might their views of actual economic conditions or of the potential effects of different policy steps.

But the authorities have other options. They can try specifically to influence the direction of private spending as between tradable and nontradable products, or they can try to regulate capital movements. We will complete our analysis of adjustment mechanisms through a review of such expenditure-switching policy methods.

Important Concepts

expenditure-switching	monetary policy instrument
demand management	sterilization (of reserve changes)
marginal propensity to import	tax-reduction multiplier
open-economy policy dilemma	elastic capital flows

1. A trade and payments deficit affects the level of income, the money supply, and the supply of goods and services in the domestic economy. These effects can be said to be disinflationary. Explain how the various disinflationary forces will manifest themselves.

2. Assume that a particular country's overriding short-term policy goal is to rebuild its official foreign reserves. Outline the various macroeconomic policy strategies available to it, and discuss their relative effectiveness. Apply the *IS-LM-FE* framework.

3. In the late 1960s and early 1970s, many German, French, and Swiss spokesmen complained about the American "export" of inflation to their countries. What exactly did they mean? Given the prevailing exchange-rate system, could the Europeans have refused to accept this inflation? How?

4. Assume that the Swiss economy is in a state of overfull employment and, by its own standards, relatively rapid inflation. Foreign reserves are embarrassingly large, but the authorities are reluctant to allow any major change in the international value of the franc. The authorities recognize that Swiss financial markets are closely integrated with those of other, larger countries and do not want to impose any new capital-flow controls. In what sense is the Swiss government in a policy dilemma? What do you propose it should do?

Further Readings

Meade, James E., *The Balance of Payments* (London: Oxford University Press, 1951), Part III.

Mundell, Robert A., "The Appropriate Use of Monetary and Fiscal Policies Under Fixed Exchange Rates," *IMF Staff Papers*, March 1962.

Stern, Robert, *The Balance of Payments: Theory and Economic Policy* (Chicago: Aldine, 1973), Chapter 10.

Whitman, Marina v. N., *Policies for Internal and External Balance*, Special Papers in International Economics, No. 9 (Princeton: Princeton University, 1970).

23

EXPENDITURE-SWITCHING POLICIES

It may seem odd that monetary and fiscal policies are regarded as major tools of international payments adjustment. Their effects are broad and general, and only indirectly find their way into the foreign trade and capital accounts. And even if there is no fundamental policy conflict in this respect, the magnitudes of the internal and external policy requirements will rarely be the same. Overall balance can then be achieved only through a carefully calibrated policy mix—one that will usually be beyond the grasp of the uncoordinated governmental authorities of democratic societies. If there are international economic problems, why not deal with them through direct international actions? Why complicate internal economic conditions unnecessarily by tailoring general economic policies to what, for most countries, is a relatively low volume of international transactions? Why let the tail wag the dog?

This line of reasoning would appear to favor expenditure-switching policies, applied so as to change the volumes or composition of trade or capital flows. We shall now examine this policy option, starting with exchange-rate changes and proceeding to controls over trade and international financial transactions. We will generally find that such policies can indeed be more powerful, but that they have side effects that may lessen their usefulness. In a separate section, we introduce the "absorption approach" to international economic policy analysis, so as to get more of a macro perspective on these policy options. We will wrap up the topic of adjustment policy by discussing the overall policy strategies pursued by different groups of countries.

REPEGGING THE EXCHANGE RATE

Naturally, if the government desires to reduce or eliminate a trade deficit, or to enlarge a trade surplus, it will want to decrease the relative amount of domestic spending on both imports and exportables. Inevitably, it will then encourage the relative amount of spending on products made strictly for home-market use. If it should desire to enlarge the trade deficit, or to reduce the trade surplus, it would want to do the opposite: encourage domestic expenditure on imports and exportables by inducing a spending shift away from purely domestic products.

The switching of expenditure could be induced in many different ways, but the most dramatic, and the most interesting, is that of adjusting or controlling the exchange rate. The government will in this case allow itself, at its own discretion, to interfere with the private exchange market, and the exchange rate will hence not be allowed to float freely. (If the authorities, contrariwise, had committed themselves to maintaining a free float, they would thereby have forsworn all use of this potential policy tool.) Nor could the exchange rate under these circumstances be permanently fixed, for the government's hands would then also have been tied, although in another way—by the obligation to support the exchange rate through intervention at its agreed-upon level.

Accordingly, the following discussion is relevant to two situations: (1) the government has pegged the exchange rate of the domestic currency to another currency—a key currency—or to some other international standard of value (historically, to gold), but it reserves the right to repeg it at another level; or (2) the government has not pegged the exchange rate, but manipulates it by changes in the amount and direction of its intervention in the exchange market, as it sees fit. The first situation is one of an *adjustable peg*; the second, one of a *managed float*. The two situations share one important feature—that of discretionary control by the national authorities over the exchange rate. Thus, what we specifically say about adjustments of the peg will apply as well to decisions to manage the exchange rate in such a way that it assumes a different value. Both situations imply intervention in amounts sufficient to produce the new, desired exchange rate. By contrast, the discussion has no relevance to the two extreme—and rare—situations of a perfectly free float and a perfectly fixed rate, since both of these preclude such discretionary exchange-rate control.

We will now evaluate the potential effectiveness of the exchange-rate tool, especially as compared with other adjustment tools. But let us first sum up the intuitive ways in which it would seem to function. A devaluation of the home currency—that is, an increase in the domestic price of foreign currency—will tend to change the home-currency price of imports and the home-currency price equivalent of exports. These are the prices relevant to domestic buyers and domestic producer-sellers. Higher import prices will discourage imports, thereby lessening the volume of imports; this is the normal demand response to such a price shift. At the same time, higher prices of exportables will encourage sales broad and increase the export volume; this is the normal business response to better profit opportunities. At first blush, there may thus seem to be no question about the ability of devaluation to both reduce imports and increase exports, and an improved trade balance would seem assured.

Yet as we showed when we dealt with the foreign exchange behavior of exporters and importers in Chapter 19, the problem is more complex. We have to consider how the prices of the traded products are determined and how they might change with the exchange rate. And we have to account for the interconnections between price and volume changes in the product markets.

Conditions in Product Markets

We thus have to examine demand and supply conditions in two product markets—that for exports and that for imports—and to trace the effects of exchange-rate changes on export revenue and import expenditure. For simplicity and clarity, it is assumed that there is only one, homogeneous export product and only one, homogeneous import product, although various nontraded products may be exchanged in purely domestic markets. We ignore capital flows for now.

Figure 23-1 follows that procedure. In each of the two panels, the pertinent product price is plotted vertically and the corresponding quantity horizontally, just as in standard microanalysis. Prices could be specified in either foreign or domestic currency; we have chosen the former alternative. Thus, the price variables are P_x^f, the foreign-currency export price, and P_m^f, the foreign-currency import price. We may think of these prices as world-market prices, or the local prices in the main trading countries. As explained in Chapter 19, the currency actually used for invoicing purposes is immaterial.

The *export* diagram in Figure 23-1a shows an initial situation in which the downward-sloping foreign demand curve, $D_x^f D_x^f$, intersects the upward-sloping domestic supply curve, $S_x S_x$, at an equilibrium export price of P_x^f and an equilibrium export quantity of Q_x. Export revenue then equals $P_x^f \times Q_x$ and is graphically represented by the broken-line rectangle placed between the intersection point and the origin.

When we draw this kind of export demand curve, we mean to say that world-market demand for the home country's exports is a declining function of their foreign-currency price, and this normally reflects a situation in

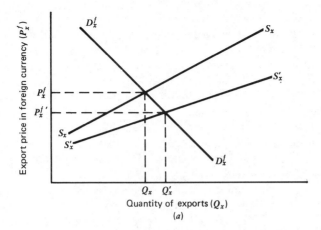

$P_x{}'Q_x{}'$: initial export revenue
$P_x{}'Q_x{}'$: export revenue after devaluation

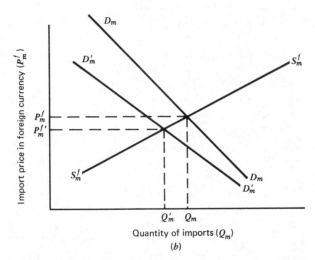

$P_{m'}Q_{m'}$: initial import expenditure
$P_{m'}Q_{m'}$: import expenditure after devaluation

Figure 23-1. Effects of devaluation on exports and imports. (*a*) Exports: demand, supply, and revenue. (*b*) Imports: demand, supply, and expenditure.

which these products are only partial substitutes for the products available abroad. The home country is, therefore, an international *price maker* in this market. (Were it a price taker, the demand-for-export schedule would have been a horizontal line.) When we draw this kind of upward-sloping export supply curve, we suggest the home-country suppliers of exportables react positively to world-market price increase. This is because their marginal production costs are rising, and it will take just such a price inducement to make additional production and export sales worthwhile for them.

But wait a minute. Exporters normally figure their costs in the domestic currency, for this is their normal means of payments. So actually, the export supply should have been related to domestic, not foreign, price shifts. Therefore, in drawing the $S_x S_x$ schedule, we tacitly assumed that there is a predetermined exchange rate that permits us to convert domestic- into foreign-currency prices. The position of the $S_x S_x$ schedule thus hinges on the level of the underlying exchange rate. A different exchange rate would produce a different $S_x S_x$ schedule, even though the basic supply function, as specified in domestic currency, remains the same. It is exactly this connection between exchange-rate levels and commodity price conditions that we want to explore.

Take an outright devaluation of the home currency, undertaken suddenly and unexpectedly. The government repegs the exchange rate of a level that it promises to maintain for an indefinite future through whatever intervention sales or purchases might be necessary. This alters the foreign-currency equivalents of the domestic-currency prices that define the potential volumes of export supply, and the $S_x S_x$ schedule will have to be redrawn. Since each unit of domestic currency (say, dollars) will now translate into fewer units of foreign currency (say, pounds) than before, $S_x S_x$ should be adjusted downward, as to $S'_x S'_x$. The downward shift of $S_x S_x$ should be proportional to the devaluation—so that, for example, a 20 percent dollar devaluation against the pound would pull it down, throughout its entire range, by 20 percent of its distance from the horizontal axis.

A new equilibrium then results, with a new, lower export price, $P_x^{f'}$, and a new, larger export volume, Q'_x. Clearly, the export revenue may now be different, as indicated by the new, longer rectangle. *Whether* the export revenue will have grown or shrunk is wholly a matter of the elasticity of $D_x^f D_x^f$; *how much* it has grown or shrunk is also a matter of the elasticity of $S_x S_x$. In the border-line case in which the $D_x^f D_x^f$ elasticity is unitary, export revenue will remain constant. If it is numerically larger than one, export revenue will grow, whereas in the opposite case it will shrink—all as measured in foreign currency.

Now consider the *import* diagram in Figure 23-1b. The foreign supply schedule, $S_m^f S_m^f$, depicts the following conditions: To be willing to produce more and sell more to the home country, foreign producers have to be offered better foreign-currency prices. The schedule will thus be upward sloping, implying that the home country is, internationally, a *price maker* in this market. (Otherwise, as when it competes with many other, or larger, nation-buyers, $S_m^f S_m^f$ would be horizontal.) The domestic demand-for-import schedule, $D_m D_m$, is actually the foreign-price equivalent of a more basic demand function originally specified in domestic currency. It presupposes a given exchange rate. Should this rate be changed through a devaluation, $D_m D_m$ will have to be lowered by a proportional fraction of its distance from the horizontal axis, as suggested by $D'_m D'_m$.

The effect of such a devaluation on import expenditure is easy to identify. Originally, import expenditure stood at $P_m^f \times Q_m$, equal to the large broken-line rectangle. The devaluation unequivocally reduces it, since both quantity and price decline, and as seen from the smaller rectangle.

We can now sum up the devaluation effects on the trade balance. In *foreign* currency, export revenue will increase or decrease, whereas import expenditure will, by necessity, decrease. The net effect on the trade balance in foreign currency is therefore ambiguous. By experimenting with differently drawn supply and demand schedules, we could conclude that the net effect is a function of the elasticities of all four schedules. Generally, if all these elasticities are reasonably high, or at least around unity, there will be an improvement in the trade balance—through a reduced trade deficit, an increased trade surplus, or a deficit turned into a surplus. By the same token, these conditions would ensure that an upward currency revaluation would decrease a preexisting trade surplus, or increase a preexisting trade deficit.

For some purposes, such as national-income accounting, the outcome of the repegging might better be expressed in *domestic* currency. The conversion will be simple to carry out. For instance, a change in the British pound rate from \$2.00 to \$2.50—a 20 percent dollar devaluation—might have lowered the U.S. trade deficit from £10 to £2 billion. From a domestic U.S. perspective, this is a trade balance improvement of \$20 billion – \$5 billion = \$15 billion. Had the pound figure remained unchanged at £10 billion, the dollar figure would actually have indicated an *increased* trade deficit, now at \$25 billion.

The exact elasticity combinations necessary for these outcomes are mathematically laid down in what is called the *Marshall-Lerner condition* (so named after Alfred Marshall and Abba Lerner, who derived these relationships). The exact mathematical formulation is too complex to be worth trying to memorize. But it can be simplified through the Keynesian-type assumption that the two supply elasticities are infinite and the special assumption that the initial trade balance is zero. The Marshall-Lerner condition then stipulates that for a devaluation (revaluation) to improve (worsen) the trade balance, the sum of the elasticities of the domestic import demand, η_m, and the foreign demand for exports, η_x, shall be larger than unity:

Conditions in the Exchange Market

We can now recapitulate and reconcile these results with our previous analysis of the exchange market (Chapter 19): Export revenue translates into foreign exchange supply, whereas import expenditure translates into foreign exchange demand. This import-generated demand unequivocally responds negatively to the exchange rate, but the response of the export-generated supply will in some cases be positive, in other cases negative.

When export revenue, because of elastic export demand, indeed reacts positively to an increase in the exchange rate, the exchange market conforms to the standard supply-and-demand model. This is shown in Figure 23-2a. Compare exchange rates R and R' along the foreign-exchange supply schedule, $S_{fe}S_{fe}$, and examine the distance between it and the foreign-exchange demand schedule, $D_{fe}D_{fe}$. AB represents the foreign exchange surplus that would emerge if the exchange were to be pushed up from R to R' by the authorities.

By contrast, if export demand is inelastic, the exchange-rate response of exports will be negative—as suggested by the backward-bending supply schedule, $S_{fe}S_{fe}$, in Figure 23-2b. In this illustration, the backward bend is so pronounced that it more than wipes out the accompanying reduction in imports, and in the associated foreign-exchange demand. Compare exchange rates R and R', and you will find that the implicit devaluation creates a foreign-exchange shortage—that is, a trade deficit—equal to BA.

This is the result of the foreign-exchange supply curve intersecting the demand curve from the "wrong side"—in which case it violates the Marshall-Lerner condition. A devaluation would then, contrary to intuition, reduce export revenue so sharply that it creates an excess demand for foreign exchange. An upward revaluation would conversely reduce that demand, or bring about a surplus in the exchange market—equally contrary to intuition. This can be seen by comparing the quantities supplied and demanded at exchange rates R and R'' in Figure 23-2b. Thus at R'', there is a trade and foreign-exchange surplus equal to DC, although one would have expected a deficit. If a trade deficit—such as that corresponding to BA—were observed in this perverse case, the home currency would seem undervalued (the exchange rate being too high). If a surplus—such as DC—were observed, one would have to interpret this as the home currency being overvalued (the exchange rate being too low). In the normal case, the conclusions would of course be the reverse.

A great deal of research has been devoted to measuring the actual demand elasticities for different countries' exports and imports. Econometrically, it has proven difficult to isolate the influence of price changes from those of other, concurrent economic changes (especially, in incomes). Until recently, there was also considerable "elasticity pessimism"—an at-

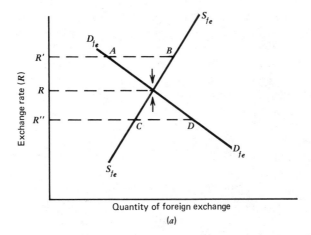

Quantity of foreign exchange

(a)

R':   an above-equilibrium exchange rate (undervalued domestic currency)
AB: market surplus of foreign exchange
R'':   a below-equilibrium exchange rate (overvalued domestic currency)
CD: market shortage of foreign exchange

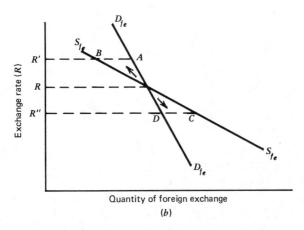

Quantity of foreign exchange

(b)

R' an above-equilibrium exchange rate (undervalued domestic currency)
BA: market shortage of foreign exchange
R'':   a below-equilibrium exchange rate (overvalued domestic currency)
DC: market surplus of foreign exchange

Figure 23-2. Disequilibrium in the private foreign-exchange market. (*a*) Normal market situation (with stable equilibrium). (*b*) Perverse market situation (with unstable equilibrium).

titude that made many countries unduly hesitant to repeg their currencies. But the best contemporary estimates nevertheless indicate that the elasticities, at least after a brief transition period, are usually high enough to satisfy the Marshall-Lerner requirements. The demand and supply schedules thus seem to intersect in the "right" way. Devaluations are then surplus-creating, revaluations deficit-creating.

In the very short run, however, export volumes tend to be rigid—in particular, because production and purchasing plans are inflexible. Both exporters and importers may need time to take full advantage of the new price relationships and adjust their trading strategies. Therefore, devaluation may at first worsen the trade balance (while the elasticities are still very low), before it gradually turns the balance around and produces the intended improvement in it. It has accordingly been suggested that following a devaluation, the trade balance (measured by its algebraic value) may over time change as if it followed a curve shaped like a **J**. In case of revaluation, the trade-balance path would then look like an upside-down **J**. There is some empirical evidence that supports these conclusions. But the shapes of such **J** curves will naturally vary among countries, along with changes in their respective export and import markets.

The Elasticity Approach

This type of balance-of-payments analysis, referred to as the *elasticity approach*, seems to give a fairly clear-cut set of policy prescriptions. Devaluation seems to have the potential for gradually restoring payments balance to a deficit country that is running out of foreign reserves. Revaluation seems to have a comparable potential for removing an undesired surplus and reserve accumulation. Yet no government could easily estimate the true elasticities of demand and supply at the moment when it considers making this policy move. It will therefore run a risk of repegging the exchange rate at much too high, or much too low, a level for the desired amount of trade-balance correction.

If, contrary to our assumptions so far, the exchange rate was allowed to *float*, it would of course settle at its market-clearing level—such as *R* in Figure 23-2*a*. If there were shifts in the positions of the demand and supply schedules (e.g., because of factor-supply changes), the market would automatically adjust and immediately restore equilibrium, usually at a different exchange rate. But this process, too, depends on the Marshall-Lerner condition, and thus on the relative shapes of the demand and supply schedules.

Yet if the market were "perverse" (not fulfilling the Marshall-Lerner condition), the free-market equilibrium would not be stable. This is the abnormal case depicted in Figure 23-2*b*. Any temporary disequilibrium would be self-aggravating. For example, an exchange rate—such as *R'*—that

accidentally turned out to be too high, would create an excess demand—
here equal to *BA*—which in turn would push the rate farther and farther
away from its market-clearing point. Market forces would hence tend to
pull the exchange rate away from its equilibrium, rather than toward it
(see arrows in the two diagrams). The market rate would then be highly
unstable. The possibility of such an unstable exchange-market equilibrium
has been used as an argument against a flexible-rate system. But how
realistic it is, we actually do not know.

The elasticity approach can be applied also to the circumstances in which
there is a *managed float*. If the authorities wish to stabilize an unpegged
exchange rate, or to modify its movements, they will of course have to
be prepared to make sufficient intervention sales or purchases to achieve
that result. What will be sufficient is partly a matter of the demand and
supply elasticities in tradable product markets. The greater the elasticities
are, the larger, normally, are the required amounts of intervention. (If
this sounds puzzling, remember that elastic market forces are highly susceptible to a changing price; if the government tries to distort the
price, the larger its market interference then has to be in order to offset
the counteracting market forces.)

In less typical situations, a government may be directing its intervention
policies toward a deliberate change in its foreign-asset portfolio. It may
wish to rebuild its reserves by some particular amount of foreign exchange.
It may then estimate the domestic currency depreciation that will result
when it adds its foreign-exchange demand to the apparent market forces. It
might find that, based on its demand-and-supply analysis, the indicated
depreciation would be unacceptably high, and it might therefore decide to
modify its intervention strategy.

The elasticity approach focuses entirely on price effects—in the tradable
product and exchange markets and, by implication, in the entire domestic
economy. It ignores other variables, including, in particular, income, major
expenditure categories, money, and lending and borrowing. As we have
described it, this approach relies on a partial-equilibrium technique, even
though the problem of payments adjustment is one of general equilibrium.
In principle, the product market analysis could be made part of a more
complete general-equilibrium framework, but it would then lose most of its
useful simplicity. Furthermore, the elasticity approach does not address
the issue of whether and how external and internal balance might coexist.

Income and Money Effects

In regard to *income* changes and more complex price effects, consider the
following complications. The technical elasticity requirements may indeed
be satisfied. A devaluation will then increase domestic income—in part
through an increase in domestic-currency export revenue, in part through

an expansion of demand for import substitutes and income increases in substitute-producing sectors. There will be additional, indirect effects on income via consumption and, possibly, investment, so that domestic income will reach even higher levels.

This illustrates a *trade multiplier*, in which increased net foreign spending on the national product, via subsequent domestic spending changes, leads to a proportionately larger ultimate income increase. The added spending will partly fall on importables and exportables—so that the net multiplier effects will actually be somewhat reduced by a so-called trade leakage—and it may also generate further price pressure. The conventional demand and supply curves do not account either for the income-induced expansion of demand for imports or for the supply contraction that these cost-price pressures can impose on exports. If we incorporated these effects into the formal analysis, the supply and demand curves in Figure 23-2 would have to be made interdependent of each other, and the job of analyzing the effects of exchange-rate shifts would be hopelessly messy.

Yet it is clear that both the income and the induced price effects will tend to undermine the effectiveness of a repegging policy. It almost seems as if a devaluation, or revaluation, will sow the seeds of its own destruction. Could it be that the trade balance correction, seemingly achieved through an exchange-rate change, will only be temporary, or even illusory?

If we consider the role of *money*, we will have further doubts about the effectiveness of the exchange-rate tool. In itself, the exchange-rate change does not seem to involve either supply or demand in regard to money, or similar liquid assets. But adjustment theory has taught us that there are important links among the markets for goods and services, securities, and money, and in an overall equilibrium, conditions in the three sets of markets must be mutually consistent. Will this really be the case, after the exchange-rate change has altered conditions in the goods-and-services market? Or will there be further complications, with feedback effects between this market and that for money?

To the last question, we probably have to say yes. If a devaluation initially removes a trade and payments deficit, there will at first be a reduced product supply at home; foreigners are now taking a larger slice of the pie. Possibly, the ensuing income increase will stimulate a higher degree of resource use, thereby expanding output and restoring part of the product supply sold abroad. But this will be only a partial offset, and if the economy was originally near the full-employment point, the devaluation-induced product "shortage" will remain. Meanwhile, there may no longer be an automatic reduction of the money supply through intervention sales of foreign currency, since intervention may no longer be called for. So the imbalance between money holdings and the product supply will worsen, and the public will again gradually expand its product demands so as to correct this situation. Additional devaluations may then become necessary.

As the reader must have realized by now, this reasoning is part of the monetary approach. Recall that in its extreme version it maintains that money is the crucial equilibrating variable. No discretionary exchange-rate change can then, except momentarily, push this rate out of line with relative money supplies and price levels in the trading countries. Devaluations and revaluations seem doomed to failure.

The more eclectic view is that the money supply will continue to exercise some pressure on the trade balance, despite the devaluation. It will therefore be easier to make the devaluation stick if money-supply growth is, at the same time, curbed. And a monetary expansion could usefully complement a currency revaluation. Whether fiscal policy changes should also be part of the policy package is another controversial question. The true monetarists would shrug off the idea; the followers of Keynes would happily accept it.

RESTRICTIONS ON TRADE AND CAPITAL FLOWS

Various other measures may be available to a government that wants to induce a switching of expenditure so as to correct an external payments imbalance. These measures include import tariffs and quotas, export subsidies, differential tax rates on the production of sale of tradable and non-tradable products, and exchange controls on product trade. All of these seem to have the potential for diverting spending from imports or exportables to strictly domestic commodities (or, when they are relaxed or removed, from the latter to the former). Similar measures might be applied on lending, borrowing, and security transactions, so as to tip the scales in favor of domestic or foreign financial transactions, or to prevent the latter altogether. All these steps may seem relatively effective. Yet appearances can be deceiving, and we should look beneath the surface.

Tariffs and Quotas

Under the topic of commercial policy, we analyzed the consequences of import tariffs and quotas at great length. We used both a neoclassical, two-commodity barter model (with offer curves) and a standard partial-equilibrium framework (with conventional demand-and-supply curves). Unfortunately, neither model is fully adequate to the general-equilibrium problem of payments adjustment. The conventional demand-and-supply analysis can, at best, give us a feeling for the direct, first-round effects—which might later cancel out. The offer-curve analysis misses the possibilities for substitution between traded and nontraded products.

The imposition or tightening of import restrictions may initially reduce the volume of the restricted imports and the nation's aggregate expenditure on them. To be sure, this is a first, positive step toward an improved trade balance. If the restrictions are in the form of tariffs, the public's tariff-inclusive spending on these goods may or may not decline, but its spending on domestically produced substitutes will usually grow. Also, if the government spends the additional tariff revenues (or reduces its borrowings by a comparable amount), there may be a further spending shift in the domestic direction.

The extent of the change in import expenditure as a result of higher tariffs depends on the home-country elasticities of demand and supply for the affected products. The higher these elasticities, the greater will be the reduction in this expenditure. Also, refresh your understanding of the relevance of the foreign supply elasticity. If it is less than infinite, a rise in tariffs or an increase in the restrictiveness of quotas will tend to lower the supply price of imports. This will lessen the reduction in import quantities and moderate the switch toward domestic spending.

Even if the foreign supply is perfectly elastic, the effects of tariffs on the balance of trade are by no means certain. With an increase in spending on import substitutes and other domestically produced goods, domestic income will be increased via the trade multiplier. Increased income, in turn, means increased imports, which will offset the initial import decline brought about by the trade restrictions. Also, trade restrictions—like exchange-rate changes—in themselves do nothing to change the money supply. If there is no expansion of output, the money may continue to leak out via the trade account. Indeed, under a strict monetarist interpretation, there can be no trade-balance or payments improvement simply because of changes in trade restrictions; monetary problems such as payments deficits or surpluses require monetary solutions. Anyhow, the net result may be a far smaller improvement in the trade balance than originally envisioned.

Suppose we also consider foreign repercussions. Decreased home-country imports mean decreased exports by foreign nations. This serves to depress foreign incomes, which in turn reduces foreign imports (the home country's exports). The net improvement in the home country's trade balance will then be even smaller.

Furthermore, increases in tariffs, particularly on the part of large, economically significant countries, may result in retaliation on the part of other countries. The reduction in import expenditure resulting from the home-country tariff must then be weighed against the possible consequent reductions in export receipts that occur because of foreign retaliatory tariff measures. In this particular respect, trade liberalization is likely to be more effective (in correcting surpluses) than trade restriction (in correcting deficits).

Financial Controls

Controls on capital outflows (or inflows) are in many ways analogous to trade controls. Their primary effect is on lending and borrowing, but there will also be secondary effects on income, spending, and commodity trade. Capital-outflow controls, such as those imposed by the United States in 1963-74, may immediately reduce the funds outflow via the capital account—unless they are circumvented through outflows via uncontrolled channels. But if they do achieve that aim, they will, at the same time, increase the domestic supply of loanable funds and generate easier domestic credit conditions. Gradually, this result could lead to larger nominal income and increased net imports. Capital-flow controls, too, may therefore set in motion counterbalancing forces that tend to negate the intended effects on capital flows and the payments balance, especially over the longer run.

Perhaps the most drastic means of payments adjustment available to a nation is *exchange control.* We have dealt with this form of payments restriction in connection with commercial policy. From a balance-of-payments standpoint, the sole purpose of exchange controls is to ration out the available supply of foreign exchange according to some predetermined set of priorities. With complete exchange control, a payments deficit could be entirely avoided, simply because foreign-exchange receipts from exports and capital inflows could be administratively allocated to payments for authorized imports and capital outflows, while all unauthorized foreign-exchange demands remained unsatisfied. Or the deficit could be set at a specific, tolerable level consistent with the government's willingness to draw down its foreign reserves.

There are also a variety of milder versions of exchange control that merely limit certain sources of demand for foreign exchange and thereby reduce their importance in the payments picture. For example, tourist expenditure and security purchases abroad by domestic residents are two payments categories particularly susceptible to restriction. One way to discriminate on the basis of the social worthiness of the transactions is to set quantitative limits on the foreign exchange allotted to them, or to make them subject to discretionary government approval. Another method is to employ *multiple exchange rates,* with separate official exchange rates for different transaction categories. Historically, partial exchange controls such as these tend to be temporary in nature. They create many bureaucratic headaches and are often scrapped after a more basic improvement in the balance of payments has occurred.

Exchange controls permit economic policy makers a certain freedom of action, not only in times of financial emergency, but in more normal times as well. Strict exchange controls insulate the national economy from world markets; in the extreme, the economy will be closed. No matter what happens internally, the balance of payments can then remain unaffected. Hence the national money supply can be expanded without limit. And government spending can be as liberal as political considerations will allow, without any trepidation about the possible balance-of-payments effects. With exchange control, the goals of full employment can be aggressively pursued, so long as the measures used remain politically acceptable.

But by insulating the national economy from payments disequilibria and providing increased freedom for domestic economic policy, exchange controls may leave the way open for a serious aggravation of inflation. As domestic prices rise relative to those abroad, the official, pegged exchange rate becomes even further removed from the equilibrium exchange rate that would prevail in the absence of exchange controls; at the official exchange rate, the home currency will be increasingly overvalued. If exchange control were suddenly removed and the exchange rate was kept unchanged, a serious payments disequilibrium would result—or, rather, the underlying disequilibrium would no longer be artificially concealed. The political reality is that the greater the overvaluation of the domestic currency, the smaller the likelihood that the exchange control will be removed. Meanwhile, the retention of exchange control may add upward pressure on costs and prices, because of (a) excessive monetary growth, and (b) the negative output effects of reduced competition from abroad.

A responsible policy maker will also keep in mind that all quantitative restrictions, be they on financial or on product markets, tend to lessen the beneficial social effects of the market mechanism. Market distortions will result. Sometimes, these could be justified on the grounds of "externalities" or "public goods"—which might have to be dealt with through government interference in some form. But there is a danger that the government will fail to make the necesary cost/benefit evaluation. It may instead take the easy way out by slapping on some form of direct controls with direct and highly visible benefits, without concern for the hidden costs to longer-run economic efficiency. Note the parallel with domestic wage, price, rent, and interest-rate controls.

ABSORPTION AND OUTPUT

We made certain reservations about the soundness of the elasticity approach and about the possibility to foresee the results of expenditure-switching policies. Some of these reservations can be appreciated even more fully via the concept of *absorption*. This term refers to the sum total of a nation's product demands, as expressed through aggregate private and government purchases in domestic or foreign markets for goods and services. It is equivalent to "domestic expenditure," as long as we measure the latter in real, price-corrected terms.

Denoted by A, absorption is accordingly defined as the sum of private consumption, private investment, and government purchases:

$$A = C_p + I_p + G$$

In conjunction with the national-income definition,

$$Y = C_p + I_p + G + X - M$$

we can further deduce that absorption will equal national income (or product) less the trade (goods-and-services) surplus, or plus the trade deficit:

$$A = Y - (X - M)$$

or

$$A = Y + (M - X)$$

This relationship should conform to our intuition: A nation can and will absorb only that part of its output not sold abroad. If it is in fact making net purchases abroad (via net imports), it can, however, absorb that much in excess of its output.

Absorption and output then become the effective constraints on the magnitude of the trade balance; in effect, they jointly determine it. For a trade deficit to be reduced, one or both of two things must happen: Either output will have to go up, so as to provide the wherewithal for additional exports and/or import reduction; or domestic absorption will have to be cut back, so as to free additional product supplies and, through changes in trade, put them at the disposal of the world market. In a relatively fully-employed economy, chances of expanding output are bound to be slim. If the trade deficit is to decline, absorption will then have to be reduced instead—approximately by the same amount. In an economy with ample idle resources, there will be more leeway in maintaining the prior absorption level, even while net imports decline. Conversely, reducing a trade surplus will normally require some efforts to expand absorption, but these efforts ought not be so painful or difficult. It could alternatively be achieved through an output reduction—generally not an appealing option.

The *absorption approach* toward the analysis of payments disturbances, therefore, stresses that it does not suffice to examine the direct effects of exchange-rate changes or trade controls on the markets for tradable products. However favorable the pertinent elasticities may look, there must ultimately be an adjustment of the relationship between absorption and output. Otherwise the trade-balance adjustment logically cannot be accomplished. The big question remains: When and how can it be done?

The most immediate possibility of correcting the absorption-output relation is through an adjustment of either private or government saving. Given aggregate output and income, larger saving will, by definition, mean less absorption. Consider a devaluation. There seem to exist two circumstances under which it may be accompanied by larger saving. First, if idle resources are mobilized through the diversion of demand to the domestic market, the expanded real income typically will entail some increase in aggregate private saving. Second, if marginal income-tax rates increase with nominal income, the added price pressure will automatically lead to a more-than-proportional increase in tax revenue for the government, and this "inflation tax" in itself implies a reduction of government dissaving (reflected in the budget deficit).

Yet devaluation certainly does not guarantee that either of these hoped-for effects will materialize. For one thing, the marginal saving propensity out of income might change. If people tried to maintain their living standards despite the higher import prices, the saving propensity would go down—and the trade-balance improvement would not materialize after all. More generally, the absorption approach underscores the fact that all expenditure-switching policies depend on the possibility of changing overall demand and supply conditions in national product markets. Like the monetary approach, it suggests skepticism toward such policies.

THE OVERALL STRATEGY

Our analysis of different adjustment policies has not led to any definitive conclusions. We have not been able to say unequivocally that some policies, or policy combinations, are better than others, or always better suited to particular countries or circumstances. On the contrary, we have stressed the diversity and unpredictability of the effects of the available adjustment tools on the external and internal balance.

Nevertheless, we have some notions about what policy makers want to do, and what can be done. One of the main lessons of neoclassical trade theory is that free trade and capital movements generally promote an efficient allocation of labor and real capital and, hence, real income growth. Adjustment policy can promote the possibilities to capture these longer-run gains—by refraining from the use of distortive trade and capital controls, and by allowing the exchange rate to reflect marginal costs and returns. A realization of this might have forestalled the disastrous protectionism that characterized payments policies in the interwar period. Adjustment policies based on this kind of reasoning might be called "supply-directed." In adopting this term, we want to touch base with the new stress on productivity and other supply issues in the current debate over domestic economic policy.

To survive in power, a government may indeed have to concern itself mostly with more transitory, short-term matters. A commitment to full, or overfull, employment may induce it to ignore international economic considerations. In other cases, governments will be tempted to adopt rigid external goals, as in the form of a balanced trade account. To do so may mean to sacrifice opportunities for socially beneficial trade deficits—beneficial in part because they can easily be financed through a drawdown of excessive foreign reserves, in part because this may be the best available method for temporarily meeting domestic economic or social goals. Sometimes adjustment toward short-term trade or payments balance will then seem uncalled for, and further "maladjustment" may actually be the best national strategy.

Portfolio Aspects

Furthermore, the international portfolio aspects of the adjustment problem deserve more attention. Nations may over the longer haul desire to be international lenders or borrowers; to accomplish either of these results, they need of course to run current-account surpluses or deficits. "Equilibrium" in the form of trade balance may then indicate a "disequilibrium" in the broader, long-term context of optimal resource allocation vis-à-vis the rest of the world. And a nation may wish to reduce potential future shocks to its import capacity by augmenting its official reserves. This, too, is a portfolio matter, involving a desire for increased international liquidity and for lessening certain international economic risks.

The portfolio view of the adjustment problem is particularly appropriate for three categories of nations. First, all borrowing and investment-receiving developing nations are, in essence, in the process of "imbalancing" their contemporary trade accounts, so as to expand absorption in accordance with their development plans. In so doing, they ought to realize the necessity for reversing these imbalances in some undefined future. For them, adjustment policy is, today, largely a problem of incurring the proper level of international indebtedness. Traditional trade theory tells us that this can be an appropriate attitude for a country with high real rates of return, relative to the going international rates of interest or to the return requirements of foreign direct investors. This analysis, however, ignores the uncertainties about whether sufficient resources will actually be available for future debt service and whether future generations will be willing to pay their ancestors' international bills. Does an aging dictator in the 1980s really care about the debt burden his policies will impose on his hypothetical successors in the beginning of the next century?

Secondly, the members of the Organization of Petroleum Exporting Countries (OPEC) are now accumulating current-account surpluses of around $100 billion a year. These surpluses result from the practical difficulties faced by the OPEC countries in quickly raising their spending levels so that they will keep pace with the exceptional increases in incomes—a matter of limited absorption capacity in nonindustrial, relatively backward nations. The OPEC countries are thus faced with a unique long-run adjustment problem—that of sharply raising investment and consumption and avoiding an excessive accumulation of external financial wealth. One option they have is to keep more of this wealth in the ground. Another is to employ it in enterprises in other countries through direct foreign investment or through aid to current or future allies. The relative returns and risks on these strategies obviously depend on a number of international political imponderables. It is an international portfolio problem of unprecedented scope.

Thirdly, the international financial problems of the United States in the 1960s and 1970s were different from those of any other nation. They centered on the appropriate amount of monetary liabilities to foreign governments—and on the desirability of playing a continued global banker role. Both the U.S. and most European governments came around to the view that those dollar liabilities should no longer grow, at least not at an unchecked inflationary rate. But the conventional corrective measures did not seem to work. Fiscal policy was dominated by domestic social programs and Vietnam War expenditure. Beginning in the mid-1960s, specific efforts were made to strengthen the U.S. payments balance, especially the capital account, through restrictive monetary policies and capital-outflow controls, but they were relatively unsuccessful. They were only half-hearted to begin with; the nation was unwilling to take the internal-balance consequences, and the rest of the world did not appear prepared to see its superbank retrench in this way. The 1972-73 steps toward floating exchange rates created a degree of additional monetary policy independence, but the United States has remained too concerned about the stability of the dollar to make full use of it.

Internal-External Conflicts

The histories of other industrial nations provide numerous examples of attemps to find the best feasible combinations of domestic monetary, fiscal, and exchange-rate policies. More than other nations, the United Kingdom has, as noted, repeatedly been caught in the dilemma of trying to stop capital outflows and reserve losses while simultaneously stimulating a sluggish domestic economy. It has frequently employed the monetary policy weapon, but during the currency crises of the 1960s and early 1970s, no practical way was found to offset the negative conequences for the internal real balance.

When the pound was devalued (as in 1967), there was a temporary respite from these opposing pressures. But as devaluation led to a renewed push on domestic prices and incomes, the external-balance gains proved short-lived. By tightening and loosening the monetary screw on and off, the United Kingdom developed a "stop-go" pattern of domestic expansion and contraction, very likely to the detriment of long-term private investment, productivity, and output growth. The floating of the pound in 1972 removed the immediate balance-of-payments constraint on domestic economic policy. Yet the British economy remains very vulnerable to the inflationary effects of higher import prices, and this realization still forces the U.K. government to keep a close watch on the external consequences of its domestic economic policies.

The situation of West Germany, Switzerland, and, at times, Japan has been almost the reverse. They all have had to continually choose between reserve accumulation and appreciation. On the one hand, intervention purchases of foreign exchange, especially U.S. dollars, accelerated the rates of monetary expansion and inflation. Especially to the inflation-averse Germans, this was a very unattractive outcome. On the other hand, currency appreciation could undermine the competitiveness of these countries' exports and their domestic full-employment policies.

Problems of Potential Key-Currency Countries

Against this background, it is understandable that both West Germany and Switzerland in the 1970s actively discouraged the growing trend among other governments to adopt their currencies as official reserve assets, as partial complements to the dollar. Reserve-currency status creates direct financial benefits through the ready access to cheap credit. These benefits are in the nature of *seigniorage*, a historical term denoting the difference between the face value of money and the unit cost of minting or printing it. Seigniorage originally accrued to the medieval money-printing lord; today, it accrues to nations that issue key currencies, or low-cost monetary debt, as in the form of treasury bills. Such a status can bring with it the risk of erratic capital inflows and outflows, in particular when other governments suddenly decide to enlarge or reduce their holdings of these currencies; in a multiple-asset world, such portfolio adjustments should actually be expected.

Maintaining the stability of its currency can therefore be a heavy burden for a reserve-currency government. It entails indirect costs that can outweigh the benefits of seigniorage income. The Germans and Swiss have felt that way. There are, however, indications that the Germans in particular are reevaluating their position in this regard. The Deutschemark weakened in 1980, and the German government took steps to encourage inflows of short-term funds from official as well as private sources. Suddenly key-currency status seemed more desirable.

Large-Country Complications

Large countries or groups of countries (such as the European Economic Community) that try to coordinate their economic policies face special problems in defining their adjustment policies: They have to anticipate the responses of world markets and foreign governments. When such a country wishes to reduce its payments deficit, it may find other nations unwilling to accept the reduction of their payments surpluses that is required for such an adjustment. From the global standpoint, payments adjustment is a "zero-sum game," and the large country can make drastic moves only at the peril of retaliatory or compensatory countermoves by other major players.

During the era of the "dollar shortage"—the 1940s and 1950s—there was no serious conflict between the United States and other nations in regard to the U.S. payments situation. The American deficits reflected the large American private capital outflows and outward transfers, and the associated buildup of foreign dollar reserves financed those deficits. At the same time, they provided the rest of the world with badly needed international liquidity, while creating seigniorage benefits to the United States. Had the United States, or the other major trading countries, insisted on adjustment in the conventional sense, world trade and global economic growth would certainly have suffered.

As the dollar shortage developed into a "dollar glut" during the course of the 1960s and 1970s, it may have seemed that the United States ought to run sufficient surpluses to absorb this glut, and to eliminate what is now called a dollar "overhang." But as we have indicated, it was not willing to undertake the recessionary domestic policies or to permit the sharp dollar depreciation needed for such a result. Foreign governments, on their part, were also not sufficiently keen on inducing the indicated deficits in their payments.

There is no well-developed mechanism for a global coordination of adjustment policies. There have even been minor "interest-rate wars" between the United States and continental European countries. These have occurred when countries on both sides of the Atlantic have tried, via monetary policy, to strengthen their capital accounts and overall payments situations. Not only will such competitive policy steps tend to cancel out the sought-for payments improvements for all concerned; they can also jeopardize attempts to revive economic growth and produce a global recessionary spiral. These conflicts underscore the lack of a basic agreement about how the "adjustment burden" should be shared. Deficit countries normally feel more pressed to adjust than do surplus countries; but a broader, more "symmetrical" acceptance of this responsibility might make adjustment both easier and fairer all around.

Cooperation has been even less successful in regard to establishing conditions that favor internal balance in these various countries. Governments are well aware of the real linkages among their economies, especially under fixed or highly managed exchange rates, and of the similarities in their respective business cycles. But it has proven difficult to reconcile their policy approaches.

Politically and economically, the distinct leadership of the United States, and its power to coordinate, has weakened. One result of this trend is that the United States has become much more cognizant of the international constraints on its monetary and payments policies. Still, there is an apparent need for leadership, perhaps of a multinational kind. When, in the late 1970s, there were signs of an impending world recession, it was suggested that the United States should act as a "locomotive" for other, less powerful nations in getting their economies going again. But the metaphor was exaggerated and unrealistic. More apropos, it was also said that the industrial nations might form a "convoy" that was to be led by the United States but in which each vessel retained some control over its own speed and direction. The need for cooperative economic management has been recognized; the appropriate mechanism and command structure have not.

SUMMARY

As tools of balance-of-payments adjustment, expenditure-switching policies aim at altering the relative portion of domestic demand that is directed toward tradable products or securities. By pushing the exchange rate to a level above or below its free-float level, a government can try to discourage or encourage imports and the sale of exportables to the home market. Or it may drive a wedge between home markets and international markets through special taxes, subsidies, tariffs, quantitative transaction controls, or foreign-exchange restrictions.

Superficially, such direct measures would seem to have dependable, clear-cut balance-of-payments effects. But as underscored by the absorption approach, there are likely to be indirect offsets, especially via income changes or secondary price changes. Many countries thus have learned that the initial trade-balance improvement achieved through devaluation or import restrictions can soon be jeopardized by accelerating inflation. In most cases, external imbalances reflect more general demand-supply imbalances in the domestic economy—and ought to be diagnosed and treated as such.

The choice of adjustment policies, especially by the largest trading nations, is a matter of general global concern. Those policies can greatly affect conditions in international markets. They help determine the nature of the international monetary-financial system—the topic that will occupy us in the last part of this book.

Important Concepts

devaluation	managed float
adjustable peg	multiple exchange rates
price taker (maker)	dollar "overhang"
Marshall-Lerner condition	seigniorage
trade multiplier	absorption

Questions

1. It has been argued that devaluations tend to set in motion forces that undermine their own effectiveness. What are these forces? Does this analysis apply mainly to fully, or to less-than-fully, employed economies? Would you classify it as Keynesian, monetarist, or what?

2. Assume the following conditions in regard to country X: Its export supply is highly elastic (because of unused capacity), and it has a virtual monopoly in its chief export markets. Its import demand is highly inelastic (because of a lack of raw materials for import substitutes), and it is a price taker in its import markets (despite its size). Its government is contemplating a currency devaluation, so as to correct its trade deficit. Is this policy likely to succeed?

3. It may seem that restrictions on capital outflows will often be the least painful method for eliminating a payments deficit. But most economists will oppose this method. Why? What social costs is it likely to entail?

4. In the 1960s, many Europeans maintained that the United States enjoyed an unfair privilege in regard to its balance-of-payments situation because of the special status of the dollar. American officials retorted that, on the contrary, this status imposed severe constraints on their international and domestic economic policies. Explain and evaluate these contradictory views.

Further Readings

Alexander, Sidney, "The Effects of a Devaluation on the Trade Balance," *IMF Staff Papers*, April 1952.

Cooper, Richard, *Currency Devaluation in Developing Countries*, Essays in International Finance, No. 86 (Princeton: Princeton University, 1971).

Grubel, Herbert, *International Economics* (Homewood, Illinois: Irwin, 1977), Chapters 14-16.

Stern, Robert, *The Balance of Payments: Theory and Economic Policy* (Chicago: Aldine, 1973), Chapters 5, 7, and 9.

V
The
International
Monetary
System

24

RESERVE ASSETS AND PAYMENTS REGIMES

Our analysis of balance-of-payments disturbances and adjustment processes underscored the high degree of economic interdependence in the world economy. Governments have learned that their possibilities to restore external or internal balance depend on market repercussions and policy reactions abroad. Policy makers hence have to anticipate the likely reactions of the rest of the world. They have to obey the rules of the game, or face the consequences if they don't. Yet if they are economically powerful, they may be able to influence these rules.

The practices, policies, and rules that have evolved over time constitute an international financial-economic "system." Since most of the actual policy issues—for example, the size of payments deficits and surpluses, and methods for their settlement—are monetary in nature, the conventional term for it is the "international monetary system." Some authors prefer the term "regime," which suggests a body of formal, supranationally enforced rules. Whatever we call it, we need a summary description of the global financial arrangements that define the national options in regard to adjustment policies and the manner in which official international debts can be settled. This is the purpose of the present chapter. It first describes the various features by which one can ordinarily define an international monetary system, whether they emerge through coordinated policy decisions or through the evolution of private practice. After that, we will give a more detailed account of each of the main systems that have existed or been proposed and contrast their modes of operation.

CHARACTERISTIC ASPECTS

Perhaps the most fundamental characteristic of any modern monetary system is the nature, amount, and uses of existing international *reserve assets*. These are monetary assets held by government authorities in anticipation of possible future payments deficits—which the authorities may have to settle. In theory or practice, a particular monetary system may be based on one or several such assets—or it may lack any such asset. If such assets exist, they will typically perform roughly the same functions among governments as do ordinary money holdings in the private domestic economy. Like all transaction balances of money, they help bridge gaps between outlays and receipts. And since these gaps will never be fully predictable, such balances in part have a precautionary purpose: They reduce the risk of being without sufficient funds. A special provision for the creation and distribution of such official international means of settlement may then be needed.

The quantity of existing reserve assets will determine the supply of official *international liquidity*, a term that connotes the degree to which temporary negative imbalances in international payments can be sustained. But the need for liquidity depends on the capacity of each nation for quick, relatively painless adjustments to potential payments disturbances. A well-functioning monetary system should facilitate both adjustment and deficit financing— the two alternative ways of coping with adverse payments changes.

All international reserve assets will have to be assigned some agreed-on values; otherwise, they could not in practice be used for discharging debts denominated in national currencies, or in intergovernmental credit transactions. They therefore need to be defined, at each point in time, in the national currencies of the nations that plan to use them, as via *exchange rates* or other price relationships between them. A broader question is how these price relationships are to be determined and maintained. It could be done through government decrees, perhaps backed up by government intervention sales and purchases in the exchange market, or through similar steps by a hypothetical supranational agency for international currency affairs. Or it could be done through the varying day-to-day pressures of private and official exchange-market activity.

Most conceivable international monetary regimes also need some rules about the *adjustment policies* that nations may undertake. Without such rules, some nations may feel free to take steps that nullify the effects of other nations' policies. There may result a veritable policy war that severely destabilizes international markets and renders national policy helpless.

At one extreme, the range of permissible policies may be very wide, so that each nation is at liberty to choose its preferred policy mix almost at will. But since the value of such national policy freedom will be reduced by the like freedom of other nations, it may be preferable to collectively restrict the available policy options. If policies with especially harmful effects on the world economy can be discouraged, the remaining options may become much more effective. For instance, it might be deemed appropriate to set up guidelines that encourage expenditure-changing over expenditure-switching policies, since the latter could severely distort trade flows and resource allocation. And the burden of adjustment might be shared more equitably among deficit and surplus nations. Or certain countries with special policy capabilities or market advantages may be assigned particular tasks and responsibilities, for the sake of a more efficient overall system.

We will now present a survey of the principal types of systems that have existed in relatively modern history or have been proposed during the contemporary international monetary debate. At first, each system is described in its extreme, pure form; later on, we will look at some compromises among them. Table 24-1 outlines the main characteristics of four basic systems. It indicates how, under each of them, reserve assets are created and distributed, how exchange rates are defined and maintained, and what adjustment methods are permitted and practiced.

THE GOLD STANDARD

For both historical and analytical reasons, our survey ought to start with the gold standard, which was an actual model for the rules and practices adopted by leading trading countries during the period around the turn of the present century (approximately between 1880 and 1914). It is often hailed as the ideal system—perhaps a solution to the problems of inflation, exchange-market crises, and irresponsible national economic policies that seem to plague us today—but it is also being derided as barbarously primitive.

As the term suggests, a strict gold standard is an international monetary system with one sole international reserve asset and one official means of debt settlement. Monetary gold thus represents the only form of official international liquidity. Along with other (nonreserve) foreign assets, denominated in national currencies, it constitutes part of each nation's wealth. Its real value stems from its ability to command goods and services (through net imports) produced elsewhere. To perform its monetary function, gold has to be *convertible* into national currencies. And the conversion rates—the price of gold in various currencies—ought in theory to be permanently fixed—or the gold equivalent of currency-denominated obligations will be subject to unpredictable changes; also, individual governments might then be tempted to influence the gold price so as to increase the gold value of their claims or decrease the gold value of their debts.

Fixing the Gold Price

Therefore, under a strict gold standard each nation will define the price of gold in its own currency, and its government must be prepared to maintain this price. It does that in either one of two ways: It can see to it that all money

Table 24-1
Typical Characteristics of Different Monetary Systems

System	Reserve Asset(s); Their Creation and Distribution	Definition and Determination of Exchange Rates	Adjustment Methods
Gold standard	Gold, purchased by governments in the private market	All currencies officially defined in gold; fixed rates maintained through gold-currency convertibility	Automatic expansion (contraction) of money supplies in surplus (deficit) countries
Key-currency standard	One (or several) national currencies (e.g., dollar, sterling), supplied through key-currency country deficits to surplus countries	Nonkey currencies officially defined in key currency; fixed rates (or adjustable pegs) maintained through exchange-market intervention in the key currency	Changes in monetary policies, possibly coupled with changes in fiscal policies or in trade and exchange controls
Centrally created asset standard	Special international reserve asset (e.g., SDR), issued by an international monetary agency (e.g., IMF)	All currencies defined in the reserve asset; fixed rates (or adjustable pegs) maintained through exchange-market intervention in the reserve asset	Changes in monetary policies, possibly coupled with changes in fiscal policies or in trade and exchange controls
Freely floating exchange rates	None	No official exchange-rate definition; actual rates determined by the exchange market	Exchange-rate movements, possibly coupled with changes in monetary and fiscal policies or in trade controls

issued within its borders consists of gold coins (so that gold and currency become virtually synonomous); or it can link the issue of debt money (cheaply made metal coins or paper money) to the size of the national monetary gold stock. The former is usually called a *gold specie standard* ("specie" = coin); the latter, a *gold bullion standard* ("bullion" = uncoined metal in bars or ingots).

Under the gold specie standard, ordinary goods-and-services prices will be directly defined in amounts of gold, and the size of the money supply will be identical to the value of the monetary gold stock. Historically, this has been the more primitive type of gold standard, often with silver or copper coins circulating as well. Under the gold bullion standard, goods-and-services prices will be directly defined in terms of debt money, yet they will be immediately translatable into gold equivalents via the official gold-money conversion rate.

The amount of money issued may or may not then be equal to the value of the gold stock. If it exceeds the gold stock, there is effectively a *fractional reserve* system, with reserves consisting of gold. The domestic money supply will then have less than 100 percent gold "backing," as was frequently the case in the early part of the 1900s.

Exchange Rates

As each currency in this way is fixed in terms of gold, the relative values of different national currencies—exchange rates—will also be fixed. For instance, country A may decide to call its currency lira and establish a gold conversion rate of 100 lire per ounce of gold. Country B issues pesos officially valued at a rate of 25 pesos per ounce of gold. Clearly, the peso is worth four times as much gold as the lira, and the implicit exchange rate will be $R_{\text{lira, peso}} = 4$.

If there is a private exchange market for lira-peso trading, the exchange rate established in it (spot and forward) cannot significantly depart from the official four-to-one *parity*. If it did, private arbitrageurs would start to engage in triangular peso-gold-lira transactions and take advantage of the inconsistency among the three price relationships. There would in effect be two methods for A residents to obtain pesos for their own lire—by buying pesos outright or by first buying gold at home and then selling the gold to B residents for pesos. The respective peso proceeds would differ, and the difference would represent a margin of potential arbitrage profit. This situation would soon be corrected, however, through demand and supply forces. Despite some transaction costs, market exchange rates would therefore always be close to the official gold parities.

Adjustment Method

In regard to payments adjustments, the fixed link between gold and domestic money inevitably places the emphasis on *monetary* mechanisms. A country may at one time be running an overall payments surplus, and its exporters and international borrowers may be generating foreign-currency claims in excess of the currency needed by importers and security buyers. These excess claims, through the assistance of private banks, will be presented to the home country's monetary authority (its central bank) in exchange for domestic gold coins or debt money. The monetary authority will cash these claims for gold at the central banks of the deficit countries against which the claims had been obtained. If there is 100 percent gold backing, the home country's money supply will then grow exactly by the amount of gold obtained through this clearing procedure. If there is, say, only a 25 percent gold reserve against the money supply, the total new money issue will be a multiple of four of the payments surplus. In neither case can there be any question of sterilizing that surplus—that is, canceling its domestic money-supply effects; to do so would be a breach of the essential gold standard rules.

Beyond the change in the money supply, a variety of money-related adjustment processes (described in detail in Chapter 21) will begin. To recapitulate briefly: Under the classical conditions of competition and price flexibility, the monetary expansion will lead to an immediate decrease in domestic interest rates, additional spending on investment and consumption, higher prices, and larger nominal (but not real) income. In turn, these developments will tend to create a capital outflow and an increase in net imports, so that payments balance gradually will be restored. Opposite tendencies will develop in the foreign deficit countries, thereby speeding up the adjustment process. Arbitrage will ensure identical product prices and returns on securities. Apart from temporary disturbances, purchasing power parity will hold. Via their mutual ties to gold, national economies in this idealized picture will be highly integrated across the borders.

Actually, it is difficult to see how any disturbances could ever come about in this smooth and efficient theoretical world. Still, changes in harvests or in industrial productivity could temporarily upset supply and demand conditions, and so could shifting tastes or misinformation about prices. Government budgetary policies might also create an internal imbalance that spills over into imports.

Monetary disturbances could occur only if there are changes in the available supplies of monetary gold. This might occur because of gold mining, or private gold hoarding or dishoarding. If a government decided to purchase gold, under the rules of the gold standard game it would have to expand the stock of money accordingly, perhaps by a multiple of its gold purchases. If the ensuing money expansion were in excess of the general growth of the economy, inflationary pressure would of course occur. A tendency toward a payments deficit would develop, unless foreign gold and money stocks were also increased at comparable rates.

Performance

How well can the gold standard be expected to operate? In other words, how quickly will payments disturbances be corrected, and how easily will internal balance be maintained? Part of the answers revolve around the assumptions of the underlying neoclassical model. In reality, transportation costs, incomplete market information, sudden changes in technology, or erratic shifts in tastes could at least slow down, if not halt, the adjustment process. And downward wage-and-price rigidity could prevent the price mechanism from leading a deficit country, via reduced domestic demand and growing exports, back to payments balance. On the other hand, if capital flows were very sensitive to the emerging interest-rate differential, the very pressure for internal adjustment would weaken because of capital inflows into the deficit country. The remaining trade deficit might then have a prolonged dampening effect on domestic output and employment.

Understandably, the gold standard has been criticized for favoring external over internal adjustment, as if the tail were wagging the dog. For example, a deficit country with only a low marginal import propensity may be forced into a long depression as it slowly, through successive money-supply reductions, works off its excess imports. While international traders and investors enjoy the benefits of easy access to all markets, this system may thus carry intolerable domestic costs. There will consequently be a temptation for countries with severe domestic economic problems to break the rules—for example, by adopting *discretionary* monetary policies or direct trade controls.

From the standpoint of global monetary management, one must also question the rationale for tying the amounts of money issued to changes in the supply of a particular commodity. This supply should, it seems, be irrelevant to the general problem of providing for adequate liquidity. Today, sudden changes in South African gold production, or in Soviet gold sales, can drastically alter the supply of monetary gold. Under a gold standard, such events could greatly alter monetary conditions throughout the capitalist West. Those who believe in deliberate global monetary planning would not want to place the provision of international liquidity at the mercy of such haphazard or hostile forces.

It has, in fact, proven impossible to establish and maintain official gold prices that are consistent with demand and supply conditions in the private international gold market. Official gold stocks have been inadequate to counter the forces of private speculation; how large they would have to be to do so is impossible to tell. This undermines the intended global monetary stability. Under the rules, when the gold price rises or falls, the monetary authorities would be obliged to automatically alter the money supplies accordingly, with worldwide inflationary or deflationary consequences.

On the other hand, severing the connection between private and official gold prices—a strategy attempted in the 1960s—would create other pitfalls. Assume that the private gold price were to rise sharply. Individual governments would then be tempted to avoid making use of their gold holdings in international settlements and, instead, to sell them at more attractive prices in the private market. There seems to be an intrinsic difficulty in letting one commodity fulfill two separate, partially incompatible functions—that of satisfying private industrial and collector demands and that of governing the global monetary system.

A KEY-CURRENCY STANDARD

Instead of gold—or silver, or other precious metals or objects—the central reserve asset could consist of a national currency, or possibly a few, specially selected currencies. The most obvious reason for preferring a national currency over a commodity is that the former may be more easily managed in regard to its supply and valuation.

The Reserve Center

The country whose currency has been selected for this role—that of *key currency*—will in principle have to carefully control its domestic money supply, and thereby its overall payments deficits. By so doing, it will effectively determine the amount of official international liquidity, for each new deficit will inject an equivalent amount of reserve assets into the international economy. To achieve this result, however, it will need the cooperation of other nations so that they will be running the surpluses implicit in its own deficits. The country thus designated as the *reserve center* will then, via its deficits, issue monetary liabilities that need to be sufficiently attractive so that other nations will want to acquire them; its liquidity supply will have to be matched by a comparable demand. It will fail in this regard if its reserve-asset issues are too small to provide for the financing of the potential growth of world trade. It will also fail if it floods the world economy with assets of questionable real value.

Ideally, then, the reserve center will pursue monetary policies that guarantee a high degree of price stability, so that the real value of its currency on the world market becomes stable—perhaps even stabler than gold. Second best, it might compensate for the erosion of its currency's purchasing power through adequate payments of interest on its monetary liabilities (e.g., on outstanding securities such as treasury bills). As long as these interest payments are lower than the domestic or international returns on the loanable funds obtained in this fashion, the reserve center will collect *seigniorage*—a term introduced in Chapter 23. From its own standpoint, the seigniorage income is its reward for shouldering the responsibility of being the world's official banker. From the view of the "peripheral" (non-reserve-center) countries, the low returns on their reserve assets may be justified by the value stability and liquidity these assets possess.

Adjustment Methods

The existence of a generally accepted reserve asset means that each peripheral nation can incur occasional payments deficits or surpluses and settle them through transfers of reserve assets. By tying its currency to the reserve asset through a fixed parity, each nation will be able to let its own economy share in the price stability provided by the reserve center. It may even cement this relationship by making reserve-asset holdings the official backing of its national money supply. Most likely, this will be done on a fractional reserve basis.

But the gain in monetary stability will represent a loss of a potential adjustment mechanism. As under the gold standard, the scope for discretionary monetary policies will be narrow, and the arsenal of economic policies will be comparatively limited. Admittedly, it might be possible to minimize internal imbalances through a judicious use of fiscal policy, or through restrictions on trade and capital flows. Yet these options may be less effective, and more costly, than a policy mix that includes more flexible adjustments of the money supply; and they may create internal imbalance abroad.

Actual Experience

The world has not actually had a monetary system of precisely this kind, but something resembling it existed for a short while in the early 1970s. The Nixon administration in August 1971 announced that official foreign dollar holdings were no longer convertible into gold at the U.S. Treasury, as they had been for decades. This step effectively demolished what remained of the previous gold exchange standard (see below). The world was then pretty much on a "dollar standard," as the dollar was then nearly the only reserve asset used worldwide both in international settlements and as a standard for currency valuation. This situation lasted until the spring of 1973, when most currencies were unpegged from the dollar and allowed to float. The dollar thereby lost at least part of its unique, key-currency status.

Throughout most of this century, however, the U.S. dollar—partly in conjunction with the British pound—has played something of a key-currency role. That experience has taught us a number of lessons. First, there will normally not be any consensus about the appropriate rate of growth of reserve assets. Conflicts will then arise about whether the reserve center should run smaller or larger deficits, and about how and where the corresponding surpluses should be generated.

Second, few countries are willing to sacrifice their monetary policy independence, their right to employ trade controls, or their general control over internal economic conditions, for the sake of payments balance. When they give priority to domestic economic goals, their trade and payments conditions will at times be severely destabilized, with negative repercussions for the entire system. The basic tensions between national autonomy and international cooperation—and between centralization and decentralization—in economic affairs will remain under this type of system.

A CENTRALLY CREATED ASSET STANDARD

For reasons indicated, it may be difficult to find one suitable key currency (or a lasting combination of key currencies), or to reach agreement with the reserve center on the amount of reserve currency creation. Most nations may prefer to handle these matters jointly and to set up a supranational institution within which they can exercise some political control. This institution, the central monetary agency, could function like a super-central bank that serves the various national governments or national central banks. And it could issue its own money.

A Global Central Bank?

If this institution became a full-scale international central bank, it might be modeled after the U.S. Federal Reserve System. It could then accept deposits from the national central banks and extend credit to national government agencies (e.g., by purchasing treasury bonds and bills, and, possibly, making short-term loans to national central banks for emergency purposes). Its deposit liabilities could be denominated in a special international *unit of account*, which would thus become the special official international currency. This currency would, realistically, be held only by government agencies, and not be circulating among the public. The balance sheet of the global central bank might look like this:

Global Central Bank

Assets	*Liabilities*
National treasury securities (denominated in the respective national currencies)	Deposits due national governments or central banks (denominated in a special international reserve unit)
Loans to national central banks	

Alternatively, the central monetary agency might be confined to *pooling* already existing reserve assets, and exchanging them for a newly created international monetary unit. It might also regulate the future use of the new reserve asset, so as not to encourage irresponsible balance-of-payments policies. Or it may simply issue an entirely artificial reserve asset not connected with any financial intermediation. It could then closely control the gradual expansion of international liquidity.

What degree of power this agency would have over national monetary authorities is an open question. But the operations of a full-scale international central bank would be facilitated if each nation were obliged to tie its money supply to its reserve position at that institution. This would be a step toward a unified international system of banking, and it would help ensure that each national currency would have a stable value. Such a system would, however, eliminate all national monetary sovereignty—as would a strict gold standard. On the other hand, individual nations may insist on retaining the right to regulate their own money supplies. There could then be no firm assurance of exchange-rate stability. Each nation may occasionally have to devalue or revalue its exchange rate vis-à-vis the central reserve asset, and hence against all other currencies, at the peril of disrupting its financial relationships with other nations.

Advantages and Disadvantages

The advantage of this system lies in the possibility that any global liquidity surplus or shortage can be avoided and any unwanted global inflationary or deflationary pressure from such a source can be prevented. Yet if national money supplies are linked to the amounts of reserve assets issued by the central reserve agency, many nations may have to severely compromise their domestic economic policies. In the opposite case, exchange-rate instability will reappear, whereas domestic policies will gain an additional degree of freedom.

Also, national governments might find ways of circumventing the monetary "discipline" that centralized reserve-asset creation and monetary control should bring about. For example, a nation that, for the sake of global payments balance or world price stability, ought to cut back its spending, might escape such an adjustment by encouraging a net capital inflow. It might accomplish this through special security issues abroad, or through capital-outflow controls. This would allow it to postpone its adjustment—and possibly to create additional adjustment problems for other countries. Conversely, surplus countries might be tempted to place some of their excess funds in nationally issued securities or bank deposits (such as Eurocurrency deposits) that offer better returns than the central reserve asset. Such portfolio practices could undercut the planned monopoly of the central monetary agency in regard to international liquidity control.

As compared with a key-currency standard, a system based on centralized reserve creation offers greater international control over the distribution of seigniorage income. The magnitude of such income will of course depend on the interest rates paid and charged by the central monetary agency. Possibly, the agency might just break even—especially if it sets its interest rates on its loans and deposit liabilities so that the interest-rate markup on the intermediation exactly covers its operational expenses. Otherwise, some scheme has to be developed for the distribution of the seigniorage profits, or for covering any losses that might be incurred. This is a problem that could invite further political controversy.

Partial Examples

The idea of central reserve creation and management is relatively modern, and it has not been implemented on any significant scale. The International Monetary Fund (IMF) in the early 1970s created Special Drawing Rights (SDRs), and this was a small step in that direction. (We will discuss this further in Chapter 25.) Yet the IMF is a far cry from a global central bank; SDRs make up only a small fraction of existing reserve assets, and there is no provision for controlling national money supplies. One might nevertheless view the creation and distribution of SDRs as an embryo of a potential "SDR standard." National governments might increasingly use SDRs for settling their mutual debts, and additional SDR issues might allow them to store more financial wealth in this form. Should this happen, an "SDR standard" might gradually become a reality.

Under consideration is also the establishment of a so-called *substitution account* within the IMF. Through it, any nation with excess dollar reserves would be able to rid itself of these assets and acquire SDR-denominated claims on the IMF instead (see Chapter 25). Should this scheme be implemented, it would lead to further partial reserve centralization. It would entail financial intermediation between nations with excess dollar holdings and the United States, via the IMF. It would transform both the maturities and the currency denominations of the financial assets available to the governments of IMF member countries. Whether it would be coupled with further steps toward coordinated adjustment policies remains to be seen.

FREELY FLOATING EXCHANGE RATES

The systems described so far are in sharp contrast to a regime of freely floating exchange rates. The latter concept denotes an absence of government control over exchange rates, whether through a rationing of available currency supplies or through intervention on the exchange market. It ought also to imply an absence of special, discriminatory taxes or subsidies on international transactions, at least when they are manipulated in response to shifting balance-of-payments conditions, for such policies would have similar consequences on the international markets.

The absence of intervention means that no official foreign reserves will be necessary, at least not for traditional settlement purposes. Since all private exchange transactions will then be cleared through the market, there will in any case be no deficits or surpluses that could require official settlement. If governments want to keep foreign reserves in anticipation of their own foreign expenditures or for general budget-management purposes, this should, however, still be possible. If they do, they will be performing functions that mostly belong in the private sector. Of course, private firms may keep "reserves" for their own transaction or investment purposes. But such "reserves" are not at the disposal of the national authorities. Contrary to official reserves, they may be as useful and as prevalent even when exchange rates float freely.

A long list of arguments have been marshaled in the intensive debate over the relative merits of pegged and floating exchange rates. Some arguments have been based on broad economic-theoretic principles; others, on more pragmatic considerations, or on observations on the mentality of businessmen or bureaucrats.

Market Efficiency

The most substantive profloat argument is that free, private markets—including the exchange market—generally are more efficient. Such markets have the capacity to allocate real and financial resources to the uses for which these resources are best suited. Their key feature is competitive pricing, which is generally the best device for inducing the resource shifts required for the maximization of real income and wealth. Or, as the so-called Austrian school of economics likes to put it: The market is the most efficient mechanism for economic "coordination," as well as for the expression of individual economic freedom. Why, then, let the government tamper with it?

To be sure, even free-market advocates admit possible exceptions. Generally, government interference might be called for in cases of demonstrated market failures, perhaps caused by "externalities" in production or consumption, or by the existence of nonmarketable "public goods." Yet it is uncertain whether the case for pegged exchange rates can comfortably be fit into any such category. Private exchange transactions surely do not pollute the environment, nor do they violate common standards of equity. If particular product or security markets are malfunctioning, these problems ought to be corrected in those particular markets (perhaps through selective compensatory taxes or subsidies), and not through exchange-rate manipulation. Money is indeed, in part, a public good; this is a fundamental justification for government control over its issue. But whether flexibility in the relative prices of national monies weakens or strengthens their public-good aspects is a question that defies easy analysis.

There is a strong risk that pegging the exchange rate will produce what from a social standpoint will be the wrong price signals. A currency that, by the free-market criterion, is internationally too cheap (i.e., undervalued) will be too readily purchased. There will be an unwarranted incentive to import products available in the cheap-currency country, or to invest in cheap-currency assets in anticipation of an upward adjustment of their value (through a future currency revaluation). This depicts a country in payments surplus, sustained through intervention purchases of foreign currencies in exchange for home currency. (The reader should by now be able to construct the opposite case, involving currency overvaluation and a deficit.)

A skeptic of this reasoning may retort that most prices are probably very distorted anyway and do not reflect actual social scarcities. One more distortion will then not make that big a difference. To him, the efficiency of the market is little more than a textbook myth. And neither side can produce definite, empirical proof on the real effects of free or controlled currency prices.

Constraints on Economic Policy

Another controversy revolves around the implications of pegged and floating rates for domestic economic policy. We discussed the sometimes conflicting policy requirements for external and internal balance in Chapter 22, and we demonstrated the loss of policy freedom for countries with pegged exchange rates: They may have to slow down the domestic economy for the sake of external payments adjustment, despite the costs in forgone real income and employment. It has usually been claimed that a country with a floating rate will retain much more policy freedom. It seems that it can put its domestic house in order and just let the exchange rate drift to its new, market-determined equilibrium. In short, floating may generally insulate the domestic economy monetarily from other economies.

A technical amplification is, however, here in order. As explained in Chapter 22, the monetary sovereignty under a floating exchange rate will not necessarily extend to the determination of interest rates. If capital flows are highly elastic, the domestic interest rate may in fact be tied to the world market level. Independence in money creation, yes; in interest-rate determination, no. In turn, volatile capital flows can, via exchange-rate movements, make for serious instability in the trade account as well. (Remember that a large capital outflow will have to be offset by an equally large current-account surplus, which may have stimulatory, inflationary consequences.) So the added domestic policy options are not without problems and costs of their own.

To gain even more flexibility, a country may want to be free to choose, at each moment, whether or not to intervene. It will then, it seems, have the best of the two worlds, and a chance to change its mind with shifting circumstances. This is actually how contemporary floating-rate experiments have operated—that is, with occasional discretionary intervention. Canada let its dollar float relatively freely in 1950-62, and so did a number of countries in 1972 and 1973 during the transition to general managed floating; even so, they did not refrain from substantial occasional intervention.

For those who trust the intentions and capability of their governments, such extra freedom of choice may appear highly valuable. For those who do not, it may just invite abuse and irresponsibility—in particular, by reducing monetary discipline and encouraging excessive or erratic monetary growth. Again, the arguments will turn on the proper role of government, and on the merits of binding policy rules and commitments versus discretion and political judgment. If governments can hardly do anything right, how in the world could they possibly establish optimal exchange rates? And how could they possibly cooperate with one another so as jointly to determine the exchange rates that satisfy the domestic requirements of each of them?

The Stability Issue

On a more technical plane, there has been some question about the ability of a floating exchange rate to clear the market in a stable fashion. If the Marshall-Lerner condition (see Chapter 23) does not hold, the market will be inherently unstable, and the rate may move sharply and unpredictably in a futile search for a market-clearing level. This, we recall, is supposed to be the result of insufficiently elastic demands and supplies in product markets. Yet empirical research has tended to reject this possibility, and the so-called elasticity pessimism seems mostly unwarranted. What remains of this argument is a fear that a large devaluation or revaluation may be necessary if the trade balance is to be restored after an initial disturbance, or that the government cannot even approximately estimate the needed exchange-rate correction.

More attention has lately been paid to short-term capital movements. If uncovered, we consider them to be speculative, and they are then predicated on anticipations of a favorable change in the exchange rate. Fixed-rate advocates have often claimed that speculation is self-reinforcing, as the greedy speculators jump on the bandwagon and intensify the exchange-rate movement that is underway. Such speculation is said to be *destabilizing*. If it occurs, it might unnecessarily aggravate the social costs of temporary payments imbalances. Figure 24-1 shows the large, exaggerated amplitude of such an exchange-rate path (path # 3).

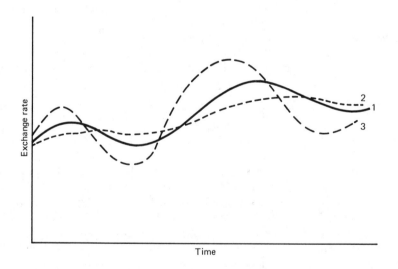

Three hypothetical paths of a floating exchange rate:

1. In the absence of speculation.
2. Under stabilizing speculation.
3. Under destabilizing speculation.

Figure 24-1.   Possible effects of exchange market speculation.

Destabilizing speculation is claimed to create added risks to traders, investors, and borrowers who operate in foreign currencies. Since they tend to be risk averse, they will respond by scaling down their international transactions. The levels of trade and capital flows will then be suboptimal, to the detriment of the trading parties and, more important, the national economies. Forward markets can, it is felt, provide only partial remedies for these risks; besides, forward cover is rarely available for longer-term contracts.

The free-floaters, with much theoretical justification, argue that speculation will normally be *stabilizing*, not destabilizing (see path #2 in Figure 24-1). Most of the time, speculators will tend to even out the ups and downs in the exchange rate by buying low and selling high. They will then usually make profits; those few who don't will incur losses and gradually be weeded out of the marketplace. This view—which has a strong Darwinian flavor—has been forcefully articulated by Milton Friedman.

Moreover, the instability that remains may merely reflect the underlying instabilities of the trading economies, especially in regard to changes in money supplies, prices, and interest rates. It will then be fallacious to treat the exchange market as an independent source of risk. Besides, if speculators sometimes make the wrong—that is, destabilizing—move, so will government officials when, under a managed float, they try to alter the course of the market. The whole debate hinges on the ways in which different market participants form their exchange-rate expectations—in part, by trying to anticipate the moves of the other players. Economists have not really come to grips with these issues of market psychology.

HYBRID SYSTEMS

Perhaps there ought to be a compromise among these systems. If the strengths and weaknesses of each of them could be identified, it ought to be possible to define the cost-benefit trade-offs that could be made through a gradual modification of one system into another. These costs and benefits would especially involve different degrees of international and domestic price stability, risks, and control over the domestic employment situation. Theoretically, one might even envision an optimal solution in which the achievable trade-off would precisely match the nation's relative preferences among these economic variables. But the potential strengths and weaknesses of the various sytems are in reality not so clear-cut. And there are deep-seated problems of consistency and compatibility among the choices open to individual countries.

The Gold Exchange Standard

By combining the main features of the gold standard with those of a key-currency standard, one obtains what is called a "gold exchange standard." The inclusion of the word "exchange" refers to the ability of governments to exchange gold for the key currency, and vice versa—something described as key-currency *convertibility*. There will thus be two (or perhaps more) officially designated reserve assets. Their mutual relationship will be permanently fixed via the key-currency price of gold and—amounting to the same thing—via the gold "content" of that currency.

The gold price must then be guaranteed or stabilized by some authority, normally the treasury of the key-currency country's government. This government will have to be ready to redeem foreign holdings of its currency (at least those by foreign governments) in gold, for it is precisely this obligation that will give the key currency the same stability and reliability as the metal itself. This government ought also to permit conversions in the other direction—of gold into its currency—so that individual nations can replenish their reserves of the key currency and use these reserves for settling their official international debts. In practice, this method of debt settlement will be cheaper, quicker, and safer than transfers of gold, especially if it is handled through the telecommunication facilities that now exist.

The advantage of a gold exchange standard lies, in part, in the increased flexibility of the supply of international liquidity. The key-currency country can supply, via deficits, the rest of the world with additional reserve assets as long as it can continue to maintain their gold convertibility. This approximately describes conditions during a large part of this century. The leading key currency, linked to gold, was at first the British pound. Later on, the pound was replaced on an increasing scale by the U.S. dollar. U.K. deficits in the 1920s and 1930s helped meet the world's liquidity needs in that period. So did U.S. deficits in the subsequent three decades, thereby supplementing existing gold reserves.

Yet both nations gradually encountered resistance to their key-currency roles and to the ways in which they carried out their global banker functions. In the 1960s, the continental European powers (notably France) started to argue that the United States was grossly abusing its power to attract low-cost international funds through continuous increases in its monetary liabilities to foreign governments. It thus seemed to collect more seigniorage than it could possibly deserve, of course at the expense of its creditor nations. Ultimately, it also did not succeed in ensuring the value of its currency or its convertibility into gold, since convertibility was suspended in 1971 and the dollar was devalued in both 1971 and 1973. Effectively, the gold exchange standard ceased functioning in 1971 under the combined pressure of global money and credit expansion, changing international price relationships, and a permanent imbalance in U.S.-European payments. In retrospect, these developments pointed to the inevitable disadvantages of a gold exchange standard: a lack of payments discipline on the key-currency country, an inequitable sharing of the adjustment burden between it and other nations, and the potential instability connected with multiple reserve assets.

Exchange-Rate Bands

All modern systems of pegged exchange rates have contained at least one small, technical concession to floating: They have had provisions for small day-to-day fluctuations in exchange rates around their official pars. There is then a stipulated *margin* of permissible spot rate fluctuations of $\pm X$ percent on each side of par, and there will be an exchange-rate *band* that has a corresponding width of $2X$ percent thereof. This is illustrated in Figure 24-2a. Provisions such as these make the practical task of exchange-rate control a bit easier, since the majority of transactions usually can be cleared through the market itself at rates falling within these margins.

More important, even these small exchange-rate fluctuations can perform a role in payments adjustment. After a change in interest-rate relations, they can help restore interest parity and equilibrium in the money markets. The relationship between spot and forward rates—and the forward premium or discount—can then more easily fall in line with the new interest differentials, and thereby calm down short-term capital flows. Whether spot-rate flexibility does or does not occasionally fuel destabilizing speculation is still an open empirical question. Spot-rate movements even of small magnitudes may of course increase short-term risks in lending and borrowing, but this added risk can normally be offset through forward-market hedging or diversification. Therefore, moderate exchange-rate margins need not significantly complicate private financial management—and perfectly fixed exchange is anyhow not a realistic alternative.

Peg Adjustments

Not even a wider band that spans a total of, say, 10 percent can be expected to solve severe, long-lived payments problems. In particular, if the elasticities in the markets for tradable products are comparatively low, eliminating a sizable trade balance might require a much larger depreciation than possible within that band. A sharp exchange-rate shock might also be needed to put a stop to a wave of aggressive speculation in the exchange market. These are some of the reasons for the historical failure to maintain fixed pars over extended periods and for the transformation of the nominal fixed exchange-rate system after World War II into a regime of *adjustable pegs*. Permanent fixity has been out of reach—essentially because of poor economic policy coordination. The adjustable-peg regime is depicted in Figure 24-2b.

By repegging its exchange rate, a country can gain more leeway in the formulation of its domestic economic policies. For example, it may get a chance to adopt an expansionary monetary and fiscal policy designed to remedy a short-term recession. Yet we recall from Chapter 23 that the freedom thereby gained can rather quickly be dissipated through a new burst of inflation, and a failure to slow the monetary expansion will most likely necessitate further devaluation along the way. As each new devaluation is seen to be approaching, speculators will take increasing long positions (net asset positions) in foreign currencies. When devaluation occurs, they will cash in their capital gains at the expense of the intervening authorities. These gains will seem socially unjust to many, and populist politicians and media figures will press for exchange controls. There may be periods of stable, credible exchange rates, when foreign-exchange risks are minimal. Yet these risks may become exceedingly large as soon as the market senses a significant probability of a devaluation. As the magnitude of the devaluation will remain a well-kept secret, no normal profit and cost calculations will be possible in international dealings.

Because of the unsettling effects of such sudden, sharp exchange-rate changes, a few countries have chosen to make their peg adjustments more frequent and gradual. This is currently true of Brazil, with its "mini-devaluations" that occur one or more times every month. The technical term is a *crawling peg*, or, alternatively, a "gliding parity" (see Figure 24-2c). If the peg adjustments are geared to accommodating rapidly shifting market pressure, they will of course be very frequent, and the path of the crawling peg will be similar to that of a free float. Even so, it can permit the policy makers to manipulate the trade and payments balance for short-term domestic purposes. Depending on how it is implemented, it may increase or decrease short-term risks and uncertainties for international firms.

Under some proposals, the maximum permissible amounts of the peg adjustments are to be predetermined, and so are the time intervals between them. For example, the exchange rate might be allowed to move by a few percent (or even less) per month, quarter, or year. Some proposals would let the government decide whether or not it will avail itself of the right to repeg; others would establish factual criteria (say, certain reserve changes or spot-rate deviations from par) that would automatically trigger a new peg.

Note that if the crawling peg has a band attached to it, a peg adjustment may actually not entail any immediate change in the going spot rate at all. The spot rate may just glide smoothly from the upper range of the predevaluation band into the lower range of the postdevaluation band; this can be seen from the fact that part of these bands in Figure 24-2c lie on the same horizontal level. The crawling peg therefore need not create the same incentives for sudden, large-scale speculation as does the ordinary adjustable peg.

Managed Floating

As compared with a crawling peg, the managed float—sometimes called the "dirty float"—seems to pose less of a constraint on domestic policy (see Figure 24-2d). The very notion of "management" suggests discretionary control, whereas all systems with formal pegs preclude such control, at least in the short run. Since under a managed float, the authorities—if they wish—can let

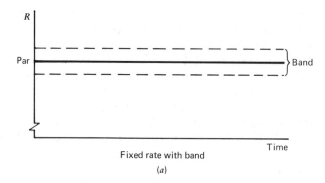

Fixed rate with band

(a)

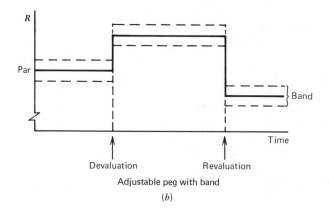

Adjustable peg with band

(b)

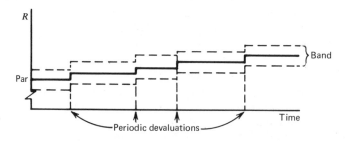

Crawling peg with band (for depreciating currency)

(c)

Figure 24-2. Permissible exchange-rate fluctuation. (a) Fixed rate with band. (b) Adjustable peg with band. (c) Crawling peg with band (for depreciating currency).

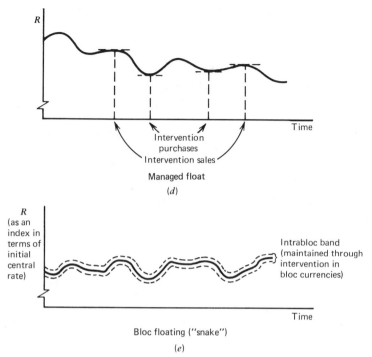

R = spot exchange rate in units of domestic currency per unit of key currency; broken horizontal lines indicate intervention points.

Figure 24-2. *(d)* Managed float. *(e)* Bloc floating ("snake").

the exchange rate drift up or down, they should not need to worry about incurring undesired imbalances in international payments. There will thus be no direct international financial barrier to domestic monetary growth, or to fiscal deficits, something that should please countries with great inclinations toward inflation. At the same time, this regime allows the authorities a chance, if they so prefer, to stabilize short-term exchange rate movements through carefully executed intervention.

Still, a choice will ultimately have to be made between (1) the exchange-rate corrections necessary if domestic money supply growth is out of step with that abroad, and (2) the monetary discipline implied in longer-term exchange-rate stability. There will be no substantial freedom to manipulate longer-run exchange-rate trends. Moreover, speculators, trying to second-guess the intentions of the intervening authorities, may be powerful enough to undo most of the intended stabilization, even in the very short run. If the government has set a particular exchange-rate target, achieving it may then require large amounts of intervention, and the intervention may jeopardize its control over domestic monetary expansion.

The managed-float practices that started in the early 1970s have produced greater flexibility for the authorities, in particular in the short-term handling of money and credit policies; but they apparently have introduced some new uncertainties and risks as well. The capital markets of the large industrial nations are now highly integrated, so that a monetary policy shift by one of them can promptly produce capital flows that offset monetary policy changes in other countries. Also, most countries sense a need to cooperate in setting mutually agreeable exchange-rate targets. Their policy options will then be quite limited, after all. Overall, the effects of the managed float have been obscured by other dramatic changes in the world economy—in particular, the accelerated global inflation, the oil price shocks, and new channels of international financial intermediation.

Currency Blocs

In a multilateral world, each nation will normally have stronger economic links to certain countries than to others, and such geographic patterns might be important to the choice of exchange-rate regime. Consider two economies that are highly integrated and also share the same priorities in regard to price stability and full employment. This situation suggests that they will pursue very similar economic policies, externally and internally—and this should make it easy for them to keep their mutual exchange rate stable. Meanwhile, they may wish to insulate their policies from those of other major nations. They might then, perhaps together with additional countries, choose to form a *currency bloc*, within which exchange rates are firmly pegged but which allows their currencies to float jointly against the currencies of third countries.

The most outstanding example of this compromise scheme is that of the European currency *snake*. This name describes the combination of (1) a narrow range of permissible internal exchange-rate movements within the European Economic Community, and (2) the legally unlimited movements of the entire group of currencies vis-à-vis other currencies (see Figure 24-2e). More details on this scheme will be presented in Chapter 25. It is based on an anticipation that monetary policies, as well as other economic policies, will be more and more coordinated within the EEC bloc, perhaps to the point of complete economic union. No such close coordination is likely to come about in relations vis-à-vis the United States and other non-European countries. The snake, it is hoped, will pave the way for a common European currency.

Robert Mundell has introduced a theoretical concept that captures some of the conflicting forces working for and against such moves toward monetary integration. The concept is that of an *optimum currency area*—an area ideally suited for a common currency, not shared by other areas. If such areas can be defined—and do not encompass the whole world—it will be because economic relations among the countries *within* them are markedly different from relations *between* them and other currency areas. They would represent a special, monetary kind of regionalism, or selective multilaterialism in monetary affairs.

Mundell's own position has been that the shape of the currency areas should be dictated primarily by the degree of resource mobility. Well-integrated areas (such as, for the most part, the United States, or parts of Western Europe) should each have a single currency—which is equivalent to permanently fixed exchange rates among the regions of that area. Poorly integrated areas (possibly even within now-existing nations) may, on the other hand, need to be divided monetarily into separate subareas, which can then enjoy the benefits of monetary independence. Other writers have elaborated on these rules and added rules of their own. No one has as yet come up with a magic formula for the optimal global currency structure.

SUMMARY

Our comparative evaluation of different monetary regimes has indicated what the principal requirements for an ideal exchange-rate system are. The world economy needs an efficient mechanism for settling private international transactions, without introducing distortions into competitive price relationships. Much, if not all, of this job can be done by the private exchange markets and the network of international commercial banks. But governments almost always play a leading role in the creation of money, and the logical extension of domestic central banking would seem to lie in an international agency charged with supplying a stable, generally accepted global currency. Responsibility for running such an agency, and such a system, would probably have to be shared by all major trading nations. Alternatively, the nation with the largest participation in world trade and finance may assume the burden—and the privilege—of supplying the rest of the world with a broadly acceptable key currency.

Yet both economic history and monetary theory show that there are costs, as well as benefits, in sharing a common means of payment. In the short run, these costs stem from the need to tailor the rates of money growth to the varying conditions of individual countries or areas—for instance, to maintain aggregate demand in the face of rigid prices and wages. A common currency, or fixed exchange rates, will often make this impossible. Trading off internationally stable, low-risk money for more jobs at home can thus be awfully tempting, despite the danger that abrupt exchange-rate changes might impair the longer-run development of international markets.

Freely floating exchange rates is a radical alternative, and an especially natural arrangement among countries with sharply different inflation rates. There are powerful arguments both for fixed and for flexible exchange rates, and for systems that contain elements of both. In the next, and final, chapter, we will examine the evolving economic-political rules that characterize the current international monetary system and reflect the tensions of contrary national interests, priorities, and capabilities.

Important Concepts

reserve asset	reserve center
gold convertibility	adjustable peg
gold bullion standard	exchange-rate band
fractional reserve system	crawling peg
gold exchange standard	optimum currency area

Questions

1. One important issue in the organization of the international monetary system is the degree of "discipline" on the conduct of national monetary policy. In this respect, compare systems of fixed, adjustable, and freely floating exchange rates. Under each of them, what can the "penalties" (internally or externally) be for defying that discipline?

2. The United States is said to play the role of a world banker. Explain this metaphorical description of financial relations between the United States and the rest of the world. What do the "bank deposits" and the "bank loans" actually consist of?

3. Foreign governments that consider the U.S. dollar an unduly risky asset can diversify their international reserves by acquiring other major currencies. If this practice became widespread, what would most likely happen to the U.S. balance of payments and the U.S. dollar?

4. Free-float advocates claim that freely floating exchange rates do not necessarily make currencies any riskier and that, even if this was the case, traders and investors could easily hedge against those risks. Evaluate both arguments, while noting the role of speculators in the exchange markets. How would the hedging be carried out?

Further Readings

Friedman, Milton, "The Case for Flexible Exchange Rates," in his *Essays in Positive Economics* (Chicago: University of Chicago Presss, 1953).

Journal of International Economics, September 1972. (Entire issue is devoted to international monetary problems.)

McKinnon, Ronald, "Optimum Currency Areas," *American Economic Review*, September 1963.

Mundell, Robert, "The Theory of Optimum Currency Areas," *American Economic Review*, September 1961.

Williamson, John, "Surveys in Applied Economics: International Liquidity," *Economic Journal*, September 1973.

Yeager, Leland, *International Monetary Relations*, 2nd ed. (New York: Harper and Row, 1976), Chapters 11-14.

25

THE EVOLVING MONETARY SYSTEM

If we made a broad sweep through international monetary history, we would not find any clear evolutionary trends. Some societies have favored metal or metal-based money; others, pure debt money. In some, the issue of money has been a prerogative of the national authorities; in others, it has mainly been the job of private commercial banks. Most monies have been used exclusively within the nations in which they have been issued; a few major ones have, in addition, assumed international functions. And throughout modern times, the existence of separate, nationally controlled currencies has posed problems and controversies in regard to the financing of international trade and capital flows.

We will not try to resolve the deeper mysteries of the zigzags of international monetary history. That it has been closely connected with political history, changing borders, and shifting economic-political alliances is, however, obvious. This impression will be reinforced as we survey in this chapter the changes that have occurred in the international monetary system during this century. We will try especially to convey one important perception: that there is an ongoing struggle between the interests of a liberal, stable world economic order and those of national economic independence and political autonomy. In this struggle, money can be an international instrument of cooperation and integration—or of conflict and fragmentation.

THE EARLY 1900s

The monetary system during the pre-World War I period can be characterized as a gold standard, which in the interwar era evolved into a gold exchange standard. Some of the crucial historical dates from this period on are listed in Table 25-1. Following the international economic disruptions of World War I, the leading international economic powers—Britain, the United States, and France, in particular—all tied their respective currencies to gold. Britain had by far the largest monetary gold reserves, and the pound was widely used in international finance, on the official as well as the private plane.

Yet the U.S. dollar (and to some extent, the French franc) played a subsidiary international monetary role. This role grew as Britain experienced increasing outflows of gold, traded for more attractive-seeming assets in the United States—an illustration of the complications arising when there exist competing international assets.

Maintaining the established gold par finally became too severe a straitjacket for the British economy, especially as the Great Depression toward the end of the 1920s sharply cut her export earnings. By going off the gold standard in 1931, Britain took a major step to reduce the international importance of the pound. In so doing, she acknowledged the new international financial weight of the United States.

By raising its official gold price to $35 per ounce in 1934, the U.S. government similarly acknowledged the growing international scarcity of gold. In regard to economic policy, this step loosened the metal's monetary rein on the domestic economy. It also disappointed all those private speculators who had gambled on the dollar's international value stability. And it helped encourage gold production and gold sales.

The remainder of the 1930s were, monetarily speaking, chaotic: Some countries (the United States, France and Switzerland, among others) kept their newly established gold pars, despite continuing deflationary pressures; Germany and Austria adopted systems of strict authoritarian exchange controls over trade and capital flows, and many nations engaged in successive, competitive currency devaluations. The latter were designed to stimulate their exports and income at the expense of their trading partners—and have been aptly described as "beggar-thy-neighbor" policies. There was neither an efficient free-market mechanism, nor a central source of financial stability and controlled monetary expansion. The United States refused to take the responsibilities being relinquished by Britain. Instead, it pursued protectionist policies that were detrimental to foreign lending, foreign investment, and imports—the most prominent measure being the Smoot-Hawley tariff (see Chapter 13). In retrospect, these policies

Table 25-1
Important Dates in Modern Monetary History

September 1931	Britain abandons the gold standard.
February 1934	The United States raises its official gold price from $20.67 to $35 an ounce.
July 1944	An international monetary conference is held in Bretton Woods, New Hampshire, and agreement is reached on establishing the International Monetary Fund (in operation in 1947).
September 1967	A plan is adopted at IMF meetings in Rio de Janeiro for creating Special Drawing Rights (with initial distributions in 1970-72).
March 1968	The industrial countries establish a two-tier gold market, following the dissolution of the London "gold pool."
August 1971	The United States withdraws its commitment to convert foreign official dollar holdings into gold.
December 1971	At a conference at the Smithsonian in Washington, D.C., the United States and other major countries agree to an increase in the official gold price to $38 an ounce, a general realignment of exchange rates, and a widening of the intervention bands (to 4.5 percent of the "central rates").
May 1972	The European Economic Community decides to limit the permissible fluctuations in its members' mutual exchange rates (to 2.25 percent of their central rates).
June 1972	Britain allows the pound to float.
January-February 1973	The Italian lira, the Swiss franc, and the Japanese yen are allowed to float.
February 1973	The United States raises its official gold price to $42.22 an ounce (in effect, devaluing the dollar by 10 percent).
October 1973	The Organization of Petroleum Exporting Countries places an embargo on exports of crude oil, thereby initiating a series of sharp increases in world oil prices.

Table 25-1
Important Dates in Modern Monetary History (continued)

January 1974	The United States abolishes its program of capital-outflow controls (adopted, in stages, in 1963-68).
April 1978	The IMF declares the official gold price abolished.
February 1979	The EEC establishes the European Monetary System, centered on the European Currency Unit (ECU).
January 1980	The private-market gold price temporarily exceeds $800 an ounce.

appear to have had severe negative spillover effects on other trading nations—via trade multipliers—and to have delayed the general international economic recovery.

BRETTON WOODS AND THE IMF

Purposes

It was apparent to the major powers that reconstruction and recovery after World War II required a reorganization of the international monetary system, and it had to be based on a cooperative effort to balance national and global interests. This was the background of the conference held in 1944 in Bretton Woods, New Hampshire, and the agreement there to establish the International Monetary Fund.

According to its charter, the IMF has a number of broadly defined purposes:

To expand world trade and investment.
To eliminate or reduce government restrictions on international payments.
To promote stable exchange rates.
To reduce deficits and surpluses in national balances of payments.
And generally, to promote international monetary cooperation.

These purposes may seem entirely unobjectionable. But we know from international monetary theory that each monetary system will always have some drawbacks and that critical trade-offs will have to be made. How does the IMF deal with these problematic issues?

The IMF charter makes no direct reference to the relative importance of internal and external balance, but the focus is clearly on the latter. Exchange-rate stability is an explicit goal; but we know that it may be inconsistent with the elimination of payments imbalances, and there is no firm rule about when it should be sacrificed on the altar of payments equilibrium. To what extent should individual countries be allowed to run moderate deficits or surpluses for the sake of facilitating their domestic macroeconomic policies? This is a critical question that the IMF charter also leaves unanswered, but that has to be dealt with in formulating a guide for concrete policy decisions. During the course of its existence, the IMF has tried to reach workable compromises on these issues, without finding clear-cut solutions to the inherent dilemmas.

Exchange Rates

The system that was initially adopted was one of fixed exchange rates, defined in terms of the two recognized reserve assets: gold and the U.S. dollar. The dollar retained its $35 official gold par, which, until the late 1960s, represented the gold price in the private market. Other currencies in turn were linked to the dollar (and thus, implicitly, to gold) via their parity exchange rates against the dollar. Graphically, the three asset categories were then chained to each other in the following way:

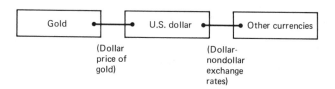

The U.S. government was to maintain the dollar's official convertibility into gold by offering to buy dollars in exchange for gold at the prescribed price ratio (and also to buy gold for dollars at this price), at the request of foreign governments. Other governments were to maintain the par values of their currencies by being ready to intervene, as necessary, in the spot exchange markets by buying or selling dollars at the established rates. They were, however, allowed to let the actual spot rates to depart by a margin of ± 1 percent from these pars; the band of permissible fluctuations was therefore 2 percent wide. The U.S. government, by virtue of the dollar's special, pivotal status, had no such obligation to intervene in the exchange markets. Technically, such an obligation would have been redundant. For example, since the French authorities were to support and maintain the French franc-dollar rate, there was no need for the U.S. authorities to duplicate those efforts.

Under the IMF rules, changes in par values were to be avoided. But such a step could be permitted in case of what the IMF called a "fundamental disequilibrium" in a country's balance of payments. Of course, a par change could involve either an upward revaluation—which would raise the official dollar price and gold content of the currency—or a devaluation—which would lower its dollar and gold equivalents. Unless the par change was very small, the IMF was to be consulted before such a step were to be taken. In practice, such consultations were not always carried out.

Quotas and General Credit Facilities

Each member of the IMF has been assigned a *quota*, which is a kind of participation share in the organization. It is determined, by the IMF, so as to reflect the member country's relative size and international economic importance. It was originally defined in dollars (and thus in gold).

The quotas have two related functions: They define the member countries' relative voting power within the IMF, and they determine the member countries' financial commitments to it. Each nation has to make a contribution, or *subscription*, equal to the value of the quota, with 25 percent payable in gold or other foreign asssets and 75 percent in its own currency. The foreign-asset subscription represents a true commitment of resources to the IMF. The domestic currency subscription, however, is merely a bookkeeping transaction. A depositlike account is set up at the member's central bank in favor of the IMF; but there is, at this point, no transfer of any real or financial assets out of the member country. This will not occur until the IMF decides to make withdrawals from this account and to permit the funds to be spent in this country by other nations. How this can come about will shortly become apparent.

The original IMF rules provide for a complex system of credit facilities for nations that appear to be in temporary balance-of-payments difficulties—difficulties that, through IMF assistance, might be overcome. They can get medium-term credit in the form of foreign currencies, which they can then use for intervention purposes or in settling international debts. The currencies are obtained through *drawings* (i.e., borrowings), and the drawing country credits the IMF with an equivalent amount of its own currency—as if it actually were purchasing foreign currencies in exchange for its own. It is through such drawings that the domestic currency subscribed by one member can be placed at the disposal of another member—the one making the drawing—and ultimately used for product or financial-asset purchases from the former. Repayments, generally to be made within a three-to-five-year period, are construed as *repurchases* by that nation of its own currency in exchange for foreign currencies—currencies that are acceptable to the IMF. Nominal interest charges and fees are levied on the borrowing countries.

There are detailed rules about how much a member can draw. Drawings equivalent to the member's paid-in foreign assets—or its *reserve-asset tranche* ("tranche" = slice of its quota)—are permitted automatically. After all, such drawings are fully collateralized by those paid-in assets. Beyond that, the IMF has a right to evaluate and possibly reject a country's credit application. In practice, it lays down conditions on the prospective borrower in the form of demands for monetary, fiscal, or exchange-rate reforms (possibly including a devaluation). These conditional borrowings represent true, net credit obtained via the IMF; and in undertaking them, the member is said to be utilizing its *credit tranche*. The larger the credit tranche drawings a member wants to make, the stricter will usually be the conditions imposed by the IMF on it. Under these rules, the maximum potential drawings that could be permitted were set at 1.25 times the quota. If a member was actually allowed such extensive drawings, the IMF's holdings of the member's currency would reach 200 percent of the member's quota.

The countries whose currencies are used in a particular drawing will obviously become indebted to the drawing country, as the drawing country receives their currencies from the IMF; remember that currencies are debt instruments. And since the IMF's holdings of these currencies will correspondingly decline, the respective debts of these countries to the IMF will also decline. For instance, when the United Kingdom (historically, the absolutely largest IMF customer) draws U.S. dollars, it gains additional claims on the United States, at least until it has sold the dollars on the exchange market. Meanwhile, the dollar liabilities of the United States to the IMF are reduced by the same amount. At this stage, the overall U.S. financial position vis-à-vis the rest of the world therefore remains intact; but should the British proceed to spend these dollars on U.S. products, the financial relationships will of course in the end be altered.

Upon Britain's repayment of her previous drawings (her sterling repurchases), the countries whose currencies are used in these transactions will conversely be debited by the IMF with the appropriate amounts. The ownership of these currency claims thereby shifts from Britain to the IMF. If, for example, Britain made repayments in dollars, U.S. monetary liabilities to Britain would decline, whereas U.S. liabilities to the IMF would increase.

The activities of the IMF become more meaningful if we think of the IMF as a kind of intergovernmental bank. Member country subscriptions are like deposits, just as drawings are medium-term loans. Some members have "deposits" in excess of their "loan" liabilities; others are in the reverse situation.

Each member has a *net position* with the IMF, similar to a person's bank deposit balance, less his outstanding loan liabilities to the same bank. For each IMF member,

its net IMF position = its foreign-
asset subscription – its net drawings (drawings less repurchases)
+ the IMF's net use of its currency
in drawings, less repurchases, by
other members.

Consequently, if a country's currency has been used in drawings by other nations, and it has not itself made any drawings, its net IMF position will exceed its foreign-asset subscription. Its right to make drawings will then be correspondingly augmented; it has become an additional creditor to the IMF and deserves the chance to withdraw these funds from the IMF at will. By contrast, countries that have already dipped into their credit tranches will tend to have negative net IMF positions.

To assure a member that credit will be available beyond the reserve-asset tranche, the IMF can enter into a *standby arrangement* with such a member. For example, a nation may commit itself to a gradual program of monetary and fiscal restraint, and perhaps a relaxation or elimination of its exchange controls. The IMF may, in return, offer a "line of credit" in this form, with actual drawings contingent on a satisfactory compliance with that program.

Additional Credit Facilities

In actuality, the currencies suitable for drawings are those of major industrial countries, and normally only those countries that do not currently have serious payments problems. Both the availability of such currencies and the IMF's need for them can vary significantly over time, especially if one or several industrial countries suddenly wish to make large drawings. A shortage of eligible currencies relative to the currency needs of deficit members might then conceivably occur. To forestall such situations, the IMF in 1962 entered into an agreement with ten leading industrial countries (the Group of Ten, as they came to be called) to make available additional amounts of their own currencies, if this should become necessary. This ten-country "credit line" in favor of the IMF was named the General Arrangements to Borrow. It was renewed in 1979.

Through various amendments to the IMF charter, certain categories of members have acquired additional opportunities for financial IMF assistance, notwithstanding the original rules about maximum drawings. In the late 1960s, the IMF adopted a special scheme for compensatory assistance to countries suffering from temporary shortfalls of export earnings—say, because of crop failures or unstable foreign demand. Several developing countries with a high dependence on individual export commodities have availed themselves of these additional drawing rights. In addition, there have been successive across-the-board increases in quotas, and new members (now numbering nearly 150) have joined the IMF, with the result that the total pool of recyclable currencies has been substantially enlarged. On the other hand, global inflation has eroded the real value of this currency pool— that is, its international purchasing power, and its capacity for financing imbalances in flows of goods and services among countries.

Nations with large, increasingly expensive oil imports have had particular difficulties in balancing or financing their international payments. The IMF in the latter part of the 1970s therefore set up a special credit facility intended to help these countries through a transition toward reduced dependence on imported oil. Yet the total amount set aside for this special purpose was severely out of proportion to the extra oil-import bills incurred by various IMF members, both in the industrial world and in Latin America. It remained for the private markets—the Euromarkets, in particular—to supply the bulk of the needed oil-import finance.

SPECIAL DRAWING RIGHTS

The most fundamental change in the IMF's functions since its inception was the decision in 1967 to create *Special Drawing Rights*. These are an entirely new kind of international reserve assets that supplement the previously existing supplies of gold and foreign exchange, as well as the original drawing rights in the IMF. Contrary to the latter, SDRs do not represent potential claims on national currencies. Rather, they represent a new form of international money with specific, limited uses. They can, so far, be held only by governments, and they are to be used exclusively for settling official payments deficits.

In some ways, SDRs are similar to national monies; in other ways, they are not. Like all modern monies, they are created, as it were, by a stroke of the pen or by pushing the printing-press button. They are bookkeeping entries (on the books of the IMF). However, they are not construed as debts of their issuer (the IMF), in this respect differing from national monies. Thus, the creation of SDRs rather oddly appears to add to the world's net financial assets.

To suggest this mysterious quality—or perhaps to invoke a suspicion of alchemy—the press likes to refer to SDRs as "paper gold." But does the production of paper gold really create wealth? Only superficially. Just as each SDR that a nation holds represents a potential claim on other nations' real resources, the SDR holdings of other nations represent potential claims on its own resources; the newly created claims are mutual. The total IMF membership is, in effect, responsible for honoring SDRs as acceptable official instruments of international payments. In this sense, outstanding SDRs can be regarded as a de facto joint liability of the IMF members. If our accounting methods were realistic, their issue would create no global net assets, and no longer seem like hocus-pocus.

Initially, the value of the SDR was made equal to one U.S. dollar—that is, 1/35 of an ounce of gold. But when the 1971 and 1973 dollar devaluations altered the gold-dollar relationship, the SDR was revalued upward in terms of dollars, while retaining its gold par. Subsequently, as the official gold price gradually became more and more unrealistic, this price lost its relevance to official international settlements, and the gold-SDR connection became practically meaningless. A new method of SDR valuation became necessary.

The IMF in 1974 decided to assign the SDR a value corresponding to a weighted average of a "basket" of 16 leading currencies, the weights reflecting the relative involvement of these currencies in international trade and finance. Starting in 1981, the number of currencies included in the basket was reduced to five: the U.S. dollar, the Deutschemark, the British pound, the French franc, and the Japanese yen, with the dollar and the mark weighted most heavily. See Table 25-2 for the precise definition and valuation of this multicurrency monetary unit. In 1980, the SDR's dollar value fluctuated within the $1.30-$1.35 range. From the valuation formula it is obvious that if the dollar should depreciate against the other four currencies, the SDR will increase in dollar value, and vice versa; but the percentage change in the SDR value will be smaller than that occurring, on average, in the four exchange rates for the dollar.

Table 25-2
Official Value of the SDR

Currency	Relative Weight (%)	Approximate Equivalent U.S. Dollar Value
U.S. dollar	42	$0.55
Deutschemark	19	0.25
British pound	13	0.17
French franc	13	0.17
Japanese yen	13	0.17
Total	100	$1.31

Note: The formula (the relative weights) is that adopted by the IMF as of January 1981. The equivalent dollar value of each currency component was calculated from the exchange and SDR rates that generally prevailed in the last quarter of 1980. Recalculated in the other four currencies, the SDR was then worth about DM2.35, £0.55, 5.45 francs or 279 yen.

Allocations and Use

The amount of SDRs initially created was 9.5 billion, *allocated* in 1970-72 in accordance with the sizes of the members' quotas. Additional allocations, totaling 12 billion, were scheduled for 1979-81. After allowance for the depreciation of the dollar against the SDR, the current dollar value of outstanding SDRs is close to $30 billion—still a fairly modest addition to overall international liquidity.

SDRs can be used in two ways. A nation in deficit can make an agreement with a surplus nation that it will transfer an appropriate amount of SDRs to the latter in exchange for the deficit country's own currency. In practice, this will be a reserve currency such as the U.S. dollar or perhaps the Deutschemark or the Swiss franc; and this could consequently occur if the United States, West Germany, or Switzerland was in deficit and wanted to finance part of its deficit in this particular way. Alternatively, a deficit nation may ask the IMF to designate a suitable surplus nation to which SDRs are to be transferred in exchange for various foreign currencies that the latter has accumulated. The deficit country will thereby be able to settle additional foreign currency debts or to intervene more extensively in the exchange markets. In either case, the IMF's SDR accounts will of course show a debit for the deficit country and a credit for the surplus country. As we showed in Chapter 20, corresponding changes in the SDR balances of these countries will show up in the official reserve accounts of their respective balances of payments.

A 5 percent interest is levied on each member's net use of SDRs, and the same interest rate is paid on net SDR accumulations above and beyond the original allocations. In either situation, the relevant "principal" on which interest is paid is the difference between total allocations and actual holdings. Rules have been set up for the gradual reconstitution by deficit countries of their SDR balances, as well as for the maximum SDRs that any one surplus country can be forced to accept.

A Numéraire

The SDR has, moreover, begun to replace the U.S. dollar as an official international unit of account—also called a *numéraire*. This is one of the traditional functions of money—to provide a yardstick for the definition and measurement of financial obligations. The IMF itself now keeps all its accounts in SDRs, including the sizes of quotas, the members' net IMF positions, and their repurchase obligations. This means that claims on and by the IMF are now fixed in amounts of SDRs even though they are generally payable in national currencies.

In this capacity, the SDR serves as a guarantee against sharp value instability in individual currencies. For example, both the IMF and its members have to compensate each other for changes in the SDR values of the currencies actually drawn. An illustration: Italy might have drawn a mix of, say, dollars, Deutschemarks, and Swiss francs, and is now, a couple of years later, ready for a partial repurchase of lire. If it pays for this repurchase in dollars, and the dollar in the interim has depreciated against the SDR, the dollar payment (even apart from interest) will be numerically larger than the dollar value of its original drawing. Should it instead make payment in appreciated Swiss francs, the opposite will of course apply.

Even though it is not available to private investors, the SDR can be used also as a private international unit of account. Bank accounts, bonds, and commodity contracts could be so denominated, if the parties agree and government regulators do not specifically outlaw such contracts. The practice has not yet caught on, but there has been a great deal of talk about the OPEC countries switching from dollars to SDRs as the unit in which they denominate their oil export contracts. Even so, actual payments will of course have to be made in plain currencies, since the SDR is not a commercial medium of exchange. The possibility that the IMF will evolve into a full-scale international bank issuing a generally circulating SDR "currency" is still remote.

A Substitution Account?

A step that would consolidate and expand the reserve-asset status of the SDR is the possible introduction of the *substitution account*, mentioned in Chapter 24. Through such an arrangement, dollar reserves could be exchanged for SDR-denominated assets issued by the IMF, most likely through a one-shot conversion. This idea has been debated extensively but not yet implemented. The main purposes behind it would be to reduce the dollar "overhang"—the excessive dollar holdings by foreign governments—that might threaten the stability of the present monetary system.

Such a scheme would make the IMF even more like an international superbank, or like a mutual fund for national governments. It would give the IMF further control over the management of international reserve assets. The assets to be created would, both de facto and de jure, be debts of the IMF. They could called "deposits" or "bonds"; their name is fairly insignificant. In their legal form, and in regard to their use, they would differ from SDRs; yet it is understood that their value would be defined in SDRs. By accepting U.S. dollars, the IMF would become an intermediary between the nations thus "depositing" dollars and the U.S. government, and it would transform the composition of governmentally held foreign assets. These results are apparent from the hypothetical balance sheet of the substitution account:

IMF Substitution Account

Assets	Liabilities
U.S. Treasury securities, denominated in dollars	Bonds issued (or deposits due) to governments, denominated in SDRs

The newly issued reserve assets would presumably be freely tansferable among governments in settlement of their mutual debts; they would thus not be subject to the restrictions that apply to the SDRs themselves. If, as is likely, they could never be cashed, there would be no problem of maintaining the solvency or liquidity of the account. Still, there is a ticklish question as to what interest rate is to be paid on these assets. It has also not yet been decided whether the U.S. government will have to issue some kind of value guarantee on the prospective U.S. Treasury securities in the account, or to replace them by specially issued long-term bonds with a more attractive coupon. Under the latter arrangement, the U.S. seigniorage income from its official international debt would decline.

THE SMITHSONIAN AGREEMENT

The weaknesses of the Bretton Woods system became increasingly apparent during the latter part of the 1960s. The official $35 gold price started to look more and more archaic, because of a growing private net demand for gold and because of the general, longer-term increase in overall price levels. The industrial countries attempted first to stabilize the private gold price through the London "gold pool," through which offsetting, stabilizing official gold sales were made. When this experiment failed in 1968, these countries established a "two-tier" gold market, with one private tier and one official tier. The latter was to be firmly controlled by the participating governments, so that at least the official price could be kept in check.

Meanwhile, the U.S. government had taken a series of actions designed to curb or conceal the U.S. payments deficits: It had, in 1963-68, introduced a complex set of *capital-outflow controls* (an Interest Equalization Tax, a Foreign Direct Investment Program, and restrictions on bank lending to foreigners); it had offered foreign governments specially designed bonds, denominated in their own currencies (partly called "Roosa bonds"), and it now actively discouraged them from exercising their right to convert dollars into gold. Critics derided these steps as financially protectionist, and as constituting a de facto devaluation of the dollar.

Major foreign countries—such as the United Kingdom, West Germany, and Japan—felt increasingly pressured to alter their parity exchange rates, so as to free their domestic economies from these shackles. The U.S. dollar came under speculative attack again and again, particularly during waves of increased gold buying. In all, contrary to what had been envisioned in 1944, exchange-rate stability could no longer comfortably be maintained— certainly not at the existing parities. Nor was there a stable, dependable reserve currency at the center of the system.

It was against this background that the leading Western governments during the fall of 1971 hammered out a new global monetary agreement, signed at the Smithsonian in Washington, D.C., in December of that year. The U.S. government had already, in August 1971, shut the "gold window." As a diplomatic pressure device intended to speed up the negotiations, it then imposed a temporary across-the-board import surcharge.

The final agreement, adopted at the Smithsonian, provided for an increase in the official gold price to $38 an ounce (implying an 8 percent *dollar devaluation* against gold) and a general realignment of nearly all important exchange rates. Some countries (including Britain and France) decided to keep their previous gold pars, thereby effecting approximately a 9 percent revaluation against the dollar. Others chose to alter their oficial exchange rates by different amounts, mostly in the direction of revaluations against the dollar—as did the notorious surplus nations West Germany and Japan. As they generally had not complied with the formal procedures for IMF consultations regarding par changes, they instead announced the new exchange rates as *central rates*—only a minor semantic innovation. The U.S. import surcharge was dropped.

In addition, most countries agreed to widen the bands within which they would keep their actual day-to-day spot rates. The new permissible rate fluctuations were to be confined to a margin of ± 2.25 percent of the central rates, making the band 4.5 percent wide. Both the readiness to undertake such extensive official exchange-rate changes and the widening of the band pointed in the same direction: toward greater actual exchange-rate flexibility.

It could fairly be concluded that the Bretton Woods system had fallen apart, even though an attempt was made to reconstitute an adjustable-peg system. Especially, the gold-dollar exchange standard had crumbled, in favor of something that looked like an unorganized dollar standard. These were constructive developments that greatly helped adjust exchange rates to actual international price relationships and to rectify payments conditions. And abolishing the unsustainable gold-dollar convertibility seems to have paved the way for a more efficient system of reserve-assist creation.

GENERAL MANAGED FLOATING

Despite the accomplishments at the Smithsonian, the financial markets did not seem fully convinced that the new exchange rates were "fundamentally" correct, or that they could remain correct for very long. The dilution of the dollar's official status must also have injected a new sense of uncertainty about the structure of the international financial system and its management. A series of speculative attacks on various major currencies

followed in 1972, and short-term capital flows had by then reached such
large magnitudes that it had become even more difficult to contain each
such crisis. On and off, Britain had to engage in extensive intervention
operations that nearly exchausted her foreign reserves and severely taxed
her short-term international credit facilities. This predicament in the summer
of 1972 prompted Britain to let the pound *float*. This step was taken
despite the risk that further pound depreciation would fuel additional
inflation in the import-sensitive British economy.

Early in 1973, several other countries (Italy, Switzerland, and Japan)
followed suit. On its part, the United States, disappointed with the absence
of a clear turnaround in its external payments accounts, announced an
additional *dollar devaluation*. It amounted to 10 percent of the nominal
official gold value—bringing the gold price, for sheer accounting purposes,
to $42.22. By March 1973, the European Economic Community announced
that its members, too, would permit their currencies to fluctuate relatively
freely in the market vis-à-vis other currencies, but they would, at the same
time, maintain strict limits on changes in their mutual exchange-rate
relations. They thus opted for pegged *intrabloc* exchange rates, combined
with floating *extrabloc* exchange rates. They would from then on permit
their currency *snake* to swim around relatively freely; the snake since
early 1972 had been trapped in the "tunnel" provided by the joint official
intervention band of the EEC currencies against the dollar, but the dollar
tunnel was now demolished. (On this technical subject, more will be said
in the next section.)

Spring 1973 thus marked the time at which the adjustable-peg system
was abandoned in favor of a general *managed float*. It is "managed" in
the sense that the authorities have been, and still are, frequently intervening
in the exchange markets. Thus, the float became "dirty." Little remains
of the Bretton Woods system, except for the credit facilities of the IMF;
little also remains of the Smithsonian agreement.

The gross amount of intervention (buying plus selling) reported by the
leading monetary authorities in the remainder of the 1970s was in the
neighborhood of $100 billion a year. Superficially, such an enormous
amount of intervention might indicate that the pressures toward exchange-
rate instability were equally enormous; and had it not been for such massive
intervention, exchange-rate movements might actually have been much
wider and more irregular. Yet the reality of the situation is not so simple.
Intervention itself is sometimes likely to encourage additional speculation,
as speculators form opinions about the extent to which the authorities will
allow the various rates to rise, or drop, and decide to take advantage
of the anticipated new constellation of rates, with destabilizing results.

What would happen today in the absence of intervention is an untestable
problem. Therefore, we cannot directly assess the effect of the current
intervention practices on the levels or stability of exchange rates. Both

in this regard and in regard to the achievement of internal balance, we cannot easily pass a fair verdict on the managed float. But given the great disparities in national monetary policies, and given the desire to avoid severe disruptions in trade and capital flows, hardly any economists would recommend a return to the fixed or adjustable pegs of the old variety.

THE EUROPEAN MONETARY SYSTEM

As already indicated, the EEC countries have undertaken to reform their own internal monetary relationships, with the ultimate aim of creating one unified EEC currency. These moves are technically unrelated to the broader global reforms within the IMF membership. But there are significant parallels. They illustrate some of the problems inherent in the choice of reserve assets and the appropriate scope and depth of monetary integration.

The long-standing plan for EEC currency unification got a shot in the arm in May 1972. The EEC countries then decided to narrow their *intrabloc band* of exchange-rate fluctuations to one-half of that permitted under the Smithsonian agreement; the width of the intrabloc band became 2.25 percent, as against the 4.5 percent Smithsonian band. This meant that while any EEC currency could in theory fluctuate by as much as 4.5 percent against the U.S. dollar, its fluctuations around its official *cross* rates vis-à-vis its EEC partners were limited to a total of 2.25 percent. For example, the Dutch guilder could move up all the way to its official dollar ceiling only if all the other EEC currencies were at or above their respective central dollar rates—otherwise, it would slip outside the intrabloc band. As a metaphor for their arrangement, a *snake in a tunnel* was apt: The 4.5 percent dollar tunnel provided a fixed space within which the EEC currencies jointly could wriggle up and down.

The adoption of a general float in 1973 did away with the dollar tunnel, while the EEC snake itself remained (refer again to Figure 24-2e). But the practice of "managing" currency movements through exchange market intervention still restricts the freedom of the snake to swim with the currents of private trade and capital flows. The authorities thus frequently hit it on the head—perhaps making it more jittery than is its natural tendency.

The EEC intervention is carried out in two ways—in U.S. dollars (in accordance with the global practice) and in the EEC currencies. If the Belgian franc is especially strong, it may be pushing against its ceiling in terms of other EEC currencies while also appreciating against the dollar. The Belgian central bank might then purchase both dollars and some of the weaker EEC currencies so as to offset both of these tendencies. At the same time, all or some of the EEC countries with weaker currencies might sell dollars to strengthen their own currencies against the dollar. Such intervention steps will tend to bring the intrabloc currencies into line with one another, as the formal EEC rules require.

In other situations, EEC intervention can be taken in order to mitigate movements of the entire currency bloc against the dollar. For example, several central banks within the EEC might sell dollars to lessen a depreciation of the entire currency group, with or without the cooperation of the U.S. authorities. This, however, is a matter of discretionary decisions by these various monetary authorities, since no formal commitments exist in this regard.

The EEC's monetary integration advanced further in March 1979. The Community then announced the formation of the *European Monetary System*, modeled partially after the IMF and intended to further centralize the creation and management of reserve assets within the bloc. The main features of the EMS are:

> Adoption of a European Currency Unit,
> defined as a weighted average of the nine
> EEC currencies (Deutschemark, French
> franc, Dutch guilder, Belgian and Luxem-
> bourg francs, Italian lira, British and Irish
> pounds, and Danish krone).

> Fixing of the central rates of each of the
> currencies (except the British pound) in
> terms of ECUs.

> Establishment of a "reserve fund," to be used
> for short- and medium-term balance-
> of-payments assistance to the EEC members.

The ECU is consequently another "artificial" currency (somewhat like the SDR). Its value in dollars—and in other non-EEC currencies—fluctuates with the daily swings in the actual dollar exchange rates of the nine participating currencies, in accordance with their respective weights. In 1980, the ECU was worth about $1.40. Furthermore, official exchange rates ("central" rates) for eight of the EEC currencies (excepting the British pound) were established not in dollars, but in ECUs. These central rates can be translated into mutual *cross rates* among these eight currencies, so that the Danish krone will be defined in Deutschemarks, or in French francs, and so on. The resulting cross rates form what has been dubbed a "parity grid"—essentially, an eight-by-eight exchange-rate matrix that shows $(8 \times 7) \div 2 = 28$ different rate relationships. But what about the British pound? The EEC has made provisions for Britain's participation in the whole scheme. Yet Britain—an EEC member—has so far refused to join the fixed-rate currency bloc. So she remains outside the snake, letting the pound float independently of the currencies of her EEC partners.

The EMS retained the 2.25 percent bands in the internal exchange-rate relationships, except that the bands now are measured around the redefined, ECU-based central rates. One further modification was made: Italy, with the worst record of currency stability among the continental countries, was allowed a 6 percent band for her currency, the lira. And it was agreed that intervention should be undertaken even before any one currency actually bounces against its ceiling or floor. A complex "early-warning" system has been set up, which signals when such precautionary intervention by the EEC authorities is in order.

The ECU will be used both as an instrument for official intercountry payments and debt settlements and for official accounting purposes. In addition, it might become a unit of account for private international bonds or other securities. Yet there remains a real possibility that the new parities will not stick and that individual EEC members will insist on formally readjusting their pegs. This has already happened a couple of times, primarily because the Deutschemark was too strong to fit inside the skin of the snake. Thus, the snake has had to be reconstituted, and the ECU value adjusted accordingly. The goal is of course to turn the snake into a thin, permanent string. But it is uncertain if the EEC countries have both the political willingness and the economic-financial capacity for surrendering that much of their national monetary independence.

The reserve fund is to expand into a future *European Monetary Fund* into which the EEC members are to transfer part of their monetary gold. It is envisioned as a forerunner of an EEC central bank. If and when these plans are realized, the EMF may gradually take over the responsibility for exchange-market intervention, and it might—somewhat like the Federal Reserve System—engage in open-market operations in the securities of the national EEC governments.

CONFLICTS AND PROSPECTS

For all the official reforms in the 1970s, and all the changes in financial market practice, no new, well-organized international monetary system has yet emerged. What exists is an uneasy mixture of unclear international rules, understandings, policies, and financial practices, with a number of unresolved intergovernmental conflicts. The system is still in transition.

On the theoretical level, there is no agreement on what the ideal monetary system should look like. International monetary theory has not yet been able to resolve the fundamental question of how to trade off the stability gains from a common currency against the freedom and flexibility associated with national monetary autonomy. On the political and institutional level, it is doubtful that the majority of countries have the will to subordinate their national interests to those of the world economy at large; neither the U.S. Congress nor, say, the French parliament is eager to take policy instructions from the IMF.

Reserve-Asset Demand and Supply

How to define, create, and distribute international reserve assets is still unsettled. To many economists, a full-fledged SDR standard seems like an appealing longer-run prospect. In particular, it could permit an orderly expansion of world liquidity and create a firmer international standard of value, not subject to national government manipulation. But it would be unrealistic today to ask governments to turn over the bulk of their foreign exchange holdings to an expanded IMF or to dispose of their hard-earned gold holdings.

For the foreseeable future, we will be living in a multiple-asset world. There will remain a broad range of options for each nation in deciding the composition of its foreign reserves, especially in regard to their foreign-exchange component. In exercising these options, governments will be motivated both by international risk-return considerations and by international obligations to cooperate in the development of a workable global "economic order." Larger countries, in particular, will have to abide by the official rules of the evolving global financial game. Certainly, they can hardly refuse to accept settlement in officially adopted reserve assets. Nor can they, with impunity, suddenly shift large amounts of reserve funds out of one financial center into another. For example, if the Deutschemark, after all, will gradually assume a greater international currency role, West Germany will need exactly these kinds of assurances from prospective official Deutschemark holders; otherwise, it may refuse to accept the burden of being a reserve-currency country.

Even so, the U.S. dollar will undoubtedly retain most of its official and private functions. Should the IMF scheme for a substitution account be implemented, the dollar's official reserve status will naturally be modified. But it will still be the major national currency in government portfolios, whether or not the trend toward currency diversification continues. Most intervention will still be done in dollars, except within the EEC currency bloc. And no other currency will be able to compete with it as the leading transaction and investment instrument, given the unparalleled size and flexibility of U.S. money and capital markets and the pervasive influence of U.S. multinational corporations.

One major question mark is the future international financial behavior of the OPEC countries. The world economy has not yet absorbed the shock of the massive, still ongoing redistribution of income and wealth in their favor. In this case, the issue of international reserve policy is closely connected with the broader questions of commodity trade, long-term investment, and intertemporal substitution: How much of their new export earnings will the OPEC countries want to spend concurrently? How much will they want to set aside for international investment in anticipation of greater absorption opportunities in the future? In what kinds of foreign assets will they want to invest? The answers to these questions will greatly influence the functioning of the global financial-economic system.

These problems center on the uncertain future *demand* for international liquidity in various forms. There is also no consensus about the appropriate liquidity *supply*. There was much academic debate in the 1960s and 1970s about the relative "adequacy" of international liquidity, but it seems to have led nowhere. In the first place, the "need" for reserves depends on many complex factors that do not fit into any simple-minded formula. These factors include national political priorities, the degree of flexibility in price formation and real resource allocation, the available policy tools for correcting payments disturbances, and the risk of influencing the financial strategies of trading partners.

In the second place, liquidity is not just a matter of actual holdings of short-term assets. Like corporations and financial institutions, governments can satisfy some of their needs for internationally usable funds by borrowing (e.g., in the Euromarkets). Unlike private parties, they have the further short-term option of putting policy pressure on financial markets so as to induce compensatory inflows of private capital. All these factors complicate the liquidity demand-and-supply picture.

Actual Reserve Holdings

Nevertheless, data on total international reserves tell an important story. According to Table 25-3, these reserves at the end of the 1960s amounted to about $80 billion (and, thus, at the going SDR value, also to about SDR80 billion). Of this, one half consisted of gold, with foreign exchange (primarily U.S. dollars) and IMF positions making up the other half. These figures reflect a succession of growing official U.S. payments deficits throughout the 1960s.

Ten years later, foreign exchange reserves had increased even further— and there was increasing talk of a dollar "overhang." But the physical amount of monetary gold had declined somewhat, so that the official value of these reserves in the noncommunist world, as measured at SDR35 per ounce, stood at only SDR32 billion ($42 billion). Yet this gold price was completely out of touch with the reality of the private gold market. Recalculated at the market price prevailing in 1980, gold reserves constituted by far the largest component of international reserves. The total supply of official liquidity then seemed out of proportion to all previous norms. On the other hand, if the bulk of this gold will never be allowed to enter the private market (instead being "frozen" in the coffers of the authorities), the more modest official liquidity data may be more relevant after all.

These data should also be amended in another way. They should somehow be made to include existing arrangements for official international credit,

Table 25-3
International Reserves

	End of 1969		August 1979		
	(In billions of U.S. dollars, or SDRs)		*(In billions of SDRs)*	*(In billions of U.S. dollars)*[a]	
Monetary gold, nationally held[b]	39	(50%)	32	42	(11%)
Net IMF positions	7	(9%)	12	16	(4%)
SDRs	—	(0%)	12	16	(4%)
Foreign exchange	32	(41%)	235	304	(81%)
Total reserves	78	(100%)	291	378	(100%)

[a]Based on the conversion rate SDR1 = $1.30.

[b]In these statistics, gold is valued at its official price of SDR35 (or, in 1969, $35) an ounce. If it is revalued at the market price quoted at the end of 1979 (approximately $600 an ounce), the revised 1979 figures will be: monetary gold, $554 billion (68%); total reserves, $813 billion (100%). Gold deposited with the IMF is included with the "net IMF position."

Source: IMF, *International Financial Statistics*, various issues.

to be used for debt settlement or exchange-rate support. Apart from IMF drawing rights, these facilities include what are called central-bank *swaps.* These are a network of reciprocal short-term credit lines among 14 central banks (and the Bank for International Settlements in Basel—a bank that, on a limited scale, serves as a central bank to national central banks). These swaps have been expanded so that they amount to over $30 billion in mutual credit facilities. They are frequently used by both European and the U.S. authorities, usually in preparation for more aggressive intervention sales. They serve to strengthen currencies subject to temporary payments pressures—in the best of circumstances, permitting more "fundamental" forces to gather momentum before the credit is to be repaid.

But the appropriate amount of liquidity is closely tied to the exchange-rate regime. What is "adequate" liquidity under one regime may be "inadequate" under another. There seems to be no possibility that the leading powers will adopt a truly free, "clean" float—under which liquidity needs would be drastically lowered. Instead, central bankers remain convinced that their own foreign exchange management can produce more of the desired stability and order, and governments are reluctant to give up the exchange-rate tool—or any other policy tool. Further political compromises may be worked out so as to better coordinate intervention policies— perhaps through stricter exchange-rate "surveillance" by the IMF. Under all foreseeable arrangements, the freedom of choice will be especially circumscribed for the United States and other emerging reserve-currency countries. This is the price they will have to pay for the seigniorage, the banking business, and the prestige that comes with this status.

The international monetary system will undergo more drastic changes if additional groups of nations in the future seek to establish new currency blocs—theoretically, so as to encompass what might be "optimum currency areas." Even the notion of a "dollar bloc"—or dollar area—is not entirely farfetched, considering the special financial-economic ties the United States has developed both with Canada and with countries in Latin America. Such a trend could make for better monetary coordination and control, at least within each bloc. It might, on the other hand, induce a return to a more fragmented world economy, with interbloc relations dominated by political rivalries and economic protectionism.

SUMMARY

International monetary history since World War II has been eventful, dramatic and—in later years—turbulent. The fixed exchange rates established at Bretton Woods in 1944 gradually evolved into adjustable pegs. Devaluations of major European currencies became increasingly disruptive to the stable flow of trade and capital. The Smithsonian agreement in 1971 at the time seemed like a big positive achievement, but private speculators and investors soon decided otherwise. Reluctantly, all major governments in 1972-73 abandoned their long-standing commitments to peg exchange rates at predetermined levels, while claiming the right to discretionary intervention. The adoption of a managed float was an emphatic concession to a fundamental monetarist principle: Exchange rates cannot be pegged for any length of time, as long as national rates of monetary expansion and inflation are sharply different.

Almost as significant are the changes in the use and value of various international reserve assets. With the gradual demonetization of gold in the 1960s and 1970s, the U.S. dollar had to carry an even larger burden as a medium of settlement and reserve management. But both economic and political pressures have since led to greater efforts toward a global centralization of reserve-asset creation—as via the SDR—and toward a diversification of reserve holdings.

The main result of all these reforms are that: (1) for most countries, payments adjustments, via exchange rate changes, has become easier, if by no means painless; (2) for the United States, the modification of its key-currency status now makes international deficit financing more difficult; and (3) the industrial nations in general are trying to devise new ways of coordinating their monetary and exchange-rate policies without sacrificing important domestic economic interests—an unavoidable, perennial conflict.

Import Concepts

Bretton Woods agreement	Special Drawing Right
IMF credit tranche	central rate
net IMF position	IMF drawings
numeraire	currency snake
General Arrangements to Borrow	EMS

Questions

1. The Bretton Woods system has been criticized for not providing for an equal, or "symmetrical," sharing of the adjustment burden among different countries. What types of "asymmetries" can you think of? Have they been remedied through the managed float?

2. Assume that Turkey draws SDR1 billion on the IMF, half of which is against its credit tranche. It receives a mixture of U.S. dollars, British pounds, and Deutschemarks. What happens to (a) Turkey's net IMF position, (b) its net foreign reserves, and (c) the IMF positions of the United States, Britain, and West Germany?

3. Imagine that gold was remonetized internationally, with a new official gold price set at, say, $500 (or SDR400) an ounce. What might be the consequences for (a) the official demand for U.S. dollar assets, and (b) the international economic policies of gold-producing and gold-hoarding nations?

4. The OPEC countries have toyed with the idea of invoicing their oil export contracts in SDRs, rather than in U.S. dollars. Why? Under what circumstances would this be beneficial to them?

Further Readings

Cooper, Richard, *The Economics of Interdependence: Economic Policy in the Atlantic Community* (New York: McGraw-Hill, 1968).

Katz, Samuel, "'Managed Floating' as an Interim International Exchange Rate Regime, 1973-75," *The Bulletin*, No. 1975-3 (Graduate School of Business Administration, New York University, 1975).

Triffin, Robert, *Gold and the Dollar Crisis* (New Haven: Yale University Press, 1960).

Yeager, Leland, *International Monetary Relations*, 2nd ed. (New York: Harper and Row, 1976), Part II.

INDEX